Fundamentals of Investments for Financial Planning

Huebner School Series

Gary K. Stone, Editor

Huebner School Series

Fundamentals of Investments for Financial Planning

Roger C. Bird
Robert S. Graber
Paul Hoffman
Lynn Hayes, Managing Editor

The American College/*Bryn Mawr, Pennsylvania*

This publication is designed to provide accurate and authoritative information about the subject covered. While every precaution has been taken in the preparation of this material, the authors, the editor, and The American College assume no liability for damages resulting from the use of the information contained in this publication. The American College is not engaged in rendering legal, accounting, or other professional advice. If legal or other expert advice is required, the services of an appropriate professional should be sought.

© 2001 The American College
All rights reserved

Library of Congress Control Number 00-134451
ISBN 1-57996-022-7

Printed in the United States of America

Contents

Preface

A basic and inescapable principle of economics is the law of scarcity: In every society, human wants are unlimited, whereas the resources available to fill those wants are limited. The available resources must somehow be rationed among the wants. This rationing problem creates the need for financial planning even in affluent societies, such as the United States, and even among the most affluent members of such societies. To put it bluntly, there is never enough money to go around.

In today's economy, available financial resources are rationed through markets, and these markets operate in a dynamic environment in which the only certainty is change. It is in this environment that financial planners endeavor to practice their profession. Volatile economic conditions create greater demand for financial planning services. They also emphasize the need for financial planners to continually monitor their clients' financial circumstances and to adjust the plans as circumstances dictate. A major part of the financial planner's challenge in today's economic environment is to help clients overcome obstacles that could impede the achievement of their financial goals. To this end, the planner needs to educate clients about managing their money so that they will derive the maximum benefit from what they earn. To accomplish this purpose, financial planners must understand the securities markets and the investment alternatives that comprise it.

This is a basic or fundamentals textbook that is designed to help both financial planners and individual investors understand the nature of the securities markets and investment opportunities. It presupposes no prior knowledge of these subjects, yet it covers all the topics that constitute the foundation for the study of more specialized aspects of investments. Those who seriously study the information contained herein should find the book to be a useful guide. Practical aspects of investing are stressed. Abstract theoretical issues are introduced only when they are relevant to actual investing.

Investing is seen by many as a worthwhile "game." Those who are going to play the game may as well play it to win. Whether or not the game is worth playing, it is certainly worth winning. This book should help both financial planners and individual investors learn the rules of the game and learn something about the strategies that are most likely to prove effective in winning the game.

The book includes numerous pedagogical features designed to help students focus their study of investments. Among the features found in every chapter of the book are

- *Learning objectives:* Statements at the beginning of each chapter are designed to provide direction to students studying the subject matter in the chapter.
- *An outline:* Following the learning objectives, the subject matter is organized and listed in the order in which it appears in the chapter.
- *Key terms:* In the margins where the terms first appear, as well as grouped together at the end of each chapter, certain terms or phrases are singled out because of their importance to the specific subject matter.
- *Examples:* Problem sets interspersed throughout the chapter are designed to help students see how difficult concepts are applied in specific situations.
- *Review questions:* Essay-style questions at the end of each chapter are designed to test the student's knowledge of the learning objectives.
- *Self-test questions:* True-false statements following the review questions at the end of each chapter are designed to provide students with a quick assessment of their grasp of the subject matter.

Features located in the back of the book are

- *A glossary:* Key terms found in each chapter are defined and included in the back of the book.
- *An answer section:* Answers to all the review questions and self-test questions are located in this part of the book.
- *An index:* The book has a comprehensive index to help identify pages on which various topics are found.

Roger C. Bird
Robert S. Graber
Paul Hoffman

Acknowledgments

We would like to especially thank Ben Branch, professor of finance in the school of management, the University of Massachusetts at Amherst, for his contributions to this book. Its foundation and starting point was the second edition of *Investments: Principles and Practices* by Ben Branch, which was published in 1989 by Longman Financial Services Publishing. Ben's specific contributions to The American College version of the book were confined to revising and/or updating parts of chapters 1, 2, 3, 4, 5, 7, 8, and 15.

We would also like to thank the following individuals for their contributions in revising and/or updating parts of the book:

- Thomas A. Dziadosz, associate professor of economics at The American College, for his contributions to chapters 12, 15, and 19.
- George W. Trivoli, professor of finance in the college of commerce and business administration, Jacksonville State University, for his contributions to chapters 9, 10, 11, 12, 13, and 14.
- C. Bruce Worsham, associate vice president and director of the Solomon S. Huebner School at The American College, for his contributions to chapters 1, 2, 3, 4, 5, and 6.

We gratefully thank members of The American College's production, editorial, and graphics departments who worked on some aspect of the book during its development. These individuals are Patricia G. Berenson, Charlene McNulty, and Evelyn Rice from production; Liz Fahrig, Lynn Hayes, Maria Marlowe, Rosemary Pagano, and Suzanne Rettew from editorial; and Joe Brennan and Andrea Parella from graphics. Two of these individuals, however, must be singled out for their noteworthy contributions to the project—Lynn Hayes, editorial director, and Charlene McNulty, production group leader.

Lynn Hayes, the managing editor of the project, spent countless hours, including evenings and weekends, pouring over the entire manuscript trying to decipher our esoteric gibberish. Her outstanding editing skills and unwavering commitment to excellence made an unmistakable imprint on the book. Lynn carried the organization and administrative responsibility of the book in a brilliantly effective manner. It is no exaggeration to say that this book could not have been done without her; such is our appreciation to Lynn.

Charlene McNulty from our production department typed the brunt of the manuscript. Typically she typed, retyped, and retyped again and again each chapter as we changed, rechanged, and rechanged again and again the wording. Her patience in following our arrows and reading our scribbles was commendable. Thank you Charlene for a job well done.

We thank The American College's librarians—Judith Hill and Debbie Jenkins—for their support in finding all the information requested.

Finally, we would like to thank Gary K. Stone, vice president of academics at The American College and editor of the Huebner School Series, for providing the support and encouragement necessary to complete this project and to keep the Series, of which this book is a part, at the highest standards.

All of these individuals made this a better book, and we are grateful. However, in spite of the help of all these fine folks, some errors have undoubtedly been successful in eluding our eyes. For these we are solely responsible. At the same time, however, we accept full credit for giving those readers who find these errors the exhilarating intellectual experience produced by such discovery. Nevertheless, each of the authors acknowledges that any errors discovered are the fault of one of the other authors.

Roger C. Bird
Robert S. Graber
Paul Hoffman

About the Authors

Roger C. Bird, PhD, is professor of economics at The American College, where he also holds the Frank M. Engle Distinguished Chair in Economic Security Research. He earned his BA degree in mathematics from Lafayette College and his MA and PhD degrees in economics from the University of Pennsylvania. Prior to his current position, he served as senior vice president of the WEFA Group (formerly Wharton Econometric Forecasting Associates), manager of economics with IBM Corporation, and economics instructor at Lafayette College. He is a member of the board of directors and a former president of the Global Interdependence Center (GIC) at Fels Institute of the University of Pennsylvania.

Robert S. Graber, PhD, is an assistant professor of finance at The American College. He obtained his BS in economics from the Massachusetts Institute of Technology and his MBA, MA in economics, and PhD in financial economics from the University of New Orleans. He also has taught at Moorehead State University, the University of Houston, and Villanova University. In addition, his experience includes serving as a financial analyst with the Securities and Exchange Commission and as a financing specialist with Louisiana Power and Light Company.

Paul Hoffman, MA, is an assistant professor of finance at The American College. He obtained his BA in statistics from the University of Rochester and his master's degree in managerial and applied economics from The Wharton School of the University of Pennsylvania, where he was a Huebner and Sloan Fellow in the Insurance and Risk Management Program. In addition, he was a Senior Fellow and program manager at Wharton's Financial Institutions Center. Earlier in his career, he served as an operations specialist for Chase Manhattan Bank.

Fundamentals of Investments for Financial Planning

1

Introduction to Investments

Learning Objectives

An understanding of the material in this chapter should enable the student to

1-1. Identify the three separate but related processes of investing.

1-2. Explain several characteristics of investments.

1-3. Describe the tax treatment of investments, and explain why tax considerations are an important factor in deciding which investments to purchase.

1-4. Explain why investors need to take account of their own psychological tendencies.

Chapter Outline

INTRODUCTION TO INVESTMENTS

The first three chapters of this book lay the groundwork for a practical approach to investment and money management. The following hypothetical case raises many of the issues with which these three chapters deal.

The Newleys: A Young Couple's Finances

Dick and Jane Newley have decided to take a careful look at their finances. They were married immediately after graduation from college 5 years ago and now have two children aged 3 and 1 1/2. Dick earns $37,000 per year as a history teacher at Metropolis High School. He expects modest salary increases if he remains a teacher. He may, however, move into school administration, in which case his income should rise somewhat faster. Jane is a CPA with the prestigious accounting firm of Earnest Anderson, earning $54,500 a year. She seems to be on a fast track and may become a partner in 10 to 15 years. Even junior partners in the firm earn in excess of $200,000.

The Newleys' principal assets are a home (estimated market value of $200,000 with a $140,000 mortgage), $45,000 in savings, and a tract of land left to them by Jane's parents. Jane's father was a real estate developer who died 3 years ago. Her mother is in ill health, and she is supported from a large trust whose principal asset is her late husband's development firm. The real estate company will be sold and the principal of the trust (after deducting taxes) will be divided between Jane and her two brothers upon her mother's death.

Dick's parents are in good health and have relatively modest assets. Dick and Jane both have small amounts of life insurance through their respective employers. They are currently adding about $7,000 per year to their savings.

The Newleys are already relatively well off financially. They have a sufficiently large combined income to meet most of their needs. They have also begun to accumulate some assets (for example, their house and savings). Nonetheless, they believe that a careful examination of their situation will reveal a variety of ways to prepare better for the future. For instance, a substantial portion of their joint income goes for taxes. They would like to reduce that tax burden. Should anything happen to Dick and Jane, they also want to protect their children. Finally, they expect their financial situation to improve over time. Accordingly, they want their personal financial management to grow as their professional careers progress.

Consider each of the following questions that relate to the Newleys' situation:

- They maintain a balance of about $3,000 in their NOW checking account. Should they switch to a super NOW, money market, or cash management account?

equity
- Their $45,000 in savings is currently in a passbook savings account at their bank. That money serves as an emergency reserve, but they could also borrow against the *equity* in their house (the excess of its market value over the mortgage is at least $60,000). Thus, they are now ready to begin investing the sum in the savings account for growth and are willing to take some risks. What might they do?

- Jane's share of her parents' estate will probably exceed $300,000. She would like to learn more about investment opportunities. What are the various types of investment media for her to consider?

- Dick has been a stamp collector since he was 8. Although he has a large collection, most of his stamps are relatively inexpensive. Therefore, the entire collection has only a modest value. He is, however, thinking of becoming more serious and using this hobby as an investment vehicle. Should he? Why or why not?

- After some thought, the Newleys concluded that they should begin to invest some of their savings in the stock market. How should they go about selecting a broker? Should they use a discount broker or a full-service broker? Or should they use the Internet?

- Having selected a brokerage firm, they now would like to buy stock in a company recommended to one of Jane's colleagues. What orders should they give their broker? Should they try to diversify? What about mutual funds?

- The Newleys have heard about such aspects of stock market trading as short selling, margin trading, and the over-the-counter market. What do they need to know about each of these issues?

Many of these questions do not have single or simple answers, and the first three chapters of this book deal extensively with these basic issues. Chapter 1 provides an overview of the investment scene, including a discussion of general investment characteristics such as return, risk, liquidity, marketability, investment effort, minimum investment size, and tax treatment.

Chapter 2 introduces a variety of specific investment types: short-term debt securities, long-term debt securities, common stock, preferred stock, pure option securities, convertibles, mutual funds, small firm ownership, venture capital, real estate, commodities, collectibles, and noncollectible investments. Most of these topics are covered in greater detail in later chapters. The coverage in chapter 2 is designed to give readers a framework in which to evaluate specific investment types.

Chapter 3 explores the workings of securities markets in considerable detail. The discussion begins with such topics as brokers, investment advisers, stock exchanges, commissions, types of orders, specialists, floor traders, the over-the-counter market, short selling, margin trading, secondary offerings, block trades, and tender offers. The chapter then examines securities market regulation, placing particular emphasis on the developing central market. The chapter focuses primarily on how securities trades of various sizes may be executed. Although it is often neglected, effective securities market execution of trades is an extremely important aspect of successful investing. Chapter 3 concludes with a discussion of the economic role of the securities market. The capital allocation, management allocation, and use in implementing economic policy are all considered.

The Investment Process

Virtually all of us are at least somewhat involved in the management of our own financial situations. Different people take different approaches to their personal finances. A few people focus entirely on their present circumstances. They spend all of their money as soon as it is available and worry about tomorrow when it comes. Children whose allowances burn holes in their pockets are examples of this type of financial (mis)management. Those who never outgrow this tendency are forever facing financial crises. Most people, however, eventually learn to plan for the future. They always keep at least one eye on the longer term aspects of their financial situations.

Effective financial management inevitably involves some investment-like decisions. We decide how much to spend on current consumption, how much to spend on durable goods like a car or stereo (which will provide long-term value), and how much to save for later. Moreover, most people do periodically put aside some portion of their current income. Often, they have accumulated, inherited, or otherwise received money or other financial assets. These individuals need to decide what to do with those assets. Choosing not to spend the money is one decision. Determining what to do with the resulting funds requires a second decision. The choices are virtually limitless. Each investment opportunity has advantages and disadvantages. Each investor has a unique set of needs, goals, attitudes, and resources that influence the relative attractiveness and suitability of particular investments.

We should realize that the purchase of durable consumer goods is an investment-like decision. For example, we choose between buying a more expensive, but long-lasting automobile, washing machine, stereo, and so on, or one that is cheaper now but is likely to involve future costs for repair or replacement. This is very similar to an investment decision, which involves the amount, timing, and riskiness of future cash flows.

Clearly, individuals with significant resources to invest need to know something about investment management. This knowledge should help them to select and manage their investments intelligently. Even those who do not now have much money to invest may well expect to have more in the future. Thus, most of us have good reasons for wanting to learn more about investments.

Investing involves three separate but related processes: selection, implementation, and timing. The investor must decide which investments to buy or sell, how to go about implementing the transactions, and when to do it. An investor who manages his or her own portfolio encounters the same basic decisions in adding to (buying) or subtracting from (selling) the portfolio over time. This book is designed to help current and prospective investors make each of these decisions.

Example: Investors often seek to convert some of their portfolio to cash. They may need to sell one or more of their investments so that they can either withdraw funds for consumption or obtain funds to make other investments. Therefore, these investors need to go through a similar process as that described above: deciding what, how, and when to sell.

The Separate Processes of Investing

- Selection: what to buy or sell
- Implementation: how to buy or sell
- Timing: when to buy or sell

This book explores various aspects of investing. Chapters 1–3 deal with investment basics: general characteristics of investments, the primary types of investments, and the mechanics of the securities markets. Chapters 4 and 7 are devoted to the theory of investment valuation. Chapters 5 and 6 deal with fixed-income securities. Chapters 8 and 9 focus on modern portfolio theory. Chapters 10 and 11 explore the various approaches to fundamental analysis. Chapters 12–14 discuss the issues involved with market timing. All of these chapters focus primarily on stocks and bonds. Chapters 15–19 consider a variety of other types of investments: mutual funds, options, convertibles, futures, and real estate.

This chapter introduces the characteristics of investments that largely determine their appeal.

CHARACTERISTICS OF INVESTMENTS

Many types of investments are available, each of which attracts at least some interest from some potential investors. Indeed, some types of investments have been tailor-made to appeal to specific types of investors. Obviously, investors themselves have a diverse array of interests and characteristics. They range from unsophisticated individual investors with modest resources to huge institutions (banks, mutual funds, insurance companies, and so on) with literally billions of dollars to invest. Individual investors differ in such dimensions as age, wealth level, income level, tax bracket, *risk tolerance,* financial sophistication, access to commission discounts, ability to spend time researching and managing their investments, need for current income, access to relevant investment information, ethical and moral attitudes toward particular investments, and a host of other dimensions. Institutional investors also differ in some of these dimensions. Accordingly, each of the very large number of types of investments may appeal to some of the many different types of investors.

risk tolerance

yields

Some assets promise nearly certain short- or long-term *yields.* More risky investments offer less certain but potentially much higher returns. Some investment areas require detailed management, whereas others are virtually trouble free. Liquid investments can be quickly converted into cash at little cost or risk while marketable assets can usually be bought and sold in quantity at the current *market price.* That market price, however, may or may not be an attractive price to the current holder. Some investment areas are open to people of modest means, while other areas require large minimum commitments. Some investments finance activities to which many people object, while other investments are much more innocuous. Finally, investment income may be subject to a variety of different types of tax treatments depending upon how the return is generated. Clearly, investments vary in a number of important dimensions.

market price

We begin this coverage of investment characteristics with a discussion of return. We then examine risk and the risk-return trade-off. Next, we discuss liquidity, marketability, investment effort, minimum investment size, socially responsible investing, and the differing tax treatments of various investment categories. Finally, we explore psychological aspects of investing.

Return

Most people accumulate at least a small amount of what might be called excess funds. These savings or reserves are not required for immediate consumption, and are therefore available for other things. Once accumulated, these excess funds can be "spent" in several ways. They can be used to finance some current expenditure such as a new car, vacation, cosmetic surgery, or other type of consumption spending. A second possibility is to let the funds accumulate in a bank (checking) account where they earn little or no interest. Finally, the owner of such funds could apply them to one or more investments.

Those who choose to invest do so because they hope—and expect—to earn a satisfactory return on their investment. Why invest to earn an unsatisfactorily low, break-even, or negative return? Virtually everyone prefers profits to losses and prefers higher profits to lower profits. Investors who invest rather than consume currently available funds do so because they expect the investment to generate a positive return. Thus, by investing some money now, they hope and expect that they will eventually have more money to spend later.

**dividends
interest**

The expected profit, or return on an investment, is a key factor in determining its relative attractiveness. Profits generally take two forms: current income and price appreciation. Many investments are structured to yield periodic and relatively dependable income payments (such as *dividends, interest,* or rents). Some investments (such as a savings account or CD) have a market value that remains very near to the purchase price. Many other investments (such as shares of stock) have market values or prices that may either increase or decrease substantially over time.

Clearly, an increase in value adds to the investment's overall return, whereas a decrease in value reduces its overall return. Therefore, a determination of the profit or return on an investment needs to take into account both periodic payments (income, which may be either positive or zero) and gains or losses in market value (appreciation, which can be either positive or negative).

Determining an Investment's Overall Return

- Periodic payments: positive income or no income
- Changes in market value: gains or losses in value

While investments are expected to yield a positive return, their actual return may turn out to be very different from the expected level. Indeed, many investments do not produce a positive return, even though that was the investor's expectation when he or she purchased the asset. This discussion raises the issue of risk, which we shall address shortly.

First, however, we need to explore the mechanics of defining and computing returns.

The Holding Period Return

holding period return

holding period return relative

The overall profitability of an investment is often expressed in the form of a relatively simple concept called the *holding period return* (HPR). The HPR relates the profit on an investment directly to its beginning value. A concept called the *holding period return relative* (HPRR) is useful in its own right, as well as being helpful in introducing the HPR. The HPRR is the ratio of the current value of the investment (including any income received during the holding period) relative to its initial cost:

HPRR = Current value of investment / Initial value of investment

---

Example: If an investment is purchased for $10 and is now worth $20, its HPRR is computed as follows (assuming no income payments from the investment):

$$\text{HPRR} = \frac{\$20 \text{ (current value)}}{\$10 \text{ (initial value)}} = 2$$

In other words, this investment is now worth twice its initial cost.

The HPR is the profit for the holding period relative to the initial investment. Mathematically the HPR is simply the HPRR less 1. The "1" reflects the initial amount invested. Thus, the HPR is the total profit or gain on the investment as a percentage of the amount initially invested:

HPRR − 1.00 = HPR = Holding period profit / Initial value of investment

---

Example: Suppose an investment purchased for $100 is sold for $130 and made no income payments during the holding period. The HPRR would be

HPRR = $130/$100 = 1.30

The HPR itself would be 1.30 − 1.00 = .30, or 30%

Alternatively, suppose an investment that cost $1,000 made a payment of $100 during the holding period and was sold for $1,500.

The total holding period profit would be the sum of the appreciation of $500 ($1,500 − $1,000) and the income payment of $100. Thus, the total income would be $600 ($500 + $100 = $600). Dividing this sum ($600) by the initial cost ($1,000) is one approach to computing the HPR.

$$HPR = \$600/\$1,000 = .60, \text{ or } 60\%$$

Alternatively, we could first compute the HPRR and subtract 1 as follows:

$$HPRR = \$1,600/\$1,000 = 1.60$$

$$HPR = HPRR - 1.00 = 1.60 - 1.00 = .60, \text{ or } 60\%$$

The holding period return, or HPR, reveals how much more (or less) an investment is worth than when it was initially purchased. A profitable investment will have an HPR that is greater than 0. An investment with an HPR of less than 0 is showing a loss.

The HPR return has one principal drawback: It does not reflect the length of time that the investment is held. Therefore, an HPR of 1 might be considered quite good if the investment has been held for only a relatively short time (2 years, for example). Conversely, that HPR would be very poor if the holding period is very long (20 years, for example).

The Per-Period Return

per-period return

The *per-period return* (PPR), in contrast, provides a more standardized concept for computing returns. An asset's PPR is defined as the sum of that period's income payments and price appreciation divided by its beginning-of-period market value or price:

$$PPR = \frac{\text{Per period } (\text{Income} + \text{Price change})}{\text{Beginning Value}}$$

Computing a single-period return with the PPR formula produces the same value as a one-period return computed by the HPR formula. The two formulas, however, produce different return values when the holding period differs from one standard-length holding period. PPRs are generally expressed for standard periods of one year's length. Thus, a one-year PPR is the same as an HPR for a one-year holding period. In contrast, a PPR earned for 2 years corresponds to a different and higher HPR value. Indeed, if the PPR equals x, the 2-year HPRR is $(1 + x) (1 + x)$, and the HPR is this value less 1. That is, the 2-year PPR $= (1 + x) (1 + x) -1$. Returns based on a one-year period are called annual, or annualized, returns.

Example 1:   A stock that was bought a year ago for $100 per share, paid a $5 dividend, and now trades for $108 would have the following annual return:

$$PPR = HPR = (\$5 + \$8)/\$100 = 13\%$$

The investor would have received a $5 dividend and have earned appreciation of $8 (the $108 current value less the $100 cost) on the stock. The sum of the two return components equals $13. This $13 in turn is equivalent to 13 percent of the initial cost of $100.

Example 2:   Obviously, returns can also be negative. If the price of the stock in the previous example had declined by $10 (as opposed to appreciating by $8) the result would have been

$$(\$5 - \$10)/\$100 = -\$5/\$100 = -.05 = -5\%$$

Thus, the investor's return (in dollars) would be the result of subtracting the $10 decline in the stock price from the $5 received in dividends ($5 – $10 = –$5). Relating this –$5 to the initial investment of $100 results in a return of –5 percent.

These two examples represent simple one-year returns. Clearly, earning a given return for 6 months will produce a very different result from earning that same return for 6 years. The longer the investment earns a given (positive) PPR, the greater its ending value. Accumulating returns over time and earning a return on the return of prior periods is called *compounding*. An investment's value will grow through the process of compounding.

compounding

Impact of Compounding

Stated returns, particularly for longer holding periods, generally reflect the impact of compounding. Returns are compounded when an investment earns a return for more than one period. After each period, the return from that period is credited to the account and thereby increases the amount on which the subsequent return is earned. The investment earns a return on both the initial sum invested and on the returns that accumulate from earlier periods. In other words, compounding reflects the impact of earning a return on both the amount initially invested and the returns that have been earned on the initial investment in prior periods.

Example: Consider an investment that yields 10 percent per year for 2 years. It earns 10 percent during the first year. At the end of that first year the investment will show an HPRR of 1.10. Earning another 10 percent during the second year will generate an HPRR of 1.21 for the 2 years. This compound value results from earning 10 percent on the initial principal in the first year, another 10 percent on principal during the second year, and 10 percent on the first year's 10 percent return (.10 x .10 = .01, or 1%). The sum is 10% + 10% + 1% plus the initial investment, or 121 percent of the original amount. A simpler way of making this computation is to take 110 percent of 110 percent (1.10 x 1.10 = 1.21).

We can also work backward from the appreciated value to the interest rate that produced it. Therefore, an investment that, after one year, was worth 110 percent of its initial value is said to have yielded a return of 10 percent. Similarly, an investment that appreciated by 21 percent over a 2-year period is said to have generated a 10 percent annual return compounded annually.

PPRs are usually stated on an annualized basis with annual compounding. That is, the standard period for stating returns and for computing compound values is generally one year. Returns can, however, be compounded more frequently than once a year.

Example: A return might be described as 10 percent compounded semiannually. An investment earning such a return would receive one-half of the annual rate of 10 percent each 6 months (5% per 6 months, or .05). Such an investment would appreciate to 121.55 percent of its initial value after 2 years: (1.05 x 1.05 x 1.05 x 1.05 = 1.2155). Had the return been compounded annually, the compound value after 2 years would, in contrast, be only 121 percent. Thus, the semiannual compounding increases the compound value by .55 percent compared with annual compounding.

For a given stated rate per year, the more frequently an investment's returns are compounded, the more rapidly it will grow. Thus, an investment earning a 10 percent return will grow faster with semiannual compounding than annual compounding, and still faster with quarterly compounding. Accordingly, the complete description of a stated return must include both the PPR return and the frequency of compounding.

Example: Ten percent compounded quarterly is equivalent to 10.38 percent compounded annually (1.025 x 1.025 x 1.025 x 1.025 = 1.1038). A return of 10.5 percent compounded annually, therefore, is preferable to 10 percent compounded quarterly. Still, 10 percent compounded quarterly produces a higher rate of return than 10 percent compounded annually. The rate of compounding *does* matter.

mean return

Measuring the Mean Return

Mean (or average) returns often need to be computed for two different types of circumstances: an investment (single asset or portfolio) over time and a group of investments over the same time. We may, for example, know the PPRs for each year and wish to know the average return for the entire holding period. That is, we might have an investment that earned 10 percent, 7 percent, and 12 percent per year over a 3-year period. Alternatively, we may know the individual returns for the components of a portfolio and wish to compute the portfolio's overall return. For instance, if we have a portfolio of five investments that individually had annual returns of 3 percent, 7 percent, 9 percent, 11 percent, and 15 percent, we may then want to compute its overall or mean return.

The Mean Return of a Portfolio. The mean return for a portfolio can properly be represented as the arithmetic average of the returns of the individual components. If equal amounts are invested in each component, the portfolio's overall return is a simple unweighted (or equally weighted) average of its components. To compute the mean return of the five-investment portfolio noted above, we need to add the five separate returns and divide by 5:

$$(3\% + 7\% + 9\% + 11\% + 15\%) / 5 = 45\% / 5 = 9\%$$

If different amounts are invested in the various investments, a weighted average (with weights equal to the relative amounts invested in each asset) must be computed.

Example: Suppose a portfolio consists of 50 percent of investment R that earned 10 percent, 25 percent of investment S that earned 6 percent, and 25 percent of investment T that earned 9 percent. The weighted arithmetic averaging would be

$$(.5 \times 10\%) + (.25 \times 6\%) + (.25 \times 9\%) = 8.75\%$$

Such an arithmetic average return (weighted or unweighted) has a very desirable property. If that arithmetic average return were earned on each investment in the portfolio, the total value of the portfolio would be the same as it was for the returns actually earned.

The Mean Return for a Single Investment. We may also know the returns for a single investment over several periods and wish to compute its mean, or average, return over the entire period. Clearly, if the same per-period return were earned in each period, that PPR would also be the mean return. Frequently, however, the investment will produce different PPRs during different periods. An arithmetic average of these returns can be computed by adding the PPRs and dividing by the number of periods. This average is simple to compute and reasonably useful when the individual returns are similar.

**arithmetic mean
return**

Example: An investment that earned successive returns of 7
percent, 7.5 percent, and 8 percent would grow to a
compound value equal to 1.24227 times its initial
level. The arithmetic average of these three returns is
7.5 percent. Had the investment actually earned 7.5
percent per period for 3 years, its compound value
would be 1.24230. Thus, the actual compound value
and the value derived from using the *arithmetic mean
return* are very similar.

When the separate returns vary over a wide range of values, however, the
arithmetic average of returns earned over time presents a relatively
unrealistic picture. Conceptually, the number reported for the overall return
should be one that, if earned every period, would produce the same end-of-
period value as has resulted from the separate per-period returns actually
earned. The arithmetic mean does not have that property.

Example: To see just how misleading the use of this arithmetic
mean can be, consider an investment of $1,000 that
doubles in value (to $2,000) in the first period (a
return of 100 percent) and then falls to half of its
value (to $1,000) during the next period (a return of
–50 percent). This investment would have the same
value at the end of the second period ($1,000) as it
had at the start of the first ($1,000). Most people
would agree that an investment with the same
beginning and ending value (an HPR of 0) would
generate an average return of 0 percent over the two
periods. Yet if we average +100 percent and –50
percent, we obtain +25 percent. Thus, we see that
using the arithmetic mean can yield a misleading
return figure.

The Geometric Mean Return

**geometric mean
return**

Unlike the arithmetic mean return, the *geometric mean return* (GMR)
has the desirable property that an investment that earns its GMR each period
will grow to the same end value as it would have from earning the separate
returns used to compute that mean. The GMR is obtained by first computing
a sequence of holding period return relatives. The HPRRs may be determined

in either of two ways. We can simply divide the current values by the initial values. Sometimes, however, we may have access only to the PPRs. In this circumstance, we can form the product of each of the individual HPRRs (1 plus the PPRs) for the entire set of periods. Then the nth root is taken of the result (the HPPR), where n is the number of periods. Remember, that taking the nth root of a number is the same as taking that number to the 1/n power. For example, suppose we want to take the fifth root of 7. The calculation is as follows:

$$\sqrt[5]{7} = 7^{1/5} = 7^{.2} = 1.4758$$

On a typical hand-held calculator, we simply input "7," then hit the "y^x" key, then enter ".2." This result minus 1 is the geometric mean return (GMR):

$$HPRR_i = PPR_i + 1.00; i = 1, \ldots n$$

$$HPRR = HPRR_1 \times HPRR_2 \times \ldots \times HPRR_n$$

$$GMR = \sqrt[n]{HPRR} \qquad 1.00$$

(Note : Symbols "$\sqrt[n]{}$" are to be read as "the nth root of ....")

$$\text{where} \quad PPR_n = \text{PPR for period n}$$
$$HPRR_n = \text{HPRR for period n}$$

Thus, in the previous example where n = 2:

$$HPRR = 2.00 \times .50 = 1.00$$

$$GMR = \sqrt[2]{1.00} - 1.00 = 1.00 - 1.00 = 0\%$$

This is exactly the result that we would expect for an investment that doubled and then lost half of its value. The value of the investment would be back where it started. Thus, a 0 percent return is consistent with our expectations.

Example: Now let us consider a more complicated example. Suppose we want to determine the GMR for an investment that generated annual returns of 13 percent, 17 percent, 2 percent, 8 percent, and 10 percent. We could start the search by computing its HPRR:

$$HPRR = 1.13 \times 1.17 \times 1.02 \times 1.08 \times 1.10 = 1.60$$

To find the GMR we must take the nth root of the HPRR. In this instance n is 5:

$$GMR = \sqrt[5]{1.60} - 1.00 = 1.10 - 1.00 = .10, \text{ or } 10\%$$

Note that in this relatively straightforward case the arithmetic and geometric means are approximately equal. The arithmetic mean is

$$(13\% + 17\% + 2\% + 8\% + 10\%) / 5 = 10\%$$

Whenever no negative returns are present and all of the individual returns are of similar magnitude, the two means (arithmetic and geometric) will have relatively similar values.

Risk

risk

In popular usage the term *risk* refers to the probability of some undesirable and uncertain event. Thus, a risky investment is one that might well produce a return substantially less than is expected. Most people would probably agree that an investment with significant chance of producing a substantial loss is a risky investment. Investors may talk of the downside risk (that an investment's return will be less than anticipated) perhaps coupled with the upside potential (that the return will exceed expectations). No doubt such statements convey information. The element of risk that troubles investors is the possibility of downside fluctuations in value and return. Yet using the term risk in this way is imprecise. Where does the downside risk end and the upside potential begin? What units are used to measure the amount of risk? How is the risk of one investment compared with another?

pure risk
speculative risk

To help clarify the meaning of risk, we can begin by classifying risk as either *pure risk* or *speculative risk*. Pure risks involve only the chance of loss or no loss, whereas speculative risks involve the chance of loss, no loss, or gain. Pure risks are "pure" in the sense that they do not mix both profits and losses. Insurance is concerned mainly with the economic problems created by pure risks. This text deals primarily with speculative risks, which involve an element of both profit and loss.

The more serious experts in finance and economics have another view of risk. They use the term to refer to the dispersion of potential variation in possible returns.[1] We will follow their usage. Thus, we relate risk to the likelihood that realized returns will differ from those that were expected. An asset with a wide range of possible returns is considered risky, while one with a narrow range of potential returns is considered more secure. For example, an asset that could easily double its value or become worthless in a year would be viewed as quite risky. On the other hand, a one-year U. S. government bond with a 5 percent yield would be viewed as having practically no risk. The government bond is viewed as having no risk of *default*. A person who holds the government bond until it matures is virtually certain of receiving the promised yield.

default

The range of returns is generally measured in terms of the distance or dispersion from the mean or expected (per-period) return. An asset's *expected return* is the average of its possible returns weighted by their respective likelihoods. Thus, the probabilities of below-expectation and above-expectation returns balance out. The actual yields of risky assets are often well above or well below the market's expectations. Low-risk assets, on the other hand, usually generate returns that are very close to their expected values. The owner of a (relatively risky) asset whose return is expected to be between 2 percent and 18 percent bears the "risk" that the actual return could be anywhere within this range. The investor who owns a (relatively secure) asset with a 99+ percent of earning exactly 7.5 percent has very little risk to be concerned about.

expected return

In subsequent chapters we will explore how the range or dispersion of returns can be measured, as well as the role of portfolio formation and diversification in the assessment and reduction of risk. For now, however, we will work with the simplified concept that risk refers to the magnitude of the range of possible returns.

The Risk-Return Trade-Off

A few people may thrive on speculative risk. They love to gamble even when they know the odds are heavily against them. Most, however, prefer to limit their exposure to unpleasant surprises. The popularity, profitability, and success of the insurance industry illustrate the demand for risk reduction.

Insurance companies are in the business of selling protection from pure risk. The insurer and the insured, in effect, "wager" on the possibility of a significant casualty loss.[2] For most families the loss of their one and only house to a fire or other disaster would be catastrophic. The insurance company, in contrast, has insured thousands of houses. Having to reimburse the policyowner for the loss on a particular policy (even yours) is for the insurer just part of being in the insurance business. In a given year, claims are likely to be filed on only a small portion of the homes the company covers. The one exception occurs when a natural disaster, such as a hurricane, destroys a large number of homes in a particular area. An insurance company with many policyowners in such an area may face huge claims and losses. This risk has led many insurance companies to limit or eliminate their exposure in areas where such disasters are thought to be most likely to occur. The payoff odds on homeowners insurance must be structured to favor the insurer. That is, the amount that the insurance company pays out in claims in a typical year must be well below the amount it collects in premiums. Otherwise, no company would want to be in (or could long survive in) that business. Indeed, homeowners insurance premiums in the aggregate must exceed the sum of expected claims, administrative costs, and commissions by a sufficiently large margin to keep the insurance company interested in the business. Thus, the individual policyowner's premium needs to be structured to cover not only the risk of loss but also administrative costs, commissions, and a reasonable return for the insurer. The policyowner pays a premium that covers these extra costs to achieve the peace of mind that the protection offers. Because most homes are insured, the risk reduction must be worth the cost to a large fraction of the population. Similar arguments apply to other types of insurance (life, auto, medical, and so forth).

There is also a risk-return trade-off for investors. Most investors are willing to sacrifice some potential return if they can thereby obtain a sufficiently large reduction in risk. Accordingly, to be salable, risky assets must offer a high enough expected return to offset their risk. Thus, corporate bonds, having some risk of default, yield a higher return than otherwise similar U.S. government bonds. Similarly, higher-risk corporate bonds yield a higher return than otherwise similar low-risk corporate bonds. When an investment offers too low an expected return to justify its risk, the asset's price will fall until the market views its risk to be in line with its expected return.

Example: Suppose an asset is expected to be worth $1,000 in 6 years. That asset will generate an expected annual return of 12.25 percent if it is priced at $500. If, in contrast, that same investment is priced at $335, its expected annual return will be 20 percent. In general, the lower the price on any given investment in relation to its expected value, the higher its expected return will be.

Risky assets, however, do not automatically produce high expected returns. Rather, the market tends to set a price that is appropriate for the expected return and risk level. An appropriate price that results in a reasonable expected return for the risk is not achievable for every potential investment, however.

Example: A company or partnership proposing to exploit the moon's mineral resources would certainly be risky. With current technology, such a venture would have little chance of yielding a positive return. The expected value of any sum invested would probably be less than the amount actually invested. Thus, no price on such an investment would be likely both to allow sufficient capital to be raised to fund the project and to offer a high enough expected return to compensate investors for the risk. On the other hand, a company organized to mine the nodules on the ocean floor might very well offer a high enough expected return to justify the risk. Therefore, the nodule company could probably raise capital in spite of its high risks. The moon company's expected return, in contrast, would probably be too low to offset its risks.

By way of analogy, there are potential products that never reach the market because the highest price that potential purchasers would be willing to pay is less than the cost of producing and distributing the product. In the language of economics, we can say that the supply and demand curves do not intersect.

Liquidity

liquidity

Liquidity can generally be thought of as the ease of converting an asset into cash. The most liquid of assets is cash (paper money, checking account balances, and coins). Other types of liquid assets are close to cash—bank certificates of deposit (CDs), Treasury bills—but cannot be spent in their present form. A department store or gas station may accept currency, checks, or credit cards but will not let someone pay for a purchase with a CD or Treasury bill. These assets can, however, be readily converted to spendable form with relatively little sacrifice for the investor. That is, the owner who wishes to sell the asset in order to obtain immediately spendable cash can do

---

Other Types of Investment Risks

(It is important to consider all risks in investment analysis. The following risks are present to some degree in every monetary investment.)

- Loss-of-principal risk: the risk of losing the initial investment
- Loss-of-income risk: the risk that the investment may not provide the income anticipated
- Inflationary risk: the risk that the investment dollar will lose purchasing power
- Timing risk: the possibility of getting into or out of an investment at a disadvantageous time
- Liquidity risk: the possibility of being unable to convert an investment to cash when needed
- Management risk: need for management
- Income tax risk: the degree to which earnings and gain are taxable
- Interest rate risk: the risk associated with changes in the interest rate

Many of these risks are discussed elsewhere in this textbook. Some are discussed in other investment literature under different names.

---

so at little or no cost, inconvenience, or danger of receiving less than the sum of the purchase price and accrued interest. These "investments" are immediately redeemable or at most require a minimum amount of effort to make them so. Bonds with short maturities or the right to be redeemed upon demand are also quite liquid. The more distant the redemption date (that is, the longer until its maturity), the less liquid the investment is considered to be. Thus, long-term debt securities and nondebt investments like stocks and real estate (no maturity date) can be very illiquid.

Marketability

marketability
market value

Marketability refers to the ease of (buying or) selling an asset for its *market value*. The market value of an investment is the price that a willing buyer and willing seller would reach if neither were under immediate pressure to trade. Investments differ substantially in their degree of marketability. Shares in very large firms like Exxon or General Motors are very marketable. They trade nearly continuously at prices that vary little from transaction to transaction. Assets that are exchanged in active high-volume markets generally sell at or very close to the current market price.

Market prices may, of course, vary appreciably over time. Indeed, an investment that sells for its market price may or may not be an attractive investment.

Example: An investor who bought IBM stock at its 1987 pre-crash high of 175 might not have thought selling it at its March 1988 market price level of 115 was such a good deal. Similarly, an investor paying the April 1999 high of 213 for Amazon.com would not have been so happy when the stock fell to 102 only 2 months later. Both stocks were very marketable but not necessarily at prices attractive to the investors who had bought them at their highs.

The advantage of marketable assets is that they will sell easily for their market prices, whatever those prices might be at the time. These market prices, however, may or may not yield an acceptable return for the investor. Investments with poor marketability present their owners with another kind of problem: They are difficult and costly to sell.

Example: Difficult-to-market assets such as a house, rare painting, or certain one-of-a-kind investments appear on the market rather infrequently. Potential buyers of such investments are relatively scarce. Sellers must either be patient or be willing to trade at a substantial discount from the theoretical market value. Suppose the owner of a house that should sell for $200,000 (according to current conditions in the local real estate market) needs a lot of cash in a hurry. He or she might have to accept a sacrifice price of $150,000 to make a quick sale. To obtain a reasonable price (fair to the seller), the seller would need to be prepared for a potentially significant wait for the right customer to come along.

Although marketable assets tend to be liquid, some exceptions exist. A widely held stock can generally be sold for the current market price (marketable), but that price may vary substantially from the purchase price (illiquid). Conversely, U.S. government savings bonds and low-denomination CDs may be cashed in early at their face value plus reduced interest (liquid) but are not negotiable (unmarketable). Note that the term "liquid" is often used interchangeably with "marketable" in the press. Thus, a stock that is referred to as liquid is one for which an active competitive market exists.

Investment Effort

Selecting and managing some types of portfolios require little or no special knowledge, facilities, or time commitment. For instance, the investor need not be an expert on short-term debt securities to understand the relevant characteristics   (risk, expected return, liquidity, marketability, and tax treatment) of Treasury bills and similar securities. Moreover, the certificates of ownership can be conveniently held by a brokerage firm or in a safe deposit box. Those who invest in other assets, such as real estate, collectibles, soybean futures, or mink farms need very special knowledge, talent, and/or facilities. Similarly, some types of assets may be maintained with little or no effort (bonds), whereas others require constant management (an apartment complex). Accordingly, would-be investors need to carefully consider the expertise, talent, facilities, and time required to assemble and manage the particular type of investment portfolio effectively. Investors with little time to spare should stick to investments that require relatively little maintenance. Those in a position to invest both time and money may be able to enhance their return by the extra effort, particularly if they have some appropriately useful skills.

Minimum Investment Size

Portfolios of some types of investments may be assembled with small sums, whereas others require a much larger minimum commitment. Moreover, some investments have such low risk that a portfolio consisting of a single asset is an appropriate holding. For instance, a savings account can be opened for as little as $100 and some higher-yielding bank certificates are available in $500 denominations. Most mutual funds will accept initial deposits of $1,000. Indeed mutual funds offer an attractive way for small investors to participate in the stock and bond market with relatively small sums of money. Many collectibles sell for a few hundred dollars or less. On the other hand, several thousand dollars are generally needed to purchase a single stock or bond position efficiently. Such a holding, however, would be very much at the mercy of the market for that particular stock or bond. A reasonably well-diversified stock or bond portfolio would require several times as much of an initial investment. In a future chapter we will discuss the use of mutual funds and other investment company products that allow for well-diversified stock and bond portfolios at low cost. A single real estate purchase (to say nothing of a diversified real estate portfolio) is likely to require at least several thousand dollars (or more likely several tens of thousands of dollars) for just the down payment. Similarly, most brokers will not accept commodity accounts having less than $20,000 to $50,000 in investor capital.

Obviously, the capital requirements of different types of investments differ appreciably. Those beginning with relatively small sums are restricted to investments that are available in modest size units. Over time, however, investors may be able to shift into investments that are traded only in larger increments. For instance, a beginning investor may start with a savings account and then move into certificates of deposit. Later, he or she may buy into a mutual fund and still later begin assembling a portfolio of stocks and/or buy some rental property.

Ethical and Moral Appeal

Investments may also differ substantially in their ethical and moral appeal, particularly to certain groups of investors. Many investors take the attitude that if an activity is legal, it is a proper area in which to seek investment profits. Other investors, however, want their investment dollars associated only with activities of which they personally approve. Accordingly, the perceived social responsibility of the activity is a relevant consideration for many investors. Most investors would probably prefer not to have their investment money associated with what they consider to be objectionable activities. What is socially unacceptable for some, however, is not socially unacceptable for others. Social responsibility is largely in the eye of the beholder. Each investor has his or her own code of what is an acceptable area in which to invest. No doubt many, but by no means all, investors would draw the line at pornography and prostitution even when and where they are allowed by the law. Others would refuse to become slumlords even if all health and safety codes are adhered to and the profit potential is substantial. Still others would object to investments in companies involved with one or more of the following types of products or activities: alcohol, tobacco, armaments, war toys, major pollutants, nonunionized employees, unionized employees, child labor, misleading advertising, or poor safety records.

TAX TREATMENT OF INDIVIDUALS

Investors are able to retain only the after-tax component of their returns. The after-tax return of an investment is similar to a worker's take-home pay. It is the part of the return available to the investor after various governments take their cut. Because not all types of investment income are taxed equivalently, tax considerations are an important factor in deciding which investments to purchase. The tax treatment of an investment is particularly relevant for investors in high tax brackets. To understand how investment income is taxed, we need to examine our tax system's basic makeup.

The individual federal tax return on Form 1040 has a relatively complex structure. First, income from wages, salaries, and most other sources (including investment income) is added to compute total income. (Certain items of income, such as municipal bond interest, are excluded because they are tax free at the federal level.) Total income is then reduced by certain deductions, such as alimony paid by the taxpayer, to arrive at adjusted gross income (AGI). AGI is then reduced by personal exemptions ($2,800 per exemption in 2000) and either itemized deductions or the standard deduction. The result of this series of calculations is called *taxable income*. This sum is the amount on which tax liability is based. The actual tax liability incurred depends on both the individual's taxable income and filing status (joint, individual, head of household, and so forth). The computation uses a schedule such as that of table 1-1.

Itemizing deductions is advantageous to the taxpayer if allowable deductions exceed the standard deduction. Deductions are allowed for charitable contributions, certain employee business expenses (above a threshold), some types of interest payments, unreimbursed medical expenses (above a threshold), and casualty losses (above a threshold), as well as most state and local income and property taxes (but not sales taxes). At higher income levels, the tax shelter that itemized deductions as well as personal and dependency exemptions provides begins to be reduced, thereby effectively raising the marginal tax rate at these income levels.

Taxation of Extra Income

Additions to total income almost always increase taxable income. Moreover, for taxpayers in all but the 15 percent tax bracket, extra taxable income is taxed at a marginal rate that is higher than the average rate.

An individual's taxable income results from adding investment income to other forms of income (after subtracting appropriate deductions). Thus we can view investment income as the last increment of income. If the investment income had not been received, total income would have been less by that amount. Taxes would then be reduced by the amount of the investment income not received multiplied by the tax rate on that increment of income. The last increment of income is always taxed at the marginal rate. Therefore, the *marginal* rate is the relevant rate to use in assessing most investment decisions.

TABLE 1-1
Individual Tax Rate Schedules for 2000

Filing Status	If Taxable Income Is	The Tax Is
Married individuals filing joint returns and surviving spouses	Not over $43,850 Over $43,850 but not over $105,950 Over $105,950 but not over $161,450 Over $161,450 but not over $288,350 Over $288,350	15% of the taxable income $6,577.50 plus 28% of the excess over $43,850 $23,965.50 plus 31% of the excess over $105,950 $41,170.50 plus 36% of the excess over $161,450 $86,854.50 plus 39.6% of the excess over $288,350
Heads of households	Not over $35,150 Over $35,150 but not over $90,800 Over $90,800 but not over $147,050 Over $147,050 but not over $288,350 Over $288,350	15% of the taxable income $5,272.50 plus 28% of the excess over $35,150 $20,854.50 plus 31% of the excess over $90,800 $38,292 plus 36% of the excess over $147,050 $89,160 plus 39.6% of the excess over $288,350
Unmarried individuals (other than surviving spouses and heads of households)	Not over $26,250 Over $26,250 but not over $63,550 Over $63,550 but not over $132,600 Over $132,600 but not over $288,350 Over $288,350	15% of the taxable income $3,937.50 plus 28% of the excess over $26,250 $14,381.50 plus 31% of the excess over $63,550 $35,787 plus 36% of the excess over $132,600 $91,857 plus 39.6% of the excess over $288,350
Married individuals filing separate returns	Not over $21,925 Over $21,925 but not over $52,975 Over $52,975 but not over $80,725 Over $80,725 but not over $144,175 Over $144,175	15% of the taxable income $3,288.75 plus 28% of the excess over $21,925 $11,982.75 plus 31% of the excess over $52,975 $20,585.25 plus 36% of the excess over $80,725 $43,427.25 plus 39.6% of the excess over $144,175
Estates and trusts	Not over $1,750 Over $1,750 but not over $4,150 Over $4,150 but not over $6,300 Over $6,300 but not over $8,650 Over $8,650	15% of the taxable income $262.50 plus 28% of the excess over $1,750 $934.50 plus 31% of the excess over $4,150 $1,601 plus 36% of the excess over $6,300 $2,447 plus 39.6% of the excess over $8,650

Example: Jan Q. Investor's $65,000 per-year income is the sole support for her family of four. The three dependents (including her husband) and her personal exemption permit her to exclude $11,200, while the standard deduction for married couples filing jointly of $7,350 reduces her taxable income to $46,450. Table 1-1 shows that joint filers (Jan and her husband file jointly) with taxable incomes between $43,850 and $105,950 pay (2000 rates) $6,577.50 plus 28 percent of the excess over $43,850. This formula yields a tax liability of $7,305.50 ($6,577.50 + $728). This amount is equivalent to an average tax rate of 15.7 percent (7,305.50/46,450) on taxable income. Any additional income would be taxed at the marginal tax rate of 28 percent. If Mrs. Investor's income increased to $66,000 without changing deductions, her taxable income would increase to $47,450, and her tax would rise by $280, or 28 percent of the $1,000 income increase. Her average tax rate on the $47,450 of taxable income would increase to almost 16 percent.

Different tax brackets apply to the various filing statuses. For example, single filers reach the higher tax brackets at lower levels of income than joint filers do. Although Congress may change the tax rates from time to time, each investor's marginal rate (whatever its current level) remains the relevant rate for most investment decisions.

Tax laws are discussed in the section that follows. While tax laws are frequently revised, most revisions are relatively minor, although some, such as the Tax Reform Act of 1986, resulted in substantial changes. The possibility of tax law changes increases both the complexity and the desirability of tax planning. Serious investors need to stay abreast of the current tax laws. They may well want to change their strategy and adjust their portfolio in light of tax law changes or even in light of expected changes.

Taxation of Investment Income

Whether, and if so how, the income from an investment is taxed can have a major impact on the net return that the investor receives. Accordingly, effective tax planning is an important aspect of both investing and personal finance. The form of investment income determines how it is taxed.

Interest income on savings accounts, corporate bonds, and U.S. government bonds is taxed as ordinary income (that is, like wages and salaries) whereas state and local (municipal) government bond interest is (with a few exceptions) untaxed at the federal level. Capital gains on municipal bonds, however, are subject to capital gains tax. After any relevant expenses are deducted, rents, royalties, and most dividends are fully taxed like income from wages and salaries. Dividends not covered by current profits are considered *capital distributions*. These distributions are not taxed when received but do affect the taxable capital gains or losses on such assets when they are sold. Capital gains and losses are subject to special tax treatment.

Capital Gains and Losses

capital gains and losses

Capital gains and losses arise whenever capital assets (essentially, any assets such as stocks or bonds that are held for investment purposes) are bought and sold for different amounts. Normally, the taxable gain equals the sale price (minus commissions) less the purchase price (plus commissions). Any capital distributions must, however, be subtracted from the purchase price to determine the basis. The *basis* is the sum that is subtracted from the sale price to produce the taxable gain.

Example: Suppose 100 shares of the BDC Company are purchased for $25 per share and sold for $35 per share. The taxable gain (ignoring commissions) would normally be $1,000 ($3,500 − $2,500). Prior capital distribution dividends of $500 would, however, reduce the basis from $2,500 to $2,000. Such distributions would have the effect of increasing the taxable gain to $1,500 ($3,500 − $2,000).

Capital gains and losses are subject to rather complicated tax treatment. The basic rule is that short-term gains (gains on assets sold after being held one year or less) are taxed as ordinary income, whereas long-term gains (gains on assets sold after being held for more than a year) are generally subject to a maximum tax rate of 20 percent. Unrealized gains (appreciation on assets that have not yet been sold) are not subject to tax. Gains only become taxable if and when they are *realized*, which would normally occur only if the underlying asset is sold.

Taxes are applied to the net gain or loss. Thus, a taxpayer who has some capital losses may deduct the amount lost on some transactions from any gains on other transactions to arrive at the net gain or loss. A separate net figure is computed for both short- and long-term gains or losses.

If both short- and long-term gains are positive, the taxpayer is taxed at his or her ordinary income tax rate on the short-term gains and at the 20 percent maximum rate on the long-term gains. If, however, the taxpayer is in the 15 percent tax bracket on total taxable income, then long-term gains would be taxed at a 10 percent rate instead of a 20 percent rate. In other words, the 20 percent maximum rate can be applied to reduce tax liability but not to increase it.[3]

Things get more complicated if the taxpayer has net losses for either the short or long term. If either short- or long-term transactions result in a net loss figure, that amount is netted against the opposite gain. That is, short-term losses are subtracted from long-term gains, or long-term losses are subtracted from short-term gains. In other words, if this overall net number shows a gain, it is subject to tax based on its term. If the net gain is short term, it is taxed as ordinary income, and if it is long term, the 20 percent maximum applies.

If the overall net number shows a loss or if there are only short-term and long-term losses, the taxpayer may use the loss to offset ordinary income. Generally, up to $3,000 of capital losses may be deducted from ordinary income (married filing separately taxpayers are limited to $1,500) in any one year. If the net capital loss is greater than $3,000, the excess may be carried forward and used to offset capital gains and/or ordinary income in subsequent years.

Note that the law on the taxation of capital gains has been changed frequently in the past. At different times long-term capital gains had been fully taxed, taxed at half the ordinary rate, and subject to a 6-month or 18-month (as opposed to 12-month) holding period. Expect future changes to the tax laws.

The Alternative Minimum Tax

Individuals with large amounts of tax-sheltered income (accelerated depreciation, and so on) or high itemized deductions may be subject to the alternative minimum tax (AMT). To determine whether the AMT applies, tax liability is first computed in the regular way. Then all of the includible tax-sheltered items are added back to adjusted gross income and certain allowable deductions are subtracted to obtain the income subject to the AMT. The AMT tax equals 26 percent (or 28 percent of the taxable amount exceeding $175,000) of this sum. The individual's tax liabilities computed for the two different ways (regular and AMT) are then compared. The higher of the two tax figures is the one that must be paid. In other words, the AMT can raise but cannot lower an individual's tax liability.

State and Local Taxes

Investment income may also be subject to state and local taxes. U.S. Treasury issues are exempt from state and local taxes. State and local bonds are not taxed within the state that issued them. In contrast, those issued by other jurisdictions are fully taxed in the owner's own state and local residence jurisdiction.

Tax Treatment Summary

The four basic types of investment income for federal tax purposes are as follows:

- capital distributions on stock and the interest on state and local government bonds. These are tax free.
- unrealized capital gains. These are untaxed until the gain is realized.
- dividend and nonmunicipal bond interest income, net rents, royalties, other investment income, and short-term capital gains. These are taxed at ordinary tax rates.
- long-term capital gains. These are subject to a maximum 20 percent tax rate (2000 tax law).

Table 1-2 summarizes these tax categories.

Implications of Investment Tax Treatment

Those whose incomes put them in high tax brackets will find tax-sheltered investments particularly attractive. Table 1-3 shows the fully taxable yield that is necessary to produce a 10 percent after-tax return (2000 rates). Regardless of the tax-free rate, however, the basic point remains: A given tax-free yield is worth more to people in higher tax brackets. Note that state taxes, exemption and deduction phaseouts, and the AMT would raise the tax rates for higher income investors.

Investors are able to retain only the after-tax portion of their returns on investments. Investors focus on the portion of the return that they get to keep. For two otherwise similar investments with the same before-tax return, investors would prefer the one with the higher after-tax return. For example, a tax-free payment stream of $100 per month is worth more than an

TABLE 1-2
Tax Treatment of Investment Income

Capital distributions on stock Interest on state and local (municipal) bonds	Not subject to federal income tax
Unrealized capital gains	Tax deferred until realized
Dividend and interest income (other than municipal bond interest) Rents, royalties, and any other investment income payments Short-term capital gains and short-term capital gain distributions (net of capital losses) Payments from deferred income plans, 401(k) plans, IRAs, and so forth	Taxed at ordinary income tax rate
Long-term capital gains and long-term capital gain distributions	Maximum tax rate of 20%

otherwise equivalent payment of $100 per month that is taxable. Indeed, for an investor in a high tax bracket, a $100-per-month tax-free income stream may be worth more than a $150-per-month taxable income stream. Accordingly, asset prices generally reflect the way their returns are taxed. If other characteristics, such as risk, are the same, a tax-free or tax-sheltered

tax equivalent yield

TABLE 1-3
Tax Equivalent Yield (Joint Return 2000 Rates)

Taxable Income (joint filers)	Marginal Tax Rate	Tax Equivalent Yield (at 10%)
$0–$43,850	15%	11.8%
$43,850–105,950	28%	13.9%
$105,950–$161,450	31%	14.5%
$161,450–$288,350	36%	15.6%
Over $288,350	39.6%	16.6%

payment stream will be priced higher than a payment stream of equal size that is fully taxable. Pricing investments in this way produces a trade-off. Investments that offer a tax-free or tax-sheltered return are priced to offer a lower before-tax return than otherwise equivalent investments whose returns are fully taxed. Thus, for example, the before-tax yields of tax-free bonds are generally well below otherwise equivalent taxable bond returns. A lower tax-free return may or may not be more attractive than a higher taxable return for a particular investor. Which investment offers the highest after-tax return depends on both the level of the two pre-tax returns and on the investor's tax bracket.

The market-determined trade-off between fully taxed and tax-deferred income reflects the average tax impact on the relevant investors. Different investors, however, face different tax rates. Some investors (for example, nonprofit charities and college endowment funds) do not incur taxes on their investment income, while others pay taxes at various marginal rates (15 percent, 28 percent, and 31 percent, 36 percent, and 39.6 percent at the federal level). A fully taxable return of 10 percent might be equivalent to an after-tax return of 8.5 percent, 7.2 percent, 6.9 percent, 6.4 percent, or 6.04 percent, depending on the investor's tax bracket. State and local income tax rates further complicate the after-tax cash flow comparisons, as does the AMT and the phaseout of exemptions for higher-income taxpayers. Thus, the after-tax return on a given investment depends, among other things, on the particular investor's tax bracket.

Suppose tax-free bonds offer a 7.2 percent yield, while otherwise similar taxable bonds offer 10 percent. An investor in the 28 percent tax bracket would earn the same net return on either investment (.72 x 10% = 7.2%). Investors in higher brackets will retain more from the tax-free investment, whereas those in lower brackets will receive a higher after-tax return from the taxable investment. Thus tax-sheltered investments will normally offer those in very high tax brackets relatively higher net returns, while those in below-average tax brackets will find fully taxed investments more attractive.

In general, for an investor with a marginal tax rate of T, the tax equivalent yield on a tax-exempt bond paying a coupon of C can be expressed as

$$TE = \frac{C}{1-T}$$

where: C = coupon on tax-exempt bond
        T   = investor's marginal tax rate
      TE = tax equivalent yield

Table 1-4 lists the principal investment characteristics and types of investments that have high and low levels for each characteristic.

TABLE 1-4 Investment Characteristics		
Characteristic	High	Low
Expected return Risk Liquidity Marketability Investment effort Minimum investment size Social responsibility Favorable tax treatment	Gold mine Futures contract Money market account Actively traded stock Real estate Commercial paper Most collectibles Municipal bonds	Savings account Treasury bill Small business Collectibles Mutual fund Savings bonds Pornographic movies Corporate bonds

PSYCHOLOGICAL ASPECTS OF INVESTING

Investors need to take account of their own psychological tendencies. Otherwise, such factors may unduly influence their decisions. Investors are subject to all of the shortcomings and biases inherent in human judgment. Individuals who evaluate their own biases and tendencies may be better able to control and perhaps offset those that could otherwise lead them astray.

Example: A tendency to invest impulsively could cause the investor to trade too frequently. Overly active trading may be profitable to the broker (in commissions) but is usually rather costly for the investor. This tendency might be reduced if the investor could agree to take a day to think over each trade. That approach would allow for a cooling-off period to rethink the decision.

Paul Slovic and his coworkers at the Oregon Research Institute have pioneered in the study of human judgment biases and their impacts on investor decisions. His classic work, "Psychological Study of Human Judgment: Implications for Investment Decision Making," synthesizes the investment implications of a number of psychological studies.[4] For example, Slovic observes that the human mind frequently makes random judgmental errors. This trait may be dealt with by programming individual decision processes. The decision maker would use mathematical models of the considerations, weights, and estimates to check the logic of the decision. Random human error can cause the unprogrammed approach to yield different results from the programmed approach. The programmed result may or may not be superior to the unprogrammed one, but knowledge of the differences is generally helpful.

Slovic also reports that people usually react to new information by revising their opinions in the correct direction but more conservatively than is warranted by the new information. On the other hand, people tend to extrapolate from a small nonrandom sample to an unsupportable generalization.

Complex decisions may be divided into a series of smaller decisions, combining the judgments on each decision into a solution for the initial major problem. Systematic biases in the smaller decisions, however, may lead to a biased decision on the larger question.

Note that systematic biases are different from random errors. For example, suppose that an investor can interpret new information in an overly optimistic, overly pessimistic, or accurate manner. Someone who makes random errors will be sometimes overly optimistic and sometimes overly pessimistic, but on average will interpret new information accurately. An investor with systematic biases, however, will have either an overly optimistic or an overly pessimistic interpretation of events most of the time. This distinction will be important to remember later when the efficient market hypothesis is discussed.

Selective recall is one typical human bias. People remember some events more easily than others. People also tend to see patterns where none exist and to attribute a result to a particular cause even when there is no real correlation. The claimed success of many investment chartists may be due to such tendencies. Another common fallacy is to attach undue importance to very recent events, relative to other events that occurred in the more distant past but are relevant nonetheless.

Individuals also sometimes respond differently to the same question if it is asked in different ways. For example, an individual might simultaneously predict a 10 percent increase and a $5 price rise on a $40 stock (10 percent of $40 is $4, not $5). Questions, therefore, should be structured to elicit the most accurate approach to answering them. If available data are in percentages, for example, a question asked in terms of percentage may elicit a more reliable response.

risk aversion

Apparently, the degree of *risk aversion* is not a universally generalizable characteristic. People may be very risk averse in their investment decisions but much less so in their driving, or vice versa. Moreover, decisions made by a group tend to be riskier than individual decisions. Finally, many people tend to overrate the reliability of their own judgments. Others, however, tend to "follow the herd" and seem to have little confidence in their own judgment.

SUMMARY AND CONCLUSIONS

The expected return and its associated risk are key factors in most investment decisions. Other relevant characteristics include liquidity (the ease of converting the asset into spendable form without a sacrifice of return), marketability (the likelihood of trading at the market price without waiting), effort (the time and expertise required of a serious investor), capital requirements (the minimum sum needed to purchase one unit and/or a diversified portfolio), appeal to socially responsible investors, and tax treatment.

Investments differ appreciably in the way that they are taxed. Some investment returns, such as municipal bond interest and stock capital distribution dividends, are not taxed. Most other types of investment income are fully taxed. Long-term capital gains have at various times been taxed at lower rates than ordinary income. Currently, these gains are subject to a maximum tax rate of 20 percent after they have been recognized.

CHAPTER REVIEW

Answers to the review questions and the self-test questions start on page 737.

Key Terms

equity	arithmetic mean return
risk tolerance	geometric mean return
yields	risk
market price	pure risk
dividends	speculative risk
interest	default
holding period return	expected return
holding period return	liquidity
relative	marketability
per-period return	market value
compounding	capital gains and losses
mean return	tax equivalent yield
	risk aversion

Review Questions

1-1. Describe what is meant by return and risk. Put your description into words that an individual with little or no economic or financial background can understand.

1-2. Explain the various return concepts, including holding period return relative (HPRR), holding period return (HPR), per-period return, annualized return, compound interest, arithmetic mean return, and geometric mean return

1-3. Compute the HPRR and HPR for each of the following:
   a. an investment in land purchased for $5,000 and sold for $7,000
   b. a $3,000 noninterest-bearing note purchased for $1,800 and held until maturity, at which time it is paid off at its face value
   c. a building that is held for 9 months, during which time it generates $3,500 in rental income (in excess of costs), and then sold for a $30,000 profit. Its original purchase price was $195,000.

1-4. Compute the annual return for each of the following investments:
   a. An investment in 100 shares of stock costing $10 per share, sold one year later for $11 per share, during which time a 30-cent-per-share dividend is received. Ignore commissions in your computations.
   b. A $1,000 one-year CD with a stated yield of 7 percent compounded quarterly. To compute its return determine what an equivalent one-year investment would have to earn if its returns were not compounded.
   c. A long-term bond purchased for $890 and sold a year later for $850. The bond pays a coupon of 8 percent on its $1,000 face value. The first coupon (one-half of the annual rate) is payable in the middle of the one-year holding period. To be precise, you should compute the interest earned on the coupon payments. Assume the interest on the coupon accrues at the same rate as the bond's yield (coupon/price).

1-5. Compute the appreciated value of an investment held for 2 years with 10 percent return compounded annually, semiannually, quarterly, and monthly.

1-6. a. Compute the arithmetic mean return (AMR) of a portfolio consisting of equal amounts invested in assets yielding returns of 7.8 percent, 9.3 percent, 4.5 percent, and 11.5 percent, respectively.
   b. Now suppose the amounts invested (in a. above) were in the proportions of .2, .3, .4, and .1. What would the mean return of this portfolio be under these changed circumstances?

1-7. a. Compute the geometric mean return (GMR) for an investment with the following per-period returns: 5.6 percent, 8.9 percent, 10.0 percent, 7.7 percent, and 13.0 percent.

      b.   Compare the result (in a. above) with the arithmetic mean return (AMR).

1-8.   a.   Explain what is meant by the risk-return trade-off.

      b.   Does the risk-return trade-off imply that all risky investments offer high returns? Explain.

1-9.   a.   Define and compare liquidity and marketability.

      b.   Are liquid investments always marketable; are marketable investments always liquid? Explain.

1-10. Explain what is meant by investment effort. Give specific examples.

1-11. Describe the roles of minimum investment size and ethical and moral appeal in investment selection and portfolio management.

1-12. Explain the various ways in which investment income may be taxed at the federal level.

1-13. a.   Assume that a married taxpayer with three dependents (including the spouse) has insufficient deductions to itemize. Using the 2000 tax information from the chapter, compute the federal tax liability for this taxpayer who files jointly and receives the following income items:
- wages: $29,000
- dividends: $750
- municipal bond interest: $500
- savings account interest: $500
- short-term gain on stock: $1,200

      b.   Computed on the basis of taxable income, what is the marginal and average tax rate for this taxpayer?

1-14. a.   Assume that a married taxpayer with two dependents (including the spouse) itemizes deductions. Using the 2000 tax information from the chapter, compute the federal tax liability for this taxpayer who files jointly and has the following income and deduction items:
- profit of a sole proprietorship: $90,000
- dividend and interest income (no municipal interest): $3,000
- mortgage interest payments (which are deductible): $9,000
- state income and real estate taxes: $6,500
- gifts to charity: $800

      b.   Computed on the basis of taxable income, what is the marginal and average tax rate for this taxpayer?

Self-Test Questions

T   F   1-1. Investing involves three separate but related processes: selection, implementation, and timing.

T   F   1-2.   Marketable assets can be quickly converted into cash at little cost or risk.

T   F   1-3.   The holding period return (HPR) relates the profit on an investment directly to its beginning value.

T   F   1-4.   An asset's per-period return (PPR) is defined as the sum of that period's income payments and price appreciation minus its first-of-period price.

T   F   1-5.   Accumulating returns over time and earning a return on the return of prior periods is called compounding.

T   F   1-6.   In finance and economics, the term risk refers to the dispersion of possible returns.

T   F   1-7.   Insurance companies are in the business of selling protection from speculative risk.

T   F   1-8.   Long-term debt securities are considered to be very liquid.

T   F   1-9.   The tax treatment of an investment is particularly relevant for investors in high tax brackets.

T   F   1-10. Itemizing deductions is advantageous to the taxpayer if allowable deductions fall below the standard deduction.

T   F   1-11. Deductions are allowed for sales taxes.

T   F   1-12. The last increment of income is always taxed at the marginal rate.

T   F   1-13. The marginal rate of taxation is the relevant rate to use in assessing most investment decisions.

T   F   1-14. State and local government bond interest generally is taxed as ordinary income.

T   F   1-15. The basic rule is that short-term capital gains are taxed at a maximum tax rate of 20 percent.

T   F   1-16. If a taxpayer is in the 15 percent tax bracket on total taxable income, then long-term gains would be taxed at a 10 percent rate.

T   F   1-17. Individuals with large amounts of tax-sheltered income or high itemized deductions may be subject to the alternative minimum tax (AMT).

T   F   1-18. The lower of the regular tax or the AMT is the tax amount that a taxpayer must pay.

T   F   1-19. People may be very risk averse in their investment decisions but much less so in their driving, or vice versa.

T   F   1-20. Decisions made by an individual tend to be riskier than group decisions.

NOTES

1. Like the experts in finance and economics, statisticians have long defined risk as the degree of dispersion of values around a central position or means, and since the operation of the insurance mechanism is based on the theory of probability, it is not surprising that many insurance experts use the statistician's definition of risk. However, the notion of risk as the relative dispersion of actual from expected results places the emphasis in an aggregate context. The relative dispersion notion is based on actuarial risk theory and is concerned primarily with the variability of the insurance company's experience. It has little relevance for the individual.

   From the standpoint of the individual policyowner, risk can be defined in many different ways. One such way is to define risk in a simple, common-sense way as the possibility of loss. This is the definition adopted for use in *Fundamentals of Insurance for Financial Planning*, B.T. Beam, D.L. Bickelhaupt, and R.M. Crowe (Bryn Mawr, PA: The American College), 2000.

2. "Wager" may be a poor choice of words. Although gambling can exhibit many of the attributes of insurance, it is not insurance. Nonetheless, so many uniformed persons think of insurance as gambling and sometimes even feel that they have "lost the bet" if they fail to have a loss equal to the cost of insurance. The distinction is not in the method of operation, which may appear similar, but in the fact that insurance is concerned with an existing risk. Risk as an existing condition is what removes insurance from the category of gambling. Insurance does not create risk, but it transfers and reduces a risk that already exists. Contrast this to a bet: No risk exists before, but one is created at the time of the gambling transaction, thus putting values in jeopardy that were not in jeopardy before the bet.

3. Not all long-term capital gains of individuals are eligible for the maximum rate of 20 percent. First, the portion of long-term gain from the sale of depreciable real property that is attributable to unrecaptured depreciation claimed on the property is taxed at a 25 percent maximum rate. Second, long-term gain from the sale of "collectible" capital assets is taxed at a maximum rate of 28 percent rather than 20 percent. "Collectible" assets include works of art, rugs, antiques, stamps or coins, precious stones and metals, and alcoholic beverages. Third, to the extent that the 15 percent marginal tax rate on ordinary income would otherwise apply to the capital gain, the maximum rate on long-term gain is reduced from 20 percent to 10 percent. This means that individuals in the 15 percent tax bracket will pay a 10 percent tax on their long-term capital gains up to the point where their total taxable income, including such gains, exceeds the maximum amount subject to the 15 percent bracket. Any additional gains will be subject to the 20 percent maximum rate. Fourth, there are special rules that will apply to sales of capital assets by individuals taking place after December 31, 2000.

4. P. Slovic, "Psychological Study of Human Judgment: Implications for Investment Decision Making," *Journal of Finance*, September 1992, pp. 779–799.

2

Types of Investments

Learning Objectives

An understanding of the material in this chapter should enable the student to

---

2-1. Describe the various types of both short- and long-term debt securities.

2-2. Describe the various types of equity and equity-related securities.

2-3. Describe several other investment types, including real estate, commodities, collectors' items, and nontraditional investments.

Chapter Outline

The preceding chapter laid the necessary groundwork so that we can now effectively explore some of the more important types of investments. This chapter discusses investments in three categories: debt securities, equity investments, and less common investments including real estate, commodities, collectors' items, and nontraditional investments. The chapter is designed as an overview. A more detailed discussion of many of these investments is presented later in the book.

DEBT INSTRUMENTS

interest

Many of us are introduced to the concept of investing when a savings account is opened in our name. Such an account is a type of debt instrument, which is basically an IOU. The bank (or other type of financial institution) holding the account is in debt to the depositor for the balance in the account. The borrower, in this case the bank, is legally obligated to repay the lender (in this case the depositor) the amount deposited plus the agreed rate of periodic interest. The provisions of a savings account illustrate the nature of a debt instrument. The borrower and lender enter into a legally enforceable contract. The lender agrees to provide the borrower with a sum of money for a period of time. The borrower agrees to pay *interest* at a prespecified rate and repay principal (amount borrowed) according to the terms of the debt instrument. A savings account's principal is to be available to the depositor upon demand. Failure of the borrower to fulfill any of the contract's provisions (such as missing a scheduled interest or principal payment) constitutes a default. If the default itself is not cured, the lender may take appropriate legal action. This action may eventually result in a seizure of assets (collateral), bankruptcy, and/or liquidation of the borrower's assets.

Equity investments, by contrast, involve a share of ownership in an asset. The holder of an equity instrument (such as stock) has no more than a residual claim on the property of the instrument's issuer. The claims of the issuer's creditors have priority over those of the equity holders. On the other hand, the equity holders own all of the firm's value in excess of the creditors' claims. (Creditors in this context include employees, suppliers of raw materials, the IRS, the electric company, and so on).

Short-Term Debt Securities

securities
maturity

Debt *securities* may be classified according to the length of time until the borrower must be paid back (time until *maturity*). Securities that come due (mature) within a year are classified as short term. Short-term securities are available from a relatively large number of issuers. One of the most popular of these types of investments is the savings accounts offered by banks and thrift institutions.

credit unions

Savings accounts are both very liquid and very safe investments. Funds can normally be deposited or withdrawn at any time, and most accounts are guaranteed up to a maximum of $100,000 by a United States government agency. Accordingly, depositors need not spend much time shopping around for a "safe" bank or thrift. Rather, they should focus on convenience, service, and return. Savings institutions have generally paid similar rates. Compared with other depository institutions, *credit unions* usually offer a slightly higher government-insured return coupled with valuable borrowing privileges. Although they are safe and convenient, savings accounts generally offer very low rates to savers (compared with the market rates on other similar instruments).

certificates of deposits

FDIC

Banks also issue short-term debt instruments called *certificates of deposit*, or CDs. CDs are typically offered with maturities varying from 30 days to 5 years. Interest rates vary from bank (or other depository institution) to bank but are generally competitive with other similar instruments in the marketplace. The best CD rates banks offer are relatively attractive. Moreover, such instruments are guaranteed by the Federal Deposit Insurance Corporation (*FDIC*) up to the maximum ($100,000 per depositor per bank), as are all commercial bank and most other depository institution debt instruments.

Depository institutions were once subject to maximum rate limitations on most of their accounts and certificates (Regulation Q). Now, however, they are allowed to pay whatever rates the competitive situation calls for.

Short-Term Debt Securities (Available to Small Investors)

- Deposits in banks and thrift institutions
- Money market mutual funds
- Money market accounts
- U.S. savings bonds

Treasury bills

money market

money market funds

Money market securities (*Treasury bills*, for example) have relatively high minimum denominations ($10,000 or more). The high minimum on these securities has prevented many small investors from participating directly in the *money market*. Money market mutual funds are designed to serve small investors who want access to this market. *Money market funds* pool the resources of many individual small investors. These funds thereby accumulate relatively large sums to invest in the high-denomination money market securities that would otherwise be unavailable to small investors. Thus, money market funds assemble a diversified portfolio of money market instruments. They then package these portfolios into a form that allows small investors to participate.

After subtracting administrative expenses, money market funds yield slightly less than the rates on the money market instruments themselves. If, for example, money market returns are 6 percent, a $1,000 money market fund account would earn about 5.5 percent. These returns compare very favorably with those paid on a savings account. Money market fund deposits are readily accessible by check or wire transfer. Because most money market funds buy only high-quality short-term securities, they are considered quite safe.

The money market deposit accounts (MMDAs) offered by banks compete directly with money market mutual funds. The rates they pay are usually below those offered by money market funds. These accounts typically require a $1,000 minimum balance and allow six withdrawals (three by check) per month. They are, however, protected by FDIC insurance (up to the $100,000 maximum).

savings bonds

U.S. government *savings bonds* also compete for small investors' funds. The government issues a number of different types of savings bonds. Rates tend to be below but close to the market rates on other short-term instruments. Although they are not really short-term securities, the early redemption feature of U.S. savings bonds offers a similar degree of *liquidity*.

liquidity

Most types of savings bonds do not pay periodic interest but rather accumulate value over time. Typically, at maturity they pay $4 for every $3 invested. Early redemption leads to a yield sacrifice, however. Savings bonds do allow the investor to defer federal income taxes on their return until maturity. In addition, no state and local income taxes are assessed on interest

debt security

earned on this or any other type of federal government *debt security*.

**Money Market Debt Securities
(Available in Large Denominations That Appeal
Primarily to Large Investors)**

- Treasury bills
- Banker's acceptances
- Eurodollars
- Commercial paper
- Short-term municipals

---

municipals

A number of other types of securities also compete in the short-term market. Virtually all of these (Treasury bills, bankers' acceptances, Eurodollar deposits, commercial paper, and short-term *municipals*) are available only in large denominations. Moreover, unlike savings bonds, most do not provide an early redemption option. The owner must either hold these securities until their maturity or sell them in the marketplace. Such a sale will usually require the payment of a commission to the agent (broker) handling

face value

the sale. Moreover, as with any publicly traded security, the sale price may differ somewhat from the purchase price. The prices of these securities, however, seldom differ greatly from their cost. Their maturity and redemption at *face value* are always relatively near in time so that short-term debt securities almost always sell for a price that is relatively close to both what was paid for them and their value at redemption.

Many money market instruments are sold at a discount and mature at their face value. For example, a one-year T-bill might be sold at 95 and mature at 100, thereby earning a return of 5/95, or 5.26 percent. Other short-term instruments make periodic payments. For example, a one-year CD could be structured to pay interest each month.

In summary, short-term debt securities generally offer a very secure (sometimes government-guaranteed) return. Savings accounts are highly liquid, whereas CDs and money market instruments are somewhat less so, depending on maturity. Buying and selling these securities is seldom difficult or costly. Indeed, some issuers allow redemption prior to the securities' maturity. Little or no time commitment or special expertise is required to purchase or manage portfolios of many types of short-term debt securities. On the other hand, interest income from most of these investments is fully taxable. The returns are also often lower than those available on less liquid investments, and only the high-denomination ($10,000–$100,000) securities offer the highest short-term returns.

Bonds and Similar Long-Term Debt Instruments

bonds

Bonds are obligations to pay interest periodically and to pay principal at the end of a specified period. Bonds with a maturity date of one to 10 years in the future are considered intermediate term. Those with maturities more than 10 years in the future are called long term. The issuer's "guarantee" makes most bonds less risky than most stocks. Corporate bonds are usually as secure as the financial condition of the issuing company. Similarly, the extensive taxing power of the federal and many state and local governments

default risk

minimizes the *default risk* on their bonds. Not all cities and smaller governmental units that issue bonds are in strong financial condition, however. Also, not all municipal bonds are backed by the "full faith and

revenue bonds

credit" of the municipality. Some, known as *revenue bonds*, can be repaid only from the revenue of a particular project (such as bridge tolls).

Long-Term Debt Securities

- Corporate bonds
- Federal government notes and bonds
- State and local bonds (municipals)

risk
interest rate risk

Bond investors face two major types of *risk*: default risk and *interest rate risk*. An issuer failing to fulfill (defaulting on) its interest and/or principal obligation risks bankruptcy and possibly liquidation. Relatively few bonds default, and those that have were almost always rated as speculative shortly before their default. Thus, an investor can largely avoid default risk by investing only in nonspeculative bonds, known as investment-grade bonds, and selling any issues that get downgraded to speculative. Even in a default, the bondholder will often receive a portion of the promised principal and accrued interest. Moreover, the promised return on a bond tends to rise with its perceived risk.

The possibility of an adverse interest rate move is a major risk that long-term bond investors face. As market interest rates rise, the prices of outstanding bonds (which yield a fixed-dollar amount) decline. A bond's market price may deviate from its purchase price, but the bond will still repay its full face value at maturity. A hold-to-maturity approach, however, misses out on the higher market yields that become available when rates rise. The gain from a favorable interest rate move, on the other hand, may be limited by the call feature. *Callable bonds* permit the issuer to repurchase its issues prior to maturity, usually for a premium above their face value.

callable bonds

A bond's vulnerability to interest rate fluctuations varies directly with its maturity. The prices of debt instruments that will soon be redeemed at their face values are unlikely to fluctuate greatly. While short- and intermediate-term debt instruments are less sensitive to adverse interest rate movements, their yields are often slightly below those on otherwise comparable long-term bonds.

Major Risks of Investing in Long-Term Corporate Bonds

- Default risk: issuer fails to fulfill its interest and/or principal obligations
- Interest rate risk: as market interest rates rise, the prices of outstanding bonds decline

---

Corporate bonds are issued at $1,000 face values. Bond prices are generally quoted in percentages of 100. Therefore, a bond selling at 90 (points) is priced at $900. Bond commissions are generally set at or about $5 per bond with a $50 minimum (10 bonds). A minimum of five to 15 different companies' bonds is required for effective diversification. Thus, a diversified portfolio could easily require investing $50,000 (for at least five different positions of 10 bonds each) or more. Such a minimum sum puts serious bond investing beyond the reach of small investors.

In summary, most bonds are riskier and less liquid than most short-term debt securities, but they are typically less risky and in some cases more liquid than equity instruments. Individual bonds differ substantially in risk, *yield*, and liquidity, however. Because U.S. government bonds have no default risk, their yields are almost always below those of similar maturity corporate bonds. Moreover, corporate bond yields vary appreciably with their respective risks. Short-term bonds are more liquid than longer-term issues. Even long-term government bonds are subject to considerable interest rate risk. Bonds of well-known issuers are generally quite marketable, whereas bonds of small corporations and governmental units often trade in rather thin markets. Inexperienced investors can use bond ratings to help them select bonds that match their own risk preferences. Relatively little time or effort is required to manage most bond portfolios.

yield

EQUITY INSTRUMENTS

As previously mentioned, equity securities represent ownership shares of an asset such as a corporation. The owners have a residual claim (creditors' claims come first) on the corporation's assets and earnings. Equity-related assets include publicly traded common stock, preferred stock, options, convertibles, and mutual funds, as well as ownership positions in small firms and venture capital investments. Each of these investments represents direct or indirect ownership in a profit-seeking enterprise. Equity holders' claims are subordinate to those of all debtors but encompass all residual value and income in excess of the claims of the senior securities.

Common Stock

Common stock is by far the most important type of equity-related security. Approximately 23 percent of United States households own stock directly, while many more participate indirectly in the stock market. Such vehicles as mutual funds, trust funds, insurance company portfolios, and the invested reserves of pension funds all provide indirect access. As the residual owners, shareholders are paid *dividends* out of their firm's profits. The portion of profits not paid out (retained earnings) is reinvested in the company, thereby helping it grow. Growth in sales, assets, and particularly profits should lead to a higher overall value for the firm. The benefit of any appreciation in the firm's value accrues to its owners, the stockholders. A company's stockholders theoretically control it by electing its board of directors. The board, in turn, selects upper-level management and makes major policy decisions. Most stock ownership groups are, however, widely dispersed and unorganized. Existing management usually fills the resulting power vacuum by nominating and electing friendly slates of directors.

common stock

dividends

TABLE 2-1
Compound Annual Rates of Return by Decade

	1920s*	1930s	1940s	1950s	1960s	1970s	1980s	1990s
Large Company Stocks	19.2%	–0.1%	9.2%	19.4%	7.8%	5.9%	17.5%	18.2%
Small Company Stocks	–4.5	1.4	20.7	16.9	15.5	11.5	15.8	15.1
Long-Term Corporate Bonds	5.2	6.9	2.7	1.0	1.7	6.2	13.0	8.4
Long-Term Government Bonds	5.0	4.9	3.2	–0.1	1.4	5.5	12.6	8.8
Intermediate-Term Government Notes	4.2	4.6	1.8	1.3	3.5	7.0	11.9	7.2
U. S. Treasury Bills	3.7	0.6	0.4	1.9	3.9	6.3	8.9	4.9
Inflation	–1.1	–2.0	5.4	2.2	2.5	7.4	5.1	2.9

* Based on the period 1926–1929

Source: Stocks, Bonds, Bills, and Inflation 2000 Yearbook, © 2000 Ibbotson Associates, Inc. Based on copyrighted works by Ibbotson and Sinquefield. All rights reserved. Used with permission.

In general, stock returns compare favorably with those of most bonds and depository accounts. On the other hand, returns on particular stocks over particular periods have differed greatly from the average. Furthermore, the returns on most stocks were well below these long-term averages during much of the 1960s and 1970s (see tables 2-1 and 2-2).

Managing a portfolio of stocks effectively is not an easy task. Many books have been written on the subject, and no doubt many more will be written. Playing the stock market is and always will be a very challenging game.

Dividend payments on stocks are not assured, and common stock never matures. Thus, shareholders are particularly dependent on their firm's future profitability and market acceptance. Investors who own stocks that reduce or eliminate their dividends are likely also to see a dramatic decline in the values of their shares. Bond prices generally fluctuate much less than stock prices. Moreover, the interest that bonds promise to pay must be paid, regardless of the firm's profit picture. Bonds, therefore, almost always have less downside risk than stocks of the same or similar-risk firms.

TABLE 2-2
**Basic Series: Summary Statistics of Annual Total Returns
(From 1926 to 1999)**

Series	Geometric Mean	Arithmetic Mean	Standard Deviation
Large Company Stocks	11.3%	13.3%	20.1%
Small Company Stocks	12.6	17.6	33.6
Long-Term Corporate Bonds	5.6	5.9	8.7
Long-Term Government Bonds	5.1	5.5	9.3
Intermediate-Term Government Notes	5.2	5.4	5.8
U.S. Treasury Bills	3.8	3.8	3.2
Inflation	3.1	3.2	4.5

Source: Stocks, Bonds, Bills, and Inflation Yearbook, © 2000
Ibbotson Associates, Inc. Based on copyrighted works by Ibbotson
and Sinquefield. All rights reserved. Used with permission.

Because stocks can be bought and sold effectively in increments of as little as a few thousand dollars, the low minimum cost of a stock portfolio makes stocks relatively accessible to small investors. Commissions, however, are disproportionately high on very small transactions (less than about $1,000 and/or fewer than 100 shares).

In summary, common stock offers somewhat higher but more risky expected returns than bonds. Although some stocks are not very liquid, those of most large- and medium-size firms are quite marketable. Small investors can begin to assemble a stock portfolio with relatively modest sums. Informed stock selection requires considerable skill and time, however.

Preferred Stock

preferred stocks

Preferred stocks vary greatly in risk but, as a class, tend to be more risky than most types of debt securities. While also a form of ownership, preferred stock is generally less risky than common stock. Common dividends may be paid only after the preferred dividend requirement is satisfied. Unpaid back dividends (arrearage) on *cumulative* preferred shares must be made up before common dividends may resume. Moreover, in any reorganization of the company, the preferred shareholders must be paid the liquidation value of their stock before common stockholders receive anything. Preferred stock is senior to common, but bondholders are assured of interest income and

cumulative

principal payments before preferred stockholders receive any dividends or liquidation payments.

Preferred dividend yields are usually below the average long-term total return (dividend plus capital gains) on common stocks. As relatively fixed-income securities, preferreds are subject to the same type of interest rate risk as bonds. Moreover, most preferred shares have relatively little long-term appreciation potential. The preferred stock of a weak company may, however, be riskier and have a higher expected yield than the common stock of a stronger company.

The prices of preferreds vary inversely with interest rates. While dividends paid to individuals are fully taxed, only 30 percent of dividends paid to corporations are subject to federal tax. This special tax treatment is a particularly attractive feature for preferreds when dividends constitute most of the return.

convertible

Preferred stock is not particularly liquid, but it is generally marketable. Assembling a diversified portfolio of preferred stock requires a modest amount of time, funds, and effort. *Convertible* preferred, like convertible bonds (see below), may be exchanged for a prespecified number of shares of common stock.

Small Firm Ownership

Most people who invest in companies (for example, as shareholders) hold very small stakes in relatively large firms. Others, however, hold a relatively large stake in a small company. The small firm may be organized as a sole proprietorship, partnership, or closely held corporation. Investors may or may not take an active role in their company's affairs. Those who take an active role in their enterprise are much more involved in the management side of the business than the investment side. This management commitment may cut deeply into their time for other activities. Moreover, joint ownership can lead to troublesome policy disputes, and nonexpert part-time owner-managers may be at a disadvantage relative to specialist-competitors. Finally, valuing and ultimately selling a small business can be especially difficult.

Silent partner owners have different problems. A suitable manager may be difficult to find and/or keep. Managers may misuse their positions (legally or illegally) and, unless given a share in the firm's profits, may have less incentive than the owners to operate the business profitably. Moreover, the owners are personally liable for the unpaid debts of a partnership or sole proprietorship, and many creditors require the owners of a small corporation to cosign its loans.

Limited Partnerships and Master Limited Partnerships

Most businesses are organized as partnerships or corporations. The corporate form of organization provides limited liability for owners (shareholders) but its income is first taxed at the corporate level and its shareholders are taxed again on their income (dividends) and capital gains from the firm.

Unlike that of a corporation, the income of a partnership is taxed only once. Partnership profits, whether distributed or retained by the partnership, are treated for tax purposes as the imputed income of the partners. Partners are, however, individually and collectively liable for all of the partnership's obligations.

limited partnerships

Limited partnerships are an alternative way of organizing business enterprises. These partnerships combine the benefits of a corporation's limited liability with the single taxation advantage of a partnership. A single general partner, who is usually the organizer and may be a corporation, *does* have unlimited liability. The limited partners, however, are not generally liable for the partnership's debts and obligations beyond their initial capital contribution. Most limited partnerships have one major drawback: Because they are relatively small, their ownership units trade in very thin markets. In addition, there may be legal or contractual restrictions on the sale of a limited partnership interest.

MLP

The master limited partnership (*MLP*) is designed to overcome this drawback. Most MLPs are relatively large (compared to limited partnerships). Their ownership units are designed to trade actively in the same types of markets as stock.

MLPs have generally been organized around oil and gas holdings. Others are designed for real estate. Investing in MLPs involves many of the same advantages and disadvantages as investing in common stock. Note, however, that the stated current yields on MLPs are often inflated and unsustainable. The managers of these MLPs are depleting assets to make what appear to be attractive payouts. Moreover, the tax advantages of MLPs may well be limited by future congressional action.

Venture Capital

Venture capitalists provide risk capital to otherwise undercapitalized companies that they believe have attractive growth prospects. In exchange, venture capitalists receive ground-floor equity positions in what may turn out to be highly lucrative ventures.

venture capital

Venture capital may be used to help fund both start-up firms and undercapitalized going concerns. Most types of direct venture capital investing are available only to institutions and wealthy individuals. New ventures generally require a minimum of $500,000 or more. Investors of more modest means can, however, participate indirectly through public venture capital funds, venture capital limited partnerships, venture capital clubs, mutual funds that specialize in venturing, small business investment companies (SBICs) geared toward venture capital investing, newly public companies needing venture capital, commercial banks with venture capital components, and private venture capital funds. Regardless of how investors participate, they will find venture capital to be a risky business. Nevertheless, the potential rewards may sometimes justify the risk.

Equity-Related Securities: Direct Ownership of a Company

- Common stock: provides residual ownership of a corporation
- Preferred stock: preference over common to dividends and liquidation assets
- Small firm ownership: may be organized as corporation, partnership, or sole proprietorship
- Master limited partnership: combines the tax advantage of a partnership with the limited liability and ease of trading of a corporation
- Venture capital: gives risk capital to a start-up company

Options: Calls, Puts, Warrants, and Rights

derivative securities

Options are a type of derivative security. *Derivative securities* (derivatives) are securities whose values are related to—in fact derived from—one or more underlying securities or other assets (for example, bushels of corn).

The special feature of options is that they give the owner (holder) the choice of whether or not to engage in a particular transaction in the future. Stock options give the holder the right to acquire or dispose of an equity-related security. The owner of a *call* option has an option to buy something. The call writer sells the call buyer the right (but not the obligation) to purchase an asset, such as 100 shares of a particular stock. The contract specifies the price (called the *strike price* or *exercise price*) at which and the period over which the call may be exercised. Similarly, a *put* is a sell-option contract for a particular security, specifying the strike price, quantity, and period. Exercising the option is solely at the owner's (not the seller's) discretion. The option buyer and option writer generally have different expectations of what will happen to the price of the asset on which the option is written. For example, the call buyer will earn a profit if the price of the underlying asset rises sufficiently. Call writers, in contrast, usually profit if the asset's price does not rise above the exercise price. In that case, they earn

call

**strike price
exercise price
put**

the option premium (price paid for the option) without having to deliver the stock or other underlying asset.

Example:	Suppose an investor pays $200 for an option to buy (a call) 100 shares of stock at a strike price of 20 ($20 per share). If the stock's price subsequently rises to 30, the investor can exercise the option (buy the stock) at 20 and then immediately turn around and sell that same stock at 30. That trade would produce a gain of $1,000 ($3,000 – $2,000). After deducting the cost of the option, the set of transactions would yield a net profit of $800 (before commissions) compared with an initial cost of $200 for the call. That $800 gain amounts to a profit of 400 percent ($800/$200) of the amount invested. The same $200 could, in contrast, have purchased only 10 shares at 20, producing a $100 gain for a $10 price rise (50 percent profit). A similar profit ($800, or 400 percent) would be made on $200 invested in a put (an option to sell) at the same strike price if the price subsequently fell from $20 to $10. An adverse stock price move can, however, lead to a total loss for the option holder. The shareholder's potential loss, in percentage terms, is generally much less.

Standardized option trading began with the 1973 opening of the Chicago Board Option Exchange (CBOE) and soon spread to other exchanges. Listed options now exist for a large number of different stocks. Other options are written on stock indexes and commodities futures contracts. Most options have relatively short lives (9 months or less), and their prices are affected by random market fluctuations in their underling assets. Accordingly, successful option trading is largely the province of relatively sophisticated investors.

warrants   *Warrants*, like calls, permit their owner to purchase a particular amount of stock at a prespecified price within a prespecified period. Unlike calls, warrants are generally exercisable for relatively long periods, such as several years. Furthermore, warrants are issued by the company whose stock underlies the warrant. If the warrant is exercised, the issuing company simply issues more shares. In contrast, existing shares are used to satisfy the exercise of a call. Thus, warrants are company-issued securities whose exercise results in additional shares and generates cash for the issuer. Calls are contracts between individual investors that do not involve the underlying company. Warrants and rights are traded in the same markets that trade the stocks that underlie them.

rights   *Rights*, like warrants, are company-issued options to buy stock. Rights differ from warrants in two ways: First, rights are issued for very short-run periods. They expire in a few weeks or at most a few months from the time of their issue. Second, rights are generally exercisable at a price that is substantially less than the current market price of the stock. The issuer sets a low enough price to make immediate exercise attractive. Most rights are exercised, therefore, while the exercise of warrants is more uncertain.

> *Example:*   A right might allow an investor to buy stock at $40 when the market price is $45. Failure to exercise or sell such rights is like throwing away $5 multiplied by the number of rights. Rights are normally issued to existing shareholders on the basis of their current holdings. For instance, shareholders might receive one right for each 20 shares that they own.

Option prices tend to move in the same direction as the underlying common stock (except for puts, which move in the opposite direction from their underling stock) but with a considerably greater magnitude. As a result, options are generally considered relatively risky securities. On the other hand, writing an option on securities that are currently owned (selling a covered call) may reduce a portfolio's risk of falling in value. (This practice

hedging   of offsetting the risk of other transactions is known as *hedging*.)

Equity-Related Securities: Options

- Call: private option-to-buy contract
- Put: private option-to-sell contract
- Warrant: company-issued buy option
- Right: short-term company-issued option to buy

In summary, most listed options are quite marketable, whereas unlisted options are generally traded in thin markets. Most types of option trading are relatively risky. At least as much expertise and time are required for profitable option trading as for trading common stock.

Convertible Bonds

convertible bonds   *Convertible bonds* (convertibles) are debt securities that can be exchanged for the issuing company's stock at a preassigned ratio. Although they are technically debt instruments, their conversion feature gives them an equity-related component. Their value tends to increase with increases in the underlying stock's price. As a result, they offer a compromise between the relatively assured income of bonds and the upside potential of stock. Convertible prices tend to rise when their conversion values increase (as the underlying stock's price rises), but they are somewhat insulated from stock price declines by their value as fixed-income securities. Convertibles generally sell for more than their conversion value. Consequently, with a set amount of money, the investor can usually buy more shares of the underlying stock directly than by purchasing convertibles. Accordingly, direct stock ownership is normally more profitable in a rising market. Moreover, their conversion feature allows convertibles to be sold for lower yields than otherwise similar nonconvertible bonds. Therefore, straight bonds are generally more attractive in declining stock markets. Convertibles offer a compromise between investing in a company's stock and its nonconvertible (straight) bonds.

Convertible bonds tend to be less risky than common stock but somewhat more risky than straight bonds, since they usually are subordinated to straight bonds. Their liquidity, marketability, and minimum investment requirements are similar to those of straight bonds, but they require an amount of expertise and time commitment similar to what is required of investors in common stocks.

Mutual Funds, Closed-End Investment Companies, and Similar Investments

mutual fund

Many investors have neither the time nor the inclination to manage and monitor their investments carefully. These investors can leave most of this work to a *mutual fund*. The fund's shares represent proportional ownership of its managed investment portfolio. Funds pool the resources of many small investors. Their fund holders' money is used to assemble and manage a diversified portfolio of investments. Funds may invest in a large variety of types of investments. Most funds, however, hold portfolios of debt or equity securities. Mutual funds agree to redeem their shares at their *net asset values*

net asset values

(NAVs). A fund's NAV equals the market value of its portfolio divided by the number of its outstanding shares.

load funds
no-load funds

Some mutual funds—*load funds*—are sold by agents who receive a fee (up to 8.5 percent of the purchase price). *No-load funds*, in contrast, sell and redeem their shares through the mail, thereby eliminating the need for a sales

load

force and *load* fee. No-load fund portfolios usually offer about the same average risk-adjusted returns on their portfolios as those of load funds.

Mutual funds are classified as open-end investment companies. New shares of these funds will be issued and sold to the public if demand is sufficient. Alternatively, funds will redeem outstanding shares if their fund holders so request. Closed-end investment companies, by contrast, neither

closed-end fund

issue additional shares nor redeem them on demand. The number of outstanding shares of a *closed-end fund* is established at the time the fund is founded, and it remains relatively constant. These shares are usually listed on an exchange, although some are traded off the exchanges in the so-called over-the-counter market. (The operations of exchanges and the over-the-counter market are discussed in the next chapter.) Unlike mutual funds, closed-end share prices can vary substantially from their net asset values, and they usually trade at a discount.

unit investment trusts

Unit investment trusts and variable annuities are additional types of pooled portfolio arrangements. Unit investment trusts generally hold unmanaged portfolios. Variable annuities are much like mutual funds, but they usually offer a life guarantee component and are organized and managed by insurance companies.

Equity-Related Securities: Hybrid Debt Instruments and Indirect Equity Ownerships

- Convertible bond: debt security that may be exchanged for a prespecified amount of stock
- Mutual fund and closed-end investment company, unit investment trust, and variable annuity: pooled portfolios of securities and other types of investments

---

The investment goals and portfolio compositions of mutual funds differ widely. Portfolios may be made up of low-risk or speculative bonds or stocks, tax-exempt securities, short-term highly liquid securities, combinations of stocks and bonds, and so on. Still other mutual funds invest in such assets as options, commodities, and collectibles. Thus, mutual fund investors can choose from a wide array of characteristics. Average mutual fund performance does not differ appreciably from and is generally not superior to the average market performance.

In summary, mutual fund risks, liquidities, and tax treatments vary greatly. An investor can begin with as little as $500 or $1,000 in a mutual fund. Most mutual funds are well diversified and, as such, are considerably less risky than most individual common stocks or small portfolios consisting of a few different stocks. Investors with sufficient resources can assemble their own diversified portfolios of common stocks tailored to their own particular circumstances although the commitment of time and effort may be substantial. No-load funds are at least as liquid and marketable as individual common stocks. Load funds are more costly to trade, however. While mutual funds require less time and expertise than individually managed portfolios, selecting a suitable fund does require some effort.

OTHER INVESTMENTS

In addition to debt and equity securities, there are two other important investment types to consider: real estate and commodity futures contracts. Other somewhat less common investments (in terms of total market values) are collectibles, noncollectibles, and Ponzi schemes.

Real Estate

Many large fortunes have been built from small initial investments in real estate. Real estate investing offers the potential of large percentage profits, as well as a number of tax advantages. On the other hand, many small investors' life savings have been wiped out by the Florida land boom-bust in the 1920s and other less spectacular real estate market collapses. Many bank failures in the late 1980s and early 1990s (for example, First Republic Bank in Texas and the Bank of New England) can be traced to a collapse in real estate values.

Real estate investors have good reasons to be cautious:

- The more debt (leverage) used to finance real estate purchases, the greater the risks. Yet one of the primary attractions of real estate as an investment is the ability to use debt to finance a large percentage of the cost.
- The one-of-a-kind nature of individual real estate investments makes such properties relatively difficult and costly to buy and sell. Having to sell real estate on short notice can result in a substantial sacrifice.
- Determining a fair value for a prospective real estate investment requires considerable expertise.
- Managing improved property is a time-consuming task.
- Real estate commissions are considerably higher than those on securities. So real estate is more difficult, time consuming, and costly to buy and sell than most other types of investments.
- Most real estate purchases require a relatively large initial investment (down payment).

In summary, real estate may offer attractive returns to investors with the required talents, but securities markets demand less time and expertise, offer greater liquidity, and are generally less risky. The stock of real estate-related companies provides an interesting compromise. Real estate investment trusts (REITs) are yet another way of participating. Like MLPs, REITs offer the tax advantages of partnerships and the limited liabilities and ease of trading of the corporate form or organization. To continue to qualify as REITs, however, they must meet rather strict IRS requirements. They must derive almost all of their income from rents and mortgages on real estate, and they must pay out at least 95 percent of that income each year.

Futures Contracts

futures contracts

Futures contracts represent another major investment area. Like options, futures contracts are derivatives. Their values are derived from the values of the underlying assets on which the contracts are based. Futures speculators and hedgers buy (go "long") and sell (go "short") contracts for future delivery of a prespecified amount of some commodity, such as so many ounces of silver, bushels of corn, or thousands of dollars worth of T-bills at

commodities

the full futures contract value. Standardized *commodities* contracts are traded on various commodity exchanges.

To execute a trade, commodity market participants are required only to deposit between 5 percent and 15 percent of the contract's value. As a result, any given percentage price fluctuation is magnified 7 to 20 times in terms of profit or loss.

Example: Buying a 6-month contract valued at $100,000 (a "long" position) might require a 10 percent margin ($10,000 in earnest money). A 20 percent increase in the contract's value (to $120,000) would produce a profit of $20,000 (less commissions), or 200 percent of the original $10,000 investment. A 10 percent fall in the contract's price would, however, wipe out the original $10,000 investment. In contrast, selling such a contract (a "short" position) would result in a loss if prices rose and a gain if prices fell.

Most brokerage firms require individuals seeking to open a commodity trading account to establish a relatively large beginning balance (initial deposit of funds) and to have a substantial net worth. Commissions on commodity trades are only a tiny fraction of the potential gains or losses.

Predicting price movements generally involves outguessing the commodity market's consensus expectations of weather conditions, government intervention, consumer and producer attitudes, and any other factors that may influence the underlying commodity's supply and demand. Its risky nature and the need for a very special understanding of a complex market, therefore, make futures speculation a tough challenge for most individual investors. Some traders, however, use futures markets to hedge their risks. For example, a farmer might sell soybean futures and, in effect, tie down a price for his or her expected soybean harvest. Others may assemble relatively complicated but lower-risk combination positions that depend on relative price movements (such as straddles, which are short and long positions on related futures contracts).

In summary, commodity speculation is generally quite risky. Futures contracts are marketable but illiquid. Substantial expertise, time, and resources are required. Still, some individual investors find the fast-paced action and potential for rapid riches (coupled with at least as great a potential for disaster) very appealing.

Collectibles

collectibles

Although a relatively minor investment medium, *collectibles* have grown substantially in popularity in recent years. As an indication of their importance, both *Barron's* and *Forbes* report the Sotheby Index of prices on a variety of types of art, ceramic, silver, and furniture collectibles.

A bewildering assortment of items are now considered collectibles. Investments in such assets are usually relatively illiquid and very speculative. Collectibles are generally sold at a high markup, subject to a substantial fraud risk, and they involve all of the uncertainties present in the more traditional types of investing. Nonetheless, success stories abound. Investors should enter the collectibles market very cautiously (if at all), so that their initial mistakes are made with relatively small sums.

Coins, stamps, art, and antiques have long been of interest to collectors. For almost as long, investors have sought to profit from the price appreciation that must "certainly" follow the "inevitable" growth of the hobby. As prices have risen for established collectibles, many newer hobbies have sprung up to take advantage of the lower prices on what had until then been thought of as out-of-date junk.

New collectible areas seem to go through a relatively predictable cycle. First, everything is very cheap and most collectors are amateur hobbyists. As time passes, the hobby becomes more commercial. The entry of professional dealers and serious investors causes prices to rise. For a while all is well, as increased public interest raises the market value of everyone's material. New investors, attracted by the sharp increase in values, drive prices still higher. Eventually, however, the arrival of unscrupulous promoters increases the likelihood of fraud, unconscionable markups, and incorrectly graded (overgraded) material. Many novice investors are taken in by these people. Once they discover what has been done to them, their interest in the hobby is likely to wane.

After those most likely to enter the collectible areas have been attracted, the hobby's growth rate slows. Some collectors become bored and drop out. Higher prices further discourage potential interest. Without growing numbers of hobbyists, prices soften. Some investors who entered the hobby for its profit potential may try to sell. They soon find that buying interest will only absorb their collections at appreciably lower prices. Declining prices may lead others to sell or stop buying. The area may even experience a temporary panic. Baseball cards and Beanie Babies are examples of hobbies that have recently gone through this cycle.

Selling is one of the most difficult aspects of investing in collectibles. Investors may, of course, use the same outlets to sell as they used to buy, but this approach may not always be best. Transaction costs are likely to be quite high.

Noncollectibles and Investment Scams

Collectibles constitute one class of nontraditional investments. Additional nontraditional investments include Broadway shows, movies, California vineyards, discos, coal mines, computerized home-delivery groceries, racehorses, baseball clubs, and freight cars; and the list goes on and on. Some of these investment media may be worth pursuing, but others should be avoided entirely due to their inherent risk and lack of an efficient market mechanism to assess the value of the investments. Some of these can be quite legitimate but so specialized that only the aficionados will stand a chance of breaking even.

Dozens of examples of offbeat investments with disastrous results can be cited. Gross mismanagement, highly inflated prices, and totally unrealistic profit forecasts are all too common. Anyone considering a nontraditional investment outlet should exercise extreme caution. While most traditional investments (securities, real estate, and commodities) are risky, at least the investor has a better idea of past history and a modicum of regulatory protection. All too often investors in offbeat investments have almost no knowledge of the subject—a nearly certain recipe for disaster.

Ponzi Schemes

Ponzi scheme

The *Ponzi scheme* is not a true investment, but it is sold as one. Ponzis are a classic type of investment fraud. Promoters of Ponzi schemes attract purchasers by promising high "yields" that they secretly plan to finance from later investors' capital, at least as long as the money holds out. These schemes are inverted pyramids that need ever larger new "investments" to pay returns on earlier "investments." Eventually, not enough new money is brought in, and the scheme collapses. Those holding such "investments" are left with little or nothing.

Ponzi schemes were named after Charles Ponzi who, in 1919, promised $1.40 in 90 days for each $1 "invested." Ten million dollars were taken in before the fraud was discovered and Ponzi was sent to jail. He later died in Brazil in impoverished obscurity. Since Ponzi's time, numerous imitators have appeared.

A Ponzi scheme can utilize almost any type of investment medium. A number have involved chain letters applied to whiskey, savings bonds, and gold. Others have used the appeal of oil wells, precious metals, and gemstones. Investors should always be wary of returns that seem unrealistically high. By the time the scheme is revealed, usually almost nothing is left for the "investors."

Investments Other Than Debt or Equity Securities

- Real estate: land and property that is permanently attached to it
- Commodity futures: contracts calling for deferred delivery of some physical commodity
- Collectibles: diverse array of tangible assets
- Noncollectibles: diverse array of investments, including Broadway shows, coal mines, race horses, sports clubs, freight cars, etc.
- Ponzi schemes: frauds that secretly pay out high returns from principal

SUMMARY AND CONCLUSIONS

Generalizing about the various types of investments is difficult. Clearly, each type has advantages and disadvantages. Although this book has discussed an assortment of the more popular investment vehicles, the list is by no means complete. Such diverse investments as wildcat oil wells, equipment leases, and currency speculation were not covered.

Very conservative investors may prefer fixed-income investments, such as savings accounts, bonds, and preferred stock. Commodities futures or options may be attractive to more speculative investors. Those with the time and special expertise may find real estate, collectors' items, or small businesses appealing. Investors with limited time, funds, expertise, and willingness to take risks may find common stock and related securities (convertible bonds, convertible preferreds, warrants, mutual funds) an attractive compromise.

Investors should, however, carefully consider any investment opportunity before making a commitment. In particular, whenever an unrealistically high return is offered, the investor should be wary of a possible Ponzi scheme or other undisclosed risks.

CHAPTER REVIEW

Answers to the review questions and the self-test questions start on page 740.

Key Terms

interest	cumulative
securities	convertible
maturity	limited partnerships
credit unions	MLP
certificates of deposit	venture capital
FDIC	derivative securities
Treasury bills	call
money market	strike price
money market funds	exercise price
savings bonds	put
liquidity	warrants
debt security	rights
municipals	hedging
face value	convertible bonds
bonds	mutual fund
default risk	net asset values
revenue bonds	load funds
risk	no-load funds
interest rate risk	load
callable bonds	closed-end fund
yield	unit investment trusts
common stock	futures contracts
dividends	commodities
preferred stocks	collectibles
	Ponzi scheme

Review Questions

2-1. a. Identify the dimensions of risk, return, liquidity, marketability, minimum investment size, investment effort, and moral and ethical appeal (using L for little, M for moderate, H for high, and N for neutral) for the following types of fixed-income securities: savings deposits, savings bonds, money market mutual funds, Treasury bonds, corporate bonds, and municipal bonds.

   b. Describe any special tax treatments that apply to any of the fixed-income securities listed in a. above.

2-2. What would be the typical bond commission for each for the following trades?
   a. purchasing seven bonds for a per-bond price of 70
   b. selling 15 bonds for a per-bond price of 105
   c. purchasing three bonds for a per-bond price of 56

2-3. Compute the commission percentage for the dollar figures in question 2-2.

2-4. a. Identify the dimensions of risk, return, liquidity, marketability, minimum investment size, investment effort, and moral and ethical appeal (using L for little, M for moderate, and H for high) for common stock and preferred stock.
   b. Describe the tax treatment resulting from the ownership and sale of common stock and preferred stock.

2-5. a. Describe the major characteristics of limited partnerships that make them attractive to investors.
   b. What major drawback of limited partnerships inspired the development of master limited partnerships?

2-6. Compute the after-tax yield for a preferred stock with a before-tax return (all in the form of dividends) of 7.5 percent for an individual in the 28 percent tax bracket and a corporation in the 36 percent tax bracket.

2-7. Assume equal amounts are invested in venture capital opportunities with the following returns: 80 percent, –25 percent, –15 percent, 12 percent, 105 percent, –80 percent, 350 percent, –100 percent, and 0 percent.
   a. What would the overall return from venturing be?
   b. If these returns were earned over a 5-year period, what would the per-period (annual) geometric mean return be?

2-8. a. Compute the percentage holding-period return for an investment in a stock purchased at 20 and sold for 30.
   b. Assume that call options were bought with a striking price of 20 for the price of 2 and exercised when the stock reached 30, with the resulting stock position then sold. What would the holding period return be?

2-9. Compare warrants to each of the following:
   a. calls
   b. rights

2-10. a. Compute the holding period return for a fund purchased with a NAV of 10 and sold when the NAV reached 12. Assume an 8.5 percent front-end load is charged at purchase time.
   b. How much would the holding period return be if the fund (in a. above) were no-load?

2-11. Give several reasons why real estate investors should be cautious.

2-12. Assume an investor purchases a futures contract having a value of $150,000 with a 10 percent margin.
   a. How much would the investor be required to have in his or her margin account?
   b. Ignoring commissions and taxes, assume the investor closes out his or her position right after its value rises to $200,000. In this situation, what is the gain as a percentage of the amount originally invested?

Self-Test Questions

T F 2-1. Depository institutions are subject to maximum rate limitations on most of their accounts and certificates.

T F 2-2. Money market securities have relatively high minimum denominations ($10,000 or more).

T F 2-3. Most types of savings bonds do not pay periodic interest but rather accumulate value over time.

T F 2-4. The possibility of an adverse interest rate move is a major risk that long-term bond investors face.

T F 2-5. Approximately 75 percent of U.S. households own stock directly.

T F 2-6. Stock prices generally fluctuate much less than bond prices.

T F 2-7. Preferred stock is not very marketable, but it is generally liquid.

T F 2-8. Master limited partnerships (MLPs) have generally been organized around oil and gas holdings.

T F 2-9. Warrants are generally exercisable for relatively long periods, such as several years.

T F 2-10. Calls are sold by the company whose stock underlies the call.

T F 2-11. A mutual fund's net asset value (NAV) equals the market value of its portfolio divided by the number of its outstanding shares.

T F 2-12. Mutual funds are classified as closed-end investment companies, which neither issue new shares nor redeem outstanding shares.

T F 2-13. Futures contracts are derivatives whose values are derived from the values of the underlying assets on which the contracts are based.

T F 2-14. Commissions on commodity trades are a large portion of the potential gains or losses.

T   F   2-15. Ponzi schemes are inverted pyramids that need ever larger new "investments" to pay returns on earlier "investments."

3

The Securities Markets

Learning Objectives

An understanding of the material in this chapter should enable the student to

---

3-1. Explain the role of brokers and investment managers, and describe the markets where securities are traded.

3-2. Explain the mechanics of executing transactions, and describe the methods for minimizing trading costs.

3-3. Describe the mechanics of margin trading and short selling.

3-4. Explain the various institutional arrangements for handling new issues and large trades.

3-5. Explain the state of securities regulation, and describe the emerging central market system.

3-6. Explain how securities markets impact on economic performance.

Chapter Outline

This chapter explores the mechanics, regulation, and economic functions of the securities markets. Although common stocks are the principal focus, preferred stocks and warrants are traded in virtually identical fashions. Moreover, the listed option, mutual fund, and bond markets have much in common with the stock market. Thus, the topics this chapter covers apply to much of the investment scene.

This chapter deals largely with the mechanics of the securities market. First, the basics are covered. The broker's role is explored, followed by a discussion of investment managers, exchanges, and the over-the-counter market. Then the chapter examines commissions, bid-ask spreads, and types of orders in the context of how to minimize transaction costs. This is followed by a discussion of short selling and margin trading. Then various specialized institutional arrangements for trading stock are considered: third and fourth markets, new issues, private placements, rights offerings, secondary distributions, block trades, and tender offers.

After market mechanics have been covered in some detail, securities market regulation is discussed. This regulation is first put in its historical context, and then progress toward a competitive central market is analyzed. The third and final topic of this chapter is the function of the securities market in the economy, particularly its capital allocation role. How the securities market helps allocate managerial talent and how it helps the Federal Reserve Board (the Fed) implement monetary policy are also considered.

THE MECHANICS OF THE SECURITIES MARKETS

Unlike the purchase of a can of beans at the supermarket, buying and selling stocks and bonds frequently involve a variety of relatively complex trading arrangements. For example, brokers, exchanges, third and fourth markets, limit orders, specialists, margin purchases, stock certificates, and commissions may play a role.

Brokers and Brokerage Firms

broker
brokerage firm

registered representative

An investor's principal link to the securities market is through his or her broker. The term broker is frequently used to refer to both the individual employee and the employing firm. To minimize such confusion, here the term *broker* will mean the employee, and *brokerage firm* or *brokerage house* will refer to the employer. In securities industry jargon, the term "broker" or "broker-dealer" applies to the brokerage firm. The individual employee is referred to as a *registered representative*.

Brokers and their firms perform a number of functions, the most basic of which is linking investors to the securities markets. Stock brokers implement

dealers

their customers' trading instructions. *Dealers*, in contrast, trade for their own accounts and make markets by advertising a willingness to buy and sell.

In addition to facilitating trades, most full-service brokerage firms engage in a variety of other activities, such as offering investment advice, holding customers' securities, sending out periodic account statements, lending money on the collateral value of certain securities (margin loans), and acting as investment bankers (marketing new security issues and large blocks of already outstanding securities called secondary offerings). One easy way to remember the distinction is to think of an investment banker or underwriter as a wholesaler of securities, while a broker-dealer is like a retailer of securities. Some brokerage firms also manage and sell mutual funds, make a market in unlisted securities, sell life insurance, offer and manage various types of pension plans, manage some customer accounts individually, provide access to commodity exchanges, deal in government securities, sell tax-sheltered annuities, and so on. As brokerage firms have expanded into new areas, other types of financial service firms have expanded into their areas. The lines between brokerage and other types of financial service firms, particularly commercial banks, are quickly eroding,

Glass-Steagall Act

and the erosion is likely to accelerate with the recent repeal of *Glass-Steagall Act* (the Bank Act of 1933). Indeed, some nonfinancial firms have entered the field, mainly through acquisitions. Some of these financial conglomerates offer an entire array of financial services, including checking, credit cards, travelers' checks, personal loans, insurance, pension packages, and real estate trading and management, as well as the traditional brokerage functions.

What Should Investors Expect of a Broker?

Investors need to know what is realistic and what is unrealistic to expect from their brokers. Brokers should implement customers' orders effectively and quickly correct their own firm's errors. Full-service brokers also provide customers with investment advice. While investors should not accept this advice on blind faith, discussing prospective trades with their brokers often gives some perspective.

Many investors, particularly beginning investors, have rather unrealistic expectations. They do not understand why their brokers cannot select some surefire winners and thereby make the investors a lot of money in a hurry. They want to know which stocks are going to undergo a quick and certain increase. Individuals with crystal balls, however, would not need to earn their livings as brokers. Brokers usually act as investment counselors, not investment managers. Moreover, an individual broker can follow only a small fraction of the more than 10,000 actively traded U.S. stocks. Brokers, therefore, are often unfamiliar with the issues that interest particular investors. Accordingly, investors should either assume full responsibility for their portfolio management or hire a mutual fund or investment manager.

Indeed, many investors have switched to discount or Internet brokers who offer minimal service but low-cost executions. Although seeking investment miracles from a broker is unrealistic, investors have every right to expect financial soundness and integrity.

Bankruptcy of Brokerage Firms

SIPC
FDIC

Prior to 1971, customers of failed Big Board firms were compensated by the NYSE through membership assessments. While no failure of a NYSE member ever cost a customer money, by late 1970 the trust fund was exhausted. The solvent NYSE members opposed further assessments. Congress then set up the Securities Investor Protection Corporation (*SIPC*) patterned after the Federal Deposit Insurance Corporation (*FDIC*) that protects deposits in banks. SIPC protects brokerage customers against losses that would otherwise result from the failure of their brokerage firm. Of course, customers are not protected against losses due to market fluctuations. SIPC liquidates troubled firms at the SEC's request. Customers are insured up to $500,000, not more than $100,000 of which may be in cash. Any claims above those sums are applied against the firm's available assets during liquidation. Most brokerage firms, however, have purchased additional insurance.

In the past, the SIPC has taken as long as several months to complete a liquidation. As a result, many of the bankrupt firm's investors are locked into their portfolio until the liquidation is complete. Furthermore, the securities of bankrupt brokerage firms' margin customers are sold to pay loans. These investors must incur commission charges on the sale and repurchase (perhaps at higher prices) if they are to restore their positions.

Integrity of Brokerage Houses

NASD
SEC

Most brokers and brokerage firms are honest. The exchanges, the National Association of Securities Dealers (*NASD*) and the Securities and Exchange Commission (*SEC*), try to monitor the brokerage industry closely. Those found guilty of serious wrongdoing can even lose their license to work in the industry. Still, improprieties such as the following are uncovered with some frequency:

- conflicts of interest: Potential conflicts are raised by managing mutual funds, underwriting securities, making a market in some stocks, and advising customers. Most firms, however, take great pains to avoid even the appearance of a conflict.
- kickbacks: Order clerks may receive kickbacks to steer over-the-counter (OTC) orders to particular market makers. The cost of

paying for the kickback is passed on to the customer in the form of higher prices.

- misuse of customer assets: Brokerage firms sometimes use customers' funds and the collateral value of their securities for positioning stocks and operating expenses. As long as the firm remains solvent, the customer is not likely to be harmed, but the practice is questionable, dangerous, and illegal.
- embezzlement: Alert customers should quickly detect misappropriation of their assets by carefully monitoring their monthly statements. Because the brokerage firm is responsible for any employee's fraud, the stolen property should be easy to recover, if detected.
- improper use of discretionary authority: Sometimes brokers trade without specific customer approval. Customers who give their broker limited or complete discretionary money management powers may thereby encourage excessive buying and selling of securities for the purpose of generating commissions rather than for the customer's benefit. This practice, known as *churning*, is considered unethical, and brokers caught churning are subject to disciplinary action.

churning

Investment Managers

Professional investment management services are offered by brokerages, mutual funds, and many other financial service providers, such as banks, insurance companies, insurance agents, and financial planners. Individuals with $100,000 or more have long been able to hire a portfolio manager. Many investment advisory firms and banks will handle portfolios as small as $10,000, making professional advice available to investors of rather modest means. Accounts of less than $100,000 are generally managed as part of a pool, with a pro rata return assigned to each account. Accounts of $100,000 or more may be managed individually.

The risk-adjusted returns of the average mutual fund are generally comparable to but no higher than those of the market averages. Advisers often charge a management fee of up to 2 percent of assets (on small accounts) compared with fees of about 0.5 percent for most mutual funds. Investors can even hire someone to help select and monitor the manager. *No-load* (that is, no sales commission) *mutual funds*, however, offer small investors greater diversification and lower management fees, but less specialized attention than most investment advisers. Those who do decide to use an investment adviser may find the following questions useful in choosing one:

no-load mutual funds

- How does the firm make its money? Some base their fee on the account's assets. Others charge commissions for the work done, which can prove more costly.
- Is financial counseling the only service offered? An investor should know in advance if the firm also sells insurance, tax shelters, pension packages, or mutual funds.
- Is the firm independently owned? If it is owned by a bank or a brokerage house, how independent is it? Does it do its own research, for instance?
- Will the firm provide at least three reliable business references, such as a top local banker? (The investor should not, however, expect an adviser to supply client names.)
- What is the firm's track record? Will it list its recent market selections and fully explain its investment philosophy?
- How many accounts does one portfolio manager handle? High-quality firms assign each manager no more than 20 to 60 accounts. Some firms hesitate to answer this question, but the investor should press the point.
- Does the firm use a limited power of attorney? Otherwise, how would it handle a situation requiring quick attention when the owner is unavailable?
- Will the firm contact clients, if necessary, while they are traveling? If the account is large and the service personalized, a conscientious firm should even be willing to phone overseas.

Whether the investor wants to manage his or her own investments, hire an investment manager, or purchase mutual fund shares is an individual decision. The investor should take into account the sum to be invested, the time available, and his or her goals. Presumably, many of the readers of this book intend to manage their own investments.

TYPES OF SECURITIES MARKETS

Regardless of how the portfolio is managed, securities must be bought and sold. Potential buyers could try to find sellers themselves, but relatively few people wish to trade any one stock at a particular time. The need to bring buyers and sellers together efficiently led to centralized facilities (exchanges) for trading stocks, bonds, commodities, and options. Other trading takes place in somewhat less organized over-the-counter markets.

The Stock Exchanges

NYSE

NYSE (New York Stock Exchange) listed companies produce a large percentage of the economy's gross domestic product. Most other exchanges tend to follow NYSE rules. Only members can transact business on the exchange, and only listed securities may be traded. Large established firms are generally traded on the Big Board. The NYSE has about 2,500 listed companies and about 3,000 listed securities, including preferred shares.

New York Stock Exchange

- Only members can transact business.
- Only listed securities can be traded.
- About 2,500 companies are listed.
- About 3,000 securities are listed.

AMEX

Smaller firms may be listed on the American Stock Exchange (*AMEX*), which is the second largest in terms of primary listings (about 1,000 issues listed). Still smaller firms have their primary listing on the regional exchanges. Most of the regional exchanges' trading volume, however, involves NYSE listed securities. Some exchanges permit trading other exchanges' listings, and many stocks are listed on more than one exchange (dual listings). To become listed, a firm meeting the requirements must apply, pay a fee, and not engage in any practice prohibited by the exchange.

NASDAQ and the Over-the-Counter Market

Although most large firms are listed on a stock exchange, numerous smaller publicly owned firms, and even several hundred NYSE-eligible companies, are unlisted. Their stock trades in the over-the-counter (OTC) market, an informal network of market makers who offer to buy and sell unlisted securities. Many listed companies (which trade primarily on an exchange) are also traded *OTC*. To trade in the OTC market, an investor would have his or her broker ask the brokerage firm's trading department to contact an appropriate OTC dealer.

OTC

Until the National Association of Securities Dealers (NASD) set up the National Association of Securities Dealers Automated Quotations (*NASDAQ*), OTC stocks were relatively difficult to trade. Now, however, NASDAQ connects the quoting dealers and brokers and reports the best available prices for NASDAQ issues.

NASDAQ

NASDAQ securities are listed in one of three categories of OTC quotations. The National Market Issues (*NMI*) list contains the largest and most actively traded issues. National Market Issue newspaper quotations use

NMI

the same format as NYSE and AMEX securities. About 4,000 firms are "listed" on the NMI. More than 1,100 smaller firms appear on the NASDAQ's SmallCap List. Another group of much smaller NASDAQ OTC issues are included on the Bulletin Board.

Three Categories of NASDAQ OTC Quotations

- National Market Issues (NMI): largest and most actively traded stocks
- SmallCap List: smaller firms
- Bulletin Board: much smaller issues

Table 3-1 shows company listing requirements for the NYSE, the AMEX, and the NMI category of NASDAQ.

TABLE 3-1
Company Listing Requirements (as of 2000)

	NYSE	NASDAQ/NMI	AMEX
Pretax income (last year)	$2.5 million	$.75 million	$.75 million
Net tangible assets	None	$4 million	$4 million
Shares publicly held	1.1 million	1 million	.5 million
Market value of public shares	$100 million	$50 million	$3 million
Number of round lot holders	2,000	300	400
Minimum share price	None	$4	$3

Pink Sheets

The National Daily Quotation Service reports the bid and ask prices for all actively traded OTC issues (about 6,000 NASDAQ and 22,000 other issues). These price quotations appear daily in the *Pink Sheets*, copies of which are available at most brokerage firms. Investors who want a current quotation of a Pink Sheet stock need to have their brokers call one or more of the firms listed as making a market in the stock for a price. The phone numbers of these firms are listed in the Pink Sheets.

In 1999, NASDAQ and AMEX merged. As a result, they now have a common governance board and a common web site. Nonetheless, the two markets continued to operate much as before. The AMEX remains an exchange for medium-size companies, and NASDAQ continues to facilitate unlisted trading in the OTC market. Perhaps in time the combined operation will seek to compete more effectively with the NYSE for larger capitalization companies.

Size of the Stock Markets

In 1998, about 169 billion shares changed hands on the NYSE. NASDAQ volume was about 202 billion; AMEX was 7.3 billion. These numbers are not directly comparable, however. NYSE share prices average two to three times those of AMEX issues, and the NASDAQ average price is even lower than that of the AMEX. Moreover, the frequency with which a given share is traded varies from market to market. Finally, institutional trading makes up a much larger part of NYSE volume than that of the AMEX or NASDAQ.

Other Securities Markets

Preferred stocks, warrants, and rights are traded on the same exchanges and OTC markets as common stocks. Standardized options (specifying strike price and delivery date) are also traded on a number of exchanges. While corporate bonds may be listed on exchanges, most are traded over-the-counter. Moreover, unlike warrants and preferred stock, bonds have a different commission structure, and bond trading on an exchange is generally physically separated from equity trading. In addition to buying or selling a bond, bond trades usually include an adjustment for interest accrued on the bond since the last interest payment date. Although some U.S. government bond trading takes place on exchanges, the vast majority of trades are handled by a small number of OTC government bond dealers. Commercial paper, large CDs, municipal bonds, and other money market instruments trade primarily in similar OTC markets. Commodity exchanges differ substantially from stock exchanges.

The Ticker Tape

ticker tape

Actual transactions for listed securities are reported on the *ticker tape*. Many brokerage houses display the ticker tape on a large electronic screen in their offices. The ticker tape is also available on a few cable television stations, such as those of the Consumer News and Business Channel (CNBC). Each stock has an identifying ticker symbol. For example, the symbol "T" stands for telephone (American Telephone and Telegraph), and "XRX" is Xerox. Volume and price information for each transaction appear below the company ticker symbol. A typical ticker tape reading is shown in figure 3-1. The first entry, DCX with 6 3/4 below, reports a single round-lot (100 shares) sale of Daimler Chrysler Corporation at $66.75 per share. The second entry, X with by 2s 9 below, indicates a trade of 200 shares (2s) of USX at $29 per share. The entry LDW, with 2700 7 1/2, reports that 2,700 shares of Laidlaw traded at $7.50 each. Those who follow the tape are expected to know the general price range for the stocks they follow. The full number of shares is displayed for trades of 1,000 shares or more. Company names and the corresponding ticker symbols are contained in some investment references, such as the *S&P Stock Guide*, and most brokerage houses keep booklets with the same information.

FIGURE 3-1 **Typical Ticker Tape Reading**			
DCX	X	LDW	
6 3/4	2s 9	2700	7 1/2

TRANSACTION COSTS

Securities investing involves three basic processes:

- selection: what to trade, including how to screen a large list of potential investments to arrive at a relatively small number of candidates for more detailed study
- timing: when to trade, including economic analysis designed to forecast the market's direction
- execution: how to trade, especially how to trade cheaply and effectively

Most books and articles on investing deal with what and when to trade. How to trade effectively at the lowest costs is often ignored or treated only briefly. Nevertheless, relevant techniques are not only worthwhile but are also considerably more straightforward to apply than the various approaches to successful timing and selection. The sections that follow deal with the two major costs of executing a trade:

- commissions (broker fees)
- spreads (wholesale/retail markups)

Basic Processes of Securities Investing

- Selection
- Timing
- Execution

commissions

Commissions

Security market commission rates were long fixed by agreement among the brokerage firms. Indeed, the so-called Buttonwood agreement setting up the original New York Stock Exchange in the late 18th century had a rate-fixing clause. In the 1930s, the SEC assumed regulatory authority over the rate structure. Thirty years later, rates were still being fixed.

Deregulated Rates

By the late 1960s, institutional traders made up a large and growing percentage of stock market volume. These institutional traders began to find various ways around the high fixed commissions. The brokerage industry was forced to respond by making commission setting competitive. Since May 1, 1975, each brokerage firm has set its own schedule rather than agreeing to some common formula.

A hypothetical commission formula based on that of a large retail brokerage firm is illustrated in table 3-2. If this table is applied to a 200-share trade of a $15 stock, for example, the commission on the principal value of $3,000 would be $30 plus 1.25 percent of $3,000 ($37.50). In addition, a lot charge of $8 per round lot, or $16, is applicable. This commission of $83.50 ($30.00 + $37.50 + $16.00) is equivalent to 2.78 percent of the $3,000 principal. Commissions on trades of this size (a few thousand dollars) average about 2 percent to 3 percent of the dollar value of the trade. Commissions on larger transactions are generally less than these percentages; those on smaller trades are proportionately more.

Discount Commissions

The end of fixed commissions greatly expanded potential competition among brokerage firms. At first, this reform primarily benefited institutional customers, such as mutual funds, insurance companies, and bank trust departments. Although full-service firms are willing to negotiate discounts with their large individual customers, most do not compete openly on a price basis. Small investors will generally find more attractive rates at discount brokers—and today, Internet trading offers the least expensive (and fastest growing) method for the small investor. Some discounters' rates are a specific percentage below the old fixed rates, whereas other schedules are based on the dollar value of the trade, the number of shares traded, or a combination of factors.

In addition to executing trades, a few discounters offer services similar to retail houses. Thus, investors should shop for the combination of discounts and services (including the quality and quantity of investment information) that best suits their needs.

TABLE 3-2
Hypothetical Retail Commission Table

Stocks, Rights, and Warrants Selling for More Than $1.00

Principal Value	Commission
$0–300	11% of principal
$301–$800	$9 + 2.75% of principal
$801–$2,500	$18 + 1.75% of principal
$2,501–$20,000	$30 + 1.25% of principal
$20,001–$30,000	$125 + .90% of principal
$30,001–$300,000	$210 + .60% of principal
$300,001 and over	$1,300 + .25% of principal

Charges (Per Round Lot)

Number of Shares	Charge
100 or less	No charge
101–1,000	$8 per lot
1,001 or more	$80 + $5.50 per lot

Maximum commission charge per share	$1.00
Minimum commission for principal value exceeding $300	$35.00

Stocks, Rights, and Warrants Selling for Less Than $1.00

Principal Value	Commission
$10–$1,000	11% of principal
$1,000–$10,000	$50 + 7% of principal
$10,001 and over	$200 + 5.5% of principal

Bid-Ask Spreads

bid-ask spreads   *Bid-ask spreads* represent the second major component of transaction costs. OTC dealers and their stock exchange equivalent, the specialist, quote both a bid price at which they will buy and an ask price at which they will sell the securities in which they make a market. The difference, or spread, between the buy and sell prices is the dealer's markup. Spreads tend to represent a smaller percentage of the price for higher priced and more actively traded stocks. OTC spreads average 2 percent to 4 percent for actively traded issues but are often much higher for less actively traded issues. To understand how the impact of the spread may be reduced, we need to explore the ways to place purchase and sale orders.

Market and Limit Orders

market order

    A customer wishing to trade a security begins by placing an order with his or her broker. The investor is likely to use either a market or a limit order. A *market order* requires an immediate execution at the best available price. Normally, this type of order results in a trade at the highest unexercised bid for a sale and at the lowest unexercised ask for a purchase. If a stock is quoted 23 bid and 23 1/4 ask, a buy market order would generally result in a purchase at 23 1/4 and a sell market order in a sale at 23. Sometimes, however, a buy and sell order will arrive simultaneously and be crossed with each other, usually at a price within the bid-ask range. By contrast, customers using limit orders specify the prices at which they are willing to do business. Thus, a *limit order* is executable only at the limit price (or better). A market order ensures a transaction, whereas a limit order transaction must await an acceptable price.

limit order

    Brokerage firm representatives take their customers' orders to the section of the exchange where stocks are traded (trading stations, or *posts*) and attempt to execute the orders.

Example: A representative may seek to fill a client's limit order to purchase 100 shares of XYZ at 23. If the stock is available at 23 or less, the trade will be executed immediately. Indeed, the order will be filled at less than 23 if possible. A limit order stipulates only the least favorable price that will be accepted. Normally, a limit order is entered at a level that is more favorable to the initiator than the current price, however. Thus, the order to buy XYZ at 23 might be entered when the stock was offered at 23 3/4 (ask) and others were willing to pay 23 1/4 (bid).

    After waiting a short time, the representative will leave any unexecuted limit order with the specialist who makes a market in that stock. The order will then be put on the specialist's book for later execution, if possible.

Stop-Loss and Stop-Limit Orders

stop-loss order

    Stop orders (both stop-loss and stop-limit) are used to limit exposure to an adverse price move. Most stop orders are designed to sell a position before the stock goes any lower. A *stop-loss order* to sell implements a sale at market (which means the best immediately available price) if the price falls to the prespecified level. These orders seek to protect the investor from a further fall. Because the stock must be traded immediately after the stop price is reached, the realized price is usually relatively close (but not

stop-limit order

necessarily identical) to the stop-loss price. Therefore, a stop-loss order at 20 might result in a sale at 20, but it could result in a sale at 19 7/8 or even 19 1/2 or lower if the stock is dropping rapidly. A *stop-limit order*, in contrast, activates a limit order when the market reaches the stop level. Thus, when the stop level is reached, a stop-limit order may or may not liquidate the position. The vast majority of stop orders are set to sell a position if the price drops. Buy-stop orders, in contrast, are triggered by a price rise. Such an order might be used to protect a short position. A stop-loss buy order at 30, therefore, might be placed on a stock trading at 25. As long as the price stays below 30, nothing is done. Once it touches 30, the stock is bought.

Principal Types of Orders

- Market order: requires an immediate execution at the best available price
- Limit order: stipulates the minimum (sell) or maximum (buy) price acceptable for a trade to take place
- Stop-loss order: requires an immediate trade if the specified price is reached
- Stop-limit order: activates a limit order if a specified price is reached

---

One relatively popular use of stop orders is called the *crawling stop order strategy*. Using this approach, the investor protects his or her position with a stop order at a price a bit below the current market level. As the price moves up, the stop price is also raised. As long as the price of the stock rises or does not fall back very much, the investor continues to hold onto a position whose market value is stable or increasing. Profits can be allowed to compound without great risk of losing them in a market decline. As with any kind of mechanical strategy, however, this approach has its limitations. For example, a modest price pullback may trigger a sale just before a major advance. Moreover, the strategy can be applied only to a stock whose price rises.

A similar strategy can be used with a short position and a falling stock. After the short seller implements a short sale, a stop-loss buy order is entered at a price a bit above the current quote. If the stock's price then falls, the stop-loss price level is also reduced.

Example: Suppose the investor sells stock QUZ short at $50 a share and places a stop-loss buy order at $55 a share. Now if QUZ's price falls to $35 a share, a crawling peg strategy would follow the price down by placing a stop-loss buy order at a price level such as $40 a share. If QUZ's stock price then fell to $25 a share the crawling peg strategy would replace the stop-loss buy order at $40 a share with one at 30.

Good-'Til-Canceled, Day, Fill-or-Kill, and All-or-Nothing Orders

GTC orders

day orders

fill-or-kill orders

Because market orders require immediate execution, specifying how long to keep trying to fill the order is not normally necessary. Limit, stop-loss, and stop-limit orders, in contrast, may be entered either as *good 'til canceled (GTC)* or as executable for a specified period. An order can be placed to remain on the books for a day, a week, for some other period, or until it is executed, whichever comes first. *Day orders* are canceled automatically, whereas the broker must remember to cancel other orders on the prespecified day. *Fill-or-kill orders* must be either executed immediately or canceled.

Period for Which an Order Is Executable

- GTC order (good 'til canceled): executable until filled or canceled
- Day order: executable only during the day the order is placed
- Fill-or-kill order: canceled if not immediately executed

all-or-nothing orders

Commission charges are based on trades of the same security that take place during the same day. If an order to purchase 500 shares is executed in several pieces throughout the same day, the commission will (or should) be computed for a single 500-share trade. If that same trade took several days to be executed, however, the commissions would be computed separately on each day's trade. The total commission on a stretched-out trade would appreciably exceed that on a single 500-share transaction. A customer who wishes to trade more than one round lot may either allow the order to be filled a bit at a time or stipulate an all-or-nothing order. *All-or-nothing orders* must trade as a unit incurring a single commission (with any volume discount applying) but can be executed only when sufficient volume is simultaneously available. A regular order might be filled in pieces because insufficient volume exists for a single fill. Moreover, all-or-nothing orders are automatically superseded by any other limit orders at the same price. Thus, those who would use all-or-nothing orders need to realize that the potentially lower commission is accompanied by a reduced likelihood of execution.

Orders for More Than One Round Lot

- All-or-nothing order: must be executed as a block
- If not specified: may be executed in pieces as small as one round lot

---

Versus Purchase Orders

Investors frequently sell only a portion of their holdings of a particular issue. For example, an investor might sell 200 shares from a 1000-share position. The holdings may themselves have been accumulated at different prices over an extended period. The tax implication of the trade will depend heavily on the price applied to the purchase side of the trade. The higher the cost basis, the lower the gain or the higher the loss that is reported to the IRS. Normally, the shares purchased earliest are recorded as the ones sold (first in, first out: FIFO). The seller may, however, prefer to utilize a trade with a different purchase price. Identifying securities that were purchased at a later date as the ones that were sold may produce a higher basis (reducing the profit or increasing the loss for tax purposes). Making the order *versus purchase* allows the seller to specify which block of shares is to be sold.

versus purchase

Sales of Only a Portion of an Investor's Holdings of a Particular Issue

---

- Versus purchase order: allows the seller to specify which block of stock within his or her holdings is to be sold
- If not specified: identifies as sold the shares that were purchased earliest (FIFO)

The Internet

Beginning in the late 1990s, on-line trading over the Internet became an increasingly important means of trading stocks. Until the late 1990s, when the Internet and e-commerce emerged as a major force, most investors undertook stock trades by contacting and instructing their brokers to implement the desired transactions. Usually, contact is made by a phone call. With on-line trading, in contrast, the trade is initiated via the Internet. The investor simply goes to the Internet broker's web site and enters an order. Commissions on Internet trades are as low as $7 for a trade, even a very large trade (although there may be a required minimum balance). The Internet is becoming an increasingly important factor in security market trading, just as e-commerce is becoming an increasingly important factor in the overall economy. *Business Week* compiled lists of recommended online brokers (see table 3-3) and Internet resources to help investors (see table 3-4).

**TABLE 3-3
Online Brokers**

Broker	Limit Order	Comments
Datek www.datek.com	$9.99	Quick, low-cost trades through its own electronic communications network, when service isn't disrupted
E*Trade www.etrade.com	$19.95	Special high-speed trading services for active investors; orders executed through own electronic communications network; market maker
Web Street www.webstreet-securities. com	$14.95	Site features "trading pit" designed for trading and little else; bargain prices on NASDAQ Level 2 screen
Discover www.discover-brokerage.com	$19.95	Excellent trade execution. easy-to-use screens; access to Morgan Stanley research for a fee
Suretrade www.suretrade.com	$9.95	Budget-price division of Quick & Reilly offers quick trades, low margin rate, and access to a range of research
DLJ Direct www.dljdirect.com	$20	Easy-to-use screens, diverse investment tools, and access to IPOs
Fidelity www.fidelity.com	$30	Broad product selection, good fund screening and phone support; IPOs available; slow to update holdings
Charles Schwab www.schwab.com	$29.95	Strong in advice and information, links to investment advisers, IPOs available; special services for those with $100,000
Waterhouse www.waterhouse.com	$12	Low prices, good basic investing tools and wide fund selection; web site could be faster

Reprinted from May 24, 1999, issue of *Business Week* by special permission. Copyright © 1999 by The McGraw-Hill Companies, Inc.

TABLE 3-4
Internet Resources

Site/Address	Comments
ADR.com www.adr.com	The skinny on American depository receipts as provided by J. P. Morgan
BigCharts www.bigcharts.com	A bevy of performance and comparisons and technical analysis charts—for free
Bridge.com www.bridge.com	Excellent global charts and quotes
Business Week Online www.businessweek.com	Charts, quotes, portfolio tracker, news analysis, asset allocator.
CBS Marketwatch www.cbsmarketwatch.com	Fine overall investment news site
Cents Financial Journal 1p-11c.com/cents/	Daily market commentary from leading economists and strategists at Moody's, Morgan Stanley, and others
Financenter www.financenter.com	Free on-line calculators for stocks, bonds, and mutual funds
FreeEdgar www.freeedgar.com	Unlimited access to SEC filings, plus e-mail alerts
IPO Maven www.ipomaven.com	Lives up to its name with historical and current data on initial public offerings
Market Guide Investor www.marketguide.com	Good collection of free fundamental data and earnings estimates
Morning.net www.morningstar.net	Not just mutual funds but also a database of more than 8,000 stocks
NASDAQ www.nasdaq.com	Free InfoQuotes feature gives delayed quotes and bid-ask spreads on NASDAQ
Quote.com www.quote.com	Streaming live charts to enable investors to watch the market move while they work in other programs
S&P Personal Wealth www.personalwealth.com	Asset allocation, stock picks and pans, fund screens (costs $9.95/month)
10K Wizard www.10kwizard.com	A powerful search engine for SEC filings
Wall Street City www.wallstreetcity.com	Telescan's comprehensive site with free and fee-based fundamental and technical analysis

Reprinted from May 24, 1999, issue of *Business Week* by special permission. Copyright © 1999 by The McGraw-Hill Companies, Inc.

The Specialist

Specialists manage the markets in listed stocks. They do so primarily by quoting bid and ask prices on the securities assigned to them. They maintain an inventory of their assigned stocks and buy for and sell from that inventory. A given specialist may make markets in a dozen or so securities, and a few actively traded securities are handled by more than one specialist. Most securities, however, are assigned to a single specialist. Securities that are traded on more than one exchange have an assigned specialist for each exchange.

Specialists record limit and stop orders in their order books. They are responsible for executing these orders whenever the prespecified limit prices are reached. If the bid dropped from 23 1/4 to 23 1/8, for example, a limit order to buy at 23 would still be below all buy orders at 23 1/8. Once all orders to buy at 23 1/8 are filled, the bid will fall to the next highest unexercised order—in this case, 23 (assuming there are no orders at 23 1/16). Orders entered at the same price level are executed chronologically.

Example: A particular order to purchase 100 shares at 23 may be preceded by another buy order at 23 for 500 shares and another 300 shares at 23 may follow the 100-share buy order. Once the 500 shares at 23 are purchased, the 100-share order will be crossed with any incoming market sell order or limit order to sell at 23 or lower. However, if any offer to pay more than 23 should arrive prior to the 100-share order's being executed, it would immediately supersede the 100-share order.

Individual specialists are members of specialists' firms. These firms may handle up to 70 stocks. Under most types of market conditions, these specialists' firms perform their jobs effectively. They are supposed to ensure that the market for each of their stocks is always orderly and well managed. In an orderly and well-managed market, someone is always supposed to be prepared to buy and someone is always supposed to be prepared to sell at prices that are reasonably close to recent levels. Similarly, prices are not supposed to swing too widely from transaction to transaction.

The specialist is expected to fill any temporary gaps by offering to buy and/or sell as necessary. Specialists are supposed to be net buyers when the public wishes to be net sellers. Under normal circumstances, specialists' firms may be managing a few stocks that are under selling pressure while others have more public buyers than sellers. During the October 1987 crash, however, almost all of the public orders were on the sell side. Most of the specialists' capital was quickly committed. Some firms were unable to provide an orderly market as they were hit with more and more sell orders at lower and lower prices.

Floor Traders or Registered Competitive Market Makers (RCMMs)

Specialists, who make markets, and unexecuted limit orders, which represent potential demand and supply, both have a major influence on stock prices.

floor traders
RCMMs

Individuals called *floor traders* or registered competitive market makers (*RCMMs*) also have a modest role in the price-formation process. RCMMs own exchange seats and trade for their own account. They benefit from quick access to the market and the information that is available at the center of the action at very low incremental trading costs (although they must pay the high fixed cost of exchange membership). As recently as the 1960s, a substantial fraction of NYSE members were floor traders. Since that time, however, various restrictions have substantially reduced their ranks. By 1982, only 23 were registered, and only 10 of them were active on the NYSE. The decline continued into the late 1990s. In 1999, only 10 floor traders remained. The options and commodity exchanges, however, continue to have many floor traders.

TRADING AT THE MOST ATTRACTIVE PRICE

Investors should always seek to trade at the best available price. Why should an investor pay 23 1/4 for a stock that can (with a little additional effort) be bought at 23? Because future prices are very likely to be both higher and lower, the current level is seldom the best obtainable price. Nonetheless, between 75 percent and 85 percent of all transactions utilize market orders that require immediate execution at the current level (including the adverse impact of the bid-ask spread). Limit orders, on the other hand, are structured to take advantage of short-run imbalances in supply and demand. Most buy limit orders are set for execution slightly below the current price level. Similarly, sell limit orders normally await somewhat higher prices. While saving a fraction of a point on a single small trade will not make an investor rich, enough small savings could easily be the difference between outperforming and underperforming the market.

If limit orders are so useful, why are they not more widely employed? First, brokers may be reluctant to explain limit orders' more complicated mechanics to their clients. The broker's commission is certain to be realized when a market order is used. But a limit order might not result in a trade and therefore might not generate a commission for the broker. Also, many investors may prefer execution of an order with certainty to a possible fraction of a point savings or no execution of the order at all.

Unlike a limit order, a market order can result in an appreciably less favorable price than the investor expects. With a current bid price of 23 1/4 and an ask price of 23 3/4, for example, a buy market order on 100 shares would normally be executed at the quoted ask price of 23 3/4. But the price could move above 23 3/4 between the time the quote is obtained and the time the order reaches the floor. Alternatively, the displayed quotation itself could be incorrect. The quotation services make no guarantee as to the accuracy of the information that they transmit. Prices seldom change markedly in the short time required for an order to reach the post, but an eighth or quarter of a point move is not uncommon. A dramatic news event such as an assassination rumor could cause a much greater change. A good-till-canceled (GTC) buy limit order at 23 3/4 would either be executed at the current ask price if it is less than or equal to 23 3/4 or be held for possible later execution. Thus, a limit order set at or near the reported market price protects the trader from both a temporary price change and a trade based on an incorrect quote. In ordinary circumstances, however, it is executed at the same price as a market order. A limit order, therefore, combines the advantage of a market order's very high probability of being executed with the protection from an adverse price movement that might occur with a market order in a fast-moving market.

Setting the Limit Price

A limit order placed at or close to the current price (bid for a sell and ask for a buy) incurs little nonexecution risk, but it is unlikely to result in a better price than a market order. Setting a more favorable limit level than the current quote increases both the nonexecution risk and the potential for gain from a more attractive price. The three rules that follow are helpful for striking a favorable balance between the probability of execution and the possibility of obtaining a better price.[1]

First, if an imminent development is expected to affect the price, the limit should be set to assure a quick execution. For example, if year-end tax-loss selling temporarily depresses the price, the limit might be set very near or equal to the current level.

Second, when the trade is not dictated by imminent developments, the limit price should be set near the expected forthcoming low for a buy or expected high for a sale. Past trading ranges may help identify the expected highs and lows. For example, suppose a stock has a 2-week high of 24 5/8, a low of 22 1/2, and a last trade of 23 1/2. The stock would seem to be trading in a range of a point above and a point below the current price. Thus, the investor might try to buy close to 22 1/2 and sell close to 24 1/2. Setting the limit closer to the last trade of 23 1/2 would reduce the nonexecution risk but would also limit the profit potential.

Third, the investor should take advantage of the tendency for prices to cluster at focal points. More trades occur and more prices are quoted at whole numbers than at halves, and both are more common than quarters. Quarters, in turn, are more common than eighths. Most investors prefer to think and trade in what they view as round numbers. Their placement of limit orders reflects this preference. More sophisticated investors can place their own limit orders to take advantage of this tendency. The investor should bear in mind that when several orders are entered at the same price, they are executed on a first-come first-serve basis. If, for example, the bid is at 23, each buy order at 23 will be executed in the chronological order in which it was placed. The bid could easily move above 23 before all orders at 23 are filled. The tendency of prices to cluster at round numbers implies that far fewer unexecuted limit orders will be entered at 23 1/8 or 22 7/8 than at 23. A buy at 23 1/8 or sell at 22 7/8 is considerably more likely to be executed, therefore, than an end-of-the-line order at 23. Accordingly, investors should normally set limit orders to buy at 1/8 and sell at 7/8. Indeed, where allowed, orders should utilize sixteenths. Thus, a buy order at 23 1/16 and a sell order at 22 15/16 could be used when allowed. Generally, investors should not change the limit price on a limit order once it is entered because doing so will cause the trader to lose his or her place in line.

Rules for Setting a Limit Price

- If an imminent development is expected to affect the price, set the limit price to assure a quick execution.
- When no imminent development dictates the trade, set the limit price near the expected forthcoming low (high) for a buy (sale).
- Take advantage of the tendency for prices to cluster at focal points, such as whole numbers.

An investor who wishes to acquire a relatively large block of stock might effectively utilize several limit orders placed at varying prices. Orders near the current quote would be very likely to be executed, while orders entered further away would produce a lower average price if the stock reached their level. Only round-lot orders should be used, however. The total commission on below round-lot (odd-lot) orders is generally too large to justify the price savings.

In summary, investors should generally use limit rather than market orders. In doing so, they should refer to past trading ranges and take advantage of the tendency of prices to cluster at round-number values.

pricing points

Pricing Points

Historically, stocks, bonds, options, and similar securities have been priced in dollars and fractions of a dollar. Until recently, most stocks were priced in eighths. Thus, investors encountered prices like 21 1/8, 25 1/2, and 30 3/4. Very low-priced stocks (for example, under one dollar) were priced in sixteenths and finer gradations. As this textbook is written, however, most stocks are now allowed by the major markets to be priced in sixteenths.

Pricing in fractions is increasingly complicated in a world where decimals rule. Most people just do not think in eighth parts of a dollar (12.5 cents) or sixteenth parts of a dollar (6.25 cents). How many people can quickly compute 13/16 of a dollar as equal to 81.25 cents? Accordingly, a shift to using a decimal system to price securities has long been proposed and in fact is scheduled to occur in the summer of 2000. Under a decimal system, prices would be quoted in tenths, twentieths, and perhaps hundredths of a dollar (for example, 23.1 or 23.15 or 23.11).

OTC versus Listed Stocks

Listed stocks are generally more marketable (have lower bid-ask spread) than those traded over-the-counter. On the other hand, the local issues that are most familiar to many individual investors are usually unlisted. Furthermore, a disproportionate percentage of the numerous small companies traded OTC may be misvalued. A market tends to be most efficient when the greatest attention is paid to each stock. So many analysts follow actively traded large capitalization companies (AT&T, IBM, GM, GE, and Coca-Cola, for example) that very little relevant information is likely to be overlooked. The prices of their stocks probably closely reflect whatever publicly available information can reveal about the true intrinsic values of the stocks. Less actively traded stocks, in contrast, are more likely to be ignored by analysts. Similarly, portfolio managers, business writers, and individual brokers generally pay much more attention to the actively traded issues. As a result, the prices of securities that receive little attention are much freer to stray appreciably from their underlying values.

The Third and Fourth Markets

Most trading and virtually all trades involving individual investors take place on an exchange or in the traditional OTC market for unlisted issues. Institutional investors, on the other hand, make significant use of two other markets. OTC trading of listed stocks takes place in what is called the *third market*. The *fourth market* is an informal arrangement for direct trading between institutions. Both third and fourth markets involve off-exchange trading of what are usually large blocks of exchange-traded stock. The third

third market
fourth market

market grew up in response to the exchanges' then-fixed commission schedules. The fixed commission rate on a large institutional transaction (over $500,000, for example) could result in a commission that exceeded $10,000 for paperwork, similar to the commission for a single round lot. NYSE members could not obtain discounts from these rates.

Two Other Markets Institutional Investors Use

- Third market: OTC trading of listed stocks
- Fourth market: direct trading between institutions via an informal arrangement

Third-market dealers were not bound by exchange-set commissions. Thus, they were usually able to (and, in fact, did) charge high-volume institutional traders much less than the commissions charged on the exchanges. By the time the exchanges stopped setting commissions, the third market was already established. Third-market dealers often offer a more attractive overall price (stock price and commission) than is available on the exchanges.

The fourth market provides its institutional participants with an even less costly way of trading. Because the institutions trade directly with each other, no commission is incurred. Those who help put the two sides of the trade together usually receive a finder's fee. This finder's fee is, however, much lower than the commission on a trade of equivalent size.

Dually Traded Securities

arbitrageurs

Many high-volume stocks trade simultaneously on the NYSE, several regional exchanges, and OTC (including the third and fourth markets). Each market's bid and ask prices may differ somewhat. *Arbitrageurs* seek profits from price disparities. While they do tend to drive the prices on different markets together, frictions permit some disparities. Moreover, the quantities available on a single market may be more limited than needed. Shopping around, therefore, may be worthwhile for traders who seek to execute large orders.[2]

MANAGING EQUITIES

Buying on Margin

Marketable securities provide excellent collateral for lenders. The Federal Reserve Board allows collateralized margin loans on almost all listed and on many OTC securities. A margin requirement of x percent permits marginable stock to be purchased with x percent cash and (100 – x) percent borrowed funds (called the initial margin). Thus, a 60 percent margin requirement would allow the purchase of $10,000 worth of stock with as little as $6,000 in cash. The margin requirement on stocks has typically been set at between 50 percent and 90 percent. In the past, the Fed lowered and raised the margin requirement on stocks as part of its economic policy. More recently, however, it has left the margin requirement on stocks at 50 percent where (as of 2000) it has been since 1974.

margin account
buying power

A *margin account* is said to have *buying power* based on the net equity in the account and the amount of margin borrowing already outstanding. Buying power equals the maximum dollar value of marginable stock or other securities supportable by the account's equity minus the current value of marginable securities in the account.

Example 1:	An investor with $20,000 worth of marginable stocks and no margin debt outstanding could, with a 50 percent margin rate, buy another $20,000 worth of marginable stocks with the account's buying power. At that point the account would have $40,000 worth of stock and equity of 50 percent ($20,000 in equity out of a $40,000 total).
Example 2:	An investor with $35,000 in marginable stocks and an outstanding margin balance of $10,000 would be able to purchase another $15,000 worth of marginable stock with the account's buying power. In other words, this account has an equity of $25,000 ($35,000 – $10,000) and could support $50,000 worth of marginable securities, including a margin balance of $25,000 ($25,000 in equity and $25,000 in borrowing, which equals the overall account value of $50,000). With a current value for the account of $35,000, another $15,000 ($50,000 – $35,000) in buying power is available.

To be marginable, an OTC stock must have at least 1,200 shareholders and a market value of $5 million or more. Listed companies are marginable unless specifically excluded by the SEC. However, most brokerage firms will not extend margin loans on low-priced shares (below $5). Moreover, the customer must have at least $2,000 in equity both to open and to maintain a margin account.

The formula relating the equity value of a portfolio of marginable stocks to the maximum value that equity can support is as follows:

$$MAV = \frac{E}{MR} \qquad \text{(Equation 3-1)}$$

where: MAV = Maximum amount value
E = Equity (marginable stocks)
MR = Margin requirement

Borrowing power is equal to the difference between the equity in the portfolio and the maximum amount value.

$$BP = MAV - E \qquad \text{(Equation 3-2)}$$

where: BP = Borrowing power

Example: A portfolio with $10,000 in equity and a 50 percent margin requirement (MR) would be able to support a maximum amount value (MAV) of $20,000.

$$MAV = \frac{E}{MR}$$

$$\$20,000 = \frac{\$10,000}{.5}$$

This portfolio with an MAV of $20,000 would have borrowing power (BP) of $10,000.

$$BP = MAV - E$$
$$\$10,000 = \$20,000 - \$10,000$$

Buying power is equal to the borrowing power of the account less the amount already borrowed:

$$BYP = BP - AB \qquad \text{(Equation 3-3)}$$

where: BYP = Buying power
AB = Amount borrowed

margin calls

Margin Calls

Margin loans may remain outstanding as long as the borrower's equity position does not fall below the maintenance margin percentage. Maintenance margin requirements are set by the brokerage firms and are generally less restrictive than initial margins. Margin borrowers are not required or expected to make payments according to any particular schedule. The only time that the borrower may be required to make a payment is when the equity in the account falls to too low a level to support the loan against it. A margin account's equity will rise and fall as the price of the securities in the account rises and falls.

Margin accounts are structured to limit the danger of becoming undercollateralized (having an outstanding loan balance close to or greater than the value of the securities collateralizing it). As long as the value of the collateral comfortably exceeds the amount of the loan, the outstanding loan is considered to be relatively secure. If the cushion becomes too small, however, the lender begins to risk incurring a loss on the margin loan. The margin borrower remains personally liable for any deficit in a margin account.

Brokerage firms, however, much prefer to satisfy the outstanding balance on the loan from the collateral and avoid the problems that tend to occur when they must seek recovery from a customer's personal assets. These efforts often result in countersuits alleging various wrongdoings (for example, poor advice) by the broker. If a general market decline leads to substantial margin account losses for brokerage firms, the stock market and economy could suffer. Clearly, neither the regulators nor the brokerage industry wants to risk incurring such losses, particularly if the losses are substantial. Financially weak and failing brokerage firms could trigger a financial panic leading to major problems for the overall economy.

Ways to Satisfy a Margin Call

- Add more money to the account.
- Add more marginal collateral to the account.
- Sell stock from the account and use the proceeds to reduce the margin debt.

In each case, the result must raise the equity percentage above the margin maintenance minimum in order to remove the margin call.

Accordingly, the Federal Reserve Board sets a minimum maintenance margin percentage (25 percent as of this writing). This maintenance margin provision is designed to force investors to deal with problems quickly while the account still has positive equity. Most brokerage firms set a somewhat higher maintenance margin percentage for their customers. Thirty-five percent is typical. An investor whose equity falls below this percentage of the value of his or her portfolio (counting only marginable securities) will receive a margin call.

Example: A 50 percent initial margin requirement allows $10,000 in marginable stocks to be purchased with $5,000 in cash and $5,000 in credit. Any fluctuation in the portfolio's value will be reflected in a change in the equity position (equity equals portfolio value less margin debt). If the value of the portfolio rises to $12,000, the equity rises to $7,000 ($12,000 − $5,000). If, however, the value of the margined stock falls to $7,700, the equity position declines to $2,700 ($7,700 − $5,000) or 35 percent ($2,700/7,700). If the brokerage firm has a 40 percent maintenance margin requirement, the investor will then receive a margin call. Unless the loan value is reduced or additional collateral is deposited, the brokerage firm must sell some of the borrower's stock. In this example, a $1,000 stock sale would reduce the loan from $5,000 to $4,000, increasing the equity position to 40 percent ($2,700/$6,700). Note that the sale increases the percentage by reducing the loan amount relative to the equity amount.

A margin call can be either a "house call" or a "Fed call." The brokerage firm has the option of enforcing or waiving the enforcement of a house margin call. However, a Fed call must be enforced. In either instance, the brokerage house may give the customer a modest amount of time to restore the account to the compliance level.

Types of Margin Calls

- House call: occurs when the equity percentage falls below the minimum maintenance level set by the brokerage firm
- Fed call: occurs when the equity percentage falls below the maintenance level set by the Fed for margin accounts

Concentrated Positions

Most investors with margin accounts have a relatively well-diversified portfolio of marginable stocks. These accounts are vulnerable to a general market decline, but they tend to be rather well protected against price declines limited to a few individual stocks within a larger portfolio. If one or two stocks in a diversified portfolio decline sharply, the overall account value will generally be able to withstand the pressure and thereby avoid a margin call.

Example:	If a single stock position representing 10 percent of a portfolio's value falls to half its previous value, that fall would cause the portfolio's overall value to fall by 5 percent. If the account had met the initial margin requirement (50 percent) prior to the stock's decline it should still be considerably above the maintenance level (35 percent).

If, however, a large percentage of the account's value is concentrated in one or a very few stocks, the risk to the margin borrower (and the margin lender) goes up. If the one or a few stocks on which most of the account value is derived suffer a serious decline, the danger of a margin call becomes much greater than with a well-diversified portfolio.

Example:	Suppose a stock representing 50 percent of the portfolio's value falls to half its previous value. The portfolio's value would fall by 25 percent (.5 x .5 = .25), which could easily trigger a margin call.

Not only does the concentration in the portfolio increase the impact of an adverse price move, but it also makes sales from the portfolio more problematic. The need to sell a large position in a stock whose price is already dropping is all too likely to produce selling pressure that causes the stock's price to fall still further. Margin calls that are triggered by a price decline in an issue already under selling pressure can cause its price to drop further. A further price decline can lead to more margin calls and still more selling pressure. Margin lenders (brokerage firms) aware of this potential danger are likely to limit the percentage of margin borrowing for concentrated accounts.

The Leverage of Margin Borrowing

Margin loans are normally used to allow the investor to purchase more stock than cash alone could buy. The use of such leverage tends to magnify both gains and losses. With $5,000, the investor could buy 50 shares of a marginable stock outright or (with a 50 percent margin rate) 100 shares by borrowing the additional $5,000. Table 3-5 illustrates some possible results (neglecting the impact of dividend payments and interest charges) from a cash versus a margin purchase. Clearly, margin purchases increase both the upside potential and the downside risk.

TABLE 3-5
Margin Example: $5,000 Available to Invest in Stock
Selling for $100 per Share

Stock Price Moves to	Purchase 100 Shares Using 50% Margin at $100 per Share		Purchase 50 Shares for Cash at $100 per Share	
	Change in Holding's Value	Change Relative to Equity	Change in Holding's Value	Change Relative to Equity
70	–$3,000	–60%	–$1,500	--30%
80	–2,000	–40%	–1,000	--20%
90	–1,000	–20%	–500	--10%
100	0	0	0	0
110	+1,000	+20%	+500	+10%
120	+2,000	+40%	+1,000	+20%
130	+3,000	+60%	+1,500	+30%

To examine the impact of margin interest charges, assume the margin loan costs 9.5 percent. If a year later the stock illustrated in table 3-5 had risen to 120, the cash purchase would have appreciated by $1,000 ($20 x 50), compared with a $1,525 gain on the margin purchase ($20 x 100 = $2,000; 9.5% x $5,000 = $475; $2,000 – $475 = $1,525). Should the stock fall to 80, the losses would be $1,000 and $2,475, respectively. Interest costs on the margin position would, however, be at least partially offset by dividend payments. Commissions and taxes also affect the amounts modestly but leave the basic point unaffected. The use of margin credit to purchase stock tends to magnify both gains and losses. As long as the stock's return (net of commissions and taxes) exceeds the financing cost of the loan, leverage will enhance the overall return.

Using margin credit may also provide some tax advantages. Interest costs are fully deductible (but only against investment income) as incurred, whereas any price appreciation is taxable only when the asset is sold. Thus, the interest charges incurred on margin borrowing may shelter other investment income, while the price appreciation goes untaxed until realized.

Brokerage firms finance some of their margin lending from other customers' credit balances, such as those generated through short sales. A positive balance in a customer's account is called a *credit balance*; a negative one (a margin loan) is referred to as a *debit balance*. Additional loan funds are obtained from commercial banks at the *broker call-loan rate*. Interest charges on margin loans are based on the exact length of each part of the loan. If, for example, $10,000 is borrowed and then $750 is repaid a week later, interest will be calculated on $10,000 for a week and on $9,250 thereafter. Margin loan interest rates are usually determined by a sliding scale added to the broker call-loan rate. Table 3-6 is typical.

credit balance

debit balance

broker call-loan rate

TABLE 3-6
Typical Margin Loan Rates

Net Debit Balance	Call Rate Plus
$ 0 – 9,999	2 1/4%
$10,000 – 29,999	1 3/4%
$30,000 – 49,999	1 1/4%
$50,000 and over	3/4%

Banks generally set their broker call-loan rate equal to or below their prime rate (the lowest advertised business rate). Margin loan rates are normally no more than 2 percent above the prime business rate. Relatively favorable interest rates and flexible payment schedules make margin loans an attractive credit source.

Preferreds, warrants, and convertibles are subject to the same margin requirements as common stocks. Margin restrictions also apply to corporate bond purchases, although their proportional collateral value is typically higher (25 percent margin rate on most nonconvertible bonds). A 10 percent margin requirement applies to government bonds with a 10-year or greater maturity. The margin requirement is lower for shorter-term governments.

While brokerage houses specialize in margin loans, banks and other financial intermediaries also accept securities as collateral. If these loans finance other security purchases, the Fed's margin restrictions apply. Otherwise, the lender can determine the maximum loan value on such collateral.

short selling

Short Selling

Selling short involves selling an asset that is not owned but borrowed and later buying an equivalent asset to replace the borrowed asset that was sold.

To understand the concept of short selling, consider the following situation. A friend stops by and mentions that he badly needs a particular CD for a party that he is having that night. Unfortunately, he had to work late and all of the record stores are closed. When he sees the CD he needs in your CD rack, he offers to pay double the retail price. That particular CD, however, belongs to your roommate who has left for the weekend. You know that your roommate would not mind if you sold his CD, as long as you replace it. So you sell the CD in the rack and replace it with a new copy before your roommate returns. You made a profit and your roommate still has his CD. The new copy of the CD is at least as good as the one you sold. The trade that you made is, in effect, a short sale. You sold something that you did not own, but you had the (implicit) permission of the owner to make the sale and you intended to replace what you sold. Short sales are not uncommon in the securities markets.

Most stock trades involve the purchase and sale of securities that the seller owned prior to the transaction. Unlike offering to sell the Brooklyn Bridge, however, an investor who sells stock that he or she does not own (short selling) is involved in a perfectly legal practice. The short seller's broker simply sells someone else's shares. The short seller then owes the lender the shorted shares. The customer whose stock is borrowed is as secure as a bank depositor whose funds are loaned. If the lender wishes to sell the loaned stock, the brokerage firm will simply borrow replacement shares from another customer or brokerage firm.

Sometimes a trader will try to use his or her own trades to influence the market price of a particular security. For example, someone may try to cause a stock's price to run up by buying large quantities on the market. Alternatively, he or she might try to drive a price down through excessive selling. Traders are entitled to buy or sell, even in large quantities, when the purpose is simply to accumulate or liquidate a position. Large trades often influence the market price.

downtick

Any type of effort to manipulate the market, however, is illegal. Thus, for example, using short sales to drive a stock's price down is considered an illegal attempt to manipulate the market. To forestall such attempts, traders are not allowed to sell short after a negative price change (*downtick*) in a stock. If the last price change was a decline, therefore, a would-be short seller must wait until the price begins to rise again (two or more successive trades at rising prices, which is called an uptick) before implementing a short sale.

The short seller hopes the price will fall far enough so that when the stock is repurchased, he or she will make a profit after covering expenses. This gain would be reduced somewhat by commissions on the short sale and covering (repurchase) transactions. Furthermore, the short seller must pay any dividends accruing on the borrowed stock. Moreover, the short sale proceeds and an additional percentage (margin) of the sale price must be left in a non-interest-bearing account at the brokerage house. A still larger margin deposit may be required by an adverse price move.

Example: Shorting 100 shares at 50 and then repurchasing them (covering the short position) at 35 produces a gross profit of $1,500 (100 x [$50 – $35]) less commissions and accrued dividends. However, should the stock price increase to 65, the seller would show a loss of $1,500 ($100 x [$50 – 65] plus commissions and accrued dividends.

The short seller may legally remain short indefinitely. The dividend payment and margin deposit requirements, however, make such positions costly to maintain. Moreover, stock prices have no ceiling. Thus, losses are technically unlimited on a short sale.

Clearly, short selling is a relatively risky practice. Amateur investors should probably avoid short sales.

One limit to short selling is the brokerage firm's ability to obtain stock that can be used to facilitate the short sale. For widely held stocks, this need to find shares to sell is generally not much of a problem. Sometimes, however, the interest in selling a less widely held stock short is so great relative to the shares available to short that brokerage firms run out of available shares. This situation is particularly likely for small companies in which the shares are closely held by a few people or the shares' price has dropped to such a low level that it is not marginable. Investors tend only to hold stock in the name of the brokerage house, referred to as street name (where it is available for shorting) if the stock is marginable. Investors who wish to sell short shares of a stock that is in short supply may not be able to do so. Similarly, an investor who sells such a stock short may be required by his or her brokerage firm to close the position if the firm finds that it can no longer borrow the shares needed to maintain the short position.

As the preceding discussion indicates, to short stock is to sell stock that is not owned with the intention of covering (buying it back) later—ideally, at a profit. The act of executing a short sale may be described as shorting or, in the past tense, as having shorted the stock. To be short or have a short position is to have executed such a trade and not yet covered. Similarly, an investor can be long or go long or have a long position. This is just another way of saying that the investor owns the stock.

Personal Financial Management Accounts

Most full-service and many discount brokerage firms offer a flexible type of personal financial management account that combines checking, credit card, money fund, and margin accounts into a single framework.

These types of accounts transfer funds back and forth to minimize interest costs on debit balances and/or maximize short-term yields on credit balances. When an account holder writes a large check, his or her checking account is first drained of funds. Then, if necessary, the money fund balance is tapped. If still more funds are needed, a margin loan is extended. Credit card balances are handled in a similar fashion. Alternatively, a large deposit will first be applied to loans and then put into the money fund. These accounts relieve the investor/money manager of some of the cash management burdens.

Street Name

street name

Margined securities must be left on deposit with the shareholder's brokerage house, and unmargined securities may be. Broker-held securities are generally registered in the *street name* (name of the brokerage house) although the customer retains beneficial ownership. Street-name registration offers secure storage and allows securities to be traded without having to reissue the certificates. Furthermore, a customer who holds a diversified portfolio of securities and who changes addresses needs to file only one change of address notice with the brokerage firm, rather than notifying all the companies separately.

Advantages of Street-Name Registration

- Offers secure storage
- Lets securities be traded without having to reissue the certificates
- Allows customers who move frequently to file only one change of address with brokerage firm instead of notifying all companies separately

---

Street-name registration has a number of disadvantages. Assets held in street name may be tied up during a bankrupt brokerage firm's reorganization. Moreover, dividends and interest on street-name securities are sometimes credited to an improper account. The customer must discover and report the error before it is likely to be corrected. Even a properly credited dividend may be retained by the broker in a non-interest-bearing account for up to a month before being sent to the shareholder. Furthermore, all company reports (annual reports, quarterly reports, proxy materials, class-action suit notices, and so on) for street-name securities are sent initially to the brokerage firm. Thus, street-name holders will receive their company reports only after the brokerage firm has forwarded them. Investors who want to be sure of receiving all company mailings may retain a small portion (say, 10 shares) of each security in their own names. Clearly, street-name registration has both advantages and disadvantages.

Disadvantages of Street-Name Registration

- Assets may be tied up during the reorganization of a bankrupt brokerage firm.
- Dividends and interest may be credited to an improper account.
- Properly credited dividends may be retained by the broker in a non-interest-bearing account for up to a month before being sent to the shareholder.
- Because all company reports are sent to the brokerage firm, the shareholder will receive them only after they have been forwarded.

The Stock Certificate

stock certificates

In this day of computerized accounting and electronic transfers, using *stock certificates* to prove ownership is similar to a cash-only payment system. Stock certificates must be issued whenever a stock is registered in an individual's name. Because the certificates require a great deal of paperwork and may be stolen or forged, many experts have advocated substituting computer cards or bookkeeping entries. Individuals might still receive a stock certificate upon request or at least be given some proof of ownership, such as a receipt or a bill of sale.

Institutions are involved in a large percentage of securities transactions as either the buyer or seller or both. Many other trades involve individuals who leave the stockholding function to their brokerage firm. With such trades, appropriately safeguarded bookkeeping entries have largely eliminated the need for stock certificates. Stock certificate reissues are minimized by the National Securities Clearing Corporation (NSCC). It records all members' transactions, verifies the consistency of their accounts, and reports net positions daily. NSCC members settle within the clearinghouse rather than between individual brokerage firms. Moreover, the Depository Trust Company (DTC) immobilizes many certificates by holding member firms' securities. Securities traded between members can be handled internally by simply debiting one account and crediting another. Although institutional and street-name accounts benefit from these facilities, investors with non-street-name securities continue to experience all the inconveniences inherent in a stock certificate transfer system.

OTHER TRADING MECHANISMS

The vast majority of security trades take place in modest-sized lots on an exchange or OTC (including the third and fourth markets). Special mechanisms have, however, been devised both for newly issued securities and for trades whose size would strain everyday market facilities.

Trading in Already Issued Stock (Secondary Market)—Small- to Moderate-Size Blocks

---

- Exchanges: organized trading in shares of medium- to large-size firms
- OTC: informal hookup of market makers trading small- and medium-size companies
- Third market: OTC trading in listed securities
- Fourth market: direct trading between institutional investors

---

primary market

The Primary Market

The primary or new-issues market handles initial sales of securities; subsequent exchange and OTC trading take place in the secondary market. Some shares of a primary distribution may already be actively traded in the secondary market. Alternatively, the stock of the issuing firm may have heretofore been privately held (owned by a very few people). A private firm that sells a substantial block of additional shares and thereby creates a more active and diverse ownership is said to *go public*. Normally, an *investment banker* (usually also a brokerage firm) is retained to assemble a syndicate to *underwrite* the issue.

go public
investment banker
underwrite

Investment bankers facilitate new-issue sales of debt and equity by agreeing to buy the securities for resale (underwriting). Together, the issuing firm and its investment banker compose a registration statement and a *prospectus* detailing all of the relevant material information. These statements must be filed with the SEC and supplied to every buyer. The investment banker deducts its underwriting fee from the offering price. The investment-banking syndicate generally guarantees to sell the issue, although the job might be taken on a *best-effort basis*, in which case the investment banker acts as an agent for the issuing firm. Most underwriting is done on a *firm-commitment basis*, which means the investment banker buys the securities from the issuer and then sells them to the public.

best-effort basis

firm-commitment basis

Shelf Registration

shelf registration

While most primary sales are marketed quickly after their registration, *shelf registration* is permitted by the SEC's Rule 415. Under this rule, a firm can file one registration statement for a relatively large block of stock and then sell parts of it over a 2-year period. The shelf registration option tends to reduce red tape and expenses, and because the stock can be sold directly to institutional investors it often eliminates the underwriting fee.

Private Placements

private placement

lettered stock

New issues are sometimes sold in large lots to a small group of buyers in what is called a *private placement*. These placements allow start-up firms to demonstrate viability by successfully raising some capital on their own. Additional shares may subsequently be marketed to the public through an underwriter. The private placements are usually sold below the public offering price. In exchange for a favorable price, the initial investors may agree to accept *lettered stock*. Under SEC Rule 144, such securities can be resold only after a reasonable holding period (such as 2 years) and in a gradual manner that does not disrupt trading markets.

Debt issues may also be placed privately, usually to large buyers such as insurance companies.

Rights Offerings

rights offering

preemptive rights

As discussed earlier, shares may be bought and sold through an underwriting syndicate, private placement, or the ordinary channels of trade (exchange or OTC). Firms may also sell additional shares of their stock in a *rights offering*. Indeed, a preemptive rights clause, if part of the corporate bylaws, ensures shareholders of the right to maintain their proportional ownership of the company. In a 5 percent stock sale, stockholders with *preemptive rights* would have the right of first refusal on one new share for each 20 shares that they owned. Stocks sold through rights offerings are generally priced sufficiently below the market level to make the rights attractive to exercise before they expire. Normally, stockholders may sell their rights for a price that reflects the savings offered. If 20 rights are required to buy one share of a $50 stock at $40, rights will sell for about 50 cents each: ($50 − $40)/20 = $.50. While some companies still use rights offerings, many have persuaded shareholders to give up their preemptive rights.

A sale of additional stock through an underwriting or a rights offering inevitably increases the number of shares outstanding. Any stock sale that increases shares outstanding beyond the number authorized must first receive the stockholders' approval. Suppose a company wished to sell 200,000 shares when 400,000 are authorized and 300,000 are already issued. The sale would require an additional 100,000-share authorization. Most companies try to maintain a substantial cushion of authorized but unissued shares so that they can issue additional shares as needed without having to seek shareholder approval.

Indirect Stock Sales: Warrants and Convertibles

Firms may need equity capital but consider the current stock price too low to undertake a direct sale. A company that sells additional shares of its stock immediately increases the number of shares outstanding. This increase dilutes the ownership position of existing shareholders. The sale is likely to drive the stock's price down further. Accordingly, management may choose to raise the needed funds by selling other securities, such as convertible bonds or a package of bonds and *warrants*. With the sale of either *convertibles* or bonds plus warrants, the firm raises the needed funds by initially selling securities that are mainly or exclusively debt but have the potential of becoming equity. This indirect sale of similar magnitude to a stock sale causes less dilution because exercise (conversion or purchase of stock at a prespecified price) is attractive only if the stock's price rises above the specified exercise price. If the exercise does eventually take place, fewer shares will be issued than had the same sum been raised through an immediate stock sale. Clearly, the stock's price must rise above the exercise level, or the warrants will not be exercised and the convertibles will not be converted.

Thus, an indirect stock sale is an uncertain approach to raising equity. If the stock price remains below the exercise level, the firm has ended up selling debt rather than equity securities.

warrants
convertibles

Initial Stock Sales (Primary Market)

- New issues (public sale): sold through a syndicate of investment bankers organized to underwrite the issue
- New issues (private placement): sold to one or a few buyers who may agree to take lettered stock
- Rights offerings: give existing shareholders the opportunity to maintain their proportional ownership by purchasing stock from the company at below-market prices
- Warrants and convertibles: indirect, uncertain, and delayed stock sales, depending on exercise by holders, usually in conjunction with the sale of debt securities

LARGE SECONDARY MARKET TRADES

The vast majority of secondary market trades can be handled comfortably by the specialists or OTC market makers who earn their living positioning the stock. Other institutional arrangements are, however, used to handle trades that would strain the specialist's or market maker's capital resources. Very large amounts of stock usually require a secondary distribution (sale) or tender offer (buy); intermediate-sized trades may go through a block trader or be handled as a special offering.

block trades

Block Trades

Attempting to buy or sell 10,000 shares or more in the ordinary channels might result in a very unfavorable price for the trader. For example, an attempt to purchase 10,000 shares of a less actively traded stock could temporarily raise its market price appreciably while the buying is under way. Similarly, a large sale could cause the price to decline. Therefore, these trades are often implemented by a professional who specializes in handling large quantities in ways designed to minimize the market disruptions: the block trader.

For a large sell order, the block trader first obtains buyer commitments for part or all of the shares. He or she then offers to buy and resell the lot slightly below the current price, charging commissions to both sides of the trade. The block trader may purchase some of the lot to facilitate the transaction. This facilitating purchase may ultimately have to be sold at a loss. While block traders are usually given the task of selling large quantities of stock, they sometimes are asked to assemble large blocks for single buyers.

Special Offerings

special offerings

Special offerings or spot secondaries are also sometimes used to sell relatively large blocks of stock. Brokers who buy the securities for their clients receive a special incentive fee. The exchange must approve the offering, which is then announced on the ticker. It must remain open for at least 15 minutes. The offering price must generally equal or exceed the current bid but not exceed either the last sale price or the current ask.

Secondary Distributions

Block traders do not want to hold a large position long enough for an adverse price movement to offset their commission revenues. Moreover, very large blocks generally require relatively long periods to be sold at reasonable

secondary distributions

(non-distress-level) prices. These very large blocks are generally sold in *secondary distributions* that are handled in much the same way as new issues. A syndicate or the original seller directly markets the issue over time at a price somewhat below the previous level. The offering price includes a discount to the selling syndicate. No direct commission is charged.

Tender Offers

go private
tender offer

Large investors sometimes seek to make a substantial stock purchase, acquire control, or buy out most of the smaller shareholders (*go private*). A *tender offer* is generally used for these large purchases. For a limited period, the buyer offers to purchase a substantial block of stock, normally at a premium price. The tenderer usually pays an additional fee to brokers who handle their customers' trades. If the offer is oversubscribed and the buyer does not want the excess, stock may be bought on a pro rata basis. If too little is tendered, the buyer may reject all bids or purchase what is offered.

Large Blocks of Stock

- Block trade: trades of 10,000 shares or more with the passive side assembled by a block trader
- Special offerings: offerings that pay special incentive commissions to brokers who buy for their customers
- Secondary distributions: offerings of very large blocks of stock through a syndicate of investment bankers
- Tender offers: offers to purchase large amounts of stock almost always at a premium over the preoffer market price

---

SECURITIES MARKETS REGULATION

Because they are "clothed with the public interest," the securities markets are regulated. Investors need to understand the nature and direction of the regulation in order to take maximum advantage of any resulting opportunities.

Historical Background

Big Board

For many years the securities markets were operated largely in the interests of *Big Board* (New York Stock Exchange) members. Typical of a rational monopolist, the NYSE responded to potential competition by seeking to combine with, destroy, or limit the power of the rival exchange. In its first serious threat, the NYSE merged with the Open Board and Government Bond Department (1869). In the late 19th and early 20th centuries, the Consolidated Board (or "Little Board") provided a challenge. After the NYSE responded by forbidding its members to deal with the rival exchange's members, disreputable elements took control of the Little Board. The Consolidated Board soon withered away. The outdoor traders of the *New York Curb Exchange* traded only unlisted stocks. When the Curb went indoors (1921) and eventually changed its name to the American Stock Exchange (1953), it did so with the NYSE's blessing.

More recent forces have been draining the NYSE of its power and authority. Institutional investors have forced some changes. Commodity exchanges have invaded the NYSE's presumed turf by listing options and financial futures. The Securities and Exchange Commission, under pressure from the Justice Department's Antitrust Division, has taken a harder line against the exchange's quasi-monopoly position. Finally, competition from the third and fourth markets and the regional and foreign exchanges is being felt over, under, around, and through the exchange's regulations.

Current State of Securities Regulation

The exchanges, led by the NYSE, engage in a great deal of self-regulation. The NYSE maintained three monopolistic rules into the mid-1970s: fixing commissions, prohibiting exchange members from trading listed shares off the exchange, and prohibiting the AMEX from trading NYSE-listed securities. After a long struggle and rearguard action to preserve them, fixed commission rates were ended by SEC order in 1975. While the AMEX no longer automatically de-lists companies that obtain NYSE listings, only a relative handful of the NYSE's listings are dually traded with the AMEX, and most of the volume in those issues takes place on the NYSE. Therefore, the two New York exchanges still do not compete head-on. Off-exchange member trading of listed securities is no longer prohibited *per se*, but restrictions still discourage such activity.

Some NYSE regulations help both the exchange and its customers. For example, protecting customers from fraud or bankruptcy of member firms inspires public confidence.

The SEC has been diligent in protecting investors against fraud, misrepresentation, financial manipulation, and trading on inside information. Full and frank disclosure is also a top priority. Public security offerings must be accompanied by a prospectus that fully discloses all pertinent information. Publicly owned firms must file periodic financial statements with the SEC, the exchanges where they are traded, and their stockholders. Trading by insiders must be reported to the SEC. In spite of the SEC's efforts, however, substantial insider-informed trading continues. Any attempt to manipulate security prices runs afoul of both SEC regulations and the antitrust laws. The SEC has also extended its jurisdiction to many nonstock investments and has pushed for greater corporate disclosure. The major remaining security regulation controversy involves the central market.

THE DEVELOPMENT OF A CENTRAL MARKET

Congress has mandated that all of the exchanges and other securities markets (third and fourth) be fully linked. If and when that mandate is realized, buyers and sellers in all submarkets will be able to trade directly with each other. The more numerous alternatives should move buying and selling prices closer together (narrower spreads), and the greater diversity of reachable markets should allow larger blocks to be absorbed. Not surprisingly, this vision requires a number of difficult changes.

Consolidated Reporting

Until the mid-1970s securities trading was highly segmented. To obtain the best available price, each market had to be checked separately, and NYSE members could not trade in the third market. Most NYSE brokers simply funneled their orders to the market with the greatest volume. In 1974, consolidated trades began to be reported on a common ticker tape. The financial press initiated consolidated quotation reporting in 1976.

Composite Limit Order Book (CLOB)

Consolidated reporting without fully consolidated trading is confusing, however. Investors expect a buy limit order to be executed if the subsequent low falls below the limit price. If, however, the limit order is entered on the Big Board, and the low (high) occurs on the third market or another exchange, the trade may not take place. A *Composite Limit Order Book (CLOB)* and free order flow would allow all orders to be executed in any market where the security is traded. Thus, investors would always have access to the best available price regardless of where the order was entered. Not surprisingly, however, NYSE specialists, regional specialists, and third-market dealers are each interested in preserving their existing advantages. The various submarkets cannot be linked without exposing the participants to some additional competition. These conflicts coupled with the SEC's unwillingness to impose a solution has slowed the pace of reform.

Rule 390

Rule 390

As with the CLOB and market-link controversy, rules barring member off-exchange trading of listed securities have been fiercely defended by the securities profession. NYSE Rule 394, which prohibited such trading, was replaced with *Rule 390*, which restricts such trading. In 1977, the SEC announced that it intended to require the repeal of Rule 390 by January 1,

1978. That deadline was moved forward a number of times until December 2, 1999, when the NYSE finally voted to repeal Rule 390.

Industry sources had argued that if Rule 390 were repealed prior to the complete establishment of a central market, off-exchange markets made by the larger brokerage houses would cause some exchanges to close and others to shrink. According to this argument, brokerage houses too small to make markets for their customers would be unable to obtain competitive prices on the exchanges. Some industry sources went so far as to advocate concentrating trading on a single exchange. Similar self-serving arguments were used to oppose the end of fixed commissions. In actuality, the repealed fixed commission rates left the overall security trading system largely intact. In any case, it might prove beneficial to hasten the linkup of the various markets. Easy access to the third and fourth markets should increase competition and lead to more efficient pricing.

The intermarket information system, which facilitates an exchange of price quotations, is a small step toward centralized trading. Fortunately, Congress has mandated that trading on and off the exchanges be unrestricted and that orders be allowed to flow freely from market to market.

THE ECONOMIC FUNCTIONS OF THE SECURITIES MARKETS

Securities markets play an important role in the economy. They assist with capital and managerial allocation. They also provide a vehicle for the Fed to transmit monetary policy to the economy. Thus, the securities markets have a significant impact on both short- and long-run economic performance.

Shifting technology, evolving tastes and preferences, and the introduction of new and improved products lead to changes in consumer spending patterns. Increasing demand frequently outstrips existing capacity and bids up prices in some areas. Overcapacity tends to drive prices down elsewhere. Profits increase where demand is strong at the expense of firms with excess capacity. The securities markets tend to react to these shifting spending patterns. Generally, more capital is allocated toward firms that appear to have bright prospects and away from firms where the outlook is poorer. Clearly, this market-based reallocation of capital is an uncertain process. Let us consider how effectively the task is performed.

Sources and Uses of Funds

Companies need to finance their plant, equipment, and working capital (particularly inventories). Funds can be obtained in the form of either debt or equity. Corporate debt sources include bonds, notes, trade credit, bank loans, accrued expenses, and all other firm borrowings. Stock sales and retained earnings (profit after taxes and dividends) are the primary ways of raising equity capital. Retained earnings supply most equity capital for most firms over most time periods. Stock sales generate only a modest portion of total new equity funds.

Debt security sales average perhaps 10 times the amount of new capital raised from new stock sales. The stock market's capital availability impact is much greater, however, than that suggested by the relatively modest amount of equity capital raised through stock sales. Most firms try to maintain what they view to be an appropriate balance between debt and equity capital, depending on the relative costs of the different kinds of capital.

On the one hand, debt allows firms to leverage their shareholders' equity positions. In addition, the interest payments on debt are tax deductible so the effective cost to the issuing firm can be relatively low. If the operating profits earned with the borrowed funds exceed the cost of the loan, the return attributable to the owners (shareholders) is enhanced. Shareholders, therefore, will benefit from an effective use of debt.

Advantages of Using Debt

- Debt allows firms to leverage their shareholders' equity positions.
- The interest payments on debt are tax deductible; therefore, the effective cost to the issuing firm is relatively low.
- If the operating profits earned with the borrowed funds exceed the cost of the loan, the return attributable to the owners is enhanced.

On the other hand, firms have several reasons for limiting their reliance on debt. First, a borrower firm is contractually obligated to make principal and interest payments on its debt or risk legal action that could lead to its bankruptcy. Equity is, in contrast, permanent capital supplied by the owners. Thus, the issuing company may suspend, reduce, or freeze its payments to shareholders (dividends) without violating any legally enforceable commitment.

debt-equity ratio   Second, a high *debt-equity ratio* tends to increase the interest rate on all of the company's borrowings, as well as the discount factor applied to all future (expected) earnings. As the firm's debt-equity ratio rises, therefore, its interest expense increases and its stock value may decline, other things being equal. This rise in financing costs is due to two factors: the greater amount borrowed and the higher cost of the funds borrowed. Lenders demand higher interest payments of firms that are highly levered and therefore more risky to lend to. Financial analysts also take such risks into account when assessing the long-term prospects of the firm.

Third, if the borrowing rate exceeds the return on the additional investment, debt will depress the firm's earnings. The greater the percentage of debt, the greater the adverse impact of leverage. The target ratio is likely to vary with the industry, the firm, and over time. Nonetheless, efforts to stay within the desired debt-equity range still limit borrowing and encourage equity sales to support additional borrowing.

Reasons a Firm Limits Reliance on Debt

- A borrower firm is contractually obligated to make principal and interest payments on its debt.
- A high debt ratio tends to increase the interest rate on all the company's borrowings and the discount factor applied to all future earnings.
- If the borrowing rate exceeds the return on the additional investment, debt will depress the firm's earnings.

Role of the Securities Markets in Allocating Capital Funds

The amount of equity capital that a firm can raise is constrained by the price it can get for its stock. Firms are expected to avoid selling additional stock when these sales would adversely affect their existing shareholders' interest. Although the long-term impact of a stock sale is very difficult to judge, some attention is given to the effect of stock sales on per-share book value (accounting value of equity). Book value is one, admittedly imperfect, measure of the firm's own resources (as opposed to borrowed resources). Per-share book value measures the resources attributable to each share. Thus, a stock sale that increases per-share book value tends to raise the amount of resources attributable to each share, whereas a sale that decreases (dilutes) per-share book value has the opposite effect. The higher a stock's price relative to its per-share book value, the easier equity capital is to raise. A high relative share price allows a given sum to be raised without dilution.

Example: The BCD Company has a total accounting (book) equity value of $5,000,000 and 1,000,000 shares outstanding selling for $10 per share. To raise $1,000,000 (ignoring underwriting costs), it could sell 100,000 shares. The sale would increase shares outstanding by 10 percent. Its per-share book value would rise from $5 ($5,000,000/1,000,000) to $5.45 ($6,000,000/1,100,000). Now contrast this situation with that of the CDE Corporation. CDE also has a total accounting equity value of $5,000,000 and 1,000,000 shares outstanding, but its stock sells for $2.50 per share. To raise $1,000,000, CDE would need to sell 400,000 shares. As a result, shares that are outstanding would increase 40 percent and per-share book value would fall to $4.29 ($6,000,000/ 1,400,000). Many of its shareholders would likely object to a sale of the firm's stock at a price below its per-share book value.

Both the BCD and CDE examples assume, for the sake of simplicity, that the sale of additional shares would not affect the share price. In fact, however, selling additional shares might very well depress the stocks' prices at least temporarily. Because the increase in shares outstanding would be proportionately greater for CDE, its per-share price is likely to decline by the greater amount.

Companies like BCD, therefore, with high stock prices relative to book values, can usually raise additional equity more easily than those like CDE, with lower relative stock prices. Moreover, because debt is considered less risky when the capital structure contains proportionately more equity, a high relative stock price indirectly contributes to the success of a debt offering. Thus, both debt and equity capital tend to be more available to firms with the greatest perceived potential.

return on equity

Another important consideration in the sale of equity capital is the firm's current *return on equity* (ROE). A firm that is earning a high return on its existing equity is likely to be able to earn a high return on additional equity. On the other hand, a firm that has a low ROE currently is less likely to be able to earn an attractive return on any new equity. The market is likely to be much more receptive to a stock sale from a high ROE firm than from a low ROE firm. Stocks of companies with high ROE values tend to sell at high prices relative to book values, whereas low ROE companies tend to sell at low prices relative to book values.

The stock market also has an impact on a firm's ability to retain earnings. Stockholders of rapidly growing firms are less likely to object to a large retention ratio (percentage of earnings not paid out in dividends) than are those of slower growth firms. Increased per-share earnings are generally associated with rapid growth. Rapid growth (particularly rapid growth in profits) tends to raise stock prices sufficiently to offset the forgone dividends. Other firms may maintain a higher payout (percentage of earnings paid as dividends), however, to compensate for their slower growth. Alternatively, companies with excess funds may repurchase and then retire their own stock.

Allocating Management Talent

The stock market also helps allocate managerial talent. Stock prices of poorly managed firms often do not fully reflect their potentials. These undervalued firms attract investors who may try to take control, put in more effective managers, and profit from the improved operation. Sometimes the mere threat of a takeover is enough to motivate better management. In the past, such well-known investors as T. Boone Pickens, Saul Steinberg, Carl Icahn, Irwin Jacobs, the Bass family, Sir James Goldsmith, and a host of others have found these strategies to be very profitable.

leveraged buyout   Takeover artists sometimes utilize a technique called the *leveraged buyout* or LBO. The acquisition target's own asset values are used to finance much of the acquisition costs. Once in control, the acquirer may replace ineffective management and sell company assets in order to increase profitability and generate cash. LBOs were very popular in the 1980s. In some instances, however, too much debt was piled upon too little equity, and the enterprise failed. The market has tended to be more cautious of LBOs since that time.

While takeovers have many motivations, almost all stem at least in part from the acquirer's belief that the current market price of the proposed acquisition is undervalued relative to its potential. This potential can best be exploited (even in a friendly takeover) by bringing in fresh ideas, resources, and faces. Takeovers and potential takeovers, therefore, help weed out deadwood and keep managers on their toes. These acquisitions are often accomplished through tender offers. Proxy fights have, however, become increasingly popular because, compared to tender offers, they are generally less costly for the acquirer.

The stock market may also play a significant role in facilitating the hiring of individual managers. Senior-level managers are often compensated with a package of benefits, including a base salary and pension benefits coupled with possible bonuses and stock options that depend on performance. Because the value of stock option packages tends to increase with the firm's growth potential, the options of promising firms may help attract managerial talent that other firms could hire only with higher salaries. Start-up companies, especially high-tech start-up companies, are particularly likely to use option packages to attract new management.

Criteria for Efficient Capital Allocation

To distribute capital and management talent effectively, the stock market needs to reflect each firm's earnings potential accurately. Otherwise, funds and talent may flow toward overvalued firms and away from undervalued firms. Moreover, high transaction costs would raise barriers to resource flows.

In a classic study, Irwin Friend (1972) carefully considered pricing efficiency and transaction costs.[2] He concluded that the stock market has been markedly unsuccessful in forecasting firm performance, although its record has improved since the 1920s. He also found that underwriting fees have declined since the 1920s but that commission rates have tended to increase. More recently, the end of fixed commissions has reduced trading costs for some while raising them for others. The rise of low commission Internet trading has tended to make the securities market even more competitive. Friend also believed that increased security regulation contributed to improved market performance, although he offered no suggestions for facilitating further improvement.

G.J. Benston (1973), in contrast, contended that the Securities Exchange Act of 1934 did not improve market efficiency. He found no evidence that trading on fraudulent and misleading reports decreased with the act's passage.[3]

OTHER ROLES OF THE MARKET

Consumers' spending is influenced by both their current income and their financial resources. One of the important types of household financial assets is holdings of stocks and related assets (common stock mutual funds, pension funds with stocks, insurance policies with reserves invested in stocks, and so on). A rising stock market tends to increase investor wealth and spending, whereas a declining stock market has the opposite effect. The Federal Reserve Board needs to take account of the impact of the stock-market-induced wealth effect. That is, when the Fed seeks to influence the economy through changes in monetary policy, the stock market is likely to transmit part of the impact to consumers. Although the Fed may also adjust the margin rate to encourage spending or discourage speculation, it rarely does so.

Figure 3-2 illustrates the relationship between stock prices and consumer spending.

irrational exuberance

A recent debate concerns the degree to which the stock market's perceived overvaluation (*irrational exuberance* in the 1996 words of Fed chairman Greenspan) has contributed to excessive consumer spending and an abnormally low household personal savings rate. Some have argued that this means that the Fed should target the stock market in its policy initiatives. Others argue that targeting is not in the mandate of the Fed as delineated by Congress.

This debate is expected to go on for some time and is beyond the current scope of this book.

FIGURE 3-2
How Stock Values Move Consumer Spending

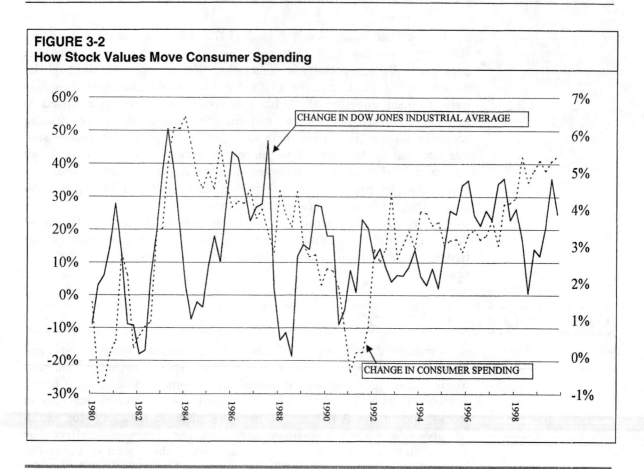

SUMMARY AND CONCLUSIONS

This chapter explores the trading mechanisms, regulation, and economic functions of the securities markets. A wide array of mechanisms may be used to buy and sell securities. Most trading involves the larger companies listed on an exchange. Smaller companies are generally traded OTC. Newly issued securities may be sold through a rights offering, underwriting syndicate, or private placement. Large blocks of already issued securities are normally marketed through a block trader, special offering, or in a secondary offering. A tender offer is generally used for a large purchase. Short sales are employed by investors seeking to profit from a price decline while margin purchases leverage investors' equity positions.

A variety of orders are used in securities trading. Market orders require immediate execution, whereas limit orders await an acceptable price. Stop orders (stop-loss and stop-limit) offer protection from adverse price moves.

The chapter provides six stock-trading rules for investors: First, for a large transaction, shop for the best price on the third market, regional exchanges, and principal exchange. Second, use discount (or Internet) brokerage firms to obtain reduced commissions. Third, take careful account of the advantages and disadvantages of the OTC market. OTC spreads are usually wider than those on listed stocks. Furthermore, some unlisted stocks are not marginable. On the other hand, local OTC stocks may be more familiar to individual investors and more likely to be undervalued. Fourth, use limit orders, which offer flexibility and protection from adverse price moves, rather than market orders. Fifth, use margin credit, a flexible source of funds available at relatively low interest costs, to magnify profit potential. Sixth, if a stock is held in a street name, retain a portion in the customer's name to ensure his or her promptly receiving company reports.

Six Stock-Trading Rules

- For a large transaction, shop for the best price on the third market, regional exchanges, and principal exchanges.
- Use discount (or Internet) brokerage firms to get reduced commissions.
- Take account of OTC market advantages and disadvantages.
- Use limit orders instead of market orders for greater flexibility and protection from price moves.
- Use margin credit to magnify profit potential.
- If a stock is held in a street name, retain a portion in the customer's name to ensure timely receipt of company reports.

As for the development of the central market, reform forces are quite powerful, much progress has been made, opposition to additional reform is intense, and further reforms have been recommended and will probably be enacted. The principal unresolved issues involve the consolidation of trading and limit order access.

Finally, the securities markets play an important role in allocating capital and managerial talent, as well as in facilitating the Fed's implementation of economic policy.

CHAPTER REVIEW

Answers to the review questions and the self-test questions start on page 742.

Key Terms

broker
brokerage firm
registered representative
dealers
Glass-Steagall Act
SIPC (Securities Investor
   Protection Corporation)
FDIC (Federal Deposit Insurance
   Corporation)
NASD (National Association of
   Securities Dealers)
SEC (Securities and Exchange
   Commission)
churning
no-load mutual funds
NYSE (New York Stock Exchange)
AMEX (American Stock Exchange)
OTC (over the counter)
NASDAQ (National Association of
   Securities Dealers Automated
   Quotations)
NMI (National Market Issues)
Pink Sheets
ticker tape
commissions
bid-ask spreads
market order
limit order
stop-loss order
stop-limit order
GTC orders
day orders
fill-or-kill orders
all-or-nothing orders
versus purchase
specialist
floor traders
RCMMs
pricing points
third market

fourth market
arbitrageurs
margin account
buying power
margin calls
credit balance
debit balance
broker call-loan rate
short selling
downtick
street name
stock certificates
primary market
go public
investment banker
underwrite
prospectus
best-effort basis
firm-commitment basis
shelf registration
private placement
lettered stock
rights offering
preemptive rights
warrants
convertibles
block trades
special offerings
secondary distributions
go private
tender offer
Big Board
New York Curb Exchange
Composite Limit Order Book
   (CLOB)
Rule 390
debit-equity ratio
return on equity
leveraged buyout
irrational exuberance

Review Questions

3-1. Explain the purpose of the Securities Investor Protection Corporation (SIPC).

3-2. Explain the purpose of the National Daily Quotation Service.

3-3. Using table 3-2, compute the following commissions:
    a.   the commission on a single trade of 1,500 shares at $7 per share
    b.   the commission on 15 separate 100-share trades at $7 per share
    c.   Compare the two commissions from a. and b.

3-4. In the OTC market, RST stock is quoted as bid 80 and ask 81. Assume that an investor buys 500 shares of RST stock in this market.
    a.   What is the commission for this trade (using table 3-2)?
    b.   What is the purchase cost (cost of stock plus the commission) of this trade?
    c.   What is the spread for this stock?
    d.   What is the percentage spread for this stock?

3-5. Assume that the investor in question 3-4 above sells the 500 shares of RST stock when it is quoted as bid 90 and ask 91. What is the investor's holding period return for RST stock?

3-6. Explain the four principal types of orders.

3-7. Assume that over a period of time, an investor purchases XYZ stock in five 300-share blocks at prices of $15, $18, $31, $23, and $40 per share, respectively.
    a.   If the investor then sells 700 shares of XYZ, how would the basis in these shares normally be determined?
    b.   Explain how the investor could achieve a much higher basis for the 700 shares of XYZ than would normally be the case as determined in a. above.

3-8. a.   Describe three rules that are helpful for setting a limit price.
    b.   Under what circumstances should an investor ignore the three rules and use a market order?

3-9. Explain the roles of the third and fourth markets.

3-10. a.   Describe the two types of margin calls.
    b.   Explain the various ways in which a margin call can be satisfied.

3-11. Jo Ann Investor uses $5,000 plus maximum margin (50 percent) to buy stock in the Up Up Corporation at $10 per share. The stock is a clear winner. It rises to $15 per share after one month, and she continues to hold it. It then splits three for two (that is, for every two shares owned by Jo Ann, she will now have three shares) and continues rising in price until it reaches $20 per share after another 4 months have passed. Jo Ann then buys as many more shares as her position allows. Six months later, the stock pays a 25 percent

stock dividend and rises to $30 per share. Jo Ann again increases her holdings to the maximum allowed by her equity. Up Up then goes to $50 per share one year later. Ignoring the impact of taxes, regular dividends, interest, and commissions, answer the following questions about Jo Ann's position after 23 months' experience with the Up Up Corporation stock.
a. How many shares does Jo Ann own?
b. What is the value of Jo Ann's stock?
c. How much does Jo Ann owe in margin?
d. What is Jo Ann's equity position?

3-12. Joe Investor uses $50,000 plus maximum margin (50 percent) to buy stock in the Down Down Corporation at $50 per share. After 6 months, the stock falls to the point where he gets a margin call (35 percent equity). To satisfy the call, he sells enough of his position to bring his equity back up to 50 percent. Two months later, Joe gets a second margin call (35 percent equity) and repeats the process. When he gets the third margin call (35 percent equity) one month later, Joe liquidates his position. Ignoring the impact of taxes, dividends, interest, and commissions in answering this question, how much of Joe's original $50,000 investment is left?

3-13. Assume the broker call-loan rate is 8 1/2 percent and that the margin loan rates of table 3-6 apply. Compute the cost of margin for each of the following, using monthly compounding:
a. $53,000 borrowed for 6 months
b. $27,000 borrowed for 3 months
c. $7,000 borrowed for 10 months

3-14. Investment bankers facilitate new-issue sales of debt and equity securities. Describe the two underwriting approaches they use to accomplish this objective.

3-15. Explain what the creation of a central market for securities would accomplish.

3-16. a. Describe the advantages to a firm of using debt capital.
b. Explain why firms may want to limit their reliance on debt capital.

3-17. The ABC Corporation has 5 million shares outstanding and a total net worth of $60 million. If it sells an additional 750,000 shares for a price of $18 per share (15 percent of which are flotation costs), what will happen to its net worth and per-share book value?

3-18. a. Explain the role that securities markets play in allocating management talent.
b. Explain the role that corporate takeovers play in allocating management talent.
c. Describe the role of stock options in attracting managerial talent.

Self-Test Questions

T   F   3-1.   The most basic function that brokers and their firms perform is the linking of investors to the securities markets.

T   F   3-2.   The lines between brokerage and other types of financial service firms, particularly commercial banks, are quickly eroding, and the erosion is likely to accelerate.

T   F   3-3.   The Securities Investor Protection Corporation (SIPC) protects brokerage customers against losses due to market fluctuations.

T   F   3-4.   The New York Stock Exchange (NYSE) has about 5,000 listed companies and about 10,000 listed securities, including preferred shares.

T   F   3-5.   The National Daily Quotation Service reports the bid and ask prices for all actively traded over-the-counter (OTC) issues.

T   F   3-6.   Institutional trading makes up a much larger part of the AMEX or NASDAQ volume than that of the NYSE.

T   F   3-7.   Although corporate bonds may be listed on exchanges, most are traded over the counter.

T   F   3-8.   The two major costs of executing a trade are commissions (broker fees) and spreads (wholesale/retail markups).

T   F   3-9.   Security market commission rates are fixed by agreement among the brokerage firms.

T   F   3-10. Bid-ask spreads tend to represent a larger percentage of the price for higher priced and more actively traded stocks.

T   F   3-11. A limit order ensures a transaction since it requires an immediate execution at the best available price.

T   F   3-12. A stop-limit order activates a limit order when the market reaches the stop level.

T   F   3-13. The total commission on a trade that takes several days to be executed would be far less than that on a single transaction involving the same number of shares.

T   F   3-14. An all-or-nothing order must be either executed immediately or canceled.

T   F   3-15. Specialists maintain an inventory of their assigned stocks and buy for and sell from that inventory.

T   F   3-16. Floor traders or registered competitive market makers own exchange seats and trade for their own account.

T   F   3-17. In 1999. more than 100 NYSE members were floor traders.

T   F   3-18.   Between 75 percent and 85 percent of all stock exchange transactions utilize limit orders.

T   F   3-19.   A limit order might not result in a trade and therefore might not generate a commission for the broker.

T   F   3-20.   Stocks traded over the counter are generally more marketable than those listed on an exchange.

T   F   3-21.   The third market involves informal arrangements for direct trading between institutions.

T   F   3-22.   Many high-volume stocks trade simultaneously on the NYSE, several regional exchanges, and over the counter.

T   F   3-23.   As of 1999, the Federal Reserve Board set the margin requirement on stocks at 25 percent.

T   F   3-24.   To be marginable, an OTC stock must have at least 1,200 shareholders and a market value of $5 million or more.

T   F   3-25.   Margin loans may remain outstanding as long as the borrower's equity position does not fall below the maintenance margin percentage.

T   F   3-26.   Preferreds, warrants, and convertibles are subject to the same margin requirements as common stock.

T   F   3-27.   Traders typically use short sales to drive a stock's price down.

T   F   3-28.   Margined securities must be left on deposit with the shareholder's brokerage house.

T   F   3-29.   Stock certificates must be issued whenever a stock is registered in an individual's name.

T   F   3-30.   Investment bankers generally agree to sell a new issue on a best-effort basis where they act as agents for the issuing firm.

T   F   3-31.   A preemptive rights clause ensures shareholders of the right to maintain their proportional ownership of the company.

T   F   3-32.   In 1921, the New York Curb Exchange went indoors and eventually changed its name to the New York Stock Exchange.

T   F   3-33.   Off-exchange member trading of listed securities is strictly prohibited.

T   F   3-34.   Congress has mandated that trading on and off the exchanges be unrestricted, and that orders be allowed to flow freely from market to market.

T   F   3-35.   Stock sales supply most equity capital for most firms over most time periods.

T   F   3-36.   Debt security sales average about one-half the amount of new capital raised from new stock sales.

T   F   3-37.   The higher a stock's price relative to its *per-share* book value, the easier equity capital is to raise.

T   F   3-38.   A firm that is earning a high return on its existing equity is likely to be able to earn a high return on additional equity.

T   F   3-39.   Tender offers have become increasingly popular because they are generally less costly for the acquiring firms than proxy fights.

T   F   3-40.   To distribute capital and management talent effectively, the stock market needs accurately to reflect each firm's earnings potential.

NOTES

1. B. Branch, "The Optimal Price to Trade," *Journal of Financial and Quantitative Analysis,* September 1975, pp. 497–514.
2. I. Friend, "The Economic Consequences of the Stock Market," *American Economic Review,* May 1972, pp. 212–219.
3. G.J. Benston, "Required Disclosure and the Stock Market: An Evaluation of the Securities Exchange Act of 1934," *American Economic Review,* March 1973, pp. 133–155.

4

Valuation of Investments: Fixed-Income Securities

Learning Objectives

An understanding of the material in this chapter should enable the student to

---

4-1. Explain the time value of money and how it enters into the valuation of investments.

4-2. Explain the various factors that affect the discount rate.

Chapter Outline

market price

Most prices (including the prices of investment assets) are established and maintained by market forces. That is, the interplay of supply and demand sets prices at levels that allow the relevant markets to clear. At the *market price*, all would-be buyers have bought, and all would-be sellers have sold. Additional purchases would be desired at lower prices, and more sales would be offered at higher prices. Market prices fluctuate as market forces vary over time. That is, market prices change as new buyers (demand) or new sellers (supply) enter or leave the marketplace. Underlying the determination of the market price is a more complex set of processes. Understanding these

cash flow

processes and the implications of these prices is an important step in any comparative valuation process.

Investments trade largely on the basis of their expected *cash flow* and price appreciation. Accordingly, this chapter examines how these expectations influence market values. First, the chapter introduces time value and assesses its investment valuation role. It also discusses the role of several factors, particularly risk and inflation, in establishing the appropriate discount rate.

TIME VALUE

time value

Time value is crucial to expected income stream valuations. Suppose you were offered the choice of receiving $100 now or $100 a year from now. Which would you choose? Almost everyone would choose to have the money now rather than later. Even those who did not intend to use the money for a year would not want to wait for it. Any funds that are available now but not needed until a year from now can be invested. For example, the funds could earn a year's interest in a government-guaranteed savings account. Clearly, a sum of money that is available now is worth more than that same sum to be received at a later time. In other words, money has what is called time value. The concept of the time value of money is central to the valuation of investments. Investments are expected to pay a return over time.

To understand how time value enters into investment valuation, consider the value of a commitment to pay $100,000 a year for 20 years. Such a commitment could arise in a number of ways. For example, an individual could sell or lease a business to a buyer who commits to such a payout. Alternatively, it could arise when a university chair is endowed. The benefactor of a chair must supply the university with enough money to pay the professor's salary and other expenses (secretarial, and so on) until retirement. If the professor is now 45 years old, he or she can be expected to continue to hold the chair for another 20 years. The giver might offer to make a separate $100,000 payment each year. However, few, if any, universities would be comfortable with such an arrangement. The university would have committed itself to make the payments to the chaired professor until he or she retires. What would happen if the benefactor died, went broke, or changed his or her mind? Presumably, the university would be expected to stand behind its promise to the chaired professor even if the donor did not. Because of these uncertainties, the university, no doubt, would rather have the chair funded up front.

How much funding would be required to assure the university that it would be able to cover the payments? Although a total of $2 million in payments is promised over the 20-year period, the present value of the commitment is considerably less. Suppose there were a 5 percent annual interest rate; a $2 million CD would yield $100,000 a year forever. If the university could earn 8 percent on its investments, it could generate a $100,000 payment each year with an investment of $1.25 million (8% x $1,250,000 = $100,000). It could make the required payments with even less than $1.25 million if it also liquidated the principal over the period. With this strategy, at the end of 20 years, the initial sum would be depleted. On the other hand, if the payments were to be raised each year to offset the impact of *inflation*, the initial sum would need to be greater.

inflation

Clearly, problems like this one have a number of dimensions. They involve relating current stocks of money to flows of money through time. How much, for example, is a promise to pay X dollars a year for Y years worth in current dollars? The answer turns out to be relatively straightforward.

As we have already seen, a current dollar can begin earning interest immediately. Thus, a currently payable dollar should be worth more than a promise to pay a dollar in the future. How much more should the current dollar be worth? The *present value* of a future payment depends on three things: how much is to be received, when it is to be received, and how much of a discount is applied to future values compared to present values. Similarly, the value of a stream of payments to be received over time depends on the amounts, timings, and discount rate applied to the payments.

present value

The Present Value of a Future Payment or Stream of Payments Depends On . . .

- How much is to be received
- When is (are) the payment(s) to be received
- How much of a discount rate is to be applied to the payment(s)

Discounting to Take Account of Time Value

Valuing an expected stream of future payments involves placing a present value on each individual expected future payment. That valuation should enable someone to compare each such future payment to an immediate payment. The current or discounted value of a future sum is called its *present value*. For example, saying that the present value of a $1,000 payment 3 years from now is $860 means that an investor would be indifferent to receiving $860 now or the expectation of receiving $1,000 in 3 years. Once the present value of each expected future payment is determined, the individual present values can be added. The resulting sum is the present value of the expected future payments. The rate at which the present value of future cash flows is determined is called the *discount rate*. Think of discount

discount rate

rates as interest rates in reverse. Just as an interest rate determines what a present amount of money will be worth in the future, a discount rate determines what an expected future cash flow is worth in the present.

The appropriate discount rate will vary substantially with the economic environment and the specific circumstances of the expected cash flow to be evaluated. If a present dollar is viewed as equivalent to $1.06 a year from now, the appropriate discount rate is 6 percent. Using a 6 percent discount rate, $1.00 received today is equivalent to $1.1236 received 2 years from now (1.06 x 1.06 = $1.1236). Similarly, a promise to pay $1.00 next year is worth $.943 today (.943 x 1.06 = $1.00).

Example 1:   Discounting an asset promising three annual payments of $100 at a discount rate of 6 percent yields a present value of:

$$PV = \frac{\$100}{1.06} + \frac{\$100}{(1.06)^2} + \frac{\$100}{(1.06)^3} = \$267.30$$

where: PV = present value of the income stream

Discounting the first year's payment at 6 percent is equivalent to dividing it by 1.06. The second year's payment is discounted at 6 percent twice, which means dividing it by (1.06 x 1.06) or $(1.06)^2$. Similarly, the third year's payment is divided by (1.06 x 1.06 x 1.06) or $(1.06)^3$.

Example 2:   Valuing an asset (again using a 6 percent discount rate) that yields successive annual payments of $100, $300, $50, $100, and $300 and a resale price of $1,000 involves a little more complicated arithmetic, but the principle is the same:

$$PV = \frac{\$100}{1.06} + \frac{\$300}{(1.06)^2} + \frac{\$50}{(1.06)^3} + \frac{\$100}{(1.06)^4} + \frac{\$1,300}{(1.06)^5}$$

$$= \$100(.9434) + \$300(.8900) + \$50(.8396) + \$100(.7921) + \$1,300(.7473)$$
$$= \$94.34 + \$267.00 + \$41.98 + \$79.21 + \$971.44$$
$$= \$1,453.97$$

Note that the resale price and final payment are both discounted by $(1.06)^5$ because both are to be paid 5 years later.

Present value tables or a financial calculator is often employed to simplify present value computations. Also, using a hand-held calculator, the computation in the previous example would be as follows:

$$(1.06)^{-1}\$100 + (1.06)^{-2}\$300 + (1.06)^{-3}\$50 + (1.06)^{-4}\$100 + (1.06)^{-5}\$1,300$$

In general, dividing by x^n is equivalent to multiplying by x^{-n}.

Present Value Applied to Bonds

Let us see how the concept of time value can be applied to the income stream of a bond. Bonds are debt securities that make periodic interest (coupon) payments and then return their *face value* at *maturity*. For the vast majority of bonds, the periodic interest payment is fixed at a set amount, called the *coupon rate*. Most of these bonds pay interest every 6 months.

face value

maturity

coupon rate

Example: A 10-year, 8 percent, $1,000 bond would promise the following income stream: coupon payments of $40 every 6 months (1/2 x 8% of $1,000) for 10 years, and at the end of 10 years a principal payment of $1,000.

An investment promising a constant income stream, known as an annuity, can be valued by the present value formula:

$$PV = \frac{CF_1}{(1+r)} + \frac{CF_2}{(1+r)^2} + \frac{CF_3}{1+r^3} + \frac{CF_n}{(1+r)^n} \qquad \text{(Equation 4-1)}$$

where: CF_n = cash flow per period
r = appropriate discount rate
n = total number of periods

As the example shows, investment assets can be viewed as streams of expected cash flows. Clearly, the discount rate plays a central role in the valuation of these expected cash flows. The higher the discount rate, the lower the present value of the stream of cash flows.

Example: A $1,000 (face value) bond paying annual coupons of $50 (5 percent) and maturing in 7 years at an 8 percent discount rate is worth

$$PV = \frac{\$50}{1.08} + \frac{\$50}{(1.08)^2} + \frac{\$50}{(1.08)^3} + \frac{\$50}{(1.08)^4} + \frac{\$50}{(1.08)^5} + \frac{\$50}{(1.08)^6} + \frac{\$1,050}{(1.08)^7}$$

$$= 46.30 + 42.87 + 39.69 + 36.75 + 34.03 + 31.51 + 612.66 = 843.81$$

Or we can calculate

$$= \$50 \left(\frac{1}{1.08} + \frac{1}{1.08^2} + \frac{1}{1.08^3} + \frac{1}{1.08^4} + \frac{1}{1.08^5} + \frac{1}{1.08^6} + \frac{1}{1.08^7} \right) + \$1,000 \left(\frac{1}{1.08^7} \right)$$

$$= \$50 (.9259 + .8573 + .7938 + .735 + .6806 + .6302 + .5835)$$

$$= \$843.81$$

Note: For simplicity, we assumed a single annual payment. With semi-annual payments, the calculation would be $\$25/1.04 + \$25/(1.04)^2 + ... + \$25/(1.04)^{14} + \$1,000/(1.04)^{14}$

Note that the present value of the bond in the example is less than its $1,000 face value. Indeed, any bond with a coupon rate below the discount rate is worth less than its face value. In the example, the promised coupon rate is $50, or 5 percent of $1,000 (50/1,000 = .05), which is below the discount rate of 8 percent.

Now suppose that the bond in the example is valued using a 4 percent discount rate. The bond's present value at this discount rate is $1,060, or $60 above its face value. The lower discount rate results in a higher valuation. Indeed, at a 3 percent discount rate, the bond's present value would be $1,125. Table 4-1 illustrates the relationship between present value and discount rate. Notice that when the discount rate is equal to the bond's interest rate, the present value of the bond is equal to its face value.

TABLE 4-1
Market Price of 7-Year, 5 Percent Bonds
at Various Discount Rates
(Rounded to the Nearest Dollar)

Discount Rate	Market Price
2%	$1,194
3%	$1,125
4%	$1,060
5%	$1,000
⋮	⋮
10%	$757

In general, the discount rate on a bond can be thought of as the market-determined interest rate that would be paid on a bond of comparable risk and maturity that trades at par and has a present value equal to its face value. To see this clearly, calculate the present value of any bond whose discount rate and coupon rate are equal.

When a constant amount is to be paid forever (a perpetuity), a simpler formula relates the market price to the discount rate:

$$PV = CF/r \qquad \text{(Equation 4-2)}$$

where: PV = present value of the income stream
CF = each period's cash flow
r = appropriate discount rate

A perpetual $50 annual payment divided by a discount rate of 5 percent has a present value of $1,000. Put another way, $1,000 invested at 5 percent can earn $50 per year forever. If the market interest rate changes, the present value of the $50 payment stream also changes.

Example: Interest rates rise from 5 percent to 10 percent. Dividing the $50 per-year payment stream by 10 percent produces a $500 value. A fall in interest rates has the opposite effect. At 4 percent, the $50 payment stream is worth $1,250 ($50/.04).

---

preferred stock

Britain has issued some infinite-maturity bonds called consols. The vast majority of debt obligations, however, promise to repay principal at some future date. On the other hand, most *preferred stock* issues are perpetuities (that is, they have no maturity date), so their present value can be determined by dividing their annual dividend by the coupon rate.

Why Bond Prices Vary from Their Face Values

Most bonds are initially sold for a price close to their par, or face, values. Their coupon rate is generally set to yield a return very close to the market interest rate on such bonds. The subsequent market interest rate and price, however, seldom stay very close to that level. Economic forces cause market interest rates to fluctuate over time. These economic forces also lead to changes in the prices on existing bonds. In addition, the riskiness of the issuing company can change over time, which will also change the discount rate and market price of the bonds.

A 6 percent bond will pay $60 per year and return $1,000 of principal at maturity regardless of future market rates. If otherwise similar (risk, maturity, and so forth) newly issued 7 percent bonds ($70-per-year coupon) sell at their face values, the 6 percent bond must also be priced to return 7 percent. No one will pay $1,000 for a bond yielding $60 per year when otherwise similar bonds yielding $70-per-year trade for $1,000. Rather than sell for its face value, the 6 percent coupon bond must offer a *yield to maturity (YTM)* equivalent to its discount rate.

yield to maturity (YTM)

The YTM is the discount rate that makes the present value of the coupon and principal payments equal to the market price of the bond. The YTM is analogous to the internal rate of return concept used in capital budgeting. Thus, a bond whose present value at a discount rate of 7 percent is $950 will have a 7 percent YTM if it sells for $950.

Bond prices and, indeed, most security prices move inversely with market interest rates. If interest rates rise, bond prices decline, and vice versa.

DETERMINANTS OF THE DISCOUNT RATE

Discount rates clearly play an important role in investment valuations. The appropriate discount rate varies both over time and from investment to investment. Many factors influence discount rates.

Changing economic conditions in the market can affect the general level of interest rates, as previously noted. These changes will, in turn, cause individual bond prices to move up and down as market interest rates move down and up. What causes market rates to change?

At times, the supply of funds available for borrowing (relative to the demand) is tight, while at other times loanable funds are more plentiful. Market interest rates vary inversely with the relative supply of loanable funds. More money in the system looking for borrowers leads to lower interest rates, whereas more borrowers looking for money to borrow leads to higher rates. Interest can be regarded as the "price" of loanable funds. The state of the economy and the government's economic policy (covered in detail later in this book) play a major role in determining conditions in the credit markets, and thus the general level of interest rates. The discount rate applied to a particular expected income stream will vary up and down as general market interest rates move up and down.

In addition to the general impact of the credit markets, a particular asset's appropriate discount rate will depend on several other factors, especially its risk. The more certain the expected outcome, the lower the appropriate discount rate. Because a lower discount rate increases the value of an expected future income stream, low-risk expected income streams are valued more highly than high-risk expected streams of equivalent magnitude and timing. For example, the bonds of very secure companies are discounted at lower rates than those of less secure companies. That is why the interest rates on lower-rated bonds (bonds of riskier companies) tend to be higher than the interest rates on bonds with better ratings.

Interest Fluctuation and Default Risk

default risk
interest rate risk

A bond's risk may be decomposed into two categories. The likelihood that the issuer's obligation will not be fulfilled (for example, bankruptcy or repudiation) is called *default risk*. *Interest rate risk*, in contrast, stems from sensitivity to changing market interest rates.

The government guarantee of savings accounts essentially eliminates their default risk (few people can imagine the federal government not honoring its guarantee), while the ability to withdraw part or all of the account without penalty eliminates their interest rate risk. Similarly, short-maturity Treasury bills have very little default or interest rate risk. Indeed, all federal government-guaranteed investments have minimal default risk although those with longer maturities have interest-rate risk. The market trusts the guarantee because the government has extensive taxing power, and the Federal Reserve Board (The Fed) can facilitate sales of government securities.

The default risk of municipal and corporate debt securities is always considered greater than that of Treasury issues. How much greater depends on the income-producing and/or liquidation values of the issuers' assets and on the amount of other debt they have outstanding. Some issues with strong financial positions are only slightly more risky than federal government securities, while default is much more likely for others.

Interest-fluctuation risks also vary substantially. The prices of longer-maturity debt issues are much more sensitive to interest rate shifts than are the prices of shorter-term debt issues.

Example: A one-year bond that will pay $1,000 in principal and $70 in interest is worth about $1,000 if discounted at 7 percent. Similarly, a long-term bond that has a coupon rate equal to 7 percent of face value will sell for its face value if discounted at 7 percent. If relevant interest rates move up to 8 percent, the value of the short-term bond will fall by about $9 to $991 ($1,070/1.08 = $991). On the other hand, a long-term 7 percent bond (that is worth $1,000 when valued with a 7 percent discount rate) will fall by a much greater amount if long-term rates rise to 8 percent. In the case of a (no maturity) consol, its price would fall $125 (from $1,000) to $875 ($70/.08). A long-term but finite life bond would fall by almost as much. For instance, a 20-year 7 percent bond would fall to $902 (or by $98) if the discount rate rose to 8 percent.

Therefore, we might well expect the market to demand higher discount rates for longer-term issues to compensate for the uncertainty of interest rate fluctuations. While the term structure of interest rates, which will be discussed in detail in chapter 6, often has this pattern (higher rates for longer maturities), the relationship between maturities and discount rates is more complex.

A Bond's Risk Depends On . . .

- Default risk
- Interest rate risk

The Discount Rate for a Risky Asset

risk-free rate

risk premium

The discount rates applied to risky investments can be viewed as determined by two basic forces: general credit conditions and the risk of default. Credit conditions in the marketplace determine the general level of interest rates, including the rate for riskless assets. The appropriate rates for risky assets are scaled up from the current market rate (the *risk-free rate*) on riskless assets. Yields on government bonds are often used to proxy for the risk-free rate. A risk-free rate of 5 percent plus a *risk premium* (inducement required to attract risk-averse investors, or compensation for bearing risk) of 2 percent would imply a 7 percent (5% + 2%) discount rate. If the risk-free rate should fall to 4 percent, the appropriate discount rate for this risky asset would become 6 percent (assuming the 2 percent risk premium remains unchanged). The appropriate rate for discounting any income stream equals the risk-free rate plus a risk premium associated with the asset's risk.

The Discount Rate for a Risky Investment: A Combination Of . . .

- The risk-free rate: yields on government bonds used as a proxy
- The risk premium based on risk of default

The Role of Inflation

Interest rates, including the interest rate for riskless assets (risk-free rate), are thought to reflect the impact of inflationary expectations. Investors who supply funds to borrowers by buying debt instruments such as bonds (even government bonds) expect and demand a yield that not only will compensate them for forgoing present consumption but will also compensate them for any loss in purchasing power.

Example: Bond investors expect a 3 percent average rate of inflation during the life of the bond. They will expect a market interest rate that will fully compensate them for the expected loss in purchasing power (3 percent), as well as an additional increment to compensate them for forgoing present consumption (real risk-free rate). Why lend money out if you can't get back more purchasing power than you lent out?

nominal interest rates
real interest rates

Nominal interest rates are stated in current dollar terms, whereas *real interest rates* are stated in inflation-adjusted terms. Nominal rates are the rates that are quoted in the newspaper and elsewhere. Real rates take out the effect of inflation. The two rates are related as follows:

Nominal interest rate = Real interest rate + Inflation rate

The risk-free rate is generally thought to equal the expected rate of inflation plus the real risk-free rate, which is related to the real long-term growth of the economy. Accordingly, assuming a real risk-free rate of 2 percent, an expected rate of inflation of 3 percent would correspond to a nominal risk-free rate of 5 percent (3% + 2%). A rise in inflationary expectations to 6 percent would cause the nominal risk-free rate to rise to 8 percent (6% + 2%).

These relationships are approximate. Depending on the credit markets' relative tightness or looseness (determined by the interaction of the strength of the economy and the Federal Reserve System's monetary policy), the actual level of nominal and real risk-free rates can vary. For example, in some market environments the nominal rate may be only 1 percent above the expected inflation rate, while in other markets the difference may be as much as 4 percent. Moreover, inflationary expectations are not directly observable. Therefore, the difference between nominal and real interest rates cannot be known with certainty.

The Risk Premium

A bond's coupon rate and principal repayment terms are fixed by the indenture (the written contract between the borrower and leader) encompassing all of the commitments that the company makes to its bondholders. If a bond does default, the indenture trustee (usually a bank identified in the bond's indenture) is obligated to take appropriate legal action to protect the bondholders' interests. With the income stream fixed in the indenture, the risk premium set by the market is directly observable as the difference between the bond's yield to maturity and the risk-free rate. For example, a medium-grade corporate bond yielding 9 percent has a risk premium of 3 percent if government bonds with similar maturities yield 6 percent.

Examples of Risk Premiums

Table 4-2 shows some estimated risk premiums for early 1982 (a period of relatively high interest rates), late 1987 (a period of lower interest rates), and June 24, 1999 (a period of still lower rates). This table illustrates the wide range in risk premiums (defined here as the difference between the yields on risky securities and those on otherwise similar risk-free assets such as U.S. Treasury securities). For example, the Public Service of New Hampshire (PSNH) 14 1/2 percent bonds due in 2000 were priced to yield 18.1 percent, compared with similar maturity Treasury bonds yielding 8.9 percent. The PSNH bond's risk premium of 9.2 percent reflects the very real threat that the utility would be forced to declare bankruptcy. PSNH was the lead utility (with the largest percentage of ownership) in a troubled project to construct a nuclear power facility at Seabrook, New Hampshire. Indeed, shortly after this particular set of quotations was compiled, PSNH did declare bankruptcy.

Similarly, the Texas Air 15 3/4 percent bonds due in 1992 had an 8.2 percent risk premium. Texas Air was also experiencing major difficulties as its various subsidiary airlines were having problems reaching their breakeven load factors (the percentage of seats filled on an average flight). Coincidentally, one of Texas Air's subsidiaries was Eastern Airlines, whose 17 1/2 percent bonds due in 1998 were priced to yield 18.1 percent in 1982. Texas Air acquired Eastern and exchanged its own debt securities (at a discount) for those of Eastern. Subsequently, Eastern filed for bankruptcy protection in 1989 and ceased operations in 1991.

On the other hand, the AT&T and Citicorp bonds were low-risk instruments in 1982 and remained so in 1987 and beyond. These bonds were priced to yield very little more than comparable maturity Treasuries. Thus

TABLE 4-2
Yields to Maturity for Selected Bonds

January 4, 1982

Issuer	Coupon Rate	Maturity	Price	Yield	Risk Premium*
U.S. Treasury	13 1/4	1991	94 7/16	13.8%	0%
AT&T	13	1990	94	14.1	.3
Citicorp	14 3/8	1986	97 1/4	14.5	.7
Pacific Telephone	15 1/8	1988	100	15.0	1.2
Alabama Power	14 3/4	1995	95	15.5	1.7
Montgomery Ward	16	1986	98 1/4	16.3	2.5
Georgia Pacific	16.9	1987	97 1/4	17.3	3.5
Eastern Airlines	17 1/2	1998	96 7/8	18.1	4.3

December 30, 1987

Issuer	Coupon Rate	Maturity	Price	Yield	Risk Premium*
U.S. Treasury	11 3/4	2001	121 5/8	8.9%	0%
AT&T	8 3/4	2000	94 1/8	9.3	.4
Citicorp	8 1/8	2007	83 5/8	9.7	.8
Alabama Power	8 7/8	2003	89 1/4	9.9	1.0
Georgia Power	11	2009	100 1/4	11.0	2.1
GAF	11 3/8	1995	94 3/8	12.1	3.2
Ramada Inns	11 5/8	1999	88 7/8	13.1	4.2
Pennzoil	14 5/8	1991	101	14.5	5.6
Texas Air	15 3/4	1992	92	17.1	8.2
Public Service of NH	14 1/2	2000	80	18.1	9.2

June 24, 1999

Issuer	Coupon Rate	Maturity	Price	Yield	Risk Premium*
U.S. Treasury	5 5/8	2006	97	6.1%	0%
Chase Manhattan	6 1/4	2006	98	6.5	.4
AT&T	7 1/2	2006	103 3/4	6.9	.8
Dole	7 7/18	2013	101 5/8	7.9	1.8
RJR	8 3/4	2015	101 1/8	8.5	2.4
Revlon	8 1/8	2006	96	8.9	2.8
HMH Properties	7 7/8	2007	91	9.4	3.3
Nextel	0	2007	72	10.6	4.5
Advantica	11 1/4	2008	96	12.0	5.9
Trump AC	11 1/4	2006	90	13.5	7.4
Integrated	9 1/4	2008	72 1/2	15.1	9.0

* The risk premium is the yield to maturity less the risk-free rate.
  (Note: The computed risk premiums are approximations that ignore the impact of
  differential tax rates and maturity differences.)

the market persisted in thinking that the issuers of these bonds were very unlikely to default.

The risk premium on a debt security, as the term is used here and as it is commonly understood, reflects both the expected loss from default and an additional increment called the *pure risk premium*. The pure risk premium is the part of the risk premium needed to compensate investors for the anxiety they experience due to uncertainty.

pure risk premium

Example: Consider the Georgia Power 11 percent bonds due in 2009. On December 30, 1987, they were priced at 100 1/4 to yield almost 11 percent. This pricing corresponded to a risk premium of 2.1 percent. Suppose the market estimates that the Georgia Power bond's probability of default is 1 percent and that the expected loss from a default (if it occurs) is 50 percent of the payment stream's present value. (The market's actual expectations are not directly observable, and these particular numbers may or may not be reasonable estimates. For the sake of the analysis, however, let us use them as if they are accurate estimates of the true market expectations.) The corresponding expected loss from default would equal .5 percent (.01 x .5) of the principal. Subtracting this expected default loss of .5 percent from the total risk premium of 2.1 percent leaves a pure risk premium of 1.6 percent. According to this analysis, the pure risk premium needed to induce risk-averse investors to purchase this risky security was 1.6 percent.

Although the decomposition of the risk premium into its two components cannot be observed directly, inferences can be drawn from historical default experience. For the vast majority of bonds (particularly those rated medium risk or better) the default loss has, in fact, since the end of World War II, been very much lower than the risk premiums actually charged for the various risk classes. Thus, either the market does not trust the forecast value of past default experience, or expected default losses are a relatively small component of risk premiums. On the other hand, the 1989–1991 experience with risky bonds (often from failed leveraged buyouts) may suggest greater risk than had been the case previously.

As shown in table 4-2, the risk premium spreads for June 24, 1999, have remained close to their December 30, 1987, values following the shaky credit crunch of late September 1998. This episode was driven by both foreign and domestic turmoil in capital and credit markets. In other words, even though the particular risks of the late 1980s may have dissipated, other risks appeared in the late 1990s, and the financial markets priced them (establishing risk premiums) accordingly.

Other Factors Affecting the Discount Rate

As discussed earlier, both general credit conditions and the risk of default play a large role in determining the appropriate rate for discounting a bond or other asset's expected income stream. While these issues are not discussed in detail until a later chapter, note that relations between interest rates for equivalent risk bonds having different maturities (the term structure) are determined by the market. Finally, various special characteristics, such as whether or not a particular bond can be called (repurchased by the issuer at a specified price prior to maturity), may affect its price and thus its discount rate.

SUMMARY AND CONCLUSIONS

The valuation of securities, like the valuation of all assets, is based on the market forces of supply and demand. To understand how the value of securities is determined, therefore, it is necessary to examine the factors that influence the supply of, and the demand for, various securities.

The two factors that influence the value of any investment are their cash flows and their price appreciation, or capital gain. To determine these values, it is necessary to understand the time value of money. The intuition behind time value is rather straightforward. All else equal, people would rather have money sooner than later. Time value, or present value, is a measure of what an expected future cash flow is worth now.

There are three components to the discount rate. The first is known as the real risk-free rate. This is the compensation that investors need to induce them to forgo current consumption. The second is the inflationary component. This is compensation for the loss in purchasing power due to inflation. It is determined not only by the present rate of inflation but also by expectations about what the rate of inflation will be during the time that the cash inflows are expected. The real risk-free rate plus the inflationary component is the risk-free rate. The rate on U.S. government debt is considered the risk-free rate, since there is virtually no risk that the United States government will default on its debt obligations. The third component of the discount rate is the risk premium. It is applicable when there is some risk, however slight, that the borrower might default on the debt obligation. The existence of a risk premium explains why there is a higher interest rate on corporate bonds than on U.S. government bonds and why the interest rate is higher on bonds issued by riskier companies.

Once the discount rate is known, the present value of a stream of expected future cash flows can be calculated. The three types of present-value calculations are a perpetuity, an annuity, and a lump sum. Preferred stock is an example of a perpetuity, which is the same amount of money at regular intervals. An annuity is the same amount of money at periodic intervals for a specified term. A bond is an example of an annuity plus a lump sum, since the investor receives both periodic interest payments and the face value of the bond at maturity.

When the rate of inflation changes over time, market interest rates change. When market interest rates rise, the value of an outstanding bond decreases, since the coupon interest rate it pays is below that paid on comparable bonds currently issued. Therefore, the existing bond sells at a discount in the secondary market. Likewise, when market interest rates decline, the value of existing bonds increases. Such bonds sell for a premium on the secondary market.

There are two major sources of risk with respect to long-term bonds. The greatest risk is the risk that the borrower will be unable to make the interest and principal payments when due. That is known as default risk, and is reflected in the risk premium, which is one component of the discount rate. The second major risk is interest rate risk. This is the risk that, because of an unexpected increase in market interest rates, the value of the bond will decrease, and the future cash flows will have less purchasing power than expected. Even long-term government bonds, which have no default risk, have some interest rate risk.

CHAPTER REVIEW

Answers to the review questions and the self-test questions start on page 747.

Key Terms

market price	preferred stock
cash flow	yield to maturity (YTM)
time value	default risk
inflation	interest rate risk
present value	risk-free rate
discount rate	risk premium
face value	nominal interest rates
maturity	real interest rates
coupon rate	pure risk premium

Review Questions

4-1. Explain what is meant by time value. How does the concept enter into investment valuation? Define and distinguish present value and compound value.

4-2. Compute the present value (PV) for the following income streams:
   a. $50 annually, forever discounted at 10 percent
   b. $200 annually for 20 years, discounted at 20 percent
   c. bond with a $150 annual coupon for 12 years, maturing at $1,070, discounted at 16 percent
   d. payment stream of
   - year 1: $200
   - year 2: $300
   - year 3: $400
   - year 4: $500
   - subsequent years: 0
   - discounted at 8 percent

4-3. Compute the price of a 20-year bond with a par value of $1,000 and a 10 percent annual coupon when comparable market interest rates are
   a. 7%
   b. 9%
   c. 10%
   d. 11%
   e. 13%

4-4. Look at the following income streams:

Year	A	B	C
1	$100	$500	$200
2	$200	$400	$300
3	$300	$300	$500
4	$400	$200	$300
5	$500	$100	$200

   a. Which of these will have the greatest present value and why? Which will have the least present value?
   b. Find the present value of the income streams discounted at 12 percent.
   c. What would the present value of the income streams be if they were discounted at 0 percent?

4-5. Compute the price of the following bonds. Assume a principal payment of $1,000 and annual interest payments.

	Coupon Rate	Years to Maturity	Discount Rate
Bond A	8%	10	12%
Bond B	16%	10	12%
Bond C	8%	2	12%
Bond D	16%	10	10%

4-6. How is an approach based on the present value of the expected future income stream used to value investment assets?

4-7. Explain how a 20-year bond with a $1,000 face value could sell for $600 or $1,200. What would cause such bonds to rise or fall in value?

4-8. Discuss the various components of risk:
   a. default
   b. interest rate fluctuation
   c. pure risk premium

4-9. Explain the various ways that inflation might affect the value of a bond.

Self-Test Questions

T   F   4-1. For the vast majority of bonds, the periodic interest payment varies directly with the current market rate of interest.

T   F   4-2. Any bond with a coupon rate below the discount rate is worth more than its face value.

T   F   4-3. The yield to maturity (YTM) is the discount rate that makes the present value of the coupon and principal payments equal to the market price of the bond.

T   F   4-4. Bond prices move inversely with market interest rates.

T   F   4-5. Market interest rates vary directly with the relative supply of loanable funds.

T   F   4-6. The prices of longer-maturity debt issues are much less sensitive to interest rate shifts than are the prices of shorter-term debt issues.

T   F   4-7. Yields on government bonds are often used to proxy for the risk-free rate.

T   F   4-8. The appropriate rate for discounting any income stream equals the risk-free rate plus a risk premium associated with the asset's risk.

T   F   4-9. Nominal interest rates are stated in inflation-adjusted terms, and real interest rates are stated in current dollar terms.

T   F   4-10.   The risk-free rate is generally thought to equal the expected rate of inflation plus an increment of about 2 percent, which is related to the real long-term growth of the economy.

T   F   4-11.   The risk premium set by the market is directly observable as the difference between the bond's yield to maturity (YTM) and the coupon rate.

T   F   4-12.   The risk premium on a debt security reflects both the expected loss from default and an additional increment called the pure risk premium.

T   F   4-13.   The decomposition of the risk premium into two components is directly observable.

Types of Fixed-Income Securities

Learning Objectives

An understanding of the material in this chapter should enable the student to

---

5-1. Describe the characteristics of the various short-term debt instruments that trade in the money market.

5-2. Describe the characteristics of the various long-term debt instruments and preferred stock issues that trade in the financial market.

5-3. Describe several different methods for calculating yields, and explain their relationship to each other.

Chapter Outline

TYPES OF FIXED-INCOME SECURITIES

Fixed-income securities provide the principal investment alternative to common stocks. The same brokers and similar markets are used to trade them, and many companies issue both types of securities. Oftentimes, fixed income securities are very competitive with common stocks because of their diversity and higher yields (particularly when compared with the low dividend yields of many stocks). Their volatility, attention, number of types, ways of participating, and small investor involvement have all increased in recent years. Bonds may not belong in every portfolio, but all serious investors should at least consider investing in them.

fixed-income securities

The federal government, state and local governments, corporations, foreign governments, and international organizations all issue *fixed-income securities*. Most debt securities promise to pay a fixed periodic coupon amount and return their face value at a prespecified time. They vary in a number of ways, including length to maturity, coupon rate, type of collateral, convertibility, tax treatment, and restrictions placed on the borrower.

This chapter explores the characteristics of the various types of short- and long-term debt instruments, along with the mutual funds that invest in these securities. It first considers money market and other short-term securities: T-bills, commercial paper, large CDs, acceptances, Eurodollars, federal funds, repurchase agreements, discount loans, money market funds, short-term unit trusts, and low-denomination bank-issued securities. The chapter then discusses various long-term securities, including governments, agencies, mortgage-related securities, municipals, corporates, long-term bank CDs, income bonds, floating-rate securities, zero-coupon bonds, Eurobonds, private placements, and preferred stock.

THE MONEY MARKET AND OTHER SHORT-TERM DEBT SECURITIES

money market

Securities maturing in a year or less are considered short term. High-quality, short-term debt obligations trade in what is called the *money market*. Money market instruments are highly liquid, quite marketable, and very secure. The principal money market instruments are Treasury bills, commercial paper, large bank CDs, bankers' acceptances, and Eurodollar deposits. Very short-term lending and borrowing in the federal funds market, repurchase agreements, and the Fed's discount window round out this market. In addition, money market mutual funds, short-term unit investment trusts, and certain securities and accounts of banks and other financial institutions also compete in the short-term debt security market.

Treasury Bills and Other Short-Term Governments

Treasury bills (T-bills)

Short-term U.S. government securities (governments) make up one of the money market's largest segments. This market consists of bills and other securities maturing within a year. *Treasury bills (T-bills)* are issued at a discount and mature at par (face value), whereas other governments are sold initially at or near par and pay a semiannual coupon.

Most short-term governments are issued in $10,000 minimum denominations. Short-term governments are frequently offered for sale (original offerings) and possess excellent OTC (over the counter) marketability, very low perceived risk, and competitive yields. Moreover, governments are not subject to state and local taxes. This feature enhances their relative after-tax yield, particularly for investors in high tax states. A number of non-Treasury U.S. government agencies also issue short-term securities.

New issues of T-bills can be bought through a broker or bank for a commission, or they can be purchased directly from the nearest Federal Reserve bank at the weekly auction. Bills with maturities of 13 weeks and 26 weeks are offered each week, while 52-week bills are typically offered once every fourth week. Bids may be entered on either a competitive or a noncompetitive basis. All noncompetitive bids are accepted by the Treasury, and buyers who enter these bids agree to pay the price (yield) that corresponds to the lowest price (highest yield) of all the competitive bids that are accepted. Buyers entering competitive bids state a price (yield) they are willing to pay and the Treasury accepts these bids, taking the highest prices (lowest yields) first until the issue is sold out. However, the price (yield) that all buyers who have accepted competitive bids actually pay is the same as the price (yield) that noncompetitive buyers pay. In other words, once the lowest price (highest yield) that the Treasury is willing to accept is determined, then all buyers (both competitive and noncompetitive) pay that price (yield).

Example 1:	Suppose the Fed wants to sell $8 billion of 13-week T-bills. It receives $14 billion in bids, $5 billion of which are noncompetitive. The $5 billion of noncompetitive bids are accepted. The remaining $9 billion in bids are put in order, from the highest price (lowest yield) to the lowest price (highest yield). The Fed then accepts $3 billion worth of these competitive bids (to round out its goal of $8 billion), taking the highest prices (lowest yields) first. It is the very last bid in this group, which is the lowest price (highest yield) bid accepted that determines the price paid (yield received) by all. All bids are provisional until this final step of the auction when the price (yield) is determined.
Example 2:	A buyer enters a competitive bid for a 13-week T-bill at a rate that translates into a price of 98.552 (5.79 percent). If this bid is accepted and happens to coincide with the auction price, the buyer will pay $9,855.20 for a $10,000 (face value) bill. If the bill is held until it matures 13 weeks later, the buyer will receive $10,000 for an investment of $9,855.20.

Dealers in government securities maintain an active secondary market in T-bills. The terms offered by these dealers are reported daily in the financial section of most major newspapers, as well as online at the Federal Reserve's web site. Dealers buy and/or sell T-bills prior to maturity by bidding and/or asking discount percents. The actual dollar prices for which a dealer will buy and/or sell a T-bill are obtained from the discount.

Example 1:	A T-bill with 60 days left to maturity is listed as 5.62 percent bid and 5.58 percent asked. Both of these

discount percents were computed by multiplying the actual discount by 360/60 (the reverse of the portion of a 360-day year involved). To obtain the actual discount associated with the 5.62 percent bid, the bid is multiplied by 60/360. This results in .963 percent. In other words, the dealer is bidding 99.037 percent of face value (100.00% − .963%). This translates into a price of $9,903.70 that a dealer is willing to pay for a T-bill that matures in 60 days for $10,000.

Example 2:   A dealer will sell the T-bill in Example 1 at a discount of .930 percent [100.00% − (5.58% x 60/360)]. In dollar terms, the dealer is willing to sell the T-bill for $9,907.00 [$10,000 x (100.00% − .930%)], a discount of $93 off the $10,000 face. The difference between the price that a dealer is willing to sell the T-bill for and the price the dealer is willing to buy the bill for (that is, $9,907.00 − $9,903.70 = $3.30) is called the dealer's spread, and it compensates the dealer for maintaining an inventory of bills, taking the associated risks, and incurring the necessary costs.

Besides the bid and asked discounts, *The Wall Street Journal* and several other media provide an equivalent yield that is based on the asked price. The equivalent yield is computed by first dividing a security's dollar discount (based on its asked price) by its purchase price (what a dealer will sell it for). The resulting figure is the rate of return associated with buying the security. This rate is then annualized by multiplying it by 365, and dividing the product by the number of days until maturity. This gives the equivalent yield.

Example: The equivalent yield for the T-bill in Examples 1 and 2 is calculated by taking the $93 discount (from Example 2) and dividing it by its purchase price of $9,907.00 (from Example 2). The result of .938% is the rate of return associated with purchasing the security ($93/$9,907 = .938%). This rate of .938% is then annualized by multiplying it by 365 (.938% x 365/60 = 5.70%), and then dividing it by 60, the number of days until maturity. The answer of 5.7% is the equivalent yield.

**Treasury Bill Quotations
(Sample Quote from the OTC Market as Presented in
the Financial Media on 4/13/2000)**

Maturity	Days to Mat.	Bid	Asked	Chg.	Ask Yld.
Jun 01 '00	49	5.64	5.60	−0.04	5.72

- Maturity: the date when the T-bill will be paid off
- Days to Mat.: the number of days remaining (from the previous trading day) until the T-bill matures
- Bid: the price (in 100ths) that a dealer is willing to pay for the T-bill (as of mid-afternoon of the previous trading day)
- Asked: the price (in 100ths) that a dealer is willing to sell the T-bill for (as of mid-afternoon of the previous trading day)
- Chg.: the change (in 100ths) between the bid price as listed in bid column (see Bid above) and the bid price from the previous trading day (which is really two trading days previous) (for instance, a + 0.05 means an increase of 5/100 and a − 0.04 indicates a decrease of 4/100)
- Ask Yld.: the yield to maturity for the T-bill based on its asked price

Commercial Paper

commercial paper

Corporations that seek to raise short-term debt capital in the public markets often sell what is called commercial paper. *Commercial paper* is usually issued by large corporations with solid credit ratings to finance their short-term needs. The paper is secured only by the issuer's good name. The issuer does, however, usually have a backup line of credit at a bank. This credit line is available to repay the commercial paper issue when due if sale of new paper is not possible in the existing market environment. Commercial paper issuers are generally able to pay slightly less than bank rates (the prime rate) on their borrowings. They will also incur a fee on their backup credit lines. Even adding in this fee, the commercial paper issuer's borrowing costs are typically below the alternative cost of bank borrowings. Similarly, eliminating the intermediary's (that is, the bank's) compensation allows those who issue commercial paper to pay investors a slightly higher interest rate than they would get by buying a bank's CDs.

Commercial paper is rated, but as a practical matter, only high-grade issues are marketable. Paper is marketed in round lots of $250,000 and is seldom available in smaller than $100,000 denominations. Some paper is registered; most is payable to the bearer.

Large CDs

**CDs (certificates
of deposit)**

The interest rates on bank and thrift-issued negotiable *CDs (certificates of deposit)* of $100,000 and above usually exceed the rates payable on smaller balances. Several New York-based CD dealers handle most secondary market trading. CDs are subject to the same government guarantee up to $100,000 as other bank and thrift institution issues. Most of the principal of very high-denomination CDs ($1 million or more) is uninsured, but most CDs are considered quite safe. Those issued by troubled banks may be risky, however. Troubled banks generally have difficulty selling uninsured CDs even at high interest rates. *Moody's* rates the quality of some CDs. Most CDs have short-term maturities.

Their relatively high minimum denomination ($100,000) puts large CDs beyond the range of small investors. Funds for one large CD may be assembled from several investors, however. Moreover, many banks will lend individuals the funds needed to reach the minimum. Typically, the loan rate slightly exceeds the CD rate, but the holding's net yield may still be relatively attractive. Other types of securities and accounts that banks offer have, however, greatly reduced small investors' need to find ways to purchase large CDs.

Banker's Acceptance

banker's acceptance

A *banker's acceptance* involves an obligation to pay a certain amount at a prespecified time. Once the obligation is accepted (guaranteed) by a bank, it becomes an *acceptance*. The acceptance is a liability of the bank. As such, the bank is required to redeem it whether or not the issuer funds the redemption. With this possibility in mind, banks are inclined to check very carefully the credit standing of the issuers of these obligations.

Example: An American firm wishes to finance the importation of Widgets using a banker's acceptance. After negotiating with the foreign exporter of Widgets, the American importer arranges with his or her U.S. bank for the issuance of an irrevocable letter of credit (L/C) in favor of the foreign exporter.

The L/C specifies the details of the shipment and states that the exporter may draw a time draft for a certain amount on the U.S. bank. In conformity with the terms of the L/C, the foreign exporter draws a draft with his or her local bank, receiving immediate payment. The foreign bank forwards the draft and the shipping documents conveying title to the Widgets to the U.S. bank that issued the L/C. The U.S. bank stamps the draft accepted (accepts an obligation to pay the draft at maturity), and an acceptance is created.

The new acceptance is either returned to the foreign bank or sold to a dealer with the proceeds credited to the foreign bank's account. The shipping documents conveying title to the Widgets are released to the American importer so that he or she can take delivery of the Widgets for resale to customers. The proceeds of the Widget sales are deposited by the American importer at the accepting U.S. bank in time to honor the acceptance. At maturity, the acceptance is presented for payment by its owner, whether that be the foreign bank or someone else who purchased it from a dealer, and the transaction is completed.

The purpose of an acceptance is to substitute the credit-worthiness of a bank, which is known and respected either nationally or internationally, for that of a local merchant, who may be relatively unknown, especially in the international market. While most acceptances arise in the course of foreign trade, they may also result from domestic trade.

Once an acceptance is created, it trades like other money market securities. Acceptances are available in a wide variety of denominations and maturity dates. A small number of dealers buy and sell acceptances, quoting spreads of about 1/4 of 1 percent. Acceptances, like most money market securities, can be purchased through a stockbroker.

Eurodollar Deposits

Eurodollar deposits

Eurodollar deposits are dollar-denominated liabilities of banks located in Europe or anywhere else outside the United States. Most Eurodollars are held as fixed-rate time deposits of $250,000 to $5 million with maturities from one day to several years.

Eurodollar yields are quite competitive with other money market rates. Indeed, they typically offer a bit more than other components of the money market. On the other hand, Eurodollar deposits of U.S. investors may occasionally be difficult to repatriate. Moreover, disputes between borrower and lender must be settled without reliance on the protections of the U.S. legal system. Finally, the issuing bank's depositors are rarely as protected by insurance and government regulation as those of U.S. banks. In fact, one reason that many foreign banks can afford to pay a higher interest rate than

U.S. banks is that they do not have the reserve requirements and other costs of complying with government regulations that U.S. banks face. Many issuers are subsidiaries of U.S. banks, and others are large institutions with long histories of sound operations. Thus, risks in the Eurodollar market should not be overrated. Defaults have been very rare.

Short-Term Debt Securities: Money Market

Type	Issuer	Minimum Denomination
Treasury bills	U.S. Treasury	$10,000
Commercial paper	Secure corporations	$250,000
Large CDs	Banks and thrifts	$100,000
Acceptances	Export/import companies; but bank guaranteed	Varies
Eurodollars	Foreign-based banks	$250,000

Federal Funds, Repurchase Agreements, and Discount Loans

federal funds market

Banks and other types of financial institutions also participate in several very active short-term debt markets. The *federal funds market* arose to facilitate overnight bank borrowing and lending of excess reserves. Subsequently, other financial institutions and even some foreign banks and government security dealers entered the market. This federal funds market, in fact, encompasses all unsecured overnight loans in immediately available reserve-free funds. The federal funds rate is the interest rate that banks charge other banks for these overnight loans.

repurchase agreements (repos)

Repurchase agreements (repos) are sales of securities with guaranteed repurchase at a prespecified price and date (often one day later). The relation between the purchase and sales prices establishes the instrument's return. For example, a guaranteed resale in 6 months at 5 percent above the purchase price would generate a 10 percent return. This is an indirect way for banks to borrow from other banks, using the security as collateral. Payment is generally required to be in immediately available reserve-free funds transferred between financial institutions. These arrangements generally are considered quite safe.

discount loans

Discount loans, another part of the money market, are extended by the Fed to member banks and certain other institutions. These loans are designed to cure a short-term reserve deficiency. The Fed sometimes signals monetary policy shifts with changes in the rate charged on such loans (discount rate) or by its willingness to make such loans.

Except for retail repos, this part of the money market is almost exclusively restricted to depository institutions, such as commercial banks and savings and loan (S&L) associations. Moreover, the instruments involved generally are for very large amounts and, therefore, would not be suitable for most individual investors if they could invest in them.

Short-Term Debt Securities:
Intra-Institutional Market

Type	Institutions Involved
Federal funds	Loans between Fed members
Repurchase agreements	Sale and guaranteed buy-back of securities by banks and other depository institutions
Discount loans	Loans from Fed to Fed members

Money Market Mutual Funds (MMFs)

money market mutual funds

Money market mutual funds and short-term unit investment trusts (discussed next) were developed several years ago in response to interest rate ceilings on many bank savings instruments coupled with generally higher money market rates. These money funds invest resources from many small investors in a large portfolio of money market securities. While some funds have no minimum account size, many funds set a $1,000 or larger minimum. Still other funds have implemented a rate structure that pays higher rates for larger balances. The net income of the portfolio is distributed to the fund's owners and may be paid monthly or reinvested.

The returns paid to small investors are generally about one-half of a percentage point below the prevailing rates in the money market. Because these money market funds concentrate on very liquid short-term instruments, adverse interest rate moves are unlikely to affect the fund's share prices significantly. Most money market instruments (CDs, T-bills, and so on) must be sold at the prevailing market price (less commissions) in discrete and relatively large units.

Money market funds can, in contrast, be redeemed in whole or in part on very short notice without a redemption charge. Most funds permit several types of redemption: The fund holder can write, e-mail, or call toll free for an immediate check-mailing or wire transfer into the fund holder's bank account. Most funds also permit checks to be written on the fund holder's account. Use of this feature allows the investor's funds to earn interest until the check clears.

Individual money market funds have somewhat different risk, return, and marketing characteristics. Some invest only in Treasury bills (governments only), whereas other portfolios contain slightly riskier (for example, Eurodollar, commercial paper) money market investments. Some funds hold only very short-term instruments. Others are willing to incur the somewhat reduced liquidity of slightly longer maturities. Still others vary their average maturity on the basis of their interest rate expectations. Some short-term municipal funds offer (lower) tax-free yields. Thus, different types of money market funds appeal to various types of investors.

Most money market funds of a given class (general, governments only, or municipal) offer very similar risks and returns, but they do differ somewhat. In addition, there are organizations that rate the safety and performance of these funds.

Short-Term Unit Investment Trusts

unit investment trusts

Short-term *unit investment trusts* offer many of the same advantages as money market funds: low-risk, low-denomination investment and money market yields. On the other hand, the money funds are managed and perpetual, whereas unit trusts are unmanaged and mature. Furthermore, unit trusts are less convenient than money market funds, but their expenses are appreciably below those of the money funds. Units must be held until maturity (generally 6 months) or sold in a relatively inactive secondary market. Because short-term unit trusts invest in longer-term securities than most money funds do, they are somewhat less liquid.

Unlike money market funds, unit trust yields are established when they are purchased. Yields on existing units will not increase when market interest rates rise.

If, for example, market rates move up subsequently, the trustholder continues to earn the rate originally promised. He or she must wait until the units mature to reinvest at the higher rate available in the market. On the other hand, if interest rates decline, the holder will receive an above-market rate until the trust matures. The principal advantage of unit trusts, compared with money market funds, is the lower administrative costs and therefore, other things being equal, higher yield. Unit trusts are, however, less convenient for investors and more exposed to interest-fluctuation risk than most money funds.

Low-Denomination Short-Term Securities of Banks and Other Intermediaries

In the past several years, banks and other financial intermediaries have been permitted to offer a variety of low-denomination securities. The relevant regulations have and will, no doubt, continue to change. Banks and thrifts continue to offer traditional passbook-type savings accounts that allow immediate withdrawals and generally pay minimal interest. Money market rates have, however, usually been well above the passbook rates.

To compete with money market funds, banks and other deposit institutions offer an account that is federally insured up to $100,000. These so-called money market deposit accounts typically are limited to a specified number of withdrawals per month. The rates paid on these accounts are not regulated. Thus, the depository institutions can compete for funds by offering whatever yields they like. Banks also sell short-term certificates of deposit with a variety of maturities. Rates on these instruments are also unregulated.

The investor response to money market deposit accounts has been quite favorable. Unlike Treasury bills, bank and thrift institution certificates and accounts are subject to state and local income taxes. Thus, the after-tax yield on T-bills is generally higher than the yield on equivalent depository institution certificates. While most debt securities may be sold prior to maturity, small denomination CDs are generally nontransferable. Holders can redeem their CDs before maturity at the issuing bank, but they sacrifice up to 90 days' interest. Alternatively, holders may borrow up to the amount represented by the investment using the CD as collateral, even though the rate of interest charged exceeds the interest rate paid on the CD. Before redeeming a CD early, therefore, the holder should compare the interest sacrifice with the net cost of such a loan.

FDIC (Federal Deposit Insurance Corporation)

As with all debt securities other than municipals, CD interest income is fully taxable at the federal level. On the other hand, the risk of loss through bankruptcy is virtually nil. The *FDIC (Federal Deposit Insurance Corporation)* guarantees the security up to $100,000 per depositor. Thus, small short-term CDs appeal to safety-oriented investors.

Money Market Rates

The rates on CDs, bankers' acceptances, and commercial paper tend to move together. Treasury bills generally offer a slightly lower yield because of their somewhat greater security and marketability. Eurodollar rates tend to exceed other money market rates by a modest increment, reflecting their slightly greater risk as well as the avoided costs of complying with U.S. banking regulations.

Money rate quotations for key U.S. annual interest rates are found in the financial section of most major newspapers. At a minimum, these sources provide the latest quote from the previous or most recent business day. Some sources also provide rates from 6 months and/or one year ago for comparison purposes. In addition, the Federal Reserve provides daily updates of selected rates on its web site.

Short-Term Debt Securities: Small Investor Market

Type	Term	Minimum Denomination
Money market funds	On demand	None to higher
Short-term unit trusts	Six months	$1,000 (typically)
Low-denomination bank CDs	Varies	Varies
Money market deposit accounts	Typically a limited number of withdrawals per month	$1,000 (typically)

Implication of the Money Market for Individual Investors

The market for short-term debt instruments has grown dramatically in recent years. Some individuals may buy money market securities directly, but their large denominations ($10,000 for Treasury bills, $100,000 for negotiable CDs, $250,000 for commercial paper) put this market out of reach for investors of modest means. Money market funds, short-term unit trusts, and banks' certificates of deposit and money market deposit accounts do, however, offer a viable alternative for those desiring a highly liquid low-risk instrument.

LONG-TERM DEBT INSTRUMENTS

In addition to the wide variety of short-term debt securities available to investors, several types of long-term debt securities are also available. Most of these securities fall into three categories: government bonds (including agencies), municipals (also called state and local securities), and traditional corporate bonds. Other categories include mortgage loans and mortgage-related securities, bank CDs, bond funds, income bonds, floating-rate securities, zero-coupon bonds, Eurobonds, and private placements. Preferred stock also competes for the same income-oriented investor dollars that might otherwise go into long-term debt securities.

Before reading on, it may be helpful to remember that for all its complex language and provisions, a bond or other debt instrument is basically an IOU. That is, it is a contract by which one party (which may be a business corporation, bank, municipality, or even the federal government) borrows money from another party or group of parties. The contract may, in some cases, be rather complex. It specifies the amount of the loan, when the loan must be repaid (maturity date), the rate of interest, and the frequency with which interest payments are to be made. The contract may specify whether certain particular property of the borrower is to serve as collateral to guarantee repayment, what is to happen in case of default, the priority of repayment obligations when the borrower has multiple debts (subordination), whether the borrower has the option of repaying the debt before it is due (call provision), whether the lender has the option of exchanging the financial obligation for an ownership interest in an agreed upon percentage of the borrower's net assets (conversion provision), and any number of other provisions. Still, for all its potential complexity, a bond is basically just an IOU between two parties or groups of parties.

Treasury Notes and Bonds

notes

Besides short-term (T-bills) debt instruments (covered earlier in this chapter), the U.S. Treasury Department also auctions debt instruments that have intermediate (*notes*) and long-term (bonds) maturities. Notes are issued with maturities from one to 10 years; bonds have maturities greater than 10 years at the time of issuance. Both notes and bonds are issued in denominations of $1,000 or more, and both are traded in an active secondary market made by dealers in U.S. government securities. Price quotations for notes and bonds in the over-the-counter market are contained daily in *The Wall Street Journal* and other media sources for financial information. Unlike T-bill quotes, which are in hundredths, note and bond quotes are expressed in 32nds.

Example: A bond has bid and asked price quotes of 99:31 and 100:01, respectively. Since these quotes are expressed in 32nds, they correspond to 99 31/32 and 100 1/32, giving the bond a spread of 2/32 or 1/16. In dollar terms, the bid is equivalent to $999.6875 per $1,000 of par value. Alternatively, the asked quote is equivalent to $1,000.3125 per $1,000 of par value.

**Treasury Note and Bond Quotations
(Sample Quote from the OTC Market as Presented in
the Financial Media on 4/13/2000)**

Rate	Maturity Mo./Yr.	Bid	Asked	Chg.	Ask Yld.
6 5/8	Jun 01n	100:06	100:08	−1	6.40

- Rate: the coupon rate at which interest is paid as a percentage of par value
- Maturity Mo./Yr.: the month and year in which the note/bond will be paid off (a small n after the maturity date identifies the security as a note, while a range of years given as the maturity date identifies the security as a callable bond)
- Bid: the price (in 32nds) that a dealer is willing to pay for the note/bond (as of mid-afternoon of the previous trading day)
- Asked: the price (in 32nds) that a dealer is willing to sell the note/bond for (as of mid-afternoon of the previous trading day)
- Chg.: the change (in 32nds) between the bid price as listed in the bid column (see Bid above) and the bid price from the previous trading day (which is really two trading days previous) (for instance, a +5 means an increase of 5/32 and a −4 indicates a decrease of 4/32)
- Ask Yld.: the yield to maturity for the note/bond based on its asked price

bearer bonds

Since mid-1983, all newly issued Treasury notes and bonds are in registered (payable only to the registered owner) form. Prior to mid-1983, some notes and bonds were issued in bearer (payable to bearer) form. All notes that were issued in bearer form have long since matured, but some *bearer bonds* still remain outstanding. An advantage to having securities issued in the registered form is that if they are lost or stolen, they will be replaced by the issuer.

Treasury notes and bonds generally make coupon payments semiannually with the par or face value paid at maturity. Unlike notes, some bonds have call provisions that allow them to be called during a specified period prior to maturity (although none have been issued since 1984). This period usually begins 5 to 10 years before maturity and ends at the maturity date. This means that at any scheduled coupon payment date during the callable period, the Treasury can force the bondholders to sell the bonds back to the government at par value.

The yield-to-maturity for Treasury securities typically is calculated using the asked price. However, if the asked price for a callable bond is greater than par, then the yield-to-maturity is calculated on the assumption that the bond will be called at the earliest allowable date.

Treasury notes and bonds are generally traded in an over-the-counter market composed of about two dozen dealers. Most of these dealers are New York investment or commercial bankers. Treasury notes and bonds are also traded on the NYSE. Finally, the Treasury conducts an active original-issue auction for notes and bonds. Banks and others may bid for newly issued notes and/or bonds at this auction.

Treasury securities (that is, bills, notes, and bonds) will continue to be considered secure as long as the government is willing and able to raise sufficient tax revenues to finance the debt. Because of their lower risk, these securities generally yield less than highly rated corporate securities. Moreover, they are not subject to state and local income taxes.

Agency Issues

In addition to the Treasury department, several federal agencies, as well as federally sponsored agencies, also issue debt obligations. The federally sponsored agencies are privately owned agencies that issue securities and use the proceeds to support the granting of certain types of loans to farmers, homeowners, and others. Although the securities of these federally sponsored agencies typically are not guaranteed by the federal government, federal control does ensure that these securities are relatively safe. Moreover, it is generally presumed that federal assistance would be forthcoming if there were any danger of defaulting on these securities. For the sake of analysis, all federal and federally sponsored agencies are lumped together and simply referred to as federal agencies. Like Treasury securities, most federal agency issues are not subject to state or local taxes, although there are some notable exceptions, including securities of the Federal National Mortgage Association (FNMA or Fannie Mae) and the Government National Mortgage Association (GNMA or Ginnie Mae).

agency securities

Agency securities generally bear a slightly higher interest rate than Treasury securities of comparable maturity. Their somewhat lower marketability accounts for part of the yield differential. Also, because the trading volume for most agency issues is less than that for Treasury securities, the market is thinner and spreads are wider. This results in greater trading costs for agency issues and forces investors to demand a higher return. In addition, although default risk is virtually nonexistent, there is some prepayment risk associated with mortgage-based agency issues.

The wide assortment of agency issues is a bit confusing for many relatively unsophisticated investors. However, taking time to learn about agencies is a small price to pay for the higher return they offer. As with Treasury notes and bonds, the prices of agency issues are quoted in parts of

100 and then 32nds of a percent. Moreover, an investment's degree of marketability concerns only those who may need to sell prior to maturity. Holding for a substantial period spreads the buying and selling costs over several years.

Government Agency and Similar Issues Quotations (Sample Quote from the OTC Market as Presented in the Financial Media on 4/13/2000)

Rate	Mat.	Bid	Asked	Yld.
5.88	4–04*	95:16	95:19	7.15

- Rate: the coupon rate at which interest is paid as a percentage of par value
- Mat.: the month and year in which the issue will be paid off (an asterisk (*) after the maturity date identifies the issue as callable)
- Bid: the price (in 32nds) that a dealer is willing to pay for the issue (as of mid-afternoon of the previous trading day)
- Asked: the price (in 32nds) that a dealer is willing to sell the issue for (as of mid-afternoon of the previous trading day)
- Yld.: the yield-to-maturity for the issue based on its asked price (if the issue is callable, yields are computed to the earliest call date for quotes at par or above and to the maturity date for quotes below par)

Mortgage Loans and Mortgage-Backed Securities

mortgage-backed securities

mortgage

Many agency and some types of nonagency securities are either backed by or represent ownership in a pool (portfolio) of *mortgage* loans. The vast majority of outstanding mortgage debt is collateralized by a first claim (first mortgage) on developed real estate, such as single family homes, apartments, or commercial property. Most such mortgage loans require a minimum initial down payment of 10 percent to 20 percent. These mortgages are generally amortized with level monthly payments over an extended period (20 to 30 years is typical). Thus, the amount owed usually declines over time. Moreover, the property securing the mortgage loan usually appreciates as time passes, as inflation drives up real estate prices. As a result, the ratio of

collateral

collateral value to mortgage debt that remains tends to rise as time passes. Accordingly, first mortgages are usually declining-risk investments. Even in a default and distress sale of the property, the mortgage holder is likely to recover a high percentage of the outstanding debt.

Financial intermediaries, such as banks, savings and loan associations, and insurance companies write the vast majority of mortgages. Some

VA (Veterans Administration)
FHA (Federal Housing Administration)

mortgages are backed by the federal government through the *VA (Veterans Administration)* guarantee program or the *FHA (Federal Housing Administration)* insurance program, which adds further protection. Several federal agencies and some other groups promote mortgage lending by purchasing mortgage loans from the originator.

FNMA (Federal National Mortgage Association)

Virtually all actively traded mortgage-backed or mortgage-related securities are issued by federal agencies and a handful of large banks. The oldest and largest of these is the *FNMA*. It purchases mortgages from original mortgage lenders (mortgage bankers, commercial banks, S&Ls, and savings banks) with the proceeds of its own debt security sales. Its bonds have fixed coupons and maturities and trade in a secondary market much like other bonds.

GNMA (Government National Mortgage Association)

The *GNMA* bundles together packages of similar mortgages. These mortgage packages are created by certain private institutions (mortgage bankers, commercial banks, S&Ls, and savings banks) and are permitted to contain only individual mortgages insured by the FHA or guaranteed by the VA. Once a package is bundled together, an application is made to GNMA for a guarantee on the pass-through securities. Once guaranteed, GNMA

pass-through

pass-through securities are backed by the full faith and credit of the U.S. government and therefore are very secure debt instruments.

The principal drawbacks of GNMA pass-throughs are a relatively high minimum denomination ($25,000, but they may be bought in $5,000 units thereafter) and an uncertain amortization rate. Pass-through owners literally own a part of a mortgage pool. They receive monthly interest and amortization payments (less a small service fee to GNMA and the financial institution that administers the mortgage).

Mortgages written for specific periods are often prepaid, and the prepayment rate cannot be predicted with certainty. As a result, a typical GNMA pass-through security with a stated life of 30 years may actually have a much shorter life. This can cause a loss for an investor who buys an existing GNMA pass-through that is selling at a premium. If, for whatever reason, homeowners decide to prepay their mortgages, the investor will then receive par value on the security, thereby incurring a loss. In spite of this drawback, GNMA's relatively secure high yields make GNMA pass-throughs quite attractive to income-oriented investors.

Freddie Mac (Federal Home Loan Mortgage Association

The *Freddie Mac (Federal Home Loan Mortgage Association)* also sells mortgage-related securities. Freddie Mac purchases conventional (not government-backed) mortgages, pools them, and sells participations that have much in common with GNMA pass-throughs. Freddie Mac participations trade in $100,000 minimum denominations. Substantial collateral generally underlies the mortgages, and Freddie Mac guarantees them; therefore, participations are also considered quite safe.

Because of the success of FNMA, GNMA, and Freddie Mac, several large banks also started packaging and marketing their own mortgage pools. These pools offer somewhat higher yields and are a bit more risky than the agency securities. While not government backed, these private pass-throughs are backed by the underlying mortgage collateral, and most have a partial guarantee from a private insurer.

Some depository institutions also sell mortgage-backed bonds. These securities are, however, just another type of corporate bond that happens to have mortgages as collateral. Finally, many mutual fund families manage mortgage-backed security portfolios, thereby allowing small investors relatively easy access to the mortgage market.

Securitization

securitization

The various categories of mortgage-related securities are an example of a broader phenomenon called *securitization*. Securitization involves taking assets that heretofore were not easily traded in a secondary market and structuring a marketable security or group of securities from them. The goal of the process is to convert assets with poor marketability into assets with much greater market acceptance. If the effort is successful, the institution doing the converting will be able to acquire the less marketable assets for appreciably less than the corresponding securitized assets can be sold for.

The difference, less the cost of the conversion, represents the fee or profit paid for the conversion. Looked at from another perspective, securitization allows an institution to turn over its capital much more frequently than is possible with the more traditional buy-and-hold approach to the intermediation process. Thus, a bank that is only able to make and service loans equal to a fraction (less than 100 percent) of its deposit base can securitize, earn an origination fee, and earn a service fee on a multiple (many times 100 percent) of its deposit base.

One major benefit of securitization, from the standpoint of the investor, is that it effectively creates a diversified pool of loans, thus reducing the overall risk to the investor (risk reduction through diversification will be discussed in greater detail in chapter 8). While the risk of default would deter most investors from providing a large loan to an unknown individual, investing in a diversified pool of such loans is relatively safe.

Most of the activity in securitization has been based on first mortgage real estate loans. More recently, however, other types of assets have been securitized. For example, auto loans, credit card loans, second mortgages, sovereign loans to Third World countries, student loans, and a variety of other types of loans are (or are suggested as) the basis for securitization. Moreover, real estate mortgages themselves are coming in for further securitization, as discussed in the following section.

Collateralized Mortgage Obligation (CMO)

CMO (collateralized mortgage obligation)

A basic feature of mortgages and traditional mortgage pass-throughs is their uncertain rate of repayment. When the underlying property is sold or refinanced, the original debt instrument is generally paid off. The borrower may also have the option of prepaying part of the principal. Thus, a typical 25- or 30-year mortgage may, on average, actually be paid back in 12 years. The rate of prepayments will, however, vary with a number of factors, including market interest rates compared to the stated rate on the mortgage, the amount of labor mobility (and the divorce rate) in the community, inflation, the stage of the business cycle, economic conditions (for example, the bankruptcy rate) in the area originating the mortgages, and so on. Many investors prefer a more certain time frame of payments than is provided by the typical mortgage. The CMO *(collateralized mortgage obligation)* was devised to deal with this problem. CMOs are multiclass pass-through securities. They offer a potentially improved way of securitizing mortgage loans.

Owners of the various classes of CMO securities are paid out at different but defined rates. Thus, one class might receive payments equivalent to a one-year zero-coupon bond, a second class might receive payments equivalent to a 5-year zero-coupon bond, and a third class might receive payments equivalent to a 10-year zero-coupon bond. The CMO issuer would be left with the residual cash flow, which might itself be sold as another security. In this way, the uncertain cash flows of a pool of mortgages are restructured into a series of bond-like predictable cash flows and a residual. Virtually all of the uncertainty of the payment timing is impounded into the residual security. Because of the market's general preference for predictable payment rates, the total value of a mortgage pool subdivided into CMOs can be substantially higher than as a single class pass-through.

The Residuals

The securities formed from the residuals of CMOs have been the source of major problems in the marketplace. Their cash flows are very uncertain, depending on such things as default rates and, particularly, the rate of prepayments. Prepayments are, in turn, largely a function of refinancing, which is very sensitive to changes in interest rates. Accordingly, a major change in interest rates can have a dramatic effect on the residuals' value because of the impact on the amount of the security's cash flows, and on the discount rate applied to the residual security's expected stream of cash flows. Moreover, the secondary markets for residuals are very imperfect and at times almost cease to operate. Accordingly, these investments are viewed as extremely risky.

Direct Mortgage Investment

Individuals can also participate directly in the mortgage market. Rising housing prices have led some property owners into seller financing, particularly at times when traditional mortgage money is scarce. Individual investors can extend collateralized loans much like those originated by financial intermediaries. All that is required is a legal document setting forth the rights and obligations of the borrower and lender. The mortgage may be a first mortgage, or it may be junior to some other obligations.

The mortgage agreement contains the borrower's pledge to pay principal and interest at a prespecified rate. Normally, the mortgage payment is set to amortize the loan. Some types of mortgages are interest only or only partially amortized. Thus, the periodic payments do not pay off the loan over its life. The remaining balance is called the balloon. The balloon is payable in a lump sum at the loan's maturity.

If any of the mortgage payments are not made promptly, the lender has the right to enforce the default provisions of the mortgage contract. Ultimately, the borrower's failure to make the required payments when due allows the lender to seize and dispose of the collateral and apply the proceeds of the sale to pay off the debt owed. The proceeds would first be used to repay any outstanding property taxes, the mortgage loan plus accrued interest, and collection expenses (plus any other liens on the property). The lender would still have a claim against the borrower for any remaining deficit. Only after all creditors' claims are satisfied will anything be left for the property's former owner.

Unlike "firsts," most second mortgages are generally written for relatively short periods (for example, 5 years) and may require only principal repayment at maturity (the balloon). With a second mortgage, the lender generally has the right, if it is not repaid, to assume the borrower's position. Thus, the second mortgage holder may make up back payments and, when the first mortgage is paid off, take full possession of the property. Alternatively, the second mortgage holder can sell or let his or her interest lapse.

Second mortgages are usually written for an appreciable fraction of the asset's remaining value (after subtracting the first mortgage), and those who need to use them are often overextended. Moreover, second mortgage holders are frequently asked to extend the repayment dates when the mortgagee cannot pay the balloon. Such instruments are therefore often quite risky and generally trade in a relatively thin secondary market.

Finally, another type of second mortgage is the home equity loan, which is promoted by banks and finance companies. This lending against homeowners' residual equity above and beyond their first (and second) mortgages does not create any debt instruments available to individual investors, even though the interest rates charged on home equity loans are generally much higher than mortgage rates.

Mortgage Investment Assessment

The advantages and disadvantages of indirect mortgage ownership are, in general, similar to those of bonds. Nonetheless, the various pass-throughs and participations offer a less certain maturity and payout rate than most bonds do. Direct mortgage participations (especially second mortgages if priced competitively) usually bear a high interest rate, which reflects the greater risk and trouble involved. Clearly, potential investors should approach direct mortgage lending cautiously.

State and Local Government Debt Obligations

municipals

A large number of state and local government securities are also part of the debt security market. These securities are called *municipals* or municipal bonds. Municipals may be revenue bonds (which are backed by revenues from a designated project, authority, or agency, or by the proceeds from a specific tax) or general obligation bonds (which are backed by the taxing power of the issuing government). The issuing government or authority may be as well known as the State of New York or the New York Port Authority, or as obscure as a small rural water district. Obviously, the adequacy of the tax or revenue bases of these units varies enormously. A major determinant of municipal bond quality is the unit's ability to pay, as measured by its tax or revenue base.

Even well-known, long established issuers of municipals can default. Investors concerned about possible default can purchase insurance to cover any losses that they would incur if coupons or principal are not paid in full and on time. Alternatively, the issuers of municipals can purchase this insurance for the benefit of investors, with the municipalities benefiting from lower interest costs due to lower default risks. A lower default risk on a bond would cause an increase in its rating, as well as its marketability. In fact, while many municipal bonds are rated by Standard & Poor's and Moody's investor services, effective municipal investing, nevertheless, involves substantial individual monitoring. Investors in these securities should carefully evaluate the financial resources of the issuing municipal units.

Municipal bond interest is not subject to federal income tax or state and local tax in the state of issue (except for a small number of taxable issues). Capital gains on municipal holdings are taxable, however. The tax advantage of municipals allows issuers to offer lower before-tax returns than otherwise-similar taxable bonds. The relative after-tax return depends on the individual's tax bracket and the differential yields.

Obviously, tax-free income becomes more attractive to those in higher tax brackets. Those with marginal tax rates of 28 percent or more will often find their after-tax return on municipals above that of similar-risk taxable bonds. For investors with marginal tax rates of 15 percent, taxable bonds tend to offer the higher after-tax yield, but not always. Investors should evaluate the situation on an individual basis because relative interest rates vary over time and with maturity.

Tax-Equivalent Yields

Comparing after-tax returns on taxable and tax-free investments is quite straightforward. First, the investor determines his or her marginal tax rate for federal tax purposes. As explained in chapter 1, an investor's taxable income results from adding investment income to other forms of income. Following this approach, the last dollar of investment income is then viewed as the last increment of income, and the last increment of income is always taxed at the marginal rate.

As the last increment of income, the last dollar of taxable investment income may be taxed in one of five tax brackets: the 15 percent, 28 percent, 31 percent, 36 percent, or 39.6 percent bracket. The after-tax return corresponding to these tax brackets equals 85 percent, 72 percent, 69 percent, 64 percent, and 60.4 percent of the taxable income, respectively. Therefore, a 10 percent taxable return from a bond would be equivalent to an 8.5 percent, 7.2 percent, 6.9 percent, 6.4 percent and 6.04 percent tax-free return for an investor in the 15 percent, 28 percent, 31 percent, 36 percent, and 39.6 percent tax brackets, respectively. The impact of the alternative minimum tax, the phaseout of itemized deductions and personal exemptions, and state and local income taxes, if applicable, further complicate the comparison between taxable and tax-free investments. The presence of these other complicating factors, however, can appreciably enhance tax-free returns. A New York City resident, for example, escapes federal, state, and city income taxes on any interest income from bonds issued by New York municipal units.

Example: An investor's income puts him or her squarely in the 15 percent tax bracket. Any additional income the investor receives will be taxed at the marginal rate of 15 percent. Assuming this investor wants to purchase a bond, which bond would provide the highest after-tax return: a corporate bond or a tax-free municipal bond? The 8.125 percent tax-free municipal bond matures in 2023 and is currently selling for 101. This bond, being tax free, provides both a before-tax and after-tax return of 8.04 percent. The 8.80 percent corporate bond matures in 2012 and is currently selling for 94½. It provides a before-tax return of 9.31 percent. The after-tax return for this corporate bond is computed as, follows: Before-tax return x (1 – marginal tax rate). Filling in the numbers, the equation is as follows: 9.31% (1 – .15) = 9.31% x (.85) = 7.91%. Thus, ignoring capital gains taxes and state taxes for simplicity, the after-tax return on the 9.3 percent corporate bond (7.91 percent) is slightly lower than the (tax-free) return on the municipal bond (8.04 percent) for the investor in the 15 percent tax bracket. Most investors who invest in municipals, however, are in higher tax brackets. For an investor with a marginal tax rate of 28 percent, the after-tax return on the corporate bond is 6.70 percent [9.31% (1 – .28) = 9.31% x .72 = 6.70%]. This return is substantially lower than the 8.04 percent return on the municipal bond.

Municipal Bond Funds

A rather large investment would be required to spread the risks of a municipal bond portfolio effectively. A reasonable degree of diversification would not be achieved with less than five separate bond issues, each from a different governmental jurisdiction. Ideally, an investor would not want to purchase such bonds in smaller than 10-bond units. Five-bond units would be possible, although the per bond commission would be higher. Thus, a minimum of 25 to 50 bonds would be required for a diversified portfolio. Such a portfolio would cost $25,000 to $50,000. An investment of this magnitude would put a diversified municipal bond portfolio out of reach for most investors.

municipal bond funds

Fortunately, investors who have relatively limited resources have an alternative to assembling their own municipal bond portfolios. *Municipal bond funds* assemble and manage well-diversified portfolios. These funds appeal to investors with moderate means who seek tax-exempt income. Many portfolios of these funds are, however, weighted toward high-risk securities. Prospective investors may have to do a substantial amount of digging through a fund's prospectus to determine the fund's average risk level.

Like the money market mutual funds, municipal bond funds compete with unit investment trusts that assemble and hold portfolios of municipals. There are several similarities. The risk-adjusted yields of municipal unit trusts are somewhat higher, but the units are somewhat less convenient to own than municipal bond funds. A number of funds invest only in the securities of a single state. Thus, their residents can take full advantage of the tax-free status of the income at the federal, state, and local levels.

Corporate Debt Obligations

debentures

Corporations constitute yet another category of bond issuers. They issue both secured bonds (backed by specific collateral) and *debentures* (backed only by the issuer's full faith and credit). Corporate bonds, like government bonds, bear interest and mature on a specified date. In addition, some corporate bonds may, at the owner's option, be exchanged at some fixed ratio for stocks of the issuing corporation. These corporate bonds, known as convertibles, are discussed in greater detail in a later chapter.

Most bond trades involve both the price of the bond and an adjustment for accrued interest. The buyer pays and the seller receives a sum to reflect the portion of interest that has already been earned but not yet paid.

Example: A bond that is quoted at 93 would initially cost the buyer $930 in principal plus the prorated amount of accrued but unpaid interest. If the bond has a 10 percent coupon and made its last coupon payment 3 months ago, unpaid interest would have accrued as follows:

$$3/12 \times (.10 \times \$1,000) = 1/4 \times \$100 = \$25$$

That is, the bond pays interest every 6 months. Since 3 months have elapsed, half of one coupon payment has arrived. This corresponds to 3/12 (or 1/4) of one year's interest. One year's interest at 10 percent of a $1,000 bond corresponds to .10 x $1,000 = $100. One fourth of $100 is $25.

As with dividends on stock, interest is paid to the one who holds the bond on the day of record. When the issuer makes the coupon payment, the new owner will receive and get to keep the entire amount of interest for that period.

flat

Bonds trading for a net price that does not reflect any accrued interest are said to trade *flat*. Typically, bonds that are in default or whose interest payments are considered very uncertain trade flat. While the number of bonds that are traded flat is relatively small, if these bonds do make their interest payments, the full amount of the payments goes to the holder of record on the record date. Thus, the owner of these bonds on the day of record receives all of that period's interest payments, regardless of length of ownership. In the bond quotations, bonds that trade flat have an "f" following the abbreviation for their name.

Many corporate bonds are listed on an exchange, but most of the trading takes place in a very active OTC market. Investors who wish to buy or sell a large amount of bonds should obtain several quotations to see which market maker offers the best price. In addition to NYSE listings, small amounts of bonds are also traded on some other exchanges, including the AMEX.

Corporate Bond Quotations
(Sample Quote for Bonds listed on the New York or American Exchanges as Presented in the Financial Media on 4/13/2000)

Bonds	Cur. Yld.	Vol.	Close	Net Chg.
Att6s09	6.6	4	90 1/2	– 1/8

- Bonds: the name of the company issuing the bond, the interest or coupon rate as a percentage of the face or par value (typically $1,000), and the year in which the bond will be paid off (the s that sometimes appears between the interest rate and the year of maturity has no significance other than to separate the interest rate from the year of maturity when the interest rate does not include a fraction—read the explanatory notes given in the financial media for the meaning of other letters used)
- Cur. Yld.: the current yield or annual percentage return to the purchaser at the current price (as of 4 p.m. Eastern Time of the previous trading day when the exchanges closed, calculated by dividing the coupon rate by the current price)
- Vol.: the volume in terms of thousands of dollars (to be read by adding three zeros) traded (as of 4 p.m. Eastern Time of the previous trading day when the exchanges closed)
- Close: the price (in 32nds), which is a percentage of par value (as of 4 p.m. Eastern Time of the previous trading day when the exchanges closed) (A bond trading for less than 100 is selling at a discount from its par value; one selling for more than 100 is trading at a premium.)
- Net Chg.: the difference between the closing price as listed In the close column (see Close above) and the closing price from the previous trading day (which is really two trading days previous) (for instance, a +1/2 means an increase of 16/32 and a –1/4 indicates a decrease of 8/32)

Corporate bond quotations, like other bond and stock quotations, are presented in the financial media. Perhaps the best known and most comprehensive media source for financial information is *The Wall Street Journal.*

High-Risk Corporates (Junk Bonds)

junk bonds

Bonds were once thought of as very secure low-risk investments. More recently, since the 1980s' merger and acquisition wave led by risk arbitrageurs and certain take-over "artists" and corporate raiders, the issue volume and marketability of *junk bonds* have increased manyfold. Many of these bonds are viewed as very risky, and thus bear commensurate risk premiums, even though most junk bonds will pay off. Table 5-1 illustrates some yield differentials from May 19, 1982. This was a time of relatively high rates. Risk premiums also tended to be high at that time. For comparison, the table also shows some rates for January 18, 1988, and June 24, 1999.

Clearly, these substantial yield differentials reflect appreciable differences in risk. Indeed, the higher the "promised" yield, the greater the default risk is likely to be. Although junk bonds are ill-suited to the needs of cautious investors, many risk-tolerant or risk-neutral investors are attracted to them. Risk and potential return can be as great as with many stocks. Indeed, a risky firm's bonds sometime offer a more attractive way of speculating than its stock does, since the bonds represent a stronger claim on the firm's assets in case of liquidation or bankruptcy. To realize an attractive return, the junk bond investor only needs the troubled firm to avoid bankruptcy or to maintain substantial value in a reorganization. The stockholder's return, in contrast, may not be attractive unless the firm becomes relatively profitable, since stocks represent only a residual claim on the firm's assets.

Note that not all bonds that offer high yields are "junk." Sometimes a new company whose performance is unproven will have to offer a high interest rate on its bonds in order to obtain capital to fund its activities. As time goes on and the company develops a track record of good performance, it will then be able to obtain capital at a lower cost.

During the late 1980s' and early 1990s' returns on junk bonds were often low and sometimes even negative. Poor junk bond performance, when it occurs, may be due to the interaction of two factors: First, high prior returns for junk bonds tend to attract new investors who bid prices up to levels that, once reached, are unlikely to allow superior returns for new investors. Second, a weakening economy tends to push marginal companies into bankruptcy, causing their bonds to default. Thus, a period of high junk bond returns and a strong economy (that is, the mid 1980s) followed by a weaker

TABLE 5-1
Differential Bond Yields

May 19, 1982				
Company	Coupon	Maturity	Price	Current Yield
Very Secure:				
AT&T	13 1/4	1991	96 1/4	13.7
GE Credit	13 5/8	1991	97 1/4	14.0
Risky:				
Eastern Airlines	17 1/2	1998	92 7/8	18.8
Rapid American	11 1/4	2005	57 5/8	18.9
World Airlines	11 1/4	1994	52 7/8	22.3
Very Risky:				
International Harvester	9 1/4	2004	28 1/2	31.6
In Default:				
Braniff	10 1/4	1986	32 1/2	30.8 (if paid)

January 18, 1988				
Company	Coupon	Maturity	Price	Current Yield
Very Secure:				
AT&T	8 5/8	2026	89 1/2	9.6
General Motors	8 5/8	2005	91 1/2	9.4
Risky:				
Bethlehem Steel	8 3/8	2001	74 1/2	11.3
Commonwealth Edison	11 3/4	2015	103 1/2	11.4
Very Risky:				
Texas Air	15 3/4	1992	94 1/2	16.7
Resorts International	11 3/8	2013	62 1/4	18.3
In Default:				
LTV	8 3/4	2004	25 1/4	35.0 (if paid)

June 24, 1999				
Company	Coupon	Maturity	Price	Current Yield
Very Secure:				
AT&T	7 1/2	2001	103 3/4	7.2
Chase	6 1/4	2001	98	6.4
Risky:				
RJR	8 3/4	2015	101 1/8	8.7
Revlon	8 1/2	2001	96	8.5
Very Risky:				
Trump	11 1/4	2006	90	12.5
Integrated	9 1/4	2008	72 1/2	12.8

economy (the early 1990s) is just the type of situation that is likely to produce poor returns for junk bond investors.

While always an important investment goal, diversification is crucial for junk bond portfolios. A defaulting issue may eventually pay off, but the wait can be long and nerve-racking. Having a diversified bond portfolio substantially dilutes the impact of a single default. Risk spreading is especially advisable for junk bond investors. Junk bond funds provide small investors with an effective diversification vehicle. In fact, the growth of these funds has encouraged some firms with relatively low credit ratings to return to the market.

Corporate Bond Funds

corporate bond funds

Corporate bond funds have existed for many years. With the stock market depressed and interest rates at historic highs, bond fund yields became increasingly attractive in the early 1970s. The very high interest environment of the early 1980s further enhanced their yields and attractiveness. Markets are, of course, always changing. Later in the 1980s, interest rates fell, making bonds and bond funds somewhat less attractive. Their yields were still lower throughout the 1990s as the stock market boomed. As a result, bonds have lost some of their luster.

Long-Term Debt Securities: Primary Types

- Treasury notes and bonds: lowest risk category
- Agency issues: slightly higher risks and yields than Treasuries
- Mortgage-related securities
  - FNMA: mortgage-backed (VA and FHA)
  - GNMA: mortgage pass-throughs (VA and FHA)
  - Freddie Mac: conventional mortgages, with Freddie Mac guarantee
  - Bank issued: conventional mortgages, often with a private guarantee
- Direct mortgage, seller financing: risk varies; seconds are usually quite risky
- Municipals: tax-free; risk varies
  - Municipal bond funds
  - Diversified: may be open- or closed-end
- Corporates: vary greatly in risks and yields
  - Corporate bond funds: diversified; may be open- or closed-end
  - Junk bond funds: high-risk portfolios

As with other types of mutual funds (the subject of a later chapter), bond funds may be load or no-load, open-end or closed-end, and managed or unmanaged (unit trusts). As they do with stock funds, most investors will find the no-load type of fund a generally preferable way of buying into a bond portfolio. Most closed-end funds sell at a discount from their net asset value (NAV). Both open-end and closed-end bond funds have similar advantages and drawbacks vis-à-vis direct bond ownership, as do common stock mutual funds relative to investor-assembled stock portfolios. The bond funds offer diversification, convenience, and low-denomination purchase. On the other hand, the expenses incurred in marketing and managing the funds reduce their yields somewhat (as compared with individually managed bond portfolios). As with other types of funds, unmanaged funds have lower expenses. Thus, more of the portfolio's yields flow through to the funds' investors.

Long-Term Certificates of Deposit

We have already seen that commercial banks and other financial intermediaries offer a number of different types of short-term debt instruments, including CDs. They also sell a variety of longer-term debt instruments, including CDs. Some of the longer-term CDs have maturities of 10 years or more, with denominations up to $100,000. Although most CDs are insured by federal deposit insurance, investors should verify this fact at the time of purchase. Moreover, the rate of return earned on CDs is typically higher than the rate paid on savings accounts because the funds are being committed for a specified time period. If an investor decides to redeem the CD before the time period expires, a penalty in the form of forfeited interest may be assessed. Some CDs offer special rates for IRA and Keogh accounts.

Income Bonds

income bonds

Most bonds must either pay the agreed-upon sums (coupon rate) or go into default. *Income bonds*, on the other hand, pay interest only if the issuer earns it. Passed coupons may or may not accumulate. Bonds with large unpaid arrearage may offer attractive speculation opportunities. Specific indenture provisions indicate when earned income is sufficient to require an interest payment.

Most income bonds originate in a reorganization exchange. Some, however, are sold initially as income bonds. Income bonds offer issuers about as much flexibility to withhold payments as preferred stock does. Moreover, the issuer has the right to deduct the (interest) payments from taxable income. Nonetheless, the volume of income bonds outstanding is negligible in comparison to preferred stock.

Floating-Rate Securities

floating-rate securities

Bonds can be issued with variable or floating rates of interest. These instruments are a form of long-term debt, but they are subject to short-term rates. The floating or variable rate feature of these bonds generally causes their prices to remain relatively close to their par values. Just how close their prices remain to their par values is a function of how frequently the coupon rate is adjusted, as well as the rate to which it is pegged. By adjusting the coupon rate up or down with the inflation rate, floating rate bonds keep their *real* rate of return relatively constant. They are structured so that their yields adjust to market conditions. Thus, their prices can stay relatively constant as interest rates fluctuate. However, the more distant the maturity date of these bonds, the more risky they are likely to be (greater default risk) than otherwise similar short-term debt instruments.

The characteristics of these floating-rate bonds vary somewhat. Some adjust their coupon rates once every 6 months; others adjust them weekly. Some peg the coupon rates to one percent over the base rate; others peg them to .75 percent over the base rate or even lower. Some peg the coupon rates to 90-day T-bills; others use the prime rate or the federal funds rate as the base rate. Although floating-rate bonds do appear in the United States, they appear more often in the international market, especially in Asia. A few companies even issue floating-rate preferred stock.

Zero-Coupon and Other Types of Original-Issue Discount Bonds

Most bonds' coupon rates are initially set so that the price of the bonds will be close to their face or par value. Original-issue discount bonds are sold for appreciably less than their value at maturity (par). These bonds have either a zero-coupon rate or a coupon rate that is well below the market rate. As a result, such bonds initially sell for a market price that is substantially below their face value.

Bonds that do not make coupon interest payments are called zero-coupon bonds, or zeros. The return on these securities is derived from the difference between their purchase price and maturity value. Treasury bills and certain other government securities such as U.S. savings bonds have long been sold on a discount basis. For example, a one-year T-bill might be priced at 95. This means that a bill with a $10,000 face value would initially cost $9,500 and pay an additional $500 ($10,000 − $9,500) at maturity. In addition to government zero-coupon securities, a number of long-term corporate zeros have also been issued.

Zero-coupon bonds may also be created from some types of coupon bonds. The coupons are simply separated from the principal portion and the two components sold separately. Most bonds pay interest to the registered owner, but some of the older bonds have attached coupons that may be

strip bond

clipped and sold to an investor who seeks periodic income. The bond without its coupons attached is called a *strip bond*.

The Treasury recognized the popularity of stripping Treasury securities and in 1985 introduced a program call STRIPS (Separate Trading of Registered Interest and Principal Securities). Under this program, the Treasury prestrips certain interest-bearing Treasury securities so that investors who purchase them can keep whatever cash payments they want and sell the rest. For example, a 20-year coupon bond could be stripped of its 40 semiannual coupons, and each of these coupons would then be treated as a stand-alone zero-coupon bond. The maturities of these 40 bonds would range from 6 months to 20 years. The final payment of principal would also be treated as a stand-alone zero-coupon bond.

U.S. Treasury Strips Quotations
(Sample Quote from the OTC Market as Presented in the Financial Media on 4/13/2000)

Mat.	Type	Bid	Asked	Chg.	Ask Yld.
May 06	ci	68:15	68:19	– 10	6.29

- Mat.: the month and year in which the principal will be paid off
- Type: ci—indicates stripped coupon interest; bp—indicates Treasury bond, stripped principal; np—indicates Treasury note, stripped principal
- Bid: the price (in 32nds) that a dealer is willing to pay for the security (as of 3 p.m. Eastern Time of the previous trading day)
- Asked: the price (in 32nds) that a dealer is willing to sell the security for (as of 3 p.m. Eastern Time of the previous trading day)
- Chg.: the change (in 32nds) between the bid price as listed in the bid column (see Bid above) and the bid price from the previous trading day (which is really two trading days previous) (for instance, a +2 means an increase of 2/32 and a –3 indicates a decrease of 3/32)
- Ask Yld.: the yield to maturity for the security based on its asked price

---

zero-coupon bonds

Zero-coupon bonds have precisely identifiable maturity values. This feature has an appeal for IRA and Keogh accounts. Investors in zeros know at the outset exactly what the value will be at maturity. The end-period value of funds invested in coupon-yielding bonds, in contrast, is not nearly so certain. The actual compounded value of such a portfolio will depend, in part, on the rate earned on the reinvested coupon payments.

The uncertainty associated with the return on reinvested coupon payments is called reinvestment rate risk. Because of their lack of reinvestment rate risk and relative scarcity, zero-coupon bonds have tended to sell for somewhat lower yields than equivalent-risk coupon bonds.

Like other long-term bonds, long-term zero-coupon bonds lock both the buyer and the issuer into a long-term rate. If rates go up after the purchase, the buyer will end up receiving a below-market return. The issuer, in contrast, will pay an above-market rate if market interest rates decline after the issue is sold. Moreover, for a given change in interest rates, the prices of zeros change proportionately more than those of coupon bonds do. Owners of coupon bonds are at least able to reinvest their coupon income at higher rates when market interest rates rise. Owners of zeros receive no coupon payments and thus have no interim payments to reinvest.

Even though zeros pay no coupons they nevertheless impose an annual tax liability on their owners (assuming the investors are subject to income tax). Determining a zero-coupon bond's tax liability first involves determining the relevant amount of imputed interest, which is the bond's yield to maturity. This is the amount that the government assumes is accrued but not received each year. The imputed interest rate is computed as if the bond made annual coupon payments equal to its yield-to-maturity rate at the time of its purchase. Thus, a zero-coupon bond that was sold to yield 8 percent would be treated for tax purposes as if it did, in fact, earn 8 percent each year. The issuer is allowed to deduct the imputed interest cost each year, while the owner incurs an equivalent tax liability. As a result, the issuer obtains an early tax deduction, while the owner must pay taxes prior to receiving the associated income.

The tax computation on coupon-paying original-issue discount bonds is even more complex. The owner is, of course, liable for taxes on the coupon payments. In addition, taxes are assessed on the appropriate imputed interest (amortization of the discount) as the bond moves closer to maturity. The basis on both types of original-issue discount bonds is increased each year by the amount of the accumulated imputed interest. Therefore, the basis on an original-issue discount bond would equal the initial purchase cost plus the sum of the imputed interest amounts.

Eurobonds

Eurobonds

Eurobonds are bonds that are offered outside the country of the borrower and outside the country in whose currency the bonds are denominated. Therefore, if a U.S. corporation issues bonds that are denominated in U.S. dollars (or in Japanese yen for that matter) but sold in France (and perhaps some other countries as well), the bonds would be considered Eurobonds. These foreign bonds differ from U.S. or foreign bonds that are traded in only one country. The Eurobond issuer benefits from the wider distribution and the absence of restrictions and taxes that are placed on single-country bonds. Eurobond buyers may obtain greater diversification than is available from U.S. bonds alone. Moreover, bonds denominated in a foreign currency offer investors an opportunity to speculate against the dollar.

One of the most attractive features of Eurobonds (at least for some investors) is the ease with which some of these bonds allow investors to avoid taxes. Two features of many Eurobonds facilitate tax avoidance. First, unlike domestic bonds, no backup withholding is applied to unregistered Eurobond interest and principal payments. Second, many Eurobonds have been issued in bearer (unregistered) form. Without either registration or backup withholding, Eurobond owners find that taxes are relatively easy to avoid. Because of this appeal, Eurobonds tend to yield less than domestic bonds of comparable risk. More recently, however, Eurobonds have generally been issued in registered form, and thus the tax avoidance opportunity has disappeared for newer issues.

Most Eurobonds are issued by multinational corporations, governments, and international organizations, and most are denominated in dollars, yen or d-marks. They may take on any of the forms of regular bonds: straight bonds, convertibles, floating-rate notes, zero-coupon bonds, and so on.

Private Placement

private placement

Approximately one-third of the debt instruments sold are placed privately to a few large buyers (often insurance companies) and publicly announced in the financial press. Announcements are generally referred to as "tombstones" because of the large amount of white space and small amount of lettering. Even if the size (tens of millions of dollars) of typical private placements rules out direct purchases, individuals may participate indirectly through one of the closed-end funds that specialize in such investments.

Private placements generally yield 1/2 percent to one percent more than equivalent-risk bonds because they lack marketability. Private placements offer greater flexibility to issuers. They can be tailored for specific buyers and do not require a prospectus. Moreover, the underwriting cost savings largely offset their somewhat higher coupon. Finally, the relatively small number of owners makes terms easier to renegotiate if necessary.

Preferred Stock

Although preferred stock is a type of equity security, it has much in common with debt instruments. The issuer of the preferred stock is not required to declare dividends. However, the payment of preferred stock dividends is required before common stock dividends can be paid. Moreover, most preferreds are cumulative, which means that accumulated (unpaid) dividends must be made up before any common stock dividend can be paid. Thus, most companies' preferred stock dividends are almost as dependable as their bond interest. In addition, many preferred stock charters call for the preferred stockholders to gain voting rights if two consecutive dividend payments are missed, giving preferred stockholders some control over the management of the company. The preferreds of a weak company may, however, be almost as risky as its common stock. Some preferreds (participating) may receive an extra dividend payment if earnings or common stock dividends are high enough.

Preferred stockholders are residual claimants only one step ahead of common stockholders. Unless the creditors' claims are fully satisfied, nothing will be left for either class of stockholders. Unlike corporate interest payments, 70 percent of the dividends received by a domestic corporation from another (incorporated in the United States) domestic corporation are tax deductible. This tax preference applies not only to common stock dividends but also to preferred dividends. Moreover, the deduction may be either 80 percent or 100 percent of dividends received if the receiving corporation owns specified percentages of the stock of the paying corporation. For a corporation in the 34 percent tax bracket eligible for the 70 percent dividends-received deduction, a 9 percent preferred yield is equivalent to an after-tax yield of 8.08 percent. In contrast, a fully taxable yield of 12.25 percent would be needed to generate the same after-tax yield of 8.08 percent.

Preferreds have become very popular with corporate investors. Because their tax advantage is available only to corporations, most individual investors will not find preferreds attractive. Preferred dividends are not tax deductible to the issuer so, all other things being equal, corporations would generally choose to issue bonds rather than preferred stock.

Implications of the Long-Term Bond Market for the Investor

Investors may choose from a large number of long-term debt security types. Governments and agencies offer very secure yields. Municipals are tax sheltered. Corporates and municipals can be bought in a wide array of risk and expected return categories. Specialized types have coupons that vary with earnings or market rates. Still others have no coupons but pay substantially more than their current market price at maturity.

THE MATHEMATICS OF YIELDS

The term yield is often used as if its meaning were unambiguous, but it can actually be taken to mean a number of different things. For example, the current yield reported in the newspaper quotation is simply the coupon rate divided by the current price. Thus an 11 percent coupon on a bond quoted at 85 would have a current yield of:

$$\text{Current yield} = 110/850 = 12.94\%$$

Such a computation does not, however, take account of the discount or premium from par. A more complex concept, the yield to maturity does consider the impacts of premiums or discounts. To compute the yield to maturity one would solve for the rate that would make the present value of the income payments equal the price of the bond.

Since some bonds are likely to be called before maturity, the yield to earliest call is often computed for such issues. The computation is similar to that for the yield to maturity except the earliest call date and the call price are used rather than the maturity date and face values.

Those who sell their investment prior to maturity may compute yet another yield: the holding period or realized yield. This is the rate that makes the present value of the payments and sale price equal the purchase price.

Most yields, especially long-term yields, are quoted in coupon-equivalent terms. Short-term yields, in contrast, are often stated in what is called the discount basis. The two yields are computed differently and can produce rather different numbers. Coupon-equivalent yields assume that interest payments take place semiannually and are based on a 365-day year. Discount yields, in contrast, work with a 360-day year and assume that the interest is deducted at the outset. As a result, stated discount-basis yields are somewhat below the coupon-equivalent yield computed for the same security.

The formula for a discount-basis yield of a one-year security is

$$d = D/F$$

where: d = discount-basis yield
 F = face value
 D = discount in face value

Thus, a $1,000 face value one-year bond selling for $900 would be priced at a $100 discount and offer a discount yield of 10 percent ($100/$1,000). A slightly more complicated formula is required for maturities of less than one year:

$$d = (D/F)(360/M)$$

where: M – number of days to maturity

Accordingly, the yield for a Treasury bill with 250 days until maturity selling for $9,500 would be computed as follows:

$$\$500/\$10,000 \times 360/250 = 7.20\%$$

We can compute the simple-interest yield from the discount-basis yield with the following formula:

$$i = (365\ d)/(360 - dM)$$

where: i = simple-interest yield

Applying this formula to our previous example produces

$$i = 365\ (.072)/[360 - (.072)\ (250)] = 7.68\%$$

Thus, we see that the simple-interest yield (7.68 percent) appreciably exceeds the discount-basis yield (7.20 percent) for this security. Table 5-2 illustrates the differential in the two yields.

TABLE 5-2 **Comparisons at Different Rates and Maturities between Rates of Discount and the Equivalent Simple Interest Rates on the Basis of a 365-Day Year**			
	Equivalent Simple Interest		
Rate of Discount	30-Day Maturity	182-Day Maturity	364-Day Maturity
4%	4.07%	4.14%	4.23%
6	6.11	6.27	6.48
8	8.17	8.45	8.82
10	10.22	10.68	11.27
12	12.29	12.95	13.84
14	14.36	15.28	16.53
16	16.44	17.65	19.35

The simple-interest yield approximates but does not equal the coupon-equivalent yield. The two yields differ because the simple-interest formula assumes that the interest payments are received at maturity whereas the coupon-equivalent yield takes account of semiannual interest payments. When a security has less than 6 months to run, the two rates are equivalent. For longer maturity instruments, however, the following formula is employed to compute the coupon-equivalent yield on a security that is priced on a discount basis:

$$r = \frac{\dfrac{2M}{365} + 2\sqrt{\left(\dfrac{M^2}{365}\right) - \left(\dfrac{2M}{365} - 1\right)\left(1 - \dfrac{1}{p}\right)}}{\dfrac{2M}{365} - 1}$$

where: r = coupon-equivalent yield
p = price as a percentage of face

Thus, a 6-month Treasury bill selling at $9,506.53 with 190 days to run would be handled as follows:

$$r = \frac{\dfrac{2(190)}{365} + 2\sqrt{\left(\dfrac{190}{365}\right)^2 - \left(\dfrac{2(190)}{365} - 1\right)\left(1 - \dfrac{1}{.950635}\right)}}{\dfrac{2(190)}{365} - 1} = 9.95\%$$

SUMMARY AND CONCLUSIONS

At a minimum, investors should consider the wide variety of risks, returns, marketabilities, liquidities, and tax treatments the bond market offers. A well-diversified portfolio that contains both equity and debt securities is likely to be less risky than a well-diversified portfolio of stocks or bonds alone. Investors should have little difficulty finding issues bearing risk/expected return characteristics that correspond to their own preferences.

The money market provides relatively attractive short-term rates on high-quality securities, such as T-bills, commercial paper, large bank CDs, bankers' acceptances, and Eurodollar loans. Small investors can participate in this market through money market mutual funds, short-term unit investment trusts, and the money market certificates and accounts of commercial banks and thrift institutions. Larger investors can assemble their own money market portfolios.

Treasury and federal agency securities make up a large part of the long-term debt security market. Most of these issues are untaxed at the state and local level. The agencies tend to offer slightly higher yields but are somewhat less marketable than Treasury issues. A large part of the agency security market is mortgage related. The various bonds, pass-throughs, and participations of FNMA, GNMA, Freddie Mac, and the large bank pools offer high, safe, monthly income combined with a somewhat uncertain maturity.

State and local issues, whose interest payments are untaxed at the federal level, form another major segment of the debt security market. Most municipals offer relatively low before-tax yields. These securities appeal primarily to investors in high tax brackets. Municipal bond funds and municipal unit investment trusts give small investors various ways to enter this market. Municipal bonds are also generally exempt from state income tax in their state of issue, making them even more attractive to investors in high tax brackets.

Long-Term Debt Securities: Specialized Types

- Long-term CDs: limited variety
- Income bonds: interest paid only if earned
- Floating-rate securities: coupon varies with market rates
- Zero-coupon bonds: sold at a discount; pay no coupon
- Eurobonds: traded internationally
- Private placements: large and flexible
- Preferred stock: 70% tax sheltered to domestic corporations

---

Corporate securities vary greatly in risk. Some high-risk issues offer very high yields. Corporate bond funds (including high-risk bond funds) and closed-end bond funds permit small investors to own part of a diversified debt security portfolio.

Other types of debt securities include income bonds, floating-rate securities, zero-coupon bonds, Eurobonds, privately placed issues, and preferred stock (an equity asset but paying a fixed amount periodically). Each of these securities appeals to specialized segments of the marketplace.

Thus, the debt security market offers a wide array of risk-return tradeoffs, maturities, and tax treatments. Moreover, in the past few years, a variety of new instruments have improved small investors' access to these markets. A number of mutual funds and short-term unit trusts facilitate investing in money market, municipal, corporate, high-risk corporate, and various other more specialized types of debt securities. Access is therefore no longer restricted by the difficulty of diversifying across a variety of high-denomination securities.

CHAPTER REVIEW

Answers to the review questions and the self-test questions start on page 749.

Key Terms

fixed-income securities
money market

Treasury bills (T-bills)
commercial paper

CDs (certificates of deposit)
banker's acceptance
Eurodollar deposits
federal funds market
repurchase agreements (repos)
discount loans
money market mutual funds
unit investment trusts
FDIC (Federal Deposit Insurance
    Corporation)
notes
bearer bonds
agency securities
mortgage-backed securities
mortgage
collateral
VA (Veterans Administration)
FHA (Federal Housing Administra-
    tion)
FNMA (Federal National Mortgage
    Association)

GNMA (Government National
    Mortgage Association)
pass-through
Freddie Mac (Federal Home Loan
    Mortgage Association)
securitization
CMO (collateralized mortgage
    obligation)
municipals
municipal bond funds
debentures
flat
junk bonds
corporate bond funds
income bonds
floating-rate securities
strip bond
zero-coupon bonds
Eurobonds
private placement

Review Questions

5-1.   Compute the equivalent yield for a 52-week T-bill priced at 95.

5-2.   Compute the equivalent yield for a stripped T-bond with 180 days until maturity. The strip is quoted at 97.31.

5-3.   Construct a table that briefly itemizes the advantages and disadvantages of T-bills, commercial paper, federal funds, and money market mutual funds.

5-4.   How much would the equivalent yield in question 5-2 decline if the strip's price increased by $10.00?

5-5.   Describe the three principal types of bonds by issuer. How do they differ? In what ways are they similar?

5-6.   In relation to mortgages and mortgage-related securities:
    a.   What is meant by securitization?
    b.   What is the advantage to the issuer, individuals, and to the marketplace of the securitization of assets?

5-7.   Explain how to compare municipal bond yields with those of other types of debt issues.

5-8.   You have a choice between a taxable bond yielding 7.94 percent and a nontaxable bond yielding 5.41 percent.

   a.   Calculate the tax-equivalent yields for the 15, 28, 31, 36, and 39.6 marginal tax rates.

   b.   At what marginal tax rate does the taxable bond offer a return equal to the taxable bond?

5-9.   Summarize the characteristics of

   a.   income bonds

   b.   floating-rate notes

   c.   zero-coupon bonds

5-10.   Discuss the relevance to individual investors of

   a.   Eurobonds

   b.   private placements

   c.   preferred stocks

5-11.   Discuss alternative ways (to direct investment) that the individual investor can participate in the various fixed-income investments introduced in this chapter. Briefly indicate advantages and disadvantages.

Self-Test Questions

T   F   5-1.   T-bills are sold initially at or near par value and pay a semiannual coupon.

T   F   5-2.   New issues of T-bills can be purchased directly from the Federal Reserve.

T   F   5-3.   New issues of T-bills come with maturities of 13 weeks, 26 weeks, or 52 weeks.

T   F   5-4.   All auction bids for new issues of T-bills are entered on a competitive basis.

T   F   5-5.   Dealers in government securities maintain an active secondary market in T-bills.

T   F   5-6.   Commercial paper is usually issued by large corporations to finance their short-term needs.

T   F   5-7.   Commercial paper is typically secured by real estate or high-quality securities.

T   F   5-8.   Commercial paper issuers usually have to pay 1 or 2 percent above the prime rate on their borrowings.

T   F   5-9.   The principal of negotiable CDs issued by bank and thrift institutions does not qualify for protection by government deposit insurance.

T   F   5-10.   The relatively high minimum denomination of $100,000 puts negotiable CDs issued by bank and thrift institutions beyond the range of most individual small investors.

T F 5-11. A banker's acceptance is a contingent liability of the bank that guaranteed it.

T F 5-12. Once a banker's acceptance is created, it trades like other money market securities.

T F 5-13. In the case of Eurodollar deposits, disputes between the bank and the depositor must be settled under the U.S. legal system.

T F 5-14. The federal funds rate is the interest rate that banks charge other banks for overnight loans.

T F 5-15. Discount loans are extended by the Federal Reserve to member banks for the purpose of covering a short-term reserve deficiency.

T F 5-16. Adverse interest rate moves are likely to affect a money market fund's share prices significantly.

T F 5-17. Most money market funds permit checks to be written on the fund holder's account.

T F 5-18. Short-term unit investment trusts are managed and perpetual.

T F 5-19. The yields on existing short-term unit investment trusts increase when market interest rates rise.

T F 5-20. Small-denomination CDs issued by banks are generally transferable.

T F 5-21. For all its potential complexity, a bond is basically just an IOU between two parties or group of parties.

T F 5-22. U.S. Treasury bonds are issued with maturities from one to 10 years.

T F 5-23. Treasury note and bond price quotations are expressed in hundredths.

T F 5-24. All newly issued Treasury notes and bonds are in bearer form.

T F 5-25. Some Treasury bonds have call provisions that allow them to be called during a specified period prior to maturity.

T F 5-26. The yield-to-maturity for Treasury securities typically is calculated using the asked price.

T F 5-27. Treasury securities are subject to state and local taxes.

T F 5-28. Most federal agency issues are not subject to state and local taxes.

T F 5-29. Agency issues generally bear a slightly higher interest rate than Treasury securities of comparable maturity.

T F 5-30. The principal drawbacks of Government National Mortgage Association (GNMA) pass-through securities are their relatively high minimum denomination and an uncertain amortization rate.

T   F   5-31.   The Federal Home Loan Mortgage Association (Freddie Mac) purchases only FHA and VA government-backed mortgages for its pools.

T   F   5-32.   The goal of the securitization process is to convert assets with poor marketability into assets with much greater market acceptance.

T   F   5-33.   The category of municipal bonds, known as revenue bonds, is backed by the taxing power of the issuing government.

T   F   5-34.   Corporate bonds known as debentures are backed by specific collateral.

T   F   5-35.   Bonds that are in default or whose interest payments are considered very uncertain typically trade flat.

T   F   5-36.   Income bonds must pay the coupon rate of interest or go into default.

T   F   5-37.   Original-issue discount bonds are sold for appreciably less than their value at maturity (par).

T   F   5-38.   A bond that is separated from its coupons is called a junk bond.

T   F   5-39.   The maturity value of a zero-coupon bond is difficult to calculate.

T   F   5-40.   There is no annual tax liability associated with zero-coupon bonds.

T   F   5-41.   Eurobonds are bonds that are offered outside the country of the borrower and outside the country in whose currency the bonds are denominated.

T   F   5-42.   Debt instruments that are privately placed lack marketability.

T   F   5-43.   The payment of preferred stock dividends is required before common stock dividends can be paid.

T   F   5-44.   Preferred stockholders' claims to corporate assets receive the lowest priority.

T   F   5-45.   Corporations would generally prefer to issue preferred stock rather than bonds.

T   F   5-46.   Discount yields assume that interest payments take place semiannually and are based on a 365-day year.

T   F   5-47.   The simple-interest yield equals the coupon-equivalent yield when the security has less than 6 months to maturity.

6

The Determinants of Fixed-Income Security Yields

Learning Objectives

An understanding of the material in this chapter should enable the student to

6-1. Describe the parameters of the default risk facing debt security instruments, and explain how rating services assess the risk.

6-2. Describe the term structure of interest rates, and explain the investment implications of the term structure.

6-3. Describe the concept of duration, and explain how immunization is used to achieve a desired duration level.

6-4. Describe several factors that affect bond prices and yields.

6-5. Describe several aspects of assembling and managing a bond portfolio.

Chapter Outline

The terms *fixed-income security* and *debt security* are often used interchangeably. This is because the initial interest rate or *coupon rate* on debt instruments, such as bonds, is stated in a contractual agreement at the time that the debt instrument is issued. This differs from other investments, such as common stock, whose actual rate of return is unknown at the time the stock is sold. It is also different from the actual yield on a debt instrument that will be achieved if the debt instrument is sold and/or bought after the issue date and/or before the redemption or maturity date. Although there are other types of debt instruments, most debt takes the form of bonds. Therefore, unless stated otherwise, the terms *bond yield, debt security yield,* and *fixed-income security yield* can be used interchangeably.

yield   The *yield* or actual return on a debt security instrument is based on its market price and coupon rate. The coupon rate on a debt security instrument is initially determined by the general level of interest rates and by the factors specific to the particular instrument, such as its level of risk. As discussed in chapter 4, the general level of interest rates is determined both by the real (purchasing power) rate of interest and by inflationary expectations. The real rate of interest is determined by the supply and demand for loanable funds (credit), which in turn are, respectively, determined by consumers' willingness to forgo present consumption in return for greater consumption in the future (time preference for consumption) and by the production and investment opportunities in the economy.

coupon rate   Aside from general credit conditions, the yield and the *coupon rate* on an individual bond are influenced by a variety of other factors. The most significant factor that influences the required rate of return on a bond is the risk premium. Although there are different types of risk related to bonds, the **default**   most important is the risk of *default*. While other factors are important to bondholders, it is crucial that they be confident of receiving their interest payments and return of principal when due. Therefore, any risk of default will have a major impact on a bond's market price and required rate of return.

bankruptcy proceedings   Near-default workouts and *bankruptcy proceedings* are important in assessing the extent of the riskiness of bonds that clearly have a high degree of default risk. In general, bond ratings are used to assess the credit risk of bonds, and they have a considerable impact on the required rate of return.

Other factors, such as the term structure of interest rates, duration, marketability and liquidity, call features, sinking fund provisions, priority of debt, and nature of collateral all affect the price of a bond and its required rate of return. It is also important to consider bond portfolios as a whole and the relative risk and expected return characteristics of bonds and stocks.

This chapter explores the impacts of a variety of factors that affect individual debt security yields. Default risk, a primary determinant of yields, is given considerable attention. Near-default workouts, bankruptcy proceedings, and bond rating are each discussed. The chapter also explores the impacts of term structure, duration, coupon effect, seasoning, marketability, call protection, sinking fund provisions, priority of debt, industrial classification, condition of collateral, and listing status. It concludes with a discussion of bond portfolio management and the relative performance of bonds and stocks.

DEFAULT RISK

No investor wants to buy bonds in what appears to be a secure company and later see the company get into financial difficulty. The market price of these bonds would adjust downward to reflect their increased risk. Unless the financial problems facing the firm are corrected quickly, the issuing company may default on its debt obligation. The bonds might eventually pay off part or all of the principal amount plus accrued interest, but that is uncertain when default occurs. It is even possible that the bondholders will be left with nothing.

As discussed in the previous chapter, it is possible for an investor to achieve high yields from investing in a portfolio of risky bonds. Some investors are even willing to bear the risk of investing in a diversified portfolio of bonds that are near default, since they can purchase these bonds at a substantial discount below their face value. Such a strategy, while potentially very profitable, is quite risky. Most bond investors would prefer just to collect their principal and interest payments when due and not worry about the risk of default. These risk-averse investors should avoid investing in bonds with high default risk, and focus on maximizing their expected return for whatever level of risk they find acceptable.

The challenge is to determine the different degrees of risk of different bonds. This function is, to a large extent, performed by rating agencies such **bond ratings** as Moody's and Standard & Poor's. The market uses these *bond ratings* to determine the appropriate risk premium for bonds of each level of risk.

In evaluating the risk characteristics of different bonds, we now turn to **indenture** the bond *indenture*, which is the issuer's contract with the bondholders.

Indenture Provisions

Bond indentures are contracts and, as such, contain a variety of provisions. Most important are those specifying the interest rate and the maturity date. The borrower agrees to make specified coupon payments at specified intervals (generally every 6 months) until the *maturity* date, at which time the face value and accrued interest must be paid to the bondholder.

maturity

The indenture may also contain a number of other provisions. For example, some debt obligations are backed by specific *collateral*. The indenture for such a security will specify the nature of the collateral obligation. The provision will typically state that the issuer agrees to maintain any pledged assets or acceptable substitutes in good repair.

collateral

Most corporate bonds, known as *debentures*, do not have specific property serving as collateral but, rather, are backed by the *full faith and credit* of the issuer. In the event of bankruptcy, holders of debentures are treated the same as any other creditors of the issuer.

debentures

full faith and credit

Some other fairly common indenture provisions include *subordination*, a sinking fund, call or conversion provisions, and restrictions on the company, such as restrictions on the amount of dividends that can be paid. Subordination means that the company's obligation to the bondholders is subordinate to certain other financial obligations—called *senior debt*—such as its obligation to pay interest and principal to other bondholders. This means that if the company becomes insolvent and unable to pay all of its debts, the holders of the subordinated bonds will not be paid until after the holders of senior debt are paid.

subordination

senior debt

A *sinking fund* is a fund into which the company periodically deposits a portion of its debt obligation to the bondholders. The purpose of this fund is to make certain that when the bonds mature, the company will have sufficient money available to repay the principal amount of the bonds. In order to meet the sinking fund requirements, the company may buy back some of the bonds on the open market, call some of the bonds (assuming the indenture contains a call provision), or put funds into an *escrow account*.

sinking fund

escrow account
call provision

A *call provision* gives the issuer the option of redeeming the bonds prior to maturity, usually at a specified amount above the par value, called a *call premium*. When a bond has a call provision, the indenture generally specifies when the company may call the bond and what the call premium will be at any given point in time.

call premium

Example: A hypothetical bond has an initial maturity of 30 years. The indenture specifies that the issuer may call the bond 20 or more years after the date of issue and that the call premium is 1 percent of the face value for each remaining year until the bond matures. If the company issued a $1,000 bond in 1999, the soonest the bond could be called is 2019, in which case the company would have to pay bondholders $1,100 per bond. If the company were to redeem the bonds in 2024, it would have to pay $1,050 per bond.

Usually, a company will call bonds prior to maturity only if market interest rates decline sufficiently that it will be cost effective for the company to call the bonds, even with a call premium, and refinance at a lower interest rate. Although less likely, there are also situations in which a company will become less risky over time, so that even if market conditions do not change, the company will be able to issue bonds with a lower risk premium than before.

Example:	Imagine a start-up company with very little operating history. Since the company's financial performance is uncertain, the market may require a substantial risk premium on the company's debt obligations. But 20 years later, if the company establishes an admirable track record of profitable operations and financial stability, its debt might be regarded as quite safe, and therefore it may be able to borrow money at a much lower interest rate. It might then make sense for this company to call its outstanding bonds and issue new bonds at a lower interest rate.

An investor who is considering purchasing a bond should be careful of call provisions, especially if the bond is paying a high coupon rate and trading at a substantial premium above par. An early call would cost the bondholder the difference between the bond's market price and the *call price* (par value plus call premium). Therefore, an investor considering purchasing a bond at a premium should check for call provisions and never pay more than the present value (based on prevailing interest rates on comparable bonds) of the stream of payments until the first call date plus the call price.

call price

Some restrictions contained in the indenture are intended to ensure that the company remain solvent and be able to make interest and principal payments when due. For example, an indenture may specify that a company limit its dividend payments to a specified percentage of its net income. The indenture may also specify that the company maintain at least a certain current ratio (current assets divided by current liabilities) or that its total debt be limited to a specified percentage of its total assets.

A trustee, usually the trust department of a large bank, is appointed to represent the bondholders and ensure that the company abides by the provisions of the indenture.

Indenture Provisions

- Principal and maturity: specifies amount and timing of principal payment
- Coupon: specifies amount and timing of each coupon payment
- Collateral (equipment trust certificate or other collateralized bond): identifies pledged collateral and specifies obligation of the issuer to maintain collateral's value
- Full faith and credit (debenture): backs bond with the "good name" of the issuer
- Subordination: gives liquidation priority to other specified debt issues
- Sinking fund: provides for periodic redemption and retirement over the life of the bond issue
- Call provisions schedule: specifies length of no-call protection and call premiums payable over life of the bond
- Dividend restrictions: restrict dividend payments, based on earnings and amount of equity capital
- Current ratio minimum: requires that the ratio of current assets to current liabilities not fall below a specified minimum
- Me-first rule: restricts the amount of additional (nonsubordinated) debt that may be issued
- Trustee: specifies the institution responsible for enforcing the indenture provisions
- Grace period: specifies the maximum period that the firm has to cure a default without incurring the risk of a bankruptcy filing

---

Defaults and Near-Defaults

Firms rarely fail to pay required interest and principal when they have a choice. Sometimes, however, they have no choice. The 1980s saw a large number of financially troubled firms: Braniff, Chrysler, AM International, International Harvester, Saxon Industries, Wicks, Mego, Manville, World Airways, LTV, Bethlehem Steel, A.H. Robins, Texas Air, Pan Am, Continental Illinois Bank, Continental Airlines, First City Bank, First Republic Bank, Texaco, and so on. The experiences of these firms heightened interest in the default issue in the late 1980s and early 1990s.

The recent years of prosperity have tended to lower this level of concern, but since the economy tends to move in cycles, understanding some of the aspects of defaults is still important.

A firm is in technical default whenever any of the indenture provisions of its bonds are violated. Similarly, a violation of any of the terms of its other debt agreements constitutes a technical default.

Many defaults, however, involve relatively minor matters. For example, if the working capital ratio falls below the stipulated minimum, the firm is technically in default of the relevant debenture provision. Rarely, if ever, does a default in such a matter in and of itself lead to a bankruptcy filing. The trustee may grant a waiver for the violation, or the matter may be quickly cured.

Even a failure to make an interest payment on time does not necessarily lead to bankruptcy. The firm may rectify the situation with a late payment; the indenture usually provides for a grace period. In addition, defaults and near-defaults generally result in a mutually acceptable resolution that stops short of bankruptcy and liquidation.

When a few large creditors (such as banks who have extended substantial loans) can be identified, the troubled borrower may seek concessions that will give it a reasonable chance of avoiding a bankruptcy filing. Big lenders have an important stake in their debtors' survival. An interesting oversimplification of the borrower-lender relationship is seen in the following two sentences:

- A borrower who owes $1,000 and cannot pay is in trouble.
- A borrower who owes $1 million and cannot pay puts the lender in trouble.

The weakness of a troubled borrower is, in fact, a strength in any negotiations with the lender. Accordingly, lenders with large exposures are likely to be asked to accept a payment stretch-out, an interest rate reduction, a swap of debt for equity or tangible assets, a reduction in loan principal, and a change or waiver of certain default provisions. Lenders often agree to such restructurings in the hope of eventually recovering more than they would in a formal bankruptcy.

Because obtaining concessions from all the numerous bondholders would be difficult, they are only rarely asked to make them. Accordingly, the bondholders obtain the benefit of the large lenders' concessions without making any corresponding sacrifice. If the effort fails, the bondholders still have the option of initiating formal bankruptcy proceedings in the hope of recouping some of their principal and interest.

Bankruptcy Filings

indenture trustee

Even though bankruptcy should be avoided if at all possible, the reorganization of a financially troubled firm is not always possible without filing for bankruptcy. Bankruptcy proceedings may begin with a petition from a creditor, a creditor group, an *indenture trustee*, or the defaulting firm itself.

If the firm chooses to file for reorganization under Chapter XI, it intends to emerge from bankruptcy as a continuing entity. Chapter XI permits the firm to retain its assets and to restructure its debts under a plan of reorganization. A Chapter XI proceeding can give the firm respite from creditor claims since it will have 120 days after filing the petition to formulate a plan of reorganization. Reorganizations under Chapter XI, however, are often not successful in salvaging financially troubled firms, plus they are very expensive. An unsuccessful Chapter XI reorganization effort usually leads to Chapter VII liquidation proceedings.

liquidation
bankruptcy trustee
**absolute priority of
 claims principle**

If a defaulting firm is thought to be worth more dead than alive, bankruptcy proceedings may begin as a Chapter VII *liquidation*. Under Chapter VII, the *bankruptcy trustee* is responsible for selling the firm's assets and distributing the proceeds according to the *absolute priority of claims principle*. Under this principle, the valid claims of each priority class are fully satisfied before the next class receives anything. The marginal priority group receives proportional compensation. The classes below the marginal priority class receive nothing since the funds available for distribution will have already been exhausted.

A few companies do successfully emerge from Chapter XI bankruptcy proceedings after a careful review of their financial and competitive situation. The process is designed to preserve the potentially profitable elements of their businesses in a recapitalized form. Unproductive assets are liquidated. The bankruptcy trustee and courts seek to preserve as much value as is possible for distribution to the creditors. They also try to minimize the risk that the firm will have to return for court protection or seek additional lender concessions.

Many troubled firms would be financially viable if their debt load were sufficiently reduced. Thus, an objective of many Chapter XI bankruptcy proceedings is to reduce the company's debt load, and since bankrupt firms generally have little or no excess cash to distribute to creditors, most creditors are prevailed upon to accept lower priority securities of the reorganized firm. Senior creditors may receive debentures or preferred shares, whereas junior creditors could be given common stock and warrants. The distribution of these securities typically is governed by the absolute priority of claims principle.

Several factors, however, limit the applicability of the absolute priority of claims principle. The going-concern value of a firm experiencing a bankruptcy process is quite subjective. The securities to be issued by the reorganized firm will not have an established market price until it emerges from bankruptcy. Therefore, the relevant values are rather uncertain when (in the course of the bankruptcy proceeding) the securities distribution is being set. Not surprisingly, the ability of these securities to satisfy claims is often subject to dispute.

Generally, the lower priority claimants argue for a higher overall valuation for the company and its securities. In this way, they seek to increase the estimated value of the securities that are available for distribution to their priority class. The greater the firm's overall estimated value, the greater the proportion of that estimated value available to satisfy the lower-priority claimants.

Example: Suppose a company's high-priority claimants have claims of $95 million and the company's value is estimated at $100 million. The high-priority claimants will be awarded securities representing 95 percent of the firm's value. Only 5 percent will be available to the lower-priority claimants. Now suppose that the lower-priority claimants are able to get the company's estimated value raised to $110 million. At that valuation, the higher-priority claimants will receive about 86 percent (95/110) of the firm's value. The lower-priority claimants will, in contrast, see their share rise to about 14 percent (15/110).

Clearly, the lower-priority claimants will prefer the higher valuation estimate. The higher-priority claimants, in contrast, will argue for a more conservative valuation. They want to concentrate the distribution of the assets toward the senior claimants. Unless the low-priority claimants are given something, however, they may use various legal maneuvers to delay the proceedings. As a result, most informal workouts and reorganizations ultimately allocate lesser-priority claimants somewhat more than what the absolute priority of claims principle requires. In practice, unsecured and subordinated creditors can usually make enough noise to obtain some share of the assets even when senior creditors' claims exceed the firm's remaining asset value.

The reduced debt burden generally permits the reorganized firm to remain solvent. New equity holders, however, may have a long wait before receiving any common or preferred dividend payments.

Bond Ratings

The best way to avoid the uncertainty and potential losses from a default and possible bankruptcy is to invest in low-risk bonds. This strategy requires a method for assessing the risk level. Bond ratings offer a risk-assessment method. The default risks of both municipal and corporate bonds are rated by several rating services. The best known services are *Standard & Poor's* and *Moody's Investor Service*. Each service's ratings are based on its evaluation of the firm's financial position and earnings prospects. Table 6-1 describes the primary rating categories of the two principal agencies. Pluses and minuses are used to discriminate within a rating category.

Standard & Poor's Moody's Investor Service

Rating services do not release their specific rating formulas or analysis, but a number of academic studies do reveal a rather predictable pattern. Ratings tend to rise with profitability, size, and earnings coverage (earnings before interest and taxes divided by total interest expense). They decrease with earnings volatility, leverage, and pension obligations; they vary with industry classification. Ratings sometimes differ among the rating agencies; these differences usually reflect a close call on fundamentals. Moody's tends to be more conservative than Standard & Poor's.

For issues of the same company, a subordinate issue usually receives a lower rating than a more senior security. The rating agencies follow the fortunes of issues over time, but rating changes occur relatively infrequently and often take place long after the underlying fundamentals change. Accordingly, several services now offer more up-to-date analyses, including a prediction of rating changes. Moreover, many brokerage firms are paying attention to bond analysis.

Investors can use financial ratios and bankruptcy-prediction models to perform their own bond analysis. Such an examination would probably include an analysis of the level and trend in a variety of financial ratios: current, quick, debt-equity, return-on-equity, times-interest-earned, and other relevant ratios. These ratios can be compared with industry and national averages to reveal current deficiencies and/or significant long-term risks. Clearly, high debt-equity ratios and low times-interest-earned percentages are not reassuring. Unfortunately, this analysis can provide only part of the story. Bondholders should also be interested in the firm's future prospects. For example, a seemingly shaky current financial position may be offset by an upcoming product introduction. Alternatively, a firm with a solid financial position may be trapped in an industry that is slowly being eliminated by a changing technology.

The risk that a bond may be downgraded is also an important consideration for investors. Many investors sell their bonds in the secondary market, rather than holding them until maturity. Therefore, even if a bond makes all of its interest payments on time, downgrading may mean that the

TABLE 6-1
Bond Rating Categories

	Moody's	Standard & Poor's	Definition
Highest grade	Aaa	AAA	An extremely strong capacity to pay principal and interest
High grade	Aa	AA	A strong capacity to pay principal and interest but lower protection margins than Aaa and AAA
Medium grade	A	A	Many favorable investment attributes but possible vulnerability to adverse economic conditions
Minimum investment grade	Baa	BBB	Generally adequate capacity to pay interest and principal, coupled with a significant vulnerability to adverse economic conditions
Speculative	Ba	BB	Only moderate protection during both good and bad times
Very speculative	B	B	Generally lacking characteristics of other desirable investments; interest and principal payments not safe over any long period of time
Default or near-default	Caa	CCC	Poor-quality issues in danger of default
	Ca	CC	Highly speculative issues often in default
	C		Lowest rated class of bonds
		C	Income bonds on which no interest is being paid
		D	Issues in default with principal and/or interest payments in arrears

Adapted from *Bond Guide* (New York: Standard & Poor's Corporation, monthly); Bond Record (New York: Moody's Investor Services, monthly).

bondholder who seeks to sell the bond in the secondary market will be forced to sell it for a lower price than would be available otherwise. This is because the coupon rate paid on the bond is based on its former rating, so comparably rated bonds pay a higher coupon.

Bond Ratings and Performance

How well do bonds of the various risk classes perform? Bonds in the top four rating categories (Aaa, Aa, A, or Baa) are considered investment grade. Bonds with ratings below investment grade are referred to as junk bonds or, euphemistically, as high-yield bonds. In principle, the lower the rating, the higher a bond's interest rate, since investors require a risk premium that is roughly proportional to the riskiness of an investment. It can be argued that a diversified portfolio of Baa-rated bonds is a sensible investment, since the likelihood of any bond's defaulting is very low and the expected return is higher than that of safer (Aaa-rated) bonds.

At least down to Baa-rated bonds, some have argued that differences in default risk do not justify the return differentials. That is, even after subtracting default losses, investors can achieve a significantly higher return with Baa than with Aaa issues. Although the average yield differences accurately reflected default experience in the 1920s and 1930s, with recent default experience as low as it has been, the slight additional safety margins of highly rated issues may not be worth the interest sacrifice. In other words, short of a major depression, A-rated (or perhaps even Baa-rated) bonds are probably safe enough for most investors. The additional safety of investments in Aaa and Aa bonds is rarely worth the yield sacrifice.

The issues are less clear for lower-rated bonds. The realized (after default loss) yield experience of below-Baa bonds is of considerable interest in light of the growing numbers of these issues. Since many institutional investors are not permitted to own below-Baa bonds, these securities may well offer superior risk-adjusted yields. Thus, diversified portfolios of medium-to-high-risk bonds might outperform similarly diversified high-quality bond portfolios. Diversification across industries would spread the default risk, and the higher indicated yield might more than offset any default losses. In fact, extensive studies in the mid-1980s found that the yield premium on junk bonds substantially exceeded the loss from default.[1] These results, however, were derived from studies that covered relatively prosperous times. Experience during severe recessions might be quite different.

TERM STRUCTURE OF INTEREST RATES

term structure   Length to maturity is one of three major determinants of a debt security's yield to maturity. (The other two are general credit conditions and default

yields to maturity

yield curve

risk.) *Yields to maturity* tend to vary systematically with length to maturity. This relationship can be illustrated with a *yield curve*. A yield curve is the graphical representation of yield versus term to maturity for issues with otherwise similar characteristics (risk, coupon, call feature, and so on). The yield curve reveals a pattern that at various times rises, falls, does not vary, or rises and then falls (see figure 6-1).

FIGURE 6-1
Types of Yield Curves

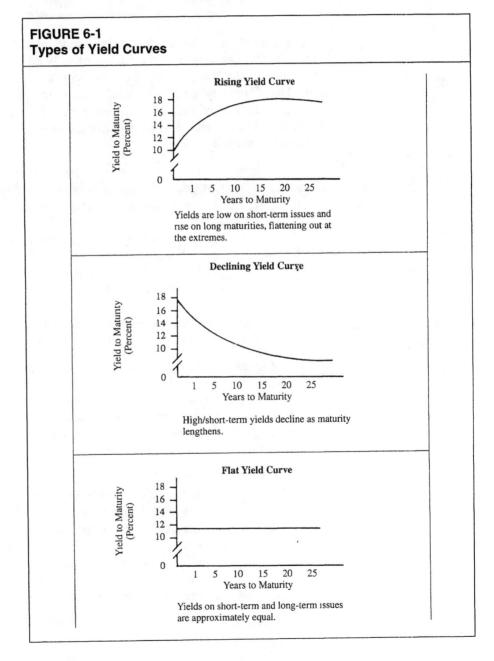

Rising Yield Curve

Yields are low on short-term issues and rise on long maturities, flattening out at the extremes.

Declining Yield Curve

High/short-term yields decline as maturity lengthens.

Flat Yield Curve

Yields on short-term and long-term issues are approximately equal.

**Major Determinants of a Debt Security's
Yield to Maturity**

- length to maturity
- general credit conditions
- default risk

The market price of a bond is inversely related to prevailing market interest rates. The longer the maturity of a bond (all other things being equal), the greater the bond's price sensitivity to changes in market interest rates. Therefore, any change in market interest rates, such as an overall increase in the rate of inflation, will have a larger impact on the price of a bond with 10 years remaining to maturity than on a bond with only one year remaining to maturity.

Example: Consider a 100-year bond with a $100 coupon rate. For such a far-off maturity, this simplified formula is a very close approximation: Price = coupon/discount rate. Accordingly, when corresponding market rates are 10 percent, this bond will sell for $1,000 ($100/.10). If market rates on equivalent-risk issues rise to 11 percent, this bond's price will fall to $909 ($100/.11). On the other hand, a 9 percent market rate will price the bond at $1,111 ($100/.09).

Since most investors are risk averse, the possibility of an interest rate rise and the consequent capital loss generally causes them great concern. Furthermore, a bond's call feature limits its upside potential.

Both short- and long-term bond prices respond to changes in market interest rates. The imminent return of principal limits the interest rate sensitivity of short-term issues, however.

Example: A one-year issue with a $100 coupon rate (assuming interest is paid annually) should sell for $1,000 when interest rates are 10 percent. If rates rise to 20 percent, the issue must be priced to offer a 20 percent return. In other words, using the discount formula (100/1.20 + 1000/1.20 = $916.66), a one-year 10 percent coupon note selling at $916.66 would yield about 20 percent by providing $100 in interest and $83.33 in capital gains (183.33/916.66 = .20). A very long-term bond with an equivalent $100 coupon would, in contrast, need to fall to about $500 ($100/.20).

As the example shows, a doubling of interest rates would cause the price of the very long-term bond to fall by nearly half its previous value, while the price of the shorter-term issue would decline by much less. Thus, in a sense, short-term issues are less risky to investors than longer-term securities are. On the other hand, borrowers (bond issuers) may prefer the security of a fixed long-term rate and therefore find distant-maturity issues less risky. Some investors may also prefer longer-term issues since they offer an assured long-term rate. Clearly, the relative risk of a particular maturity depends on the investor's perspective (investment horizon, timing of cash needs, and so on).

Example 1:   Consider a hypothetical bond that pays an annual coupon of 8 percent, or $80 per year. For simplicity, assume that interest payments are made once a year. Assume that because of an increase in the inflation rate, the market-determined interest rate of bonds of comparable risk is now 10 percent. The bond with one year to maturity has one more interest payment of $80 plus the principal amount of $1,000, both due in one year. Since the discount rate of future cash payments is equal to the required rate of return, or required interest rate of 10 percent, the present value of future cash flows is $80/1.1 + $1000/1.1 = $1,080/1.1 = $981.82, which would be the market price of the bond if the bondholder were to sell it in the secondary market rather than hold it to maturity. In other words, a 2 percent increase in the market interest rate would cause the market value of the bond to decrease by $18.18 or 1.82 percent ($1,000 − 981.82)/1,000).

Example 2:   Now consider a similar 8 percent coupon bond that has 10 years to maturity in an environment in which the required rate of return on comparable bonds is 10 percent. Again, for simplicity, assume that interest is paid only once a year. The present value of the stream of cash flows is now $80/1.1 + $80/1.1^2 + $80/1.1^3 + $80/1.1^4 + \ldots + $1,080/1.1^{10} = $72.73 + 66.12 + 60.11 + 54.64 + 49.67 + 45.16 + 41.05 + 37.32 + 33.93 + 416.39 = $877.12, which should also be the market price of the bond in the secondary market. Therefore, for a bond with 10 years to maturity, a 2 percent increase in market interest rates causes the value of the bond to decrease by $122.88 or 12.29 percent ($1,000 − 877.12)/1,000). (To make the same calculations with semi-annual coupon payments, double the number of payments, let each coupon payment be $40 instead of $80, and use 5 percent as the discount rate instead of 10 percent, since only half a year elapses between each payment. The result should be similar.)

Sensitivity to interest rate changes implies upside potential as well as downside risk. To see this, assume that market interest rates decline by 2 percent, and compute the market value of both the 8 percent bond with one year to maturity and the bond with 10 years to maturity. While both will now trade at a premium above par, the premium on the bond with 10 years to maturity will be much higher. This calculation should also demonstrate how the call feature could work to the detriment of bondholders. To see this clearly, assume that the bond with 10 years to maturity has a call feature, allowing the issuer to redeem the bond in 2 years at a 5 percent premium over par ($1,050). The present value of the stream of cash flows will now be $80/1.06 + ($80 + $1,000 + $50)/1.06^2 = $75.47 + $1,005.70 = $1,081.17. Although this bond will still trade at a premium, its market value will be far less than the $1,147.20 it would be worth if there were no call feature and the bondholders were assured of receiving the $80 annual coupon for 10 years while bonds of comparable risk paid 6 percent.

Term Structure Hypotheses

The following term structure hypotheses are all designed to explain the various shapes of the yield curve:

- market segmentation
- preferred habitat
- liquidity preference
- unbiased expectations

In this discussion of the term structure of interest rates, we are considering only differences in maturity and assuming away the risk of default. Government securities are a good example.

market segmentation hypothesis

The *market segmentation hypothesis* asserts that supply and demand within each market segment determine interest rates for that maturity class. According to this hypothesis, the yield curve simply reflects the supply and demand for each maturity class. Some investors are thought generally to prefer to lend short, whereas many borrowers prefer to borrow long term. Thus, rates are often lower for short maturities.

preferred habitat hypothesis

A related but somewhat less restrictive form of the segmented markets hypothesis is the *preferred habitat hypothesis*. According to this hypothesis, borrowers and lenders prefer certain maturities. They can be induced to other maturities only if the rates are significantly more attractive. As with the market segmentation hypothesis, preferred habitat assumes that investors often prefer the short end and borrowers usually tend to prefer the long end of the market.

The difference between the two theories is that the market segmentation hypothesis states that there are completely separate markets for debt instruments of different maturities, so the interest rates of bonds of a particular maturity should have no effect on the interest rates of bonds of another maturity. By contrast, the preferred habitat hypothesis allows for the possibility of substitution if the interest rates on debt instruments of different maturities differ sufficiently. Under the preferred habitat hypothesis, investors may wish to invest for a particular period of time, but they can be persuaded to invest for a different time period if the interest rate is sufficiently higher. Likewise, borrowers may prefer to borrow for specific time periods, but they can be persuaded to borrow for different time periods if the interest rate is sufficiently lower. Therefore, the preferred habitat hypothesis allows for differences between interest rates of different maturities, but it recognizes that there are limits to the extent by which those rates can differ. The market segmentation hypothesis treats the markets for debt of different maturities as separate and distinct. Therefore, under the market segmentation hypothesis, there should be no limit on the amount by which the interest rates on bonds of different maturities can differ.

As long as there is an active secondary market for bonds and other debt instruments, it is difficult to argue that the markets for debt instruments of different maturities are distinct, and that investors cannot be attracted to bonds of different maturities by interest rate differentials.

Example 1:   Imagine an investor with an extra $10,000. She knows that she will need the money in 5 years, but in the meantime, she wants to obtain the best possible rate of return with very little risk. Suppose 5-year bonds pay 5 percent interest and 10-year bonds pay 8 percent interest. Suppose further that there is no expected change in interest rates in the future. She could invest in 5-year bonds, receive $500 a year, and get the principal amount of $10,000 in 5 years when the bonds mature. Alternatively, she could buy 10-year bonds, receive interest payments of $800 a year, and sell the bonds in 5 years. As long as market interest rates do not change and 5-year bonds still pay 5 percent, she should be able to sell the bonds at a premium; they should have an intrinsic value (present value of expected future cash flows) of $11,298.83. (Furthermore, by taking advantage of the futures market, the investor can protect herself from unexpected changes in interest rates.)

Example 2: Now imagine the opposite scenario. Suppose 5-year bonds pay 8 percent interest, and 10-year bonds pay 5 percent interest. We now have an investor with $10,000 to invest, but this investor will not need the money until 10 years from now. He can buy 10-year bonds, receive $500 a year for 10 years, and then receive the principal amount of $10,000. Or he can buy 5-year bonds, receive $800 a year for 5 years, and receive the principal amount of $10,000 in 5 years. At that time, he can again buy 5-year bonds, receive $800 a year (as long as market interest rates stay the same), and then receive the $10,000 principal amount. He will have the $10,000 when he needs it, and in the meantime, he will have received $800 a year instead of the $500 he would have received with 10-year bonds.

Of course, the same logic applies to the borrower. If 5-year rates pay substantially lower interest than 10-year rates, it makes sense to issue 5-year bonds, repay them in 5 years, and then issue 5-year bonds again. (Of course, there are some expenses involved with issuing new bonds, so the interest rate differential must be sufficient to compensate for the additional expenses.) Therefore, as long as there are a substantial number of buyers and sellers of bonds of various maturities, it is difficult to argue that the market is truly segmented. The forces of supply and demand should bring the interest rates of bonds of different maturities into alignment unless there are other factors that prevent them from doing so, such as expectations of interest rate changes in the future.

liquidity preference hypothesis

The *liquidity preference hypothesis* assumes that markets are not segmented *per se* but that some lenders (especially commercial banks with their short-term capital sources) generally *prefer* to lend short. One reason for this preference is that, even though lenders have formed expectations about future interest rates, there is no assurance that those expectations are correct. Therefore, investors in long-term debt instruments take the risk that interest rates will rise in the future, reducing the purchasing power of their future interest payments and repayment of principal. (Although we have assumed that there is no default risk, interest rate risk is still present.)

Also, individual depositors may prefer to have access to their money sooner, rather than later. After all, people still keep money in passbook savings accounts, checking accounts, and money market accounts, even though they often could obtain a higher rate of interest with no risk of default with long-term CDs or government bonds. Some investors, however, prefer not to have their money tied up over long periods of time, and they may require a higher rate of return to compensate them for the inconvenience. Thus, a rising yield curve is generally observed, as higher interest rates are often needed to compensate lenders for their greater time commitment.

On the other hand, many borrowers prefer to borrow money for longer periods of time. If borrowers borrow on a short-term basis, they face the risk that when they need to repay the loan, they will not be able to obtain new financing on equally favorable terms. Market interest rates may rise. In addition, there are transaction costs associated with issuing new debt. For all these reasons, borrowers might be willing to pay a slightly higher rate of interest to borrow for longer periods of time. Therefore, considering the motives of both borrowers and lenders, rates on long-term debt may be higher than rates on short-term debt, even when prevailing interest rates are not expected to change. This difference between long and short rates due to liquidity preference is called the liquidity premium.

unbiased expectations hypothesis

The *unbiased expectations hypothesis* asserts that long-term rates reflect both current short-term rates and the market's expectation of future short-term rates. Thus, the one-year rate is simply the geometric average of the current 6-month rate and the expected rate 6 months later. Suppose that the 12-month rate is Y percent. The unbiased expectations hypothesis asserts that current rates have embedded within them the market's anticipated 6-month rate 6 months from now. That anticipation is, in fact, the rate necessary when coupled with the current 6-month rate to yield a 12-month return of Y percent.

Example: Consider 6-month and 12-month yields of 8 percent
                  and 9 percent, respectively. Taken together, these
                  yields imply a specific value for the expected 6-
                  month yield for a security whose life begins in 6
                  months. Thus, the rate for the second 6-month period
                  will cause an investment that yields 8 percent for the
                  first 6 months to generate an overall 12-month return
                  of 9 percent.

                  An (annualized) 8 percent return that is earned for
                  6 months corresponds to a return relative of 1.04. (A
                  return relative is one plus the rate of return.) A 9
                  percent return that is earned for 12 months
                  corresponds to a return relative of 1.09. Thus, we first
                  seek the return relative for the second 6 months that
                  will produce the appropriate 12-month return relative.
                  Once we obtain the return relative, the corresponding
                  annualized return is easy to compute. The appropriate
                  formula is as follows: $1.04 \times X = 1.09$. Therefore,
                  solving for X is $1.09/1.04 = 1.048$.

                  A return relative of 1.048 for 6 months
                  corresponds to a 12-month return relative of 1.096.
                  This, in turn, corresponds to an annualized return of
                  9.6 percent. Thus, the implied yield for the second 6
                  months is 9.6 percent. In other words, an investment
                  that earns 8 percent in the first 6 months must earn
                  9.6 percent in the second 6 months to produce an
                  overall 12-month return of 9 percent.

The unbiased expectations hypothesis asserts that the market's
expectations for future interest rates are reflected by the rates it establishes
for debt securities of various maturities. According to this view, potential
arbitrage activity (riskless buying and selling to gain a profit) always drives
the yield curve into the shape that is appropriate for that set of expectations.

If long-term rates seem too high vis-à-vis expected future short-term
rates, some short-horizon investors will move toward longer-term issues
while some longer-horizon lenders will switch toward shorter-term
borrowing. This activity should quickly drive rates into the appropriate
relation. Although the preferred habitat, liquidity preference, and unbiased
expectations hypotheses all recognize the existence of this arbitraging
activity, only the unbiased expectations hypothesis asserts its overriding
power.

Term Structure of Interest Rates Hypotheses

- Segmented markets: Yields reflect supply and demand for each maturity class.
- Preferred habitat: Investors and borrowers can be induced out of their preferred maturity structures only by more attractive rates.
- Liquidity preference: Lenders generally prefer to lend short and borrowers prefer to borrow long, tending to produce an upward-sloping yield curve.
- Unbiased expectations: Long rates reflect the market's expectation of current and future short rates.

Each hypothesis explains the various yield curve shapes slightly differently and has somewhat different implications. According to liquidity preference, yield curves are typically rising because, on balance, lenders prefer the short end and borrowers the long end. Segmented markets and preferred habitat are also consistent with a tendency for yield curves to rise. Lenders may be relatively more numerous at the short end.

The unbiased expectations hypothesis, in contrast, asserts that yield curves only rise when interest rates themselves are expected to increase. A flat yield curve indicates neutral expectations—that is, expectations that interest rates will remain constant. A falling yield curve reflects an expectation that rates will fall. This expectation causes borrowers (bond issuers) to rely on short-term financing until the expected fall occurs. Accordingly, borrowers anticipating a decline in interest rates tend to shift demand from the long- to the short-term market. As a result, short rates tend to be bid up relative to long rates.

Lenders' expectations have a similar effect. Lenders (bond buyers) want to profit from the expected interest rate decline by owning long-term bonds. Falling rates would cause the prices of outstanding long-term bonds to rise relative to shorter-term issues. Thus, investors who expect rates to fall will tend to favor the longer maturities, thereby pushing downward on long-term rates and upward on short-term rates.

In summary, when rates are expected to fall, the actions of both lenders and borrowers will tend to shift the yield curve downward, causing short-term rates to exceed long-term rates. The very tight monetary policy in 1974 and again in 1980–1981 created just such circumstances: very high short-term rates with lower long-term rates.

None of the term structure hypotheses has gained overwhelming acceptance or been completely ruled out of contention. On theoretical grounds, the unbiased expectation hypothesis is generally favored. Liquidity preference may have a slight edge in explaining the data. Most academicians believe that modern debt markets are not segmented *per se* but that appreciable numbers of borrowers and lenders may have preferred habitats. From the investor's viewpoint, the relative strengths and weaknesses of the hypotheses are less important than understanding the relationship between yield and maturity.

Investment Implications of the Term Structure

Yield curve relationships may give bond traders two opportunities. First, securities whose yields are some distance from curves plotted with otherwise-similar issues may well be misvalued. Thus, bonds whose yields exceed their respective yield curve values may be underpriced. If their market prices adjust more quickly than the curve itself shifts, the strategy could produce an above-market return. Of course, a trader who detects such underpriced bonds will need to act very quickly since other investors will be following the same strategy, thus driving the price of undervalued bonds up to their intrinsic value.

riding the yield curve

A second strategy involves what is called *riding the yield curve*. A steeply rising yield curve may offer an attractive trading opportunity. If an investor believes that the market's expectation of a future increase in interest rates is incorrect, then he or she can make money by buying long-term bonds and later selling them at a premium. Of course, for such a strategy to be effective, the investor must be better at predicting interest rate changes than the competition is. That is a rather risky proposition, since yield curves are based on the collective wisdom of a variety of analysts who use rather sophisticated models of macroeconomic and other variables in order to forecast interest rate changes.

Example: Suppose that one-year T-bills yield 7 percent, compared with 5 percent (at an annualized rate) on 6-month securities. Both the 6-month bill and a 12-month bill, when sold 6 months later, would generate a 6-month return. Suppose that 6-month T-bills are still yielding 5 percent 6 months later. If the discount rate on 6-month T-bills is 5 percent, then a T-bill yielding 7 percent with 6 months to maturity should sell at a premium in the secondary market. Therefore, the return for holding the 12-month T-bill for 6 months and then selling it in the secondary market will exceed 7 percent, since a capital gain will also be realized on the sale. However, riding the yield curve does incur the risk of an adverse interest rate move. If

6-month rates rise to 8 percent, the 6-month return on the 12-month bill would only be around 3 percent.

DURATION

A 12-year bond is a bond that promises to return principal in 12 years. Not all 12-year bonds are alike, however. Measuring their length by maturity or the amount of time remaining before principal is to be repaid may be a bit misleading. The term to maturity does not fully reflect the timing of a debt security's payment stream. The final payment on a debt security is only one of the promised payments. Most debt securities also make periodic coupon payments. Each of these coupon payments may be viewed as a partial maturity of the instrument, and the higher (lower) the coupon rate is, the smaller (larger) the percentage of the total cash flow the principal represents.

The greater the proportion of the return coming from the coupon, the more of the debt security's promised cash flows will be paid prior to its maturity. Thus, a higher coupon is somewhat akin to a shorter maturity. The owner of such a security will receive a higher proportion of his or her investment back prior to the return of principal at maturity.

Bonds with coupons close to market yields sell near par. Others having coupon rates that are very low or very high compared to market rates will be priced far from par. Computed yields to maturity will have somewhat different implications for each such issue.

On the one hand, a high coupon reduces vulnerability to adverse interest rate moves. At least the coupon payment of such a bond can be reinvested as received. On the other hand, high coupon payments cannot, in a period of falling yields, be reinvested at rates as high as the bond's initial yield. Thus, for equivalent maturities, a high-coupon bond has less interest fluctuation risk but greater reinvestment rate risk than one with a lower coupon; therefore, maturity alone cannot measure a bond's total sensitivity to interest rate changes. Maturity describes only the time until the principal is repaid but tells nothing about the interest payments.

duration   The concept of *duration* allows the investor to make an appropriate adjustment for different maturities and coupon rates. Like maturity, duration is a measure of time. Duration is defined as the weighted average of the lengths of time until all remaining payments are made. In other words, it is the weighted average time until recovery of the present value of the bond's future cash flows (principal and interest). The weight of each of the promised payment's time to receipt is based on its present value relative to the sum of the present values of the entire payment stream (the intrinsic value of the bond). That is, each weight equals the present value of that payment divided by the bond's market price. The total of the present values equals the bond's market price. Duration thereby captures the impact of differing coupon rates and recognizes that the earlier coupon payments have a higher present value than later coupon payments. For a bond paying annual interest, the general formula for the duration (D) of a bond with N remaining payments left in its life is as follows:

$$D = \frac{\sum_{t=1}^{N} PV(C_t) \times t}{P_0}$$
(Equation 6-1)

where: $PV(C_t)$ = the present value of the cash flow
        t = the time period when the cash flow is to be received
        P_0 = the current market price of the bond

Besides being the current market price of the bond, P_0 is equal to the sum of the present values of the cash flows, $PV(C_t)$, and can be expressed as

$$P_0 = \sum_{t=1}^{N} PV(C_t)$$

where: the discount rate = the bond's yield to maturity

Consider the durations of two bonds maturing in 7 years. Bond A has a 6 percent coupon, whereas bond B has a 10 percent coupon. Table 6-2 shows the results of computing the durations of both bonds when the market-determined interest rate for new bonds of comparable risk is 8 percent.

Dividing the total in table 6-2 column 4 by the total in table 6-2 column 3 gives us the duration of each bond, which is approximately 5.84 years for Bond A and 5.44 years for Bond B. Thus, although both bonds have maturities of 7 years, they have durations of only 5.84 years (Bond A) and 5.44 years (Bond B).

Bond A's lower coupon rate corresponds to a duration of about 5 months longer than Bond B's. For equivalent maturities, the lower the coupon, the longer the duration. The sensitivity of bond price movements to interest rate changes varies proportionately with duration, and when market interest rates change, the duration of all bonds changes in the opposite direction. Thus, a bond's duration reflects its sensitivity to interest rate changes more accurately than the bond's time to maturity does.

The mathematical link between bond price and interest rate changes involves the concept of modified duration, which is discussed later in this chapter.

TABLE 6-2
Durations of Two Bonds Maturing in 7 Years

Bond A

(1) Year(s) Until Receipt t Where N = 7	(2) Cash Flow	(3) Present Value at 8%	(4) Year(s) x Present Value [Column (1) x Column (3)]
1	$ 60	$ 55.56	$ 55.56
2	60	51.44	102.88
3	60	47.63	142.89
4	60	44.10	176.40
5	60	40.83	204.15
6	60	37.81	226.86
7	1,060	618.50	4,329.50
Total	$1,420	$895.87	$5,238.24

Duration for Bond A is equal to $5,238.24/$895.87 = (5.8470984 years rounded to) 5.84 years

Bond B

(1) Year(s) Until Receipt t Where N = 7	(2) Cash Flow	(3) Present Value at 8%	(4) Year(s) x Present Value [Column (1) x Column (3)]
1	$ 100	$ 92.59	$ 92.59
2	100	85.59	171.46
3	100	79.38	238.14
4	100	73.50	294.00
5	100	68.06	340.30
6	100	63.02	378.12
7	1,100	641.84	4,492.88
Total	$1,700	$1,104.12	$6,007.49

Duration for Bond B is equal to $6,007.49/$1,104.12 = (5.4409756 years rounded to) 5.44 years

An equivalent method for calculating the duration of Bond A and Bond B is shown in table 6-3 by rewriting equation 6-1 as follows:

$$D = \sum_{t=1}^{N} \left[\frac{PV(C_t)}{P_0} \times t \right]$$
$$\text{(Equation 6-2)}$$

where: • The present value of each cash flow [PV(C$_t$)] is expressed as a proportion of the market price (P$_0$) (table 6-3, column 2).

• Each proportion is multiplied by the amount of time (t) until the cash flow is received (table 6-3, column 3).

• The products in column 3 are summed, with the sum being equal to the bond's duration (table 6-3, column 3 is summed).

TABLE 6-3
Durations of Two Bonds Maturing in 7 Years

	Bond A	
(1) Year(s) Until Receipt t Where N = 7	**(2)** PV(C$_t$)/P$_0$	**(3)** [Column (1) x Column (2)]
1	$ 55.56/$895.87 = .0620179	.0620179
2	$ 51.44/$895.87 = .0574190	.1148380
3	$ 47.63/$895.87 = .0531662	.1594986
4	$ 44.10/$895.87 = .0492259	.1969036
5	$ 40.83/$895.87 = .0455758	.2278790
6	$ 37.81/$895.87 = .0422048	.2532288
7	$618.50/$895.87 = .6903903	4.8327321
Sum	$895.87/$895.87 = 1	5.8470980

Duration for Bond A is equal to (5.8470980 years rounded to) 5.84 years

	Bond B	
(1) Year(s) Until Receipt t Where N = 7	**(2)** PV(C$_t$)/P$_0$	**(3)** [Column (1) x Column (2)]
1	$ 92.59/$1,104.12 = .0838586	.0838586
2	$ 85.59/$1,104.12 = .0775187	.1550374
3	$ 79.38/$1,104.12 = .0718944	.2156832
4	$ 73.50/$1,104.12 = .0665689	.2662756
5	$ 68.06/$1,104.12 = .0616419	.3082095
6	$ 63.02/$1,104.12 = .0570771	.3424626
7	$ 641.84/$1,104.12 = .5813136	4.0691952
Sum	$1,104.12/$1,104.12 = 1	5.4407221

Duration for Bond B is equal to (5.4407221 years rounded to) 5.44 years

Note that the proportions shown in table 6-3 column 2 for both Bond A and Bond B sum to 1, which means that they can be interpreted as weights in calculating a weighted average. To calculate the average maturity of the payments associated with Bond A and Bond B, each of the weights in table 6-3 column 2 (for both Bond A and Bond B) is multiplied by the amount of time until its corresponding payment is to be received. The resulting products are then summed to give the durations for both Bond A and Bond B.

A zero coupon bond will always have a duration equal to its remaining life N because it has only one payment, the principal, associated with the bond. In other words, since $P_0 = PV(C_t)$ for a zero coupon bond, equation 6-2 reduces to

$$D = \frac{PV(C_t)}{P_0} \times N = 1 \times N = N$$

The duration of a bond that has coupons will always be less than its remaining life N because in equation 6-2 the largest value that t can have is N, and since each value of t is multiplied by a weight equal to $PV(C_t)/P_0$ (as is done in table 6-3, column 3), it follows that D must be less than N.

From the calculation of the duration of individual bonds like Bond A and Bond B, it is a simple matter to calculate the duration of a whole portfolio of bonds. The duration of a bond portfolio is equal to the weighted average of the durations of the individual bonds in the portfolio.

Example: If a portfolio has one-fourth of its funds invested in Bond A with a duration of 5.84 years and three-fourths in Bond B with a duration of 5.44 years, then the portfolio itself has a duration of 5.54 years [DP = (1/4 x 5.84) + (3/4 x 5.44) = 1.46 + 4.08 = 5.54 years, where DP is the duration of the portfolio].

Major Characteristics of Duration

- The duration of a zero coupon bond is equal to its term to maturity.
- The duration of a coupon bond is always less than its term to maturity.
- There is an inverse relationship between coupon rate and duration.
- There is an inverse relationship between yield to maturity and duration

One of the most important uses of the duration concept is in a strategy that is known as bond portfolio immunization. This strategy is discussed next.

Immunization of a Portfolio

immunization

Minimizing the interest rate risk on a bond portfolio—the risk of losing purchasing power when interest rates change—is called *immunization*. Immunization allows an investor to earn a specified rate of return from a bond portfolio over a given period of time, regardless of what happens to market interest rates. In other words, the investor is able to "immunize" his or her bond portfolio from the effects of changes in market interest rates over a given planning horizon.

To understand why an investor would want to immunize his or her bond portfolio requires an understanding of how changes in the market interest rate affect a bond portfolio. If the market interest rate decreases, coupon payments get reinvested at this new lower rate, but existing bonds in the portfolio increase in value and thus can be sold at a premium because the coupon rate they pay is now above the prevailing market rate for bonds of comparable risk. If the market interest rate increases, the value of existing bonds in the portfolio decreases, but coupon payments get reinvested at this new higher rate. In other words, a decrease in the market interest rate has a positive effect on the price of bonds and a negative effect on the reinvestment of coupons, while an increase in the market rate has a negative effect on the price of bonds and a positive effect on the reinvestment of coupons. Regardless of the direction in which the market interest rate moves, the price effect and the reinvestment effect, also knows as the *price risk* and *reinvestment rate risk*, work in opposite directions. The objective of immunization is to have these opposing effects or risks exactly offset each other, and this is accomplished by frequently rebalancing the portfolio so that its duration is always equal to the investor's planning horizon—that is, when the investor needs to receive funds from the portfolio.

price risk
reinvestment rate risk

Components of Interest Rate Risk

- Price risk: the risk of an existing bond's price changing in response to unknown future interest rate changes. If rates increase, the bond's price decreases, and if rates decrease, the bond's price increases.
- Reinvestment rate risk: the risk associated with reinvesting coupon payments at unknown future interest rates. If rates increase, the coupons are reinvested at higher rates than previously expected, and if rates decrease, the coupons are reinvested at lower rates than previously expected.

There are three methods available to the investor for immunizing his or her portfolio. The easiest of these methods is to purchase a series of zero-coupon bonds that mature at times and in amounts that correspond to the investor's need for funds. This strategy encounters two basic problems, however. First, the need for funds can rarely be forecast precisely, and second, zero-coupon bonds may not be available in the exact maturities needed.

The typical method of immunizing involves assembling and appropriately managing a diversified portfolio of bonds. The portfolio is structured and managed with the objective of keeping its duration equal in length to the investor's planning horizon. This requires continual portfolio rebalancing on the part of the investor because every time interest rates change, the duration of the portfolio changes. Since immunization requires that the portfolio have a duration equal to the remaining time in the investor's planning horizon, the composition of the investor's portfolio must be rebalanced every time interest rates change. When an imbalance occurs, the investor may have to replace some portfolio components with others whose durations more closely match the planning horizon target. When the portfolio is perfectly immunized, gains from reinvesting coupon payments should exactly offset losses on the sale of bonds, and vice versa.

Immunizing a portfolio once does not ensure that it will remain immunized for all time. Even in the absence of market rate changes, immunization is an ongoing process. The mere passage of time can unbalance a portfolio since duration declines more slowly than term to maturity. This means that the investor must periodically rebalance the portfolio to reduce its duration to equal the remaining time horizon.

Example: An investor's planning horizon is presently 5 years. Assume that the investor's bond portfolio has only one coupon bond and that its duration is computed at 5 years when the market interest rate for new bonds of comparable risk is 10 percent. One year later with the market rate unchanged at 10 percent, the duration of the bond is computed to be about 4.2 years. In other words, although the bond's term to maturity declined by one full year, its duration declined by only 0.8 years. Thus, assuming no change in the market interest rate, the investor must rebalance the portfolio by reducing its duration to 4 years so that it will again equal the remaining time horizon. As noted in the previous section on duration, only a zero-coupon bond's duration decreases at the same rate as its term to maturity.

Moreover, as cash flows are received from coupon payments, the proceeds are used to purchase new bonds to maintain the target duration. These cash inflows, however, may not be adequate to rebalance the portfolio. To accomplish rebalancing under these circumstances, the investor may have to sell some bonds in the secondary market to obtain the additional funds.

Example: Jane Smith plans to retire in 7 years (her planning horizon). At retirement, she plans to use her savings to buy an annuity so that she will have a guaranteed lifetime income. Her savings are invested in a portfolio of coupon bonds that currently has a 7-year duration.

Even though the portfolio's duration currently equals Jane's planning horizon, she will have to sell some bonds and buy others to maintain the desired immunization for the next 7 years. These transactions will be necessary for two reasons. First, every time market interest rates change, the duration of the portfolio will change. Second, in the absence of market rate changes, the mere passage of time will unbalance the portfolio since duration declines more slowly than term to maturity except in the unique case of zero-coupon bonds

The third and most sophisticated approach to immunization combines a portfolio of debt securities with interest rate futures positions to achieve the desired duration target. Interest rate futures are contracts to buy or sell bonds of a prespecified maturity at a prespecified time. That is, contracts that call for the subsequent delivery of debt instruments, such as short- or long-term governments, are used to lock in a yield on future cash inflows. As coupon payments are received, the funds are immediately reinvested in the debt securities whose delivery was assured through the prior purchase of the interest rate futures contracts. In other words, the investor simply purchases interest futures contracts in amounts and maturities that correspond to the portfolio's forthcoming coupon payments. These cash inflows are immediately reinvested at known rates by taking delivery of the debt securities promised by the interest futures contracts.

This ongoing process should keep the duration of the portfolio balanced with the planning horizon target, regardless of when and by how much market interest rates fluctuate.

Immunizing a Portfolio

- Purchasing a series of zero-coupon bonds whose maturities correspond with the planning horizon
- Assembling and managing a bond portfolio whose duration is kept equal to the planning horizon
- Combining a portfolio of debt securities with interest rate futures positions to achieve the desired duration target

---

Whatever immunization method is chosen, the purposes are to ensure that the duration of the bond portfolio matches the planning horizon and that the price and reinvestment effects of changing market interest rates exactly offset each other. The investor's task in accomplishing these purposes is to ensure that the portfolio is balanced and perfectly immunized. As is evident from the discussion, portfolio immunization is a powerful investment tool that is clearly not a passive strategy. Under the typical immunization method, a portfolio requires frequent rebalancing to keep its duration equal to the remaining time horizon. Finally, it must be mentioned that the effectiveness of immunizing a portfolio must take into account transaction costs. Frequent rebalancing is very expensive.

Estimating a Bond's Price Volatility

modified duration

An adjusted measure of duration called *modified duration* can be used to estimate the interest rate sensitivity of a noncallable bond. That is, modified duration can be used to estimate the percentage change in a bond's price resulting from a relatively small (no more than 100 *basis points*) change in market interest rates. To find a bond's modified duration, calculate its duration using equation 6-2 and adjust it for the bond's yield to maturity as follows:

basis points

$$MD = \frac{D}{1 + YTM} \qquad \text{(Equation 6-3)}$$

where: MD = the bond's modified duration
D = the bond's duration
YTM = the bond's yield to maturity

Once having determined a bond's modified duration, it is relatively easy to estimate the bond's percentage price change resulting from a small change in the market interest rate. Thus, the bond's modified duration is first multiplied by −1 (to reflect the inverse relationship between bond prices and interest rates) and then by the amount of change in the market rate. In equation form, this is expressed as follows:

$$\text{Percent change in bond prices} = -1 \times MD \times r \qquad \text{(Equation 6-4)}$$

where: r = the amount of change in the interest rate

Example 1:   Continuing with the previous discussion of duration, Bond A's modified duration would be

$$MD = \frac{5.84 \text{ years}}{1+.08} = 5.41 \text{ years}$$

where 5.84 years is Bond A's duration, calculated using a YTM of 8 percent (the market-determined interest rate for new bonds of comparable risk) even though its coupon rate is lower at 6 percent.

Assuming the market interest rate for new bonds of comparable risk increases from 8 to 8.5 percent, the price of Bond A will decrease by $24.19 from $895.87 to $871.68, a fall of 2.70% in value. This is computed as follows:

$$\text{Percent change in bond price} = -1 \times 5.41 \times 0.5\% = -2.70\%$$

Example 2:   Continuing with the previous discussion of duration, Bond B's modified duration would be

$$MD = \frac{5.44 \text{ years}}{1+.08} = 5.04 \text{ years}$$

where 5.44 years is Bond B's duration, calculated using a YTM of 8 percent (the market-determined interest rate for new bonds of comparable risk) even though its coupon rate is higher at 10 percent.

Assuming the market interest rate for new bonds of comparable risk increases from 8 to 8.5 percent, the price of Bond B will decrease by $27.82 from $1,104.12 to $1,076.30, a fall of 2.52% in value. This is computed as follows:

$$\text{Percent change in bond price} = -1 \times 5.04 \times 0.5\% = -2.52\%$$

If a bond's coupon payments occur more frequently than annually, then equation 6-3 needs to be adjusted by dividing the YTM by the number of payments in a year as follows:

$$MD = \frac{D}{1 + YTM/n}$$
(Equation 6-5)

where: n = the number of payments in a year

As the discussion about modified duration has indicated, the concept is a useful tool for bond investors. It enables them to estimate bond price changes for very small changes in market interest rates. The accuracy of price change estimates deteriorates with larger changes in interest rates because the modified duration calculation is a linear approximation of a bond price-yield relationship that is convex in nature.

Tax Implications of the Coupon Effect

The relative amounts of coupon and price appreciation in the return on a bond also have tax implications. Most bond interest income is fully taxed as received by individuals. For bonds originally sold at par, capital gains are taxed only when they are realized as the bonds either mature or are sold in the secondary market. Thus, price appreciation income on such bonds is tax deferred. An investor in a high tax bracket may therefore prefer to buy bonds that pay a below-market coupon rate of interest and are sold at a discount. Note, however, that the imputed yield from price appreciation on zero-coupon and original-issue discount bonds is taxed as if it were received periodically. Only bonds originally issued at or near par generate a capital gains tax break. Still, the market generally contains many low-coupon bonds that were initially sold at par but are now priced at a deep discount—*deep*

deep discount bonds *discount bonds*. Whenever interest rates rise above some past levels, bonds that were issued in the lower interest environment will sell for a discount from par. If they are purchased at a deep discount and held to maturity, they will produce a substantial capital gain. Moreover, bonds priced well below par (and therefore below their call price) are much less likely to be called than those trading near or above par.

Accordingly, private investors in high tax brackets tend to prefer deep-discount bonds to higher-coupon issues. The before-tax yields to maturity on low-coupon, deep-discount issues are usually somewhat below yields on otherwise similar issues trading nearer to par. This relationship is called the

coupon effect *coupon effect*. When capital gains are taxed at a lower rate than ordinary income, as is the current situation, the coupon effect has an even greater impact.

One caveat to this discussion is that interest on municipal bonds is not taxable, but capital gains are. So even a high-tax-bracket investor would prefer to purchase municipal bonds that trade at par, or even at a premium, to those that trade at a discount.

OTHER FACTORS THAT AFFECT BOND PRICES AND YIELDS

The characteristics already discussed (general interest rate levels, risk of default, maturity/duration, coupon effect, tax status) constitute the principal price/yield determinants of specific bonds. Other relevant characteristics include marketability, seasoning, call protection, sinking fund provisions, and "me-first" rules.

The vast majority of bond trading takes place in high-volume markets with narrow spreads and supply and demand created by numerous investors. Many lower-volume issues, however, trade in thin markets with spreads of five and even 10 points. A quote of 75 bid to 80 asked implies a 6.67 percent spread. Trading such an issue is extremely costly. Other things being equal, the less marketable the issue, the higher the yield required to make the bond attractive to investors.

Factors Affecting Bond Yields

- General credit conditions: Credit conditions affect all yields to one degree or another.
- Default risk: Riskier issues require higher promised yields
- Term structure: yields vary with maturity, reflecting expectations for future rates.
- Duration: The average wait till payback is calculated using the duration formula.
- Coupon effect: Low-coupon issues offer yields that are partially tax sheltered.
- Seasonings: Newly issued bonds may sell at a slight discount to otherwise-equivalent established issues.
- Marketability: Actively traded issues tend to be worth more than otherwise-equivalent issues that are less actively traded.
- Call protection: Protection from an early call tends to enhance a bond's value.
- Sinking fund provisions: Sinking funds increase demand and reduce the probability of default, thereby tending to enhance a bond's value.
- Me-first rules: Bonds protected from the diluting effect of additional firm borrowings are generally worth more than otherwise-equivalent unprotected issues.

Seasoned issues are established in the marketplace. They have been traded for at least a few weeks beyond completion of the initial (offering) sale. As with new stock issues, new issues of bonds tend to be priced a bit below equivalent seasoned issues.

yield to earliest call

Call protection varies appreciably from issue to issue. Some bonds are callable when sold. Many others may not be called for the first five or 10 years of their life. Callable issues that are reasonably likely to be redeemed due to their high yields should be evaluated on their *yield to earliest call* rather than their yield to maturity. In marginal cases, both yield figures should be computed and compared. Call protection tends to increase a bond's price, but the market may tend to overvalue call protection. Therefore, some callable issues may be superior investments.

A sinking fund's presence increases demand slightly and reduces the probability of default. Thus, a sinking fund generally adds modestly to the value of a bond.

Me-first rules are designed to protect existing bondholders. These rules prevent their claims from being weakened by the issuance of additional debt with a priority higher than or equivalent to theirs. Research has found that these rules significantly enhance the market values of the protected bonds.[2]

ASSEMBLING AND MANAGING A BOND PORTFOLIO

Diversified bond portfolios should be managed to meet their owner's needs. A half dozen different bond issues are usually sufficient to achieve relatively effective diversification of a portfolio of bonds. Bonds should also be selected to produce the desired level of maturity/duration, default risk/quality rating, coupon/price appreciation. The particular owner's tax status should also be taken into account in deciding whether to include municipal bonds and bonds trading at a discount in the secondary market. Moreover, bonds are usually part of a larger portfolio that also includes stocks and perhaps some other types of assets. Thus, bonds should usually be viewed as providing liquidity, dependable income, and relative safety in the context of the overall portfolio.

Bond Swaps

bond swaps

Portfolio managers frequently finance a bond purchase with the funds freed up by liquidating another position. *Bond swaps* may be designed to increase yield to maturity or current yield, to adjust duration or risk, or to establish a tax loss.

Many swaps are not executed simultaneously. Thus, swap traders risk making one side of the swap (say, the sell) only to encounter an adverse price move before the other side of the swap is accomplished. Moreover, transaction costs absorb some of what would otherwise be the expected benefits of the swap. Nonetheless, a variety of circumstances make swaps attractive.

Example 1:	A low-coupon, deep-discount issue might be sold and the proceeds used to purchase a higher-coupon issue. The sale would normally generate a tax loss. Presumably, the purchased issue is designed to offer a higher yield. On the other hand, the swap would probably increase both the call risk and the reinvestment rate risk.
Example 2:	In another type of swap, a bond originally purchased as a long-term issue may be approaching maturity. Swapping it for a longer-term bond would restore the desired duration level and possibly enhance yield as well (if long-term rates are above short-term rates).
Example 3:	In yet another type of swap, an investor might sell one bond issue that had been held at a loss and then purchase another very similar issue. Such a pure *tax swap* establishes a tax-deductible capital loss while leaving the basic character of the portfolio unchanged.

tax swap

However, under the wash sale tax rules, a loss sustained on the sale of a bond issue is not allowed if the investor purchases a "substantially identical" issue within a period beginning 30 days before the sale and ending 30 days after the sale. An issue is substantially identical if it is not substantially different in any material feature or in several material features considered together. If a bond purchased as a replacement was issued by a different company than the bond being replaced, it will not be considered substantially identical, no matter how similar it is. Care must be taken, however, to not run afoul of the wash sale rules if the bond purchased as a replacement was issued by the same company.[3]

Other Aspects of Bond Portfolio Management

Managing a bond portfolio effectively can involve much more than the simple types of swaps mentioned above. The investor might, for example, speculate on a bond upgrade by buying an issue that the market views pessimistically. Margin borrowing may be used to magnify potential gains and/or to leverage a high yield. Some bonds may have higher promised long-term yields than the current cost of margin money. Whether such apparently attractive yield spreads should be exploited depends on both the likelihood that they will persist and the default risk of high-yielding issues. If market interest rates rise, the margin borrowing rate will increase and bond prices will decline.

Still more complicated maneuvers involve the use of interest rate futures and hedging between a company's bonds and its other securities. (In general, hedging means entering into a transaction in order to offset the risk of one or more other transactions.) For instance, a long position in a company with a high default risk might be hedged with a short position in the firm's stock. If the firm goes bankrupt, the stock could become almost worthless, while its bonds might still retain some value in a reorganization or liquidation. If the company survives, the bonds will eventually pay off, although the stock may not do well unless the company prospers. Finally, portfolio managers can trade on the basis of their interest rate forecasts. If interest rates are expected to decrease, portfolio maturities should be lengthened. An expected rise should cause the manager to shift toward near-cash (very short-term) securities. This strategy assumes, however, that the manager can accurately forecast interest rate changes.

Transaction Costs for Bonds

The cost of trading bonds is affected by broker's commissions and the bid-ask spread. Accrued interest also needs to be taken into account.

Compared to commissions on stock trades, commissions on bond trades are relatively low as a percentage of the principal amount involved. This is because most bonds are fairly liquid, which makes it easier for brokers to find counterparties to the trades. Bonds that trade at or near their par values are generally less costly to trade.

Small trades may be particularly costly to an investor. Brokers generally have a minimum commission that they charge. For a particularly small trade, this minimum charge could be a sizable percentage of the value of the bonds traded. Also, a trade involving deep-discount bonds may incur a high commission relative to the dollar value of the trade.

Bid-ask spreads are important to consider as well. On actively traded bonds, these spreads tend to be quite narrow. For example, on government bonds, the spread can be less than 0.1 percent of the price of the bonds. On the other hand, a small, inactively traded corporate bond may have a spread of 5 percent of the bond's price.

accrued interest

When buying and selling bonds in the secondary market, it is also important to consider the *accrued interest*. Coupon payments are usually made every 6 months, but interest is generally assumed to accrue at a linear (uniform) rate.

Example:	Suppose a $1,000 bond has a coupon rate of 8 percent and pays interest twice a year. Each coupon payment is equal to $40. Now suppose an investor buys the bond in the secondary market when 3 months have elapsed since the last coupon payment. The bond will have accrued 3 months' worth of interest, or $20. It is standard trading practice that the buyer pay the seller the accrued interest along with the market price of the bond. If the bond is trading at par, the buyer will be expected to pay $1,020. Of course, the buyer will be entitled to receive the entire $40 coupon payment when it is paid 3 months later.

flat

Although most bonds are traded with accrued interest, some are traded *flat*. This means that the buyer is not obligated to pay the accrued interest. Usually, bonds are traded flat only when there is uncertainty as to whether the company will make the next interest payment when due. For instance, if a company has defaulted on a previous interest payment, the bond is likely to trade flat.

Remember that the buyer does not earn interest on the accrued interest itself, while the seller, in effect, receives the interest payment in advance of the regularly scheduled payment date. It could be argued that this is like an interest-free loan from the buyer to the seller. Normally, on a small trade, the amounts involved are too small to matter. However, in the above example, suppose that instead of a single bond, $1 million worth of bonds is traded. The accrued interest would amount to $20,000. The seller will gain from investing the $20,000 accrued interest, and the buyer will, in effect, have forgone 3 months' worth of interest on the $20,000, or $400. (Since the bonds are traded at par, we can assume that market interest rates have not changed, so the coupon payments can be reinvested at 8 percent per year.)

Another concern is that if the company defaults on its next interest payment, the buyer will lose the accrued interest and have no legal recourse against the seller. Accrued interest is not returned in the event of default. During the payment period in which the bond defaults, the accrued interest will be lost to the buyer. Since the default on the coupon payment causes the market price of the bond to drop, the new buyer of the bond suffers both the loss of the accrued interest and the loss in the market value of the bond.

Bond Returns Compared with Stock Returns

Many investors keep both stocks and bonds in their portfolios. There are advantages and disadvantages to each. Stocks' expected returns are higher, but bonds are less risky. A balanced portfolio of stocks and bonds may offer the risk-expected return tradeoff appropriate to the needs and risk-tolerance levels of many investors.

The comparative certainty of bonds, especially high-grade bonds, may be most desirable for an investor with a specific time horizon who is seeking a cost-effective means of ensuring that adequate money will be available at the right time. Using the strategy of duration matching, the investor can correct for the risk of interest rate changes. An investor in a high tax bracket may find tax-exempt municipal bonds particularly attractive. Investors with a high degree of risk tolerance might choose a diversified portfolio of high-risk, high-yield bonds as an alternative to stocks.

SUMMARY AND CONCLUSIONS

There are a number of factors that influence bond yields. General market conditions, especially the inflation rate and expectations about inflation rate changes, affect both the level of yields in general and the term structure of interest rates. For any given market environment, default risk plays the largest role in determining the interest rate of a particular issue of bonds. Rating agencies assign ratings to bonds based on their assessment of the financial strength of the issuer and the default risk of the bonds.

Four hypotheses attempt to explain the term structure of interest rates. The unbiased expectations hypothesis holds that long-term interest rates are based on the average of present and expected future short-term rates. The liquidity preference hypothesis argues that investors prefer to invest short term, while borrowers prefer to borrow long term, so long-term interest rates tend to be higher than short-term rates in order to attract investors. The preferred habitat and segmented markets hypotheses argue that both borrowers and lenders (investors) have specific planning horizons, so there are, in effect, different supply-and-demand functions for bonds of different maturities.

Duration is the weighted average of the time it takes to receive the present value of the bond's expected stream of future payments. It is a measure of a bond's sensitivity to interest rate changes. Duration matching is a strategy that investors can use to immunize their bond portfolio by matching the duration of their portfolio with their planning horizon, thus allowing the price risk and reinvestment rate risk to offset each other.

Tax treatment is a factor that investors should consider when purchasing bonds. Coupon payments on municipal bonds are tax exempt, which may make these bonds particularly attractive to investors in high tax brackets. Because of their tax-exempt status, municipal bonds can pay lower coupon rates than corporate bonds and still be attractive to investors. In addition, investors may prefer to purchase bonds at a discount in the secondary market, since coupon payments are taxable when they are received, while the capital gain on a bond purchased at a discount is not taxable until the bond matures.

Other factors that influence the price and yield of bonds are marketability, call provisions, priority in the event of default, collateral, and sinking funds. Managing a bond portfolio includes ensuring that there is adequate diversification, rebalancing the portfolio to match the portfolio's duration with its desired time horizon, and using bond swaps when appropriate. Although the expected return to a portfolio of stocks is higher than that of a bond portfolio, stocks are also a more risky investment. A balanced portfolio that contains both stocks and bonds is considered to have good risk/expected return characteristics suitable to the needs, desires, and risk-tolerance level of most investors. A bond portfolio may be particularly desirable to an investor who has a specific time horizon and seeks the relative certainty of bonds' cash flows. Tax-exempt bonds are also attractive to many investors. Finally, high-risk bonds may well offer expected returns similar to those of stocks.

CHAPTER REVIEW

Answers to the review questions and the self- test questions start on page 752.

Key Terms

yield	sinking fund
coupon rate	escrow account
default	call provision
bankruptcy proceedings	call premium
bond ratings	call price
indenture	indenture trustee
maturity	liquidation
collateral	bankruptcy trustee
debentures	absolute priority of claims principle
full faith and credit	Standard & Poor's
subordination	Moody's Investor Service
senior debt	term structure

yields to maturity	reinvestment rate risk
yield curve	modified duration
market segmentation hypothesis	basis points
preferred habitat hypothesis	deep discount bonds
liquidity preference hypothesis	coupon effect
unbiased expectations hypothesis	yield to earliest call
riding the yield curve	bond swaps
duration	tax swap
immunization	accrued interest
price risk	flat

Review Questions

6-1. List and discuss the principal provisions of bond indentures. Which are most important to the bondholder?

6-2. What is a default? How does it relate to bankruptcy?

6-3. What is meant by the absolute priority of claims principle? What is its relevancy to most bankruptcies? How is it generally applied in practice?

6-4. a. What is the function of a rating service? Discuss bond ratings and default risks.
    b. What are the principal bond rating agencies?
    c. What are the principal drawbacks to relying on bond ratings to assess default risks?

6-5. a. How do yields vary with bond ratings?
    b. Do any categories of bonds typically generate higher after-default returns than other categories?

6-6. Describe the four proposed explanations for the term structure of interest rates. How would each explain the normal (rising) yield curve?

6-7. Recompute the duration for bonds A and B in table 6-2 using an appropriate discount rate of 20 percent. Compare the results with those derived from the 8 percent rate.

6-8. Compute the durations for the following bonds:

Bond	Coupon	Length to Maturity
A	7.5%	5 years
B	8.5%	10 years
C	9.5%	15 years

Assume that the next semi-annual interest payment is due in 6 months, the appropriate annual interest rate is 7 percent, and the principal is $1,000 for all the bonds.

6-9. a. Explain the coupon effect.
      b. What is immunization? Explain the various methods of immunization.

6-10. Using the bond information in question 6-8, assemble two immunized bond portfolios for an 8-year time horizon. Use weights of .6 and .7 on bond C. Which of these portfolios has the higher yield? Assume that the bonds sell for par, making their yields equal to their coupon rates.

6-11. Using the information in question 6-8, assemble an immunized bond portfolio with a 6-year time horizon. Use weights of .5 and .6 on Bond A. Assume that the bonds sell for par. Which of these portfolios has the higher yield? Compare your results with those of question 6-10.

6-12. Discuss the impacts on yields of
      a. marketability
      b. seasoning
      c. call protection
      d. sinking fund provisions
      e. How should an investor assess the importance of these factors?

6-13. a. What should be considered when assembling a bond portfolio?
      b. What are bond swaps?
      c. What trading costs are involved in buying and selling bonds?

Self-Test Questions

T   F   6-1. The terms *fixed-income security* and *debt security* can be used interchangeably.

T   F   6-2. The current yield is the contractually stated interest rate on a bond.

T   F   6-3. A bond's coupon rate and yield to maturity are always equal.

T   F   6-4. The yield to maturity on a debt instrument is based on both its market price and its coupon rate.

T   F   6-5. Aside from general credit conditions, the most significant factor that influences the coupon rate of a bond is duration.

T   F   6-6. The market uses Moody's and Standard & Poor's ratings to assess the riskiness of bonds.

T   F   6-7. The indenture is a detailed contract between the bond's issuer and the bondholders.

T   F   6-8. Debentures are bonds backed by specific collateral.

T   F   6-9.   In the case of liquidation, the claims of senior creditors must be satisfied before any money is paid to the holders of subordinate debt.

T   F   6-10. A call provision gives the bondholder the option of receiving the principal amount of the bond prior to maturity.

T   F   6-11. A call provision is most likely to be exercised if market interest rates decline appreciably while the bond is outstanding.

T   F   6-12. In the case of bankruptcy, preferred stockholders have priority over unsecured creditors.

T   F   6-13. A bond with a rating of A has greater risk of default than a bond with a rating of B.

T   F   6-14. The term structure of interest rates describes the relationship between maturity and market interest rates.

T   F   6-15. The yield curve is a graphical representation of the term structure of interest rates.

T   F   6-16. Under the liquidity preference hypothesis, borrowers prefer to borrow short-term rather than long-term.

T   F   6-17. Under the unbiased exceptions hypothesis, if long-term interest rates are higher than short-term interest rates, one can conclude that the consensus expectation is that interest rates will increase in the future.

T   F   6-18. Maturity is a better measure of a bond's sensitivity to interest rate changes than duration.

T   F   6-19. For bonds of the same maturity, the lower the coupon rate, the greater the duration.

T   F   6-20. The duration of a zero-coupon bond is equal to its maturity.

T   F   6-21. Immunizing a portfolio reduces the portfolio's interest rate risk.

T   F   6-22. Interest rate futures can be used to immunize a bond portfolio.

T   F   6-23. All other things being equal, investors in high tax brackets are likely to prefer to purchase bonds at a discount in the secondary market (even though they pay a lower coupon rate) and hold them to maturity rather than purchasing bonds at par.

T   F   6-24. Capital gains on municipal bonds are not taxable.

T   F   6-25. A bond's sinking fund reduces the risk of default.

T   F   6-26. As a percentage of the market value of the asset (stock or bond) purchased or sold, commissions on bond trades tend to exceed those on stock trades.

T   F   6-27.   When a bond is traded flat, the purchaser does not receive the accrued interest on the bond.

T   F   6-28.   The expected return to stocks tends to be higher than the expected return to bonds, but stocks also tend to be more risky than bonds.

NOTES

1. E. Altman and S. Nammacher, "The Default Rate Experience on High-Yield Corporate Debt," *Financial Analysts Journal* (July/August 1985, pp. 25–41; J. Fons, "The Default Premium and Corporate Bond Experience," *Journal of Finance* (March 1987), pp.81–97.
2. G. Brauer, "Evidence of the Market Value of Me-First Rules," *Financial Management* (spring 1983), pp. 11–18; M. Brody, "Controversial Issue: A Leveraged Buy-Out Touches Off a Bitter Dispute," *Barron's* (September 19, 1983), p. 15, 19–22.
3. *See* I.R.C. §1091(a)

7

Valuation of Investments: Common Stock

Learning Objectives

An understanding of the material in this chapter should enable the student to

---

7-1. Describe the relationship between a stock's value, its expected earnings per share, its expected payout ratio, and the discount rate.

7-2. Describe the types of earnings forecasts and their implications for investment analysis.

Chapter Outline

In chapter 4 we discussed how to find the present value of a stream of cash flows. We discussed how this valuation technique can be applied to fixed-income securities such as bonds. Now we will explain how the value of common stock can be determined by finding the present value of its expected stream of future cash flows.

A frequently encountered question is, "Why should I care what the total stream of future cash flows of the stock will be, when I only plan to hold it for a short time and then sell it?" The answer is that in order to sell an asset, the seller must find a buyer who is willing to pay the price the seller is asking. The buyer of the stock will be concerned with the risk-adjusted stream of future cash flows. The capital gain the shareholder can realistically expect to receive is based on the discounted value of the stock's expected future cash flows from the time of the purchase. Therefore, whether an investor is planning to hold a stock for one day or for many years, the same valuation techniques are appropriate.

The stream of cash flows from stocks differs from that of bonds. Unlike interest payments on bonds, dividend payments on stock tend to increase over time. Moreover, stocks do not have a specified maturity date, but they are assumed to have a perpetual life with a perpetual stream of cash flows.

discount rate
required rate of
return
risk premium

Also, the determination of the *discount rate*, or *required rate of return*, differs somewhat for stock. While the required rate of return for both stocks and bonds is the risk-free rate plus the *risk premium*, the risk premium for stock is not determined in isolation but is based on the stock's risk and correlation with the market portfolio, as will be discussed in later chapters.

present value
dividend discount
model (DDM)

Nonetheless, there are also some similarities between the valuation of stocks and bonds. In both cases, the value of a security is the discounted *present value* of its expected stream of cash flows. The *dividend discount model* is a model for calculating the present value of a stock's expected stream of cash flows (dividends).

DETERMINING THE APPROPRIATE DISCOUNT RATE

Ascertaining the appropriate discount rate requires identifying the risk-free rate, assessing the asset's risk, and estimating the appropriate risk premium. The market rate on federal government securities approximates the risk-free rate. Assessing risk and determining the appropriate risk premium (pure and default) are, however, rather complicated topics requiring more detailed treatment.

Applying Present Values to Stocks: The Dividend Discount Model (DDM)

dividends

A share of stock represents fractional ownership of a corporation. Shareholders are able to participate in the firm's performance in two ways. First, most firms pay out a portion of profits to shareholders in the form of *dividends*. Not all firms pay dividends in a given year, but all are expected to do so sooner or later. Second, profits not paid out as dividends are retained earnings and are plowed back into the company. The additional resources acquired with these *retained earnings* lead to growth and should help increase future earnings and dividends. If all goes according to plan, the firm's growing assets and sales will be accompanied by increases in earnings, dividends, and its stock price. Stockholders can then sit back and enjoy the higher dividends and the rise in the value of their portfolio.

retained earnings

Alternatively, they can take advantage of the higher stock price by selling some or all of their shares at a profit. Thus, stock returns may take the form of both dividends and price appreciation.

Obviously, not all stocks experience rising earnings, dividends, and stock prices. Some companies experience losses, pay no dividends, and sustain declines in their stocks' price. In extreme cases, a company may be forced to declare bankruptcy. The shareholders may be left with nothing but some worthless stock certificates and a tax write-off. Nevertheless, those who buy stock expect, at the time that they make the investment, to receive a return in the form of dividends and/or price appreciation. In principle, therefore, as implicitly, its future market value, should yield its present value:

$$P_0 = \frac{d_1}{(1+k)} + \frac{d_2}{(1+k)^2} + \frac{d_3}{(1+k)^3} + ... + \frac{(d_n + P_n)}{(1+k)^n}$$

(Equation 7-1)

where: P_0 = present value of share
d_n = expected dividend for year t
k = appropriate discount rate
P_n = expected stock price for year n

Moreover, P_n can be evaluated by discounting subsequent dividends. Note that P_n's value, as shown in equation 7-2, stems entirely from the future dividends that its owners expect to receive into the far future (effectively, infinity):

$$P_n = \frac{(d_{n+1})}{(1+k)^{(n+1)}} + \frac{(d_{n+2})}{(1+k)^{(n+2)}} + ...$$

(Equation 7-2)

Thus, equation 7-1 can be restated as follows in equation 7-3:

$$P_0 = \frac{d_1}{(1+k)} + \frac{d_2}{(1+k)^2} + \frac{d_3}{(1+k)^3} + ... + \frac{d_n}{(1+k)^n} + ...$$ (Equation 7-3)

Remember that when valuing common stock, the first dividend of interest is d_i, the next period's dividend. This is because an investor is only concerned with future cash flows, not past cash flows.

Constant Growth Model

constant growth model

A much simpler formula applies to stock valuations when dividends can be assumed to grow at a constant rate. When g represents the expected growth rate of dividends, $d_1 = d_0(1 + g)$, $d_2 = d_1(1+g) = d_0(1+g)^2$, and so on. Equation 7-3 then becomes

$$P_0 = \frac{d_0(1+g)}{(1+k)} + \frac{d_0(1+g)^2}{(1+k)^2} + \frac{d_0(1+g)^3}{(1+k)^3} + ... + \frac{d_0(1+g)^n}{(1+k)^n} + ...$$

or

$$P_0 = \frac{d_1}{(1+k)} + \frac{d_1(1+g)}{(1+k)^2} + \frac{d_1(1+g)^2}{(1+k)^3} + ...$$

When n approaches infinity, this formula reduces to the following:

$$P_0 = \frac{d_1}{(k-g)} \quad \text{for } g < k \qquad \qquad \text{(Equation 7-4)}$$

Equation 7-4 yields a value for a stock when its dividends are expected to grow at a constant rate g. In other words, the equation says that a stock's price should equal its next dividend divided by the difference between the appropriate discount rate and its growth rate. According to this formula, the price of a stock rises with both its dividend and its growth rate and falls as the discount rate is increased. This relationship is exactly correct when the growth rate g is a constant value. It is approximately correct when g represents an appropriately weighted average value and each year's actual value is not expected to deviate greatly from that average. This relationship is the basis for the dividend discount model. The model and various modifications of it provide investment analysts with a tool for evaluating relative stock values. These models can be helpful in identifying misvalued securities because the formula yields the *intrinsic value* of the stock.

intrinsic value

The formula applies only when expected growth rates are below the discount rate. Stocks whose dividends have expected growth rates that are forever above the discount rate would have infinite prices. That nonsensical result would occur because each successive expected dividend would have a higher present value than the one before it. Because the dividend payments would be expected to continue forever, their sum would grow without bound. Clearly, stock prices are finite. Thus, we need not consider the possibility that long-term expected growth rates might exceed the appropriate discount rate. For short periods, companies may grow more rapidly than their market-determined discount rate. These growth rates are, however, temporary phenomena that exist only when a company is in an early stage of rapid growth. In the long run, dividends grow more slowly than the rate at which they are discounted.

Example 1:   Assume that Acme Corp. experiences constant dividend growth at a rate of 5 percent per year. Its required rate of return (discount rate) is 15 percent. The dividend that was just paid is $2/share. Using the dividend discount model, we can find the fair market price of Acme Corp. common stock as follows: The price formula is Price = P_0 = d1/(k − g). Remember that the most recent dividend is d_0, not d_1. To find d_1, we multiply d_0 by (1 + g). Therefore, d_1 = $2 x 1.05 = $2.10. The price of the stock should equal $2.10/(.15 − .05) = $2.10/.1 = $21 per share.

Example 2:   Use the same assumptions as in the Example 1, except assume that Acme's dividend growth rate is now 7 percent. To find the fair market price, note that d_1 = $2 x 1.07 = $2.14. Thus, P_0 = $2.14/(.15 − .07) = $2.14/.08 = $26.75. Therefore, when the dividend growth rate increases and everything else remains the same, the market price of stock should increase.

Example 3:   Use the same assumptions as in Example 1, except assume that now Acme's required return is 20 percent. To find the fair market price, we use the formula Price = $2.10/(.2 − .05) = $2.10/.15 = $14. Thus, as the required return increases and all else remains the same, the price of a stock decreases. Since required return is a function of risk, the riskier a company is, the lower the price of its stock for a given expected income stream.

Example 4:   Assume Baker Company just paid a dividend of $3/share. It is expected to pay $3.15/share next year and to maintain a constant rate of growth. The price of Baker stock is $25/share.

To find the required rate of return (discount rate) for a company, we first evaluate its dividend stream. If the current dividend (d_0) = $3 and next year's dividend d_1 = $3.15, then g = ($3.15 − $3)/$3 = $.15/$3 = 5%. Next, we know that P_0 = d_1/(k − g). Multiplying both sides of the equation by (k − g), P_0 x (k − g) = (P_0 x k) − (P_0 x g) = d_1. Adding (P_0 x g) to both sides of the equation, we see that $P_0 \times k = d_1 + (P_0 \times g)$. Finally, we divide both sides of the equation by P_0, obtaining the equation: $k = (d_1/P_0) + g$. Applying that equation, the required rate of return, $k = (\$3.15/\$25) + .05 = .126 + .05 = .176 = 17.6\%$.

Example: Finally, let's look at a company that does not have constant dividend growth. Data Corp. pays no dividend currently, but it is expected to pay $.50 in year 1 (next year), $1 in year 2, $1.50 in year 3, $2 in year 4, and to start paying dividends at a constant growth rate of 10 percent thereafter. Data has a required rate of return of 20 percent. We can find the fair market value of Data common stock by using successive periods of evaluation of the different dividend streams. This type of two-phase DDM is quite common among security analysts. We cannot use the dividend discount model directly to find P_0, but we can use it to find P_4, since constant growth is expected to begin in year 4. Therefore, $P_4 = d_5/(k - g) = (d_4 \times [1 + g])/(k - g) = (\$2 \times 1.1)/(.2 - .1) = \$2.20/.1 = \$22/\text{share}$. Next, we compute the value of P_0 as the discounted present value of the expected future stream of cash flows, keeping in mind that $P_4/1.2^4$ represents the discounted present value of P_4, which is the discounted present value of all expected future cash flows from year 5 on. Therefore, $P_0 = d_1/(1 + k) + d_2/(1 + k)^2 + d_3/(1 + k)^3 + d_4/(1 + k)^4 + P_4/(1 + k)^4 = \$.50/1.2 + \$1/1.2^2 + \$1.50/1.2^3 + \$2/1.2^4 + \$22/1.2^4 = \$.42 + \$.69 + \$.87 + \$.96 + \$10.61 = \$13.55$.

Stock Prices and PE Ratios

PE ratio

Investors and investment analysts often focus on the price of a stock in relation to its earnings per share (EPS). The per-share price divided by the per-share earnings is called the price earnings or *PE ratio*. The PE ratio puts stock prices into perspective by relating the stock's price per share to its earnings per share. The more optimistically the market views the prospects for a particular stock, the more it is prepared to bid up the price of the stock relative to its current earnings. Thus, the stocks of companies with favorable growth opportunities (often called growth stocks) tend to have high PE ratios. Stocks with more mundane earning potentials have lower PEs.

Equation 7-4 as restated in equation 7-5 below illustrates the relation between PE and growth. By dividing both sides of equation 7-4 by earnings per share (e_1) we obtain the following:

$$P_0/e_1 = \frac{d_1/e_1}{k-g}$$

or

$$PE = \frac{p}{(k-g)} \qquad \text{(Equation 7-5)}$$

where: e_1 = expected earnings per share next year

PE = P_0/e_1, the price earnings ratio

p = d_1/e_1, the expected payout ratio (assumed to be constant)

Therefore, the PE ratio is a function of three variables: the expected growth rate g, the expected payout ratio p (the percentage of earnings that are paid to shareholders), and the discount rate k. It rises with g and p and falls as k is increased. When g and p are constant, the PE model leads to the same results as the dividend discount model.

Applying the Dividend Discount Model: An Example

The pricing of AT&T stock gives us a useful opportunity to see how the dividend discount model might be applied. At year-end 1987, AT&T's common stock was priced at 27. Its indicated dividend rate was $1.20 per share per year. Earnings per share (EPS) through the first 9 months of 1987 were $1.42. These 9-month earnings extrapolated to a 12-month EPS estimate of about $1.89 (4/3 x 1.42). (AT&T's actual 1987 EPS turned out to be $1.88, but the market did not know this until several weeks past year-end 1987.) The estimated earnings corresponded to payout of .63 (1.20/1.89). Long-term Treasury bonds were at this time yielding about 8.9 percent, while AT&T's own bonds were yielding in the range of 9.3 percent to 10 percent. As is the case for virtually all companies, AT&T's common stock was by its very nature considerably riskier than its bonds. Thus, the risk premium of AT&T's common stock should therefore have been appreciably higher than that of its bonds. Perhaps a risk premium for the common stock in the area of 4 percent would have been appropriate. This is approximately the difference between the average long-term return on stocks and T-bills. That would imply an appropriate discount rate of 12.9 percent. AT&T's expected annual EPS of $1.89 implied a PE of 14.3. Applying these numbers to the PE ratio equation yields the following:

$$14.3 = \frac{.63}{(.129 - g)}$$

(continued on next page)

or

$$g = .129 - \frac{.63}{14.3} = .085$$

Thus, the market at year-end 1987 appeared to be pricing AT&T's common stock at a level that implied an expected growth rate in the range of 8.5 percent. This result is, however, sensitive to our assumed values for dividends, EPS, inflation and the risk premium.

Suppose, for example, we thought a 3 percent risk premium was more appropriate than the initial assumption of 4 percent. That change would imply an expected market growth rate of 7.5 percent. Alternatively, suppose our annual EPS estimates were changed to $2. This EPS would change the payout to .6 and the PE to 13.5. Curiously, the resulting expected growth rate would remain almost unchanged at 8.5 percent. The impact of the decline in the payout would largely offset the impact of the lower PE. A change in the stock price, however, would have a more significant impact. A week earlier, AT&T's common stock had been priced at 29. That implied a PE of 15.3, which in turn implied a market expected growth rate of 8.8 percent.

These estimated growth rates in the range of 7.5 percent to 9 percent may or may not have been accurate, but they did seem reasonable. The economy generally grows at a rate of about 3 percent to 4 percent in real terms (adjusted for inflation), and inflation may add about another 4 percent to 5 percent (viewed from 1987). Therefore, in nominal terms, the economy generally grows in the range of 7 percent to 9 percent. Presumably, AT&T would grow at approximately the growth rate of the economy.

Reapplying this analysis to mid-year 1999 (June 25) reveals the following: AT&T was priced at 55 with a prior 12-month EPS of $2.32 and a consensus forecast for $2.40 in 2000. Its dividend rate was 33 cents a quarter, or $1.32 for 12 months. This corresponds to a payout of .57:

$$\text{Payout} = \frac{\text{Dividend}}{\text{EPS}}$$

$$= \frac{\$1.32}{\$2.32}$$

$$= .57$$

Using the $2.40 forecasted EPS results in a PE of 22.9:

$$\text{PE} = \frac{\$55}{\$2.40}$$

$$= 22.9$$

Long-term Treasuries were yielding about 6.1 percent. Accordingly, for a 3 percent risk premium (now lower due to a more optimistic view in the market) we have an estimated discount rate of 9.1 percent. Using the dividend discount model results in an expected growth rate of 6.6 percent:

(continued on next page)

$$22.9 = \frac{.57}{(.091 - g)}$$

$$g = .091 - \frac{.57}{22.9}$$

$$= .091 - .025$$

$$= .066 \text{ or } 6.6\%$$

Thus, At&T's market price in mid-1999 implied an expected growth rate of 6.6 percent, because inflation rates and expectations were much lower than they were in 1987. Inflation was expected to be in the 1 percent to 2 percent range and real economic growth in the 3 percent to 4 percent range, implying overall economic growth of 4 percent to 6 percent in nominal terms. For AT&T's earnings and dividends to grow at a rate of 6.6 percent or more would require that the company grow faster than the economy. The market demonstrated through its pricing, therefore, that it was relatively optimistic on AT&T's future.

While interesting, none of this analysis has indicated whether AT&T is an attractive investment (underpriced), an unattractive investment (overpriced), or fairly priced. Such a determination requires us to take a further step. We must compare the market's expectations with our own. In other words, we must assess the accuracy of the market price.

Market Price of an Investment

Investment prices implicitly reflect their discounted expected cash flow streams. Yet very few traders explicitly compute these discounted expected earnings streams. Nonetheless, an implicit analysis of future return prospects and the associated risk is an integral part of the investment pricing process. The more efficient the market, the more accurately the price will reflect available risk-return information and will be regarded as a true measure of intrinsic value.

The promised future income stream of bonds (coupon plus principal) is directly observable. For investors who hold their bonds until they mature, the discounted promised return generally differs little from the discounted promised future earnings stream. Only if the bond defaults or is called early will the actual return be different from the promised yield. Similarly, preferred stocks normally have observable promised future income streams (dividends) that are close to their expected values (expected dividends). However, some preferreds mature and most are callable.

Common stocks, in contrast, do not promise a future earnings stream or redemption and are not callable. Thus, expected income streams of common stock are much more difficult to determine than those of fixed-income securities. Although investors may use market analysts' *forecasts* or historical experience to estimate future cash flows, the market's true

forecasts

market price

(unobservable) expectations may differ. The market does, however, almost always generate a price. The *market price* does not reveal the market's earnings stream expectations *per se*. Rather, the price is jointly determined by the expected payments and the rate used to discount them. Nevertheless, the price, which is observable, does provide some insight into the market's earnings stream expectations, which are not observable.

Implications of the Market Price

The market's weighted average opinion of a particular investment (as reflected by the price that the market determines from the interplay of supply and demand) is, by itself, of little help in investment selection. Market expectations may or may not be accurate. The investment selection process as typically performed by fund managers or security analysts can be viewed largely as a search for assets that the market has improperly valued. In other words, investment analysis generally involves an attempt to understand and find errors (overvaluations or undervaluations) in the market's evaluation. Security analysts and other professional investors can compare their own discounted dividend forecasts with the market's or compare their assessments of the company's growth prospects with the market's expectations. The two approaches are mathematically equivalent. With either approach, investors identify "undervalued" and "overvalued" securities by contrasting their valuations with the market's. Selections based on this analysis can fail to produce the expected result for a number of reasons:

- The income stream forecasts can be inaccurate. If the investor's income stream forecast is too high, the investment is likely to do less well than expected.
- Even if the income forecasts are on target, errors in the assumed discount rates can account for the apparent difference between the investor's and the market's evaluations.
- The anticipated earnings increase can be offset by an increase in risk. An increase in risk will cause the discount rate to rise, thereby tending to decrease the investment's value.
- The investor may need to sell the asset before the market (favorably) reevaluates it. The investor may be correct on value but incorrect on timing.
- The investor may correctly identify undervalued securities whose subsequent revaluations are offset by a general market decline.

Therefore, a security identified as undervalued may not necessarily earn a superior return for its owners, relative to other investments of comparable risk.

If the investor's analysis proves to be both timely and more accurate than the market's analysis, the selections should show superior risk-adjusted returns. Where the market's expectations are essentially correct, the selections will tend neither to outperform nor underperform the market. Frequently, however, both the market's and the investor's analysis of the particular investment are too optimistic. As a result, the selections underperform the market. Equally frequently, a general market decline pulls down the prices of even many "undervalued" securities. Investment analysts hope that their evaluations are more accurate than the market's often enough to outweigh the times that either they are too optimistic or the market declines.

Because average market performance reflects the weighted-average performance of all participants, however, the average investor/analyst cannot outperform the market average. This basic fact illustrates the difficulty of abnormally successful investing (that is, beating the average). Only a minority of stock market participants can outperform the market averages, and only a still smaller minority can do so consistently. Even so, many investors continue to try.

FORECASTING THE INCOME STREAM

Evaluating an investment involves forecasting its income stream and assessing the corresponding risk.

Relationship between Dividends and Earnings

earnings per share (EPS)

Most stock valuation models call for dividend forecasts. In practice, however, *earnings per share (EPS)* are usually forecast instead. EPS is, at best, an imperfect substitute for dividends. Only for a constant dividend payout will the value of the expected dividend stream be precisely linked to the value of that firm's expected earnings stream. Thus, stock values based on earnings streams are only an approximation. The appropriateness of such an approach depends on the relation between expected dividends and earnings. Earnings are a useful proxy for dividends if the two variables tend to move up and down together. The more closely they move together, the better proxy earnings are for dividends.

Many firms try to maintain a stable, long-term relationship between dividends and earnings (payout). Payouts do, however, tend to vary from firm to firm and over time for the same firm. More specifically, they tend to move inversely with growth, risk, and earnings volatility. A company with rapidly growing, volatile, and uncertain earnings, therefore, tends to pay out a smaller fraction of its income than a slower-growth firm with a more dependable earnings stream. Most mature companies have a relatively high,

payout ratio

stable long-run *payout ratio*, however. Typically, between 50 percent and 60 percent of corporate after-tax earnings are paid out as dividends. In other circumstances there may be constraints on payouts because many bond indentures (contracts) set a ceiling on a firm's allowable dividend payout to protect the bondholder's interests.

Types of Earnings Forecasts

Investment analysts base their earnings predictions on relevant available data. Management forecasts generally utilize at least some nonpublic information. In addition, annual earnings predictions can be based on already reported quarterly earnings. Past earnings can be extrapolated mechanically.

Although the short-run relationship between dividends and earnings is variable and uncertain, the longer-run relationship is relatively stable and certain. Moreover, companies are often slow to adjust dividend rates to a change in profitability. Thus, a given year's dividends may not reflect the firm's long-term ability to pay dividends as well as the firm's earnings do.

profits

Finally, that portion of *profits* not paid out as dividends (retained earnings) is plowed back into the company. These retained earnings should, if used effectively, enhance subsequent growth, profits, and dividends. According to M. Miller and F. Modigliani in a *Journal of Business* article that discusses dividend irrelevancy, the payout rate is not relevant to the long-term valuation of a stock. Firms that pay out more of their earnings as dividends in the current period will grow more slowly in the future because they have less to reinvest. The net effect for shareholders is a wash. Others argue, however, that dividends signal the company's future prospects. The company's managers know more about the future prospects of the company than the public does, and they would not be increasing dividends unless they were optimistic about the company's future earnings prospects. Accordingly, security evaluation often begins with earnings predictions. Accurate earnings predictions should facilitate reliable dividend forecasts. These dividend forecasts should, when appropriately discounted, yield meaningful value estimates. Figure 7-1 illustrates the relationship between earnings and stock prices.

Investment Analysts

The predictions and recommendations of investment analysts are notoriously uneven. Two basic problems with most investment analysts are their tendency to utilize similar approaches and their reluctance to recommend sales. Thus, those rare analysts who do not follow the herd and sometimes recommend selling may deserve close attention.

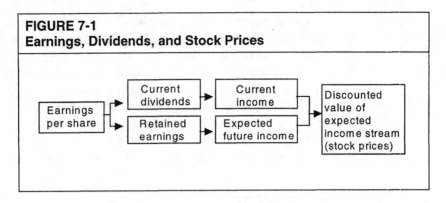

FIGURE 7-1
Earnings, Dividends, and Stock Prices

One study that examined five financial institutions covering 185 companies found that the growth rates analysts predicted highly correlated with past growth but not with the actual growth rates that the analysts were attempting to forecast. According to the study, earnings growth in past periods was not a useful predictor of future earnings growth. Careful estimates by the security analysts participating in the survey, the bases of which were not limited to public information, performed only a little better than past growth rates. Furthermore, the market price-earnings ratios themselves were not better than either analysts' forecasts or the past growth rates in forecasting future earnings growth. Follow-up studies have generally concluded that analysts do slightly better than naive models of simple **extrapolation** *extrapolation* of past growth rates.

In addition to the level of errors in analysts' forecasts, it is helpful to know the nature of the errors. Are some situations more likely to lead to large forecast errors? Do analysts learn much from experience? Does a wide range in forecasts indicate anything about the likely error? A study by E. Elton, M. Gruber, and M. Gultekin addressed these types of issues and they reached the following conclusions:

- Analysts' forecast errors tend to decline monotonically as fiscal year-end approaches.
- Analysts tend to forecast overall earnings for groups of stocks accurately.
- Errors in forecasting industry earnings were appreciably less than those for individual companies.
- Most analysts tend to overestimate the growth in those earnings that they expect to be strong and underestimate the growth that they expect to be weak.
- Difficulty in forecasting earnings in one year is associated with similar difficulty in the following year.
- Divergence of earnings forecasts is attributable to individual forecaster error.

Research on the accuracy of analysts earnings forecasts continued throughout the 1980s and 1990s. The basic conclusions drawn from that research did not, however, alter the major findings of the earlier work.

Even though there are errors in analysts' forecasts, because they have more information on which to base a forecast, analysts can still do a better job at forecasting earnings than a simple mechanical model based on past earnings growth can do. Moreover, as forecasters become more sophisticated in their modeling and in their knowledge about past forecast errors, we can expect earnings forecast accuracy to slowly improve in the future.

Corporate Forecasts

For a number of years the SEC has encouraged corporations to make their own internal earnings predictions public. Corporate officials have direct access to nonpublic corporate information and special expertise in analyzing expected profit impacts. Thus, their estimates should be relatively accurate. Stockholders are not likely to forgive a poor forecasting record. Accordingly, managers usually have greater means to forecast effectively, but the incentives are mixed. Thus, in spite of SEC encouragement, relatively few corporations have released earnings forecasts for their firms. Moreover, the firms that have disclosed their forecasts tend to have more stable and therefore more predictable earnings streams than those that have not.

Stockholders utilize announcements of dividend changes to assess management's confidence in future earnings. A dividend increase is interpreted as evidence that management expects earnings to remain at current levels or to rise. A dividend reduction or suspension is viewed as indicating a lack of management confidence in the future. Studies on the efficacy of corporate forecasts report the following: (1) Unexpected dividend changes accompany stock price changes, and dividend changes tend to forecast earnings changes. (2) Both dividend change announcements and management earnings forecasts reflect management expectations. (3) Corporate forecasts of substantial earnings increases, coupled with insider purchases around the time the forecasts are released, are associated with strong subsequent performance.

Quarterly Earnings Extrapolations

Investors often implicitly extrapolate interim results into annual estimates. If the first quarter's earnings are up by 20 percent, for example, does this imply the annual earnings are likely to improve by a similar amount? Tests of the reliability of making inferences from interim results show mainly that delay in an earnings report may be taken as a forecast of unfavorable results.

Past Earnings Growth

Can we expect a high correlation between past and future rates of growth in earnings? Can able managements generate consistently above average performance? Similarly, do ineffective managements tend to produce consistently poor performances? Are past growth rates useful guides to the future? A classic study of British corporations and subsequently of United States firms found very little relation between past and subsequent growth rates. According to another study, however, firms with the most stable first-quintile relationship between growth, income, and production showed a significant positive correlation (.40) between successive growth rates. Other studies have found somewhat greater association between future earnings growth and more sophisticated extrapolations of past growth. Nonetheless, past growth is of no more than modest help in forecasting future earnings.

An Integrated Forecasting Approach

The largely unsuccessful results of past forecasting efforts suggest the need for a more comprehensive approach. Although simple extrapolations of past earnings may not produce especially reliable forecasts, perhaps a more insightful use of past earnings data could facilitate superior predictions. One study of the predictability of corporate behavior indicates that earnings' past business cycle sensitivity reflects future earnings relationships. That is, earnings may be more accurately forecast when the firm's relationship to its economic environment is considered. Other work utilizing leading indicators has produced encouraging results. As yet, however, forecasts based on leading indicators are not publicly available.

Implications for Investment Analysis

Analysts' forecasts are of modest value; corporate forecasts are largely unobtainable and, when available, may not be appreciably more reliable; interim earnings have very little explanatory power; past growth rates are poor forecasters except when the growth rates have been stable; and forecasts based on leading indicators are not publicly available. The relative inaccuracy and/or unavailability of most types of year-ahead earnings predictions suggests that longer-term forecasts may be especially unreliable. Year-to-year fluctuations may be smoothed, but the uncertainties of the more distant future tend to compound the inaccuracies of long-term forecasts. Indeed, few analysts even make such forecasts.

The shortcomings of earnings forecasts should be put in perspective. Anyone seeking to analyze investment opportunities encounters substantial difficulties and uncertainties. Success relative to others may lead to satisfactory results even when everyone must rely on rather inaccurate forecasts.

SUMMARY AND CONCLUSIONS

The price of an investment represents the market's assessment of the present value of the investment's expected future income stream. Observing bonds' expected income streams and implied discount rates is relatively straightforward. Stocks' expected income streams and discount rates are, in contrast, appreciably more difficult to observe. Investment analysis seeks to generate estimates of future income streams and appropriate discount rates that are superior to the market's. Thus, investor/analysts compare the present value implied by their estimates of an asset's future income stream and appropriate discount rate with its market price. An undervalued asset is a good buy—particularly if it is more undervalued than the available alternatives. This analysis is, however, only as reliable as the inputs on which it is based. The approach may be useful when the estimates are relatively accurate, as for bonds. For stocks, however, forecasting difficulties make a straightforward application of present-value estimates very difficult. Valuing assets on the basis of their discounted expected income streams provides a useful framework, but identifying undervalued securities requires a much more comprehensive approach.

CHAPTER REVIEW

Answers to the review questions and the self-test questions start on page 755.

Key Terms

discount rate	intrinsic value
required rate of return	PE ratio
risk premium	forecasts
present value	market price
dividend discount model (DDM)	earnings per share (EPS)
dividends	payout ratio
retained earnings	profits
constant growth model	extrapolation

Review Questions

7-1. The American Pig Company (ticker symbol PORK) currently pays a dividend of $3.00 per share, which is expected to rise by $.25 per share for the next 5 years. The stock currently sells for $36 per share, a ratio of 12 times its current dividends. The same ratio of dividends to price is also expected at the end of 5 years. Compute the present value of PORK's expected income stream for discount rates

a.   of 8 percent
b.   of 10 percent
c.   of 12 percent
d.   of 15 percent
e.   of 18 percent
f.   at a stable dividend of $3.00 (at 8 percent)

7-2.   Evaluate the stock of ZYX Corporation using the following information:
   • current dividend rate: $1.00
   • dividend rate over next 5 years: $1.10, $1.20, $1.30, $1.40, $1.50
   • current discount rate: 16 percent
   • current and future market price/dividend rate: 6.5

7-3.   Repeat question 7-2 using discount rates of
   a.   10 percent
   b.   20 percent

7-4.   Using the dividend discount model, compute the market price for the following sets of information:
   a.   d = $1; k = 12%; g = 10%
   b.   d = $2; k = 12%; g = 11%
   c.   d = $1.50; k = 12%; g = 8%

7-5.   Assuming a payout of 55 percent, what would the PE ratios in question 7-4 be?

7-6.   a.   Discuss how the market's evaluation and our own evaluation may be used to identify misvalued securities.
   b.   What are some of the errors that can be made in such an approach to investment evaluation?

7-7.   Compute the market-implied expected long-term growth rate for the following information:
   a.   PE = 8; p = 40%; k = 12%
   b.   PE = 10; p = 50%; k = 12%
   c.   PE = 15; p = 60%; k = 12%

7-8.   a.   Suppose that you believe the firm described in question 7-7a will earn $1 and pay a dividend of $.40 next year. In fact, it will earn $1 but only pays out $0.25 and continues with that payout ratio. What is the new PE ratio that is consistent with that dividend, assuming the growth rate remains unchanged? Alternatively, how much higher must its expected growth rate be to justify the current PE and $0.25 dividend? Which is more realistic? Explain.

b. Repeat, this time assuming that the dividend increases to $0.75 and that earnings are maintained.

7-9. Why do investment analysts concentrate on earnings predictions rather than dividend predictions?

7-10. Compare earnings forecasts based on analysts' predictions, past earnings growth, management forecasts, interim earnings, and an integrated approach.

Self-Test Questions

T   F   7-1. An investor who is planning to hold stock only for a short time need not be concerned about the stock's expected dividend stream after the time he or she plans to sell the stock.

T   F   7-2. The required return on stock is equal to the risk-free rate plus the stock's risk premium.

T   F   7-3. The discount rate used to evaluate the expected future dividend stream is the same as the required return.

T   F   7-4. Dividend payments on common stock tend to remain constant over time.

T   F   7-5. A share of stock represents fractional ownership of a corporation.

T   F   7-6. The price of common stock should reflect the present value of its expected future stream of dividends.

T   F   7-7. When using the constant growth model, the price of a stock should equal its current dividend divided by $(k - g)$.

T   F   7-8. For the constant growth model to apply, the discount rate must exceed the growth rate.

T   F   7-9. In equilibrium, the price-earnings model should yield the same result as the dividend discount model.

T   F   7-10. The expected income stream from common stock is much more difficult to determine than that of bonds.

T   F   7-11. A security that is undervalued will always earn a superior return for its owners, relative to other investments of comparable risk.

T   F   7-12. An appropriate dividend payout ratio for a rapidly growing start-up company may be too low for a mature company.

T   F   7-13. Any net earnings not paid out in dividends are retained earnings, which should be used to finance the company's future growth and future income.

T   F   7-14.   Dividend increases are often interpreted as a sign of management's confidence in the firm's future prospects.

T   F   7-15.   Past earnings growth is an excellent predictor of future earnings growth.

8

Risk and Modern Portfolio Theory

Learning Objectives

An understanding of the material in this chapter should enable the student to

---

8-1. Explain what is meant by investment risk and risk aversion.

8-2. Explain the difference between individual and portfolio risk.

8-3. Describe the risk-reduction potential of diversification.

8-4. Explain the parameters of portfolio risk determination.

8-5. Explain what is meant by choosing an efficient portfolio.

Chapter Outline

Most investors have a basic understanding of the risk concept. They generally (1) realize that risk is related to the confidence placed in return expectations, (2) are willing to accept a lower expected return to obtain a reduction in risk, and (3) understand that the discount rate applied to the valuation of any expected income stream should vary directly with its risk. This chapter expands on that base, focusing primarily on risk's role in investment analysis and portfolio management. First, the definition of risk is explored and then its primary forms (individual and portfolio) are introduced. Next, portfolio risk is analyzed. Finally, a simplified approach to portfolio risk is introduced and analyzed.

SIMPLE EXAMPLE OF INVESTMENT RISK

Consider the following investment alternatives. Suppose investment A guarantees a return of precisely 5 percent. Now consider investment B with a 90 percent chance of a 5 percent return, a 5 percent chance of 0 percent return, and a 5 percent chance of a 10 percent return. B's expected return is 5 percent [(.90 x .05) + (.05 x .00) + (.05 x .10) = .045 + .00 + .005 = .05], which is the same as A's. B's actual (or realized) return is less likely to equal its expected return than A's is. Ten percent of the time investment B will not earn 5 percent. Investment A offers an equivalent expected return and lower risk than investment B does. Thus, risk-averse investors would prefer A to B.

risk averse

To be *risk averse* simply means that, for a given expected return, an individual would prefer less risk to more risk. A vast majority of people fit that definition. A full discussion appears later in this chapter. Comparing A to B is very straightforward.

Now consider asset C with a 90 percent chance of a 5 percent return, a 5 percent chance of a 3 percent return, and a 5 percent chance of a 7 percent return. Like A and B, C offers an expected return of 5 percent [(.90 x .05) + (.05 x .03) + (.05 x .07) = .05]. Because B's actual return is uncertain, risk averters would prefer A. On the other hand, because C's return variation (or range of possible returns) is less than B's, C is less risky than B, yet still riskier than A. That is, the possible returns for B are 0 percent, 5 percent, and 10 percent; for C, they are 3 percent, 5 percent, and 7 percent. B's actual return could be 5 percent above or below its expected value, whereas C's can differ only 2 percent from its mean in either direction.

Return possibilities such as these are often illustrated graphically, as shown in figure 8-1, a *histogram* of investment C's return possibilities. The vertical axis in figure 8-1 reports the probability of each event; the horizontal axis identifies the event (such as the realized return). Similar histograms could be constructed for investments A and B.

histogram

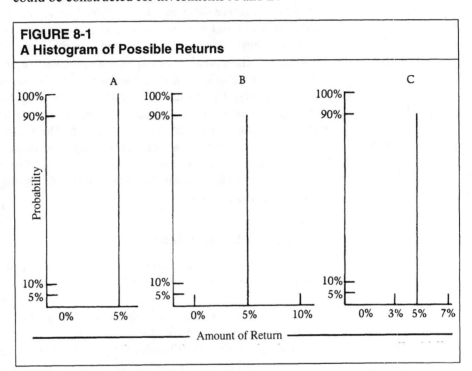

FIGURE 8-1
A Histogram of Possible Returns

RISK OF A DISTRIBUTION OF POSSIBLE RETURNS

Although determining the expected (average) value of a distribution of returns is rather straightforward, measuring its risk is more complex. B's return could vary from 0 percent to 10 percent, compared with 3 percent to 7 percent for C. Because B's range of possible returns is greater, most people would rate B as riskier. This comparison suggests that a measure of risk could be based on the difference between the maximum and minimum possible returns. Such an approach would capture at least some of the flavor of what people mean when they talk about an investment's risk. Viewed in isolation, the magnitude of the range of possible returns, however, ignores possible differences in the shape of the distribution between the two extremes. For example, imagine an investment D with a 50 percent chance of a 10 percent return and a 50 percent chance of a 0 percent return. It has the same range as investment B, yet it is clearly a riskier investment. Moreover, in the real world, many investments do not have cleanly defined minimums and maximums.

Rather than use the range of possible returns, a risk measure could be based on the deviations from the expected return. The simple average deviation from the mean is precisely zero (the negative differences exactly offset the positive differences). The absolute value of the deviation could be calculated without regard to positive or negative signs. The average of the absolute values of the deviations from the mean would measure the average distance of the actual return from the expected return. This mean absolute deviation is statistically difficult to work with, however. Thus, the deviations are generally first squared (producing nonnegative values) and then averaged. The result is called the *variance*. Statisticians have found the variance a convenient statistic to work with. The variance and its square root, the *standard deviation*, are frequently employed as descriptive statistics for a distribution of random variables. To understand how the standard deviation serves as a risk measure, we first need to explore its relationship to probability distributions.

variance

standard deviation

Probability Distributions

Histograms such as figure 8-1 relate possible discrete events to their likelihoods or frequencies. Probability distributions are used for continuous phenomena. Figure 8-2, a probability distribution, illustrates the relation between a large number of expected returns and their probabilities. The probabilities rise to a peak at return r_m and decline symmetrically thereafter. With a symmetrical distribution, the probabilities for returns equidistant from r_m are equal. The simple average of these paired returns is r_m. The weighted average of all of these averages must also be r_m.

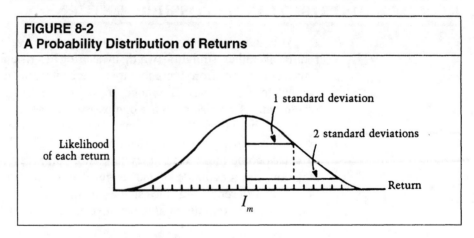

FIGURE 8-2
A Probability Distribution of Returns

Figure 8-2 also illustrates one and two standard deviations from the average. For most commonly encountered distributions, the actual value will be within one standard deviation of the mean approximately two-thirds of the time; about 95 percent of the time it will be within two standard deviations. Thus, the standard deviation of the return distribution is a useful measure of a distribution's spread. It may be used as an index of the degree of confidence (or risk) in the expected return (expected return variability).

Simple Example

mean
expected return

Suppose we had N equally likely returns denoted by R_t where time t ranges from period 1 to period N. The *mean* or *expected return* for R_t is shown in the following formula:

$$E(R) = \sum_{t=1}^{N} R_t / N \qquad \text{(Equation 8-1)}$$

Similarly, the formula for the variance is

$$\sigma^2 = \sum_{t=1}^{N} [R_t - E(R_t)]^2 / N \qquad \text{(Equation 8-2)}$$

$\sum_{t=1}^{N}$ followed by a formula such as R_t/N means "the sum of" that

formula for each value of t; $\sum_{t=1}^{N}$ means $R_1/N + R_2/N + R_3/N + \ldots R_n/N$.

The standard deviation is the square root of the variance:

$$\sigma = \sqrt{\sigma^2} = \text{standard deviation} \qquad \text{(Equation 8-3)}$$

For unequal weights, the mean and standard deviation computations are somewhat more complex. Rather than take the simple (unweighted average) of returns, a weighted average is computed as follows where $P(R_t)$ = probability of return R_t:

$$E(R) = \sum_{t=1}^{N} P(R_t) R_t \qquad \text{(Equation 8-1a)}$$

Similarly,

$$\sigma_r^2 = \sum_{t=1}^{N} P(R_t)[R_t - E(R_t)]^2 \qquad \text{(Equation 8-2a)}$$

In a simple example, we might have equal probabilities of returns of 0 percent, 4 percent, 10 percent, and 14 percent:

$$P(R_1) = P(R_2) = P(R_3) = P(R_4) = .25$$

R_1	R_2	R_3	R_4
.00	.04	.10	.14

We begin by computing the average or expected return for this set of possible returns:

$$E(R) = \left(\frac{.00 + .04 + .10 + .14}{4} \right) = \frac{.28}{4} = .07$$

Next, we form the deviations of each possible return from its expected value:

$$X_t = R_t - E(R); \quad X_1 \quad\quad X_2 \quad\quad X_3 \quad\quad X_4$$
$$(.00 - .07)\ (.04 - .07)\ (.10 - .07)\ (.14 - .07)$$
$$-.07 \quad\quad -.03 \quad\quad .03 \quad\quad .07$$

These values are then squared:

$$(X_t)^2 = [R_t - E(R)]^2; \quad X_1^2 \quad\quad X_2^2 \quad\quad X_3^2 \quad\quad X_4^2$$
$$(-.07)^2\ (-.03)^2 \quad (.03)^2 \quad (.07)^2$$
$$.0049 \quad .0009 \quad\quad .0009 \quad\quad .0049$$

The results are then totaled and averaged. (Had the probabilities not been equal, a weighted average would have been taken.) The result of this computation is the variance (σ_r^2):

$$\text{Sum} = .0049 + .0009 + .0009 + .0049 = .0116$$
$$\sigma_r^2 = \frac{.0116}{4} = .0029$$

The standard deviation is simply the square root of the variance:

$$\sigma_r = \sqrt{.0029} = .054 \text{ or } 5.4\%$$

Thus, investment R has an expected return of 7 percent and a standard deviation of 5.4 percent. This means that the best guess for R's return is 7 percent. About two-thirds of the time R should yield between 1.6 percent ($1.6\% = 7\% - 5.4\%$) and 12.4 percent ($12.4\% = 7\% + 5.4\%$). This range of possible returns is relatively large (that is, the investment is risky). For a typical distribution, the actual value will be within one standard deviation of the expected value about two-thirds of the time, within two standard deviations 95 percent of the time, and within three standard deviations 99 percent of the time.

Suppose investment Y had an expected return of 6.5 percent with a 2 percent standard deviation. About two-thirds of the time Y's investors could expect to earn between 4.5 percent and 8.5 percent (6.5% ± 2%) compared with 1.6 percent to 12.4 percent (7% ± 5.4%) for R's investors. In spite of Y's slightly lower expected yield (6.5 percent versus 7 percent), many investors might prefer Y to R. Let us now explore why.

RISK AVERSION

Most people are thought to be risk averse. As investors, they will always prefer investments with less risk when the investment's expected returns are equivalent. Therefore, when two investments offer the same expected return, risk-averse investors will choose the investment that has the lower risk. The choice becomes more difficult when the riskier asset also offers the higher expected return. The investor's attitude toward the two investments will depend on the relative differences in expected return and risk. Risk-averse investors are willing to invest in risky assets only if the incentives (higher expected return) are sufficient to offset their preference for a more certain return.

Example: Two assets (A and B) have the same expected return but different risk levels. Both investments have an expected return of 10 percent, but investment A has a 2 percent standard deviation and investment B has a 4 percent standard deviation. Thus, investment A's return is expected to be between 8 percent and 12 percent about two-thirds of the time, while investment B's is expected to be within the 6 percent to 14 percent range two-thirds of the time. The riskier asset, B, will have a higher probability of achieving a lower return (6 percent versus 8 percent) but also a higher probability of earning a higher return (14 percent versus 12 percent). The probability that its return will be near the mean expectation is correspondingly lower for the riskier asset. Mathematically, the upside potential and the downside risks offset each other. As a result, both the higher-risk and the lower-risk assets have the same expected return (10 percent). Yet, risk-averse investors will prefer the asset with the more dependable return (investment A). Risk-averse investors are, by definition, investors who prefer lower risk to higher risk when other investment characteristics are equal.

Risk-averse investors dislike the prospect of an unexpectedly low (perhaps negative) return more than they like the possibility of a favorable return of similar magnitude above the mean. For example, if the mean return is 10 percent, they view a −10 percent return (20 percent below the mean) as more undesirable than they view a return of +30 percent (20 percent above the mean) as desirable. To avoid the possibility of experiencing the pain of an unexpectedly low return, risk-averse investors prefer assets whose expected returns are more certain.

Individual investor circumstances can differ greatly from investor to investor. These different circumstances tend to affect investors' attitudes toward risk. Most, but not all, investors are risk averse. Their degree of risk aversion varies, however. Some have very good reasons for being cautious about their investments. For example, many retired couples depend upon their investments for a substantial fraction of their income. Their own budgeting decisions are relatively simple if they have a dependable source of investment income. Their finances would, in contrast, be much more difficult to plan if their investment income varied substantially from month to month.

Similarly, a younger couple saving for a down payment on a house or for their children's college education would much prefer a relatively known rate of return. This couple would have a better idea of how much they need to save if they knew how much they would earn on what they were able to save. No doubt, many other circumstances also incline investors toward risk aversion. These investors do not necessarily prefer safe, secure investments, no matter what the trade-offs, but they do prefer less risk to more for a given level of expected return. The degree of risk aversion, however, varies from investor to investor. For example, a young unmarried professional with a substantial income and some money to invest may well be less risk averse than the average investor. This individual may believe he or she is better able to absorb losses and therefore is more willing than a more typical investor to take large risks for large potential gains. Still, even this type of investor would probably prefer less risk to more risk.

Different individual investor circumstances can explain some, but by no means all, differences in investor risk aversion. A second major factor is the investor's personal preference. Some individuals are, by their very nature, risk takers. These individuals may be quite comfortable taking large risks when the expected gains are modest (compared with a lower-risk investment). They may still be risk averse but only modestly so. Other individuals may be much more cautious in their approach to risk taking. Notwithstanding their circumstances, these investors are willing to tolerate only a very low level of risk and only if the potential reward from risk taking is substantial.

Although most investors would prefer investments that contain little or no risk, most investments contain a significant degree of risk. That is, most investments offer the possibility of a wide range of outcomes (possible returns). Such (risky) investments must be priced low enough relative to their prospective payoffs to attract risk-averse investors. In practice, this means that a higher discount rate is applied to the investment's expected income streams. The market accomplishes this process as follows: In order for the market to clear—the point at which the quantity available for sale equals the quantity purchased—an equilibrium price must be established. This principle applies to investments, just as it applies to goods and services. If a particular investment with very little or no risk (for example, a Treasury bill) is priced to yield 5 percent, an otherwise similar investment with more risk (for example, a short-term corporate bond) must be priced to yield a higher expected return, such as 6 percent or 7 percent. A still riskier but otherwise similar investment would need to offer a still higher expected return, such as 8 percent or 10 percent in order to attract enough buyers for the market to clear.

Example: An investment that is expected to be worth $1,000 in 5 years could now sell for $700, $500, or $300, depending on its risk and the corresponding discount rate. At $700, the market is applying (approximately) a 7 percent discount rate; $500 corresponds to a 15 percent rate, and $300 implies a rate of 27 percent. The greater the risk, the higher the discount rate applied to the investment and the lower the current (present) value.

The riskier the investment, the higher the discount rate applied to it and, thus, the lower its market value.

Example: Suppose an investment is projected to produce an income of $1,000 a year for the foreseeable future. If this expected return is discounted at 5 percent, the investment is valued at $20,000. At a 10 percent discount rate, the value falls to $10,000, and at 20 percent its value is only $5,000.

INDIVIDUAL VERSUS PORTFOLIO RISK

As discussed earlier, the standard deviation is a useful measure of an individual investment's risk. The standard deviation of an individual asset's expected return is an inadequate risk measure, however, if the asset is part of a larger portfolio. For example, an investment with an expected return of 12 percent and a standard deviation of 3 percent will, on average, earn between 9 percent and 15 percent two-thirds of the time and between 6 percent and 18 percent 95 percent of the time—statistics that indicate the particular investment's downside risk and upside potential. The standard deviation of the individual asset's expected return does not, however, reflect the potentially important impact of diversification within a portfolio.

An investor's wealth and investment income stems from his or her entire portfolio. If poor performance by some parts of the portfolio tends to be offset by more favorable performance in the rest of the portfolio, the investor's overall wealth position may not suffer. The investor is unlikely to know ahead of time which investments will do well and which will not, but he or she will know that some investments will do better than others. The more diversified the portfolio, the more likely individual problems in the portfolio are to be offset by other components that are doing well. Accordingly, investors should concern themselves primarily with portfolio risk, rather than the risks of each of the portfolio's individual components. If the values of two investments fluctuate by offsetting amounts, the owner is no poorer or richer than if neither had varied.

The return variabilities of a portfolio's components are usually somewhat offsetting. Thus, the portfolio's overall return variability is almost always below the components' average variabilities. Moreover, different assets may contribute disproportionately to a portfolio's total risk. Risk measures of the components of a multi-asset portfolio, therefore, need to reflect how their diversification affects the entire portfolio. The following example illustrates the benefits of diversification.

Example: Imagine a sunscreen business and an umbrella business at the beach. Let's say there's a 50 percent chance that it will rain and a 50 percent chance that it will be sunny. The sunscreen business will have a 20 percent return if it is sunny but a 0 percent return if it rains. The umbrella business will have a 20 percent return if it rains but a 0 percent return if it is sunny. Each business will have an expected return of 10 percent (.5 x 20%) and a standard deviation of 10 percent. Now imagine a diversified portfolio consisting of equal weights of the sunscreen and umbrella businesses. It will still have an expected return of 10 percent, but the standard deviation is now zero since there will be a 10 percent return whether it is sunny or rainy.

As the simplified example above shows, diversification is used to create a riskless portfolio out of two risky investments. Note that risk has been eliminated without any reduction in the expected return.

TWO-ASSET PORTFOLIO RISK

The simplest type of portfolio contains a single asset, such as stock in one company. This portfolio is totally undiversified. The next simplest portfolio contains two separate assets, such as stock in two different companies. A two-asset portfolio begins to take advantage of the risk-reduction potential of diversification. First, we define the expected return of the two-asset portfolio:

$$E(R_p) = X[E(R_x)] + Y[E(R_y)] \qquad \text{(Equation 8-4)}$$

where: X = portfolio weight of asset x
   Y = portfolio weight of asset y

The risk of the portfolio depends on both the individual risk of its two components and the degree to which the two components' return variations are related. The formula for a two-asset portfolio's variance is shown in equation 8-5:

$$\sigma_p^2 = X^2\sigma_x^2 + 2XYC_{xy} + Y^2\sigma_y^2 \qquad \text{(Equation 8-5)}$$

where: X = portfolio weight of asset x
   Y = portfolio weight of asset y
   σ_x^2 = variance of asset x
   σ_y^2 = variance of asset y
   C_{xy} = covariance of asset x with y

For simplicity, the weights X and Y are restricted to the 0–1 range (ruling out short selling and borrowing). The terms $X^2\sigma_x^2$ and $Y^2\sigma_y^2$ are the squares of each component's weight multiplied by its respective variance. Recall that X and Y are the proportions of the portfolio invested in assets x and y. Therefore, both X and Y are fractions less than one. If, for example, half of the portfolio is invested in each asset, both X and Y equal 0.50. Squaring numbers less than one results in a lower number than the number being squared. For example, 0.50 squared is .25. This relationship tends to reduce the impact of the components' variances on the portfolio variance.

The remaining term, $2XYC_{xy}$, requires further explanation. The first part of the term, 2XY, is twice the product of the proportions X and Y. The key—indeed a central aspect of portfolio risk in general—is the covariance term C_{xy}. The covariance reflects the impact of portfolio diversification.

Covariance

covariance

The *covariance*, like the mean and standard deviation, is a statistic that may be estimated from past values of the relevant variables. It measures the comovement or covariability of two variables. Thus, the covariance of two assets' returns is an index of their tendency to move relative to each other. For example, the market prices of stocks of two similar companies that operate in the same industries would probably tend to move together. On the other hand, stock prices of two very different types of companies would probably tend to move largely independently of each other. The former pair of stocks would have a relatively high covariance with each other; the latter pair would have a relatively low covariance. Stocks with low covariances with each other are better diversification vehicles than those with high covariances.

To understand how the covariance statistic is defined, first consider the difference between asset x's period t return (R_{xt}) and its mean value $E(R_x)$. Because a mean value is generally located near the center of the distribution, this difference $[R_{xt} - E(R_x)]$ may be either positive or negative, and it is about equally likely to be one as it is to be the other. The same is true for the difference $[R_{yt} - E(R_y)]$. Now consider the product of the differences $[(R_{xt} - E(R_x)][R_{yt} - E(R_y)]$. When the two asset returns are either both above or both below their means together, the product is positive. The product of two positives is positive, as is the product of two negatives. The product of these two differences is negative when one deviation is above its mean and the other below. The covariance is defined as the average of the products $[R_{xt} - E(R_x)][R_{yt} - E(R_y)]$ and reflects the relatedness of the two assets' returns.

Using the original symbols of equations 8-1 and 8-2, the covariance of a two-asset portfolio is defined as

$$C_{xy} = \sum_{t=1}^{N} [R_{xt} - E(R_x)][R_{yt} - E(R_y)]/N \qquad \text{(Equation 8-6)}$$

Correlation

correlation coefficient

    An analogous statistic to the covariance, the *correlation coefficient* of x and y, denoted as ρ_{xy}, is their covariance divided by the product of their standard deviations. The divisor scales the correlation coefficient between a maximum of $+1$ and a minimum of -1. The following discussion will utilize the covariance, but it could all be recast in correlation terms with the substitution:

$$\rho_{xy} = C_{xy}/\sigma_x \sigma_y$$

    As is true of the variance, the correlation between assets x and y, ρ, is a measure of the degree to which the returns of these two assets change together. If the returns change at the same time and in the same direction, then $\rho_{xy} = 1$. If the returns change at the same time but in opposite directions, then $\rho_{xy} = -1$. If there is no relationship between the two returns, then $\rho_{xy} = 0$. Therefore, the range of possible values for ρ_{xy} is $-1 \le \rho_{xy} \le 1$. The following example illustrates the effects of correlation on two-asset portfolios.

Example: Assume that asset A has a return of 4 percent and a standard deviation of 1.5 percent. Asset B has a return of 6 percent and a standard deviation of 2 percent. Assets A and B have a correlation of 1. Also assume that asset C has the same return and standard deviation as asset B, but its correlation with asset A is -1. If an investor holds a two-asset portfolio that is composed of 50 percent of asset A and 50 percent of asset B, then the return on the portfolio is 5 percent, and the portfolio's standard deviation is 1.75 percent. However, if the two-asset portfolio is composed of 50 percent of asset A and 50 percent of asset C, the portfolio's return remains at 5 percent, but its standard deviation is now .25 percent. Therefore, the second portfolio is substantially less risky than the first. As the correlation approaches $+1$, the more correlated the returns of the two assets, the larger the portfolio standard deviation; as the correlation approaches -1, the portfolio standard deviation becomes smaller. This is a very important point in portfolio theory because this effect allows portfolios to reduce exposure to risk through diversification of portfolio assets.

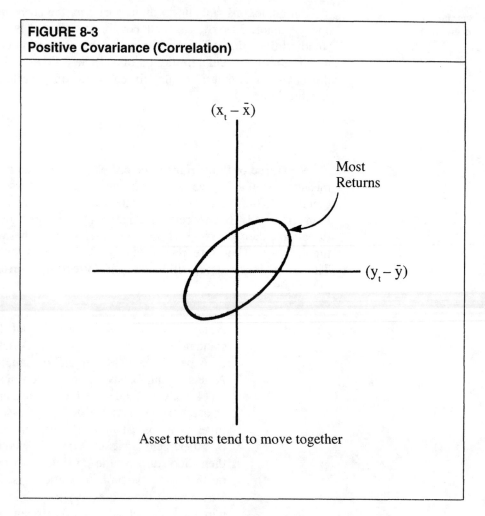

FIGURE 8-3
Positive Covariance (Correlation)

$(x_t - \bar{x})$

Most
Returns

$(y_t - \bar{y})$

Asset returns tend to move together

Figures 8-3, 8-4, and 8-5 help illustrate the meaning of the covariance. Suppose we are interested in the comovements of assets x and y. We might explore this relation by plotting $(x_t - \bar{x})$ and $(y_t - \bar{y})$ over time. Whenever investments x and y are above their averages together, we would plot the point in the upper right-hand quadrant. When they are simultaneously below their means, we will plot the point in the lower left-hand quadrant. Investments that tend to vary together will largely plot in an area concentrated in those two quadrants (figure 8-3). Most asset pairs exhibit this so-called positive covariance.

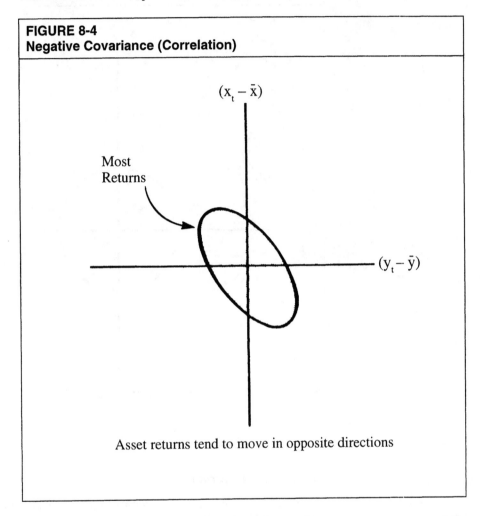

FIGURE 8-4
Negative Covariance (Correlation)

$(x_t - \bar{x})$

Most Returns

$(y_t - \bar{y})$

Asset returns tend to move in opposite directions

An investment may, however, experience above-average returns while another is below average (upper left and lower right quadrants). If the returns move in opposite directions more than they move together, the covariance will be negative (figure 8-4). Finally, if the returns move in a totally independent fashion, a zero covariance will result (figure 8-5).

Remember our earlier example of umbrellas and sunscreen. That is an example of two assets whose returns (sales) are negatively correlated. On the other hand, suppose the two assets under consideration were bread and butter. We would expect their return (or sales) to have a high positive correlation.

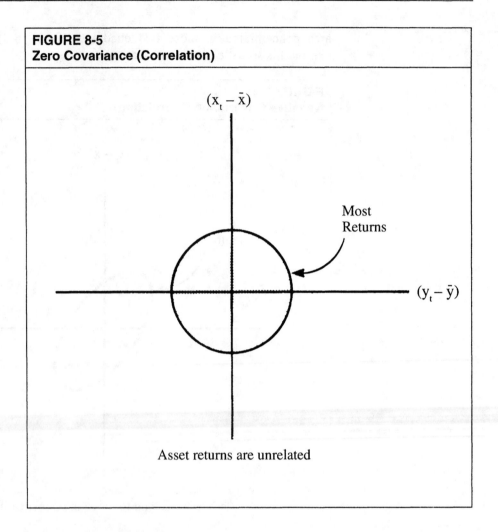

FIGURE 8-5
Zero Covariance (Correlation)

$(x_t - \bar{x})$

Most
Returns

$(y_t - \bar{y})$

Asset returns are unrelated

Computing a Covariance

To explore how a covariance of two variables is computed, suppose we have the following five observations on variables x and y:

$$
\begin{aligned}
(x_1,\ y_1) &= (1,\ 3) \\
(x_2,\ y_2) &= (2,\ 7) \\
(x_3,\ y_3) &= (3,\ 8) \\
(x_4,\ y_4) &= (4,\ 10) \\
(x_5,\ y_5) &= (5,\ 12)
\end{aligned}
$$

First, we must compute the average values for x and y:

$$\overline{X} = \left(\frac{1+2+3+4+5}{5} \right) = \frac{15}{5} = 3$$

$$\overline{Y} = \left(\frac{3+7+8+10+12}{5} \right) = \frac{40}{5} = 8$$

Next, we must compute the value for the differences $(x_t - \overline{x})$ and $(y_t - \overline{y})$ for each t value:

$(x_t - \overline{x})$			$(y_t - \overline{y})$		
$(1-3)$	=	-2	$(3-8)$	=	-5
$(2-3)$	=	-1	$(7-8)$	=	-1
$(3-3)$	=	0	$(8-8)$	=	0
$(4-3)$	=	1	$(10-8)$	=	2
$(5-3)$	=	2	$(12-8)$	=	4

Then, we must compute $(x_t - \overline{x})(y_t - \overline{y})$ for each pair of values:

$(1-3)$	$(3-8)$	=	-2	x	-5	=	10
$(2-3)$	$(7-8)$	=	-1	x	-1	=	1
$(3-3)$	$(8-8)$	=	0	x	0	=	0
$(4-3)$	$(10-8)$	=	1	x	2	=	2
$(5-3)$	$(12-8)$	=	2	x	4	=	8

Finally, we can determine the covariance by averaging these values:

$$\frac{(10+1+0+2+8)}{5} = 4.2$$

Note that in this example, the x and y values tended to move together, producing a positive covariance. The result is a relationship like that in figure 8-3.

Example of a Two-Asset Portfolio's Risk

Returning to equation 8-1, consider a simple example. Suppose x and y have standard deviations of .10 and .15 respectively, and a covariance of .01. We could form a portfolio composed half of x and half of y. If the expected returns of x and y are .09 and .11, the portfolio's expected return would be .10, an average of the component returns. This is calculated as follows: First, we multiply .5 by .09 and by .11:

$$.5 \text{ x } .09 = .045$$

$$.5 \times .11 = .055$$

Then we add the two values to determine the expected return for the portfolio:

$$
\begin{array}{r}
.045 \\
+\underline{.055} \\
.10
\end{array}
$$

We might think that the portfolio's standard deviation would also be a weighted average of .10 and .15 (.125). The formula for the variance, however, reveals a different result. Consider:

$$\sigma_p^2 = X^2\sigma_x^2 + 2XYC_{xy} + Y^2\sigma_y^2$$

$$\sigma_x = .10$$

$$\sigma_y = .15$$

$$X = .5$$

$$Y = .5$$

$$C_{xy} = .01$$

Thus, the variance is calculated as follows:

$$X^2\sigma_x^2 = (.5)^2(.10)^2 = .25(.01);$$
$$2XY\sigma_{xy} = 2(.5)(.5)(.01) = .5(.01);$$
$$Y^2\sigma_y^2 = (.5)^2(.15)^2 = .25(.0225); \text{then,}$$
$$\sigma_p^2 = .25(.01) + .5(.01) + .25(.0225), \text{or}$$
$$= .0025 + .0050 + .005625, \text{or}$$
$$\sigma_p^2 = 0.013125$$

Since the standard deviation is the square root of the variance, the portfolio's overall risk is

$$\sigma_p = \sqrt{0.01325} = .115$$

In this case, diversifying the portfolio has clearly reduced the risk below the two components' average risk. The average risk (as measured by this standard deviation of the expected return) of the two components is .125 compared with the portfolio's overall risk of .115. The next section will consider the issue in greater detail.

Two-Asset Portfolio with Equal Weights and Variances

The two-asset portfolio variance depends upon the variance of each asset and the covariance between them. As shown in equation 8-5a, if weights X and Y are equal and variance σ_x^2 and σ_y^2 are equal, equation 8-5 reduces as shown in the equation below:

$$\begin{aligned}\sigma_p^2 &= (1/2)^2\,\sigma_x^2 + 2(1/2)(1/2)C_{xy} + (1/2)^2\,\sigma_y^2 \\ &= (1/2)^2\,\sigma_x^2 + (1/2)C_{xy} + (1/2)^2\,\sigma_y^2 \qquad \text{(Equation 8-5a)} \\ &= (1/4)\left(\sigma_x^2 + 2C_{xy} + \sigma_y^2\right)\end{aligned}$$

But since $\sigma_x^2 = \sigma_y^2$ we have the following:

$$\begin{aligned}\sigma_p^2 &= (1/4)\left(2\sigma_x^2 + 2C_{xy}\right) \\ &= (1/2)\left(\sigma_x^2 + C_{xy}\right)\end{aligned}$$

Although a proof is beyond the scope of this text, in this example, C_{xy} can be no larger than $+\sigma_x^2$ and no smaller than $-\sigma_x^2$. If $C_{xy} = \sigma_x^2$, the two assets' returns x and y move in precise lockstep. Stocks of two firms planning to merge (by exchanging the stock of the target company for a prespecified amount of stock in the acquiring company) might approach this degree of relatedness. Equation 8-5b shows what happens in this extreme case:

$$\sigma_p^2 = (1/2)\left(\sigma_x^2 + \sigma_x^2\right) = \sigma_x^2 \qquad \text{(Equation 8-5b)}$$

This result implies that when the covariance of two assets in an equal weighted two-asset portfolio is at its maximum and the component variances are equal, the portfolio variance equals the component variance.

If $C_{xy} = -\sigma_x^2$ the returns of the two assets always vary inversely by precisely proportional magnitudes. Few, if any, such asset pairs exist, but otherwise equivalent (underlying stock, maturity, terms to exercise, and so on) puts and calls come close. As the underlying stock fluctuates, the puts and calls move in opposite directions.

When $C_{xy} = -\sigma_x^2$, equation 8-5a becomes

$$\sigma_p^2 = (1/2)\left(\sigma_x^2 - \sigma_x^2\right) = 0 \qquad \text{(Equation 8-5c)}$$

When the returns of two risky assets move precisely inversely, portfolio risk can be entirely eliminated by an appropriate choice of weights. A covariance that is at its minimum theoretical value is extremely rare. Indeed, even negative covariances are unusual. A covariance at or near zero (the assets' return fluctuations are unrelated), however, is more likely to be encountered. Therefore, it is an interesting special case.

$$\sigma_p^2 = (1/4)(2\sigma_x^2 + 0) = \sigma_x^2/2 \qquad \text{(Equation 8-5d)}$$

When the assets are unrelated, the portfolio's variance is equal to half of the components' variance. For this condition to occur, the portfolio must contain equal weights of each asset, and each asset must have the same standard deviation (variance). Even a zero covariance of returns is relatively uncommon, however. Most covariances are positive, reflecting the tendency of stocks to move together. Thus, a typical two-asset portfolio's covariance will lie between zero and $+ \sigma_x^2$ (its maximum possible value). As a result, the typical two-asset portfolio's variance will be between $\sigma_x^2/2$ and σ_x^2.

Examples:

Suppose $\sigma_x^2 = \sigma_y^2 = .1$ and $C_{xy} = .06$. Equation 8-5a reveals

$$\sigma_p^2 = (1/2)(\sigma_x^2 + C_{xy})$$

$$= \frac{(.1 + .06)}{2} = \frac{.16}{2} = .08$$

Now suppose $\sigma_x^2 = \sigma_y^2 = 1$ and $C_{xy} = 0$. From equation 8-5a we then have

$$\sigma_p^2 = (1/2)^2 (\sigma_x^2 + \sigma_y^2) = (1+1)/4 = .5$$

If $\sigma_x^2 = \sigma_y^2 = .1$ and $C_{xy} = -.1$, from equation 8-1c we have

$$\sigma_p^2 = (1/2)(\sigma_x^2 - \sigma_x^2) = (1/2)(.1 - .1) = 0$$

To verify these formulas, compute portfolio risk for the above examples from equation 8-5:

$$\sigma_p^2 = X^2\sigma_x^2 + 2XYC_{xy} + Y^2\sigma_y^2$$

Two-Asset Portfolio with Unequal Weights and Variances

portfolio variance

The relationships are similar to those stated when the equal weights and equal component variance assumptions are relaxed. The covariance for a given pair of assets will be some specific value. In general, however, it can range from its maximum value ($\sigma_x \sigma_y$) to its minimum value ($-\sigma_x \sigma_y$). Whenever C_{xy} is at its maximum, the *portfolio variance* equals the weighted average variance of the components. If C_{xy} is at its minimum value, an appropriate choice of weights can eliminate the portfolio's variance. If C_{xy} equals zero, the portfolio variance equals one-half the weighted average variance of the components. Figure 8-6 illustrates this relationship. Table 8-1 summarizes the various possibilities for the two-asset case.

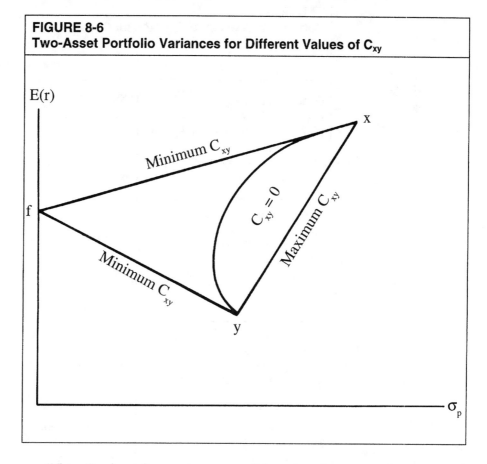

FIGURE 8-6
Two-Asset Portfolio Variances for Different Values of C_{xy}

When C_{xy} is at its maximum possible value, the expected returns and standard deviations of a portfolio of x and y will be a simple weighted average of individual expected returns and standard deviations of x and y, and no diversification benefit is derived from combining the two assets. This risk-return relationship is illustrated by a straight line from x to y. The relative proportions of x and y will determine where on line xy the portfolio lies. When C_{xy} is at its minimum possible value, the portfolio risk/expected-return levels lie on lines xf and yf. Note that $\sigma_p = 0$ at point f. That is, for the particular combination of x and y, the portfolio's risk is totally eliminated. When $C_{xy} = 0$, the portfolios of x and y lie on a curve connecting x and 7 that lies partway between the line for C_{xy} at its maximum and the line for Cxy at its minimum. Indeed, for every other value of C_{xy}, a curve between x and y represents the possible-risk/expected-return levels The closer C_{xy} is to its maximum value, the closer the curve approaches line xy.

TABLE 8-1
Portfolio Variances for Two-Asset Cases

Case	Portfolio Variance σ_p^2
General Formula	$X^2\sigma_x^2 + 2XYC_{xy} + Y^2\sigma_y^2$ (Equation 8-5)
Equal Variances and Weights General case	$\frac{1}{2}(\sigma_x^2 + C_{xy})$ (Equation 8-5a)
Perfectly related assets $\left(C_{xy} = \sigma_x^2\right)$	σ_x^2 (Equation 8-5b)

Perfectly inversely related
    assets
    $\left(C_{xy} = -\sigma_x^2\right)$
	0 (Equation 8-5c)

Unrelated assets $(C_{xy} = 0)$	$\sigma_x^2 \div 2$ (Equation 8-5d)
Normal case $\left(0 \leq C_{xy} \leq \sigma_x^2\right)$	$\sigma_x^2 \div 2 \leq \sigma_p^2 \leq \sigma_x^2$

Unequal Variances and Weights
  Perfectly related assets
    (C_{xy} at maximum level)
  Perfectly inversely related
    assets
    (C_{xy} at minimum level)
	$X\sigma_x^2 + Y\sigma_x^2$
	
	0 (possible to choose weights to make
	    variance = 0)

Unrelated Assets $C_{xy} = 0$	$\frac{1}{2}\left(X\sigma_x^2 + Y\sigma_y^2\right)$
Normal Case $0 > C_{xy} > \left(X\sigma_x^2 + Y\sigma_y^2\right)$	$\frac{1}{2}\left(X\sigma_x^2 + Y\sigma_y^2\right) \leq \sigma_p^2 \leq \left(X\sigma_x^2 + Y\sigma_y^2\right)$

(Note: This discussion oversimplifies some of these concepts. Proof and derivation of these formulas and equations are beyond the scope of this text.)

N-ASSET PORTFOLIO RISK

portfolio risk

The N-asset equivalent of equation 8-5 contains variance and covariance terms for every asset and asset pair in the portfolio. A thorough analysis of this case is beyond the scope of this book, but the logic of the matter is as follows. Think of the two-asset portfolio as a single asset. Then imagine combining it in a portfolio with another asset. For the reasons discussed above, the variance of the new portfolio should be less than the average variance of its components. By repeating this process $(N - 1)$ times, we can construct an N-asset portfolio, for any number N. Figure 8-7 illustrates the fact that risk declines as the number of portfolio components increases, and then gradually approaches the average covariance $\overline{C}$ of the components.

For randomly selected stocks, a large portfolio will have about two-thirds to one-half of the risk of a typical one-stock portfolio. Once the diversified portfolio's risk is reduced to this level, it cannot be reduced much further by

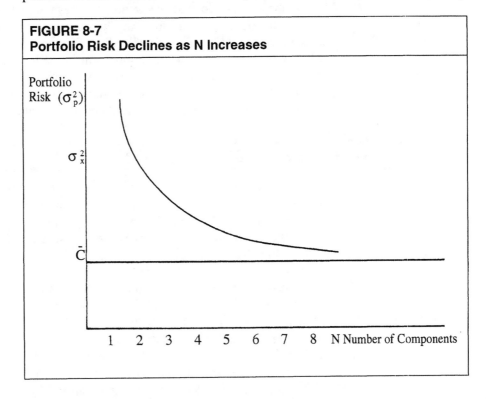

FIGURE 8-7
Portfolio Risk Declines as N Increases

adding still more stocks. As discussed more fully in the next chapter, a relatively small number of stocks (about 20) is sufficient to obtain most of the risk-reduction potential of diversification.

Estimating Variances and Covariances

Covariance and variance statistics can be estimated from past (historical) data. That is, a data series for the past returns of a group of investments can be used to compute variance and covariance estimates. When possible, however, these estimates should also utilize future-oriented information. For example, the stock of a firm whose future environment is expected to be similar to its past is likely to behave much as its historically estimated variance and covariance statistics imply. On the other hand, some firms have recently experienced a major change, such as a merger, new product introduction, changed regulatory environment, or large capital infusion. These firms are more likely to behave differently from their history than firms that have not had major changes. If the change has tended to increase risk, historically based risk measures should be adjusted upward. For example, when AT&T divested itself of its telephone operating companies, it lost a major and dependable source of revenue. The company became appreciably riskier as a result. Any computations based on predivestiture-returns data would have been misleading. Similarly, a change that decreased risk should lead to a downward adjustment in the historically based measure. In general, new companies tend to be riskier than seasoned firms. Therefore, all other things being equal, it is reasonable to expect that a firm's stream of earnings will become less volatile as its business matures.

SIMPLIFYING PORTFOLIO RISK DETERMINATION

We could estimate a portfolio's risk by applying all the relevant weights, variances, and covariances to the N-asset equivalent of equation 8-1. We could assess possible composition shifts by reapplying the formula. Mutual funds and other institutional investors—those best situated to utilize the methodology—rarely evaluate portfolio risk in this way, however. First, the required amount of data [N variances and $N(N - 1)/2$ covariances] grows exponentially with N. Most institutional investors consider investing in large sets of securities. For example, a 100-asset portfolio would require estimation of $100(100 - 1)/2 = 4950$ covariances plus 100 variances plus 100 means—a total of some 5150 parameters. Thus, making and continually updating the required estimates for such large portfolios would be costly and time consuming. Second, like earnings forecasts, historically based variance and covariance estimates are rather unreliable. Moreover, adjusting them to reflect future-oriented information is an uncertain process at best. Third, several simplified approaches give risk estimates that are about as reliable as those of equation 8-5, particularly for a large N.

Using the full form of the portfolio risk equation to assess a portfolio's risk is a relatively difficult task. A portfolio with many components requires as many variance estimates as it has components, as well as many times that many covariance estimates. For a large N, the incremental impacts of the component variances on σ_p^2 are usually small enough to ignore. The covariance of the component, in contrast, cannot be ignored. Indeed, a very large number of covariances need to be estimated. The covariances largely determine the portfolio risk of a large well-diversified portfolio, and the number of covariances grows geometrically with the number of portfolio components, N. The complete equation requires estimating the covariability of each component return with every other component return. Fortunately, other approaches for estimating the portfolio risk simplify the process.

We could, for example, restrict the analysis to the covariability of each component's return with the market as a whole. This approach might be acceptable if the influence of the overall market is the primary source of return covariability and other sources of return variability are largely random (and therefore diversifiable). Generalizable factors (business cycles, interest rates, energy availability, inflation, or threat of war, for example) do tend to affect the market and most firms similarly. Moreover, the impact of these factors on the market and the firms making it up is systematic (nonrandom). Thus, these influences cannot be diversified away. Random firm-specific and industry-specific influences, in contrast (strikes, weather impacts, or competitor moves, for example), will largely offset each other in a portfolio made up of many different assets, if the firms included in the portfolio are diversified with respect to industry, size, geographical location, and other firm-specific characteristics that may lead to a high covariance of returns.

Estimating Market Covariability: Betas

All methods for portfolio risk assessment depend on the estimated relatedness of the component returns. Decomposing return variability of individual assets into two categories of relatedness greatly simplifies the analysis of portfolio risk: that associated with the general market and that not associated with the general market. To observe an individual security's degree of market relatedness, we may plot its returns S_{it} relative to the market M_t (figure 8-8).

Most securities experience positive returns when the market rises and negative returns when it falls (positive covariance with the market). A line centered through the data would illustrate the average tendency of the security to move with the market (figure 8-9). The slope of that line, called

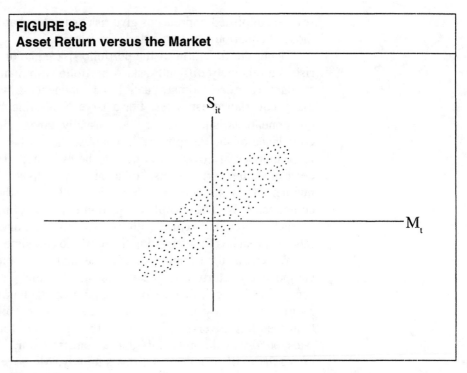

FIGURE 8-8
Asset Return versus the Market

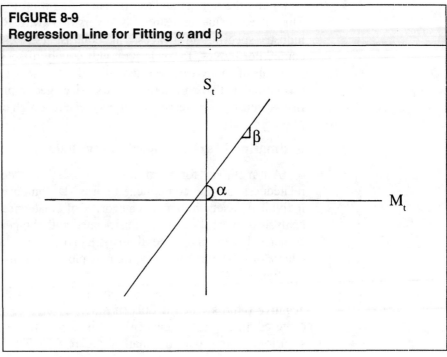

FIGURE 8-9
Regression Line for Fitting α and β

beta

the *beta*, measures the degree of proportionality between movements of the security's returns and those of the market. An asset with returns that tend to be proportional to the market will have a beta close to unity. A beta greater than 1 indicates that the asset's returns tend to exceed the market's when the market's return is positive and tend to be lower when the market's return is negative. Similarly, a beta between 0 and 1 implies that the asset's returns tend to fluctuate proportionately less than the market. Negative betas reflect a tendency for the asset's returns to move inversely with the market. Table 8-2 summarizes these probabilities.

TABLE 8-2
Expected Asset Returns for Different Betas and Market Returns

Range	Expected Asset Return for Positive Market Return	Expected Asset Return for Negative Market Return
$\beta \geq\, = 1$	Above market	Below market
$\beta = 1$	Market	Market
$0 < \beta < 1$	Below market	Above market
$\beta < 0$	Negative	Positive

Estimating the Market Model for Stocks

A beta may be estimated for any investment type. Most applications, however, have been to stocks. If future relationships are like the past—an assumption that will be discussed in later chapters—a given stock's beta may appropriately be estimated from past data (daily, weekly, or monthly stock and market index returns). The following type of equation is often used in the estimation:

$$S_t = \alpha + \beta M_t + e_t \qquad \text{(Equation 8-8)}$$

where: S_t = percentage return of stock for period t
M_t = percentage return of market for period t
β = beta coefficient or slope (to be estimated)
α = intercept (to be estimated)
e_t = random error term (to be minimized in estimation process)

market model
characteristic line

The generalized form of equation 8-8 is called the *market model*. Each stock's own specific equation is called its *characteristic line*. Separate alphas and betas can be estimated for each relevant stock. The resulting alpha forecasts the stock's return for a zero percent market return (that is, independent of market return). Its beta estimate reflects the tendency of the stock's returns to vary with the market.

least squares regression analysis

A statistical estimation technique called *least squares regression analysis* is used to determine alpha and beta estimates. The regression of equation 8-8 is illustrated graphically by a straight line through a scatter diagram of S_{it} and associated M_t values (figure 8-9). The regression line estimated by ordinary least squares minimizes the squares of the distance of S_{it}, M_t to the regression line. The line's alpha is its intercept, and beta is its slope coefficient.

The formula for beta is

$$\beta = \text{Cov}(S,M)/\sigma_M^2 \qquad \text{(Equation 8-8a)}$$

Then the formula for alpha is

$$\alpha = \overline{S} - \beta\overline{M} \qquad \text{(Equation 8-8b)}$$

where: $\overline{S}$ and $\overline{M}$ are the mean (average) returns for stock S and market M

Capital Asset Pricing Model

capital asset pricing model

Based on the availability of an estimated β for any given security, an alternative formulation of the security return/market return relationship called the *capital asset pricing model* (CAPM) is often used in more advanced security market work. The CAPM specifies a more specific relationship between security and market returns. Rather than allowing the intercept to take on an estimated value (the α), the risk-free return R_{ft} is brought explicitly into the model as the intercept:

$$S_t = R_{ft} + \beta(M_t - R_{ft}) + e_t \qquad \text{(Equation 8-9)}$$

Therefore, the CAPM intercept equals the risk-free return, and the market return variable $(M_t - R_{ft})$ is measured in deviations from the risk-free rate. Since the expected value of e_t is zero,

$$E(S_t) = R_{ft} + \beta(M_t - R_{ft}) \qquad \text{(Equation 8-9a)}$$

The CAPM model yields some interesting results. If the market return is 0, the stock's expected return becomes $R_{ft} - \beta R_{ft}$. In this circumstance, if $\beta = 1$, the stock's expected return is also 0 ($R_{ft} - \beta R_{ft} = R_{ft} - R_{ft} = 0$). Thus, when the market return is 0, a stock with a β of 1 (the market's β) will also be expected to have a 0 return. More generally, if $\beta = 1$, the stock's expected return will equal the market return:

$$E(S_t) = R_{ft} + \beta(M_t - R_{ft}) = R_{ft} + 1(M_t - R_{ft}) = R_{ft} + M_t - R_{ft} = M_t$$

A stock with the same beta as the market will therefore have the same expected return as the market. This relationship is probably consistent with what most people would expect.

Although the market model and CAPM are conceptually similar, they do have some significant differences. CAPM may be derived precisely from theoretical specifications. The market model includes the CAPM as a special case where $\alpha = (1 - \beta)R_{ft}$. The market model is more general than the CAPM. Accordingly, we shall use the market model exclusively. (The discussion could be recast in CAPM terms, however.)

Market versus Nonmarket Risk

Most investors hold stocks and other investment assets in a portfolio that contains a number of different components. Thus, the risk of their investments depends on the joint impacts of their holdings. Return fluctuations peculiar to one security tend to be offset by unrelated return fluctuations of other securities. As a result, the nonmarket component of most assets' risks can be largely eliminated through diversification. About two-thirds of a typical stock's risk stems from nonmarket sources. That

market risk

leaves about one-third due to *market risk*. These market-related return fluctuations cannot be diversified away by simply increasing the size of the portfolio. Dealing with this residual risk requires a more complex approach than simple diversification.

nonmarket risk

Because a well-diversified portfolio contains little or no *nonmarket risk*, analysis of its remaining risk focuses on its market risk or beta. A portfolio's beta equals the components' weighted average betas. Thus, the only way to reduce a portfolio's beta is to reduce its components' average beta. Moreover, the expected returns of individual assets tend to vary directly with betas. Therefore, reducing a portfolio's beta tends to sacrifice its potential return.

Four Approaches to Portfolio Risk Estimation

Now that we have introduced the simplification that the market model facilitates, we can discuss four specific approaches to estimating portfolio risk. The first effort to deal systematically with a portfolio's risk was introduced in Harry Markowitz's classic 1952 article in which he proposed estimating a portfolio's risk from an extensive analysis of each component

Markowitz model

asset. The *Markowitz model* requires estimating a mean return and variance for every asset in the portfolio, as well as estimating a covariance for every pair of assets.[1] Many estimates are required even for a relatively small portfolio. Each possible two-security combination in a 100-stock choice set would require 4,950 unique covariance estimates. Indeed, a 1,000-stock universe (a factor of 10 larger) would call for $N(N-1)/2$ or 499,500 (or a factor of 100 more) separate covariance estimates. Estimating thousands of such parameters is time consuming, expensive, and likely to produce unreliable inputs. Fortunately, a number of techniques that require less information and effort have been developed.

single-index model

W. Sharpe's 1963 *single-index model*[2] (a particular version of which is mentioned above) is much simpler to apply than the full Markowitz model. Each portfolio asset's estimated alpha, beta, and corresponding characteristic line's goodness-of-fit (or R^2) are used to analyze each relevant portfolio's risk. For a 100-stock universe, the Markowitz model requires more than 5,000 estimates, counting covariances as well as means and variances, whereas Sharpe's model needs only 300. Furthermore, the Sharpe model requires only conditional forecasts (the model implies different return forecasts for each possible market return). These forecasts tend to be easier to construct and may well be more meaningful than the absolute forecasts needed for the full covariance model.

multi-index model

The *multi-index model*'s complexity lies between that of the single-index Sharpe model and the full variance-covariance Markowitz model. This model uses separate indexes for estimating the alphas and betas of related assets, such as stocks in the same industry. Then a covariance matrix between the indexes is formed and used in the portfolio risk computation. A more sophisticated form of the multi-index model—called the Arbitrage Pricing Theory (APT)—will be introduced in the following chapter.

Finally, Sharpe's linear model (1967), the simplest of the four approaches, requires only alpha and beta estimates.[3] If each security represents only a small proportion of the portfolio (less than 5 percent, for example), the linear model is a close approximation to the single-index model. Table 8-3 summarizes the four approaches.

TABLE 8-3
Approaches to Portfolio-Risk Estimation

Model	Requirements
Markowitz's full model	Utilizes full complement of estimated returns, variances and covariances for each component
Sharpe's single-index model	Requires only α, β, and R^2 for each component
Multi-index model	Uses separate indexes for groups of stocks to estimate their α and β values
Sharpe's linear model	Requires only α and β for each component

Price Impact of Market and Nonmarket Risk

Note that the linear model computes portfolio risks with only component alphas and betas. After an estimation of the characteristic lines, the alphas should have average values close to zero and therefore not affect the portfolio's return. As a result, security alphas should have no impact on portfolio risk and thus can be largely ignored in portfolio work. Moreover, nonmarket risk, which is fully diversifiable, should be irrelevant to investors who can diversify effectively. Accordingly, a well-diversified portfolio's risk should depend exclusively on its component's market risks (betas). Furthermore, the trading activities of well-diversified investors (those institutional and other large investors who make up a substantial fraction of the market) may well largely determine market prices. If separating risk into market and nonmarket components and then ignoring the nonmarket portion is justified, an asset's risk would be fully reflected in its beta. Thus, the risk premium contained in market discount rates should be based only on market risk (beta). In other words, nonmarket risk should not affect asset prices in well-diversified portfolios.

CHOOSING AN EFFICIENT PORTFOLIO

A brief summary of the chapter so far is as follows:

- A security's total risk can be defined as the standard deviation (or variance) of its expected income stream.
- Total risk can be decomposed into market and nonmarket components.
- Beta may be used to measure market risk.
- A diversified portfolio's risk is largely a function of its component's beta.
- If most market participants can diversify effectively, nonmarket risk should not have an impact on an asset's risk premium.

In light of these findings, how should an investor go about assembling a portfolio? Assume that portfolios may be assembled from a group of risky securities, that short selling and borrowing are not allowed, and that risks and expected returns (for any given market return) may be estimated from historical data. How should these data be used to assemble the most attractive portfolio? In principle, the expected returns and risks could be plotted for every possible combination of securities. Because the number of possible portfolio combinations is infinite, an efficient search requires some shortcuts.

Market Portfolio

market portfolio

The so-called *market portfolio* offers a useful starting point. The market portfolio includes each asset class in the relevant universe of possible investments. Each component is weighted in proportion to its share of the value of that universe. For example, the relevant investment universe might be divided as follows: real estate, 40 percent; stocks, 25 percent; bonds, 15 percent; and other, 20 percent. The market portfolio would then represent each asset class in these proportions. Moreover, within each class, the proportions assignable to each specific asset would be so allocated.

The market portfolio is the appropriate index to apply to the market model. As such, it has a beta of exact unity. Moreover, the market portfolio is fully diversified and, as such, contains no nonmarket risk. Finally, if securities have been accurately priced relative to their expected performances, the market portfolio will be efficient in the sense that all other portfolios will offer either a lower expected return, a higher risk, or both. Figure 8-10 illustrates an efficient market portfolio's risk and return. Portfolio M, the market portfolio, has a beta of 1 and an expected return of m. All portfolios with lower betas also have lower expected returns; all portfolios with higher expected returns also have higher betas.

FIGURE 8-10
An Efficient Market Portfolio

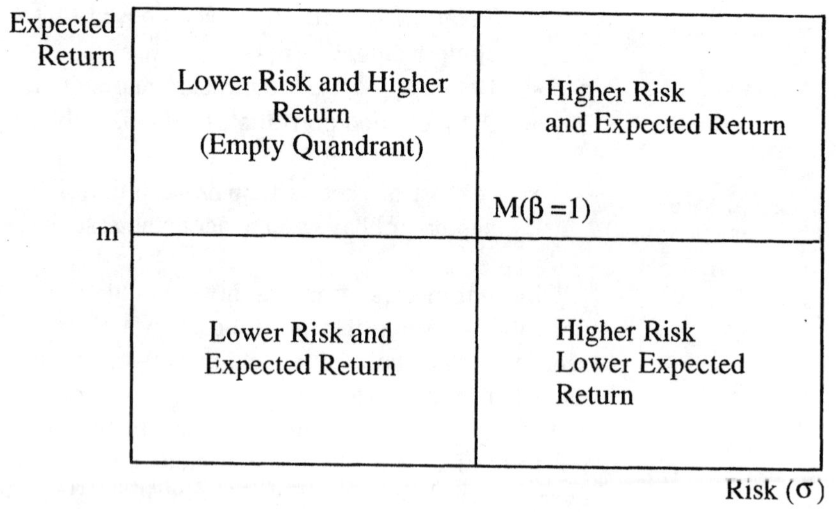

Efficient Frontier

efficient frontier

A given universe of assets contains many portfolios that are efficient. That is, a large number of different portfolios may be constructed to offer the highest expected return for their particular level of risk. Mathematical procedures can identify all the efficient portfolios from any given set of assets. Figure 8-11 illustrates a set of efficient portfolios. Plotting each of these efficient portfolios creates a relationship called the *efficient frontier*. All efficient portfolios lie on the efficient frontier. For any given risk, no higher return can be achieved from any other feasible portfolio. Similarly, for any given return, no lower risk can be achieved for any other feasible portfolio. All other feasible portfolios are inefficient. A portfolio is inefficient if a more attractive risk/expected-return trade-off is available at the frontier. The concave shape of the efficient frontier indicates that increasing risk increments must be sacrificed to gain additional expected return increments.

FIGURE 8-11
The Efficient Frontier (No Lending or Borrowing)

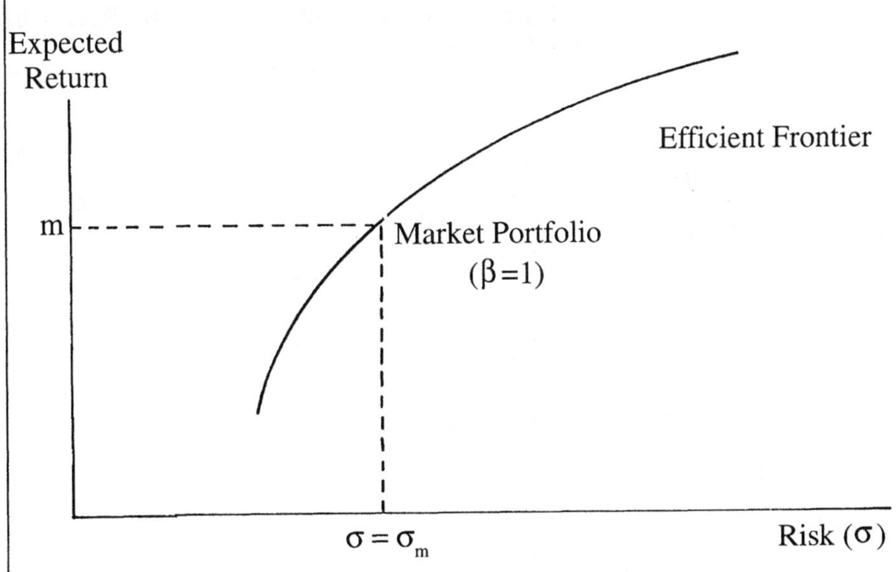

risk-return trade-off   *Choosing the Most Attractive Risk-Return Trade-off*

Each efficient portfolio offers the highest expected return for its risk level. Rational risk-averse investors might, depending on their degrees of risk aversion, legitimately choose any efficient portfolio. A very risk-averse investor would opt for a low risk point/low return, while a less risk-averse investor would accept greater risk to achieve a higher expected return. The rational investor would choose a portfolio whose risk/expected return trade-off equals his or her own willingness to trade off expected return for risk (the investor's risk tolerance).

risk-free (interest) rate   *Efficient Frontier with Lending at the Risk-Free (Interest) Rate*

So far we have assumed that investors assemble portfolios by purchasing risky securities. Additional trading options such as using leverage, selling short, and purchasing a risk-free asset have not been addressed. If one or more of these options is used, the efficient frontier takes on a different shape. The effect of lending risklessly (for example, investing in a riskless asset such as inflation-protected government bonds) is illustrated in figure 8-12.

FIGURE 8-12
The Efficient Frontier with Lending and Borrowing at the Risk-Free Rate

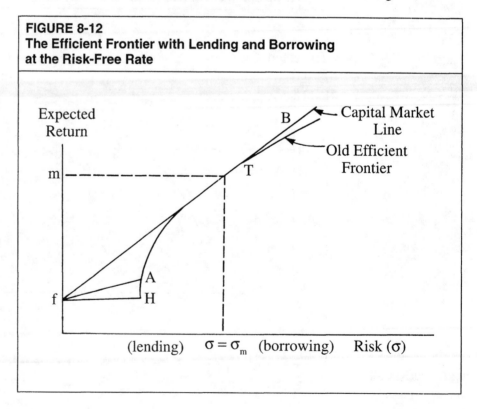

Asset F yields a riskless (or risk-free) return f that is below the expected market return m. A horizontal line from f to the efficient frontier (fH) contains all portfolios that offer an equal expected return and higher risk than F. Clearly, fH is superior to all portfolios below it. Still more attractive risk-return trade-offs are possible with asset F, however. By definition, risk-free return f has a zero covariance with all other risky returns. Thus, the risk of a portfolio containing F equals the weighted average risk of the risky components and F's own zero-risk component. Similarly, the portfolio's expected return equals the weighted average of the expected returns of the risky and riskless components. In fact, the most efficient risk and expected return combinations of any portfolio that combines F with risky portfolios lie on a straight line between the two portfolios (fT) that is tangent to the efficient frontier of all risky, feasible portfolios. (A derivation of these relationships can be found in more advanced textbooks.) Only combinations of F and efficient portfolios (on the old efficient frontier) should be considered. Moreover, a line from f to the tangency point on the efficient frontier can be found by rotating a ray beginning at f. The risk/expected-return combinations along that ray from f to the tangency point T are superior to those of any rays or combinations below it. Moreover, because fT is tangent to the efficient frontier, no ray (beginning at f) above fT intersects the efficient frontier.

Efficient Frontier with Borrowing at the Risk-free Rate

Suppose we could borrow at rate f (for example, margin borrowing at the riskless rate) to invest in some efficient portfolio G. In effect, asset F would be sold short and the proceeds invested in G. How does allowing borrowing or short selling affect the efficient frontier? Clearly, the additional funds should be invested only in otherwise efficient portfolios. As with the case permitting riskless lending, the risks and expected returns of the leveraged portfolio (portfolio with borrowing) equal a linear combination of the risks and expected returns of its components. With borrowing or short selling, however, the weight on the risky component is greater than unity, whereas the riskless component's weight is negative. In fact, financing additional investments (at rate f) in a risky portfolio simply extends the line of risk-expected return combinations of F and the risky portfolio. Again, an infinite number of lines begin at f and pass through the efficient frontier. The one passing through the tangency point (fTB) reflects the most attractive available set of risk/expected-return combinations. Accordingly, the efficient frontier, when both lending and borrowing are possible at the riskless rate, is formed by drawing a line from point f through the tangency point T on what would have been the efficient frontier had lending and borrowing not been allowed.

Borrowing at the risk-free rate is, of course, an oversimplification of real life. Although it is possible to buy stock on margin, an individual investor will have to pay an interest rate higher than the risk-free rate. This is because there is (from the perspective of the lending institution) some small risk of default and also because the lending institution needs to recover its transaction cost. However, the underlying principle is valid. There are ways that investors can increase their expected returns, if they are willing to accept more risk. One way is to buy on margin. Another way is to purchase a portfolio of high-risk (high-beta) securities, such as a portfolio of small capitalization growth companies. A third way is to purchase options, which will be discussed later in this text.

Capital Market Line

capital market line

When all marketable assets are considered part of the choice set, the relationship (fTB) is called the *capital market line*. For the assumptions used to derive it, the capital market line identifies the market's optimal risk/expected-return combinations. Thus, the individual should invest in the tangency portfolio and F in the proportions (either positively or negatively) that produce the desired risk/expected-return trade-off. Investors will maximize their expected returns by leveraging (lending or borrowing at the risk-free rate) the tangency portfolio to the desired risk level. They should, regardless of their risk preferences, hold risky assets in the proportions of the tangency portfolio. Only if the weights are the same as those of the market portfolio will the market clear (the quantity demanded will precisely equal the quantity available). Indeed, asset prices would adjust so that investors would hold assets in proportion to their relative market values. If, for example, investors wished to hold too much (relative to supply) of some assets and too little of others, the prices of the former would be bid up and the latter bid down. This process would continue until the prices reached the level at which the market would clear. Indeed, market prices generally adjust up or down to bring supply and demand into balance. Therefore, the market portfolio is the only sustainable tangency portfolio consistent with the stated assumptions.

The portfolio return at any point along the line fTB is defined as follows:

$$E(R_p) = W_f f + (1 - W_f) E(R_m)$$

where: $E(R_p)$ = expected return on portfolio
W_f = percentage of portfolio invested in risk-free asset
(negative if investor is a borrower)
f = risk-free return (the price of forgone consumption)
$E(R_m)$ = expected return of market

Suppose that

σ_p = standard deviation of the portfolio, including borrowing or lending

σ_m = standard deviation of the market

Then, the equation for the capital market line (the straight line emanating from f on the vertical axis) is

$$E(R_p) = f + \sigma_p[E(R_m) - f]/\sigma_m \qquad \text{(Equation 8-10)}$$

where: $[E(R_m) - f]/\sigma_m$ is the slope of the CML and may be interpreted as the market price for risk

Note that

$$\sigma_p = [W_f\sigma_f + (1 - W_f)\sigma_m]$$

$$= (1 - W_f)\sigma_m$$

because by definition $\sigma_f = 0$. Thus, the expected return can be rewritten:

$$E(R_p) = f + (1 - W_f)[E(R_m) - f]$$

The type of theoretical analysis presented above allows us to hypothesize a situation in which the investment decision is separate from the financing decision. Investors are assumed to invest in the market portfolio that represents the most rational mix of risky assets (the investment decision) and to choose their desired risk level by leveraging that portfolio (lending or borrowing at the risk-free rate) to the desired risk/expected-return level (the financing decision). Particularly risk-averse investors will choose risk-return trade-offs that lie on the lower portion of the capital market line. More risk-tolerant investors will choose a financing level that offers a higher expected return coupled with a higher risk. This division of the investment and **separation theorem** financing decision is called the *separation theorem*.

In theory, the separation theorem or two-mutual-fund theorem implies that investors can achieve optimal efficient diversification with just two assets. Therefore, in a practical application, an investor who can buy into a governments-only fund (money market mutual fund that buys only T-bills) and a well-diversified common stock mutual fund (including the right to buy on margin) can construct a series of risk/expected-return-efficient portfolios from varying combinations of these two assets. In theory, any risk/expected-return combination on the efficient frontier can be reached with these two assets. Moreover, since the two assets already allow the investor to reach the efficient frontier, no other portfolio (even one constructed from a larger number of securities) can produce a more attractive risk/expected-return trade-off.

Security Market Line

security market line

The *security market line* (SML) extends our analysis to the pricing of individual assets as distinct from the overall capital market. If individual assets are priced efficiently, their expected returns should be linearly related to their market risk or beta (figure 8-13). Because the expected return for a zero-beta asset is the risk-free rate, the equation of the security market line may be expressed as follows:

$$E(R_i) = f + \beta_i [E(R_m) - f] \qquad \text{(Equation 8-11)}$$

where: β_i = β of asset i
$E(R_i)$ = expected return of asset i
f = risk-free return
$E(R_m)$ = expected return of market

Notice that this is mathematically equivalent to equation 8-9a for the CAPM.

Determining the Expected Rate of Return Using the Security Market Line

The security market line provides a convenient formula for determining the expected return for any risky asset. To do so, we need to know the risky asset's data, as well as the risk-free rate and the market portfolio's return.

Example: If beta $\beta = 1.3$; $f = 5.0\%$, and $E(R_m) = 10.0\%$, applying the SML formula yields

$$E(R_i) = 5.0\% + 1.3(10.0\% - 5.0\%)$$
$$= 5.0\% + 1.3(5.0\%)$$
$$= 5.0\% + 6.5\%$$
$$= 11.5\%$$

Thus, a stock with a beta of 1.3 would be expected to return 11.5 percent when the risk-free ratio is 5 percent and the market portfolio's return is expected to be 10 percent.

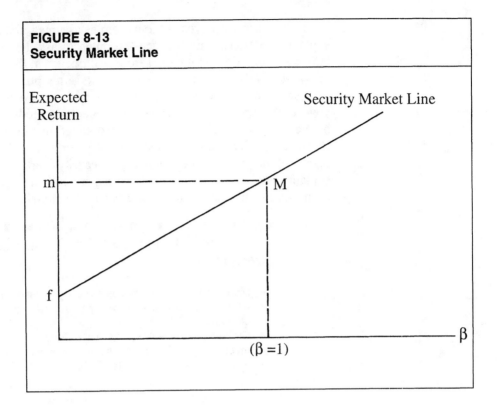

FIGURE 8-13
Security Market Line

Assumptions

To review, the assumptions that were used to derive the capital market and security market line relationships are as follows:

- Market-equivalent portfolios may be assembled, bought, and sold as easily as any other investment asset. That is, all investment assets are available in very small units; transaction costs (commissions, bid-ask spreads) can be ignored; no individual investor or group of investors can appreciably affect market prices; no institutional or psychological barriers retard the free flow of investable funds.
- Investors are rational risk averters who want to maximize their expected return and minimize its standard deviation. Moreover, they are unconcerned with any other properties of expected returns.
- Differential tax treatments are, in the aggregate, irrelevant to investment decisions.
- Investors have access to the same body of public information and analyze it in identical fashions so that they have equivalent asset return expectations.
- Investors may borrow and lend without limit at the riskless rate.

If the market behaves at the margin as assumed, the model will precisely explain its actions. This is much too much to ask, however. All models are built on assumptions that depart from reality even at the margin. The best test of a model's value is not the realism of its assumptions but the reliability of its predictions. A model whose assumptions are severely violated may still yield useful predictions. For example, Kepler's model of planetary motion heroically assumes all masses are concentrated in a single point and that the universe is frictionless. Nonetheless, Kepler's model accurately explains planetary motions. In like manner, the security market line might accurately explain asset prices in spite of its unrealistic assumptions. Thus, we need to examine the empirical evidence relating to the model's predictions.

Assumptions Used to Derive Capital and Security Market Lines

- Market equivalent portfolios are easy to assemble.
- Investors seek to maximize expected return and minimize its standard deviation.
- Differential tax treatments are irrelevant.
- Investors have identical asset return expectations.
- Investors may borrow or lend all they want at the riskless rate.

SUMMARY AND CONCLUSIONS

The modern portfolio theory discussed in this chapter yields a number of interesting conclusions: An asset's total risk may be defined as the standard deviation of its expected return distribution. Portfolio risk depends crucially on the covariance (covariability between component returns). The market model offers a simplified way of analyzing portfolio risk and expected return. This model assumes that market risk (return variability associated with that of the market portfolio) justifies a risk premium, whereas nonmarket risk (return variability unrelated to market return variability) is fully diversifiable and therefore irrelevant to asset pricing. The efficient frontier of portfolios each offer the highest expected return for a given risk level. When borrowing and lending at the risk-free rate are allowed, the efficient frontier becomes a straight line. This line stretches from the point of the risk-free rate on the vertical axis through the tangency position at the market portfolio and beyond. This capital market line implies that investors should obtain the highest risk/adjusted-expected-return for their risk preferences by leveraging the market portfolio to the desired risk/expected-return level. The security market line implies that expected asset returns are a linear function of β. The real world should behave as the model implies if at the margin investors act according to the assumptions used to develop this framework. Thus, it is not really necessary that all investors think alike. Some may overestimate a security's expected return, while others may underestimate it. As long as expectations in the aggregate are correct (unbiased expectations), we can expect securities to be accurately priced.

CHAPTER REVIEW

Answers to the review questions and the self-test questions start on page 757.

Key Terms

risk averse	capital asset pricing model
histogram	market risk
variance	nonmarket risk
standard deviation	Markowitz model
mean	single-index model
expected return	multi-index model
covariance	market portfolio
correlation coefficient	efficient frontier
portfolio variance	risk-return trade-off
portfolio risk	risk-free (interest) rate
beta	capital market line
market model	separation theorem
characteristic line	security market line
least squares regression analysis	

Review Questions

8-1.   Contrast the common concept of risk with the definition introduced in this chapter.

8-2.   Compute the expected return and standard deviation for the following:
   a.   equally probable returns of –5%, 0%, 5%, 10%
   b.   10% chance of a 0% return
         15% chance of a 5% return
         25% chance of a 10% return
         25% chance of a 15% return
         15% chance of a 20% return
         10% chance of a 25% return
   c.   100% chance of a 10% return

8-3.   a.   State and explain the formula for two-asset portfolio risk.
      b.   How does the covariance enter into the picture?
      c.   What role do the individual weights play?
      d.   When is risk zero, and when is it at a maximum?
      e.   How does the formula change as the number of assets is increased?

8-4.   Compute the covariance estimate for the following observations (assume equal probabilities):

$(X1, Y1) = (.03, .05)$
$(X2, Y2) = (.05, .03)$
$(X3, Y3) = (-.01, -.05)$
$(X4, Y4) = (.10, .08)$
$(X5, Y5) = (0, 0)$
$(X6, Y6) = (.01, -.01)$

8-5.   Compute the portfolio variance for the following:
      a. $X = Y = .5$
$$\sigma_x^2 = \sigma_y^2 = .05$$
$$C_{xy} = 0$$
      b. $X = .3, Y = .7$
$$\sigma_x^2 = .03, \sigma_y^2 = .05$$
$$C_{xy} = .8$$
      c. $X = .1, Y = .9$
$$\sigma_x^2 = .08, \sigma_y^2 = .06$$
$$C_{xy} = -.05$$

8-6.   Discuss the three simplifications for estimating portfolio risk.

8-7.   For three separate stocks having alphas and betas of .01, .7; .05, 1.1; and –.02, 1.5, respectively, compute their expected returns for market returns of .05, .10, .15, –.05, and –.10.

8-8.   Define alpha and beta, and discuss their utility in portfolio management.

8-9.   Explain and compare the market model and capital asset pricing model.

8-10.   a.   Define market and nonmarket risk.
       b.   How are the two types of risk related to diversification?

8-11.   a.   Define the efficient frontier, first without borrowing or lending allowed and then with both allowed at the risk-free rate.
       b.   What does the efficient frontier look like with riskless lending only (no borrowing)?
       c.   What happens if the two rates differ?

8-12. For efficient portfolios (100 percent invested in the market portfolio) with risk-free rates and market rates of .07 and .14; .09 and .16; and .05 and .1 respectively; what would be the expected returns with betas of .7, 1.0, 1.3, and 1.6?

Self-Test Questions

T   F   8-1. The realized return from an investment is subject to uncertainties that may or may not occur.

T   F   8-2. The realized return received by an investor is, by itself, the appropriate measure to assess and compare the performance of several investments.

T   F   8-3. Risk can be defined as the chance that the actual outcome from an investment will be less than the expected outcome.

T   F   8-4. The standard deviation is a measure of an asset's riskiness.

T   F   8-5. The riskiness of a portfolio is greater than the riskiness of the securities it contains.

T   F   8-6. A portfolio's return is the average of the returns of the assets included therein.

T   F   8-7. A correlation coefficient of −1 between two assets would result in an increased variability of the portfolio's return.

T   F   8-8. Market risk is the risk caused by factors independent of a given security or property investment.

T   F   8-9. The total risk of an investment is the sum of the general (market) risk and the specific (nonmarket) risk.

T   F   8-10. If investors are to hold only risky assets, they would hold a portfolio of assets that lies only on the efficient frontier line.

T   F   8-11. The introduction of risk-free assets enables every investor to choose the same risky portfolio.

T   F   8-12. Any portfolio on the capital market line is an undiversified portfolio.

T   F   8-13. If the beta of a stock is 1.1, the risk-free rate is 4 percent, and the return on the market is 10 percent, then according to the security market line model, the expected rate of return for the stock is 15.4 percent.

NOTES

1. H. Markowitz, "Portfolio Selection," *Journal of Finance* (March 1952), pp. 77–91.
2. W. Sharpe, "A Simplified Model for Portfolio Analysis," *Management Science* (January 1963), pp. 277–93.

3. W. Sharpe, "A Linear Programming Algorithm for Mutual Fund Portfolio Selection," *Management Science* (March 1967), pp. 499–510.

9

Efficient Market Hypothesis

Learning Objectives

An understanding of the material in this chapter should enable the student to

---

9-1. Explain the difference between fundamental analysis and technical analysis.

9-2. Explain the three forms of the efficient market hypothesis.

9-3. Explain the relationship between risk premiums and nonmarket risk.

9-4. Explain the usefulness of beta estimates as a guide to subsequent performance.

9-5. Explain arbitrage pricing theory and distinguish it from modern portfolio theory.

Chapter Outline

Modern portfolio theory (MPT) provides an elegant theoretical framework. Like most such theoretical constructs, the primary features of MPT may be derived from a relatively short list of assumptions. For instance, the assumptions that underlie MPT are that large numbers of well-informed investors hold similar views of risk and return over a similar time period, and that investors are risk averse and seek to optimize their portfolio returns. Like most such constructs, these assumptions represent substantial departures from reality. A theory is, however, much better judged by the accuracy of its predictions than by the realism of its assumptions. Accordingly, this chapter considers three interesting and important implications of modern portfolio theory:

- First, no trading method can consistently generate risk-adjusted returns that exceed those implied by the efficient market MPT model.
- Second, nonmarket risk does not affect the discount rate (required rate of return) applied to risky assets.
- Third, returns tend to vary linearly (the security market line) with (nondiversifiable) market risk.

Therefore, most returns should approximate their corresponding market model-simulated estimates. If these implications hold well enough for practical use, then practitioners in the fields of investment analysis and portfolio management have a powerful theoretical and scientific underpinning upon which to base their studies and recommendations. It is, in fact, because of these wide-ranging practical implications that several Nobel Laureates have been awarded to some of the most famous names in these fields over the last decade or so (Harry Markowitz, James Tobin, Merton Miller, Franco Modigliani, William Sharpe, and Myron Scholes).

TYPES OF INVESTMENT ANALYSIS

efficient market hypothesis (EMH)

fundamental analysis

To discuss the *efficient market hypothesis (EMH)* in a meaningful fashion we need a basic understanding of the two primary types of investment analysis: fundamental analysis and technical analysis. *Fundamental analysis* consists of analyzing the factors that affect the worth of expected future income streams. Thus, fundamental security analysts assess a firm's earnings and dividend prospects by evaluating such factors as its sales, costs, and capital requirements. Fundamental commodity analysts base their futures forecasts on the relevant demand and supply factors. Fundamental real estate analysts generate price and rental value expectations from anticipated future construction costs and demand growth estimates.

technical analysis

Technical analysis, in contrast, concentrates on past price and volume relationships of a security or commodity (narrow form) or technical market indicators applicable to that security or commodity (broad form). Both types of technical analysis attempt to identify evolving investor sentiment, but neither has a very sound theoretical base. Most technicians are not, however, particularly concerned with a theoretical justification for their method. They are more inclined to argue that results are what ultimately matter. A wealth of available data facilitates the application of technical analysis to the security and commodity markets. Technical analysis is discussed in chapters 13 and 14.

THE EFFICIENT MARKET HYPOTHESIS

The efficient market hypothesis questions the usefulness of technical analysis and, in some versions, fundamental analysis. Many natural

random walk

phenomena follow a *random walk*, or what the physical sciences call Brownian motion. A drunk in the middle of a large field who is as likely to move in one direction as another follows a random walk. Similarly, it can be argued that the next price change of a randomly moving stock is unrelated to past price behavior. Obviously, if prices move randomly, the repeating price patterns that technical analysts claim to observe have a predictive ability. Of course, stock prices tend to rise over time, so it might be more accurate to describe their movement as "random walk with drift." In other words, it seems pretty safe, based on historical evidence, to predict that the market will be higher 10 years from now than it is today, but it might not be safe to predict that the market will be higher (or lower) tomorrow than it is today.

Price movements need not be precisely random for past price data to be useless. Marginally associated relations between past and future price changes may be either too small or too unreliable to generate gross returns that consistently exceed transaction costs. Indeed, commissions, search costs, and bid-ask spreads would generally offset any expected price change of less than 2 percent or 3 percent.

Weak Form of the Efficient Market Hypothesis

weak form EMH

The random walk hypothesis, as the *weak form of the efficient market hypothesis* is sometimes called, implies that knowledge of past price behavior has no value in predicting future price movements. That is, such knowledge cannot be used to construct a portfolio that consistently outperforms the market on a risk-adjusted basis. The weak form implies that once we know the most recent price quote, we know as much about possible subsequent returns as those who know the full price history up to that point. In other words, prices do not move in predictable patterns. Weak form adherents argue that, if prices did move in dependable patterns, the reactions of alert market participants would rapidly eliminate any resulting profit opportunities. If a particular price pattern was thought to forecast a rise, some market participants might react before other investors could take advantage of the move. Such actions by some traders would frequently prevent the full pattern from occurring. Eventually, the action of traders who acted first would eliminate the value of any recognized patterns.

| *Example:* | Suppose a stock sells for $6 per share. Also suppose that based on some technical formula, it is possible to predict that next month the price of the stock will be $10 per share. Other people would also use that formula and make the same prediction. Therefore, everyone would want to buy the stock, and nobody would want to sell it. Thus, the forces of supply and demand would very quickly (perhaps within one hour of active trading) drive the price of the stock up to almost $10 per share. (To be exact, we would have to subtract the interest forgone by buying the stock now rather than next month.) |

In other words, if it were really possible to find trends and predict future stock prices, the forces of supply and demand would immediately bring present prices in line with expected future prices. Therefore, an investor cannot earn an abnormal return by using technical analysis, and we can conclude that the market is weak-form efficient.

Semistrong Form of the Efficient Market Hypothesis

The weak form of the efficient market hypothesis implies that technical analysis is useless, but it does not address the effectiveness of fundamental analysis. The *semistrong form*, on the other hand, asserts that the market quickly and correctly evaluates all relevant publicly available technical and

semistrong form EMH

fundamental information. Thus, market prices should accurately reflect all relevant public information.

Tests of the semistrong form must distinguish between anticipated and unanticipated information. Investors may correctly anticipate new information that has not yet become public. For instance, based on careful fundamental analysis, an investor may anticipate an increase in a firm's dividend. Generally, anticipated information will already be incorporated into security prices.

Unanticipated information, although not incorporated in a security price, will be quickly assimilated as soon as it is publicly available. If markets are semistrong form efficient, then risk-adjusted returns can exceed those of the market only due to unexpected developments. Therefore, some (lucky) investors may do the right things for the wrong reasons, while other (unlucky) investors may suffer from unexpectedly unfavorable developments, but none of the investors can consistently earn abnormal returns.

Strong Form of the Efficient Market Hypothesis

strong form EMH

According to the *strong form of the efficient market hypothesis*, the market also incorporates information that so-called monopolists of information (sometimes called insiders) have about security prices. There are generally three groups of information monopolists: Professional money managers, such as mutual funds or investment advisory services, are one group alleged to have special knowledge about companies they follow. Specialists who make a market in stocks on the organized exchanges are also supposed to have knowledge of their stocks. Since they are granted a monopoly in making a market in specific stocks, they have short-term knowledge of the flow of buy and sell orders on those stocks.

Corporate insiders comprise the third group of information monopolists. Corporate insiders—defined as managers, board members, and those who own 10 percent or more of the stock of a company—certainly have access to information that is not yet made public. However, SEC rules and federal law prohibit them from profiting from that information or sharing it with outsiders prior to a public announcement. Insiders are permitted to trade the stocks of their own companies, but they are subject to some restrictions. For example, they are prohibited from engaging in short-term trading. Strong-form efficiency maintains that even the information of these monopolists quickly gets reflected in security prices, thus eliminating the potential for abnormal gains.

Forms of the Efficient Market Hypothesis

- Weak form: Future returns are unrelated to past return patterns. (Charting does not work.)
- Semistrong form: Future returns are unrelated to any analysis based on public information. (Fundamental analysis does not work.)
- Strong form: Future returns are unrelated to any analysis based on public or nonpublic data. (Inside information is useless.)

Adjusting Returns for the Impacts of Risk and the Market

Theoretical and empirical studies of market efficiency need to take proper account of the impact of both risk and market returns. We have already seen how a tendency toward risk aversion causes investors to expect higher returns on more risky investments. Virtually everyone who studies the securities markets realizes that actual returns generally do increase with risk. Thus, any type of market performance study needs to take account of the impact of risk on expected and actual returns. Similarly, individual security returns tend to be higher when the overall market is strong than when it is weak. Failing to adjust for the impacts of risk and the market could lead to very misleading results. Calculation of differential returns and risk-adjusted returns are standard methods that are used to adjust actual returns for these effects.

Differential Returns

differential returns

An adjustment that produces what are called *differential returns* can be performed:

$$D_{it} = R_{it} - M_t$$

where: D_{it} = differential return for firm i during period t
R_{it} = actual return for firm i during period t
M_t = market return for period t

This simple calculation, if validly applied, then enables an assessment of whether or not the differential returns are significant enough to warrant a premium or discount on the security's or other investment's market price.

Risk-Adjusted Returns

risk-adjusted returns

To adjust for both risk and the market, *risk-adjusted returns* are computed. Recall from chapter 8 that the security market line (SML) can be written as

$$\overline{R}_{it} = R_{ft} + \beta_i(M_t - R_{ft})$$

expected return

where: $\overline{R}_{it}$ = the equilibrium or *expected return* of security i

R_{ft} = the risk-free rate of return

Actual returns R_{it} in this framework are then described in equation 9-1 as composed of three components:

$$R_{it} = \overline{R}_{it} + \overline{\alpha}_{it} + \varepsilon_{it} \qquad \text{(Equation 9-1)}$$

where: R_{it} = actual return

$\overline{R}_{it}$ = the expected return

$\overline{\alpha}_{it}$ = the average difference between actual returns and expected returns

ε_{it} = a random error term with expected value of 0

Jensen's alpha

Sometimes α_{it} is called *Jensen's alpha*. It is a measure of how well or poorly a particular security or portfolio performs compared with expected performance, considering the market-related risk characteristics of the security or portfolio. Then, the estimate of alpha, as shown in equation 9-2, is a measure of the risk-adjusted performance of the security:

$$\overline{\alpha}_{it} = R_{it} - \overline{R}_{it} = (R_{it} - R_{ft}) - \beta_i(M_t - R_{ft}) \qquad \text{(Equation 9-2)}$$

Two other measures are also commonly used for risk-adjusted performance evaluation in studies of market efficiency: the Sharpe ratio and the Treynor ratio.

Sharpe ratio

The *Sharpe ratio*, or the *reward to variability* as it is sometimes called, is defined as follows in equation 9-3:

$$R_{VAR} = \frac{R_{it} - R_{ft}}{\sigma_i} \qquad \text{(Equation 9-3)}$$

Note that the numerator of this ratio is one of the terms in equation 9-2, while the denominator is simply the standard deviation of the security's

Treynor ratio

returns (noted first in chapter 8 as the Markowitz model's measure of risk). Here, actual returns adjusted by the risk-free rate are compared with *total risk*.

The *Treynor ratio*, called the *reward to volatility*, shown in equation 9-4 is also used:

$$R_{VOL} = \frac{R_{it} - R_{ft}}{\beta_i} \qquad \text{(Equation 9-4)}$$

Note that the numerator is the same as in the Sharpe ratio, but the denominator's measure of risk is now the beta of the security—which means that only *market-related risk* is considered. Note as well that the Treynor measure is the same as the *slope* of the security market line (refer to the SML equation in chapter 8), whereas the Sharpe measure is the same as the slope of the ex post capital market line (refer to the CML equation in chapter 8).

All three measures of risk-adjusted performance—Jensen's alpha, and the Sharpe and Treynor ratios—are commonly used to evaluate security or mutual fund performance, and they are also used in studies of market efficiency.

Essentially, all the measures of risk-adjusted performance relate the actual return to some measure of the level of riskiness of the investment. Virtually all serious securities market research utilizes risk- and market-adjusted returns such as those described.

Example of Performance Measurement

Suppose the following data were available for the 1975–1989 period for several mutual funds (the S&P 500 Index and the 90-day T-bill rate will serve as proxies for the market return and the risk-free rate, respectively):

Mutual Fund	Average Return	Standard Deviation	Beta	R^2
Dreyfus Growth	19.20	18.50	.83	.472
Fidelity Magellan	31.92	18.57	1.08	.532
Wellington Fund	15.19	9.57	.65	.877
S&P 500 Index	17.16	13.18	1.00	1.000
90-day T-Bill rate	8.31	2.56		

Then, using the formulas for the Sharpe and Treynor ratios and Jensen's alpha, we can derive the following (we assume the estimates derived are statistically significant):

Mutual Fund	Sharpe	Treynor	Jensen's Alpha
Dreyfus Growth	.589	13.116	1.783
Fidelity Magellan	1.272	21.866	14.989
Wellington Fund	.719	10.585	.656
S&P 500 Index	.671	10.277	–0–

The interpretation is that Fidelity Magellan is clearly superior among the three funds on all three measures of risk-adjusted performance. Dreyfus Growth and Wellington Fund have different rankings, depending on the measure chosen. When total risk is considered as measured by the standard deviation, as with the Sharpe measure, the Wellington Fund appears superior. However, when the beta measure of risk is chosen, which reflects market risk only, Dreyfus Growth is better. All three funds are superior to the S&P 500 Index in this period on a risk-adjusted basis but this is not the usual result if one considers the averages for all equity mutual funds. Moreover, it is important to note that the Wellington Fund did not achieve as high an average return as the market, but because the return it did achieve involved less risk by any measure, on a risk-adjusted basis its performance was superior.

coefficient of determination (R^2)

The meaning of the R^2 (R-squared), the *coefficient of determination*, is as follows: It is the square of the simple correlation coefficient between the mutual fund's returns and the S&P 500 Index returns. An R^2 can range between zero and one. As such, it measures the degree of "goodness of fit" of the relationship between the fund and the market index. It also indicates the percentage of the variation in the fund's return that is "explained by" the market index. The greater the degree of diversification of the fund, the closer it approximates the market and the higher both the correlation coefficient ρ and the coefficient of determination R^2 will be. Conversely, the lower the R^2, the less diversified the fund is and the more the fund is subject to nonsystematic or nonmarket risk. In the case shown, Wellington Fund appears to have the highest degree of coincidence with the market as measured by R^2 (or by its square root, the correlation coefficient).

Outperforming the Market

As we have seen, the returns generated from applying both technical and fundamental analysis should be judged relative to the returns on the market. If the market is rising, most investment strategies will produce positive returns: a declining market tends to have the opposite effect. The market return may be used as a benchmark against which to judge the usefulness of a particular type of analysis. To be judged successful, a trading strategy needs to generate returns that, after an appropriate adjustment for risk, must, in the aggregate, exceed the market returns of the corresponding periods. Thus, the techniques of both technical and fundamental analysis need to be tested against real-world data. These data can be used to generate hypothetical returns for various investment strategies and then compared with the market's returns for the same period. Normally, a conformable stock market index such as the S&P 500 Index or the New York Stock Exchange Composite (a weighted average of all NYSE listings) is used to represent overall market performance. If the technique to be tested leads the investor to assemble a portfolio whose average market risk (average beta) differs appreciably from that of the market's (hence a beta appreciably different from one), the market benchmark should be chosen to better represent the types of investments in the portfolio. Differential or risk-adjusted returns (or some other adjustment) should be used to examine the effectiveness of any strategy based on fundamental or technical analysis. Virtually all academic studies utilize such risk-adjusted returns data.

Weak Form Tests of EMH

Technical market influences have been explored empirically in two basic ways. First, the relationship between past and future price changes has been tested for statistical dependence (relatedness) or independence (unrelatedness). Second, filter rules analogous to technical trading rules have been applied to historical data. If past price patterns help forecast future price change, past and future price changes should be related, and technically inspired filter rules should help identify profitable trading opportunities.

run

Some studies have examined serial correlation (relationship between past and present price changes); others investigated runs of prices. A *run* is an uninterrupted series of price increases or an uninterrupted series of price decreases. Many different studies have consistently failed to find any important dependence relation in price changes. Thus, past price patterns do

chartists

not appear to forecast future price movements. *Chartists* point out that these statistical tests look largely for linear relations and say that the tests are much too crude to capture subtleties. Moreover, chartists assert that their "craft" is as much art as science since it depends heavily on judgment, interpretation, and experience; that is, beneath the apparent randomness of stock price movements is a distinct nonrandom pattern that can be discerned from charts. They argue that these patterns are very difficult to quantify by standard statistical methods. Nonetheless, most nonlinear dependencies that they claim to see should show up in the tests as linear approximations. Chartists have offered no convincing counterevidence (to academicians) as to why standard statistical proofs of forecast reliability cannot be applied.

filter rules

A second set of tests has explored technical analysis using what are called *filter rules*. Filters attempt to reflect the momentum/resistance-level factors that technical analysts claim are important. (Technical terms, such as momentum and resistance level, are discussed in greater detail in later chapters.) Momentum indicates the tendency of a stock price to continue to rise; whereas resistance level refers to a stock price at which there is alleged to be either a large number of sell orders (upper resistance) or a large number of buy orders (lower resistance). Filter rules mechanically identify supposed buy-and-sell situations.

relative strength criterion

One type of filter rule flashes a buy signal whenever a stock increases by x percent. After an x percent decline from a subsequent high, a sell signal is given. For instance, a 5 percent filter would signal to buy whenever a stock rose 5 percent from the previous high. Another type of filter rule—the *relative strength criterion*—identifies stocks that have recently outperformed the market as buys and underperformed the market as sells. For instance, a stock that rises 10 percent when the market rose only 5 percent would have outperformed the market and thereby exhibited relative strength. When transaction costs are included, none of the various types of filter rules have been shown to outperform a buy-and-hold strategy.

Semistrong and Strong Form Tests of EMH

General tests of the semistrong and strong form are difficult to devise and perform. Moreover, test procedures are not very powerful in discriminating between efficient and inefficient markets. The market pricing process generates so much "noise" that prices can stray quite a bit from their intrinsic values without detection by tests that are commonly used. Nevertheless, various subhypotheses of the efficient market hypothesis have been examined. Many studies have found market imperfections or anomalies that suggest that specific types of fundamental analysis are useful and potentially profitable earning above normal returns.

For instance, a number of studies suggest that stocks with low price earnings ratios, small market capitalizations, low per-share prices, or related characteristics tend to outperform the market. Another study on the impact of splits on performance, found the market to react rather efficiently. Prior to the split announcement, the stocks tended to outperform the market, but after the announcement, performance was random.

With so much conflicting evidence, the extent of semistrong-form efficiency is decidedly mixed. Some academicians suggest that, since institutional investors—with all their professional expertise—rarely outperform the market on a risk-adjusted basis, individual investors are unlikely to do better. Others claim that there are enough market imperfections that talented investment analysts can outperform the market. Even if the market eventually evaluates public information accurately, they claim some investor/analysts may be able to take advantage of lags in the price adjustment process.

Many strong-form supporters concede that insider information is sometimes useful, but they contend that such instances are rare and therefore the conclusions of the strong form generally hold up. Research on the profitability of insider information is somewhat mixed. Several of the early studies found little evidence of excess returns to insiders. More recent studies showed that insiders earned more than outsiders on the same purchase or sale transaction in the same company's stock; results also indicated that, as the information became public knowledge, excess insider returns decreased as the length of the holding period increased.

Market Efficiency Debate

Although some academicians hold extreme positions, few who have examined the issue believe that the market is strong-form efficient or is always semistrong-form efficient. On the other hand, virtually all serious finance scholars agree that the weak form of the efficient market hypothesis is essentially correct. The principal disagreements relate to the importance, extent, and causes of the imperfections of the semistrong form. These imperfections are largely viewed as departures or exceptions to normal behavior defined by MPT.

Causes of Persistent Market Imperfections

market imperfection (anomaly)

Why, if the market contains many talented rational investors, do imperfections persist? As yet, there is no consensus on the issue. A *market imperfection or anomaly* exists whenever any group of investors can consistently earn risk-adjusted returns that are above market returns. These imperfections can have numerous causes.

Brokers, investment advisers, and the financial press continually pull investors in many different directions. Most investors have difficulty discriminating between valid and invalid analyses. (Why else do so many investment newsletters prosper in spite of the random and often conflicting nature of their advice?) Eliminating market imperfections requires that the reaction to an observed mispricing be of sufficient magnitude to force prices back into line. If the transactions of investors who act on valid mispricing evidence are overwhelmed by trading based on incorrect analysis, observable mispricings will persist. Because investors are often led into shared errors by their reliance on a common body of information, investors and analysts who erroneously project abnormally high past earnings growth into the future may bid prices up to the point where investors pay too much for "growth stocks." This process would allow other investors to outperform the market by avoiding these stocks or selling them short. Subsequent growth rates that differ from expected rates should lead to price corrections. These scenarios could occur frequently enough for some investors to profit from their ability to "predict" the resulting price moves. Mispricings will continue as long as trading by investors who recognize these mispricings is insufficient to bid prices back into line. Moreover, the investors who do recognize such mis-valuing tendencies have an incentive to keep quiet.

As discussed in chapter 8, modern portfolio theory, as it is generally formulated, assumes that market prices are formed by a homogeneous group of investors who analyze the same sources of information in identical fashions. Although market efficiency does not require perfect homogeneity of investor expectations, marginal investors must behave as if they accurately analyze all relevant public information and are unaffected (or identically affected) by such matters as tax status, costs of trading, risk orientation, borrowing power, liquidity preference, familiarity with local markets, and total available funds. In the real world, however, the resources of investors who are best positioned to profit may be insufficient to eliminate some mispricings.

Because investment analysts and periodicals concentrate on the larger, better known firms, the security prices of many smaller firms may depart from the values that a careful analysis would yield. These firms generally trade in localized markets, and therefore few investors are positioned to observe the mispricings. Other types of mispricings may be exploited only by investors who can purchase control. An investor who acquires control of a firm that is worth more out of business than it is in business could liquidate its assets for more than the firm's value as a going concern. Such takeovers, however, are not usually easy to accomplish. The effort tends to bid up prices and provoke vigorous defensive efforts by those whose interests are threatened. Thus, investors with the necessary resources to eliminate the mispricing may frequently have inadequate incentives to do so. Still other imperfections (arbitrage opportunities) may require very quick and low-cost access to several markets. Only if enough investors are able to take advantage of these imperfections will their actions right the price imbalances.

Finally, market efficiency assumes that investors rationally pursue the highest available risk-adjusted returns. In a broader context, however, investors are not merely maximizers of risk-adjusted returns but are also consumers with multidimensional goals. Thus, investors who choose to maximize their total well-being by devoting more of their resources to leisure time, education, or earning extra income may seem indifferent to investment management. As a result, some apparent market imperfections may not be fully exploited because investors best positioned to take advantage of them are unaware of or unconcerned with the potential gains. Far from being irrational, however, these investors are simply addressing other goals. Concentrating exclusively on the risk-adjusted return of their portfolios would not be rational.

Reasons for Persistent Market Imperfections

- Difficulty in discriminating between valid evidence and useless advice
- Different investor circumstances: tax status, trading costs, risk orientation, borrowing power, liquidity preferences, wealth level, familiarity with local markets, and so on
- Investors' pursuit of overall goals rather than only on maximizing their portfolios' risk-adjusted return

---

THE RISK PREMIUM ON NONMARKET RISK

According to modern portfolio theory, the risk premiums applied to the expected returns of individual investments should be solely determined by each asset's market risk. Thus, two assets with the same level of market risk should have equal expected returns even if they have very different levels of nonmarket risk. A number of studies have found, however, that risk premiums are also related to nonmarket risk. This apparent conflict between MPT and the evidence has spawned a number of hypotheses.

If, for instance, effective diversification were relatively difficult or costly, many investors would diversify incompletely rather than incur the high costs of achieving a fully diversified portfolio. Because nonmarket risk would contribute to overall portfolio risks for these investors, they would consider it relevant. The next section of this chapter, therefore, explores the relative ease of individual investor diversification.

Practical Diversification

Risk-neutral investors maximize expected returns without regard to risk. Although few investors are truly risk neutral, those with adequate financial protection provided by insurance, retirement benefits, appreciable holdings of low-risk investments, and other means may view their remaining portfolio through approximately risk-neutral eyes. Thus, some investors may put part of their wealth in less risky assets, such as well-diversified mutual funds, preferred stocks, or convertible bonds, and manage the remainder for maximum return.

Investors with long time horizons may focus most of their attention on an attempt to maximize their portfolio values 10 or 20 years in the future. These investors may be relatively unconcerned with their portfolios' interim values. For instance, investors may start with small positions in one or two stocks and periodically expand their portfolios' size and diversity. They might initially opt for high-risk securities with high expected return in the hope that the "winners" will eventually make the strategy pay off. This approach, however, risks what is called gambler's ruin: A streak of bad luck may wipe out the investor's limited resources even though the chosen strategy might eventually pay off with unlimited resources.

Investors who are neither risk neutral nor have long time horizons may either diversify their own portfolios or let mutual funds or other institutional investors do the job. Efficient portfolio diversification requires purchasing a number of different securities. Although commission and search costs may not be worth the resulting risk reduction for a small portfolio, a rather modest number of stocks may yield substantial diversification. Effective bond diversification also requires few issues.

When portfolios are assembled nonrandomly, however—for example, by following brokerage firm recommendations—diversification may be rather difficult. Under these circumstances, eliminating most nonmarket risk requires substantially more than eight to 10 stocks, although modern conglomerate firms such as GE tend to offer greater diversification value than single-industry firms and may thereby reduce the diversification requirement somewhat. Effective diversification, however, is not easy or automatic, and even partially diversified portfolios will contain a substantial amount of nonmarket risk. Also, while risk declines, administrative costs increase appreciably with portfolio size. Furthermore, portfolios whose components are concentrated among firms or industries that are likely to be affected by similar factors (for example, steel companies and automobile companies) may not be effectively diversified. All firms are affected by economic fluctuations. Industry-specific and firm-specific impacts are averaged over the securities represented in the portfolio. These industry-specific and firm-specific factors are diversified away only if the portfolio itself does not systematically overrepresent certain of these factors.

Example:	Consider the investment impact of a breakdown of price discipline by OPEC and other oil-producing nations, similar to what occurred in 1986. A well-diversified portfolio of U.S. stocks would not be greatly affected by such a breakdown. Some of its investments (for instance, the stocks of heavy energy

users such as airlines) might be helped, while others (for instance, those who sold fossil fuels or serviced the companies in the oil patch) would be hurt. On the other hand, a portfolio with a large representation of Texas banks would be very sensitive to such a development. Most of the banks in the Southwest are dependent on the health of their local economy, which in turn is dependent on energy prices. A decline in oil and natural gas prices would therefore adversely affect not only the profit outlook for oil companies but also for local real estate investments, the companies that service the oil industry, and the employees of both the oil companies and the oil service companies. Inevitably, the banks in that region would have to make extensive loans to local borrowers. The ability of most of these borrowers to service and repay that debt depends on the health of the local economy.

Some investors' diversification difficulty might not by itself account for the price effect of nonmarket risk. If small investors' aversion to nonmarket risk caused some securities to be underpriced (vis-à-vis their market risk), large investors could exploit that aversion by constructing well-diversified portfolios of these securities. Indeed, the market might well contain enough of these large investors to keep security prices in line with their market risks. Since, however, the empirical evidence points to a nonmarket risk effect, we need to search further.

Additional Reasons for a Nonmarket Risk Effect

Studies have found that various possible sources of estimation error could account for the price effect of nonmarket risks. The results suggest two factors: inefficiently estimated betas and a positive correlation between estimated betas and nonmarket risk. If betas are inefficiently estimated, the true effect of market risk will not be fully captured by the beta estimate. If the true beta and the estimate for nonmarket risk are correlated, the nonmarket risk variable may act as a second proxy for market risk.

Another explanation for the apparent premium paid for nonmarket risk relates to the borrowing and lending assumption: If investors cannot borrow and lend at the same riskless rate, effective diversification of nonmarket risk may be impossible.

The possibility that returns are not normally distributed provides yet another possible explanation. The mean and variance completely specify the shape of normal distributions. All normal distributions have the same basic shape. Like circles, normal distributions differ from each other only in scale. **skewed distributions** Nonsymmetric or *skewed distributions*, in contrast, may have identical means and variances and yet have very different shapes. Portfolio theory generally assumes that expected returns are normally distributed. When expected returns are not normally distributed, the model's implications may not apply. For example, distributions A and B (figure 9-1) have the same mean and standard deviation; yet they offer markedly different return possibilities.

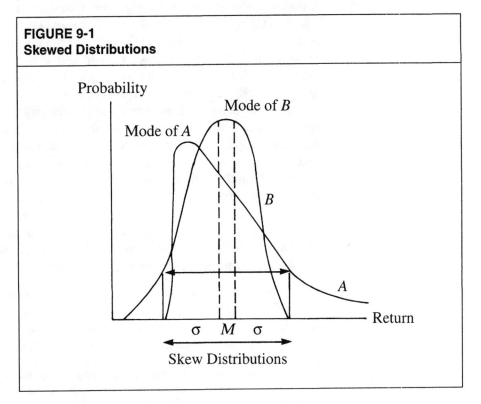

FIGURE 9-1
Skewed Distributions

Distribution A's returns have some probability of being very large but with almost no chance of being more than one standard deviation below the mean. Distribution B's returns could well be more than one standard deviation below but are unlikely to be even one standard deviation above its mean. The mode (point of greatest probability) of B exceeds the mode of A, however. While individual preferences vary, most investors seem to prefer some possibility of a very large gain. Stocks with highly variable returns also tend to have highly skewed returns that, on average, are lower than those of less risky stocks. An investor preference for skewness may cause very high-risk stocks to be priced to offer a lower expected return than less risky stocks. Moreover, investors who seek to achieve their desired skewness level must hold too few securities to be fully diversified.

Real-world distributions may differ from the normal form in several respects. We have already discussed the degree and direction of skewness. Normal distributions are symmetrical; skewed distributions are not. Another area of potential difference relates to the relative distribution of the probabilities. All normal distributions have the same probability associated with each distance (scaled in standard deviations) from the mean: 68 percent plus or minus within one standard deviation; 95 percent within two deviations; and 99 percent within three deviations. Two other classes of distributions have somewhat different shapes. *Leptokurtic* distributions are skinnier and more spread out at the extremes; that is, they are relatively more dense in the peaks and the tails and relatively less dense in the intermediate zones than normal distributions are. *Platokurtic* distributions, in contrast, are relatively more dense in the intermediate zones.

leptokurtosis

platokurtosis

The distributions of expected returns for any particular asset are not directly observable. No doubt, some are close to normal, others are highly skewed, and still others exhibit lepto- or platokurtosis. We can, however, observe actual return distributions. Presumably, expected returns are distributed similarly to actual returns. The longer the holding period, the more nearly actual returns tend to approach the normal, thus providing a reasonably accurate working hypothesis for monthly returns of both portfolios and individual securities. Daily returns may be somewhat leptokurtic and skewed. Most nonnormal behavior, however, often occurs at the beginning and end of the trading day or during after-hours trading.

Factors Contributing to Nonmarket Risk

- Most investors' portfolios contain significant amounts of nonmarket risk.
- Errors in estimated betas may be correlated with nonmarket risk contributing to an apparent empirical relationship.
- Investors who are unable to lend and borrow risklessly may find that inefficient portfolios are the most effective way of achieving their desired risk levels.
- Nonnormal expected return distributions, coupled with an investor preference for skewness, may further compound the difficulty of assembling efficient portfolios and thus increase the relevance of nonmarket risk.

ESTIMATED BETAS AND SUBSEQUENT PERFORMANCE

Estimated betas are potentially useful statistics. Investors who expect the market to move in a particular direction would like to assemble a portfolio that will take full advantage of the expected market move. If the market is expected to rise, the portfolio manager would like to be concentrated in high beta stocks. Alternatively, if a market decline is anticipated, the portfolio manager would prefer to be invested in low beta stocks. A large number of advisory services seek to service these investors. They sell their lists of beta estimates to investors and portfolio managers. Betas are normally estimated by regressions of historical securities returns on market returns. Investors who use these beta estimates as a guide to sensitivity to market moves need to know how well they explain individual security performance. A number of tests have been developed to assess the usefulness and accuracy of beta estimates. One approach is to compare actual returns with those implied by the market model estimates and actual market returns.

A security's performance can be simulated by adding its estimated alpha to the product of its estimated beta and the corresponding period's market return. Equation 9-5 determines the simulated risk-adjusted return as follows:

$$SRAR_{it} = \alpha_i + \beta_i (M_t) \qquad \text{(Equation 9-5)}$$

where: $SRAR_{it}$ = simulated risk-adjusted return
α_i = estimated α for firm i
β_i = estimated β_i (M_t)
M_t = market return

and: α_i and β_i are estimates from the fitted characteristic line of the security

This simulated return is the amount that is subtracted from an actual return to produce the corresponding risk-adjusted abnormal return. In an efficient market, risk-adjusted abnormal returns should have an average value very close to 0. In other words, the actual returns and the simulated risk-adjusted returns should be approximately equal. The accuracy of any individual security return simulation is related to both random nonmarket influences and the appropriateness of the simulation process. A sufficiently sizable sample, however, should largely eliminate individual random influences and reveal any biases and inefficiencies in the estimation process. Thus, a comparison of actual returns with simulated risk-adjusted returns should shed light on the accuracy of estimated betas. Therefore, we will now consider some properties of estimated betas.

Properties of Beta Estimates

For most publicly traded stocks, estimated betas have an average value of 1. Moreover, most beta estimates are relatively close to unity. Less than 10 percent have values greater than 2 and less than 2 percent have negative values. Betas estimated from historical data are generally similar to risk estimates based on fundamental analysis (financial ratios, and so on). Individual beta estimates have been found in several different tests to be relatively unreliable. Portfolio betas, in contrast, appear to be much more dependable. Thus, mutual fund portfolios are usually near both the efficient frontier and the risk-return trade-off indicated in their prospectuses. Growth-oriented funds have high-risk efficient portfolios, while more conservative funds are less risky and have lower expected returns. These funds tend to perform as their betas imply. Moreover, hypothetically constructed portfolios generally perform close to their predicted levels.

Apparently, errors inherent in individual company beta estimates are largely offsetting. The inconsistency between actual returns and those implied by individually estimated betas could be due to instability in the underlying betas and/or errors in the estimation process. Does the estimation process introduce systematic errors, and if so, can an improved process be devised?

Improved Beta Estimates

A number of different phenomena, including beta estimates, exhibit a tendency for extreme-value estimates to move toward the grand mean (regression toward the mean). For example, in baseball, individual high and low first-month batting averages generally move toward the overall all-player average. Note, however, that this phenomenon describes the behavior of extreme values, not the entire population. Thus, batting averages and betas near the mean tend to move randomly away from the mean with sufficient frequency to repopulate the extremes as the prior-period extremes move in. Several estimation techniques take account of the regression-toward-the-mean phenomena.

adjusted beta

M.E. Blume suggests adjusting the beta for next year as follows: *Adjusted beta* = .35 + .68 (average unadjusted beta estimate based on data for the past 3 years).[1] Others have proposed more sophisticated adjustments. Extensive study of these various beta adjustment techniques shows that they are clearly superior in explaining both future betas and future security return correlation matrices. On the other hand, beta adjustments appear to be less necessary for large portfolios even though several mutual fund advisory services create adjusted betas for each fund as a regular part of their service. Substituting fundamental factors for or combining them with historically estimated betas is a further effort to generate more reliable beta estimates. Although all of these efforts may have improved the resulting beta estimates, the best estimates are still not especially reliable. Instability in the underlying betas and a variety of other factors probably contribute to this unreliability.

Barr Rosenberg was able to predict betas for companies using fundamental operating data—that is, accounting numbers taken from either historical or projected income statements and balance sheets.[2] Rosenberg argues that the problems with applications of CAPM arise from the unrealistic assumptions of the simple model based on the EMH. For instance, the standard version of EMH is based on the clearly unrealistic assumption that investors have immediate access to all information needed to establish a security's price.

uncertain information hypothesis (UIH)

K. Brown, S. Tinic, and V. Harlow present a modified version of the EMH called the *uncertain information hypothesis (UIH),* that attempts to extend efficient market theory to show how investors respond in a situation of major uncertainty.[3] Greater uncertainty among investors leads to heightened price volatility and thus greater risk for investors. Since investors require higher returns for bearing increased risk, they tend to respond to unexpected information by setting stock prices below their expected values. As the uncertainty over an expected outcome is clarified, subsequent price changes tend to be more favorable, regardless of whether the initial unexpected event was good or bad. The UIH theory sets forth the following propositions:

- On average, stock return variability will increase following the announcements of major unanticipated events.
- The average price adjustments following the initial market reactions to both "negative" and "positive" events will be positive (or at least nonnegative).
- To the extent that the market's risk aversion decreases as the level of stock prices increase, post-event price increases will be larger for negative events than for positive ones.

The main point is that portfolios are priced rationally in both situations; thus, based on anticipated changes, there are no opportunities for investors to earn riskless or abnormal returns from alleged price overreactions or under-reactions. Therefore, markets only appear to *consistently* overreact to bad news and underreact to good news.

mean reversion

Another type of market efficiency test focuses on the "mean reversion" of security prices. The *mean reversion* process can be visualized by picturing a path of stock prices that swing excessively back and forth across some trend line that somehow measures the underlying or intrinsic value. Hence, the theory suggests a long-run pattern of overreactions followed regularly by market corrections. The general conclusion drawn from recent evidence is that there appear to be predictable return components in securities prices. It has been shown that 25 percent to 45 percent of the variability of stock returns over a 3-to-5-year time period can be predicted from returns in previous periods. These results can be explained in two different ways: (1) Investors are irrational and thus prices often depart from fundamental values that may provide an opportunity for abnormal profits, or (2) both the risks borne and risk premiums demanded by rational investors change with varying levels of uncertainty, which is consistent with the UIH discussed above.

The most recent important attack on the use of market beta was posited in an article by Fama and French in 1991.[4] They found evidence that the capital asset pricing model (CAPM) and security market line (SML) do not explain why returns of different types of risky stocks differ, and argued that beta is not a reasonable way to explain the risk-return relationship in markets. They examined transactions by major U.S. stocks exchanges between 1963 and 1990, and found that better predictors of stock returns were size of the firm and the ratio of the firm's accounting book value to its market value. Critics of the Fama French results argue that investors may simply have a preference for large capitalization firms not explained by economic rationality, or that investors may not have sufficient capital to diversify risk completely so that systematic risk may not fully explain market returns. Other researchers, using different empirical techniques and looking at different time periods, found evidence of a risk-return relationship that Fama and French found.

The Market Index

The market index used in the beta estimating equation may also introduce error into the estimation process. The theoretical model (of MPT) assumes that betas are estimated with an index that reflects all capital assets in proportion to their relative contribution to investor wealth. In practice, however, the NYSE composite or an even less broad index (such as the Standard and Poor's 500 Index) is usually employed. The NYSE index is an acceptable measure of U.S. stock movements. NYSE-listed securities are a large part of the total U.S. stock market, and NYSE, NASDAQ, AMEX, regional, and OTC stocks all tend to move together. Moreover, option, warrant, and convertible prices also tend to vary with stock prices. Thus, the NYSE composite reflects the movements of U.S. stocks relatively well.

The NYSE index's acceptability declines, however, as the relevant universe expands progressively to include U.S. debt securities, real estate, futures contracts, foreign securities, collectibles, precious metals, and so on. Even though many of these assets are influenced by the U.S. equity market, the correlations are relatively weak for most assets and essentially zero for others. Investments other than U.S. stocks (especially home ownership) represent an appreciable part of most investors' total wealth. Accordingly, using only U.S. stocks in the market index may bias the resulting beta estimates. Indexes of varying quality do exist for debt securities, foreign securities, commodities, some collector's items, real estate, and non-NYSE equities.

Although no one has yet been able to make all the arbitrary assumptions needed to assemble a complete, broad-based market index, the inclusion or exclusion of a particular asset class seems to have relatively little impact on an expanded index.

International Diversification

The stock markets in different countries appear to have a large component of independent variability. That is, a large part of the variability in their returns is unrelated to fluctuations in domestic markets. Thus, a strategy of adding foreign securities to a portfolio of domestic securities can be used to reduce the impact of the home country's market cycle. An international portfolio of debt and equity securities offers even greater diversification gains. Figure 9-2 shows the risk-reduction potential of international diversification.

American Depository Receipts (ADRs)

Investors can diversify internationally in a variety of ways. They can purchase shares in an international mutual fund, a U.S.-based multinational company, a foreign company's stock, or *American Depository Receipts (ADRs)* representing ownership of such securities. Well over 500 foreign firms are tradable as ADRs. Many mutual fund families (Fidelity, Vanguard, and so on) offer mutual funds composed of foreign stocks and bonds. With the exception of foreign index funds, international mutual funds are managed professionally. Their costs and expenses tend to be somewhat higher than domestic funds because transaction costs abroad are higher, and it is more difficult to obtain information on the securities of foreign firms. The securities of U.S-based multinational firms continue to fluctuate with those of other domestic firms, but they may offer slightly higher risk-adjusted returns.

Brokerage houses now pay closer attention to foreign investment opportunities and foreign business news, but data on most foreign firms are still not readily available or easy to interpret. Furthermore, offshore mutual funds are less closely regulated than U.S. funds. Finally, investing in foreign securities exposes the investor to exchange rate and political risk.

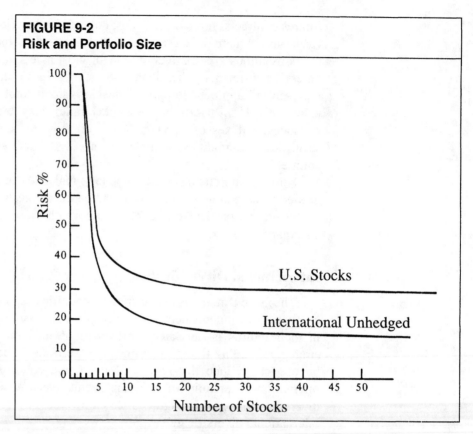

FIGURE 9-2
Risk and Portfolio Size

Empirical evidence indicates that despite the increased market integration that occurred in the 1987 to 1996 period, there are still ample opportunities for international portfolio diversification. Obstacles to international portfolio diversification include higher transaction costs, legal impediments to investing, and foreign exchange and political risks.

Diversification across Types of Investments

Buying international assets is not the only way of diversifying beyond the U.S. stock market. Nonsecurity assets such as commodities and real estate also have considerable diversification appeal. Similarly, government bonds can be effectively used to diversify a stock portfolio. Thus, international stocks and bonds and domestic nonstock assets may all be useful diversification vehicles.

Implications of Modern Portfolio Theory Tests

As a whole, the research presents a relatively discouraging picture for these implications of modern portfolio theory: (1) The markets are not as efficient as MPT assumes; (2) contrary to the theory, nonmarket risk may affect prices; and (3) relative return forecasts based on the market model are unreliable. In view of these shortcomings, why does MPT continue to receive so much attention? The answer to this question has three parts.

First, MPT is an elegant simplification of very complex phenomena. The defenders of MPT can make useful explanations of a great deal of portfolio behavior, and there is a huge amount of literature (and correspondingly huge human capital investment) behind the theory. Not surprisingly, MPT proponents would prefer to preserve as much of that investment as they reasonably can.

Second, MPT offers a useful point of departure. Economists, for example, need to understand the competitive model even though very few markets are truly competitive. Similarly, most physicists are quite familiar with the properties of a frictionless world and perfect gas. These idealized models yield interesting insights and testable predictions. A particular nonidealized effect may be observed in the difference between the model forecast and the actual event (ex post forecast analysis) and thereby yield useful information for the next (ex ante) forecast period. Remember, for rational investment, forecasting is unavoidable. Therefore, finance theorists and empiricists are expected to know the implications of MPT even if the real world often behaves differently.

Third, although the model's predictions are not uniformly accurate, some of the evidence is approximately consistent, and insights provided by the theory are useful:

- Individual inefficiencies notwithstanding, the market appears to be relatively efficient.
- Although market prices may take nonmarket risk into account, the rational investor may be able to profit from the observed price effects.
- Some inaccuracies in relative-return forecasts based on the market model may result from inadequate estimation techniques and data errors, rather than shortcomings of the model.

Of course, we need to keep in mind one of the original reasons for developing the MPT—especially the CAPM—is to evaluate the risk-adjusted past performance of professional portfolio managers. Prior to the CAPM approach, there was no formal way of evaluating the performance of a portfolio of securities by comparing its returns to the risks taken to earn those returns. Thus, the CAPM approach may be best suited to evaluating past performance, not as a predictive model. In this respect, the model performs admirably.

Finally, the beta estimates for diversified portfolios are relatively reliable. Until a demonstrably superior theory is devised, therefore, the standard form of MTP will continue to provide the foundation for the study of finance.

ARBITRAGE PRICING THEORY

arbitrage pricing theory

For all its shortcomings, modern portfolio theory has only one meaningful competitor: the *arbitrage pricing theory* (APT).[5] The APT model expands the traditional portfolio theory's number of return-generating factors from one (the market index) to several. APT was introduced by S. Ross in 1976. It begins with the idea that returns vary from the expected because of unanticipated changes in various basic economic forces. The equation form of APT is as follows:

$$R_{it} = \alpha + \beta_1 F_{1t} + \beta_2 F_{2t} + \beta_3 F_{3t} \cdots + B_n F_{nt} + E_{it} \qquad \text{(Equation 9-6)}$$

where the F_{it} are the relevant economic factors whose influence on R_{it} is to be estimated. Note that with only one factor (for example, the market index) this model is identical to the single index model (CAPM). Like MPT, APT assumes that when other things are equal, investors seek to construct portfolios that are expected to produce the highest returns. MPT assumes that investors assemble their portfolios to maximize return subject to the impact of market risk. APT, in contrast, assumes that investors seek to maximize expected return subject to simultaneously seeking to minimize the portfolio's sensitivity to unexpected changes in economic variables (industrial production, interest rates, unemployment rates, inflation rates, balance of payments, exchange rates, energy prices, and so on). In other words, MPT focuses exclusively on market risk, whereas APT sees risk as a multidimensional force emanating from a variety of economic factors. According to APT, investors would substitute securities in their portfolio whenever the expected return could increase without increasing sensitivity to unanticipated changes in economy-wide factors.

MPT can in fact be viewed as a special case of APT in which only one economic factor, market risk, is relevant. However, the more general form of APT makes it considerably more complex than the standard form of MPT. The main problem with APT is that the key factors of the model are not uniquely specified in an ex ante sense. APT is based on the economic principle that perfect substitutes must have the same price, or arbitrage profits will be available to traders. Through the action of arbitrage, all prices of financial assets remain in equilibrium. APT is appealing in that it (1) allows for different expectations by market participants, (2) does not require the use of the market portfolio, and (3) yet can result in a pricing result identical to the SML of the CAPM. In order to implement the APT model, we need to know the specific factors that account for the differences among various security returns. But the APT is unclear about exactly which factors are important to pricing securities. Moreover, empirical investigation for relevant factors has been inconclusive. In contrast, with the CAPM, the primary factor that matters to the investor is the market portfolio. This concept, although unobservable directly, is understood conceptually, and it clearly has empirical counterparts in the form of various market indexes.

The important question in comparing the two approaches is, Does the greater complexity of APT add appreciably to our understanding of markets and our ability to explain real-world prices? The initial tests of APT failed to demonstrate clear superiority over the more standard MPT. Nonetheless, the APT model has continued to generate much interest. More recent empirical work, however, continues to be mixed. Some studies are relatively favorable. The results of others are inconsistent with APT. These results do not necessarily imply that standard MPT is preferable. No doubt, work will continue toward a more satisfactory model of asset pricing. For now, however, the standard version of MPT seems likely to remain the basis for comparison.

SUMMARY AND CONCLUSIONS

We have explored predictions of modern portfolio theory dealing with market efficiency, nonmarket risk, and the properties of estimated betas. Some of the evidence appears to be in conflict with the theory's predictions. Various inefficiencies are observed; nonmarket risk does appear to affect prices; and the relationship for securities between market risk and expected return is not demonstrably linear. The chapter discusses a number of real world violations of the model's assumptions. Too few investors may be appropriately situated to eliminate some mispricings; different investors borrow and lend at differing rates; return distributions may be nonnormal; some investors may be concerned with skewness; most empirical work with the market portfolio utilizes an index that excludes everything but U.S. equity securities; and imperfections such as taxes and transaction costs influence market prices. In spite of the drawbacks, MPT continues to be studied and utilized. Most researchers have a substantial human capital stake in the theory; the current model seems appreciably ahead of whatever is in second place (APT); it offers a useful point of departure; and it fits some aspects of the real world reasonably well. APT, the primary alternative to MPT, has generated a great deal of interest but has yet to demonstrate that its much greater complexity yields superior results.

CHAPTER REVIEW

Answers to the review questions and the self-test questions start on page 759.

Key Terms

efficient market hypothesis
(EMH)
fundamental analysis
technical analysis
random walk
weak form EMH
semistrong form EMH
strong form EMH
differential returns
risk-adjusted returns
expected return
Jensen's alpha
Sharpe ratio
Treynor ratio

coefficient of determination (R^2)
run
chartists
filter rules
relative strength criterion
market imperfection (anomaly)
skewed distributions
leptokurtosis
platokurtosis
adjusted beta
uncertain information hypothesis (UIH)
mean reversion
American Depository Receipts (ADRs)
arbitrage pricing theory

Review Questions

9-1. Compare the two principal types of investment analysis.

9-2. Discuss the three forms of the efficient market hypothesis. What do each imply about the types of investment analysis? Summarize the relevant evidence on each.

9-3. For the following series of prices, test the effectiveness of a 5 percent filter rule (for change in price, change from previous high, and change from previous low): 51, 51 1/4, 52, 51 1/2, 50 7/8, 49, 48 1/4, 49, 50 1/2, 52, 52 3/4, 53, 53 7/8, 55, 57, 56 1/2, 57 7/8, 58 1/2, 60, 62, 61 1/2, 59, 57, 58 1/2, 59. Specifically, the filter rule is to buy when there is a 5 percent increase from the previous price or previous high. Similarly, you should sell if there is a 5 percent decrease from the previous price or low. Ignore the impact of commissions.

9-4. Repeat question 9-3 using a 3 percent filter.

9-5. Discuss the possible causes of persisting market imperfections.

9-6. a. Compare the theoretical price impact of nonmarket risk with real world experience.

   b.   Discuss the possible explanations for the apparent inconsistency.

9-7.   Discuss the difficulties and remedies of diversifying.

9-8.   a.   What does portfolio theory usually assume for return distributions?
       b.   How are actual returns generally distributed on a daily basis and on a longer term basis?
       c.   How do most investors feel about skewness?

9-9.   a.   Plot the following histogram of possible returns: returns of less than 5% have a probability of .05; 10%, .10; 15%, .25; 20%, .20; 25%, .15; 30%, .10; 35%, .08; 40%, .05; 100%, .02.
       b.   Compute the mean and standard deviation.
       c.   Describe the distribution's skewness.

9-10. a.   How are betas estimated?
       b.   What problems arise?
       c.   How may betas be adjusted?

9-11. Compute Blume-adjusted betas for each of the following unadjusted betas: 1.34, .57, .78, 1.20, 1.47, 1.73, .45, 1.44, .89, .95, 1.80, 1.11, .69, .87, 1.15.

9-12. a.   What is the impact of international diversification?
       b.   How might a portfolio be diversified internationally, and what are the disadvantages of these methods?

9-13. a.   Summarize the problems of MPT.
       b.   Compare MPT with APT.

9-14. A diversified portfolio of stocks is expected to generate a return of 15 percent with a beta of 1. A diversified portfolio of long-term bonds offers an expected return of 11 percent and has a beta of .3. A diversified portfolio of short-term debt securities has an expected return of 8 percent and a beta of .1. How can you combine investments in these choices to

       a.   maximize expected return
       b.   minimize risk
       c.   provide beta of .5 and a maximum return for that beta level (ignore portfolios consisting of all three investments)

Self-Test Questions

T   F   9-1.   Overall, market risk is the most important risk that affects the price movements of common stock portfolios.

T   F   9-2.   The weak form of the efficient market hypothesis (EMH) states that the past history of price information is of no value in assessing future changes in stock prices.

T   F   9-3.   The efficient market, as the term is used in investments, is concerned with making security transactions at the lowest unit cost.

T   F   9-4.   Characteristics of efficiency in the market are that information is widely available and is generated in a random fashion.

T   F   9-5.   A market that is semistrong-form efficient is also weak-form efficient.

T   F   9-6.   The semistrong form of the EMH states that stock prices reflect all public and nonpublic information.

T   F   9-7.   In a semistrong efficient market, investors cannot act on new public information after its announcement and expect to earn above-average returns.

T   F   9-8.   The semistrong form of the EMH refutes technical analysis but supports fundamental analysis.

T   F   9-9.   The reward-to-variability (RVAR) measure assesses a portfolio's total return relative to its total risk.

T   F   9-10. The reward-to-volatility (RVOL) measure assesses a portfolio's excess return relative to its alpha.

T   F   9-11. When comparing large, broad-based equity mutual funds, both the RVAR and RVOL measures generally provide identical or almost identical rankings of the funds.

T   F   9-12. Tests of technical trading rules generally conclude that past price and volume strategies cannot consistently outperform a simple buy-and-hold strategy.

T   F   9-13. Results of studies concerning the trading activities of corporate insiders generally support the validity of the strong form of the EMH.

T   F   9-14. A market anomaly is an exception to what is expected in a totally efficient market.

T   F   9-15. If the stock market is efficient, then money (portfolio) managers need not be concerned with portfolio diversification and risk.

T   F   9-16. A portfolio's beta differs depending on the benchmark portfolio used in its determination.

T   F   9-17. Arbitrage models are based on using various factors to determine security returns and profitable trading situations.

NOTES

1. M.E. Blume, "On the Assessment of Risk," *Journal of Finance,* March 1971, pp. 1–10.
2. Barr Rosenberg, "The Capital Asset Pricing Model and the Market Model," *Journal of Portfolio Management* (Winter 1981), pp. 5–16.
3. K. Brown, S. Tinic, and V. Harlow, "Risk Aversion, Uncertain Information, and Market Efficiency," *Journal of Financial Economics*, vol. 22, 1988, pp. 355–358.
4. E. Fama and K. French, "The Cross-Section of Expected Stock Returns," *Journal of Finance,* June 1992, pp. 427–465.
5. S. Ross, "The Arbitrage Theory of Capital Asset Pricing," *Journal of Economic Theory,* 1976, pp. 341–360; R. Roll and S. Ross, "An Empirical Investigation of the Arbitrage Pricing Theory," December 1980, pp. 1073–1104; H. Floger, K. John, and J. Tipton, "Three Factors, Interest Rates Differentials and Stock Groups," *Journal of Finance,* May 1981, pp. 323–335; G. Oldfield and R. Rogalski, "Treasury Bill Factors and Common Stock Returns," *Journal of Finance,* May 1981, pp. 337–350.

10

Traditional Approaches to Fundamental Analysis

Learning Objectives

An understanding of the material in this chapter should enable the student to

---

10-1.   Explain the components of fundamental analysis and how they influence stock performance.

10-2.   Explain how macroeconomic analysis is used to evaluate the economy's effect on industry and firm fundamentals.

10-3.   Explain how industry analysis assesses the outlook for particular industries.

10-4.   Explain how company analysis examines a firm's relative strengths and weaknesses within its industry or industries.

10-5.   Explain the dichotomy between fundamental analysis and market efficiency as they relate to stock market prices.

Chapter Outline

As discussed in chapter 7, the value of an investment can be estimated by discounting its expected income stream. Both the theory and the evidence supporting this approach to valuations are unimpeachable. Applying this approach, however, requires obtaining or generating estimates of that future income stream, as well as assessing the risks associated with these projections. Unfortunately, any estimates of these required inputs are subject to a high degree of error. Forecasting earnings even one year ahead is difficult enough, to say nothing of projecting both earnings and the dividend payout ratio a number of years into the future. Although explicit long-term income-stream forecasts can be generated by several types of investment analysis, most analysts do not attempt to go that far. Rather, most of the practical efforts at fundamental analysis take a much more qualitative approach.

This chapter surveys the issues that are typically treated in the fundamental analysis section of traditional investment courses. It discusses macroeconomic analysis. Industry analysis and how it relates to investment selection is explored next; specific approaches to economic and industry analysis are discussed. Then company analysis is considered, giving particular attention to the evaluation of a company's competitive position, management quality, financial situation, and profitability. Finally, the chapter examines the relevance of this analysis to the market price and the efficient market hypothesis (EMH).

OVERVIEW OF FUNDAMENTAL ANALYSIS

fundamental analysis

macroeconomic analysis

Fundamental analysis is traditionally divided into three categories: (1) macroeconomic analysis, (2) industry analysis, and (3) company analysis. *Macroeconomic analysis* seeks to evaluate the current economic setting and its effect on industry and firm fundamentals. Industry analysis assesses the outlook for particular industries, whereas company analysis examines a firm's relative strengths and weaknesses within its industry or industries.

These three categories correspond to the three principal influences on stock performance. Clearly each is important, and past studies show that, in terms of both firm profits and stock returns (dividends plus price changes), market/economy and firm-specific factors are the dominant influences, with industry factors accounting for only about 10 percent of the variability.

Three Categories of Fundamental Analysis

- Macroeconomic analysis: evaluates current economic environment and its effect on industry and company fundamentals
- Industry analysis: evaluates the outlook for particular industries
- Company analysis: evaluates a company's strengths and weaknesses within its industry(ies)

MACROECONOMIC ANALYSIS

Publicly held firms make up a very large part of the economy. Profit rates, a major determinant of share prices, are closely tied to the nation's economic health. When the economy is depressed (as in a recession), most firms operate well below their capacities. Companies can meet a short-run downturn in the economy by laying off workers, reducing raw material orders, working down inventories, and reducing expansion and modernization spending. They are, however, unlikely to scrap fixed plant and equipment, and they can do little to reduce property taxes and interest payments to meet a temporary decline in the demand for their output. As sales decline, these so-called fixed costs absorb a larger proportion of revenues, thereby squeezing profits. For example, in the 1982 recession, which had an inordinate effect upon the agriculture sector, John Deere's sales fell by 14 percent, while its profits declined by 97 percent. At the same time, many of its competitors (International Harvester, Allis-Chalmers, and Massey-Ferguson) were losing money and, in International Harvester's case, threatened with bankruptcy.

Example: The experience of Coca-Cola in recent years may prove instructive regarding the impact of changing macroeconomic conditions on company profits. Between 1988 and 1991, the price and profit performance were extraordinary. From $10 per share in 1988, the stock reached $45 in 1992 and Coke's stock far outperformed the S&P 500 Index. But this dramatic increase in Coke's stock price between 1988 and 1992 reduced the margin of safety between Coke's market price and its intrinsic value if all macroeconomic risks were taken into account as described below.[1]

For most of the 1990s, Coke's marketing strategy produced impressive results. In search of new markets to sustain its growth, Coke moved aggressively as former centrally planned economies, such as Russia, opened up. Coke's stock price and earnings grew at a compound annual rate of 19.9 percent from 1992 to 1997. Then Coke's total return dropped dramatically from 27.8 percent to 1.4 percent in 1998. Economic crises throughout Southeast Asia, Latin America, and Russia all contributed to Coke's dramatic decline. Following some bad publicity in Europe over contaminated products earlier in 1999, Standard & Poor's placed some of its credit ratings for Coke and two of its bottlers on "credit-watch" for a possible downgrade in September of 1999. The debt-rating agency cited concerns about Coke's third consecutive profit warning in as many quarters during 1999. The fall from profitability grace by Coke is a lesson in how quickly a company's fortunes can be affected by changing macroeconomic conditions (as well as some local firm-level mishaps). With Coke's high and increasing exposure to foreign economies and the lack of potential growth opportunities in the U.S., its performance is inexorably tied to its overseas markets and to the risks in these markets.

The general tendency for profits to drop more than economic activity in a recession is illustrated in table 10-1. During these recessions personal consumption generally increased (an average of 4.62 percent), employment dropped modestly (–.92 percent), while profits fell appreciably (–15.91 percent). A rapidly growing economy, in contrast, leads to above-average employment, sales, and profit increases. Although investors generally fare better in booms than recessions, the relationships are complex. The economy's primary impact on stock prices relates to its effect on their expected income streams. The dividend decisions made by corporate managements tend to reflect long-term (not annual) earnings trends. Investors do, however, expect that earnings increases will eventually lead to higher dividends. Thus, an earnings increase is still a favorable sign even if the dividend response is slow. If profitably employed, retained earnings should produce still higher earnings. Eventually, these higher earnings should lead to both increased dividends and a higher stock price. Similarly, losses or reduced earnings are likely to lead to reduced dividends and stock prices. Figure 10-1 illustrates these linkages.

TABLE 10-1
Percentage Changes in Economic Activity for Postwar Recessions: Change in Profits, Civilian Non-Farm Employment, and Personal Consumption Expenditure

Year (Period)	Change in Profits	Change in Civilian Non-Farm Employment	Change in Personal Consumption Expenditure
1948–1949	−18.4%	−.66%	+.01%
1953–1954	−1.8	−2.47	+3.16
1957–1958	−22.3	−1.91	+1.27
1960–1961	−12.2	−.9	−.64
1970–1971	−11.4	+.08	+8.27
1973–1975	−34.2	+.71	+12.60
1979–1980	−17.8	−.83	+6.38
1981–1982	−24.3	−1.40	+7.05
1990–1991	−0.8	−0.9	+3.5
Average	−15.91	−.92	+4.62

Source: Economic data obtained from the Economic Report of the President for various years.

FIGURE 10-1
Links Between the Stock Market and the Economy

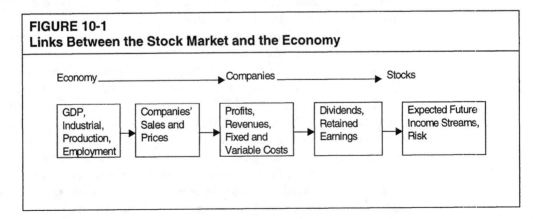

As figure 10-1 shows, causation runs from the economy to companies and then to stocks. That is, the state of the economy affects the performance of individual companies. Company performance, in turn, is the major determinant of the stock price. Economic activity is reflected in such data as the gross domestic product (GDP), industrial production, and the employment (or unemployment) rate. The level of economic activity has a major impact on the sales and prices of individual companies. Their sales revenues minus their costs then determine profits. A portion of these profits is paid out in the form of dividends and the remainder is retained earnings. Dividends provide immediate income to investors, while retained earnings are used to finance the resources needed to produce future growth. Thus, current profitability coupled with an understanding of its relationship to costs and revenues may be used to formulate a guide to the company's expected future income stream and level of risk.

Relationships between Stock Market and Economic Outlook

Because macroeconomic activity has a major impact on company sales, profits, and dividends, the investment community pays close attention to the business cycle. According to conventional Wall Street wisdom, stock values reflect the expected status of the economy approximately 6 months later. Indeed, the National Bureau of Economic Research rates the stock market as one of the primary leading indicators of economic activity. The economy generally moves in the same direction for much longer than 6 months, with the result that the economy and the stock market often move together. They may, however, move in opposite directions just before a turning point in the business cycle. At still other times, the market may incorrectly forecast business behavior and move perversely until there is a correction. However, in the last three decades, stock prices do tend to decline in reaction to increased inflation, high interest rates, and Federal Reserve credit tightening during the so-called boom-bust phase of the business cycle.

Not all market moves are related to changes in the economic outlook. What might be termed emotional factors sometimes influence the market. For example, unfavorable news such as the fall of France in 1940, the Cambodian invasion in 1970, the energy crises of 1974 and 1978, and the Iranian hostage crisis of 1980 were shocks to the stock market. Such noneconomic influences are superimposed on the basic stock market-economy relationship. More recently, the Iraqi invasion of Kuwait in 1990 and the default on foreign debt by Russia in 1998 are further examples of how external factors can dramatically affect securities markets. Indeed, the Fed reacted dramatically to the Russian default with several successive interest rate reductions to prop up panic-stricken markets.

Forecasting Economic Performance

Accurate business cycle forecasts might well facilitate profitable investment decisions. Only economic forecasts that are superior to the view of the market (6 months ahead) offer any real advantage. An ability to foresee a business downturn one year in advance, therefore, might afford 6 months' prior notice of a market move. Accurately forecasting economic behavior is very difficult, however. Indeed, the market itself would probably anticipate the economic outlook by more than the traditionally assumed 6 months if more reliable forecasts were available.

The various methods of predicting economic activity are discussed in chapter 12. These forecasts can be employed to anticipate how the industries and companies of interest are likely to perform. That is, past relationships among economy, industry, and company could be analyzed to determine how sensitive particular investments are to such matters as the general level of economic activity, interest rates, inflation, exchange rates, and so on. Investors could then use that economic forecast to assess the likely profit-dividend performance of an investment. Finally, this estimated performance could be compared with the market's view as reflected in its price.

Investors should keep in mind that investment values are relative. To demonstrate this point, suppose that the economic outlook is quite favorable for a particular firm. This outlook will make the firm's stock an attractive investment only if its price does not already reflect the favorable outlook. Similarly, a very poor economic outlook may so depress the market that many stocks are underpriced relative to their potentials.

A Specific Approach to Economic Analysis

Investment analysts do economic analysis when they use their knowledge of the economic environment to assess the outlook of the stock market. One approach to this task begins with the basic valuation models. Recall the dividend discount model and the PE (price earnings) ratio model that were introduced in chapter 7. As we have already seen, the price of a stock or other investment equals the present value of its expected income stream. When the growth rate of that income stream can be approximated by a constant defined as g, the (dividend discount) valuation formula may be expressed as follows in equation 10-1 (a repeat of equation 7-4):

$$P_0 = \frac{d_1}{(k - g)} \qquad \text{(Equation 10-1)}$$

where: P_0 = stock price at time $t = 0$
d_1 = anticipated dividend over forthcoming year

g = expected long-term growth rate for dividends

k = the appropriate discount rate for dividends

PE ratio

earnings multiplier

Most investors prefer to relate stock prices to per-share earnings (*PE ratio*) in what is also known as the *earnings multiplier*. Thus, a more usable form for this relationship brings in the expected earnings per share for next year e_1, anticipated long-term dividend payout ratio p (= d_1/e_1), and the PE ratio as shown in equation 10-2 (a repeat of equation 7-5):

$$PE = \frac{p}{(k - g)} \qquad \text{(Equation 10-2)}$$

Both equations will generate relatively accurate valuations when reliable long-term average values for p, k, and g are used (assuming that the values for individual years are generally relatively close to these averages). We can in many circumstances, therefore, use the two equations to express the determinants of the price and PE of a stock.

Although equation 10-2 is expressed in the form of a single share of stock of a single company, the same basic relationship can be applied to the entire stock market. The market is usually represented by an index value, which is designed to represent a diversified portfolio of stocks. For example, the New York Stock Exchange (NYSE) constructs an average of stock prices called the NYSE Composite Index. All stocks traded on the New York Stock Exchange are represented in proportion to the market value of their shares outstanding. The Standard & Poor's 500 Index (S&P 500) is another broad-based index of stock. A number of other popular indexes are also reported in the financial press.

When applied to the market, equation 10-2 implies that aggregate stock prices relative to aggregate earnings (as reflected by the PE of a broadly based market index) are a function of the overall payout ratio, the expected growth rate for aggregate dividends, and the appropriate discount rate for the stock market.

The level of stock prices is the product of the market's average PE ratio and its average earnings per share (or the corresponding earnings for the index). Using economic analysis to forecast the market can thus be decomposed into two tasks: forecasting the earnings of the market (or an index) and forecasting its corresponding PE ratio.

Forecasting the Market's Earnings

The per-share earnings attributable to a market index are computed according to the same principle as the value or price of the index. The individual earnings of each of the component stocks making up the index are assigned the same weights as they have in the index itself. The per-share earnings of the index then are the weighted average of the component's earnings.

The earnings on individual companies can be forecasted in a number of different ways. Similarly, forecasting the earnings of the market or a market index can be approached from a number of different directions. One logical approach is to forecast the relevant index's sales and expenses and then take the difference. A forecast for sales can be obtained from a prediction of the *gross domestic product (GDP)*. GDP reflects the sale of final output, whereas total corporate sales also include the sales of intermediate products (for example, the steel that goes into automobiles would be counted at least twice; once as a sale in the steel industry, and then again as part of the sales of the auto industry). The two types of sales numbers (final and intermediate) do tend to move together. Thus, aggregate corporate sales bear a close relation to GDP. Moreover, the stocks traded on the NYSE represent a very large percentage of the economy's overall production. Accordingly, sales attributable to the firms represented in the NYSE index are very closely related to total corporate sales.

To utilize this approach, we would need a forecast of GDP. Constructing this forecast is, however, beyond the scope of this chapter. Such a forecast could be obtained from one of the professional economic forecasters. Additionally, specific methods for forecasting GDP are discussed in chapter 12.

Determining Percentages of Profits and Expenses. The average ratio of GDP to NYSE index sales can be combined with a GDP forecast to obtain a forecast for the sales attributable to the NYSE index. The next step in this process is to determine what percentage of these sales represents profits and what percentage represents expenses. The most fruitful approach is generally believed to be first to estimate the gross profit (sales minus the cost of goods sold). Then operating and administrative expenses are subtracted to obtain the net operating income (income before interest and taxes). Then an estimate for the net profit margin (after-tax profit as a percentage of sales) is generated. The earnings of the NYSE index can be forecast as the product of forecasted sales and estimated net margin. First, however, an estimate for *gross margin* is needed.

Gross margin is largely a function of two forces: how intensively productive capacity is utilized *(capacity utilization)* and how efficiently labor is utilized *(unit labor costs)*. The overall state of the economy plays a large role in determining both capacity utilization and unit labor costs.

gross domestic product (GDP)

gross margin

capacity utilization
unit labor costs

A strong economy implies a high rate of capacity utilization, which in turn means a large amount of output relative to productive facilities. High capacity utilization tends to produce a high gross profit margin. Sales revenues tend to increase proportionately more than costs as capacity is utilized more intensively. On the other hand, as the economy weakens (and perhaps moves into a recession), capacity utilization declines and profits fall disproportionately.

Unit labor costs reflect the joint impact of two forces: wage rates and labor productivity. Aggregate wage rates often rise as time passes. The rate at which they rise depends on a number of factors:

- overall tightness of the labor market. The unemployment rate is a useful measure of labor market tightness.
- rate of inflation. Rapidly rising prices lead workers to press for compensatory wage increases.
- strength of the economy. Employers may be more inclined to grant wage increases when demand for their output is strong, but much depends upon the level of competition in their markets.
- amount of foreign competition. Strong price competition from imports encourages employers to keep down their own prices and costs, including labor costs.

Long-run productivity is largely responsive to the rate of implemented technological change. The change is brought about by investments in education and research and development, as well as the net new capital required to take advantage of these technologies. Although important in the longer-run context, this activity is largely ignored by those who are trying to forecast short-run profit and stock market performance. In the short run, labor productivity is mainly responsive to how it is combined with capital using existing up-to-date technology.

Gross margin, therefore, is principally a function of capacity utilization and unit labor costs (which, in turn, are largely determined by labor productivity and wage rates). The overall state of the economy, including unemployment and inflation rates, plays a large role in determining these factors.

depreciation

Forecasting Percentages of Depreciation and Taxes. The next step is to forecast the percentage of sales attributable to *depreciation* and taxes. Depreciation expense bears a relatively stable relation to the amount of depreciable plant and equipment. In a growing economy, plant and equipment typically expand each year by about 7 percent. Similarly, depreciation on plant and equipment increases each year by about 7 percent.

The actual forecast can be a bit above or below 7 percent, depending on circumstances for the particular year. Dividing the depreciation forecast by the aggregate sales forecast yields the percentage of sales attributable to depreciation.

Subtracting the estimated percentage of sales attributable to depreciation from estimated gross margin gives an estimate of before-tax profits as a percentage of sales. Generally, next year's ratio of corporate taxes to before-tax income will be rather similar to the current year's ratio. Sometimes, however, tax rates and rules change. At those times, the ratio tends to move in the direction indicated by the change in rates or rules. For example, if corporate tax rates go up or allowable deductions go down, the ratio of corporate taxes to profits will rise. Thus, we can start with the current ratio and adjust it for the effect of statutory changes. Once the proportion of the gross margin going for taxes is subtracted, what remains is *net margin,* which includes interest expense.

net margin

The forecasted earnings for the NYSE index may be obtained by multiplying the estimated net margin by the forecasted sales attributed to the index. The final step is forecasting the PE of the market or index.

**Steps to Forecast Market Earnings
Using Economic Analysis**

- Make or obtain a forecast for GDP, and use the result to derive a forecast for total corporate sales. Use past relationships and this forecasted sales figure to obtain a specific sales forecast for the index.
- Estimate the gross profit margin on sales. This margin can be estimated from past gross margin data and its relation to capacity utilization, unit labor costs, and the inflation rate.
- Estimate depreciation expense and the percentage of before-tax profit going to taxes. Past data and the impact of changes in tax rates can be used to form these estimates.
- Combine the gross margin, depreciation, and tax estimates to obtain a net margin estimate. Multiply net margin by forecasted sales to predict earnings for the index.

Forecasting the Market PE

Many analysts predict the market's earnings and then derive a forecast for the market's price level by applying their earnings forecast to the current market PE ratio.

> **Example:** In mid-1987, the NYSE Composite Index stood at about 180 with a PE of about 21 and most recent 12-month earnings of $8.60. If year-ahead earnings are expected to be $10, a PE of 21 implies an index value of 210.

Such a simplistic approach, however, ignores the possibility that the market PE may change. It often does. Indeed, the market did change dramatically shortly after June 1987. The great stock market crash of October 1987 saw the market fall by more than one-third in the space of a few weeks. By late November, the NYSE index was down to around 135. That level corresponded to a PE of 16. Had the NYSE index generated 1988 earnings of $10, a PE of 16 would imply a value for the index of around 160. Clearly, market forecasts need to explore the factors that may cause the average PE to change.

Recall the determinants of the PE reflected in equation 10-2:

$$PE = \frac{p}{(k-g)}$$

Thus, the market PE ratio is largely a function of p, the dividend payout ratio; k, the appropriate discount rate; and g, the expected growth rate in dividends. The overall market payout ratio has averaged close to or somewhat above .5. A given year's variations relative to that average are largely a response to departures from the normal growth in earnings. Dividends tend to adjust to changes in earnings after a lag. Therefore, if earnings or stock prices grow rapidly, dividends will not immediately rise in proportion and the payout ratio will fall.

> **Example:** During the late 1990s many companies replaced dividend increases with stock buybacks as a way of enhancing shareholder wealth. Indeed, as of mid-February 1999, the S&P 500 Index evidenced a dividend yield of only 1.3 percent, compared to 4 percent in 1990. The main reason for the drop in dividend yield during the late 1990s was the rapid run-up in stock prices. The payout ratio is also affected by the inflation rate. More rapid inflation encourages companies to retain more of their profits to offset the higher costs and taxes of operating in an inflationary environment.

The long-run growth rate in the economy is around 3 percent to 4 percent in real (noninflationary) terms. Although the growth in earnings will vary greatly from year to year, the long-term growth rate will be similar to that of the economy. The growth rate in nominal terms would tend to be increased by the inflation rate. That is, the expected nominal growth rate should approximately equal the long-term real rate plus the expected inflation rate. In periods of rapid inflation, however, the nominal growth in earnings is likely to be somewhat less than the inflation rate plus the long-term real growth rate. Rapid inflation tends to depress the real value of earnings.

The appropriate discount rate is a function of several factors. Suppliers of capital seek a return that will compensate them for both risk and the expected rate of inflation. Thus, k should equal the real riskless rate plus a premium for risk and an amount to compensate for the expected inflation. According to many theorists and analysts, market discount rates tend to be set to compensate investors fully for expected inflation. Thus, a real riskless rate of 3 percent and risk premium of 4 percent would produce a market discount rate of 7 percent plus the expected inflation rate.

One of the likely causes of the great crash of 1987 was a rise in interest rates. Long-term government bond rates rose from slightly above 7 percent in mid-1986, to slightly below 9 percent at the market's August 1987 peak, to over 10 percent just before the crash in October. This rise in market interest rates translated into a higher discount rate applied to the expected income stream of the dividends. The result was a much lower appropriate level for the market PE. The crash in stock prices brought about that decline.

Inflation plays a role in all three components of the PE equation. A rise in the inflation rate tends to depress p, thereby reducing the PE. That is, the higher the inflation rate, the larger the fraction of reported earnings represents unsustainable profits. For example, profit sources, such as sales from inventories carried on the books at long out-of-date cost levels, tend to be greater at high inflation rates. Firms are unlikely to increase their dividend rates when their earnings increases are expected to be temporary.

A rise in the inflation rate also tends to increase both k and g, but the greater impact is on k. Thus, (k − g) tends to increase as inflation rises, thereby reducing the PE. Overall, an increase in expected inflation tends to decrease the numerator and increase the denominator of the PE ratio equation, thereby tending to lower its overall value.

The inflation outlook appears to have had a minor role in the crash of 1987. Inflation was running at 4 percent to 5 percent both before and after the crash. The rise in interest rates was largely due to the government's efforts to deal with the international situation, particularly the large deficit in the balance of trade. The United States was importing far more than it was exporting and running a large payments deficit in the process. The Fed is thought to have engineered the interest rate rise at least in part to protect the dollar's international standing and to reduce the trade deficit.

Steps to Obtain the Market PE Multiple

- Estimate the market's overall dividend payout ratio p from past data, the stage of the business cycle, and expected inflation rates.
- Estimate the aggregate stock market discount rate k as the sum of the real risk-free rate, the market risk premium, and the expected inflation rate. Alternatively, add the appropriate risk premium to the current nominal (no inflation adjustment) riskless rate (for example, the rate of return on T-bills).
- Forecast the nominal long-term growth rate in the market's earnings g. The real long-term growth rate is largely a function of the stage of the business cycle. The nominal rate is the sum of the expected long-term real growth rate and a percentage (close to but probably less than 1) of the expected inflation rate.
- Apply the values for p, k, and g to equation 10-2 to obtain the forecasted market PE.

The value for the market index forecast, then, is the product of forecasted earnings and PE of the index. The steps summarized above represent a rather ambitious approach to assessing the market's outlook. Relatively few market analysts are likely to undertake such an extensive analysis. No doubt, some shortcuts are possible. Nonetheless, this type of analysis is a reasonable, logical approach to assessing the outlook for the stock market. (See section titled "Using the PE Ratio Model to Examine the Crash of 1987," which demonstrates how a related type of analysis might have helped anticipate the 1987 stock market crash.)

One question that often comes up, especially during market run-ups as occurred during the late 1990s, is whether the stock market is overpriced. Perhaps we can gain some guidance from Benjamin Graham, a money manager, professor, and noted author who is widely regarded as the father of **Graham and Dodd** modern security analysis. *Benjamin Graham and David Dodd* in their classic 1930 textbook, *Security Analysis*, maintained that the true measure of the market could be made only by relating the price of a stock to the underlying earnings of companies.

According to Graham, the stock market should be analyzed in the context of two fundamentals that determine value. Graham defined a company's stock as "a share of a business," and said that stocks ultimately derive their value from one source: the expected earnings that the firm can produce.

The other major factor that affects the value of stocks and the market in this model is the interest rate—specifically, the rate on 30-year government bonds. This rate is equivalent to the risk-free return on long-term money. Inflation also plays a role in security valuation, but the market should reflect the anticipated inflation rate in the market rate of interest. Of course, a risk premium for a specific firm's stock is included in its expected return. Graham implicitly assumed no significant change in the firm's risk premium in this approach.

Example: To explain how the two fundamental factors interact, consider an enterprise called Stable, Inc. This firm is unusual in that it is guaranteed to earn $6 per share every year, but no more. Some years it may decide to retain its earnings; another year it may pay it all in dividends. Thus, the investor can depend on earning $6 per year in either dividends and/or capital gains. The return to the investor can be determined simply by dividing the $6 by whatever the investor paid for his or her share—that is, earnings divided by price, or "earnings yield."

If 30-year U.S. Treasury bonds are yielding 6 percent, then the share of Stable, Inc., ought to be trading close to $100 per share. At that price, the earnings yield ($6/$100) would match the return on U.S. Treasuries. No investors would want to pay more for Stable, Inc., since they would end up making less than the yield on 30-year Treasuries.

The point of this simple illustration is that the stock market, as a whole, tends to be priced much like Stable, Inc. Of course, real companies are much more difficult to predict. Companies may have a tendency to grow rapidly over time; on the other hand, they can have some nasty earnings declines. Also, sometimes investors are more attuned to the earnings growth, and during tougher times they are more wary of the risks of the market. But, on average, the overall market, which is a blend of stocks with varying degrees of uncertainty and potential growth, tends to be relatively stable in the long run around the trends utilized in the Graham model.

Fundamental Factors That Affect Stock Value

- Company's expected earnings
- Interest rate on 30-year Treasury bonds

Using the PE Ratio Model to Examine the Crash of 1987

The PE ratio model can be used to examine how the stock market is viewing the future. Transforming the model to solve for the implied growth rate g yields the following:

$$g = k - p/PE$$

Thus, with estimates k, p, and PE (appropriate discount rate, expected long-term average payout ratio, and PE using expected earnings for next year) we can solve for the implied market expected growth rate in dividends g.

Data from the stock market crash of 1987 can be used to illustrate how the growth expectations vary. Doing so requires obtaining reasonable estimates for the needed inputs. Only one of these inputs is directly observable: the market price on the index. Everything else must be estimated. Ideally, we should use the market's expectations for the long-term future discount, payout, and earnings data. Presumably, however, current values of these data are reasonably close to the market's expectations. That is, the current long-term riskless interest rate is close to what the market believes to be the appropriate rate for discounting riskless assets. Adding a reasonable amount for the risk premium should produce a relatively accurate value for the appropriate discount rate for stocks.

The current payout ratio should be relatively close to what the market expects to be the long-term average. Similarly, the most recent 12-month earnings figure should be reasonably close to what the market expects for the following year. The market would normally expect next year's earnings to grow by about the long-term growth rate g. Thus, current earnings would generally differ from expected earnings for next year by only a modest scale factor.

Accordingly, our estimate for the appropriate discount rate is scaled up 3 percent from the current value for the long-term government bond rate. The actual risk premium could be somewhat different. Any differences would (assuming a relatively constant risk premium for the period of analysis) have similar impacts on each of our estimated discount numbers. The actual payout ratio p can be used for the market's long-term estimate. Similarly, the PE computed with the most recent 12-month earnings can be used as a proxy for the market's actual expectation. Although these proxies are imperfect, they are probably reasonably close to the market's actual (unobserved) expectations. Relying on these estimates will not lead to systematic errors over the time of this analysis.

Our objective is to use market data on PEs, interest rates, and payouts to assess the change in market expectations. Minor errors in estimating the expected payout, discount rate, and next year's expected earnings will have similar effects on our analysis of expectations for each date. Thus, any errors in our inputs will have little impact on the observed changes in market expectation.

Table 10-2 reports relevant data on the state of the market (using the S&P 500 index) at various dates around the time of the crash of 1987. Using these values produces the implied earnings growth rates reported in the table.

TABLE 10-2
The S&P 500 around the Time of the 1987 Crash

Date	30-year Bond Rates	S&P 500 Index	PE	Payout Ratio	Implied Growth Expectation
May 30, 1986	7.47%	247.35	16.93	56%	7.17%
December 12, 1986	7.73	247.35	16.86	56%	7.41
June 12, 1987	8.75	301.62	19.66	58%	8.80
August 21, 1987	8.90	335.90	22.42	58%	9.31
October 16, 1987	9.84	282.70	21.17	64%	9.82
October 24, 1987	10.13	248.22	17.92	62%	9.67
December 31, 1987	8.97	247.08	15.64	57%	8.33

These data reveal an interesting picture. Long-term interest rates varied from about 7.5 percent to over 10 percent, while the market PE ratio varied from under 16 to over 22. The dividend payout ratio was relatively stable in a range around 59 percent. The implied expected growth rate varied from somewhat over 7 percent to almost 10 percent. Clearly, the market's growth expectations changed substantially over this period.

Consider first the market situation on May 30 and December 12, 1986. These dates precede the major market rally that began in early 1987. The S&P 500 stood at about 250 on both dates. Long-term government bonds were yielding around 7.5 percent to 7.75 percent, and the S&P's PE was around 17. These numbers implied an expected long-term growth rate in the range of 7.2 percent to 7.4 percent. These expectations are consistent with recent historical experience of real growth of 3 percent to 4 percent and inflation in about that same range or perhaps a bit higher. We expect aggregate dividends to grow at about the same rate as the economy.

By June 12, 1987, the S&P 500 index was up substantially (over 50 points, or 22 percent) from the end of 1986. At that point, the PE had risen to almost 20 while long-term government bonds were yielding 8.75 percent. Both the PE ratio and interest rates had gone up. Normally, the two numbers move in opposite directions. These values for the market's PE and interest rates implied an expected long-term growth rate of 8.8 percent. This implied expectation was more than a full percentage point above the growth expectation of just 6 months earlier. A 1 percent difference in growth expectations may not seem like a lot. Over a period of years, however, these differences have a very substantial impact.

Example: A sum growing at 8 percent will double in 9 years. A sum compounding at a 9 percent rate will, in contrast, double in 8 years. A 1 percent difference in growth rate results in a year's difference in the time required to double.

From June to August 1987 the market continued to rise. On August 21 (near the market top), the S&P index stood at 335.90. This was almost 90 points, or 36 percent, above its 1986 year-end value. The PE exceeded 22. Had interest rates been falling, such a rise might not have been unusual. Interest rates had been continuing to rise, however. At this point, the long-term government bond rate was 8.9 percent. These values combine to produce an implied growth expectation of 9.31 percent. This expected growth rate was one-half of a percent higher than the already high implied expectation for June 1987.

Stock prices fell slightly as the crash date approached. The Friday before the crash (the crash itself occurred on Monday, October 19, 1987) the S&P 500 had fallen to 282.70. Compared with its August 21 level, this represented a decline of more than 50 points, or about 16 percent. Nonetheless, the market in retrospect was clearly poised for a further fall. Interest rates had continued to rise (reaching 9.84 percent), while the S&P's PE remained quite high (21.17) by recent standards. These values implied a growth expectation of 9.82 percent just before the crash. This expectation exceeded the corresponding expectation for mid- to late-1986 by 2 percent or more. This represents a huge change in expectations. Returning to our earlier example, at 10 percent, a sum will double in 7 years (compared to 8 years at 9 percent and 9 years at 8 percent). Thus, a 2-point increase in growth expectations implies a 2-year difference in the time required for a sum to double. Clearly, the market's growth expectations were very different just before the crash than they had been a year earlier.

A week later (October 24, 1987) the S&P had fallen 35 more points (12.2 percent) and the PE was down to 17.92. The market had actually fallen even more from Friday (October 16) to Monday (October 19), but by the end of that week it had recovered somewhat. Interest rates were, however, still continuing their rise (to 10.13 percent). As a result, even after the crash, the implied growth expectation remained very high by historical standards (9.67 percent). As the remainder of the year unfolded, interest rates declined modestly. On December 31, 1987, long-term government yields were a bit under 9 percent, and the S&P's PE was below 16. The S&P index itself was in very nearly the same range that it had been in during May and December 1986. The implied growth rate expectation was 8.33 percent.

In retrospect, the market was very overpriced at its August 1987 peak and even more overpriced just before the October crash. If the market's growth expectations in late 1986 were realistic, its expectations in mid-1987 clearly were unrealistic.

Economic analysis of the market is not at all easy. Nonetheless, the analysis demonstrated here could have been helpful in analyzing the overall stock market around the time of the 1987 crash.

INDUSTRY ANALYSIS

Economic analysis assesses the general environment and its impact on firms and industries. Industry analysis, in contrast, examines the specific environment of the markets in which they compete. Investors might begin a search for attractive investments by either evaluating the component companies of a selected industry or analyzing a particular firm first and then its industry and competitors. With either scenario, both company and industry analysis are undertaken. In the discussion that follows, the process is assumed to begin with industry analysis.

Before proceeding, we should establish the relevance of industry analysis to investors. The evidence is rather clear on one point: Individual industries have, over time, provided very different returns to investors. Consider, for example, the returns of the banking industry in the late 1980s and early 1990s versus the software industry and the telecommunications industry. Over specific periods, therefore, some industries show much higher returns than others. On the other hand, there is wide dispersion in the performance of individual firms within particular industries.

Michael E. Porter's research indicates that a critical factor affecting the profit potential of an industry is the intensity of competition in the industry.[2] He believes that the competitive environment of an industry determines the ability of the firm to sustain above-average rates of return on invested capital. Porter discusses five competitive forces that determine the intensity of competition among firms; these factors can vary greatly among industries: rivalry among existing competitors, threat of new entrants, substitute products or services, bargaining power of customers, and bargaining power of suppliers.

Looking at industry analysis from a global prospective, firms active in foreign markets will be affected by global competition. Clearly, the U.S. automobile industry faces competition from firms in Japan, Germany, and Korea. Thus, any analysis of the auto industry must be extended to include global factors.

Their independent movements notwithstanding, attractively performing industries contain a disproportionate number of profitable investments. Therefore, we would like to know how to identify industries that will show the highest future returns. One possibility might be to select industries with strong recent records. This assumes that the same forces that produced the past record will continue, at least for a while longer. Projecting past industry performance, however, involves uncertainties similar to those of extrapolating past earnings growth. Past growth may imply some momentum but also establishes a higher base. The central issue is whether past growth reflects the industry's stage of development or isolated circumstances. Thus, identifying an industry's development stage may help assess its growth prospects.

Stages of Industry Development

Industries are thought typically to pass through several developmental stages. Initially, many new firms are established (start-up stage), and growth is rapid. A shakeout then reduces the number of firms (consolidation stage) as the less efficient firms tend to merge or go bankrupt. After the adjustment, growth slows to that of the economy (mature stage). Finally, new industries begin to grow at the expense of the existing industry (declining stage). Predicting evolution from one stage to another is not easy. In fact, some industries follow different schemes from the typical one just described. For example, the solid waste disposal industry experienced modest performance until the ecology movement brought it to life.

A firm moving from one stage to another usually experiences substantial stock price volatility. For example, firms and industries introducing new products or concepts (start-up stage) will eventually see growth slow (mature stage) to the level of replacement demand. Examples include automobiles in the 1920s, black and white televisions in the 1950s, and biotechnology in the mid-1980s. Future candidates include personal computers, the Internet, proprietary hospitals, and genetic engineering. Rapid growth should never be projected beyond a reasonable saturation point. Stock prices usually suffer once the market realizes that growth is slowing.

Some experts question the validity of the life cycle approach to industry analysis. They note, for instance, that the Coca-Cola Company has been a successful competitor, deriving much of its revenues from a product that has changed relatively little in 100 years. However, Coca-Cola has achieved its most recent profit momentum through the effects of globalization and international growth. As of 1999, Coke derived over 60 percent of its revenues from outside the United States.

Life Cycle of an Industry

- Start-up stage: many new firms; grows rapidly (example: genetic engineering)
- Consolidation stage: shakeout period; growth slows (example: video games)
- Mature stage: grows with economy (example: automobile industry)
- Declining stage: grows slower than economy (example: railroads)

Differential Industry Risk

Although past industry growth offers little guide to the future, several studies have found that individual industries exhibit rather different risk characteristics. Moreover, the risks of each industry have tended to be relatively stable over time. In other words, relative risk differentials between, say, the airline industry and the auto industry, have remained relatively stable, even though risk levels tend to widen during rising and falling market cycles. The trend levels maintain their relative dispersion of risk. This is the main basis for generating industry beta coefficients for use in certain versions of the capital asset pricing model (CAPM).

A Specific Approach to Industry Analysis

The same basic methodology that was examined in the section on economic analysis can be used to analyze an industry. That is, the market performance of an industry can be forecast from an analysis of its earnings and PE potentials. This analysis is easier to perform when the industry is represented by an index. In addition to the broad stock indexes, a number of indexes are compiled for the stocks of individual industries. Data on these indexes and the stocks that make them up allow investors to forecast their earnings and PEs. If no industry index is readily available, a quasi-index can be formed from the stocks of the principal companies that make up the industry.

Analysts want to forecast both sales and the profit margins on the sales. The first step in forecasting industry sales is to find one or more economic data series that move closely with the industry's revenues. GDP is a possibility. Personal disposable income might be a better choice for industries that are consumer oriented. In some instances, the sales forecast may be based on several variables. For example, many industries are especially sensitive to interest rates. Others may be particularly affected by the strength of the dollar, the cost of energy, or changing demographics. Still others may be very dependent on the level of government spending (for example, defense) or regulatory action (for example, telecommunications).

The industry sales forecast should be based on whatever relationships have been established from past experience and an understanding of how the industry is structured. The analyst could either incorporate these factors into an ad hoc forecast or develop an equation using linear regression techniques that related the explanatory variables to industry sales. In the latter case, estimates of the future values of these variables would be applied to the equation to generate a forecast for industry sales.

To the extent possible, the gross profit margin for the industry should be estimated from past historical relationships, knowledge of the industry's capacity utilization, and unit labor costs. Industry (as opposed to aggregate) data may or may not be available on these factors. Trade associations and trade publications are potential sources for these data (both historical and expectational).

As with the value for the overall economy, industry depreciation is relatively easy to estimate. The analyst simply adds a percentage to the prior year's depreciation figure. The size of the percentage to be added depends on the past average value and any factors specific to that year. Thus, in a "normal" year the average rate of increase would be added to the prior year's depreciation level. In years when some special factor was expected to have an impact, the added increment would be adjusted to reflect that factor.

Most industries pay taxes at about the same rate as the overall average. Historical data can reveal the past relationship. Recent changes that withdraw or add tax advantages to firms in the industry, such as energy tax credits, should be factored into the analysis.

The resulting industry earnings forecast must be scaled to the index value and compared with the most recent historical earnings number. How does the forecast of this industry's percentage change in earnings compare with that for the economy? As a general rule, industries that are expected to grow more rapidly than the average should have higher PEs than the market average PE.

Steps to Forecast the Industry's Outlook Using Economic Analysis

- Make or obtain a forecast for GDP, personal disposable income, or some other factor or group of factors that has in the past been highly correlated with industry sales. Use the result to derive a forecast for the industry's sales. Use past relationships and the forecasted sales figure to generate a specific sales forecast for the industry index.
- Estimate the industry's gross profit margin on sales. This estimated margin can be derived from past gross profit margin data and its relation to capacity utilization, unit labor costs, and the inflation rate.
- Estimate depreciation expense and the percentage of before-tax profit going to taxes. Past data and the impact of changes in tax rates can be used to form these estimates.
- Combine the gross profit margin, depreciation, and tax estimates to obtain a net profit margin estimate. Multiply net margin by forecasted sales to obtain forecasted earnings for the index.

A fuller picture of the industry's prospects can be obtained by examining its current and potential future PE ratio. Equation 10-2 helps us understand the current PE level and forecast the industry's future PE. Historical experience can give a rather dependable idea of the likely payout ratio p. Some adjustments may be made in the light of the industry's expected growth g and the national inflation rates expected to prevail in the foreseeable future.

The appropriate discount rate k for the industry will differ from the rate for the overall market by the amount that the two risk premiums differ. The historical relationship between the risk premiums would provide a relatively accurate guide to the difference. Unfortunately, these premiums are not directly observable but must be inferred from other data, such as relative PE ratios or direct data on relative risks. More volatile industries, such as technology-intensive industries, can be expected to be riskier than the national average (high beta). On the other hand, there are relatively safe industries, such as food stores, drugstores, and public utilities, that tend to have fairly stable performance despite fluctuations in the overall economy. These low-beta industries are sometimes referred to as defensive industries.

The industry's expected growth rate g is related to the overall growth rate of the economy and the specific circumstances of the industry. The rate of growth of the industry's earnings is largely determined by the amount of new capital invested in the industry and the return on new and old invested capital. The amount of new capital is closely related to the industry's retention rate, which is 1 minus its payout rate p. Return on equity is related to a number of factors, such as capacity utilization, leverage, and product prices.

The estimated values for p, k, and g can be applied to the PE equation to forecast the industry's PE. A second approach relates movements in the market's PE ratio to the industry's ratio. Thus, expected changes in the market ratio can be applied to the current industry ratio. Both approaches may be used, and the results averaged. The product of the industry's forecasted earnings and PE can then be used to forecast the future value of the industry index. The predicted percentage change in the industry index may be used as a guide to whether the industry represents an attractive place to look for investment opportunities.

Steps to Obtain the Industry PE Multiple

- Estimate the industry's overall dividend payout ratio p from past data, the stage of the business cycle, and expected inflation rates.
- Estimate the aggregate stock market discount rate k as the sum of the real risk-free rate, the market risk premium, and the expected inflation rate. Adjust that figure to reflect the differential risk premium for the industry.
- Forecast the nominal long-term growth rate in the industry's earnings g. The real long-term growth rate is largely a function of the stage of the business cycle. The nominal rate is the sum of the expected long-term real growth rate and a percentage (close to but probably less than 1) of the expected inflation rate.
- Apply the values for p, k, and g to equation 10-2 to obtain forecasted industry PE.

Industry Analysis: Assessment

Industry analysis could be discussed in much greater detail. Analysts would like to be able to accurately forecast future levels of industry sales, costs, and profits. Relevant governmental policies should be assessed. The interrelationships with competing and complementary, supplier and customer industries should all be considered. This analysis is relatively difficult to perform effectively. Nonetheless, industry analysis is helpful only when it is superior to the market's assessment.

As with economic analysis, investors should bear in mind the relative nature of the process. Although the prospects of individual industries need to be evaluated, the most attractive industries for investment are not necessarily the ones with the brightest profit and growth prospects. Rather, investors seek investments with greater potentials than the market recognizes. In other words, the market may have already taken account of these prospects in the price of stocks of companies in that industry, so that investors cannot earn superior risk-adjusted returns by investing in that industry. Thus, an industry with bleak prospects may contain attractive investments if the market is even more pessimistic than the true outlook justifies.

COMPANY ANALYSIS

Once industry analysis has identified a potentially attractive area for investment, the companies within that industry need to be evaluated. Three important company characteristics are competitive position, management quality, and financial soundness. Each relates to how successful a firm is likely to be within its industry or industries.

Competitive Position

While somewhat more difficult to evaluate than its financial strengths and weaknesses, the company's competitive position is an important performance determinant. How able is the firm to withstand competitive pressures? How vigorous are its rivals? What is the government's attitude? Clearly, these are interesting questions.

A company's ability to compete within its industry depends on how its resources compare to those of its rivals. Scale economies in production, distribution, and advertising generally give larger companies an advantage. On the other hand, difficulties in exercising effective control increase with size. For example, since its inception, U.S. Steel (now USX) has been described as a lumbering dinosaur too large for effective control.

Antitrust vulnerability is yet another disadvantage of size. Every competitive move of high-market-share companies, such as Exxon, IBM, Microsoft, and AT&T, risks antitrust scrutiny. Mere size does not constitute an offense, but a company whose own sales represent a very large percentage of its market has difficulty avoiding actions that may be deemed illegal. Antitrust pressure led AT&T to agree to spin off its operating companies. Even when within-market expansion is legal, a dominant firm may have little opportunity to grow other than in line with its industry or by diversifying. For the giants, even diversification-inspired mergers may provoke an antitrust suit. Procter & Gamble's acquisition of Clorox and General Foods' acquisition of S.O.S were both undone by government action. More recently, the Burlington Northern Railroad's attempt to merge with the CNR (Canadian National Railroad) was denied by the government—even though railroading is a low-growth industry and both firms might have been strengthened. The market share argument was the dominant issue.

Some companies may be too small to compete effectively, whereas the existing size of others may limit further growth. Within a wide range of viable sizes, however, other factors have greater impacts on differential performance.

Management Quality

A perceptive, aggressive, forward-looking management improves the odds of realizing a company's full potential. The following characteristics are relevant: motivation, research and development activity, willingness to take risks, success in integrating merged firms, effectiveness in delegating authority, use of information systems, use of a board of directors, relations with financial analysts, and social responsibility. Other studies note that managers who are especially interested in stockholder welfare generally outperform those more concerned with their own well-being. Still other studies imply that highly rated managements generally do not produce high returns for their shareholders, but they do tend to reduce risk.

A broad array of information on managerial quality is probably relevant, but few investor/analysts have the resources to evaluate most of these factors effectively. Past performance is one useful guide, although it is of less help when it is needed most—that is, when leadership shifts. Investors can normally do little more than read the financial press or the online investor news services. A few, however, may contact some managers directly (particularly those of small local companies).

Financial Position

An attractive industry environment, strong competitive position, and effective management are all important components of a company's fundamental position. Only companies with adequate financial resources, however, can fully exploit their opportunities. Accordingly, much of fundamental analysis involves assessing the company's financial strengths and weaknesses.

Basic Accounting Concepts Used in Fundamental Analysis

Because accounting data are utilized extensively in financial analysis, we shall briefly review the principal types of financial statements. First, a

balance sheet

balance sheet provides an instantaneous picture of a company's resources and obligations as of its most recent reporting date. A classified listing of assets appears first, or on the left. Plant and equipment are valued at cost less depreciation, whereas most other assets are valued at the lower of either cost less depreciation or market value. Liabilities (both long- and short-term debts) and net worth (the stockholder's residual ownership position) appear next, or on the right. Because net worth equals assets minus liabilities, the two sides of the balance sheet are always equal; hence, its name (see table 10-3).

TABLE 10-3
Basic Balance Sheet

Assets	Liabilities and Net Worth

Current Assets
  Cash
  Inventories
  Accounts receivable
  • • •
Long-Term Assets
  Plant
  Equipment
  Land
  Market value of patents and
    royalties
  • • •
	Current Liabilities
	  Accounts Payable
	  Short-term notes
	  • • •
	Long-Term Liabilities
	  Corporate debt
	  • • •
	Net Worth
	  Stockholders' equity

Total Assets = Total Liabilities and Net Worth	

Think of the balance sheet as identifying the firm's key assets and how those assets are financed. The liabilities and net worth or equity section indicates how the firm's assets are financed. That is, basically the firm's assets are financed by debt (liabilities) and equity (net worth). The greater the percentage of the firm's assets that are financed by debt, other things being equal, the greater the firm's financial leverage and risk. The primary risk of too much debt or financial leverage is the risk of default.

income statement

The *income statement* is a flow statement that begins with total sales or revenues. Various expenses are then subtracted until only the company's earnings remain. The income statement helps answer questions such as, How much did the company make or lose in the recent period? How much of its earnings went to its stockholders? How do current earnings compare with past results? Every year (unless the company sells or buys back some stock) the company's net worth will change by that year's retained earnings (profit after taxes less dividends). The income statement and balance sheet are thus connected by changes in net worth.

**change in financial
position statement**

The *change in financial position statement* (sources and uses), the third of the principal statements, helps to analyze the company's liquidity/cash flow position.

Types of Accounting Statements

- Balance sheet: instantaneous picture of resources (assets) and obligations (liabilities)
- Income statement: revenues less expenses equal earnings
- Change in financial position: liquidity/cash flow position

Preparing accounting statements necessarily involves many subjective judgments, and subjectivity opens up opportunities for abuse. Unfortunately, the temptation may be too great for some unscrupulous managers. Permissible accounting conventions may be misused to alter a company's financial appearance. Nevertheless, the vast majority of accounting statements probably reflect a consistent and meaningful financial picture.

ratio analysis

Ratio Analysis

Relative magnitudes of financial data are generally more revealing than absolute levels. A company with a bank balance of $1 million dollars could be very rich or very poor, depending on its overall size. Accordingly, ratios of financial aggregates have long been used to assess the financial positions of various sized companies.

Ratios may be grouped into four categories. Liquidity ratios measure the company's ability to meet its short-run obligations. Debt ratios measure the company's leverage. And profitability and efficiency ratios are designed to reflect the firm's productivity.

**current ratio
current assets**

current liabilities

Liquidity Ratios. The *current ratio* is an index of the short-run solvency or liquidity picture. It is defined as *current assets* (cash, short-term investments, accounts receivable, prepaid expenses, and inventories) divided by *current liabilities* (accounts payable, notes due in one year, and the current portion of long-term debt). According to conventional wisdom, the current ratio should be two or greater—that is, two dollars of current assets for every one dollar of current liabilities. As with all ratios, however, the optimal value varies from company to company, industry to industry, and over time. Stable incomes and reliable sources of short-term credit lessen the need for liquid assets and therefore reduce the optimal current ratio level. Indeed, a high current ratio may indicate that resources are being tied up unnecessarily. A ratio slightly below two is generally less worrisome than a major decline in the ratio.

acid test ratio

The quick ratio, or *acid test ratio* is defined as liquid assets (current assets less inventories) divided by current liabilities, including interim debt. Therefore, inventories, which may be relatively difficult to liquidate, are part of the current ratio's numerator but excluded from the quick ratio. Most analysts recommend a quick ratio greater than 1. 5—that is, liquid current assets matching dollar for dollar with current liabilities. The appropriate level, however, varies from industry to industry, over time, and with special characteristics of the company.

inventory turnover ratio

The *inventory turnover ratio* equals the cost of goods sold divided by average yearly inventory. The reciprocal of the inventory turnover ratio, multiplied by 360, represents the average number of days that goods are held in inventory. The ideal inventory level differs with the industry and in some cases with the season and business cycle. A high turnover suggests brisk sales and well-managed inventories. However, a very high ratio might indicate inadequate inventories. A low turnover, in contrast, reflects idle resources tied up in excess inventories and/or a large obsolete inventory component. A low inventory turnover, relative to the firm's competitors, might also be indicative of a marketing problem.

Liquidity Ratios

- Current: Current assets/current liabilities
- Quick (or acid test): (Current assets – inventories)/current liabilities
- Inventory turnover: Cost of goods sold/average yearly inventory

The average collection period (ACP) is the weighted average life of outstanding accounts receivable. It should be compared with the company's stated credit policy. For example, a manufacturer might have a credit policy based on an expectation of receiving payments within 30 days of billing. If the ACP is longer than 30 days, the firm may have a problem with credit extensions. Perhaps the firm needs to tighten credit standards or improve its collection policy. On the other hand, too low an average collection period, relative to the industry, might suggest that the firm is losing potential customers by maintaining an overly stringent credit policy.

Unless substantial losses or a major adjustment (that is, a large merger) have clouded the picture, most established companies' short-run financial pictures will be satisfactory. Small, less-experienced companies, in contrast, frequently encounter short-run financial difficulty either because of poor capitalization or low rates of profit/cash flow.

debt-equity ratio

Debt Ratios. Debt-equity and times-interest-earned ratios are used to assess the prospects for a company's continued success and stability. *Debt-equity ratios* (liabilities divided by net worth), also known as leverage ratios, vary considerably from industry to industry, company to company, and over time. A public utility with highly predictable earnings, a bank with very liquid assets, or a construction company that undertakes very large projects relative to its equity base may have a relatively high ratio. This ratio could be as high as 2:1 or even 20:1. Companies with volatile earnings (for example, computer manufacturers) may choose to have a much lower target ratio, such as 1:10. A high debt ratio can be profitable to shareholders, but it also represents a type of risk, known as financial risk. As a general rule, a firm whose cash flows are relatively stable, and that experiences very little business risk, can afford to take on a fair amount of financial risk. On the other hand, a firm that is in an early stage of development, or that is engaged in a risky type of business, should avoid adding to its business risk by taking on a substantial amount of financial risk.

Companies that borrow generally do so in an effort to increase their profit relative to their net worth (that is, return on equity). This is the principle of financial leverage mentioned above. A company that can borrow at X percent and earn (X + Y) percent on the money gains the difference. Financial leverage is, however, a two-edged sword. The company that borrows has thereby incurred debts that must be serviced, regardless of the returns earned with the borrowed funds. Thus, companies that are planning to be heavy borrowers need to be relatively confident that the return that they earn will exceed their borrowing costs. Moreover, interest payments must be made when due whether or not a profit was made in that period.

Accordingly, a company with a stable return is better positioned to borrow than one with a similar average but less stable profit rate. In difficult times, burdensome debt obligations may force a company with favorable long-run prospects to liquidate needed assets and, in an extreme case, to file for bankruptcy. A substantial amount of leverage (high debt-equity ratio) is therefore both potentially profitable and risky. The more secure the company, the greater the percentage of debt that it may safely accept.

A company's appropriate debt-equity ratio varies primarily with its earning stability. A comparison of debt-equity ratios over time and within the industry may help assess the adequacy of the current level. A rapid rise in the ratio can suggest potential problems. It is of less concern if the increased debt still leaves the firm with a substantial cushion of equity and profitable operations; the company may simply be taking advantage of heretofore unused debt capacity. If the firm is experiencing losses or only modest profits, however, its increased reliance on debt suggests possible problems. It may well be taking on additional debt to finance a risky strategy. This debt may, for example, be designed to finance a program that the borrowing firm hopes will eventually show sufficient profits to finance that additional debt. These hopes, however, may not be realized. Even if the firm's greater debt is accompanied by increased profits, the investor needs to be cautious. The recent profit growth may not be sustainable. At a minimum, further growth would be difficult to finance if it required a still greater proportion of debt. In addition, creditors are likely to charge a substantially higher rate of interest to firms that have experienced unstable cash flows. Like stockholders, creditors require a risk premium when they are uncertain about the borrower's ability to service the debt in a timely manner. The higher the interest rate, the lower the potential gains from leverage.

Debt is not the only type of fixed payment obligation. In particular, leases may further complicate accounting statement analysis. Purchasing assets with borrowed funds increases the debt-equity ratio, whereas leasing the same assets does not increase debt *per se*. The long-term obligations are very similar, however, whether the assets are leased or purchased. Thus, debt-equity ratios do not always accurately reflect a company's total financial commitments. Investors need to look beyond simply the debt ratios of companies that lease a large fraction of their assets. Companies must show their capitalized long-term lease obligations on their balance sheets. Leases that call for payments of less than 80 percent of the asset's value need not be capitalized.

The absence of an allowance for unfunded pension liabilities can also distort a corporation's reported financial picture. Rising values on pension fund portfolios are expected to pay a substantial part of the promised benefits. When the portfolio does not produce the expected gains, pension funds may be inadequate to cover pension obligations. Moreover, many pension funds are underfunded by the corporation. Pension reform legislation now requires that many benefits be paid even if the employee leaves well before retirement age (vested benefits) or the company leaves the industry. These unfunded pension liabilities have a high priority claim in any bankruptcy proceeding.

Some financial analysts prefer to use the debt-asset ratio rather than the debt-equity ratio. As mentioned above, assets equal debt plus equity. Thus, the two ratios are closely related. They have the same numerator. Moreover, both have equity in the denominator. The debt-equity ratio's denominator is equity, whereas the debt-asset ratio's denominator is assets, which are the sum of debt and equity. Therefore, the debt-asset ratio's denominator is increased by the same number that appears in each ratio's numerator. The main difference in the two ratios is in their scales. Equity can be a small percentage of assets, a large percentage of assets, or something in between. Therefore, the debt-equity ratio can vary from a number close to 0 (almost no debt) to a very large number (almost no equity). The debt-asset ratio, in contrast, generally lies between 0 (almost no debt) and 1 (almost no equity). Because the debt-equity ratio varies over a larger range, some analysts prefer it to the debt-asset ratio.

times-interest-earned ratio

The *times-interest-earned ratio* (earnings before tax and interest payments divided by current interest payments) also reflects a company's debt risk. Unlike the debt-equity ratio, however, it relates the company's interest obligation to its earning power. Obviously, the higher the ratio, the greater the probability that interest will be paid promptly.

Debt Ratios

- Debt-equity: Total debt/shareholders' equity
- Times-interest-earned: Profit before tax and interest payments/current interest payment

---

return on equity (ROE)
return on assets (ROA)
return on investment (ROI)
return on sales (ROS)

Profitability and Efficiency Ratios. Five important and related profitability-efficiency (or activity) ratios are (1) *return on equity (ROE)*, (2) *return on assets (ROA)*, also sometimes called *return on investment (ROI)*, (3) *return on sales (ROS)*, also sometimes called profit margin, (4) asset turnover, and (5) debt margin. One other efficiency ratio is the average collection period. It reflects how long accounts receivables remain outstanding.

Annual averages are generally used to compute profitability and efficiency ratios. A shorter time frame can be used, but seasonal influences may distort the results.

$$ROE = \frac{After\text{-}tax\ profit}{Shareholders'\ equity}$$

$$ROS = \frac{After\text{-}tax\ profits}{Total\ revenues}$$

$$Asset\ turnover = \frac{Total\ revenues}{Total\ assets}$$

$$\text{Debt margin or leverarge} = \frac{\text{Total assets}}{\text{Shareholders' equity}}$$

asset turnover
debt margin
  (leverage)
Dupont formula

Note that ROE is the product of ROS, *asset turnover*, and *debt margin (leverage)*. This is known as the *Dupont formula* and is useful for troubleshooting when return on equity is below expectations:

$$\text{ROE} = \text{ROS} \quad \text{x} \quad \text{Asset turnover} \times \text{Debt margin}$$

$$\frac{\text{After-tax profit}}{\text{Shareholders' equity}} = \frac{\text{After-tax profit}}{\text{Total revenues}} \text{x} \frac{\text{Total revenues}}{\text{Total assets}} \text{x} \frac{\text{Total assets}}{\text{Shareholders' equity}}$$

Thus, we can examine the source of profitability problem by looking at the components of ROE. ROE as a measure of profit relative to shareholders' equity is a major determinant of share prices. Because its denominator (equity) is smaller and more variable, ROE tends to be more variable than ROA.

Return on sales (ROS) is also called the profit margin. ROS tends to vary inversely with turnover. A high-turnover operation such as a supermarket tends to have a low profit margin, whereas a high-margin operation such as a jewelry store tends to have a low turnover.

Profitability and growth prospects are forward-looking concepts. Is the past profit and growth record likely to improve or get worse? An examination of past results helps assess various possible scenarios.

High growth rates resulting primarily from increased debt, higher capacity utilization, accounting changes, cost cutting, or price increases must eventually cease. Earnings forecasts should project a more favorable margin, debt-equity ratio, or output-asset ratio only if the projected change seems likely to persist over time.

Profitability and Efficiency Ratios

- Return on equity (ROE): After-tax profit/shareholders' equity
- Return on assets (ROA): Before-tax before-interest profit/total assets
- Return on sales (ROS): After-tax profit/total revenues
- Asset turnover: Total revenues/total assets
- Debt margin (leverage): Total assets/shareholders' equity
- Average collection period: Accounts receivables/total revenues

earnings per share

Other Ratios. In addition to liquidity, debt, profitability, and efficiency ratios, investors may find several other ratios useful. *Earnings per share* (EPS) are the company's total earnings (less any preferred dividends) divided by the number of shares outstanding. Several different earnings numbers are often reported. Fully diluted EPS accounts for the exercise and conversion of any outstanding warrants and convertibles. In other words, when fully diluted earnings per share are calculated, net earnings are divided by the number of shares of stock that would be outstanding if all warrants, convertible debt, and convertible preferred stock were exercised. In a sense, fully diluted earnings per share are a "worst-case scenario" analysis. Earnings figures may include or exclude extraordinary items and the results from noncontinuing operations.

As we have already seen, the PE ratio or ratio of the per-share market price to EPS is a measure of the relative stock price. The current annual dividend rate (usually four times the quarterly rate) divided by the price per share is the current *dividend yield*. The total return reflects both capital gains and dividends. The dividend-payout ratio (p in the PE ratio model) equals dividends per share divided by EPS. A very low payout may indicate a substantial need to finance internal growth, management's desire to expand, or abnormally high current earnings. A very high ratio may suggest few attractive investment opportunities.

dividend yield

Cash flow per share is the sum of after-tax profits and depreciation (a noncash expense) divided by the number of shares outstanding. When reported depreciation is overstated (understated profits) or depreciating assets are not replaced (funds available for other uses), the cash flow per-share figure reflects an important source of discretionary funds.

book value per share

Book value per share equals the company's net worth (after subtracting that attributable to preferred shareholders) divided by the number of its common shares outstanding. The per-share book value is typically compared with the current stock price. A high book value relative to the stock's price may indicate either unrecognized potential or overvalued assets. Railroad book values, for example, are often many times the market price of the stock. Unless the assets can be sold for close to their book values, however, the railroads' modest profit rates justify their low stock prices. Alternatively, the per-share book value may be much lower than the per-share price of the stock, perhaps reflecting some hidden or undervalued assets (patents or real estate valued at historical costs). (Book value is based on historical costs and generally fails to take into account the full impact of inflation. It also ignores intangible assets such as the quality of R&D currently being undertaken by the firm. Therefore, book value is usually substantially below market value.) Because book values that diverge appreciably from stock prices suggest that securities may be misvalued, further analysis could be indicated.

Other Ratios

- Earnings per share (EPS): Profits after taxes – preferred dividends/number of shares
- Price-earnings (PE): Price per share/EPS
- Current yield: Indicated annual dividend/price per share
- Dividend payout: Dividends per share/EPS
- Cash flow per share: (After-tax profits + depreciation/number of shares
- Book value per share: Net worth attributable to common shareholders/number of shares

Sources of Ratios. A company's ratios are most effectively analyzed by comparing them with similar companies' ratios. Thus, averages of industrywide ratios are helpful. Robert Morris Associates collects data and computes ratios for a large group of industries. Other sources include Dun & Bradstreet and Standard & Poor's. Individual industry ratios may be computed with appropriate data from several similar companies. It is also important to evaluate trends in financial ratios over time, in order to see whether a company's financial condition is improving or deteriorating.

Example: To see how important the source of a company's past growth is, consider the following companies. Each has a 5-year per-share earnings growth of about 10 percent. Firm A's sales and profits have grown proportionately, while its assets have remained nearly constant. Firm B's debt has increased from 10 percent to 40 percent of its assets. Firm C's profit margin has increased from 10 percent to 16 percent. Firm D has lengthened the useful life assumption for most of its plant and equipment. Firm E's assets, sales, and profits have all grown proportionately.

Firm A (little asset growth)

	1994	1999
Assets	$10,000,000	$11,000,000
Liabilities	3,000000	3,000,000
Sales	30,000,000	50,000,000
Profits	3,000,000	5,000,000
Profits per share	$1.00	$1.61

Firm B (increased debt)

	1994	1999
Assets	$10,000,000	$17,000,000
Liabilities	1,000,000	7,000,000
Sales	30,000,000	50,000,000
Profits per share	$1.00	$1.61

Firm C (increased margin)

Assets	10,000,000	10,000,000
Liabilities	3,000,000	3,000,000
Sales	30,000,000	30,000,000
Profits	3,000000	5,000,000
Profits per share	$1.00	$1.61

Firm D (reduced depreciation)

Assets	$10,000,000	$10,000000
Liabilities	3,000,000	3,000,000
Sales	30,000,000	30,000,000
Depreciation	3,000,000	1,000,000
Profits	3,000,000	5,000,000
Profits per share	$1.00	$1.61

Firm E (balanced growth)

Assets	$10,000,000	$17,000,000
Liabilities	3,000,000	5,000,000
Sales	30,000,000	51,000,000
Profits	3,000,000	5,000,000
Profits per share	$1.00	$1.61

Clearly, the profits of these companies have grown for different reasons. Increased capacity utilization accounts for most of firm A's profit growth. Eventually, existing capacity will be fully utilized. Once that point is reached, expanding capacity further would increase relative costs. Profit growth would suffer in the process.

Firm B's profit rise is largely due to increased use of leverage. A further increase in the debt ratio would probably raise both the cost of borrowed funds and the risk to the stockholders. Thus, a sale of additional equity may be required for continued growth. Such a sale would dilute the ownership position of existing shareholders.

Firm C has either raised prices or reduced it costs. In either case, opportunities for additional profit increases are probably limited. Increasing prices may encourage greater competition; further cost cutting could reduce quality or increase future costs. Firms D's brightened profit picture is due, at least in part, to more optimistic depreciation assumptions. As with increases in leverage, capacity utilization, and profit margins, the profit-enhancement potential of imaginative accounting is limited. The accountants may soon need to run very fast just to stand still. The growth of Firm E for the next 5 years may well be like its growth in the past. Although other factors could intervene, at least the past growth rate has been balanced and is therefore potentially sustainable.

A Specific Approach to Company Analysis

The same basic approach that was explored in the discussion of economic and industry analysis can be applied to individual companies. That is, the investor can direct his or her analysis toward forecasting a company's earnings and its PE ratio. The product of these forecasts is then a prediction of its stock price. The discussion that follows assumes that the company analysis is preceded by economic analysis and an analysis of the industry in which the company operates.

First, per-share sales are forecast. As a first pass, the company's sales can be estimated to grow at the same rate as its industry. In a more refined forecast, the company's expected growth rate is adjusted to reflect individual circumstances. A second type of sales forecast can be generated from economic data. The company's past sales are related to various economic data such as GDP, interest rates, and unemployment. These economic data are then forecast and the results used to derive a company sales forecast. The analyst can rely on either of these approaches to forecasting sales or can average them. Each forecast can be given equal weight or the one that is considered more reliable can be given greater weight.

Estimates of the company's profit margin can also be based on the corresponding industry estimate. Past data will reveal how the company's profit margin has tracked the industry average. The forecast for the change in the industry's margin can then be applied to the current margin for the company. The result is the estimated margin for the company. A second estimate for the company's profit margin can be generated from an analysis of its specific cost situation. Thus, trends in labor, raw materials, and other costs can be combined with knowledge of the company's potential product and service prices to produce this second profit margin estimate. These two gross margin estimates can then be averaged (weighted or unweighted), and the result can be adjusted to take account of estimated depreciation and taxes. Multiplying the estimated net after-tax margin by the sales per share estimate generates an estimate for the earnings per share.

Steps To Forecast Company Earnings

- Adjust the company's sales estimate from the industry's estimated growth rate to reflect individual circumstances, or make (or obtain) a forecast for GDP, personal disposable income, or some other factor(s) correlated with company sales. Use the result, along with past relationships to the company's sales figure, to generate a specific sales forecast for the company. Then use either of these forecasts or an average (weighted or unweighted) of the two.
- Estimate the gross profit margin on sales. This estimated margin can be derived from past industry margin data or their relation to the company's specific capacity utilization, unit labor costs, and the inflation rate. Again, the two estimates may be averaged.
- Estimate depreciation expense and the percentage of before-tax profit going to taxes. Past data and the impact of changes in tax rates can be used to determine these estimates.
- Combine the gross margin, depreciation, and tax estimates to obtain a net margin estimate. Multiply net margin by forecasted sales to determine forecasted company earnings. Divide the result by shares outstanding to derive the per-share earnings forecast.

Various approaches can be used to forecast the company's PE. One method examines the historical relation between the company and market PEs. The forecasted change in the market PE can then be applied to the current company PE value.

A second PE estimate can be obtained by using the predicted change in the industry PE. Finally, equation 10-2, $PE = p/(k - g)$, can, with appropriate inputs, be used to derive a prediction for the company's PE. That is, values for payout p, appropriate return k, and expected growth g can be estimated and applied to the equation to generate the forecast. Estimated values for these factors can be derived both from the industry estimates and from an analysis of the specifics of the company.

Keep in mind that this is only an approximation since it assumes that the company's dividend payout ratio, growth rate, and required rate of return remain constant over time.

Approaches to Forecast the Company's PE

- Utilize the historical relation between the company and market PEs. Then apply the forecasted change in the market PE to the current company PE value.
- Apply the predicted change in the industry PE to the current company PE.
- Use the PE equation (equation 10-2) to derive a prediction for the company's PE.

These three PE forecasts can then be averaged. The value for the stock price forecast is the product of the company's forecasted earnings and its PE.

The resulting PE for the company can be averaged with the forecasts obtained from the industry and market forecasts. That average is then multiplied by the per-share earnings forecast. The result of this process is a forecast for the company's stock price. Several of these forecasts can be obtained by using the different earnings and PE forecasts. Comparing the current price of the stock with the forecasts should indicate whether the stock is appropriately priced. A low current-to-forecast price suggests a buy; a high current-to-forecast price suggests a sale.

To summarize, one logical approach to forecasting the average level of a company's stock prices is to forecast its earnings and PE multiple and take the product of the result.

Relation of a Firm's Fundamental Position to Its Market Price

Stock prices usually reflect the company's economic and industry environment, competitive position, management quality, and financial strength. A company with a strong balance sheet, market position, profit potential, and management team operating in an industry with bright growth prospects is therefore likely to be fully priced—and may be overpriced. A weaker company, in contrast, may be underpriced if its prospects are viewed too negatively. Accordingly, stock prices should always be evaluated in relative terms.

Although stronger firms deserve higher PEs than weaker firms, a strong firm with a high PE may be fully priced, whereas a somewhat less strong firm with a low PE may not be fully priced.

FUNDAMENTAL ANALYSIS VERSUS MARKET EFFICIENCY

If markets are relatively efficient (semistrong form), the (known) fundamental strengths and weaknesses of companies are already accurately reflected in their market prices. Under these circumstances, fundamental analysis may be largely a waste of time. On the other hand, if the market sometimes (or frequently) misvalues securities vis-à-vis the available public information, fundamental analysis may be worthwhile. Although the degree of market efficiency is a controversial topic, whatever level is achieved occurs because some important market participants, such as brokerage firms and other investment houses, analyze fundamentals. In other words, fundamental analysts tend to make markets more efficient than they would otherwise be. Indeed, many investors (both large and small) devote considerable amounts of time and money undertaking or buying such research. Moreover, several firms (for example, IBES International) regularly publish consensus estimates of earnings by industry analysts. When these consensus estimates are not met, the market reacts quickly to raise or lower stock prices, depending on the direction of the surprise.

Fundamental analysts believe that, at any given time, there is a basic intrinsic value for the overall stock market, various industries, or individual securities; and that these values depend on underlying economic factors. Thus, fundamental analysis can help to determine the intrinsic value of an investment asset at a point in time by examining the variables that appear to determine value, such as current and expected earnings, interest rates, and risk variables. Fundamental analysts believe that occasionally the market price of a security and intrinsic value differ, but eventually investors recognize the discrepancy and correct it. Therefore, if investors can do a good job of estimating intrinsic value based on fundamental analysis, they can make superior market timing or allocation decisions and acquire undervalued securities, which generate above-average returns.

EMH (efficient market hypothesis) does not necessarily contradict the value of fundamental analysis, but it implies that to be successful, an investor needs to first understand the relevant variables that affect rates of return and to do a superior job of estimating movements in those valuation variables. A recent study by H. Russell Foger showed that the crucial difference between stocks that enjoyed best- versus worst-price performance during given years was the relationship between expected earnings estimates of professional analysts and the firm's actual earnings (*earnings surprises*). He found that stock prices increased if actual earnings exceeded expected earnings (positive earnings surprises), and they fell if earnings did not reach expected levels (negative earnings surprises). Thus, if investors or analysts can do a superior job of projecting earnings and their expectations differ

earnings surprises

from the consensus, then they will probably have a superior investment record.[2]

APPLYING FUNDAMENTAL ANALYSIS

The preceding discussion might be summed up as follows: Investors seeking above-average returns should acquire stocks of companies whose industry, financial, competitive, and managerial strengths are not fully reflected by the market price. Clearly, investors need more practical approaches.

SUMMARY AND CONCLUSIONS

This chapter explores traditional approaches to macroeconomic, industry, and company analysis, considering both general and specific approaches. Industries exhibit very different performances, but selecting those with the best prospects is quite difficult. Past performance offers very little guidance, whereas evaluating the industry's stage in the life cycle may offer some modest help. Company analysis involves assessing a company's relative strengths and weaknesses within its industry or industries. Ideally, a company should be large enough to compete effectively but not so large as to be constrained by the threat of antitrust prosecution. Management quality, another important company characteristic, is especially difficult to judge.

Financial statement analysis utilizes a variety of different types of ratios. Liquidity ratios reflect short-run strengths and weaknesses. Debt ratios relate to a company's longer run prospects. Profitability and efficiency ratios reflect current operating effectiveness with an eye toward the future. Various other ratios such as earnings per share, PE, cash flow per share, payout, and book value may be used to provide additional insights.

When evaluating financial ratios, it is important to look for trends. The changes in financial ratios over time can often convey more information than the ratios themselves. In addition, a company's financial ratios should be compared with those of other firms in its industry. It can be valuable to determine how a firm's liquidity, leverage, profitability, and efficiency ratios compare with those of its competitors.

Although assessing industry and company strengths and weaknesses is one way to search for attractive investments, this approach is useful only if the analysis uncovers overlooked values. An efficient market for investment analysis implies that, on balance, those paying for research receive full value for their costs.

CHAPTER REVIEW

Answers to the review questions and the self-test questions start on page 763.

Key Terms

fundamental analysis	current assets
macroeconomic analysis	current liabilities
PE ratio	acid test ratio
earnings multiplier	inventory turnover ratio
gross domestic product (GDP)	debt-equity ratio
gross margin	times-interest-earned ratio
capacity utilization	return on equity (ROE)
unit labor costs	return on assets (ROA)
depreciation	return on investment (ROI)
net margin	return on sales (ROS)
Graham and Dodd	asset turnover
balance sheet	debt margin (leverage)
income statement	Dupont formula
change in financial position statement	earnings per share
	dividend yield
ratio analysis	book value per share
current ratio	earnings surprises

Review Questions

10-1. Explain how economic analysis can be used to forecast the market's performance.

10-2. Assume that the market's dividend payout ratio is .50, the required rate of return is 13 percent, and the expected growth rate is 9 percent.
   a. Compute the market PE (price earnings ratio).
   b. What would happen to the market PE if the payout ratio fell to .45 and all else remained unchanged?
   c. What would happen to the market PE if the growth rate increased by 2 percent and everything else remained unchanged? Is such a change at all likely? Why or why not?
   d. What would happen if the required rate of return declined to 10 percent and everything else remained unchanged? Is such a change at all likely? Why or why not?

10-3. Explain how economic analysis can be used to forecast the industry's performance.

10-4. a. Forecast next year's sales per share for the XYZ High Tech Index using the following information:
- The current GDP of $8.3 trillion is expected to grow by 6 percent.
- Current index sales per share are running at an annual rate of $500 and are expected to grow by 1.7 times the growth of the GDP.

  b. If GDP actually falls by 3 percent, what would the High Tech per-share sales be?

10-5. Explain how economic analysis can be used to forecast a company's performance.

10-6. Discuss the impact of a company's competitive position on its investment attractiveness. Consider potential antitrust problems.

10-7. Estimate the PE ratio for the High Tech Index in question 10-4 using the following information:
- The current payout ratio of .50 is expected to continue through next year.
- The required rate of return on the overall market is 13 percent.
- The High Tech Index usually is accorded a 2 percent risk premium above that of the overall market.
- Growth is expected to continue indefinitely at the rate in question 10-4 (1.7 times the growth of the GDP).

10-8. The Go Go Corporation currently has a payout of .2 and is accorded a risk premium of 3 percent above the market required rate of return of 15 percent. It currently sells for 35 with EPS of $1.25.

  a. What is the implied growth rate?

  b. Suppose EPS (earnings per share) grows at a rate of 25 percent for 5 years and then declines to a rate of 10 percent—a rate that is expected to continue. What will the stock then sell for (in 5 years) if the payout rises to .4 and the required return for Go Go Corporation declines to 16 percent?

10-9. Discuss the role of management quality in investment analysis.

10-10. Briefly summarize the three principal types of accounting statements.

10-11. a. Analyze the various classes of ratios.

   b. What are the advantages and disadvantages of ratio analysis?

10-12. a. When analysts are examining the cause of past growth, which factors are likely to be temporary and which capable of producing sustainable growth?

   b. What is the relevance to investment analysis?

10-13. Refer to Firms A, B, C, D, and E in the example under the heading "Financial Position." Apply the following equation to those firms using the 1999 figures:

$$ROE = ROS \times Asset\ turnover \times Debt\ margin$$

Self-Test Questions

T F 10-1. Profits tend to be less variable than the overall growth in the economy as measured by the GDP.

T F 10-2. Fewer assumptions are necessary in order to apply the earnings multiplier approach to a firm's valuation than are required to apply the dividend discount model approach.

T F 10-3. The PE ratio used in the earnings multiplier approach can be obtained by using the dividend discount model.

T F 10-4. The earnings multiplier (or PE approach) to valuation uses the estimated 12 months' earnings.

T F 10-5. One relationship that exists when using the dividend discount model to estimate the earnings per share (EPS) for valuation purposes is the higher the expected growth rate of dividends, the lower the estimated PE.

T F 10-6. The PE ratio approach to valuation is applicable to the total market as well as to industry and company analyses.

T F 10-7. If the growth estimate for the industry of a firm rises from 6 percent to 8 percent but the risk discount for the firm rises from 10 percent to 13 percent, the intrinsic value for the firm is likely to decline.

T F 10-8. PE ratios used for the earnings multiplier model are sensitive to changes in the interest rate.

T F 10-9. The basic balance sheet equation is as follows: Assets + liabilities = net worth.

T F 10-10. The quick ratio is used to assess the capital structure of the firm's balance sheet.

T F 10-11. Raising the debt-equity ratio for a firm lowers the intrinsic value of the firm's stock price.

T F 10-12. Raising the debt margin will lower return on equity, all other things equal.

T F 10-13. Fully diluted earnings per share are not affected by outstanding convertible debt.

T   F   10-14.   Fundamental analysis rests on the premise that a security has an intrinsic value that is based on the firm's underlying variables.

NOTES

1. Robert G. Hagstrom, Jr., *The Warren Buffett Way* (New York: John Wiley & Sons, Inc., 1995), p. 157.
2. H.R. Foger, "A Modern Theory of Security Analysis," *Journal of Portfolio Management*, vol. 9, no 3 (spring 1993), pp. 6–14.

11

Operational Approaches to Fundamental Analysis

Learning Objectives

An understanding of the material in this chapter should enable the student to

11-1. Describe the various screening techniques investors use to screen out unattractive stocks so that only those deserving closer scrutiny remain.

11-2. Explain the profitability and PE ratio models designed to help investors identify stocks whose characteristics are associated with profitability or whose PE ratios are out of line with stocks that have similar characteristics.

11-3. Explain the Graham and Templeton integrated approaches to investment selection that simultaneously analyze several different selection criteria.

Chapter Outline

This chapter surveys operational approaches to fundamental analysis. Background information on these approaches, derived from both academic journals and the financial press, is summarized here. Topics covered in chapter 10 include macroeconomic, industry, and company analysis. Identifying misvalued securities, however, is quite distinct from analyzing a firm's prospects. Practical investing requires approaches to investment selection that are tangible, relevant, and cost effective. Although a full-blown analysis of the economy, industry, and firm may be useful at times, most investors are unable to undertake such an effort. Even those with the necessary time, skills, and resources require operational approaches that allow them to winnow down their lists to the worthwhile prospects. Thus, shortcuts are needed to allow the analyst to identify potentially attractive investments on a first-pass basis. That is, investors need methods for *screening* a long list of stocks and selecting those that deserve closer scrutiny. Based on the narrowed-down list, investors may then undertake more detailed analysis.

screening

First, this chapter considers a variety of narrow fundamental approaches. *Forbes* magazine, *Value Line*, and several other periodicals publish lists of interesting stocks that may be a useful starting point. Similarly, many analysts recommend stocks with low PEs (price-earnings ratios). Others prefer companies with rapid growth records (even if that means paying a high price relative to earnings). Still others concentrate on small firms, low-priced stocks, research-and-development-intensive firms, or potential takeover candidates. Because of recent innovations in balance-sheet appraisals of Internet-related stocks, the chapter also discusses a new approach to "value" investing. Another suggested screening technique is to focus on out-of-favor stocks and avoid firms with appreciable bankruptcy risks. Some investment services offer specialized investment advice, and some analysts particularly recommend firms that are stockholder oriented as opposed to management oriented. Each of the characteristics mentioned above may be used to screen out unattractive stocks and concentrate on those that may be worth a closer look.

After a survey of screening techniques, the chapter explores the investment implications of PE models. These models may help investors identify stocks whose PEs are out of line with those with similar characteristics (risks, growth rates, dividend yields, and so on). Finally, the chapter discusses two integrated methods of investment selection. These methods are based on a simultaneous analysis of a number of different selection criteria. All of these approaches are designed to start with a relatively long list of stocks and end up with a much shorter list of potentially attractive investments. Note, however, that nothing assures the realization of that goal.

NARROW FUNDAMENTAL ANALYSIS APPROACHES: SCREENING TECHNIQUES

Lists of stocks that have something unusual in common appear regularly in *Forbes*. The discussion that accompanies the lists generally implies that an appreciable number of the listings are undervalued or otherwise attractive. For example, *Forbes* lists firms that sell for a small fraction of the potential values of their underlying assets. The criteria for net-nets varies over time, but they always include firms that are underpriced relative to their tangible assets.

The procedure for identifying net-nets is as follows: First, the firm's current liabilities are subtracted from its current assets. The result is working capital. The firm's long-term debt is then subtracted from this working capital figure. The remainder is the amount of liquid assets the firm would have after paying off both short- and long-term liabilities. This amount is divided by the firm's number of outstanding shares. The result is the per-share net (of short-term liabilities) net (of long-term liabilities) of the company's liquid assets. If the firm's stock sells for less than this amount, it is called a net-net.

Note that the firm's long-term assets do not figure into the analysis. These assets are viewed as a bonus. Net-nets could use their short-term assets (assuming that these assets can be liquidated at their book values) to pay off all liabilities, have enough value to repurchase all shares at their current market price, and still have some short- and all long-term assets left. Some net-nets will outperform the market. Others, however, will stay on the list for years. Determining which stocks are truly undervalued is left up to the investor.

Net-nets are compiled only once a year. Most *Forbes* issues, however, contain at least one list of interesting stocks. Examples include stocks with low PEs and high growth rates, former institutional favorites, companies with dividend reinvestment plans, companies that are expected to emerge from bankruptcy with big profit potentials, potential growth companies, stocks disliked by the experts, cash-rich and cash-poor companies, high-yield utilities, stocks that *Forbes* analysts expect to show substantial earnings increases, and emerging growth companies in a difficult market environment.

The prices of most stocks, including those on *Forbes* lists, are likely to be relatively close to their intrinsic values. That is, most stocks are probably priced in a market that processes the public information on them efficiently. Indeed, some lists may just by chance contain a below-average number of undervalued situations. Stocks that appear undervalued by one criterion (such as tangible assets) may be accurately priced relative to a more important criterion (such as prospects for growth or survival). If identifying undervalued stocks were easy, we could all be rich. Nonetheless, *Forbes* and similar lists may very well provide investors with a useful starting point. *Value Line,* for example, compiles weekly lists for each of these characteristics:

- timely stocks I (ranked #1 for next 12-month performance)
- timely stocks II (ranked #2 for next 12-month performance)
- conservative stocks I (ranked #1 for safety)
- conservative stocks II (ranked #2 for safety)
- high-yield stocks (estimated year-ahead dividends)
- high 3- to 5-year appreciation potential
- biggest free cash-flow generators
- best-performing stocks (past 13 weeks)
- worst-performing stocks (past 13 weeks)
- widest discount from book value
- lowest PE
- highest PE
- highest annual total returns (3 to 5 years)
- highest estimated 3- to 5-year dividend yield
- highest percentage earned on capital
- untimely stocks (ranked #5 for next 12-month performance)
- highest yielding nonutility stocks
- high growth stocks
- stocks trading at a discount from their liquidation values

Low-PE Stocks versus Growth Stocks

growth stocks

Many lists are based on one of two concepts: PE and growth. Indeed, investment analysts have long debated the relative merits of low-PE versus *growth stocks*. A firm whose profits are expected to grow rapidly will command a high price relative to its current earnings. One with less bright prospects will generally command a lower PE. The PE ratio equation illustrates the relation between the PE and expected growth:

$$PE = \frac{p}{(k - g)} \qquad \text{(Equation 11-1)}$$

where: p = payout ratio in decimal form

k = appropriate discount rate or required rate of return (which varies with risk) in decimal form

g = expected growth rate in decimal form

Clearly, PEs should differ with the firms' prospects (dividend payout, risk, and expected growth). Growth expectations play a key role: For a given payout and discount rate, differing growth expectations can have a dramatic impact on how the market prices a stock relative to its current earnings.

Example: Consider a company with a payout of .5 and an appropriate discount rate of 13 percent. An expected growth rate of 5 percent would correspond to a PE of 6.25. In contrast, if an 8 percent or 10 percent growth rate is expected, the corresponding PE would be 10 or 16.7, respectively. In terms of earnings per share, a company whose EPS is expected to be $1 next year would be priced at 6 1/4, 10, or 16 5/8, depending on whether its long-term expected growth rate was 5 percent, 8 percent, or 10 percent.

No one argues with the arithmetic. High growth expectations do justify higher PEs than lower growth expectations do. The debate over low-PE versus growth stock centers on how well the market prices securities relative to their actual potentials. According to such well-known fundamental analysts as Benjamin Graham and John Templeton, the market frequently goes to extremes. These acknowledged experts believe that the market tends to overestimate the growth prospects and underestimate the risks of many stocks (especially the highly touted growth stocks). As a result, the market accords them even higher PEs than their fundamentals warrant. The stocks of less exciting companies, in contrast, may be viewed by the market as having less attractive prospects than they deserve. Stocks that the market views too pessimistically would then end up with unrealistically low PEs. Once the market realizes the true potentials of these stocks, the prices of *low-PE stocks* should rise at a faster rate than the market averages, whereas the high-PE stocks should do less well. Those who accept this line of reasoning prefer a portfolio that is heavily weighted toward low-PE stocks and largely avoid stocks with high PEs.

low-PE stocks

Growth-stock advocates, in contrast, have contended that stocks with rapid growth potentials are attractive investments even at relatively high prices. A high current PE may not seem overpriced relative to future earnings, whereas low PEs may accurately reflect poor potentials. The two views (low-PE and growth stock) have alternated in popularity. Although each viewpoint has some merit, the key question is not, Can a high PE be justified? Rather, the more important question is, Are the PEs on many so-called growth stocks justified?

High PEs can decline dramatically. For example, the Dow's composite PE rose from 12.1 on December 31, 1957, to 24.2 on September 29, 1961. It then fell to 16.2 9 months later. Since that time, the multiple has generally stayed under 20 except in the latter part of the 1980s when it rose to about 20 and in the 1990s when it rose to 30 and above. In retrospect, the high growth expectations for the soaring 1960s were unrealistic. Moreover, many individual multiples were hit hard during this period. The stock market crash of October 1987 also took place when the Dow was at a relatively high level (21.5). Analysts comparing the economic conditions in the U.S. in 1999 with those of 1987 have found some striking similarities, including relatively high equity market valuations, rising interest rates, rising oil prices, rising U.S. trade deficit, and a falling U.S. dollar in the foreign exchange market.

There were, however, also many significant differences in 1999 from the previous crash of 1987. For instance, in 1987, the federal budget deficit was about $221 billion, whereas in fiscal 1999 the federal budget was projected to be in $100 billion surplus, the first in almost 30 years. Furthermore, in 1987, the CPI was rising at about a 4 percent annual rate; from September 1988 through 1999, the CPI rose at 2.6 percent. Also, in 1987 the U.S. was yet to become the major player in the global marketplace. U.S. industry was just starting its restructuring to become more efficient, there was not a North American Free Trade Agreement (NAFTA), the Berlin wall still divided East and West Germany, and the European Monetary and Economic Union, which led to falling trade barriers and increased competition both in the U.S. and around the world, was still being created. Finally, U.S. pension and retirement funds grew in size and market impact from 1987 to 1999. In 1987, pension funds, both public and private, had 41.35 percent of their assets in equities; in 1999 they had over 66 percent of their assets in equities. Pension funds seem less likely to react to short-run market downturns than, say, the average mutual fund investor.

A best selling book of 1999 titled *Dow 36,000,* by James Glassman and Kevin Hasset, maintains that the Dow Jones Industrial Average (DJIA) was undervalued at about 10,500. Observing the total returns to a portfolio of stocks held for the previous 20 years, the authors contend that a portfolio of all stocks was no more risky than holding bonds. Therefore, they argue that stocks should be priced so that their expected return equals that of bonds. In calculating what they call a perfectly reasonable price for stocks, the authors begin with a 30-year Treasury bond that yields 5.5 percent. Interest on the bond would not grow, they note, while stock dividends would tend to rise over time. Given that advantage, the authors calculate what stocks should initially yield to match the return on bonds. To match a bond yielding 5.5 percent, they say, an investor would need the initial dividend yield on stocks and the annual growth rate of the stock dividend to add up to the same as the 30-yield bond—or 5.5 percent. Actual dividend yield on stocks has varied over time, but estimates indicate that it should average 5 percent a year. Therefore, the authors assert, to match the future return on bonds, stocks initially need to yield just 0.5 percent, which would place the equilibrium value of the DJIA at about 36,000.[1]

Of course, this claim is based on very questionable assumptions, primarily that stocks and bonds are equally risky. Jeremy Siegel, finance researcher, upon whose original research Glassman and Hasset based their model, contends that his data do not lead to their conclusions. "They are under the assumption," Siegel states, " that those people who have 20- or 30-year time horizons will totally dominate the equity markets and will continue to have faith in their long-run performance, despite poor and possibly disastrous intervening years."[2] Siegel further points out that the Glassman-Hassett model does not handle the possibility of a change in the Dow's forecasted value well. For example, suppose that investors do bid up the DJIA to 36,000 so that stocks offer the same expected return as a 5.5 percent 30-year Treasury bond, but that interest rates rise to 6.5 percent. To match this higher return, stocks would have to yield 1.5 percent. To get to that level, share prices would have to plunge 67 percent. At that point, those who had thought that stock's risk was equal to that of 30-year Treasuries would have to revise their views. This indicates that the Glassman-Hassett model is extremely sensitive to changes in the inputs, especially interest-rate fluctuations.

Finally, the model's assumption that corporate dividends would continue to grow at a 5 percent annual rate is called into question by research conducted in 1999 by William R. Emmons, research economist at the Federal Reserve Bank of St. Louis. He raises this question: What returns should investors expect on stocks in the future? According to Emmons, relatively high long-term returns on stocks in the past do not necessarily portend high future returns. The dividend yield on the S&P 500 Industrial Index in April 1999 was only 1.2 percent, which was the lowest on record up until that time. The average dividend yield between 1926–1997 was 4.6 percent, with a 5.4 percent average for the longer period 1802–1997. Emmons figures that real GDP growth will likely average 2 to 3 percent annually, with expected inflation at about 2 to 3 percent. This adds up to a forecast of 4 to 6 percent annual nominal GDP growth. He projects nominal dividend yields on stocks may average less than the historic rate of 5 percent. "The unavoidable implication of low current dividend yields and low expected nominal GDP growth," Emmons states, "is that stock investors of all kinds may be forced to accept historically subpar total returns in the future."[3]

Advocates of growth stocks recommend investments in companies with outstanding past records and/or growth potentials. They do not generally seek out stocks with high multiples but are quite prepared to pay a high price (relative to current earnings) when strong future growth is anticipated. Their arithmetic can appear quite persuasive. Earnings that grow at 20 percent will double in approximately 4 years. Should the multiple remain constant, the price will also double over the same 4-year period—but multiples must be justified by *long-term* growth prospects relative to the appropriate discount rate, which is related to the riskiness of the firm.

Those who advocate stocks with low multiples (low-PE stocks) question not the arithmetic of growth-stock proponents but rather their implicit assumptions. In fact, rapid current growth rates may simply be an anomaly. These growth rates are extremely unlikely to continue for very many years into the future. One well-known growth stock, IBM, exhibited very rapid growth during the 1950s and into the early 1960s. In many of those years it grew at rates of 20 percent or more. Some analysts seem quite willing (at least implicitly) to project growth rates such as this far into the future. Between the 1960s and 1990s, however, IBM clearly shifted from high growth to moderate growth. In 1999, IBM stock price reached a peak during July and August at about 139. Then in late October 1999, it fell about 15 percent in a single day's trading to $91 a share. The company blamed a projected profit shortfall on Y2K problems, which cut across a wide spectrum of its hardware products. Although most analysts at the time still rated IBM as a long-term buy, none projected its stock price would match the peak it reached in mid-summer 1999 anytime soon.

Although IBM is a sizable company, many of the other traditional high-multiple stocks such as Microsoft, Coca-Cola, GE, and Disney are also large. Moreover, even medium-size firms would grow to a large fraction of the economy if an abnormally high growth rate continued for several decades. If nothing else put a brake on growth, government action such as an antitrust-based divestiture (for example, AT&T's breakup) probably would. Almost always, however, the factors that allow a firm or industry to grow rapidly begin to fade long before governmental action becomes necessary. When a small entity grows faster than the economy, its overall impact remains relatively small and isolated. In contrast, as a larger entity exhibits an above-average growth rate, it may expand at the expense of other economic entities. These competitors will fight to maintain their existing shares of the economy. Firms and industries with attractive products and talented managers will eventually find themselves locked in head-to-head combat with other firms and industries whose assets are comparable to their own. Rapid growth is likely for firms that have clear advantages over their rivals. Rapid growth is much less likely when the rivals are comparably equipped to compete.

The reasoning above led Burton Malkiel in his famous study of high-growth, high-multiple stocks to assume that the growth rates of heretofore high-growth companies would eventually decline to about the national average.[4] This assumption has an interesting impact on the application of the PE formula (equation 11-1). A firm now growing at an above-average rate $g*$ should be expected eventually to have its growth rate slow to, or perhaps drop below, the economy-wide rate g'. Solving the PE formula with $g*$ would produce a PE that is too high. Similarly, using g' would yield a value for the PE that is too low. In fact, the appropriate g value to use with the formula will lie between $g*$ and g'. The longer the growth rate is expected to remain high, the closer the appropriate value will be to $g*$. On the other hand, the quicker $g*$ declines to g', the closer the appropriate g value is to g'. Much of the fluctuation in stock prices reflects a change in the consensus PE ratio. The change in PE ratio, in turn, reflects changing views within the market regarding the firm's growth potential. Let us therefore examine more closely just how much differing growth expectations can affect PE ratios. The following example focuses on the impact of growth.

Example: Assume the payout ratio p is .5 and the appropriate discount rate is 12 percent for both the stock market and individual stocks. An economy-wide, long-term growth rate of 7 percent (3 percent real and 4 percent inflation) would produce an average PE of 0.5/(.12 − .07) = 10. If a particular company's g is 8 percent, its PE would be 12.5. A g of 9 percent would produce a PE of 16.7, while a g of 10 percent would imply a PE of 25. If g is as high as 11 percent, the PE would rise to 50.

As the example shows, relatively small changes in the expected long-term growth rate g can have a dramatic impact on the PE ratio. This impact is particularly great when the PE is already relatively large. A more realistic example would take account of the tendency for higher values of g to correspond to lower payouts and greater risk premiums (and thus higher discount rates). In his extensive research on security valuation approaches, Aswath Damodaran discusses a number of problems associated with uses of PE ratios, noting that the volatility of earnings can cause the PE ratio to change dramatically from period to period.[5]

Advocates of low-PE stocks note that stock prices rise dramatically when both earnings and multiples increase. Quite possibly, a multiple may more easily increase from 5 to 10 than from 10 to 20 and will have an easier time growing from 10 to 20 than from 20 to 40. That is, the market may well become more nervous about the price of a stock as its PE rises. Thus, low-PE stocks may have a better chance of achieving truly outstanding performances than high-PE stocks, which may be more likely to be fully priced already.

Example:	Suppose that a company sells initially at a PE of 5 experiences per-share earnings growth of 20 percent per year for 10 years. Its earnings will be six times as high as when it started. Such an earnings growth is likely to lead to an increase in the PE multiple. Rapid past growth often leads to expectations of rapid future growth. If the PE of this company doubles, its stock will sell for more than 12 times its earlier price.

The advocates of low-multiple stocks further contend that high-multiple stocks are particularly vulnerable to disappointing news.

Example:	Suppose a growth stock currently earns $2 per share and sells for $50 (PE of 25). If the following year, it earns only $1.50, a continuation of its PE of 25 would correspond to a price of $37.50. On the other hand, if the poor earnings led to lower growth expectations and a lower PE, the price decline would be much steeper. Thus, for example, a fall to a PE of 10 would imply a price of $15.

Clearly, disappointing earnings can severely wound a stock that had sold for a high multiple. Certainly, such disappointments happen. For instance, as mentioned earlier, IBM's announcement in late 1999 that its profits would be negatively affected by the Y2K problem during the final quarter of 1999 had a severe negative impact on IBM stock.

Value Investing

value investing
growth investing

For 20 years, *value investing* (investing in below-average PE stocks) as measured by the S&P/Barra indices led *growth investing* (investing in above-average PE stocks) as measured by average annual return. The term value investing refers to Benjamin Graham's philosophy of investing in companies with hard assets whose stock prices are relatively cheap. For the period 1975 through year-end 1995, the average annual return for value investing came to 16.5 percent, compared to 14.0 percent for growth investing. In the latter 1990s, however, the trend shifted, and since 1995, growth stocks moved ahead of value stocks, with a 29.9 percent average annual return versus 25.9 percent for value stocks for the period 1995–1999.

One explanation for value investing's lagging performance is that the payoffs from these two investment disciplines tend to move in opposite directions as investor sentiment shifts. That is, in some years, value investing is the preferred style, while in other years, growth investing is preferred. Another more profound reason for value stocks' underperformance in recent years is the dramatic changes that have occurred in the U.S. economy. The economy is no longer driven by manufacturing and so-called smokestack industries but by rapidly changing innovations in technology and services. In this type of economy, the big winners are not the manufacturing-type firms such as General Motors, but those that are at the forefront of innovation and implementation of the new technology, such as Microsoft.

Under the new economy, the traditional measures that value investors typically use to select investments, such as low PE ratios or low price-book value ratios, tend to provide the wrong answers. A new methodology of value investing is in the process of developing. Currently, it is more a framework for analysis rather than a specific set of codified rules. The new value investing relies more on forecasting future expected cash flows than on past data. Benjamin Graham and David Dodd, who first laid down the principles of value investing in their 1930s textbook, frowned on earnings forecasts as being too speculative.

The new value investing looks more to an author of the 1960s; economist John Burr Williams. Williams believed that an investment was worth the present value of its future cash flows, which must be estimated. For "new economy" companies, such as America Online (AOL) and Amazon.com, the business models are entirely different from what value investors are used to measuring. Compared to a bricks-and-mortar retailer such as Sears, AOL and Amazon.com make relatively small capital expenditures. But more significantly, these firms collect revenues immediately as customers either charge their purchases or contract for online service. Moreover, in the case of Amazon.com, the company does not have to pay its suppliers for 45 to 50 days. Therefore, in effect, it is the suppliers, not the shareholders, that are funding the company's growth. In other words, it is the balance sheet—specifically the working capital accounts—not the income statement that generates the firm's cash flows. Another successful direct seller of desktop computers, Dell Computer Corporation, also tends to be cash rich by building PCs essentially to order. Thus, the company collects from the customer immediately, slashes inventory costs, avoids the middleman distributor, and waits to pay its suppliers.

Value investors have always looked at the company balance sheets, but more as a snapshot than as an indicator of expected cash flows. These investors focus on identifying tangible assets and value a stock that appears to be relatively cheap in relation to its assets. This is why value investors tend to end up invested in tangible-asset businesses, mainly manufacturing and natural-resource companies. Unfortunately for such investors, these types of companies make up a shrinking portion of the market and the total economy.

Using the new growth criteria, we could argue that Microsoft Corporation, one of the 1990's bull market's greatest growth performers, is really a new-value stock. The reasoning is as follows: First, if we examine the quality of earnings, about 67 percent of Microsoft's profits come from sales that are booked during the same quarter, versus only 38.9 percent for the median company in the S&P 500 Industrials. Therefore, it is the momentum of receivables and the cash flow coming from Microsoft's retailers that are key. (Of course, with receivables, there is always the risk that the firm may not be able to collect them all.) According to Microsoft's 1999 annual report, its revenue growth was 32 percent in fiscal 1997, 28 percent in fiscal 1998, and 29 percent in fiscal 1999. The company's business model evolved from selling packaged products to licensing organizations and personal computer manufacturers. Microsoft projects that in the future, more software will be delivered over the Internet; thus, the boundary between online services and software products will blur. Microsoft's PE ratio on October 22, 1999, was 61 at a price of 93 1/16.[6] The idea that cheaper stock—as measured by the PE ratio or the price-to-book ratio—is a better investment may no longer be a viable guide. Stock price relative to future cash flow (rather than earnings) may be a more appropriate gauge.

So-Called One-Decision Stocks and the Nifty Fifty

The early 1970s saw the rise and fall of the *one-decision stock* concept. According to a then popular view, certain high-quality stocks (called the Nifty Fifty) should, like Manhattan real estate, be bought but not sold. Rapid past growth led many investors to expect above-average performance for the foreseeable future. Institutional investors (mutual funds, pension funds, insurance companies, and banks) scrambled to put away additional shares of 50 (or so) one-decision companies. The "foreseeable future" lasted about a year. The one-decision (or top-tier) stocks eventually fell dramatically toward the end of the 1974 stock market crash. Avon dropped from a 1973 high of 140 to 19, Disney from 121 to 19, and Polaroid from 143 to 14. Somewhat less dramatically, Xerox fell from 170 to 54 and IBM from 365 to 150. By comparison, the Dow Jones Industrial Average declined from 1051 to 576, about a 45 percent drop. Clearly, the one-decision stocks fully experienced the ravages of the 1974 decline.

During the 9 years that followed the purchase of the Nifty Fifty in 1973, the vast majority of these stocks failed to regain their one-decision highs. Although most of the companies did well, their stocks did not. Over that same 1973–1982 period, the popular market averages advanced modestly. These stocks did better in subsequent years, but their extremely high market prices in 1973 made them relatively poor investments at the time. A study by Jeremy Siegel of the subsequent performance of the Nifty Fifty stocks of the 1970s found that 15 of them were ranked among the top 40 U.S. stocks in terms of market capitalization in 1997. Siegel concluded that the relation between the PE ratios and the earnings growth of the Nifty Fifty showed that investors were *not* irrational to pay the premium they did for those stocks in 1972. Nevertheless, there were still a number of stocks that performed poorly.

relative PE ratios

Relative PE Ratios

How well do low-PE stocks do in general? Early in the 1960s and 1970s studies of several filter tests pointed to the selection value of a low-PE ratio investment strategy, concluding that selecting companies with low price-earnings multiples, measured either relative to the whole market, or to a particular industry classification, gave superior portfolio performance. Other studies, however, failed to support the hypothesis of low-PE advocates, and some concluded that even though low price-earning stocks are resistant to short-term declines, the relative advantage dissipates significantly as the downtrend is prolonged.

Reasons for Conflicting Results

Several factors may explain the differences in low-PE stocks' subsequent performance results. First, some researchers employed more than one filter than simply low PEs. Second, low-PE ratio tests usually used the Compustat data tapes, which list firms based on their size and importance at the *end* of the period of coverage. Thus, the Compustat sample suffers from

selection (survivor) bias

what is called *selection (survivor) bias*. Because only firms that grow to

Compustat-size are included, successful firms that have low beginning PEs are overrepresented. Omitting a disproportionate share of unsuccessful stocks with low PEs at the beginning of the period overemphasizes the importance of successful stocks that had low PEs at the beginning of the test period.

Third, because low-PE stocks tend to be riskier than high-PE stocks, all other factors being equal, their apparently higher returns may simply reflect a reward for risk taking. Fourth, PE analysis relies heavily on the method of comparison. The results of those analysts who first get a "feel" for the data by experimenting with several different comparisons may fit the tested data better than future reality.

Combining PE Ratios with Other Factors

Several studies have examined the PE ratio combined with other factors. For instance, PE ratios combined with abnormal quarterly earnings or the ratio of company to industry PE ratios have been found to relate to excess returns. Most of the relevant recent work, however, has examined the relative roles of PEs and firm size.

Firm Size

Much of the evidence suggests that low-PE stocks tend to be underpriced. Nonetheless, a more basic relationship may be at work. For example, a disproportionate number of low-PE stocks may be the issues of relatively small companies. Suppose that the stocks of relatively small companies tend to outperform the market. Size, not PE, might then be the true factor to explain the apparent effect of a low PE. Indeed, Reinganum found that portfolios selected on both PE and firm size tended to generate abnormal returns (above the risk-adjusted market level). The PE effect largely disappeared, however, when size was controlled.[7] Other studies found similar results.

small firm effect   The studies hypothesized that the *small firm effect* was due to a misspecification of the capital asset pricing model (CAPM) because the CAPM formed the basis for adjusting returns for risk. The positive abnormal returns may simply have been a reward for the extra effort of analyzing small firms (the basis of the "neglected firms" hypothesis discussed below). The apparent abnormal returns may have been due to underestimating their risks, or due to lower trading activity (a measure of marketability). Still other researchers reported that the magnitude of the small firm effect was reduced but could not be fully explained away when adjustments were made for the impacts of risk premium, tax effects, benchmark error, incorrect assumptions about investor risk aversion, nonsynchronous trading, or earnings yield.

analyst neglect (neglected firm effect)

Analyst Neglect (Neglected Firm Effect)

The abnormal returns of small firms could be due to either of two reasons: (1) superior performance relative to their fundamentals (current profitability, apparent growth potential, current leverage, per-share book value, and so on) or (2) underpricing relative to those fundamentals.

The evidence of pervasive scale economies argues against small firms consistently managing their assets more effectively than large firms. On the other hand, most institutional investors prefer to invest in large firms. They can make meaningful investments in large firms without having an undue effect on the companies' stock prices. With smaller firms, in contrast, a relatively small amount of dollars may represent too much of the total capitalization to be absorbed easily by the market. Thus, any attempt to invest significant sums into the stock of such a company is likely to drive the stock price up (and attempts to sell significant amounts of stock are likely to drive prices down). Similarly, analysts tend to concentrate on larger firms and therefore draw attention to such stocks. Institutions' and analysts' disproportionate attention may well cause the issues of large firms to be overpriced relative to the rest of the market. Several studies have found that stocks that analysts ignore (whether large or small) tend to outperform the more closely followed issues. Accordingly, a number of mutual funds have sought to exploit this small firm/neglected firm effect by assembling portfolios of these companies. Another factor that may be at work is referred to as the low price effect.

The Low Price Effect

low price effect

The results of several studies imply that stocks with low per-share prices tend to generate returns above the market averages. Moreover, this *low price effect* may well be stronger than (and may even swamp) both the PE and the size effects. Exactly why low-priced stocks seem to perform so well is subject to much debate. Low-priced stocks are generally believed to be more risky than the average stock. Thus, their higher average return may reflect greater risk. Still, the returns of these stocks continue to be higher when standard risk adjustment procedures are applied. Perhaps low-priced stocks are even more risky than their estimated betas imply. In particular, they may contain a substantially greater amount of nonmarket, and thus diversifiable, risk. We have already seen that, capital market theory notwithstanding, nonmarket risk is generally accorded a premium. That is, stocks with high levels of nonmarket risks are priced to offer higher expected returns than otherwise similar stocks with lower levels of nonmarket risk.

Second, low-priced stocks are also more expensive to trade. Commissions tend to be set on the basis of both the dollar value and the number of shares traded. A given dollar amount invested in a low-priced stock will correspond to more shares. Trades of low-priced stocks, therefore, typically incur higher commissions as a percentage of the amount invested than equivalent size trades of higher priced stocks. Also, the bid-ask spread of low-priced stocks tends to be relatively high. Spreads cannot be less than 1/16 on most stocks. The NYSE, for example, will not allow finer gradations for quotes on stocks priced at $1 per share or more. One-sixteenth may represent a large percentage for a stock priced at $2 or so. Stocks that are more expensive to trade probably need to offer higher expected returns to attract investors.

A third possible factor is the general aversion of many investors, especially institutional investors, to low capitalization and low-priced shares. The perceived quality of a stock is thought to be associated with the level of its per-share price. If many investors shun a significant segment of the stock market, that group of stocks may tend to be underpriced. The financial performance of some of the group may eventually lead them to achieve quality status and institutional acceptance.

Small stock performance in recent years (1995–1999) has been dwarfed by large capitalization stocks—with the possible exception of high technology small cap stocks. It was suggested that small stocks should outperform when the U.S. dollar is strong in foreign exchange, since large multinationals are hurt when they convert their foreign-currency-denominated sales and profits back to dollars. During 1997, the U.S. dollar rose 10 percent against a number of foreign currencies. Yet Prudential Securities calculated that fourth-quarter profits of large-cap companies rose by 13.1 percent from the previous year, but profits of small cap companies rose only 1.5 percent. Moreover, during 1997, the S&P 500 Industrials rose 31 percent, while the Russell 2000 index of smaller capitalization stocks rose only 21 percent.

The tendency for low-priced stocks to generate above-market returns thus has a number of possible explanations. Nonetheless, the generally favorable performance of low-priced stocks suggests that investors should at least consider their merits when low-priced stocks seem otherwise attractive. Nonmarket risk can be virtually eliminated by careful diversification. The cost of trading is less important to investors who expect to hold for a relatively long time. The higher cost of trading is more than offset by (ideally) higher returns when the investments are held for a number of years. Perceived institutional quality is irrelevant to a careful, well-diversified investor who is focusing on return. Research by Fama and French in 1995 found that stocks of small firms and those with high book-to-market ratios provided above average return. They point out, however, that there was evidence that profitability factors may have picked up risk factors left out of the simple capital asset pricing model. Fama and French suggest a three-factor model in which the expected return on a stock depends on its exposure to the market risk, size, and book-to-market value.[8] Thus, various models of risk and return have their advocates, but most financial economists continue to agree on two basic ideas: (1) Investors require extra expected return for taking on risk, and (2) they appear to be concerned predominantly with market risk that cannot be eliminated through diversification.

The Price/R&D Ratio

Long-term stock market favorites such as IBM, Hewlett-Packard, and Microsoft reflect the growth potential of technologically derived new products. The popularity of smaller but newer high-technology companies such as Cisco Systems and Sun Microsystems illustrates the market's search for a future IBM. Because most new technologies require extensive research, some analysts have suggested using the ratio of stock prices to per-share research and development (R&D) spending as an index of growth potential. Firms have been required to disclose such expenditures since 1974, but careful statistical analysis is needed to confirm (or disprove) the hypothesized relationship.

Takeover Candidates

Buying a stock just before it becomes an acquisition target is one of the few ways of making a quick profit in the stock market. Acquiring firms almost always offer a substantial premium over the preannouncement price of the target firm. Moreover, takeover candidates are sometimes bid up in a competition between would-be owners. Acquisitions have had a major impact on U.S. industrial structure. As the railroads linked the nation's local markets in the last half of the 19th century, the U.S. economy took on a national character. The resulting increase in competition led to the first great

merger wave

period of merger activity (*merger wave*). From the passage of the Sherman Antitrust Act (1890) through the turn of the century, merger activity continued at a breakneck pace. U.S. Steel, General Electric, American Can, American Tobacco, DuPont, Pittsburgh Plate Glass, International Paper, United Fruit, Allis Chalmers, Eastman Kodak, and a host of others were assembled during this period. The promoters of the amalgamations profited handsomely. J.P. Morgan, for example, received $62.5 million (1901 dollars) for putting U.S. Steel together. The stocks of the newly created giants were usually priced to reflect the monopoly power that they had just acquired. The severe recession of 1904 and an antimerger ruling on Northern Securities caused a sharp decline in merger activity. An adverse antitrust climate, a weak stock market, and a slow economy will all tend to inhibit merger activity.

A second major merger wave began during the 1920s and ended with the onset of the 1929 stock market crash and the Great Depression. During this time, the great public utility holding companies were assembled; vertical integration efforts increased; and many industries saw the growth of large "number two" firms (for example, General Motors—soon to become #1— Bethlehem Steel, Continental Can, and Allied Chemical).

Beginning slowly after World War II, a third merger wave reached a peak in the late 1960s. Relatively strict antitrust enforcement blocked most significant vertical and horizontal mergers. Nonetheless, a number of large firms such as LTV, Litton Industries, IT&T, and Gulf & Western Industries were able to emerge through conglomerate acquisitions. The acquiring company's stock was used in virtually all of the takeovers, often at inflated prices. The depressed stock market of the early 1970s abruptly halted this game. Few rode higher or fell farther than the conglomerates (LTV from 169 1/2 to 7 1/2 and Litton Industries from 94 1/2 to 2 3/4, for example).

In the mid-1970s and 1980s a new merger wave slowly began. Unlike previous merger activity, most of these more recent acquirers used cash or debt securities. The post-1973 depressed stock market discouraged exchanges for the stock of the acquiring company and also made cash acquisitions a cheap way of obtaining needed assets. Although mergers continued to take place, much of the action during the 1980s was in pure takeover plays. A large individual investor or group of investors would make a bid to take over a company. They would almost always plan to rely very heavily on debt to finance the deal and frequently intended to break up the firm once acquired.

Such leveraged buyouts (LBOs) gave the market much of its merger activity throughout the latter part of the 1980s. Eventually, however, the market's willingness to provide the debt capital waned and such deals became much rarer. Too many of the earlier LBOs and associated firms were getting into trouble (Drexel Burnam, Resorts International, Southmark, Integrated Resources, First Executive, Campeau, Eastern Airlines, and so on.)

During the 1990s with a rising stock market, there was a resurgence among companies of the use of inflated stock prices in order to purchase or merge with other companies. This process was referred to by S.C. Myers in 1976 as the bootstrap game, when during the 1960s some conglomerate firms made acquisitions that apparently offered no evident economic gain.[9] This game is not often played now, but clearly some of the mergers and acquisitions of the 1990s were accomplished with highly inflated stock prices.

In *Principles of Corporate Finance* R. Brealey and S. Myers set forth a simple analysis for estimating the cost when the merger or acquisition is financed using stock.[10] They point out that whenever a merger is financed by stock, the cost depends on the value of the share in the new company received by the shareholders of the selling (acquired) company.

The general form of the Brealey and Myers merger valuation equation is as follows:

If the sellers receive N shares, each worth P_{AB}, then the cost to the acquirer is

$$\text{Cost} = N(P_{AB}) - PV_B \qquad \text{(Equation 11-2)}$$

where: N = number of shares received
P_{AB} = value per share of combined shares
PV_B = present value of acquired firm

Example: Suppose firm A offers 325,000 (0.325 million) shares instead of $65 million in cash for firm B. Also, suppose A's share price before the deal is announced is $200. If B is worth $50 million stand-alone, then the apparent cost of the merger seems to be 0.325 x $200 – $50 = $15 million. But the apparent cost may not be the actual cost. A's stock is $200 before the merger announcement; at the announcement date the price may rise. Given the apparent gain and the terms of the merger, it is possible to calculate share prices and market values after the deal. Suppose that the combined firm will have 1.325 million shares outstanding and will be worth $275 million with a new share price of 275/1.325 = $207.55. Then the true cost is 0.325 ($207.55) – $50 = $17.45 million.

Brealey and Myers concluded that the key distinction between an all-cash merger or acquisition and a stock deal is that the cost of the merger/acquisition is unaffected by the merger gains in an all-cash deal. If stock is offered, however, the cost depends on the gains or losses per share because the gains/losses show up in the postmerger share price of the combined firm. Also, stock financing mitigates the effect of overvaluation or undervaluation of either firm. For instance, suppose in the previous example, that A overestimated B's value as a separate entity, thus making too generous an amount of stock on offer. If other things are equal, A's stockholders are better off if it makes a stock offer rather than a cash offer, since the inevitable cost of bad news about B's true value will fall partly on B's shareholders.

Brealey and Myers suggest a second key difference between cash and stock financing. Suppose A's managers have access to information about their firm's prospects that is not available to outsiders. This is referred to as asymmetric information. Firm A's managers may believe their shares will really be worth $215 after the merger, rather than the $207.55 estimated market price calculated above. If they are correct, the true cost of a stock-inflated merger with B is 0.325 ($215) − $50 = $19.88 million. In this case, B's shareholders would receive an extra "bonus" of $7.45 for every A-share they receive (extra gain of $7.45 x 0.325 shares = $2.42 million). If the market knows about the potential for overvaluation, it will immediately bid the price per share of the acquiring firm downward and view it as a dilution of stock value. The asymmetric-information phenomena explains why the buying firm's share prices often fall when a stock-financed merger is announced.

Takeover Criteria

Although the lawyers and investment bankers usually do well, often most of the merger profits have been made by those who bought their stock early. Indeed, the shareholders of the acquired firm almost always earn abnormal returns around the time of the takeover. Unless the investor is an insider (who would be legally restrained from acting on nonpublic information), identifying takeover candidates before the acquirers make their move is a difficult task.

Acquiring companies themselves seem to be paying increasing attention to estimated discounted cash flows of acquisition candidates. In essence, the would-be acquirer treats the potential acquisition as a capital budgeting problem and then assesses the prospective returns. Thus, those with attractive discounted cash flows relative to their cost may be likely acquisitions. Traders who use similar criteria may bid up many potential takeover candidates, thereby discouraging their acquisition and reducing the profit potential if the takeover proceeds. Still, an otherwise attractive stock may be even more appealing if its takeover is likely.

Raiders, Greenmail, and Risk Arbitrage

raiders

At times, stock market activity tends to focus on the possibility of a takeover. In the 1980s a number of investors (often called *raiders*) became well known for their records of attempted takeovers. Only a relatively small fraction, however, of takeover attempts actually succeed in wresting control

greenmail

from the existing management. Sometimes the target firm buys back the raider's stock at a premium *(greenmail)* over the market price. At other times, another buyer is brought into the picture by management (the white knight), or another raider eventually outbids the initial raider. At still other times, a friendly outsider (the white squire) is sold a substantial minority position. Occasionally, the target tries to acquire the raider company (the Pac Man defense).

Regardless of the buyer (white knight, target company, or another raider), the initial raider usually sells out at a profit. At still other times, the initial raider succeeds in taking control. At that point, it may do one of several things. It may, for example, seek to restructure the company in order to extract value for itself and, incidentally, the other shareholders. Such restructurings usually increase the firm's debt and use the borrowed funds to buy out the public shareholders. In other instances, all shareholders may be paid a substantial sum per share (partial liquidating dividend). Once in control, the raider may seek to sell the firm off a piece at a time or as a package. In rare circumstances, the erstwhile raider may settle in and run the acquisition as a going concern. Unless the effort fails outright (no greenmail or change in control), these investors usually find a way to take more out of their investment than they put in.

risk arbitrageurs

Another group of investors called *risk arbitrageurs* look to profit from potential and attempted takeovers. They assess the current stock price relative to the proposed or expected terms of the takeover and the likelihood of a successful acquisition. Depending on that assessment, they may purchase shares of the target firm in hopes of selling later at a profit.

Implications of Takeover Trading for Individual Investors

Several studies bear on the activities of raiders and risk arbitrageurs. One study found that, when a firm acquired enough stock (5 percent or more) to file a Schedule 13D, the target's price generally rose, probably in anticipation of a takeover attempt. Schedule 13D is required by the SEC, which discloses beneficial ownership of certain registered equity securities. Any person or group that acquires beneficial ownership of more than 5 percent of a class of registered equity securities must file a Schedule 13D, reporting the acquisition together with other information within 10 days after the acquisition. Furthermore, the market price of the stock of a target firm acts as a rather accurate predictor of the probability that the takeover attempt will succeed. The closer the attempt is to the proposed terms of the deal, the more likely it is to be successful. Thus, the activity of risk arbitrageurs generally drives the stock price toward the terms of a takeover that is likely to go through but not toward the terms of one that is likely to fail. Risk arbitrageurs are able to generate useful private information on the probability of a successful takeover and then to earn substantial returns by trading on that information. Such traders not only make profits on their own investments but also generally enhance the values of the other shareholders in the firms that they target.

Avoiding Bankruptcy Candidates

We have already seen that selecting companies that are subsequently acquired may yield attractive returns. Similarly, avoiding or perhaps even shorting the stocks of companies that are likely to go bankrupt may be another profitable strategy. E. Altman and J. Spirack's model for bankruptcy prediction facilitates such a strategy.[11] Their early warning system identifies firms with a high bankruptcy probability. Subsequent work indicates that bankruptcies are relatively predictable events. Moreover, the Altman formula seems about as accurate at forecasting failures as most of the alternatives. Whether an investor can profit from accurate bankruptcy predictions depends on the stock's prebankruptcy and postbankruptcy performance.

Studies have found significantly negative returns for risk-adjusted holding periods up to 4 years prior to a bankruptcy filing. It is also reported that shareholders experience large losses during the month of a bankruptcy filing with much of the losses concentrated during the 3 days surrounding the announcement. Taking advantage of these observed tendencies depends on having lead time relative to the market.

Using one form of risk adjustment, E. Altman and M. Brenner found predictable subsequent negative performance associated with deteriorating financial data, but the relationship disappeared when a second risk adjustment procedure was used.[12] Thus, trading signals of bankruptcy prediction models may or may not be helpful. Investors who want to try them may find a simplified form of the Altman model useful. It involves the calculation of a Z-score value of credit worthiness and financial viability from the following financial data:

Altman Z score

$$Altman\ Z\ score = 1.2A + 1.4B + 3.3C + 1D + .6E$$

where:
A = working capital/assets
B = retained earnings/assets
C = pretax earnings/assets
D = sales/assets
E = market value of equity/liabilities

A firm scoring less than 1.81 is classified as troubled.

Contrary Opinion: Investing in Troubled Firms

Far from avoiding troubled firms, some investors seek them out. Indeed, the so-called *theory of contrary opinion* advises investors to concentrate on issues that are out of favor (and therefore presumably undervalued). The market will eventually return to former favorites that are being neglected, or so the argument goes. Contrarians may differentiate their concept from what they disparagingly refer to as the *greater-fool theory:* Those who follow fads often bid prices up to unrealistic levels hoping that still greater fools will pay even more.

Like many stock market concepts, contrary opinion investing is easier to discuss in the abstract than to practice in the real world. Those who favor investments in stocks with low PEs or small capitalizations, in stocks neglected by analysts, or in stocks with low per-share prices are practicing what can be regarded as a contrarian approach.

Conceptually, the most appealing contrary opinion approach is to target troubled firms that are about to turn around. In this regard Katz, Lilien, and Nelson examined a trading strategy based on whether, according to a bankruptcy model such as Altman's, a firm was moving toward health or distress.[13] They found that the stocks of firms moving from distress to health exhibited positive abnormal returns. Stock returns of firms moving in the other direction were negative. Therefore, the changes in a firm's Z scores may offer useful trading signals.

An even more daring contrary approach concentrates on one of the most out-of-favor groups: the bankrupts. Although bankrupt companies usually decline severely around the time of their filing, a few eventually come back handsomely. Many are total or near-total losses, however. Investors who wish to invest in bankrupt companies may find their bonds a more effective vehicle than their stocks.

Another contrary approach is to buy shares in a contrary-opinion mutual fund. Still another approach is to seek out liquidation candidates and concentrate on the depressed issues favored by insiders. Stocks that sell below their liquidation values generally provide above-average risk-adjusted returns.

A study of the application of contrary opinion to short selling and short-term interest data argues against the success of the traditional short interest indicators, finding a stronger case for trading with the short sellers rather than betting against them, which the short interest indicator dictates. According to the study, stocks with short interest as a whole seem to underperform the market by a large margin.[14]

Managerial Objectives and the Agency Problem

Another approach to identifying misvalued securities focuses on the objectives of their managers. From the time of Adam Smith (circa 1776) until the 1920s, most economists believed that firms were largely motivated by the interests of their owners. With the rise of large publicly owned corporations, however, the managerial and ownership functions became increasingly separated. In 1929, 88 of the 200 largest nonfinancial firms were *management controlled;* no discernible group owned 20 percent or more of the stock and no smaller block showed any evidence of control. By 1963, the number had increased to 169; only five were controlled by a majority ownership group. Today, very few firms in the S&P 500 are controlled by a majority ownership group such as the Ford family or the Rockefeller family. The absence of identifiable ownership groups would seem to increase managers' discretion. Do managers have any reasons to sacrifice stockholder interests, and if so, how far can they go before they jeopardize their own positions?

agency problem

Corporate managers are shareholders' agents, and are paid to make decisions that maximize shareholder wealth. Sometimes, however, managers have their own agendas, and they make decisions that serve their own personal interests, rather than those of shareholders. This conflict of interest, called the principal-agent conflict or the *agency problem*, arises from the disparity between the goals of corporate managers and shareholders.

The agency problem can take rather blatant forms, such as shirking, diverting corporate funds to personal uses, or awarding contracts and hiring on the basis of personal friendship rather than seeking out those who are best qualified. It can also take rather subtle forms, such as investing in projects that enhance the manager's reputation rather than those that maximize shareholder wealth. Managers may make investment decisions that entrench their position, even though this may not be the best possible use to make of corporate funds. Managers may also take steps to block corporate takeovers in order to protect their jobs, even though, as discussed above, stockholders often benefit when a company is taken over.

Managers put their own self-interests over shareholders' interests when they adopt a short-term orientation and avoid actions that will have long-term benefits to shareholders. Because many managers stay with their employers for only a relatively short period of time, their financial incentives often emphasize short-term profits, rather than long-term growth.

Underinvestment in research and development may be another manifestation of the agency problem. As discussed above, R&D investment results in benefits to shareholders. However, in the short run, R&D investment results in expenses, and therefore lower profits, while the benefits may not be realized until years later. To the extent that managers are concerned primarily with short-term results, there will be a tendency to underinvest in research and development.

There are several market mechanisms that tend to restrict corporate managers' discretionary behavior. Internal incentives to promote shareholders' wealth maximization include stock options/ownership by managers and insider trading. External factors that encourage maximizing shareholder value include potential takeover bids, outright mergers and institutional investors voting or trading in the company's stock.

William Baumol's classic 1967 study contended that managerial salaries and prestige are more closely related to sales than to profits, and managers might therefore sacrifice income for growth.[15] The empire-building motives of many managers may reinforce this tendency. A high preference for security in the form of underinvestment in R&D and new ventures can also conflict with the shareholder wealth-maximizing goal. By doing less well than they might, managers widen the gap between the actual and potential market values of their firms. The wider that gap, the greater the risk of takeover bids, proxy fights, and bankruptcy—all of which jeopardize the current managers' jobs and may also hurt current stockholders. Outsiders, however, often have difficulty assessing managerial performance. Thus, stockholder interests may be sacrificed appreciably before management's position is threatened.

Even if managers' personal investments in their firms influence their behavior, the potential for conflicting or independent interest exists. Particularly blatant types of abuse include corporate officials overpaying themselves, trading on inside information, disposing of corporate assets at bargain prices to friends or relatives, and favoring certain suppliers.

Emphasizing growth at the expense of profits may be less blatant but more damaging to stockholders. Therefore, excessive sales promotion, setting low margins, and especially acquiring firms at inflated prices can harm current stockholders. Organizational slack is another potential problem. When not under competitive pressure, firms may allow costs to increase and overall efficiency to decline. Moreover, managers may use the corporation to promote their own social and political goals. Some social and political activity may improve the firm's public image or legal climate, but other actions may reflect the manager's own particular preferences.

Researchers, working at different points in time and utilizing different analytic techniques and data, have but one major difference: whether mergers have a neutral or negative impact on profitability. More recent studies have found that merger activity resulted in increased risk and little or no gain to stockholders of the acquiring firm (while the target firm's shareholders profit handsomely). Thus, either many corporate officials frequently misjudge merger opportunities, or merger activity has often been motivated by managerial interests. Neither of these explanations is very favorable to the managers of firms that engage in extensive merger activity.

The relevant evidence on the agency problem may be summarized as follows: Managers often substitute their own interests for those of the stockholders. Thus, firms managed in the interest of stockholders generally tend in some sense to outperform management-oriented firms. Finding a direct link between stock market performance and manager orientation has been difficult, however. Thus, manager orientation by itself may or may not be a particularly valuable selection criterion. Nonetheless, a knowledge of management orientation may be useful when the market price is slow to reflect the superior performance produced by a stockholder-oriented management.

How can an investor avoid investing in firms in which managers put their own well-being above that of shareholders? It is easier said than done, because no corporate manager is going to advertise the fact that he or she is not concerned with maximizing shareholder wealth. But there are observable clues that an astute investor can use. In general, when managers own a substantial amount of stock in a company, they are shareholders as well as managers, so they are more likely to take a personal interest in maximizing the value of the company's stock.

Another clue might be the turnover rate among senior management. (High employee turnover in general might be a warning sign. Although employee turnover is not publicly available information, firms are required to disclose the names of their top managers in their annual reports, so turnover from year to year can be detected.) A firm with high management turnover is likely to have a short-term orientation, since managers are unlikely to be concerned with the firm's well-being after their expected departure.

Accurately predicting when a firm's managers are about to become more stockholder oriented may be an especially worthwhile strategy. Management's new orientation should eventually increase earnings. Thus, purchasing the stock before these results become obvious could be particularly profitable. Moreover, investors who avoid management-oriented companies may thereby sidestep some losers.

To apply these recommendations, investors must first identify management's goals. Managerial orientation is not reported to shareholders like sales or profits. It is a subjective matter to be derived from the available evidence. One clue is provided by management statements such as the president's letter in the annual report. If growth is emphasized and profits are played down, the implications are obvious. Similarly, corporate officials can be asked to discuss goals at the annual meeting or elsewhere. Previous merger activity and management's compensation packages and portfolio composition may provide additional insight. Periodic efforts to reduce costs demonstrate that excessive organizational slack is not tolerated. A low payout ratio coupled with below-average growth suggests that management may be particularly concerned with its own interests. Management-oriented officials will vigorously oppose takeover bids or try to negotiate guarantees of their own positions. Stockholder-oriented managers will, in contrast, seek the best terms for the shareholders, confident that their past performance will protect their jobs.

Encouraging a shift toward stockholder orientation is clearly in shareholders' interests. Accordingly, shareholders might well wish to vote for the dissidents in a proxy fight. A large pro dissident vote is likely to make existing management more stockholder oriented. Asking pointed questions of management-oriented managers either by letter or at annual meetings may also signal potential stockholder dissatisfaction. Finally, a thwarted takeover bid or a new compensation scheme that ties salaries more closely to profits or stock performance may favorably affect managerial goals.

Characteristics of Possibly Undervalued Securities

- Low PE
- Small capitalization
- Neglect by investment analysts
- Low per-share price
- R&D intensity
- Unrecognized takeover candidates
- Out-of-favor stocks/bankruptcy candidates (contrary opinion)
- Stockholder (as opposed to managerial) orientation

SCREENING MODELS WITH INVESTMENT APPLICATIONS

Profitability Models

profitability models

A company's future stock price performance will be determined largely by its future financial performance, especially its profit rate. A number of industrial organization models relate profitability to various underlying factors. We have already seen that investment analysts' earnings prediction efforts are largely *ad hoc* and time-series oriented. *Profitability models*, in contrast, are fitted to cross-sectional data and have some theoretical underpinnings. In spite of the relevance of profit determinants to investments, the finance profession has largely ignored the literature. Much of investment analysis assesses potential earnings growth, risk of failure, or probability of success. Accordingly, characteristics associated with profitability might well help to judge a company's long-run potential.

Most of the research on profit determinants has focused on possible relationships (one or a few at a time). Studies of the relation of profits to company size, type of control, seller concentration, market share, buyer concentration, entry barriers, diversification, multimarket contacts, risk, product image, advertising, capital intensity, research intensity, and leverage have produced interesting findings but relatively few generalizable investment implications. The efforts of two consulting groups to derive strategic planning profitability models are potentially far more useful.

The Boston Consulting Group

Boston Consulting Group

The *Boston Consulting Group* (BCG) has asserted that business units (components of firms serving distinct markets) may usefully be grouped into four categories of cash flow generator-absorbers: cash cows, stars, question marks, and pets. The high-growth stars are expected to be net cash absorbers, whereas the cash cows generate excess cash flows. BCG suggests using some of the cows' revenue to maintain the business's dominant market position through investment and R&D. Additional sums can be devoted to the promising question marks. Most of the pets should be liquidated.

Although the BCG approach is designed to assist corporate managers, an implicit message applies to investors. Well-situated companies vis-à-vis the growth-share matrix are likely to produce more attractive profit performance than less well-positioned companies. Stocks that do not reflect such potentials are probably misvalued.

The Strategic Planning Institute

Strategic Planing Institute

The *Strategic Planning Institute* (SPI) uses a more detailed approach to business profitability than the BCG does. Also known as Profit Impact of Marketing Strategies (PIMS), SPI grew out of General Electric. Unlike the BCG approach, the SPI models are based on a statistical analysis of real economic data. SPI has hundreds of participating companies (a substantial percentage of which are among the Fortune 500). These participants supply funding and detailed product-line information on about 5,000 business units. This database was specifically assembled for structure/strategy/performance analysis. It has been used to build a number of models of product-;line performance. By far the best known and most widely utilized of these is SPI's Par ROI model.

The Par ROI model incorporates factors that explain approximately 70 percent of the ROI (return on investment or net income as a percentage of assets employed) variation across SPI businesses. Estimated from the SPI 4-year cross-sectional database, the Par equation is designed to capture the steady-state determinants of ROI. The variables of the equation were selected for their consistency with economic theory and the beliefs of knowledgeable businesspeople, statistical significance, and controllability by management.

Key Determinants of Profitability

	Effect on ROI
• Competitive-position factors	Effect on ROI
– Market share	+
– Relative share	+
– Relative product quality	+
• Market-attractiveness factors	Effect on ROI
– Growth in served market	+
– Fixed capital intensity	–
– Marketing intensity	–
– Purchase amount by immediate customers	–
• Joint competitive-position and market-attractiveness factors	Effect on ROI
– Investment/Sales	–
– Investment/Value added	–
– Capacity utilization	+
– Value added/employee	+

Competitive position factors (market share, relative market share, and relative product quality) measure strengths and weaknesses of a business within its served market. Market share reflects scale economies, while relative market share (the business's share relative to its top three competitors) examines share effects from a different perspective. A 10 percent to 20 percent market share is much more impressive if no other business has as much. The relative quality of products has a large impact on customer loyalty, repeat sales, relative price, and vulnerability to price competition.

Market attractiveness variables include growth in the served market, fixed capital intensity, marketing intensity, and purchase amount by immediate customers. These environmental factors affect the ease or difficulty of competing in a particular market. Operating successfully is easier in an expanding market than in a declining market; everyone can share in the growth rather than fight for the leftovers. Growth has only a modest ROI impact in rapid growth situations. Net book value of plant and equipment tends to reflect recent costs and thus be closer to replacement values. On the other hand, a technology that requires a high percentage of fixed (as opposed to working) capital limits flexibility.

Similarly, selling is costly in a market characterized by high marketing intensity. In addition to the accounting aspects of the relationship (marketing is a large cost component), marketing-intensive industries frequently experience fierce competitive struggles. Combining a high marketing level with a relatively low selling price is an especially damaging strategy. Moreover, customers who typically place large orders (high purchase amount by immediate customers) usually have greater buying power and price sensitivity. Having such customers tends to increase the difficulty of maintaining a high margin.

The joint competitive position and market attractiveness factors include investment/sales, investment/value added, capacity utilization, and value added/employee. They reflect both the within-market competitive position of the business and the served-market environment. For example, investment intensity (a weighted average of investment/sales and investment/value added) is affected both by how much output the business generates from its investment (its own efficiency) and by the technical nature of industry production. Similarly, capacity utilization and value added/employee are affected by both the efficiency of the individual business and the technical and cyclical nature of the industry. Clearly, high levels of capacity utilization and value added to investment (capital productivity) and value added per employee (worker productivity) contribute to business unit success. At high operating levels, fixed costs are spread over a larger output, usually reducing unit costs. Productivity and profitability go together. Businesses with heavy investment per employee tend to have higher levels of value added per employee. But those that are unable to raise value added in proportion to increased investment suffer both low productivity and low profitability.

ROIs that depart from the model values tend to move back toward their Pars, indicating that Par behaves as an equilibrium. SPI has also constructed other strategic planning models, including those for cash flow, market share, and start-up businesses. SPI members use the Par ROI equation to establish benchmarks, evaluate performance, set strategy, and estimate the potentials of acquisition candidates.

Only SPI members can utilize its proprietary models and database directly. Moreover, much of the needed data are nonpublic and, indeed, are not even assembled by most companies that are not members of SPI. Accordingly, the model is difficult to apply directly to investment decision making. However, many aspects of the model are in the public domain.

Estimating the relative levels of the key determinants of profitability listed above helps to evaluate long-run profit potentials. Thus, a low-profit company with a high investment intensity, low market share, low capacity utilization, high marketing intensity, and low product quality may be unable to improve its profitability without strengthening its strategic position. Alternatively, an equally unprofitable company that is appreciably stronger in most of these dimensions may more easily raise its profits.

The BCG approach emphasizes growth and market share, whereas the SPI approach utilizes a much broader array of profit determinants. Both assume that laws of the marketplace help investors understand profitability relations. Clearly, any superior insights that investors can gain through these models into a company's profit prospects should be helpful.

PE Ratio Models

Efforts to predict profits are based on the presumption that the market price will eventually reflect changes in profitability (current and anticipated). Attempts to establish equilibrium PE ratios for particular stocks are more direct. An effective PE ratio model could be used to generate "normal" values for a particular firm's PE. Departures from that level could be used to predict the movement of actual PEs toward their model values. PEs can change for two primary reasons: First, they can migrate toward their estimated equilibrium PE values. Second, those equilibrium values can themselves change. Depending on the relative strength of the two forces, knowledge of the equilibrium estimates could help identify misvalued securities.

Accordingly, a number of researchers have estimated equations of the "normal" or "predicted" PE ratio. A normal PE less than the actual ratio suggests that the stock is overpriced. A normal PE above the actual PE has the opposite implications.

Very little work has been published on theoretical PE ratio models since the early 1970s. The computed model parameters were fit to data from one period. They generally failed to hold up over subsequent periods. This instability suggests that the underlying equilibrium values for the PE ratio models may change too rapidly for a dependable tendency to move toward the estimated values to emerge.

INTEGRATED APPROACHES TO FUNDAMENTAL ANALYSIS

The narrow selection criteria (screening) and the profitability and PE ratio model methodologies concentrate on one or a few variables. Several other approaches integrate a variety of factors. Those of Benjamin Graham and John Templeton are particularly noteworthy.

Graham's Approach

Benjamin Graham coauthored the investment text that dominated the market from the 1930s to the 1950s, and he was a frequently quoted authority on investments. Graham advocated investment in financially strong companies with low prices relative to their underlying values. In the last years of his life (he died in 1976), Ben Graham and Dr. James B. Rea listed a set of 10 simple criteria for identifying undervalued stocks.[16] These criteria can be grouped into three categories: low price, strong finances, and growing earnings. Specifically, Graham and Rea suggested selecting securities with the following:

1. an earnings-to-price yield of at least twice the AAA bond yield. Thus, if AAA bonds yield 10 percent, EPS should equal at least 20 percent of the stock's price (PE of 5 or less)
2. a PE ratio no higher than 40 percent of its 5-year high
3. a dividend yield of at least two-thirds of the AAA bond yield
4. a stock price below two-thirds of tangible per-share book value
5. a stock price less than two-thirds of net quick liquidation value (current assets less total debt)
6. total debt less than tangible book value
7. current ratio of two or more
8. total debt no greater than twice the net liquidation value
9. compound 10-year annual earnings growth of at least 7 percent
10. two or fewer annual earnings declines of 5 percent or more in the preceding 10 years

Very few stocks ever meet all of these criteria. Those qualifying in seven or more are said to have a high reward-to-risk ratio. Graham and Rea particularly stressed criteria 1, 3, 5, and 6 (a stock price that is low relative to earnings, dividends, and book value, as well as debt that is low relative to book value). They contended that individual high reward-to-risk stocks may not necessarily perform well, but a diversified group of 30 or so such securities should produce handsome returns.

Graham and Rea also suggested that investors should sell a stock whenever any of the following occurred:

- It had appreciated by 50 percent or more.
- It had been held for more than 2 years.
- Its dividend was eliminated.
- Its earnings dropped sufficiently to make it overpriced by 50 percent or more relative to criterion 1 above (too high a PE ratio).

On the other hand, a stock that an investor would buy on the basis of the original criteria should be held. Little or no research (other than that implicit in Rea's own work) supports the value of these selling rules, however.

Templeton's Approach

If results are any indication of the value of an investment strategy, John Marks Templeton's growth fund deserves careful scrutiny. Unlike Graham and Rea, however, Templeton did not reduce his approach to a series of simple rules. Still, its major elements may be established from the published record, as summarized below:

- a world view to investing. U.S. stocks are only one component. At any one time, stocks are cheaper in some countries than in others.
- a low price relative to current earnings, asset values, and dividend yields (like Graham and a host of others)
- extensive diversification with risky stocks to produce an acceptable portfolio risk (unlike Graham's approach)
- selling when the market is particularly optimistic and buying when it is particularly pessimistic
- assessing emerging socioeconomic trends and their likely investment impact. For example, back in 1977, Templeton saw a growing economic role for government with an especially adverse impact on the visible and, therefore, more vulnerable large firms. Similarly, he saw continued high inflation rates and thus advocated investments in which the returns are most likely to move up with the price level.

Like Graham, Templeton sought conservatively priced stocks that are out of favor. In addition, he tried to assess the future. Will the country offer a favorable investment climate? Is the company well situated for forthcoming economic trends? Compared to Graham, Templeton was less concerned with individual risks: A low current ratio or high debt ratio would not necessarily have bothered him.

SUMMARY AND CONCLUSIONS

Investment analysts have suggested a wide array of fundamental approaches. *Forbes* lists offer one useful starting point. Low-PE stocks may tend to be undervalued, but small firms that investment analysts ignore seem to be a better bet to outperform the market on a risk-adjusted basis. Low per-share price may be an even better criterion. A high R&D intensity may be a modest plus, whereas an unrecognized takeover candidate could handsomely reward a timely purchase. Bankruptcy candidates and other depressed issues may be misvalued (contrary opinion) although relevant evidence is scarce. In certain circumstances, knowledge of manager orientation may help investors. The investment value of PE ratio models seems limited. The final fundamental approaches discussed in this chapter are the integrated methods of Graham and Templeton. The available—admittedly limited—evidence seems to support their methods' usefulness. Perhaps combining the components of small firm, stockholder orientation, and SPI profit potential with the basic Graham-Templeton framework would prove even more promising.

CHAPTER REVIEW

Answers to the review questions and the self-test questions start on page 766.

Key Terms

screening	low price effect
growth stocks	merger wave
low-PE stocks	raiders
value investing	greenmail
growth investing	risk arbitrageurs
relative PE ratios	Altman Z score
selection (survivor) bias	agency problem
small firm effect	profitability models
analyst neglect (neglected firm effect)	Boston Consulting Group
	Strategic Planning Institute

Review Questions

11-1.   The GRO Company has a PE of 25 and EPS of $1.00. Asset Play has a PE of 8 and EPS of $1.00.
   a.   If in the next 5 years GRO's PE falls to 20 while its EPS increases at 10 percent per year, what will its stock sell for?
   b.   Similarly, if in the next 5 years Asset Play's PE increases to 15 and its EPS grows at a 10 percent rate, what will its stock sell for?
   c.   Ignoring the impacts of dividends, taxes, and commissions, what are the rates (HPR and annual) of return for investments in GRO and Asset Play?

11-2.   Using the starting values given in question 11-1, assume that the EPS for both GRO and Asset Play has grown at a 5 percent rate (annual) for 5 years.

  a. If GRO's and Asset Play's PEs fall to 12 and 6, respectively, what will the stocks sell for?

  b. Ignoring the impacts of dividends, taxes, and commissions, what are the rates of return for investments in GRO and Asset Play?

11-3. a. Using the starting values given in question 11-1, assume that GRO's payout and its appropriate discount rate are 13 percent. What is its expected growth rate?

  b. Suppose Asset Play's payout is .5 and appropriate discount rate is 12 percent. What is its implied expected growth rate?

11-4. Summarize the track record of investing in low-PE stocks.

11-5. Discuss the small firm effect.

11-6. Summarize the neglected firm and low price effects.

11-7. Why would an investor want to be able to identify takeover candidates?

11-8. Apply the discounted cash flow approach to the following situation: The Cash Cow Corporation currently generates a net cash flow after all expenses of $3 million. This cash flow is expected to grow at a rate of 5 percent. If the appropriate discount rate is 12 percent, how much is Cash Cow worth?

11-9. a. Discuss the principal components of the Altman bankruptcy warning formula.

  b. How would an investor apply this model to investment selection?

11-10. Compute Altman Z-score values for each of the following companies (all data except per-share price are in thousands):

Com-pany	Working Capital	Pretax Earnings	Retained Earnings	Per-Share Price	Number of Shares	Assets	Liabil-ities	Sales
A	2,000	30,000	16,000	10	1,000	100,000	60,000	100,000
B	1,000	10,000	6,000	5	500	50,000	40,000	60,000
C	3,000	10,000	5,000	3	8,000	400,000	370,000	450,000
D	20,000	100,000	25,000	25	20,000	900,000	500,000	1,000,000

11-11. Compute the EPSs and PEs for each of the companies listed in question 11-10. Assume a tax rate of 33 percent.

11-12. In what ways may manager and stockholder goals differ? What is the relevance of these differences to investors?

11-13. a. Review the empirical evidence relating to manager-controlled versus owner-controlled firms.

b. What is the implication for investors?

Self-Test Questions

T   F   11-1. Screening refers to techniques to sort out stocks that will potentially earn above normal returns from average or below normal performers.

T   F   11-2. The highest P/E ratio stocks listed on the New York Stock Exchange, when held for a long period of time, often underperform the S&P 500 Index.

T   F   11-3. Low PE stocks tend to perform better than predicted by the market, and this is a sign of a market imperfection (anomaly) that can be exploited profitably by savvy investors.

T   F   11-4. Analyst neglect arises mainly because some corporations don't publish their results.

T   F   11-5. Takeovers and acquisitions usually help the stockholders of the acquired firm.

T   F   11-6. Takeover candidates can be identified using Altman's Z score.

T   F   11-7. The agency problem can be solved by paying corporate executives more.

T   F   11-8. Profitability models attempt to forecast company profits using fundamental factors in a quantitative framework.

T   F   11-9. Graham and Rea's approach to fundamental analysis requires looking at more than three key factors.

NOTES

1. J. K. Glassman and K. A. Hassett, *Dow 36,000: The New Strategy for Profiting from the Coming Rise in the Stock Market* (Times Books, 1999).

2. J. Siegel, *Stocks for the Long Run*, 2d ed. (New York: McGraw-Hill, 1998), pp.105–113; "The Nifty-Fifty Revisited: Do Growth Stocks Ultimately Justify Their Price?" *Journal of Portfolio Management,* vol. 21, no. 4 (summer 1995), pp. 8–20.

3. Williams R. Emmons, "What Can 'Buy-and-Hold' Stock Investors Expect?" *Monetary Trends,* June 1999, Federal Reserve Bank of St. Louis.

4. B. Malkiel, "Equity Yields, Growth, and the Structure of Share Prices," *American Economic Review*, vol. 53 (December 1963), pp. 1004–1031.

5. A. Damodaran, *Damodaran on Valuation: Security Analysis for Investment and Corporate Finance* (New York: John Wiley and Sons, Inc., 1994).

6. Microsoft, 1999 Annual Report, July 1999.

7. M. Reinganum, "Misspecification of Capital Asset Pricing: Empirical Anomalies Based on Earnings' Yields and Market Values," *Journal of Financial Economics* (March 1981), pp. 19–46; "Abnormal Returns in Small Firm Portfolios," *Financial Analysts Journal* (March/April

1981), pp. 52–56; "Portfolio Strategies Based on Market Capitalization," *Journal of Portfolio Management* (winter 1983), pp. 29–36.

8. E.F. Fama and K.R. French, "Size and Book-to-Market Factors in Earnings and Returns," *Journal of Finance,* vol. 50, no. 1 (March 1995), pp. 131–55.

9. S.C. Myers, ed. *Modern Developments in Financial Management* (New York: 1976).

10. R. Brealey and S. Myers, *Principles of Corporate Finance,* 6th ed. (Boston: Irwin/McGraw-Hill, 2000), pp. 952–955.

11. E. Altman, "Financial Ratios, Discriminant Analysis and the Prediction of Corporate Bankruptcy," *Journal of Finance* (September 1968), pp. 589–609; E. Altman and J. Spivack, "Predicting Bankruptcy: The Value Line Relative Financial Strength System vs. the Zeta Bankruptcy Classification Approach," *Financial Analysts Journal* (November/December 1983), pp. 60–67.

12. E. Altman and M. Brenner, "Information Effects and Stock Market Response to Signs of Firm Deterioration," *Journal of Financial and Quantitative Analysis* (March 1981), pp. 35–51.

13. S. Katz, S. Lilien, and B. Nelson, "Stock Market Behavior Around Bankruptcy Model Distress and Recovery Predictions," *Financial Analysts Journal* (January/February 1985), pp. 70–74.

14. K.S. Choie and S. Hwang, "Profitability of Short-Selling and Exploitability of Short Information," *Journal of Portfolio Management* (winter 1994), pp. 33–38.

15. W. Baumol, *Business Behavior, Value and Growth* (New York: Harcourt, Brace & World, 1967).

16. B. Graham and D. Dodd, *Security Analysis*, 3d ed. (New York: Whittlesey House/McGraw-Hill, 1951); R. Murray, "Graham and Dodd: A Durable Discipline," *Financial Analysts Journal* (September/October 1984), pp. 18–23.

The Stock Market and the Economy

Learning Objectives

An understanding of the material in this chapter should enable the student to

---

12-1.   Explain several methods of forecasting economic activity.

12-2.   Explain the economic impact of fiscal and monetary policies.

12-3.   Explain the relationship between stock performance and monetary policy.

12-4.   Explain the inflation protection of stocks and of several investments other than stocks.

Chapter Outline

Forecasting stock market movements is far from easy. Nonetheless, a number of different approaches have been suggested. One possible approach is to start by trying to predict the economy's direction. Then the investor can move from that economic forecast to a market forecast that is consistent with that expected state of the economy. While not necessarily the key to short-term trading profits, understanding stock market-economy relationships may, at a minimum, help investors avoid some unprofitable moves. Thus, under normal circumstances, a falling stock price might encourage investors to buy. If, however, the investor realized that a changed economic outlook had greatly altered profit expectations, the buy-hold-sell decision process might be very different. In addition, a solid understanding of stock market-economy relationships, coupled with an ability to forecast the economy's future, may indeed facilitate profitably timed trading in and out of the market. Accordingly, this chapter is designed to assist investors in understanding both economic forecasting and the relations between the stock market and the economy.

This chapter considers various ways of forecasting economic activity. The discussion includes econometric models, leading indicators, and investor-constructed forecasts. To help investors understand how to formulate a forecast, the chapter also examines the economic impact of fiscal and monetary policies. Then it explores the empirical relationship between stock performance and economic policy, giving particular emphasis to monetary policy. The remainder of the chapter discusses theoretical arguments and empirical evidence on the impact of inflation on returns.

FORECASTING ECONOMIC PERFORMANCE

The business cycle has a major effect on a firm's profits, dividends, and stock price. An expanding economy causes sales to rise, inventory levels to decline, working hours to expand, income to increase, and, therefore, corporate profits and dividends to rise. This economic expansion is also generally accompanied by a strong stock market. On the other hand, a weak economy tends to affect the stock market adversely. Thus, knowledge of the direction of the economy should help investors anticipate stock market moves. Accordingly, we shall now consider how to forecast economic activity.

econometric models

Econometric Models

econometrics

Econometrics is the statistical analysis of economic data, including both microeconomic and macroeconomic numbers. Microeconomics focuses on individual consumers, firms, and industries, while macroeconomics considers the overall economy's performance. Our interest here is largely in macroeconomic data and analysis. A number of econometricians have made a business out of forecasting economic activity. Their forecasts are generated by applying the latest economic information and expectations to their own models. Individuals may subscribe directly to these services, but the cost is substantial. Articles based on econometricians' predictions, however, frequently appear in the financial press. Thus, investors may, with a bit of a lag, learn about the forecasters' viewpoints for a minimal cost. But economic forecasts may not be especially useful to investors in any case.

Econometric forecasts of the economy have several noteworthy limitations. First, the predictions are made periodically and therefore do not reflect interim developments. Second, by the time the forecasts become available, stock prices may already incorporate the relevant information. Third, forecasters' past records are far from perfect, although they may be improving.

Leading Indicators

leading indicators

Leading indicators are designed to forecast economic activity. Beginning in the 1940s, the National Bureau of Economic Research (NBER) and the U.S. Commerce Department identified 10 monthly data series that tended to lead the business cycle based upon work going back to the 1920s: Today, the monthly data series are quite similar to the original selection: Stock prices themselves (500 common stocks), average weekly hours, average unemployment claims, inflation-adjusted manufacturers' new consumer goods orders, vendor performance (companies receiving slower deliveries), new building permits, interest rates spread on 10-year Treasury bonds less federal funds, and inflation-adjusted M2 (M2 includes currency and checkable deposits in the hands of the public, plus savings and small-time deposits, repurchase agreements, and money market deposit accounts), and consumer expectations from the University of Michigan Survey Research Center.

Today, these leading indicators and selected other data series are classified into three categories that reflect their timing at business cycle peaks and troughs: leading (10 series), roughly coincident (4 series), and lagging (7 series). The list of indicators by type has been expanded and revised from time to time and is now published by the Conference Board. Under normal circumstances, updates to the leading, coincident, and lagging indexes incorporate revisions to data only over the previous 6 months.

Longer-term revisions that cover changes in components that fall outside the moving 6-month window are incorporated in December of each year.

Three Categories of Data Series

- Leading (10 series)
- Coincident (4 series)
- Lagging (7 series)

Research by Wertheim and Company and by Geoffrey Moore found leading indicators quite accurate at forecasting economic turns but offering about the same amount of lead time as the stock market itself.[1] Thus, by the time the leading indicators forecast an economic turn, the stock market would already have made a corresponding turn of its own.

A study by S.B. Bulmash and G.W. Trivoli attempts to reconcile arguments regarding whether the main leading economic index—stock prices—evidences a leading, lagging, or concurrent relationship to key economic variables. The authors developed and tested a time-phased model of the business cycle and its relationship to stock prices.[2] They found that stock price increases tend to lead or accompany positive economic growth, but stock price declines tend to lag behind economic downturns that accompany rising inflation, high interest rates, or Federal Reserve tightening.

Investor-Constructed Forecasts

Both leading indicators and econometric forecasts appear to have relatively limited value in stock timing. Nonetheless, economic predictions might, if timely and accurate, facilitate more profitable performance for stock traders. Many investors seem inclined to make such forecasts at least implicitly. As they do about the weather, almost everyone has an opinion on the economy. These opinions should be based on an accurate understanding of how the economy operates, even though most investors probably prefer not to attempt the implied precision of an exact forecast of such macroeconomic data as *gross domestic product (GDP)*, unemployment, and inflation. Investors may, however, be more inclined to estimate the direction and perhaps the general magnitude of the changes in each. That is, few individuals would have felt comfortable forecasting an increase in real GDP of 4.2 percent in 1999, but many might have been more capable of correctly predicting greater growth than the prior year's 4.3 percent. Indeed, simply being relatively confident in a prediction that the economy is likely to be headed for (1) a *recession*, (2) continued growth, or (3) a pause should help in investment timing. Serious efforts to predict economic activity should take

gross domestic product (GDP)

recession

fiscal policy

account of the important role that the government's economic policy plays. Government spending and taxing policy (*fiscal policy*) and any activity that affects interest rates and the money supply (monetary policy) have important economic impacts. Let's now consider fiscal and monetary policy and their effects on the economy.

Fiscal Policy

Government spending affects the economy in several ways. First, when the economy has room to expand, increased government expenditures may call forth additional production. Thus, starting a new public works project (for example, a highway, school, or dam) will put people to work to produce the structure and the required inputs (cement, steel, and so on). These newly employed workers will likely spend most of their income on consumer goods and services, thereby creating demands that put others to work. This alleged *multiplier* process increases employment and production. At each stage, however, a portion of the extra income does not go directly back into the domestic economy. It is saved, taxed, or spent on imported goods. These *leakages* reduce the multiplier's power. Moreover, the additional spending forces the government to increase its borrowing or taxes, thereby crowding out other borrowers and/or reducing other disposable incomes. Thus, proportionately less goes to each succeeding round. In fact, leakages are so pervasive that the GDP typically increases by less than twice the amount of the government spending increase after accounting for all multiplier effects. All these assumed effects are based on the existence of neutral monetary policy—that is, no changes in monetary conditions.

multiplier

leakages

The effect of a tax decrease is similar to a government spending increase. Lower tax rates and reduced withholding increase households' after-tax income, causing spending to rise. This spending increase, in turn, leads to additional production, employment, and income, which cause further increases in spending. Thus, either a government spending increase or a tax decrease stimulates the economy, whereas a government spending decrease or a tax increase restrains the economy. According to Keynesian theory, a change in government spending has a greater economic impact than a tax change of equivalent size. The multiplier acts on the full amount of the change in government spending to affect GDP, whereas a portion of the tax change affects savings, leaving the multiplier a lesser amount on which to act.

Stimulative fiscal policy is normally applied when the economy has sufficient room to absorb the resulting increase in spending with increased output. When the economy is already operating near its capacity, however, stimulative fiscal policy can have little or no impact on output or employment. Under these circumstances, the principal effect of fiscal policy stimulation is to increase prices. As we shall soon see, inflation is not a plus for either the economy or the stock market.

How Fiscal Policy Operates through Government Spending and Taxes

- Increased government spending or decreased taxes stimulate the economy.
- Decreased government spending or increased taxes restrain the economy.

Monetary Policy: The Fed's Tools

Fed
monetary policy

    The Federal Reserve System (*Fed*) has primary authority over our nation's *monetary policy*. Its ability to influence the economy stems from its power over credit conditions. By largely determining the rate at which the money supply expands or contracts, the Fed exercises a considerable amount of influence over the supply and cost (interest rate) of credit.

money supply

    The money supply itself consists of all cash and coin in circulation outside banks, plus all accounts in depository institutions that are subject to withdrawal by check (*M1*). Most of M1 is held in the form of checkable deposits. Federally chartered banks and state banks with Fed memberships are required to maintain reserves equal to a predetermined percentage of their deposits. This percentage is called the reserve ratio. A bank's required reserve is found by multiplying its deposits by the reserve ratio.

M1

Example: Suppose a bank has $5 million in transactions deposits and the reserve ratio is 3 percent. The bank's required reserves would be $5,000,000 x .03 = $150,000. These reserves must be held either as vault cash or deposits at the bank's regional Federal Reserve Bank.

---

reserve requirement

    The Fed can cause the money supply to expand or contract by reducing or increasing the *reserve requirement* (reserve ratio). If the reserve requirement is decreased, banks need less reserves to support their existing deposits and therefore may increase their loans. An increase in the reserve requirement has the reverse effect.

Example: Suppose a bank has $5 million in transactions deposits, actual reserves of $300,000, and required reserves of $300,000 (assume the reserve ratio, unlike the previous example, is 6 percent). If the Fed lowers the reserve ratio to 4 percent, the bank is now required to have $200,000 in reserves ($5,000,000 x .04 = $200,000). It has actual reserves of $300,000—$200,000 of which are required and excess reserves of $100,000. The bank's excess reserve position is found by subtracting its required reserves of $200,000 from its actual reserves of $300,000.

To make loans, a bank must have excess reserves. By lowering the reserve ratio from 6 percent to 4 percent, the Fed required the bank to have $100,000 less in reserves behind its $5 million in deposits. The bank is now able to expand loans by an additional $100,000.

When a bank grants a loan, it funds it by creating a deposit to the borrower's account. In effect, it creates the money that it loans. The money that is thereby created is initially retained in an account at the lending bank. Checks written against these loan-created deposits will, in turn, be deposited into the accounts of the people or firms receiving the payments. In this way, most of the money flows into other bank accounts. Some of the funds will remain with the bank that made the loan, while a much larger fraction will move into accounts of other components of the banking and financial system. A relatively small portion of the loan money may go into additional cash holdings. Thus, most of the new money resulting from granting the loan ends up as deposits somewhere in the banking system. The corresponding increase in deposits throughout the banking system creates additional lending power. When this lending power is utilized, more deposits and still more lending power result.

By the time the process is complete, the money supply will have expanded by several times the amount of the initial increase in deposits. Loans outstanding will increase by a comparable amount. The ratio between the initial increase in reserves and the resulting money supply increase is called the *money multiplier*. Any reserves freed by reducing the reserve requirement will eventually be utilized to increase the money supply, loans outstanding, and investments by a multiple of the freed-up reserves.

money multiplier

Changing reserve requirements tends to disrupt the financial markets more than is desirable. Accordingly, the Fed generally prefers to exercise its influence over the banking system through what are called *open market operations*. These operations utilize the Fed's substantial portfolio of government bonds. The Fed's management of this portfolio has a major effect on the banking system.

open market operations

The Fed's portfolio management requires buying and selling substantial amounts of government bonds. When it is a buyer, the Fed pays for the bonds with drafts (checks) that increase the recipient banks' reserves. These increased reserves allow a multiple increase in deposits and loans as described above. Similarly, when the Fed sells government securities, reserves are reduced, thereby forcing deposits and loans to contract. The Fed buys and sells Treasury securities virtually on a daily basis and thereby pumps in or takes out a targeted amount of reserves. The change in reserves then affects the aggregate money supply. Many Wall Street analysts carefully monitor the Fed's open market moves and the resulting changes in the money supply.

The Fed also loans reserves (discount loans) to member banks, stressing that discounting is a privilege, not a right. It extends these loans only on a short-term basis (as a safety valve) and only to applicants that it views as not abusing this borrowing privilege. The Fed makes discounting more or less attractive by adjusting its interest rate on and its willingness to grant such loans, but it tends to keep the *discount rate* in line with the *federal funds rate*. The federal funds rate is recently the most important target rate affecting financial markets. It is the rate that banks charge each other for overnight use of excess federal reserves in the so-called federal funds market.

discount rate
federal funds
rate

Compared with the Fed's other tools, discounting plays a relatively minor role, but changes in the federal funds rate are used principally to signal changes in Fed policy. Fed policy appears to be more focused on the federal funds rate. At its meeting in February 1994, the *Federal Open Market Committee (FOMC)* began the practice of immediately disclosing its decisions upon making them, rather than waiting until the next meeting to disclose the minutes of the previous meeting. Beginning in October 1997, the Fed announced that its FOMC directive would henceforth specify an explicit target for the federal funds rate. In addition, the directive would express a bias to possible future action in terms of the rate. For a long time prior to the announcement, the Fed had implemented monetary policy by making

Federal Open
Market Committee
(FOMC)

The Fed's Principal Policy Tools

- Reserve requirement: Increasing (decreasing) the ratio reduces (raises) the amount of money that can be supported by a given reserve base.
- Open market operations: Fed purchases (sales) of government securities increase (decrease) the reserves available to support the money supply.
- Discount loans: Increasing (decreasing) the discount rate and decreasing (increasing) its willingness to grant discount loans tightens (eases) monetary policy.

discrete and frequent small adjustments to its federal funds rate target. Often, changes in the federal funds rate follow other changes in the marketplace, such as changes in market-determined interest rates. The stock market generally reacts strongly to changes in the federal funds rate. These changes are viewed as evidence of a policy shift (either in direction or magnitude).

Economic Impact of Monetary Policy

How does an increase in deposits and loans affect the economy? The supply of money in the form of transactions balances (for example, checkable deposits) and the corresponding amount of the banking system's outstanding loans play a key role in the economy. An increase in the supply of money and loans outstanding tends to reduce interest rates (at least in the short run). The increased supply and lower cost (interest rate) of loanable funds encourage many people to spend more on consumption. For example, households are more inclined to purchase a new car or a new home if it is easier to finance. Similarly, businesses are encouraged to invest more in plant and equipment expenditures and in other long-term projects (for example, research and development). These additional consumption and investment expenditures tend to create more income and jobs and to stimulate even more spending. A reduction in deposits and loans, in contrast, tends to reduce spending and income.

As with fiscal policy, stimulative monetary policy tends to increase real (noninflationary) output when the economy has slack resources, and it tends to increase prices when bottlenecks appear or when the economy is already operating near full employment or capacity utilization. Thus, stimulative monetary policy is often favorable to the economy and stock market. That is, it is likely to increase demand for goods and services and thereby increase profits. Additionally, an increase in the availability of loanable funds may reduce real interest rates. As we shall see, a decline in interest rates is particularly bullish (favorable) for stock prices. When the economy is already operating near its capacity, however, further stimulation is particularly likely to be inflationary. These inflationary pressures are bearish (unfavorable) for both the economy and the stock market. This inflation is all too likely to cause economic policy to become restrictive and thereby throw the economy into a recession.

Economic Effect of Deposits and Loans

- Increase in deposits and loans: stimulates spending and income
- Decrease in deposits and loans: restrains spending and income

Monetary and Fiscal Policy: Some Qualifications

As we have seen, the economy may be stimulated by increased government spending, lower taxes, and an increase in the money supply, and it may be restrained by the reverse processes. Now let us introduce some qualifications.

First, the impacts of changes in tax rates and government spending (fiscal policy) or in the reserve requirement, discount rate, and open market policy (monetary policy) take time to work their way through the economy. As a result, changes in the direction of Federal Reserve monetary and government fiscal policy generally precede changes in the direction of economic activity. Thus, knowledge of these changes can be used to help forecast economic behavior.

Second, monetary and fiscal policy are both subject to political pressures. Their degree of sensitivity differs, however. Monetary policy is formulated by the *Federal Reserve Board of Governors* and its Federal Open Market Committee. Members are appointed by the President and confirmed by the Senate for long (14-year) staggered terms. Furthermore, the Fed is not dependent directly on Congressional appropriations. Its own interest income is more than adequate to cover its operating expenses. The Fed, therefore, is generally able to pursue a relatively independent monetary policy. Fiscal policy, on the other hand, is formulated jointly by Congress and the President, and many diverse interest groups may directly affect the decision-making process. As a result, short-term pressures increase the difficulty of implementing long-run fiscal policies.

Third, the stock market also monitors and reacts to its perceptions of the direction of economic policy. Thus, to obtain an advantage relative to the market's own economic assessment, investors need to have a superior understanding of economic policy/economy-stock market relationships. In other words, investors need to be able to outguess the market in its forecast for the economy's future. Any economic forecasts should be based on an assessment of the probable direction for economic policy. That direction is very likely to be related to the policymakers' objectives. Accordingly, would-be forecasters of the economy need to know (and understand the nature of) what goals the policymakers are pursuing.

Goals of Monetary and Fiscal Policy

The primary economic goals of monetary and fiscal policymakers are price stability and full employment. Most people have a general idea of what price stability and full employment mean. Nonetheless, the concepts are sufficiently complex and confusing to warrant some discussion.

Price stability is the absence of either a rising (inflation) or falling (deflation) trend in overall prices. Inflation is a general rise in the price level.

(margin notes)

Federal Reserve Board of Governors

price stability

Thus, for example, a 6 percent annual inflation rate implies that $1.06 is required to buy the same diverse market basket of goods and services as could have been acquired a year earlier for $1. Deflation, in contrast, is a general fall in the price level. During most of our history, actual and potential inflation have been much more of a problem than the threat of deflation. Furthermore, policymakers (especially at the Fed) frequently state the problem of achieving price stability as a matter of lowering the rate of inflation (rate of change of prices upward), rather than the complete elimination of all price increases.

full employment

It might be logical to think that *full employment* would be defined as 100 percent of the labor force having jobs. Realistically, however, some people (not necessarily the same people) will always be unemployed, even in the best of times, because some degree of unemployment is inevitable. People change jobs (frictional unemployment), work at seasonal jobs (seasonal unemployment), or are unemployed because of location, background, or training (structural unemployment). Moreover, increasing numbers of people are either self-employed or in unreported underground economy jobs. These various classes of unemployed and unreported employees create an almost irreducible floor for reported unemployment. The height of this floor, however, changes as the economy evolves (see figure 12-1). Full employment, therefore, is generally defined as corresponding to some acceptable level of unemployment. The *unemployment rate* itself is defined

unemployment rate

FIGURE 12-1
Unemployment, Labor Force Participation, and Employment Rates

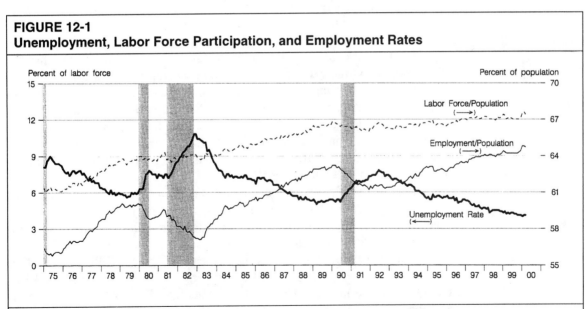

Reprinted with permission of the Federal Reserve Bank of St. Louis, *National Economic Trends.* The chart appeared on page 10 of the May 2000 issue. Lead article was written by Michael R. Pakko.

as the percentage of the labor force that is out of work and actively seeking a job. The labor force consists of those who are employed or actively seeking employment. Extensive government statistics are compiled on both employment and inflation.

Currently, the relationship of the U.S. to the international economy is increasing in importance. Thus, as the world economy has grown more interdependent, such matters as the relative exchange value of the dollar (exchange rate), the amount of imports relative to exports (*balance of trade*), and international capital flows (which may take the form of foreigners investing in U.S. securities) have become increasingly important to economic policymakers. Moreover, the actions of foreign and other international investors are having an increasingly large impact on U.S. financial markets as globalization of the world economy becomes more significant.

balance of trade

Some of the Fed's additional economic and quasi-economic goals and concerns include economic growth, freedom, and opportunity; increased productivity; a higher standard of living; environmental protection; energy independence; consumer protection; and product safety. Policies designed to achieve some of these goals may frequently conflict with other goals.

Virtually everyone agrees that price stability and full employment are desirable. Policies to reduce unemployment may, however, accelerate inflation because of the *capacity effect*. Stimulating the economy depletes the reservoir of unemployed workers, resources, and excess capacity. Eventually, those bidding for the limited supply of inputs will force prices to rise. However, some stimulation may be administered to a slack economy before bottlenecks accelerate the inflation rate.

capacity effect

The international situation adds a further complication. During the 1980s, defending the value of the dollar and seeking to attract capital to help finance both the budget and trade deficits may have led to relatively restrictive monetary policy (*tight money*). Such a policy tends to raise U.S. interest rates relative to rates abroad. However, higher interest rates usually lead to reduced domestic economic activity. Thus, policymakers may at times have to choose between doing what is best for the domestic economy or doing what is best internationally.

tight money

The trend of inflation rates in the U.S. has been basically downward from its peaks in the early 1980s, as measured by the Consumer Price Index (CPI). This trend has been matched by other leading industrial countries and regions, including the European Union, Canada, and Japan. Figure 12-2 shows the rate of inflation in the U.S. measured by the CPI and inflation expectations as measured by the quarterly Federal Reserve Bank of Philadelphia, the monthly University of Michigan Survey Research Center, and the FOMC ranges as reported to Congress in the annual Humphrey-Hawkins testimony each year. The downward trend is clearly noted in each of the time series and variables shown since 1990. The CPI inflation rate shown in figure 12-2 is the percentage change from the previous year.

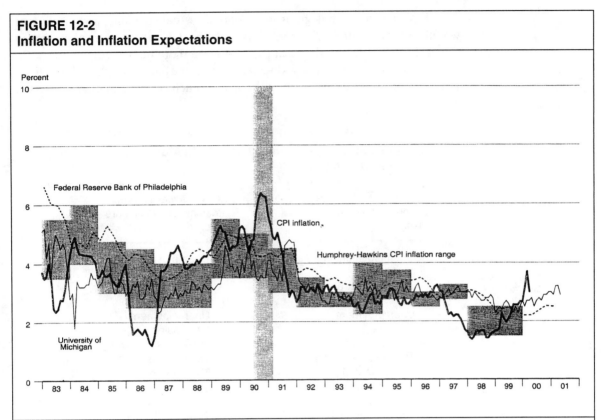

FIGURE 12-2
Inflation and Inflation Expectations

The shaded region shows the Humphrey-Hawkins CPI inflation range. Beginning in January 2000, the Humphrey-Hawkins inflation range was reported using the PCE price index and therefore is not shown on this graph.

Used with permission from Surveys of Consumers, University of Michigan. Reprinted from *Monetary Trends*, June 2000.

IMPORTANCE OF MONETARY POLICY

Stock market analysts pay particular attention to monetary (as opposed to fiscal) policy for several reasons. First, monetary policy has differential industry effects.

Second, monetary policy is often considered easier to track—and perhaps easier to predict. The Fed's weekly monetary data releases are intensively analyzed by some members of the financial press. Moreover, monetary policy can shift emphasis more quickly than fiscal policy can. Thus, Fed action may have to shoulder the entire macroeconomic adjustment burden when political pressures inhibit discretionary fiscal policy.

Third, an influential group of economists (called monetarists, many of whom are associated with the University of Chicago) assert that money drives the economy, while fiscal policy plays a more modest role.

Fourth, monetary policy directly affects the stock market through its influence on interest rates. We will consider each of these matters in greater detail.

Factors Affecting Likelihood of Shift in Monetary and Fiscal Policy

A shift toward greater stimulation is more likely if	A shift toward greater restrictiveness is more likely if
• Unemployment is far above its goal.	• Unemployment is near its goal.
• The inflation rate is near its goal.	• The inflation rate is far above its goal.
• Unemployment is increasing.	• Unemployment is decreasing.
• Inflation is decreasing.	• Inflation is increasing.
• The dollar is strong.	• The dollar is weak.
• The trade deficit is small.	• The trade deficit is large.
• The administration is liberal.	• The administration is conservative.
• The presidential election is approaching.	• The presidential election is far off.
• Substantial amounts of capital are flowing into the U.S.	• Foreign capital is threatening to withdraw from or slow its flow into the U.S.

Disproportionate Impact of Monetary Policy

Monetary policy works by rationing credit. Restrictive monetary policy not only raises interest rates (at least in the short run), but it also tends to limit availability of credit to stronger credit risks and thereby influence the allocation of funds among the financial intermediaries.

thrift institutions

Savings and loan associations and mutual savings banks (*thrift institutions*) may be particularly hard hit when money is tight. The thrifts have historically maintained a large percentage of their portfolios in long-term fixed-rate mortgages. Thus, in effect, a large fraction of their deposits has been used to fund long-term mortgage lending. Moreover, some portion has been at fixed rates.

The thrifts' deposits, in contrast, have tended to be available to their depositors on demand or to be represented by CDs with relatively short terms. This type of situation implies an imbalance between the maturity structure of thrifts' assets (long term) and their liabilities (short term). The imbalance has tended to make the thrifts more vulnerable to rising interest rates than other lending institutions that do not have a high concentration of assets in fixed-rate mortgages. As interest rates rise, the costs of funds tend to go up, while the rates that the thrifts earn on existing fixed-rate mortgage loans remain relatively constant. The larger the proportion of their assets tied up in fixed-rate loans, the more vulnerable the thrifts are to rising interest rates. Having experienced the adverse effects of rising interest rates a number of times, the thrifts have sought to limit their exposure.

adjustable rate mortgages (ARMs)

Over time, a shift to *adjustable rate mortgages (ARMs)*, as well as the use of various instruments for hedging interest rate risks (financial futures, options, and interest rate swaps), has tended to reduce this vulnerability. Nonetheless, many thrifts (particularly the smaller ones) remain vulnerable to adverse interest rate moves. Over time, the deregulation of rates that occurred during the 1970s and early 1980s has helped to offset the loss of accounts due to disintermediation (loss of deposits as savers shifted funds to direct investments or money market mutual funds), but it has done little to reduce the resulting profit squeeze.

The thrifts' sensitivity to high interest rates adds to the vulnerability to tight money of the real estate, construction, building materials, and major appliance industries. Other industries that are heavily leveraged, such as public utilities and airlines, as well as auto and farm machinery manufacturers—the bulk of whose purchases are financed—are also particularly sensitive to monetary policy. Thus, tight money affects various types of companies and their stocks differently.

Relative Ease of Tracking Monetary Policy

The financial press pays close attention to any news relating to Fed policy. Even the Fed, however, has some difficulty tracking and controlling short-run monetary aggregates. The monetary aggregates, such as M1 (primarily currency plus demand deposits) or M2 (essentially M1 plus other liquid deposits), are no longer the focus of Wall Street as they were in the early 1980s.

Nonetheless, monetary policy is easier to follow than the lengthy, uncertain path of authorizations, appropriation, and implementation of government expenditures. Tax legislation, the other side of fiscal policy, is equally difficult to follow. Moreover, the greater volatility of monetary policy leads to more signals than is the case with fiscal policy.

Monetarists versus Fiscalists

monetarists

fiscalists

Since John Maynard Keynes published his *General Theory of Employment, Interest, and Money* in 1936, the *monetarists* have debated with those who emphasize the importance of fiscal policy (*fiscalists*). Although the fiscalists dominated economic thinking throughout the 1940s and 1950s, by the early 1960s, the debate was again in full swing. The dispute continues, but the issues may be narrowing. During much of the post-1936 period, the fiscalists were far more influential in and out of government. Since the late 1960s, however, both groups have had substantial influence. Most economists now agree that both monetary and fiscal policy affect the economy but disagree on their relative importance, although the "rational expectations" school (originating at the University of Chicago, based on the work of Robert Lucas) argues that actual fiscal policy is useless in the long run.

Unless monetary and fiscal policy are working at cross-purposes, both economic schools expect the same direction (if not the same magnitude) of impact. Moreover, conflicts between monetary and fiscal policy (one stimulating and the other restraining) are usually quite short run. These conflicts usually arise because monetary policy is leading and fiscal policy will soon follow. Therefore, investors, who are principally concerned with direction rather than magnitude, need not assess the relative merits of the monetarists' and fiscalists' arguments.

Direct Effect of Monetary Policy on the Stock Market

Monetary policy indirectly influences the stock market through its effect on the economy and on corporate profits. Moreover, the impact of monetary policy on interest rates has a direct effect on the stock market in three related ways.

First, stock prices reflect the present value of their expected future income streams. The rate at which these expected incomes are discounted is affected by the market rates of interest.

Second, investors find bonds relatively more attractive as their yields to maturity increase. As a result, some investors will shift from stocks to bonds when interest rates rise and from bonds to stocks when they fall.

Finally, higher interest rates mean increased borrowing costs for margin investors. These investors will require a higher expected return to justify the greater cost of financing their margin purchases. Thus, rising interest rates should depress stock prices; they imply a higher discount rate, more attractive returns for bonds, and increased costs for margin debt. Falling interest rates have the opposite effect.

How the Impact of Monetary Policy on Interest Rates Affects the Stock Market

- The market rate of interest affects the rate at which stocks' expected future income streams are discounted.
- As bonds' yields to maturity increase, investors shift from stocks to bonds when interest rates rise and from bonds to stocks when interest rates fall.
- High interest rates result in increased borrowing costs for margin investors, who need a higher expected return to justify their greater financing costs.

As discussed earlier, Bulmash and Trivoli studied the relationship between stock prices and the economy over the period 1961 to 1987, and they developed a three-phase model of the economic cycle to describe the major factors at work in the linkages between stock prices and economic activity. The model attempts to explain the time lags that transpire between economic impact and effect on stock prices. Bulmash and Trivoli found that the interaction between stock prices and selected economic factors is reciprocal. That is, depending on the phase of the business cycle, stock prices either lead (phase I), lag (phase II), or occur concurrently (phase III). Moreover, they found that causality, feedback, and reverse causality between stock prices and selected economic variables may be categorized further into short-term, intermediate, and long-term effect. Figure 12-3 illustrates the linkages between monetary policy and stock prices related to the three phases of the business cycle.

Money-Stock Market Relationship: An Integrated Approach

Basing trading decisions on actual monetary policy changes seems unlikely to outperform a buy-and-hold strategy. Accurately predicting monetary policy changes, supplementing the analysis with knowledge of other economic influences, and concentrating on interest-sensitive securities might prove more effective. Forecasts of fiscal policy changes and other factors that have a short-run economic impact might also be considered. In particular, consumer spending and business spending for fixed plant, equipment, and construction expenditures often have substantial and sometimes unexpected economic effects. The *Survey Research Center* of the University of Michigan periodically surveys and reports on consumer sentiments. Similarly, Irwin/McGraw-Hill surveys and reports business capital expenditure plans (in the November issue of *Business Week*), as does the Commerce Department (in the December *Survey of Consumer*

Survey Research Center

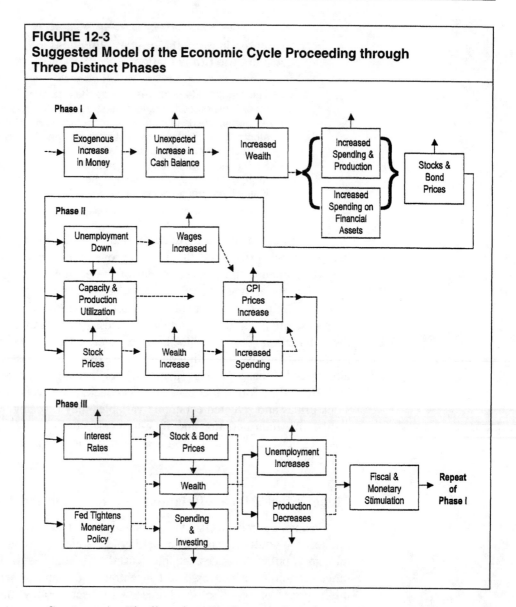

FIGURE 12-3
Suggested Model of the Economic Cycle Proceeding through Three Distinct Phases

Sentiments). Finally, the Conference Board compiles quarterly capital appropriation statistics (reported in *Manufacturing Industrial Statistics*). These forecasts are widely reported in the press.

The impact of differing economic conditions on particular firms and industries might also be considered. Banking, construction-related companies, and other interest-sensitive firms are especially vulnerable to tight money. Moreover, postponable-expenditure industries (for example, autos and consumer durables) are typically depressed by recessions, whereas other industries (for example, utilities and beer) suffer only slightly. Few industries are truly recession proof (their own claims notwithstanding), but vulnerability to the economic climate does vary. Recession-sensitive companies (for example, *smokestack companies*) may be poor performers just before a downturn, whereas they generally rally just before an upturn.

smokestack companies

The previously mentioned suggestions may seem logical, but relatively little empirical research has thus far been directed toward resolving the issues. How successful in using an understanding of economy-stock market relations will depend on investors' astuteness vis-à-vis the market consensus. If the market consensus is based on effective analysis, few investors are likely to do better. If market analysts frequently make avoidable errors, however, those with superior analytical abilities should profit. Clearly, further research is needed.

INFLATION-STOCK MARKET RELATIONSHIP

inflation

The stock market appears to be influenced by two different aspects of the economy: the business cycle and the inflation rate. Having already explored the impact of the business cycle, we now turn to *inflation* and its effect on the stock market.

Some people may see inflation as a purely monetary phenomenon. According to this view, inflationary pressures affect prices but little else. Those who accept this line of reasoning expect investors to seek to maximize their expected risk-adjusted return without regard to the inflation rate. In their view, most investors believe that inflation will reduce the real (after-inflation) return of anything that they invest in. Thus, these investors will choose their investments and manage their portfolios without taking account of the potential impact of inflation.

Most people, however, see inflation as more than a simple monetary phenomenon. Therefore, the inflation rate is thought to have an impact that goes well beyond simply affecting the price level. These people believe that inflation plays an important role in the determination of the level of economic activity and that it can have rather different effects on the various components of the economy. As a result, these investors consider the different inflation protection of various types of investments. These investors' propensities to spend (particularly on durables) may be affected by what they expect their real returns to be. In addition, different investments may offer varying degrees of long-term inflation protection. Thus, the appeal of some assets may depend on the expected long-term inflation rate. Finally, investors who are able to anticipate changes in the inflation rate may be able to shift profitably between more inflation-resistant and less inflation-resistant investments.

Wall Street View of Stocks as an Inflation Hedge

Until the 1970s, most analysts thought that the stock market offered substantial inflation protection. Stockbrokers and mutual fund salespeople argued that equity returns would tend to keep up with inflation better than the returns on *fixed-income securities* (bonds) would. Early thought often confused two rather different *inflation hedge* concepts. According to one view, the market value of an inflation hedge should rise with the general price level. Thus, the *real return* of a perfect inflation hedge should be independent of price changes. A perfect inflation hedge yielding 4 percent with stable prices would return 4 percent plus a factor for an inflation rate of x percent.

fixed-income securities

inflation hedge

real return

Although few analysts ever claimed that stocks offered complete protection from inflation, many believed that if consumer prices changed by x percent, average stocks would yield

$$r = a + b \,(x \text{ percent})$$

where: r = rate of return or yield
     a = a constant value
     b = some positive number less than unity

Thus, if a = 3 and b = .7,

then an inflation rate of 5 percent would imply a nominal (no adjustment for inflation) stock market return of

$$3\% + .7\,(5\%) = 6.5\%$$

Such a nominal return corresponds approximately to a real return of

$$6.5\% - 5\% = 1.5\%$$

A real return of 1.5 percent is positive but less than the real return would be at lower inflation rates. This type of behavior relative to the inflation rate would imply that stocks acted as a partial hedge against inflation.

A second form of the inflation hedge concept takes a much longer-range perspective. According to this viewpoint, average long-run stock returns will generally exceed the rise in the general price level. In particular short-run periods, nominal returns may be below the inflation rate. Eventually, however, nominal returns will catch up with and exceed the increase in the price level. If markets behave as this perspective implies, the real value of capital would tend to be preserved in spite of the inflation rate. This form of the inflation hedge concept is less strong because it allows for the possibility that the market will be affected adversely (if temporarily) by high and/or rising inflation rates. In spite of the experience in the 1970s with rapid inflation and poor stock market performance, and in the early 1990s when stock returns were mediocre, the view persists that stocks will still protect investors from inflation in the long run. The recent work of Jeremy Siegel at the Wharton School of the University of Pennsylvania has reinforced the view that stocks are the best investment in the long run.[3]

Theoretical Underpinnings of the Stock Market-Inflation Hedge Hypothesis

To provide effective short- or long-run inflation protection, companies must increase their profits (as measured in nominal terms) or increase their efficiency (that is, lower costs). In periods of rising prices, their own costs are almost certain to be increasing unless offset by productivity gains. Thus, one way that firms might be able to defend their profitability is by raising prices. The ability of stocks to withstand the adverse impact of an inflationary environment is very dependent on the underlying company's ability to maintain its profitability. Stocks represent ownership of real assets. The replacement value of these assets and their ability to generate income may well rise with the price level. If firms are able to raise their prices sufficiently, the real (inflation-adjusted) value of dividends and share prices may keep pace with price-level increases. A number of considerations, however, limit firms' ability to raise prices by enough to preserve investment values.

To illustrate, various aspects of our tax system tend to penalize investment income at high inflation rates. First, the IRS requires that companies use historical costs in computing their profits. As a result, they must pay taxes on sums (statutory profits) that reflect the difference between the historical cost and the replacement value of inventory, plant, and equipment.

Example: Suppose a company in a competitive environment that prevents price increases on its own products produces a widget for a recorded cost of $1, based on the company's now out-of-date materials costs. If it then sells the widget for $2, the company must report a profit of $1 ($2 – $1), even if the next widget will (based on up-to-date materials prices) cost $1.50 to produce.

A high inflation rate increases these differences between accounting costs of goods sold and the forward-looking replacement costs of goods sold. Similarly, a high inflation rate will tend to increase the tax on these reported (phantom) profits. As a result, the real after-tax component of reported profits tends to fall as prices increase. Of course, use of LIFO (last-in, first-out) accounting may reduce or eliminate the difference in accounting cost of goods and replacement costs of goods sold.

Second, inflation tends to push noninstitutional investors into higher marginal tax brackets, further increasing the tax penalty on investments. This effect was a severe problem when our tax system had 11 brackets with a top rate of 50 percent or even higher. The reduced number of tax brackets and lower maximum rate under the Tax Reform Act of 1986, somewhat reversed by the Budget Reconciliation Act of 1993, reduces but does not eliminate this effect.

Third, individuals must pay taxes on sums (dividends and capital gains) that often contain a substantial inflation component. Thus, even if the before-tax return rose point for point with the inflation rate, the after-tax return would not.

Example:	A one-third tax rate applied to a 3 percent nominal return and zero inflation (a 3 percent real return before taxes) provides a 2 percent after-tax real return. A 6 percent nominal return with a 3 percent inflation rate produces a real after-tax return of only 1 percent. A 9 percent nominal return and 6 percent inflation rate yields a real after-tax return of 0 percent. For nominal returns above 9 percent, a 3 percent before-tax real return corresponds to a negative real after-tax return.

The use of leverage makes this relationship considerably more complex, however. If the interest cost of the loan is deductible and below the return on the investment, investors can effectively use leverage to enhance their after-tax, after-inflation return. The cost of borrowing, however, tends to rise with the inflation rate.

Another complication arises due the fact that capital gains tax rates have again diverged significantly lower (at 20 percent) than marginal income tax rates (39.5 percent). This means that the real-return calculation can vary significantly between income-generating versus capital-appreciation-generating investments.

Other considerations also increase the difficulty of offsetting inflation's adverse effect. We might suspect that cost and price increases of x percent would (neglecting tax effects) approximately maintain a firm's financial position. In fact, however, higher prices and costs generally require a contemporaneous and disproportionate increase in capital to support inventories, accounts receivables, and new plant and equipment. Moreover, if higher inflation rates are associated with higher interest rates, both the amount and the cost of financing tend to increase with inflation. Thus, to offset the effect of taxes on nominal profits and to finance the increased capital requirements at higher interest rates, prices must be raised proportionately more than the direct cost increase. To offset the increased retained earnings requirement (needed to support the additional borrowings) and the investor's inflation-imposed tax burden, prices may have to rise more than proportionately.

Many firms are unable to raise prices sufficiently to recapture their increased production costs, however, to say nothing of increasing them sufficiently to offset tax and financing effects. The more rapid the inflation, the greater the likelihood of some governmental action designed to reduce demand-side pressures. This action might take the form of fiscal and monetary restraint, public pronouncements (jawboning), price controls, or guidelines. Supply-side efforts to increase efficiency and competition through regulatory reform are also possible. To the extent that these various policies succeed in restraining price increases (even if only in the short run), profits may also be reduced. Moreover, increased competition from substitutes (whose costs may be more stable) or the existence of long-term contracts from more hotly competitive firms in an environment of reduced demand and excess capacity may also limit firms' ability to raise their prices.

The fourth aspect of the tax system that may have a negative effect on investment values is that international competition tends to hold some prices down, depending on the interplay of such factors as domestic versus international inflation rates, changes in exchange rates, tariffs and import quotas, and foreign competition's pricing responses. Similar considerations influence domestic exporters ability to pass their higher costs on internationally. Thus, both governmental pressure and foreign competition constrain many firms' opportunities to raise their prices sufficiently to offset inflation's negative effect. This has been widely accepted as a major factor that kept possible price increases down in 1998–1999.

Finally, two highly regarded economists, F. Modigliani and R. Cohn, argue that investors make two basic errors in pricing securities in the presence of inflation.[4] First, investors are said to capitalize equity earnings incorrectly by comparing the current cash earnings of equity with nominal rather than real bond returns. Bond returns are fixed until maturity, whereas profits and dividends attributable to stocks tend to rise over time. Focusing on the returns on stocks as if they are expected to be constant rather than rise will cause investors to underprice them. Second, Modigliani and Cohn contend that investors have failed to take proper account of the impact of inflation on the real value of corporate debt. Over time, inflation tends to reduce the real value of outstanding debt. Thus, corporations with substantial amounts of debt outstanding will, in effect, see that debt decline (at least in real terms) in times of rapid inflation. According to Modigliani and Cohn, these two alleged mispricing effects reduced the S&P 500 Stock Index by 50 percent in 1977. In 1982, a low point for stocks, P. Cagan asserted that the market seemed to be as underpriced as it was alleged to be in 1977.[5] The market more than tripled over the next 5 years. Perhaps the market was mispriced and later realized its error. On the other hand, the crash of 1987 indicates that the market can also be mispriced on the upside.

Inflation's Adverse Stock Market Impact

- Tax impact
  - Corporate taxes are applied to historical costs of plants, equipment, and inventories.
  - Investors are pushed into high tax brackets.
  - Individual taxes are applied to nominal dividend and interest income.
- Cost impact
  - Greater capital is needed for new plant and equipment, accounts receivable, and inventories.
  - Higher interest costs are incurred on borrowings.
  - Revenues come in more slowly.
- Price impact
  - There is resistance to price increases.
  - Competition from substitutes increases.
  - International competition increases.

In summary, stocks may, for a variety of reasons, perform less well during periods of rapid inflation. Taxes tend to reduce a company's real after-tax profits because they are applied to non-inflation-adjusted, before-tax profits. Taxes may also reduce the real investment return because they are applied to the nominal returns paid to investors. Some of the higher costs caused by inflation may not be quickly recaptured even if prices are raised proportionally with costs. Cost increases may not always be passed on because of government pressure, competition from substitutes, or international competition. Finally, in an inflationary environment, the stock market itself may not price securities correctly.

All of these considerations illustrate the difficulty that companies (and their stocks) have in fully offsetting inflationary impacts. Nonetheless, stocks need to provide a positive expected real return if their issuers (firms) are to continue to attract capital. The capital markets are supposed to assure the availability of sufficient capital for market-determined expansion candidates. As consumers demand more of certain types of goods and services, the market needs to provide the suppliers of these goods and services with the capital that they need to serve their customers. Investors have no incentive to invest if they expect to lose money in the process. Thus, firms that wish to attract capital need to be able to offer positive expected real returns. If new investments yield positive real returns, the shares of firms that own equivalent existing capacity should be bid up to their replacement values. This process may not take place quickly, completely, or for all industries. It should on balance, however, operate to provide the economy with adequate expansion and modernization capital.

Normally, an industry whose capacity is outstripped by its demand will be able to raise additional capital. If, initially, the expected return is too low to attract more capital, firms in the industry will not be able to satisfy the demand for their product at current price levels. They will need to raise prices, thereby increasing the return on their existing capital. A higher return on existing capital, coupled with the prospect of a reasonable return on new investments, should make new capital easier to raise. Eventually, this process should ensure that an appreciable fraction of real returns is at an acceptable level.

Taken together, these various considerations suggest that two opposing forces may be at work. First, the short-run inflation-adjustment process of the stock market may be painful for investors. Second, however, a functioning market system must offer a reasonable expectation of positive, long-run, real after-tax returns even in an inflationary environment.

A recent study by Ibbotson Associates (2000) measures the historical performance of five asset classes of securities over a 74-year period, 1926–1999. Figure 12-4 shows wealth indices of investments in the U.S. capital markets as if $1 had been invested in 1925 in each asset, and then subsequently all dividends were reinvested in the same asset. The five asset classes are Treasury bills, long-term Treasury bonds, long-term corporate bonds, the S&P Composite Index (S&P 500), and a portfolio of smaller-firm common stocks.[6] Table 12-1 shows how $1 would have grown, adjusted for inflation between 1926 and 1999, if all dividend or interest income had been reinvested in each of the five asset classes. Of course, these investments differ in degrees of risk, which accounts for much of the differences in their respective returns. Risk aside, however, a dollar invested in the lowest risk investment, Treasury bills, would have grown to $1.67 by 1999; in long-term Treasury bonds, to $4.28; and in corporate bonds, to $6.16 in real terms. Common stocks were far and away the best inflation-adjusted investment, with $707.33 for smaller firms and $303.09 for the large-company stocks.

Ibbotson Associates also calculated the compound and average annual rate of return from the five asset classes for each year over the 74-year period. This rate reflects both cash receipts, such as dividends and interest, and capital gains or losses realized during the specific year. Table 12-2

FIGURE 12-4
Wealth Indices of Investments in the U.S. Capital Markets (Year-End 1925 = $1)

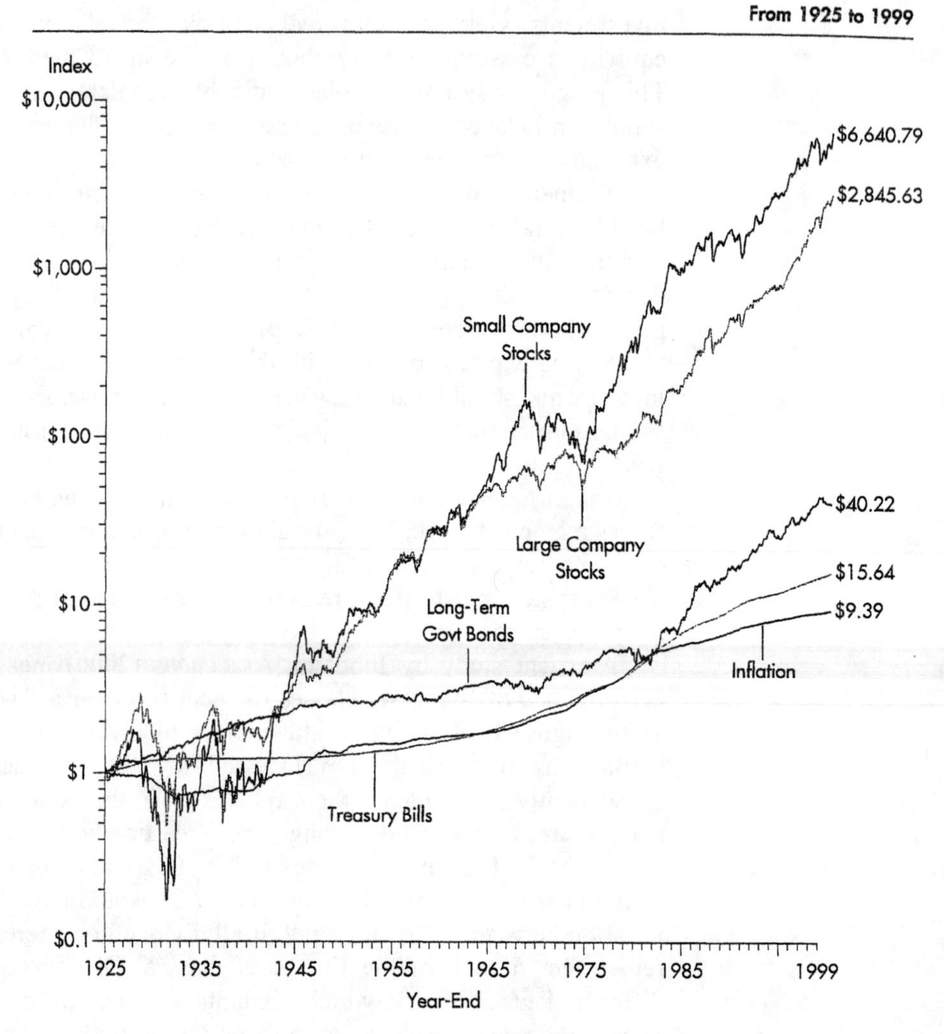

From 1925 to 1999

Index

- $10,000
- $6,640.79
- $2,845.63
- $1,000
- Small Company Stocks
- $100
- Large Company Stocks
- $40.22
- Long-Term Govt Bonds
- $15.64
- $10
- $9.39
- Inflation
- $1
- Treasury Bills
- $0.1

1925 1935 1945 1955 1965 1975 1985 1999

Year-End

Source: *Stocks, Bonds, Bills, and Inflation 2000 Yearbook,* © 2000 Ibbotson Associates, Inc. Based on copyrighted works by Ibbotson and Sinquefield. All rights reserved. Used with permission.

shows the averages of the 74 annual rates of return for each asset class. From 1926 to 1999, the Treasury bills provided 3.8 percent per year in nominal terms and 0.7 percent in real terms. The average rate of inflation over the

TABLE 12-1
Total Return: Cumulative Value of $1 with All Interest and Dividends Reinvested

	Nominal	Real
Treasury bills	$ 15.64	$ 1.67
Government bonds	40.22	4.28
Corporate bonds+	56.77	6.05
Large-company stocks	2,845.63	303.09
Small-company stocks	6,640.79	707.33
Inflation	9.39	–
+ Long term		
Derived from figure 12-4.		

period was just over 3 percent per year. Common stocks were again the winners, with the S&P 500 average annual return of 11.3 percent nominal rate and 8 percent real return, or an average risk premium of 7.2 percent. As might be expected, the nominal rate and real returns for smaller stocks were higher, with a higher risk premium of 8.5 percent. Clearly, over the 74-year period, stocks provided a good hedge against inflation. However, we cannot be certain that this period is truly representative and that the averages are not distorted by a few unusually high or low annual returns. Certainly, in some given years, such as during the high unanticipated inflation of the mid- to late 1970s, the stock market would not have outperformed the double-digit inflation rates.

TABLE 12-2
Compound Average Rate of Return (Percent) on Treasury Bills, Government Bonds, Corporate Bonds, and Common Stocks, 1926–1999 (Figures in Percent per Year)

Portfolio	Nominal	Real	Average Risk Premium (Extra Return versus Treasury Bills)
Treasury bills	3.8%	0.7%	–
Government bonds +	5.1	1.9	1.3%
Corporate bonds +	5.6	2.4	1.7
Common stocks (S&P 500)	11.3	8.0	7.2
Small-firm common stocks	12.6	9.2	8.5
Inflation	3.1	–	–
+ Long term			
Derived from table 2-2.			

Assessment of the Evidence

Overall, it seems that stocks tend to provide long-term inflation protection and possibly some short-term protection from anticipated inflation. For investors to know that stock price increases may eventually offset inflation is small comfort, however, if they must sell before the market rebounds. If unexpected inflation rate increases depress stock prices, the real value of investments falls both with the rise in the price level and with the decline in the position's nominal value. Some investors may be able to ride out these market declines, but others may not.

INFLATION PROTECTION OF OTHER INVESTMENTS

The preceding discussion implies that stocks may not be a particularly effective short-term inflation hedge; perhaps some other types of investments offer more dependable inflation protection. Stock-related securities, such as common stock mutual funds, convertible bonds, preferreds, and options, probably behave similarly to stocks. Thus, we expect inflation to affect them in much the same way that it affects stocks. Debt securities, commodities, real estate, and collectibles, in contrast, may offer different levels of inflation protection. Several studies have found that the returns on fixed-income securities tend to compensate for anticipated but not for unanticipated inflation.[7] This conclusion, while similar to that reached in a number of stock market-inflation studies, has a very different implication. Unlike stocks, debt securities mature. An inflation rate increase that depresses security prices locks in stock investors to a loss, whereas the par value of bond principal may be reinvested at maturity. This may mean a loss of real value but not of nominal value, as with stocks.

Example: Suppose an investor purchases bonds that yield 10 percent in an 8 percent inflation environment. If inflation then rises to 12 percent, equivalent debt yields might increase to 14 percent shortly thereafter. For bonds with short maturities, this rise in the unanticipated inflation rate will cause only a modest return loss. Soon the investor's bonds will mature, and the resulting principal can then be reinvested at the new higher market rates. The principal of a bond with even longer maturity will eventually become available for reinvestment.

The fact that debt securities, particularly short-term debt securities, seem to provide a degree of short-term inflation protection leads to concern about their long-run performance. For the 1926–1999 period, Ibbotson finds an average inflation-adjusted return of 8.0 percent, 2.4 percent, 1.9 percent, and 0.7 percent for common stocks, long-term corporates, long-term government bonds, and Treasury bills, respectively.[8] The recent 20-year performance of Treasury bills has been much better, however, yielding 7.2 percent (compounded) versus inflation of 4.5 percent—or a real return of 2.6 percent. Similarly, for the same period, large-company stocks, small-company stocks, corporate bonds, and government bonds have earned real returns of 12.7, 11.1, 6.1, and 6.3 percent, respectively. Thus, the securities that offered the greatest short-run protection (bills) yielded the least long-term real return, and vice versa.

Real estate might provide substantial inflation protection. Replacement costs of developed property vary with labor and material costs (which are correlated with consumer prices). Therefore, real estate construction costs should rise with consumer prices. These increased construction costs should eventually affect existing real estate values, although demand considerations may have a greater short-term effect. Since real estate, however, has its own set of drawbacks (primarily, illiquidity), its inflation-protection history is not in itself sufficient justification to invest in real estate.

The same underlying factors that cause consumer prices to rise may increase the prices of collectibles. That is, higher money incomes chasing a fixed quantity of collectibles should bid prices up more rapidly when the inflation rate is higher. Selected collectors' items did relatively well in the 1980s inflationary environment (for example, rare coins and stamps). With lower inflation, however, the 1990s have not seen a similar effect on collectibles.

Regarding precious metals, the value of gold, for instance, peaked in January 1980 at a price of $850 per ounce, but subsequently fell 34 percent to about $560 between June 1981 and June 1982. With few exceptions, the investment returns on tangible assets (precious metals) continued at a substandard pace through the rest of the 1980s. Gold prices continued to fall throughout the late 1980s and 1990s with the decline of worldwide inflation and the continued demonetization of gold. In the first quarter of 2000, it was below $290 an ounce. Like other forms of precious metals, gold is a highly speculative investment vehicle whose price tends to fluctuate widely. Whereas, historically, gold was regarded as the classic inflation hedge, the luster of gold has faded as a hedge investment since much of its recent movements have depended on relatively unpredictable policy-driven events (for example, decisions by Russia to sell gold from its official stocks or decisions by other central banks not to sell).

SUMMARY AND CONCLUSIONS

Investors who want to understand and/or forecast the market's behavior need to understand how the economy and the stock market are related. Both monetary and fiscal policy have a substantial economic impact. Macroeconomic policy generally seeks to maintain price stability and full employment. Stimulation is designed to reduce unemployment, whereas restraint is applied when inflation is the primary concern. Which is the overriding goal depends on a variety of considerations, including the relative severity of unemployment and inflation and policymakers' judgments. Understanding the likely reactions of government should help investors to forecast economic activity and perhaps stock market performance.

Investment analysts pay particular attention to relations between monetary policy and the stock market. Monetary policy affects the stock market both indirectly through its economic effect and directly via its interest rate effect. Some earlier work seemed to find monetary signals helpful, but most comprehensive recent studies have found no reliable and consistent lag between changes in monetary policy and changes in stock prices. However, trading on predicted monetary policy changes may still be profitable.

Investment analysts also consider inflation-stock market relations. According to pre-1970 Wall Street wisdom, companies could offset the adverse impact of inflation on their earnings (and stock values) by raising prices. Tax effects, government anti-inflation pressure, and international competition often make implementing the necessary price rises difficult, however. Still, to allocate capital properly, the stock market must offer the prospect of a positive real after-tax return.

Some empirical research suggests that in the short run, unanticipated rises in inflation have been associated with adverse stock market performance. In the longer run, however, average market returns may well exceed the inflation rate. Debt securities, particularly short-term debt securities, seem to provide more effective protection from the adverse near-term inflation impacts, but their long-term return only marginally exceeds the inflation rate and historically has been far inferior to equities. Both commodities and real estate offer a degree of inflation protection, but they present security market investors with a variety of other problems, such as increased risk or illiquidity.

CHAPTER REVIEW

Answers to the review questions and the self-test questions start on page 768.

Key Terms

econometric models
econometrics
leading indicators
gross domestic product (GDP)
recession
fiscal policy
multiplier
leakages
Fed
monetary policy
money supply
M1
reserve requirement
money multiplier
open market operations
discount rate
federal funds rate

Federal Open Market Committee
   (FOMC)
Federal Reserve Board of Governors
price stability
full employment
unemployment rate
balance of trade
capacity effect
tight money
thrift institutions
adjustable rate mortgages (ARMs)
monetarists
fiscalists
Survey Research Center
smokestack companies
inflation
fixed-income securities
inflation hedge
real return

Review Questions

12-1. Discuss econometric and leading indicator forecasts of economic activity. What are their limitations?

12-2. Explain how fiscal policy operates through taxes and government spending.

12-3. Discuss the Fed's three principal tools and how they are used to affect the economy. Address the degree of employment and effectiveness of each method.

12-4. Why do stock analysts generally give so much attention to monetary (as opposed to fiscal) policy? Discuss its effects on the stock market and role in investment analysis.

12-5. How would the stock market be expected to react to each of the following developments?
   a. The Fed, fearing that a recession is threatening, lowers the federal funds rate and expands the money supply. Long-term interest rates fall by over 200 basis points.
   b. Congress finally gets serious about reducing the budget deficit and raises taxes across the board by $100 billion. The Fed cushions the blow by

expanding the money supply. Interest rates fall dramatically, while the GDP continues to grow.

c. The Third World countries form a debtors' cartel and offer to negotiate. When the bargaining gets nowhere, they announce a total moratorium on interest and principal payments. The creditor nations respond by cutting off all credit.

12-6. What is the theory and evidence of inflation's effect on the stock market?

12-7. Your investment alternatives are stocks, short-term bonds, long-term bonds, and real estate. You expect their returns to follow this pattern:

- stocks: 8 percent
- short-term bonds: 3 percent + inflation rate
- long-term bonds: 5 percent + .3 (inflation rate)
- real estate: 1 percent + 1.2 (inflation rate)

You have the following inflation expectations (inflation rate, probability): 2 percent, .1; 4 percent, .3; 6 percent, .4; 8 percent, .2.
a. What is your optimal strategy for maximizing your expected return?
b. How can you best ensure yourself of the greatest expected return with no possibility of receiving less than a 2 percent real return?

12-8. In a stable price environment, investments A, B, C, D, E, and F are expected to earn 3 percent, 5 percent, 2 percent, 6 percent, 10 percent, and 7 percent, respectively. If they are all perfect inflation hedges, what will be their nominal and real expected returns for inflation rates of 2 percent, 4 percent, 6 percent, and 10 percent?

12-9. Summarize the findings of past work that links inflation and stock price performance. What are the implications for investors?

12-10. Compute after-tax real and nominal expected returns using the information in question 12-8. Assume that the tax rate on nominal returns is 30 percent.

12-11. Recompute the answers to question 12-10, except assume that the investments are only partial inflation hedges. The degree of inflation protection for each investment is of the form $a + bx$, where x is the expected inflation rate and b takes on values of .3, .5, .7, and .9. Use the real rates from question 12-8 for the values of a.

12-12. How do bonds, commodities, and real estate behave relative to inflation?

12-13. The TUV Corporation is currently selling its product for $40 per unit. Its annual sales amount to 500,000 units. Last year it earned a profit of $2 million. Because of inflationary pressures, its variable costs will increase by $5 (from $20) per unit. If it absorbs the higher inputs costs (keeping the per-unit price unchanged), it can expand sales by 20 percent with existing capacity. Alternatively, it can raise the price to cover the increased variable costs but will lose 20 percent of its unit sales.

   a. What is the profit impact of retaining the current price? (Hint: Total costs = total fixed costs + total variable costs. You must first calculate the total fixed costs, which remain unchanged this year.)

   b. What is the profit if the price is raised?

Self-Test Questions

T   F   12-1. Econometricians rely exclusively on macroeconomic data to forecast economic activity.

T   F   12-2. Data series on the average work week, average unemployment claims, and new building permits are examples of leading economic indicators.

T   F   12-3. Increases in either government spending or taxes will stimulate the economy.

T   F   12-4. The multiplier effect causes a $1 increase in government spending to increase the GDP by more than $5.

T   F   12-5. Monetary policy is a function of the Treasury Department.

T   F   12-6. The M1 definition of the money supply includes cash and coin in circulation outside the banks and checkable deposits.

T   F   12-7. Reducing the reserve requirement enables banks to increase their loans.

T   F   12-8. Cash (Federal Reserve notes) is the largest component of M1.

T   F   12-9. The money multiplier is the ratio between the initial increase in reserves and the resulting increase in the money supply.

T   F   12-10. The federal funds rate is the rate charged by the Fed when it lends reserves to banks.

T   F   12-11. Fiscal policy attempts to influence the level of economic activity by changing reserve requirements and open market operations.

T   F   12-12. Monetary policy is formulated by the Federal Reserve Board of Governors and the Federal Open Market Committee.

T   F   12-13. The primary economic goals of monetary and fiscal policy are in conflict.

T   F   12-14. Price stability implies that individual prices remain the same during the year.

T   F   12-15. The unemployment rate refers to the percentage of the labor force that is out of work and actively seeking employment.

T   F   12-16. Monetary policy affects the stock market through its influence on interest rates.

T   F   12-17. Restrictive monetary policy has no effect on the allocation of funds in the economy.

T   F   12-18. Investors who see inflation as a purely monetary phenomenon believe that inflationary pressures affect prices but little else.

T   F   12-19. If the tax rate is one-third, an investor receives a 9 percent nominal return, and inflation is 5 percent, the investor's real after-tax return is 1 percent.

T   F   12-20. Leverage will always enhance an investor's after-tax, after-inflation return.

T   F   12-21. Between 1926 and 1977, small-firm common stocks provided a higher return than large (S&P 500) common stocks.

T   F   12-22. Securities that offer the greatest short-term inflation protection also offer the greatest long-term real return.

NOTES

1. W. McConnell, *Investment Manager's Review*, Wertheim & Company, Inc., March 23, 1981, 10; G. Moore, *Business Cycles, Inflation and Forecasting*, National Bureau of Economic Research Studies in Business Cycles No. 240 (Cambridge, Mass.: Ballinger Publishing, 1980).
2. S.B. Bulmash and G.W. Trivoli, "Time-Lagged Interactions between Stock Prices and Selected Economic Variables," *Journal of Portfolio Management* (summer 1991), pp. 61–67.
3. J. Siegel, *Stocks for the Long Run*, 2d ed. (New York: McGraw-Hill, 1998).
4. F. Modigliani and R. Cohn, "Inflation, Rational Valuation and the Market," *Financial Analysts Journal* (March/April 1979), pp. 24–44.
5. P. Cagan, *Stock Prices Reflect the Adjustment of Earnings for Inflation*, NYU Monograph Series in Finance and Economics (New York: New York University, 1982).
6. Ibbotson Associates, *Stocks, Bonds, Bills, and Inflation, 2000 Yearbook*, Chicago, 2000.
7. Since 1997, there has been one notable exception to these general results. Beginning in early 1997, the U.S. Treasury began selling TIPS (Treasury inflation-protected securities). The coupon rate on these bonds is reset every 6 months. They have generally been yielding a greater than 3 percent real return, which is much above the 1 percent historical rate as reported by Ibbotson and Sinquefield (see note 9).
8. R. Ibbotson and R. Sinquefield, "Stocks, Bonds, Bills, and Inflation: Year-by-Year Historical Returns (1926–1974)," *Journal of Business* (January 1976), pp. 11–47.

13

Stock Market Timing and Forecasting

Learning Objectives

An understanding of the material in this chapter should enable the student to

---

13-1. Describe the stock market tendency to overreact to information.

13-2. Explain the use of market timing devices for identifying when to buy or sell stocks.

13-3. Describe several technical market indicators used to predict market moves.

13-4. Explain the meaning and importance of asset allocation.

Chapter Outline

We have seen that the stock market responds to economic forces such as the business cycle, money supply, inflation, and interest rates. Does the market also respond to noneconomic (that is, psychological) forces? Similarly, does it respond differently to economic information depending on the psychology of the market? In particular, does the market sometimes respond to new information (both economic and noneconomic) optimistically and at other times pessimistically?

A totally efficient market is affected only by news that has or is expected to have an impact on the underlying fundamentals. Thus, only forces that can affect earnings expectations should affect market prices. Moreover, new information that has the same basic impact on fundamentals should be given the same interpretation, regardless of the "mood" of the market. This viewpoint would seem to rule out most, if not all, noneconomic influences. Surely, an efficient market would not be described as emotional or moody. Yet most people who follow it would probably say that the market does respond to a variety of noneconomic factors. Moreover, they would probably assert that it responds differently to economic news, depending on the emotional state of its participant.

Indeed, stock prices often appear to swing between extremes of optimism and pessimism. In the crash of 1987, the Dow Jones Industrial Average dropped 508 points (23 percent) in a single day. That crash followed a very bullish market in which the Dow rose 350 percent from the 1982 low (777) to the August 25, 1987, high (2738). From this 1987 high the Dow fell to a low of 1738 on October 19. This corresponds to a fall of 36 percent in 7 weeks. These dramatic market moves clearly illustrate how market moods can appear to shift. Analysts might be able to explain the 7 weeks' decline of 36 percent as a response to significant changes in the economic environment. Interest rates had risen substantially, and the trade and budget deficits seemed to be getting worse. On the other hand, the 23 percent fall over the October 16–19 weekend is difficult to explain in efficient market terms. Many observers would agree that the crash was an example of a market in a state of panic. Efficient markets should not panic.

Regardless of how the market's swings are viewed, anyone who bought at or near the 1982 low (when the mood seemed very pessimistic) and sold at or near the August 1987 high (when optimism seemed to run rampant) would have done very well indeed. Similarly, the October 1987 low also proved to have been an attractive time to buy. A little over 2 years later, the market was 1,000 points higher, having reached a high of 2810 in early 1990. An investor lucky enough to have bought at the low of 1738 and sold at the high of 2810 would have realized a gain of over 60 percent.

Buy low and sell high is great advice, but it is useful only if the investor can identify market tops and bottoms as they are happening. Thus, we would like to know whether the market tops correspond to favorable moods for the market and bottoms to unfavorable ones. If so, can these moods be identified on a contemporaneous basis, and can knowledge of these moods be used profitably? Stock market timing and forecasting are the subject of this chapter.

The chapter first considers the stock market's tendency to overreact, and then it discusses efforts to recognize these overreactions while they are underway. Reliable timing devices are sought in declines from previous highs, such as market PE (price-earnings) ratios and their relationship to interest and inflation rates, behavior during recessions, official pronouncements, Fed margin rate and federal funds rate changes, company stock repurchases, Dow theory, and investment advisers.

The chapter then discusses various technical indicators (data series or combinations of data series that are purported to forecast market turns) in some detail. Specifically, short-interest, odd-lot trading, specialists' short selling, mutual fund cash positions, and the Barron's Confidence Index are all explored in the context of several relevant empirical studies. This chapter examines the following additional market indicators: advance-decline patterns, the short-term trading index, the January indicator, the advisers' sentiments indicator, and Monday–Friday price patterns. Finally, the chapter discusses asset allocation strategy.

STOCK MARKET OVERREACTION

stock market overreaction

When he was asked to predict stock market performance, J.P. Morgan replied, "It will continue to fluctuate." Anyone who has followed stocks understands the irony of this statement. The market's direction may be difficult to predict, but its continued volatility is not. Stock prices often change dramatically. Specific stock groups frequently go through fads. A stock may rise on a rumor that the firm is entering the Internet market, and later that same industry may be an anathema to the market. News sometimes has almost no impact, while at other times the market may appear to be looking for an excuse to move. To attribute such gyrations to a careful analysis of new information (market efficiency) seems questionable at best. Indeed, stock prices frequently change without any obvious pertinent new information entering the picture.

We have already noted that most investors believe that the market has a psychological side, and studies have come up with some supporting evidence. In this regard, Burton Malkiel examined the implications of growth stock pricing in the early 1960s.[1] Malkiel was interested in determining the growth rate in earnings and dividends needed to justify the market price. Very high growth rates must eventually decline. (We have already noted that point in our discussion of the dividend discount model.) For the purpose of his analysis, Malkiel assumed that high growth rates of growth stocks would eventually decline to the overall growth rate of the economy. He then computed how many years of abnormal growth were required to justify the PEs of growth stocks. From December 1961 to June 1962, the average PE of Malkiel's sample declined from 62.9 to 24.9. Over that same period, the average required years of abnormal growth fell from 6 to 2 1/2. Changes in the earning prospects of these companies seem unlikely to have caused the drastic reevaluations—both in Malkiel's samples and those that have been observed in past periods of downturns of the market. Further research has determined that changes in real dividends are far too modest to account for the historical pattern of real stock price changes in an efficient market; nor are news announcements about macroeconomic performance sufficient to explain stock price variation. And finally, several researchers have concluded that qualitative news, even about significant changes in financial policies, does not account for all the return variation that cannot be attributable to macroeconomic causes.

The widely held view that investors tend to overreact to information is tested directly by N. Jegadeesh and S. Titman. They found that trading strategies of buying stocks that have performed well in the past and selling stocks that have performed poorly in the past appeared to generate significant positive returns over 3- to 12-month holding periods during 1965 through 1989. The abnormal returns generated in the first year after portfolio formation, however, dissipated during the following 2 years.[2] The initial positive and later negative relative returns (returns reversals) may be evidence of overreaction and return persistence.

But there could be other explanations. For instance, one interpretation is that transactions by investors who buy past winners and sell past losers move prices away from their long-run values temporarily and this causes prices to overreact. Another interpretation is that the market underreacts to information about the short-term prospects for firms, but it overreacts to information about their long-term prospects. This is plausible since information available for a firm's short-term prospects, such as earnings forecasts, is different in nature from the more ambiguous information that is used by investors to assess a firm's longer-term prospects.

Attempts to Identify Overreactions While They Are Happening

R. Baylis and S. Bhirud followed up on Malkiel's work by suggesting that investors use as an investment tool the number of years of above-average growth needed to justify current multiples, which they called the *gamma factor*.[3]

gamma factor

Example: Suppose the market has an average PE of 15 and its earnings are expected to grow at 7 percent per year. How many years would a firm with an above-market PE have to continue to grow at its current rate to justify its PE ratio? The price that the market sets for the stock gives the answer. The gamma factor represents how long the market expects the rapid growth to continue. More specifically, it is the number of years of rapid growth in earnings that, when coupled with growth equal to the market average thereafter, would equate the present value of the stock with its market price. The gamma factor is computed as follows:

$$PE_{Market}(1+\Delta g^*)^{gamma} = PE_{Stock}$$

$$gamma = \frac{\ln(PE_{Stock}) - \ln(PE_{Market})}{\ln(1+\Delta g^*)}$$

where: Δg^* = above-average growth rate of earnings
$\ln$ = natural log

Baylis and Bhirud noted that the gamma factors for the favorite growth stocks among institutions increased markedly over the 1967–1973 period. Accordingly, in 1973 they wondered if the market was overreacting. A number of others expressed similar opinions. Soon thereafter these so-called top-tier stocks followed the rest of the market into a deep drop. Whether by superior insight, luck, or an ability to influence the market with their forecasts (self-fulfilling prophesies), a number of analysts thus correctly identified this particular emotional peak. At any specific time, however, some analysts will be predicting a decline while others will be forecasting a rise. Therefore, someone will always have correctly forecast the future. These forecasters may exhibit no more skill than a person who picks a winning lottery number.

More Evidence on Overreactions

Table 13-1, which reports the annual performance of S&P's 500 industrial index, illustrates the market's volatility. Annual price changes varied from +45 percent in 1954 to –27.1 percent in 1974 and +31 percent in 1997. Only four of 48 annual moves are within 3 percent of the overall average (10.06 percent). Clearly, stock prices fluctuate greatly from year to year. For example, the 14 percent decline in 1957 was followed by a 38 percent gain in 1958, and the 27 percent decline in 1974 was succeeded by a 29 percent rise in 1975. Fluctuations such as these reflect the market's tendency to, among other things, react vigorously to short-term factors.

TABLE 13-1
Annual Performance of Standard & Poor's 500 Industrial Index

Year	Difference between Index Value at Year End and at End of Previous Year	Year	Difference between Index Value at Year End and at End of Previous Year
1950	18.0%	1975	29.0%
1951	16.3	1976	19.2
1952	11.8	1977	−13.0
1953	−6.6	1978	1.1
1954	45.0	1979	12.3
1955	26.4	1980	25.9
1956	2.6	1981	−9.7
1957	−14.3	1982	14.7
1958	38.1	1983	17.3
1959	8.5	1984	1.4
1960	−3.0	1985	26.3
1961	23.1	1986	14.6
1962	−11.8	1987	2.0
1963	18.9	1988	12.0
1964	13.0	1989	27.2
1965	9.1	1990	−7.01
1966	−13.1	1991	26.3
1967	20.1	1992	4.4
1968	7.7	1993	7.1
1969	−11.4	1994	−1.5
1970	0.1	1995	34.1
1971	10.8	1996	20.3
1972	18.2	1997	31.0
1973	−21.1	1998	26.7
1974	−27.1	1999	19.5

Table 13-1 reports only average annual price changes. Thus, it understates the extent of the market's daily fluctuations. The long-term upward trend revealed in the table tends to mask considerable within-year movements. For example, the index recorded a low of 34.58 in January 1955 and a high of 46.41 in November of the same year (a difference of 34 percent). In 1975, the index varied from 62.28 to 79.80 (a 22 percent difference). Looking at the mean index growth of 9.88 percent for all of the years shows an upward trend, but noting the differences between highs and lows of the same and succeeding years reveals substantial short-term variability. Moreover, most individual stocks and stock portfolios experience considerably greater return variability from year to year.

This review of stock market performance illustrates the pervasive time-series variability of the market. An unemotional market reacting only to relevant newly public information should be less volatile. The observed volatility does not in itself prove that the market overreacts. It does, however, at least raise the possibility that a mood-based market timing strategy might be effective. This leads into the next topic: How can market extremes be identified, or can they?

BUY CHEAP AND SELL DEAR: WHEN ARE STOCKS CHEAP?

Buying and selling at the appropriate times is often regarded as being as important to a stock market trader as identifying misvalued securities. The relatively unspectacular performance of most mutual funds illustrates the difficulty of anticipating major market moves. Gary P. Brinson, Brian D. Singer, and Gilbert L. Beebower found that among well-qualified

market timing

institutional portfolio managers, *market timing* could account for only 1.8 percent of the average return differential, whereas security selection could account for 4.6 percent.[4] Portfolio allocation at 91.5 percent is far and away the most significant cause of the average return differential among these sophisticated investors (the residual interaction term accounts for the remainder 2.1 percent). Still, the potential rewards from accurate timing may encourage some investors to search for any useful evidence.

We should begin by lowering our sights a bit. No one should expect to be able to identify the market's tops or bottoms consistently. Some investors may succeed in developing a feel for when stocks are too high or too low, but even this level of predictability may be expecting too much. After the 1929 crash, stocks initially rebounded and then turned down again. Once they started down the second time, they continued to sink lower and lower so that what seemed like bargain prices were later shown to be extremely expensive. A similar, if somewhat shorter-run, phenomenon occurred during the market decline of 1973–1974. It was not until the previously mentioned trough of

1982 that stocks began the sustained recovery now recognized as the market phenomenon of the "booming 80s."

While declining markets may continue their decline for some time, they do eventually reverse their trend. Investors would like to buy when the market has completed most of its downward movement but has not yet risen much above its low. If the precise bottom is not usually identifiable *ex ante*, perhaps buying can at least be concentrated in depressed periods. This strategy requires some idea of when stocks are near their cyclical lows.

Declines from a Previous High

Investment analysts continually compare average stock prices with their prior levels. Some may reason that evidence of the market's past trading ranges could be used to forecast the future. Accordingly, we will now explore some recent market cycles. Because the Dow Jones Industrial Averages comprise, by far, the most closely watched index, we will use the Dow to track some of the market's history. Table 13-2 reports the major declines (greater than 15 percent) in the Dow since 1919. Purchases near these bottoms were generally superior to purchases at most other times. The problem, however, is to identify when the market is near a low.

TABLE 13-2
Major Declines in the Dow Jones Industrial Average

Year	High	Low	Percent Decline
1998	9374	7539	19%
1997	8257	7161	16
1990	3024	2344	23
1987	2722	1739	36
1983–1984	1287	1087	16
1981–1982	1024	777	24
1976–1978	1015	742	27
1973–1974	1052	578	45
1971	951	798	16
1968–1970	985	631	36
1966	995	744	25
1961–1962	735	536	27
1960	685	566	17
1957	521	419	19
1948–1949	193	162	16
1946	213	163	23
1939–1942	156	93	40
1937–1938	194	99	49
1929–1932	381	41	89
1919–1921	120	64	46

Note: Figures have been rounded to nearest whole number.

The post-1960 experience is revealing. In the 1961–1962 crash, the Dow fell from 735 to 536, whereas the 1966 decline was from 995 to 744. In the 1968–1970 period, the Dow declined from 985 to a 1970 low of 631. In 1971, the market fell from a high of 951 to a low of 798. The Dow declined from a peak of 1052 in 1973 to a low of 578 in December 1974. The 1976–1978 drop was from 1015 to 742. In 1981–1982, the Dow declined from 1024 to 777. In 1983–1984, the Dow declined from 1287 to 1087. In 1987, the Dow declined from 2722 to 1739, while in 1997 and 1998, the Dow declined from 8257 to 7161 and 9374 to 7539, respectively. In percentage terms, these declines were 27 percent, 25 percent, 36 percent, 16 percent, 45 percent, 27 percent, 24 percent, 16 percent, 36 percent, 16 percent, and 19 percent.

An investor who bought when the market was off 15 percent would have been near the low twice and far above it six times. Those who bought when the market had declined 25 percent would have missed three bottoms, been close three times, and have bought much too soon three times. An investor waiting for a 35 percent drop might buy stocks only once a decade. Apparently, past trading patterns provide very little timing insight in terms of buying at the bottom. However, the less stringent the filter (say, –15 percent versus –25), the more certain that some gain during recovery would be achieved.

Market PE Ratio as a Signal

The market average PE ratio is a measure of its relative price. As such, it might possibly be used to identify the market's tops and bottoms. The Dow PE rose from 12.1 in 1957 to 24.2 in 1961. A PE this high had been seen only once during the post-World War II period. It was clear that it was unusually high. In retrospect, the subsequent fall to 16.2 might have been expected. In 1966, the ratio rose to 18.1, only to fall to 13.5 in the same year. The ratio fell from 16.9 to 11.7 in 1969–1970; in 1971 it fell from 17.3 to 16.2. In 1973–1974, the ratio fell from 16.5 to 6.1. It rose somewhat from that low but ended the decade at 8. It stayed within the 6 to 9 range during the 1980–1981 period but exploded in 1982–1983, reflecting large losses by some of the component firms. It also reached high ground as the market ran up in 1987. It ended the decade at around 12. During the late 1990s, the Dow PE continued to rise far beyond its historic norms, and in late 1999 it was over two times its historic norms at about 30. Does this foretell a large correction?

A fluctuating market PE experience illustrates the unreliability of a multiple-based timing strategy. J. Holmes's famous 1974 study of the composite PE average of 14 for all NYSE stocks (1871–1971) provides a very rough guide at best.[5] Perhaps from an historic perspective, a PE on the

Dow of 10 or less is below average. From 1954–1973, the PE did not go lower than 9. In 1949 and 1951, the ratio was around 7, and between 1974 1982, PEs were often even lower. The low multiple value of 6 to 7 during 1974 and again in 1976–1981 was largely due to concern over high interest rates and rapid inflation. The ratio was above 13 in the 1930s, and until 1947 it was usually above 10. The 1934 multiple of almost 90 and the multiple of over 110 in late 1982 reflected abnormally low aggregated earnings. That is, large losses by a few firms (Chrysler and International Harvester, for example) offset the earnings of most of the other firms. It appears that little or no pattern is revealed. Determining when the market PE is in unsustainably high territory is equally difficult. As the multiple rises close to or above 18, a reversal seems increasingly likely. However, the market has turned down on many occasions when the Dow's multiple was well below 18. In 1987, in contrast, the Dow's PE reached 18 in January with the Dow itself around 2100. The Dow continued to rise, eventually reaching its 2722 peak. At that level, the Dow's PE stood at 21.5. Thus, investors who sold when the PE reached 18 would have missed most of the 1987 rise. Still, they would have been out of the market when it crashed.

There are several problems that have been noted in the use of PE ratios as a stock-selection criterion. One, of course, is that the denominator of the PE ratio is accounting reported earnings, which is influenced by somewhat arbitrary accounting rules, such as the use of historic cost in depreciation and inventory valuation. For instance, in periods of high inflation, historic cost depreciation and inventory costs tend to undervalue true economic values, since replacement costs of goods and capital equipment tend to rise with the general level of price. Figure 13-1 shows the relationship between PE ratios for the S&P 500 and the inflation (CPI) rate. The figure shows that with a slight lag, PE ratios tend to be lower as inflation and inflation expectations are higher, thus reflecting the market's assessment that earnings during these periods are of lesser quality. This is because the earnings are distorted by the inflation and must be discounted by higher required rates of return in order to compensate for the risk of inflation. The reverse is true as inflation and inflation expectations show a downward trend, as occurred in the 1990s. This may explain some of the extraordinary upward drift of PE ratios in this period.

Analysts should therefore be careful in using PE ratios to either select or time stock purchases. There is no way to determine that a given PE ratio is overly high or low without referring to a company's long-run growth prospects, as well as to its current earnings per share relative to its long-term trend.

In addition, PE ratios vary across different industries. PE ratios for each industry are often computed in two ways: by taking the ratio of current price **trailing earnings** to the previous year (*trailing earnings*), and by taking the ratio of current

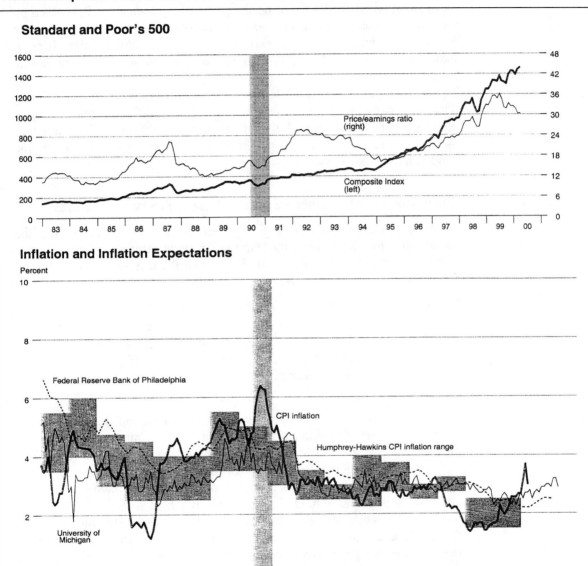

FIGURE 13-1
Relationship between PE Ratios for S&P 500 and Inflation Rate

Standard and Poor's 500

Inflation and Inflation Expectations

The shaded region shows the Humphrey-Hawkins CPI inflation range. Inflation expectations measures include the quarterly Federal Reserve Bank of Philadelphia *Survey of Professional Forecasters,* the monthly University of Michigan Survey Research Center's *Surveys of Consumers,* and the annual Federal Open Market Committee range as reported to the Congress in the February Humphrey-Hawkins Act testimony each year. CPI inflation is the percentage change from a year ago in the CPI for all urban consumers.

Source: Used with permission from Standard & Poor's Index Services and from Surveys of Consumers, University of Michigan. Reprinted from *Monetary Trends,* June 2000.

price to projected earnings for the following year. For instance, ratios based on earnings for 1997 may appear to be high, but the ratios seem more moderate when compared to forecasted 1998 earnings. Therefore, much depends on whether PEs based on the past year's earnings or PEs based on the projected year's earnings are used. Moreover, it is never certain what the following or projected year's earnings will be for any specific firm or industry. PE ratios published in the financial news almost always use trailing earnings.

Clearly, the market multiple has been an undependable basis for timing decisions. What seems like a very high (or low) multiple in one economic climate may be quite justified in another. Perhaps PE multiple analysis could usefully be combined with some knowledge of the prevailing economic conditions and expectations.

Gray approach

Gray Approach: Market PE Ratios Relative to Interest Rates

Market interest rates (with an appropriate equity premium) form the initial basis for discounting the expected income streams of investments. Similarly, market PE ratios indicate how much the market is willing to pay for a dollar of current earnings.

Example: A PE of 10 indicates that the market is willing to pay $10 for a dollar of current earnings. Similarly, a PE of 5 or 20 indicates that the market will pay $5 or $20 for a dollar of current earnings.

In chapter 7, we found that PE ratios, discount rates, and growth rates are closely related by definition if the dividend discount model and long-term growth rates are applied to a security with stable risk characteristics. The more the market will pay for a dollar of current earnings, the lower the rate at which it is discounting a firm's expected future earnings stream (or the more optimistic it is about the future growth in earnings).

Thus, in a sense, PEs also reflect a discounting of expected income. High PEs imply a low discount rate, and low PEs imply a high discount rate for stocks. From this perspective, we can see why the Gray approach is based on the proposition that interest rates and stock multiples (PEs) are related.[6] According to Gray, high interest rates should correspond to a stock market that is willing to pay only a relatively low multiple for current earnings (a low PE). Similarly, low interest rates should be consistent with high PEs in the stock market.

Gray develops the relationship between PEs and market interest rates mathematically. His basic formula is based on two relationships:

- A stock's total return is equal to its dividend yield (D/P) plus its appreciation rate (g*).
- The dividend yield equals the stock's earning/price ratio (E/P) multiplied by its payout ratio (D/E).

Total return is defined as the sum of dividend return or yield (D/P) and price appreciation (g*). Gray's first proposition, therefore, is little more than the definition of total return. Similarly, the product of the earnings/price ratio (E/P) and the payout ratio (D/E) is the ratio of dividends to stock price (D/P). Moreover, the ratio of dividends to the stock price is, in fact, the dividend yield. Again, the proposition is little more than an extension of a definition. Gray uses the following equation to express the relationship:

$$k = (D/E)(E/P) + g*$$ (Equation 13-1)

where: k = return on stock
         D = dividend per share
         E = earnings per share
         P = price per share
        g* = long-term growth rate in price per share (assumed to average 5 percent)

Note that D/E = payout ratio (assumed to average 55 percent)
           E/P = earnings-price ratio
           (D/E) x (E/P) = D/P (which is the dividend yield)

This equation is mathematically equivalent to the PE ratio equation discussed in earlier chapters if price per share appreciates at the same growth rate as dividends in the long term. The equation itself only expresses the return on a stock (or the stock market) as the sum of its dividend yield and price appreciation. Note, however, that the model does illustrate the relationship between k and the PE ratio. The model shows k to be determined by three variables: D/E, E/P, and g*. According to Gray, both g* (the long-term appreciation rate) and D/E (the payout ratio) can be treated as approximately constant (not varying by enough to matter over time). Thus, virtually all of the variability in k is thought to stem from variability in E/P. The E/P ratio is simply 1/PE (the reciprocal of PE). Thus, k should vary inversely and almost exclusively with variations in the PE ratio.

Next, Gray notes that the relationship of a variable k to a stock's price is almost identical to the relationship of yield to a bond's price. They are the returns (or, in a future-oriented context, expected returns) on the two types of investments. Clearly, the returns offered by these two types of investments should be related. If bonds, on the average, offer high expected returns (as, for example, measured by the AA utility bond yield), stocks should also, on the average, be priced to offer high expected returns (as, for example, measured by the returns on the S&P 500), and *vice versa*.

Not surprisingly, Gray found that the AA utility bond yield tended to vary with k. He also found that the higher the AA utility yield, the lower the spread between k (which he calls the "common stock sustainable return") and bond yields. The past behavior of this spread may be a guide for the future.

Example:　　　Suppose the spread between common stock sustainable return and bond yields is first regressed on the yield to estimate the historic relationship. Then the deviations from the values predicted by the regression are plotted over time. These deviations indicate the degree and direction of any tendency for stocks to be mispriced relative to bonds. If bond yields are high relative to their historic relationship to common stock sustainable returns (k), then stocks may well be overpriced relative to bonds.

The Gray approach boils down to the idea that interest rates and PEs should be in line with each other. A similar approach suggests that when interest rates and market PEs get too far out of line, the market may be about to make a major move to bring them back in line. The 1987 crash was certainly consistent with that scenario, as discussed in an earlier chapter.

Market Behavior during Recession

Stock market performance during recessions and the subsequent recoveries may follow a predictable pattern. First, there is a pattern of rising markets during recessions. Second, stock price advances tend to be more vigorous after severe than after mild contractions. Investors can often begin repurchasing 6 months after a recession has begun. Buying after the economic recovery begins does not require a forecast. The beginning of a recovery is generally observable within a few months of the bottom. Selling before an economic peak, in contrast, assumes an ability to predict the tops of economic cycles, which is inherently more difficult.

In 1991, Jeremy Siegel examined the reliability of the relationship between stock prices and the business cycle. The stock market is known to have given false signals about future economic activity, particularly with regard to impending recessions. The market has registered many false alarms. For instance, since 1946, there were seven periods during which the cumulative stock returns index fell at least 8 percent and a recession did not occur. The stock market appears to have been a better indicator of coming economic expansions, turning upward on average about 5 months before business troughs. According to Siegel, the standard deviation of the stock market's lead time before business cycle troughs is only 1.6 months—one-third of the lead time before business cycles peaks. It appears, therefore, that the stock market's ability to predict recoveries is better than its ability to predict recessions.[7]

Official Pronouncements and Company Stock Repurchases

Government officials (President, Secretary of the Treasury, Chairman of the Council of Economic Advisors, Chairman of the Federal Reserve System, and others) sometimes comment publicly on the level of the stock market. These pronouncements may either reflect nonpublic information about future macroeconomic policy or be designed to affect the securities market for political purposes. Since 1996, Fed Chairman Alan Greenspan has made comments to warn the stock market about "irrational exuberance." As they should with everyone else's advice, investors should listen to but not necessarily rely on government officials' opinions.

Another possible indicator on the state of the market relates to companies' repurchasing their own stock. Before 1960, many repurchases were made to facilitate acquisitions, stock dividends, and conversions. More recent purchases were primarily an effective use of cash; companies often repurchased their stock at bargain prices (although they seldom picked the bottom). However, during the 1980s and 1990s, many company stock repurchases were defensive maneuvers against takeovers. Thus, the use of repurchase activity as a general indicator requires close study of the motives behind it—is the stock repurchase truly undertaken in the best interests of stockholders (and is therefore a "buy" signal), or is it a defensive maneuver to preserve management's position?

Dow Theory

Dow theory

The *Dow theory* is one of the oldest and best-known approaches to market timing. Its originator, Charles Dow, was also the founder and first editor of *The Wall Street Journal*. Dow developed the key averages quoted widely in the financial pages, the Dow Jones Industrial Average (DJIA), the Dow Jones Transportation Average (DJTA), and the Utility Average. The Dow Jones Industrial Average, commonly referred to as the Dow, is composed of the stock prices of 30 leading industrial companies chosen from sectors of the economy that represent America's largest capitalization industrial (that is, nonfinancial) companies. The Dow relies on a formula resulting from the unweighted average of stock prices of the 30 industrial companies, adjusted for splits and stock dividends. The formula adds up the stock's daily closing prices and divides by a certain number to derive the average. Higher-priced stocks in the average, such as GE, have greater effect on the average when their prices change by a given percentage than lower-priced stocks, such as GM, even though the initial importance of the two stocks was the same when the current index was created.

There are two ways in which the Dow averages and other broad stock indexes, such as the S&P 500, can be useful to the average investor:

- Indexes track the long-term ups and downs of stock prices to aid the investor in determining what the present market is doing, compared with past performance.
- If a stock does not seem to follow the upward movements of the market averages, it may indicate that investigation into the health of the company is necessary.

The Dow theory asserts that a continuing trend can be identified by looking first for a new high in a market average defined as primary (such as the DJIA), and then seeking confirmation from a second high (such as the DJTA). Thus, if the Industrials reach a new high followed quickly by a new high for the Transports, the up trend is said to be intact.

Three Basic Ideas behind the Dow Theory

- To make a profit in the stock market, investors should take advantage of the primary market trend, which is the generally upward movement of the market over a period of one to 4 years.
- Whenever a primary trend is up, each secondary trend (a cycle around the basic trend) will produce a peak higher than the last one (*vice versa* for a down trend).
- Any true indicator of a primary market trend will be confirmed relatively quickly by similar action in the different stock price averages.

A recent study by S. Brown and W. Goetzmann appears to confirm the validity of the Dow theory. The original developers of the Dow theory did not provide an easily testable theory besides the simple rules listed above. The recent research, using state-of-the-art artificial intelligence software to identify the precise technical trading patterns associated with the buy-and-sell signals, applied the patterns over 70 years of data. The study found some merit in the Dow theory. For instance, a portfolio that followed the signals to buy or sell identified by the Dow theory software, using an index fund with no transaction costs, would have outperformed a buy-and-hold strategy by about 2 percentage points per year. In addition, the Dow theory portfolio would have incurred one-third less volatility (the researchers' proxy for risk).[8] Brown and Goetzmann found that their version of the Dow theory portfolio beat the market indexes during such bearish periods as the 1970s and even the 1930s. Their model, however, showed the least favorable results during strongly bullish periods, such as the 1980s and the 1990s.

According to the *Hulbert Financial Digest* (a service that monitors performance of investment advisory letters), a portfolio that switched in and out of the market on signals from Dow theorist Richard Russell in the "Dow Theory Letters" would have underperformed a buy-and-hold strategy by about 2.7 percentage points per year since 1980. *Hulbert* found, however, that a Russell-guided portfolio would also have been 35 percent less volatile than the market as a whole. Thus, on a risk-adjusted basis (using volatility as a proxy for risk), the Dow theory-guided portfolio would have beat the market.

Will the Dow theory work in the future? Only time will tell. But one feature of most timing strategies is that they appear to work for some events but not others. Moreover, they appear to diminish in usefulness over time as pricing arbitrage by investors who anticipate the timing rules eventually eliminates whatever advantage the rules initially display.

Most academics and practitioners remain highly skeptical of technical analysis. The main reason for this skepticism is that thorough tests of technical analysis techniques have failed to confirm their consistency and validity, given all the transaction costs in comparison with a simple buy-and-hold strategy. In addition, there are other troubling features of technical analysis. First, several interpretations of a particular technical tool or chart pattern are possible, giving rise to numerous different assessments or recommendations. For instance, those who interpret the signals of the Dow theory are notorious for their multiple interpretations.

A second troubling factor is if a technical trading rule (or chart pattern) proves successful, it will become widely adopted by market participants. If the rule or pattern is widely adopted, it will often prove to be self-destructive. Therefore, stock prices will reach their equilibrium value quickly, taking away profit opportunities from most market participants. Moreover, some market observers may start trying to act before the rest on the basis of what they expect to occur; thus, the prices of affected stocks will tend to reach an equilibrium even more quickly. Eventually, the value of any such rule or pattern will be negated entirely.

According to Burton Malkiel, there are three potential flaws in technical analysis. One, the information and analysis may be incorrect. Two, the security analyst's estimate of "value" may be faulty. Three, the market may not correct its mistake, and the stock price might not converge to its value estimate.[9]

It has proven difficult, if not impossible, to test all the techniques of technical analysis and their variations and interpretations. The techniques are too numerous, and new ones are developed all the time. Therefore, absolutely definitive statements about their validity cannot be made.

Market Forecasters

Rather than try to identify market tops and bottoms, many investors rely on professionals who make their living forecasting the market. But it is not easy deciding which professional to use. Similar difficulties confront investors who rely on market timing experts. Nonetheless, these services are a significant part of the investment scene.

Investors who want to know what market forecasters are saying can subscribe directly to some of the market forecasting letters, or they can read articles that report analysts' opinions on the Internet or in the popular press. Other investors may prefer to assess the data that the forecasters use. Most analysts make at least some use of technical market indicators.

Market Timing Approaches

- Declines from a previous high: Market's previous declines exhibit no consistent pattern.
- Market PE ratio: Movements in the market PE are an undependable basis for investment timing.
- Gray approach: Market PEs relative to interest rates may offer useful timing signals.
- Behavior during recessions: The market tends to turn up early in a recession.
- Official pronouncements: Administration officials may occasionally make statements that are useful to investors.
- Company stock repurchases: Large stock repurchases by many firms may signal that a market bottom is near.
- Dow theory: An up trend is confirmed when a high in the primary index (that is, DJIA) is soon followed by a high in the secondary index (that is, DJTA). Down trends are confirmed by the reverse order (DJTA high soon followed by DJIA high).
- Market forecasters: Professional advice on the market is derived from market forecasting services. Most of these services utilize some technical indicators or give some timing advice.

TRADITIONAL TECHNICAL MARKET INDICATORS

technical market indicators

Thus far we have examined market forecasts based on relative declines in the Dow, market multiples, market multiples relative to interest rates, historic relationships during recessions, official pronouncements, share repurchases, Dow theory, and market analysts' opinions. The traditional *technical market indicators* discussed below are also used to predict market moves. Specifically, many analysts claim to see timing signals in the behavior of certain data series, or combinations of data series, such as short interest, odd-lot behavior, specialist short selling, and a host of others.

Comparative Market Indices

There are over 3,000 common stock issues listed on the NYSE, not to mention thousands more traded on the American Stock Exchange, regional exchanges, and the OTC (listed in financial pages as NASDAQ). You may ask what good the Dow Jones Industrial Average is with only 30 stocks. The answer is partly historic and partly scientific. The Dow Jones Industrial Average began in 1884 with 11 stocks and increased to 30 stocks in 1928. The 30 companies listed for the Dow Jones Industrial are representative of the broad market and of U.S. industry. Except for the utility and transportation sectors, the companies are chosen because they are major players in their industries and their stocks are widely held by both individual and institutional investors. The 30 stocks in the Dow Industrials represent a fifth of the one-trillion-plus market value of all stock traded, and about a fourth of the value of stocks on the NYSE.

Research has shown that Dow averages closely mirror broader stock market indicators. By its nature, however, the Dow represents the blue chip or large-capitalization stocks such as AT&T, Coca-Cola, DuPont, GE, and IBM (and Microsoft, Intel, and Wal-Mart as of November 1999). Other broader market indexes, such as the S&P 500 Industrial Index, represent a much wider array of stocks. Whenever the broader indexes move in a direction opposite from Dow averages, there is a divergence between top-tier (blue chip), high-capitalization stocks and second-tier, lower-capitalization stocks. For instance, if the Dow average moves up while broader indexes fall or remain the same, these conflicting changes may indicate insecurity by market participants and a tendency to seek the security of larger, well-known firms (sometimes called a *flight-to-quality effect*).

flight-to-quality effect

Use of widely held and frequently traded companies in the Dow Industrial listing provides an important feature of timeliness—that is, the Dow averages represent major frequently traded stocks. Therefore, these averages represent the direction of current transactions at any point in time, which may not always be the case with broader indexes. The broader indexes, such as NASDAQ/OTC Index, include less frequently traded stocks or stocks that are not widely owned and are therefore not as timely.

Short Interest

As discussed earlier, short sellers sell borrowed stock that they hope later to replace at a profit. At one time, short sellers were thought to be sophisticated traders who were able to anticipate market turns. Thus, an increase in *short interest* (uncovered short sales) was said to forecast a market decline. Others, in contrast, argued that short interest reflects potential demand from covering short traders. According to this view, a rise in short interest forecasts a market rally.

short interest

Studies show, however, that short interest is largely unrelated to market rises and falls. In efficient markets, prices will reflect both negative and positive implications inherent in a large short position. For instance, if a high level of short interest is systematically bullish or bearish, arbitrageurs would take advantage of this news. This renders a trading rule that employs short interest information that consistently outperforms the market suspect. According to the studies, the positive cumulative excess return in the pre-announcement period indicates that investors tend to sell short in periods of rising stock prices. But investors do not benefit from selling short, since the average decline in stock price in the postannouncement period is insignificant. Short interest data are published monthly in *The Wall Street Journal*.

odd-lot activity

Odd-Lot Activity

According to some analysts, small (odd-lot, meaning fewer than 100 shares) traders tend to buy at tops and sell at bottoms. Thus, when odd-lotters are buying on balance, the market may be poised for a fall; when small investors are largely selling, the market may be ready to turn up. According to a related hypothesis, odd-lot short sellers are considered to be unsophisticated investors. When odd-lot short sales are high, therefore, the market may be near bottom and *vice versa*, because the swings of pessimism and optimism are said to be overdone by the unsophisticated.

odd-lot short ratio

The problem is how to measure this investor sentiment. Traditionally, odd-lot short selling activity has been measured by the *odd-lot short ratio*, which is calculated by dividing odd-lot short sales over some time period by total odd-lot sales. One difficulty with the ratio, however, is that both the numerator and denominator show degrees of pessimism. An alternative might be to use odd-lot purchases in the denominator. This ratio might be better at recording the differences in expectations between bullish investors (odd-lot purchasers) and bearish speculators (odd-lot short sellers).

The total odd-lot short ratio (TOLSR) can be calculated as follows:

$$\text{TOLSR} = \frac{\text{odd-lot short sales}}{\text{odd-lot purchases/odd-lot sales}}$$

Odd-lot theory suggests observing what the small investor is doing and then doing the opposite. *Barron's* breaks down odd-lot trading on a daily basis in its "Market Laboratory-Stocks" section. It constructs a ratio of odd-lot purchases to odd-lot sales. For example, on May 13, 1997, 1,944,500 odd-lot shares were purchased and 2,482,000 odd-lot shares were sold—a ratio of 0.804. The ratio has fluctuated historically between 0.50 and 1.45.

Odd-lot theory maintains that small investors actually do well most of the time but often miss key market turns—that is, reversals of trends. Thus, odd-lot traders are supposed to sell off part of their portfolios as the market rises. A net selling posture is reflected by a declining odd-lot index (purchase-to-sales ratio). As the market peaks, however, odd-lot traders believe they have an opportunity to make a profit, thus becoming strong buyers. This is supposed to predict an impending decline in the market. Odd-lot traders are also assumed to be strong sellers prior to the bottom of a bear market.

Although the odd-lot theory appeared to have some validity during the 1950s and 1960s, it has failed to be a useful predictor since then. For instance, odd-lotters outperformed many professional money managers by selling off on or before the stock market collapses of the 1970s and late 1980s, and they began buying in advance of a recovery during the early 1990s.

Specialists' Short Selling

Another insiders' theory holds that specialists are especially sophisticated investors who have access to nonpublic trading intentions information (the limit order book) and are positioned to react quickly to any emerging developments. Because their profits are largely derived from trading their assigned stocks, much of their success depends on effectively managing their inventory. Specialists generally are supposed to sell short when they expect a price decline and buy when their expectations are positive. Studies have not confirmed, however, that this is a reliable market indicator.

Mutual Fund Cash Position

Equity mutual funds usually maintain a modest cash reserve to meet redemption demands and other needs for cash. They may also hold on to cash when they are undecided about where to invest it. When the cash positions (potential buying power) of equity mutual funds rise to the point at which they become a large percentage of their total assets, the market may have some upside potential. Studies show that mutual funds attempt to time their trading to take advantage of market swings. Mutual funds do not, however, succeed in successfully altering the composition of their portfolios over the market cycles.

Barron's Confidence Index

The Barron's Confidence Index (BCI) is the ratio of 10 high-grade corporate bond rates relative to the more speculative Dow Jones Bond Index rates. A high value for the ratio indicates that high-grade yields are relatively close to the yields on more speculative issues. At such times, the market is unwilling to pay much of a premium for quality (or, stated differently, does not require a high-risk premium on lower-grade issues). Alternatively, a low ratio implies a substantial premium on quality. The ratio appears in *Barron's* "Market Laboratory" section. This section is a source of many of the underlying data used to compute market indicators. Users of the Confidence Index believe that smart money will move toward quality bonds when the market outlook is unfavorable and toward speculative bonds when the market outlook is favorable. As with most of the indicators discussed so far, the evidence is suggestive but not conclusive. Even in forecasting market peaks, the results are not especially encouraging or useful.

Traditional Technical Market Indicators

- Odd-lot activity: When odd-lot short sales are abnormally high (low), the market is said to be near a bottom (top).
- Specialists' short selling: High (low) specialist short selling is thought to forecast a market decline (rise).
- Mutual fund cash position: Mutual fund cash is an indication of potential future demand for stocks.
- Barron's Confidence Index: The ratio of high-grade to average-grade bond yields reflects confidence of "smart" investors.

OTHER TECHNICAL INDICATORS

Although various studies suggest that technical indicators may have some value, the relationships may or may not persist. If, for example, the market pays careful attention to these relationships, knowledge of them would become valueless. On the other hand, many indicators have long been touted without losing their followers. Discussing a few of the more interesting indicators is instructive, even though recent academic appraisals may not be available.

Advance-Decline Patterns

advance-decline patterns

Some analysts argue that the market's strength may be gauged by the ratio of the number of stocks advancing to the number declining, especially if there is a tendency for the ratio to persist over some time period. That is, if a particular day has many declines relative to the historic average, the next day's declines are said to be likely to lie somewhere between the last day's results and the average. Similar assertions for the London and Amsterdam stock exchanges have been cited. If the persistence characteristic is reliable, then market traders could use the ratio as a predictor of next-day market changes in a timing framework.

Short-Term Trading Index

The short-term trading index, which is derived from the advance-decline ratio, attempts to measure the degree to which volume is concentrated in declining and advancing stocks, and it is defined as the ratio of two other ratios. The first ratio (A) is the *number* of advancing stocks divided by the *number* of declining stocks. The second ratio (B) is the *volume* of advancing stock divided by the *volume* of declining stocks. The short-term trading index is A divided by B. The indicator is available on most stock quotation machines and on the Internet. A little manipulation reveals that the index is the average volume of declining stocks relative to the average volume of advancing stocks. The lower the ratio, the greater the average volume in advancing stocks. Some market participants and advisers have claimed suggestive results by using the index. To be accepted in the academic community, an index like this should be tested in a professional review in an academic journal.

The January Indicator

January indicator (January effect)

The *January indicator (January effect)* is a rather simplistic tool that often receives a good bit of attention at the beginning of each year. A market that rises in January is expected to rise during the year; a market that falls in January is expected to fall during the year. Because the market generally rises both in January and for the year, the success of the January indicator may easily be overstated. Several other months seem to do about as well. Moreover, an investor who follows a straightforward buy-and-hold strategy might have a higher-valued portfolio than an investor who uses the January indicator as a trading signal.

Regarding the January effect, Donald Keim found, in a landmark study, that small stocks outperformed large ones during the first several weeks almost every year between 1926 and the mid-1970s. One explanation for this was that hard-to-trade small stocks tend to be depressed by investors' tax-related year-end selling. But then small stocks would bounce back as investors rebought them early the next year.[10] However, according to Prudential Securities, small stocks underperformed each January for the period 1993–1998. One explanation is that fund managers buy small stock in December in anticipation of the January effect, thus nullifying investors' tax-loss selling. Keim maintains that the January effect can still be found if measured as he did in his original study, but it has weakened. However, even when the January effect does exist, it is virtually impossible to exploit because the underlying small stocks are so illiquid that trading costs (brokerage fees and so on) eliminate most or all of the profit.

The Advisers' Sentiment Indicator and Other Short-Term Indicators

Most indicators are designed to predict intermediate or long-term market trends. Day-to-day moves are not nearly as interesting to most people because of the high trading costs relative to the typically modest day-to-day moves. Nonetheless, those who trade at little cost (specialists, floor traders, and day traders on the Internet) or those who would trade anyway might as well take advantage of any predictable daily price moves.

One such market indicator is based on the investment analysts themselves. A contrary-opinion approach would expect the market to peak when adviser sentiment was most bullish and reach a bottom when sentiment was most bearish. The Monday versus Friday advance-decline ratio, and Monday–Friday price patterns are two other approaches to forecasting such short-term moves. Unusual price behavior has been found for Mondays and Fridays. In the past, the market was consistently more likely to be up on Friday than on Monday. The frequent practice of withholding unpleasant economic news until the market's Friday close may account for the phenomenon. This day-of-the-week price effect suggests that, if no overriding considerations intervene, investors might as well sell on Friday and wait until late in the day on Monday to buy. The Monday after a Friday decline may offer somewhat more attractive buying opportunities.

S. Penman's study of stock market seasonality found that the market tends to be particularly strong in the first half of the first month of quarters 2, 3, and 4.[11] This result appears to be due to a tendency for good earnings reports to be issued at that time; poor reports are released later in the first quarter after most total fiscal year results are fully known. In other words, firms act as if they are hoping to delay bad news until the last possible moment when it becomes legally impossible (due to auditing requirements) to delay any further.

Other Technical Indicators

- Advance-decline patterns: Past advance-decline patterns tend to persist.
- Short-term trading index: High (low) relative volume of advancing stocks is a sell (buy) signal.
- January indicator: January performance is said to forecast the year, but the evidence is unimpressive.
- Advisers' sentiments: Investment advisory sentiment is said to be a contrary indicator.
- Monday–Friday price pattern: The market tends to rise on Fridays and fall on Mondays.
- Monthly pattern: The market tends to rise in the first half of each month, with much of that tendency concentrated in the months of April, July, and October.

ASSET ALLOCATION

asset allocation

Market timers in their most extreme form seek to be totally in the market when it is going up and totally out when it is going down. Others, however, seek a compromise. An increasingly popular strategy called *asset allocation* has emerged. Although the concept has been around for many years based on the work of Harry Markowitz and others (see chapter 8), its name and popularity are relatively new. Investment advisers and financial planners who are asset allocators seek to vary their commitment to different types of investments based on the outlook for those investments. For example, an asset allocator may divide his or her client's portfolio into several components in some way such as the following:

- money funds for very low risk and high liquidity
- long-term, high-grade bonds for moderate risk
- junk bonds for speculative appeal in the debt market
- blue chip stocks for low-risk equity market participation
- growth and/or small-cap stocks for greater speculation in equities
- international equities for global diversification
- stock options for short-run speculation in equities

Most asset allocators stick to stocks, bonds, and cash (money market securities). Regardless of which asset categories he or she chooses, the asset allocator varies the percentages invested based on his or her assessment of the investment outlook and the use of portfolio optimizers.

***Example*:**   A neutral outlook might imply the following allocations: 20 percent in money funds, 30 percent in long bonds, and 50 percent in stocks. A more conservative stance would imply these allocations: 50 percent in money funds, 20 percent in long bonds, and 30 percent in stocks. An extremely bearish outlook might imply allocations of 80 percent in money funds and 20 percent in gold. Alternatively, a more aggressive strategy would move toward greater percentages in growth stocks, small-cap stocks, and options.

portfolio optimization   *Portfolio optimization* takes advantage of the new capability of personal computers to use a quadratic programming algorithm to find the allocations of assets that make up an approximation to the efficient frontier. Thus, with appropriate data on expected returns, expected standard deviations, and correlations among the selected asset classes, the most efficient mix of assets (highest expected returns) for any given risk tolerance level of the client can be derived. The goal of the asset allocators is to hedge risks without having to move totally in or out of the market. In this way, they hope to derive some profit from whatever the market does without leaving themselves too vulnerable to an adverse move.

SUMMARY AND CONCLUSIONS

The evidence reveals a psychological side to the market, which causes the market to fluctuate more than warranted by the fundamentals. Many efforts to identify and predict market peaks and troughs (market timing) have been proposed, but none contain a magic formula. The distribution of percentage declines from previous peaks appears to be approximately random. The market PE ratio is almost useless in isolation, but following the Gray approach, when PE ratios are low relative to their past relationship to interest and inflation rates, a market rise may be likely. Similarly, when PEs are high relative to their past relationship to interest rates, a fall is predicted. Recent data in the late 1990s confound any easy conclusions from high PE ratios, however. Stocks often rise early in a recession and move sideways (no trend) during most of the recovery period. Official pronouncements, federal funds rate changes, stock repurchases, and the Dow theory may occasionally be helpful in predicting market trends. A large number of analysts sell newsletters that attempt to forecast market trends (and make money for the analysts).

Technical market indicators that this chapter discusses include short interest, odd-lot activity, specialists' short selling, mutual fund cash positions, Barron's Confidence Index, advance-decline patterns, short-term trading, the January indicator, and the advisers' sentiment indicator. Asset allocation is also discussed as a way of hedging against strong market moves among different asset classes.

In conclusion, the market's psychological volatility seems to be very difficult—but perhaps not impossible—to predict. Clearly, this area needs more study. In any event, according to the Brinson, Singer, Beebower study mentioned at the beginning of this chapter, the return attribution to asset selection has been higher historically than the return attribution to market timing skills. Therefore, the jury is still out on whether or not stock market timing and forecasting efforts are worthwhile for the average investor.

CHAPTER REVIEW

Answers to the review questions and the self-test questions start on page 772.

Key Terms

stock market overreaction
gamma factor
market timing
trailing earnings
Gray approach
Dow theory
technical market indicators

flight-to-quality effect
short interest
odd-lot activity
odd-lot short ratio
advance-decline patterns
January indicator (January effect)
asset allocation
portfolio optimization

Review Questions

13-1. Briefly describe investor sentiment around the time of the 1987 stock market crash. What are the implications for market efficiency?

13-2. The market PE and growth rate are 10 percent and 5 percent, respectively; stock A has a PE and current growth rate of 15 percent and 14 percent, respectively; Stock B has a PE and current growth rate of 30 percent and 25 percent, respectively.
   a. What is stock A's gamma factor?
   b. What is stock B's gamma factor?

13-3. a. Using the data in question 13-2, recompute the gamma for stock A if the market PE falls to 8. Calculate the stock's PE if its gamma falls by the same percentage as the market PE.

b. Perform the same calculations for stock B.

13-4. Discuss the usefulness of market average PE ratios in forecasting the market's direction.

13-5. What is the Gray approach? On what propositions is it based?

13-6. Show the mathematical equivalence between Gray's equation and the PE equation discussed in chapters 4, 7, and 9.

13-7. What weight should investors give official pronouncements and corporate stock repurchases?

13-8. Discuss the relevance of short interest and odd-lot behavior in market timing. What is the theory, and what is the evidence?

13-9. a. Compute both the odd-lot-short ratio and the total odd-lot short ratio (TOLSR) for the following information: 10-day totals, total odd-lot sales of 1.3 million; odd-lot purchases of 1.6 million; odd-lot-short sales of .07 million.

b. Now recompute the ratios for odd-lot short sales of .24 million.

13-10. Identify the hypothesized relationships for the following indicators:
a. specialists' short selling
b. mutual fund cash
c. Barron's Confidence Index

13-11. Compute the Barron's Confidence Index for the following values for high-grade and average-grade bond rates: 5.67 percent, 6.01 percent; 7.89 percent, 8.85 percent; 9.50 percent, 11.78 percent; and 10.34 percent, 13.89 percent.

13-12. Identify the hypothesized relationships for the following indicators:
a. advance-decline
b. short-term trading
c. January
d. advisers' sentiments
e. Monday–Friday

Self-Test Questions

T   F   13-1. Stock market overreaction is inconsistent with the efficient market hypothesis.

T   F   13-2. Market timing skills have been shown to have an expected payoff about as great as stock selection skills.

T   F   13-3.   The market PE ratio used in most stock market timing studies and techniques as a technical indicator uses the same measure of earnings as the earnings multiplier model does.

T   F   13-4.   The Gray approach to market PEs can be derived from the PE ratio or the earnings multiplier model developed in chapter 7.

T   F   13-5.   The Dow theory is still used by technical analysts and chartists.

T   F   13-6.   For the purpose of the Dow theory, the most important price movement is that of day-to-day fluctuations.

T   F   13-7.   The odd-lot activity indicator is based on the presumption that odd-lotters are relatively unsophisticated investors.

T   F   13-8.   The short-interest measure as a technical predictor of the market has become distorted because of the use of arbitrage techniques.

T   F   13-9.   One problem with the short interest technical indicator is that more than one interpretation is possible.

T   F   13-10.   When mutual funds hold more of their assets in cash, this is a bearish signal, indicating that managers are expecting a downward price movement in the market and are attempting to reduce the risk of their portfolio.

T   F   13-11.   The short-term trading index and the market tend to move in opposite directions.

T   F   13-12.   The January effect denotes that abnormal returns for small-firm stocks occur largely during the first few weeks of trading.

T   F   13-13.   Asset allocators try to avoid overcommitment to any one asset class.

NOTES

1. B. Malkiel, "Equity Yields, Growth, and the Structure of Share Prices," *American Economic Review*, vol. 53 (December 1963), pp. 1004–1031.
2. N. Jegadeesh and S. Titman, "Returns to Buying Winners and Selling Losers: Implications for Stock Market Efficiency," *Journal of Finance,* vol. 48, no. 1 (March 1993), pp. 65–91.
3. R. Baylis and S. Bhirud, "Growth Stock Analysis: A New Approach," *Financial Analysts Journal* (July/August 1973), pp. 63–70.
4. G.P. Brinson, B.D. Singer, G.L. Beebower, "Determinants of Portfolio Performance II: An Update," *Financial Analysts Journal* (May/June 1991), pp. 40–48.
5. J. Holmes, "100 Years of Common-Stock Investing," *Financial Analysts Journal* (November/December 1974), pp. 38–44.
6. W. Gray, "The Application of Discount Rates in Forecasting Returns for Stocks and Bonds," *Financial Analysts Journal* (May/June 1974), pp. 53–61; W. Gray, "Developing a Long-Term Outlook for the U.S. Economy and Stock Market," *Financial Analysts Journal* (July/August 1979), pp. 29–39.

7. J.J. Siegel, "Does It Pay Stock Investors to Forecast the Business Cycle?" *Journal of Portfolio Management,* vol. 18, no. 1 (fall 1991), pp. 27–34.

8. S. Brown and W. Goetzmann, "Mutual Fund Styles," *Journal of Financial Economics,* vol. 43, no. 3 (March 1997), pp. 373–399.

9. B. Malkiel, *A Random Walk Down Wall Street,* 6th ed., (New York: W.W. Norton, 1995), chapter 5.

10. D.B. Keim, "Size-Related Anomalies and Stock Return Seasonality: Further Empirical Evidence," *Journal of Financial Economics,* vol. 12, no 1 (June 1983), pp. 13–32; "A New Look at the Effects of Firm Size and E/P Ratio on Stock Returns," *Financial Analysts Journal,* vol. 46, no. 2 (March/April 1990), pp. 56–67.

11. S. Penman, "The Distribution of Earnings News over Time and Seasonalities in Aggregate Stock Returns," *Journal of Financial Economics,* vol. 18, no. 2 (June 1987), pp. 199–228.

Individual Security Trading Strategies

Learning Objectives

An understanding of the material in this chapter should enable the student to

---

14-1. Explain the theoretical arguments and empirical evidence on technical analysis as practiced by the chartists.

14-2. Describe the numerous tendencies for prices to behave in a particular fashion.

14-3. Explain the market timing issue in brokerage share performance, dividend reinvestment plans, and dollar cost averaging.

Chapter Outline

Investment timing involves two important processes: (1) anticipating market trends and (2) formulating reliable expectations for price changes relative to those trends. The last two chapters focused on the first process. This chapter explores the second process—that is, generalizable factors that may affect individual security prices.

The chapter first considers the theoretical arguments and empirical evidence on technical analysis as practiced by the chartists. It then discusses a variety of specialized price dependencies (tendencies for prices to behave in a particular fashion). These specialized dependencies include the impact of block trades, secondary distributions, intraday dependencies, overnight price changes, tax loss trading, announcements of earnings and dividend changes, ex-dividend date behavior and dividend capture strategies, additions to Standard & Poor's 500 Industrial Index, bond rating changes, corporate crime disclosures, insider trading reports, media recommendations, splits, reverse splits, stock dividends, tender offers, mergers, liquidations, stock repurchases, rights offerings, equity sales, forced conversions, debt-for-equity exchanges, and spin-offs. Finally, it examines the timing issues related to cross-correlations, volume effects, brokerage share prices, dividend reinvestment plans, and dollar cost averaging.

TECHNICAL ANALYSIS

technical analysis

Technical analysis seeks to time stock trades by assessing the psychological state of the market. Technical market indicators (which we explored in chapter 13) are used to interpret the psychology of the overall market. A second type of tool, *charting,* is used to assess the market's mood toward specific stocks. Although controversial, chart reading (or its modern-day equivalent, momentum modeling), is still widely practiced. Accordingly, no treatment of investment timing would be complete without some discussion of the technical approach.

charting

Types of Charts

Chartists utilize two basic types of charts: bar charts and point-and-figure charts. The *bar chart* is used to show the daily price range, closing price, and daily volume. The basic format of the bar chart may be supplemented with a *moving average* line (for example, the average stock price for the past 50 days) and a *relative strength* line. The relative strength line plots the ratio of the stock's price to that of the S&P 500 average or to some other appropriate average or index.

bar chart

**moving average
relative strength**

Example:	Suppose Standard Widget's daily closing prices are as follows:

May 1, 2000	$30
May 2, 2000	$31
May 3, 2000	$32
May 4, 2000	$31
May 5, 2000	$31
May 8, 2000	$32
May 9, 2000	$31
May 10, 2000	$30
May 11, 2000	$29
May 12, 2000	$30

Assume we wish to calculate the moving average for the past 5 trading days. On May 8, our moving average would be based on the closing prices of May 1 through 5, or ($30 + $31 + $32 + $31 + $31)/5, or $31. On May 9, our moving average would be based on the closing stock prices for May 2 through 8, and so on. For the second week in May, our daily 5-day moving average would be

May 8, 2000	$31
May 9, 2000	$31.40
May 10, 2000	$31.40
May 11, 2000	$31
May 12, 2000	$30.60

Figure 14-1 shows a typical bar chart with share volume for CBS during the period of the 1987 third-quarter boom, the October 1987 stock market crash, and the aftermath through June 1988. The moving average lines (solid and dotted) trace the trend movements over selected averaging periods (typically 90-day and 360-day averages).

point-and-figure chart

A *point-and-figure chart* diagrams stock movements. This chart has no time dimension. The vertical axis measures the stock price. To construct the chart, a threshold level of price movement is determined. One point (dollar per share) is the typical threshold. Every time the stock moves past a whole number level, a mark is recorded. If the move is upward, an X is entered; a downward move calls for an O. As the price rises, Xs are stacked one on top of another. When the price direction changes, an O is entered in the next column. Additional Os are added below as the stock price falls. Point-and-figure charts give a compact presentation of price movements. Figure 14-2 shows a typical point-and-figure chart.

FIGURE 14-1
Typical Bar Chart

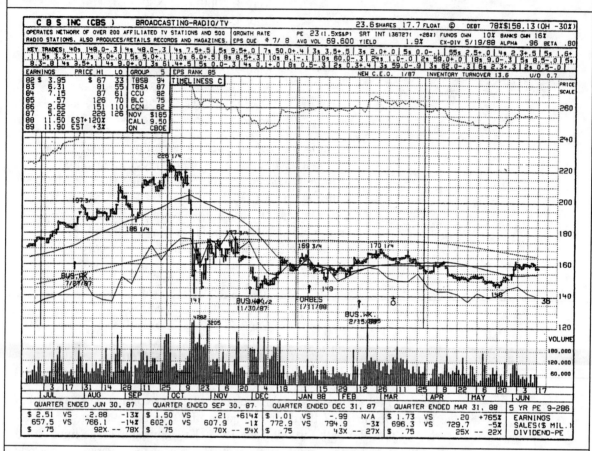

Source: Courtesy Daily Graphs and Long Term Values, P.O. Box 24933, Los Angeles, CA 90024

Major Premises of the Chartist's Approach

momentum

Chartists can illustrate price/volume patterns with either bar or point-and-figure charts. These patterns are said to reveal future demand-and-supply relationships by reflecting evolving market psychology. Much of chartism is based on one very basic premise: Stock prices follow trends. That is, chartists believe that stock prices often behave as if they have a degree of *momentum*. This momentum is expected to carry the price along in its current direction until some new force causes a change in direction.

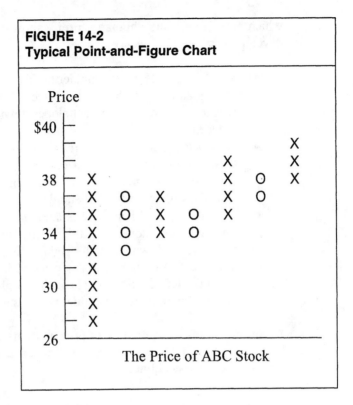

FIGURE 14-2
Typical Point-and-Figure Chart

The Price of ABC Stock

A second tenet of chartists is the belief that volume goes with the trend. Thus, in a major up trend, volume will increase as the price rises and decrease when the price declines. In a major down trend, in contrast, volume will increase as the price declines.

The third major premise of the chartist's approach hypothesizes the existence of resistance and support levels. A *resistance level* emerges as a significant number of investors look to get out when a certain price level is reached. The number of shares offered increases dramatically as this resistance level is approached. Similarly, at a *support level*, a support price may exist at about the level that the most recent rise began. Investors who missed the first move may be waiting for a second chance to buy if the stock drops back down to that level.

resistance level

support level

Chartists' Interpretations of Price Patterns

Technical analysts seek to identify favorable buying and selling opportunities from repeating price patterns. These patterns include chart formations such as triangles, coils, rectangles, flags, pennants, gaps, line-and-saucer formations, and V-formations. Perhaps the best known pattern is the *head-and-shoulders formation*, a classic pattern of chartists. This pattern,

head-and-shoulders
formation

which resembles the human form, shows the following stages of development:

- left shoulder: The left shoulder builds up when there is a strong rally, accompanied by significant volume. Thereafter, when a profit-taking reaction occurs, the shoulder slopes downward. Volume is noticeably reduced.
- head: Rising prices and increased volume initiate the left side of the head pattern, followed by a contraction, or reduced volume, which extends to the neckline. In this configuration, the head always extends well above the left shoulder.
- right shoulder: When there is another price rally, the left side of the right shoulder slopes upward; finally, when the rally breaks up and prices slide downward, the right side of the right shoulder slopes downward. Volume action is usually decidedly smaller than it was under the left shoulder and head. The right shoulder tends to be equal in height with the left shoulder and it is always well below the head.

According to this interpretation of price patterns, a trader who buys late often has an opportunity to buy a second time on a brief minor rally that pulls prices back to the neckline.

Chart Reading and Market Efficiency

The weak form of the efficient market hypothesis (see chapter 9) implies that past market behavior contains no useful investment timing information. That is, investors' efforts to find hidden values should, according to efficient market adherents, cause stock prices to reflect all relevant public information accurately and quickly (including any information implicit in past price patterns). Therefore, a stock price will follow a random walk if its present price is set at the expected discounted value of its future dividends when future dividends are supposed to be random variables.[1] Indeed, if many traders recognized repeating patterns, their rapid reaction would cause an almost immediate change to the predicted level. Eventually, some investors' efforts to react to partial patterns would probably eliminate most repeating patterns. At a minimum, these actions should reduce any repeating patterns' magnitudes to the point where they are not exploitable after the impact of commission is taken into account. On the other hand, technical analysts assert that their techniques, while not infallible, provide useful signals. Why else, they might ask, do so many investors continue to pay for and follow their advice?

The efficient market proponents respond that some successes may be the result of combining other information with charts and giving credit to the charts alone. Other technicians may simply have been lucky. Some analyses and many market turns may reveal high success rates. The relevant question is, Do these successes repeat themselves? Hearing from the winners (who are likely to be vocal) but not from losers (who are unlikely to advertise their failures) gives a distorted view.

Evidence suggests that past price behavior contains little or no generally useful information. Any generalized time series dependencies that past price behavior exhibits appear to be too weak to offset the impact of transaction costs. But a closer look suggests that the issue may not be quite so simple.

SPECIALIZED DEPENDENCIES

specialized dependencies

According to S. Smidt in his reexamination of the random walk hypothesis, researchers may find certain types of *specialized dependencies* in stock price returns for three reasons: First, the large orders of anxious traders may cause short-run price reactions that, when dissipated, produce a price reversal. Anxious traders are generally in an exposed market position, such as an outstanding short-sell position. If the market price of the stock they have shorted moves against them, these traders must move quickly to cover their short or risk a loss. Second, lags in reaction to new information may lead to short-run price trends. Third, excessive speculation may cause speculative bubbles followed by major declines.[2] Speculative bubbles are increases in stock prices that are unrelated to proportionate increases in fundamental values. These increases are the result of emotional (not rational) investor behavior. Speculative bubbles are discussed later in this chapter.

Anxious Trader Effects

anxious trader effects

Block trades, secondary offerings, intraday dependencies and tax-loss trading may lead to temporary supply-demand imbalances. Initially, the price may be disturbed away from its intrinsic value level. Later, as the *anxious trader effects* dissipate, the price may move back toward its prior level.

Block Trades and Secondary Offerings

block trades

As discussed in chapter 3, *block trades* are transactions involving 10,000 or more shares. Most block trades reflect a relatively large trader's desire to buy or sell. Sell trades may put some downward pressure on the market. If this pressure is temporary, an investor might profit from it. Most block trades, however, do not depress prices by enough to permit after-commission trading profits on the typical rebound, although those with the greatest price declines offer the most attractive trading prospects. For the first decile of trades ranked by size of open-to-block-price declines, gross profits from buying at the block price and selling at the close only slightly exceed commissions. However, specialists and floor traders, who incur much lower trading costs, may profit substantially. As discussed in chapter 3, block trades are often handled by a block trader specializing in large block trades. The block trader usually attempts to find someone to commit to all or part of the large block of shares prior to taking a position in the shares. This is often referred to as "open-to-block-price."

Several researchers have found price declines that are associated with large secondary distributions on the day of the sale and subsequently.[3] They have also found that secondary distributions of corporate insiders, investment companies, and mutual funds are followed by appreciably greater price changes than when the sellers are banks, insurance companies, estates, trusts, or individuals. Quite possibly, corporate insiders, investment companies, and mutual funds are more likely to base their decision to sell on fundamental grounds to which they are privy but others are not, whereas banks, insurance companies, and others may simply need liquidity. These secondary distribution results do not exhibit any anxious trader effects *per se*. Perhaps data on daily closing prices are too crude to reveal anxious trader effects.

intraday dependencies

General Intraday Dependencies: Specialists and Limit Orders

It has been argued that stock prices closely resemble a random walk for daily movements. However, temporary intraday barriers to price movements and nonrandom overnight (close to next day's open) price changes have been observed, which may be ascribed to the interaction of specialists' trading and publicly placed limit orders.

Specialists are charged with keeping an orderly market (that is, avoiding excessive volatility) in their assigned stocks. They rely on a combination of limit orders and buying and selling with their own inventory to keep their markets orderly. Limit orders tend to collect at even values (whole numbers, halves as opposed to quarters, quarters as opposed to eighths, and so on). A collection of these limit orders at even values may act as temporary barriers to price movements. Once the market has executed a stack of whole-number limit orders, only a few orders may restrict further movement. Continued buying (selling) activity may lead to a rather rapid price increase (decrease) until a new barrier is encountered.

Example: Buying pressure may move a stock price from 18 5/8 to 18 7/8. Once 19 is penetrated, continued buying could quickly propel the price to 19 7/8, with 20 becoming the next barrier.

Price fluctuations during regular market hours (overday) and overnight are of similar magnitude. Because overnight fluctuations involve much lower volume, smaller price fluctuations might be expected to occur overnight than overday. Perhaps the specialists influence the overnight price swings: Accumulated overnight orders and the specialists' own accounts are used to set the opening price. Price swings trigger limit orders on which specialists are paid a fee. The more limit orders that are executed, the larger the specialists' fee income from this source will be.

Investors interested in making a trade should always request complete quotes. These quotations should include the current bid and ask prices, rather than only the price of the previous trade. Complete knowledge of the current quote is particularly relevant to investors who want to place limit orders. Traders should usually also ask for a size (number of shares sought at the bid and available at the ask). For example, a large bid and small offer may well indicate that buying pressure is present and may ultimately lead to a higher price for the stock.

Informed Trading

Markets sometimes reflect the activity of informed traders executing transactions with a public that does not know what the informed traders know. For example, someone accumulating a position prior to a takeover attempt will, at the outset, generally have information that is kept secret from the rest of the market. Similarly, an insider may have a much better assessment of the company's prospects than the rest of the market does. Sophisticated traders and investors—particularly specialists—are always aware of the possibility that an informed trader may be on the other side of the market. Accordingly, they become cautious when persistent buying or selling moves a price outside of its recent trading range.

tax-loss trading

Tax-Loss Trading

Yet another area of possible anxious trader impact involves year-end selling to establish a tax loss. Tax-loss trading is believed to have dramatically affected some year-end stock prices. The end of the year, therefore, may be an attractive time to purchase stocks that are under tax-loss selling pressure.

Studies have refined our knowledge on tax-loss trading, especially, as it relates to seasonality. A number of studies have found that most of the turn-of-the-year effect—stocks that decline by the largest amounts in December are most likely to rise in January—occurs at the small-firm level.[4] Another study tests the hypothesis that tax-loss trading by individual investors is responsible for the January effect. The study examines the ownership structure of a large sample of firms over a 4-year-period and finds that the small firms that usually exhibit high January returns have low institutional ownership. Thus, the study indicates that institutional ownership is significantly related to January abnormal returns. One reason that the January effect may concentrate in small firms is because these firms are held by tax-motivated individual investors.[5]

Assessment of Anxious Trader Effects

The evidence for anxious trader effects seems somewhat persuasive. Block trading and tax-loss trading have both tended to depress prices temporarily, with a reversal generally following. Secondary offerings are also associated with modest price declines.

Intraday price dependencies related to specialist trading and limit order activity also reveal some anxious trader effects. With the possible exception of the tax-loss results, however, the magnitudes of the dependencies appear to be too small to result in trading profits after taking transaction costs into account. Moreover, what may appear to be the temporary impact of an anxious trader may actually be an indication that an informed trader is accumulating or unloading a position. On the other hand, investors who intend to trade anyway might as well take advantage of whatever forecasting value these relationships may offer.

Anxious Trader Effects

- Block trades: Prices tend to decline with block trades and regain most of the loss by day's end.
- Large secondary distributions: Prices show modest declines on the day of and following a secondary distribution.
- Intraday dependencies: Bunching orders at certain price points may slow and then exaggerate/accelerate price movements.
- Overnight price changes: Volatility may result from specialists' activity between trading sessions.
- Informed trading: Persistent buying or selling moves the price outside of its recent trading range.
- Tax-loss trading: Issues under year-end tax selling pressure may rise at the first of the year; small-firm and low-prices issues are particularly likely to be affected in this way.

---

adjustment lags

Adjustment Lags

Adjustment lags are another category of specialized dependencies. Specifically, prices may take time to react to such factors as earnings announcements, dividend changes, ex-dividend dates, additions to the S&P 500 Industrial Index, bond rating changes, corporate crime disclosures, insider trading reports, media recommendations, splits, stock dividends, tenders, mergers, liquidations, share repurchases, rights offerings, equity sales, debt-for-equity swaps, forced conversions, divestitures, and spin-offs. Moreover, cross-correlations and volume effects may also be used to identify adjustments in process.

Earnings and Dividend Announcements

According to several studies on earnings and dividend announcements, although prices may not adjust instantly to these announcements, the lags appear to be quite short. The reactions seem to be faster for firms with listed options. Firms without listed options take longer to react to quarterly earnings announcements. Moreover, several studies found a relatively slow market reaction to unexpected earnings changes.

Several different studies that focused on dividends have generally found that dividend increases often result in substantial positive price reactions that are usually completed by the day of the announcement or soon thereafter. Favorable dividend announcements tend to be made in a timely fashion, whereas delayed announcements are associated with dividend omissions or reductions.

Ex-Dividend Behavior and Dividend Capture Strategies

ex-dividend date

Ex-dividend price reactions also appear to be predictable to some extent. Dividends are paid to stockholders of record on a prespecified date. Dividends on purchases made the day after the *ex-dividend date* go to the prior owner. The price of the stock tends to fall by a bit less than the amount of the dividend on the ex-dividend date. The relationship is far from exact, however.

dividend capture

Similarly, call option prices also tend to fall on the ex-dividend day of the underlying stock. The predictability of ex-dividend price reactions suggests what have come to be called *dividend capture* trading strategies, in which corporate money managers actively trade in and out of several preferred stocks in order to capture multiple dividends. Under the Tax Reform Act of 1986, dividends received by a corporation on common and preferred stock held in other corporations, and representing less than 20 percent ownership in them, are subject to a 70 percent exclusion for tax purposes. The exclusion is 80 percent if the corporation owns between 20 and 80 percent in the other corporation paying it dividends; 100 percent of the dividends received are excluded if it owns more than 80 percent of the other company.

Both preferred and common stock may form the basis for a dividend capture. U.S. investors must, however, own the shares for at least 46 days to qualify for the special tax treatment.

Additions to the S&P Index

Additions to Standard & Poor's 500 Industrial Index are widely followed by the market. The S&P 500 Index is viewed as a much broader-based index than the Dow Jones Industrial Average. As such, the S&P 500 is the index on which many other financial instruments are based. For example, stock index futures, options on index futures, and indexed mutual funds all utilize the S&P 500. Stocks are added to and deleted from the index in order to preserve or enhance its representativeness. The announcement that a stock is to be added to the index tends to cause the stock to rise, usually within a couple of days, whereas a deletion has the opposite tendency.

Bond Rating Changes and Corporate Crime Disclosures

According to research on stock price reaction to bond rating changes, there is an appreciable reaction to rating downgrades, but upgrades have an insignificant effect. There is also a significant negative market reaction to disclosures of allegations of illegal corporate behavior. Virtually all of this reaction occurs at the time of the announcement.

insider trading

Insider Trading

Often, inside information appears to facilitate a relatively accurate stock evaluation. Noninsiders must generally wait until the information is publicly released, but traders can observe insiders' trading decisions and act accordingly.

The inside trades of CEOs and directors are a better predictor of subsequent performance than those of vice presidents and beneficial owners.[6] Apparently, CEOs and directors have better access to information.

Insiders must report their trades to the SEC. Thus, investors can consult the SEC's records to determine insiders' trading on a particular stock. Moreover, some investment services report SEC insider trading data to subscribers. Certain periodicals, including *Barron's* and *Value Line*, report on insider trades, and insider trading activity is sometimes discussed in the financial press, at least on an *ad hoc* basis. However, there can be a time lag of several days or weeks between the time insider trades take place and the time the trades become known by the investing public. During the intervening time, the market price of the company's stock might change sufficiently so that noninsiders would find it difficult to profit after taking transaction costs into consideration.

There have been several cases related to alleged misused insider information by outsiders who made trades based on it. An important Supreme Court decision in 1997 clarified what constitutes illegal insider trading. The decision upheld the so-called misappropriation theory of insider trading, which states that traders may not trade on nonpublic information even if they are not corporate insiders.[7]

Media Recommendations

According to a study of the daily "Heard in the Street" column in *The Wall Street Journal*, which highlights specific companies' and analysts' opinions of specific stocks, the market appears to react efficiently to published takeover rumors in that column. According to the study, excess returns could not be earned, on average, by purchasing rumored takeover targets at the time the rumor appeared. No significantly excess returns occurred on the day the takeover rumor was published, although a positive cumulative excess of about 7 percent occurred in the calendar month *prior* to the appearance of the rumor in the "Heard on the Street" columns.[8]

A 1992 study examined the impact of the insider information scandal related to R. Foster Winans' "Heard in the Street" column in 1984. Following the scandal, the column had a reduced impact on stock prices for both buy and sell recommendations. Several months into the postscandal period, stock price response to information prior to the column's publication day was less. The results seem to indicate that the editors of *The Wall Street Journal* may have become more cautious in guarding against information leaks concerning the column. The scandal did not appear, however, to have altered the column's impact on trading volume.[9]

Another study focused on stock price behavior of firms that were favorably mentioned in the "Inside Wall Street" column in *Business Week*. The study found positive excess returns for favorably mentioned stocks on the day prior to the publication date, the publication date, and the days immediately after publication. There were positive, significant excess returns for long-term holding periods prior to the publication date but significant negative returns for long-term post-publication holding periods.

The study's findings are consistent with the price performance of firms that might have been the subject either of rumors or recent recommendations by analysts or brokerage firms. These results, along with those of earlier studies, suggest that secondary information is valuable only to low-transaction-cost, short-term traders. Investors who buy stock for the longer term based on secondary information generally receive below-market rates of return.[10]

Stock Splits, Reverse Splits, and Stock Dividends

stock splits

Corporate managers and the investors in their firms generally prefer per-share prices of some normal range ($20 to $60, for example). Very low-priced stocks are considered too speculative, and high-priced stocks are too costly to purchase in round lots. Accordingly, *stock splits* and stock distributions are used to reduce the per-share prices of high-priced stocks; reverse stock splits may be employed for very low-priced issues. Postsplit shares usually incur proportionately higher commission charges and bid-ask spreads. Thus, splits generally increase trading costs. Moreover, stock distributions incur a number of costs: officers' time, printing stock certificates, handling fractional shares, revising the stockholder ledger, communicating with shareholders, transfer taxes, and listing fees.

stock dividend

Because the price of a stock is believed to rise prior to a split or *stock dividend* announcement, investors might trade on prior knowledge of the announcement or on the basis of accurate forecasts of the impending splits. The former strategy is illegal; the success rate of the latter is untested. Although there is significant negative price performance associated with reverse splits around the time of the proposal, approval, and ex-split dates, investors interpret stock dividends as positive signals from management on the firm's future. The larger the dividend, the greater the market reaction.

The price reactions to stock splits or dividends extend several days beyond the announcement date of the stock split or stock dividend. This implies that there must be some information associated with these distributions. Investors are constantly given a wide range of information concerning both macroeconomic events and items about specific companies. According to a recent study, stock-split announcements and revisions of analysts' earnings forecasts indicate that a firm's past history of stock splits plays a crucial role in both the design and effect of current splits. Managers appear to design splits to return their company's stock price to the level after the previous split. Moreover, managers sometimes announce a split to achieve an even lower price than with the previous split. Both investors and analysts interpret this as an especially positive signal.[11]

Tender Offers, Mergers, and Liquidations

Tender offers, mergers, and liquidations may present investors with still other attractive trading opportunities. Stockholders often profit when their stock (a target) is tendered for and/or merged into another company. The offering price almost always exceeds the previous level. Moreover, a variety of people may benefit from such transactions. For example, those who put the deals together are always well rewarded, as are the target firm's advisers. Even the acquired firm's managers are usually well compensated (the so-called golden parachute) when they are forced to leave. Those who know of planned mergers before the announcement may (illegally) trade on that knowledge. Large investors may buy a sizable position in a company and then try either to force a takeover from the inside or to get the company to pay a premium to repurchase their shares (greenmail). The company's own assets are often used as collateral to finance the full takeover (a leveraged buyout, or LBO).

Yet another strategy is to acquire a large position in an undervalued company and then have the company buy out most or all of the small public shareholders. Taking a company private in this way may buy out most shareholders at possibly depressed prices. Of course, the stock may not stay depressed if small public shareholders realize there is new demand for their shares. If the company succeeds in buying out all small public investors, it eliminates much of the stockholder relations cost. Finally, a company whose assets are worth more than the market price of its shares may be bought as a liquidation prospect.

Although these various maneuvers may yield handsome returns, traders need either inside information of planned takeovers (and a willingness to break the law) or the resources to influence the relevant firms. The only realistic strategy for investors is to try to anticipate forthcoming acquisitions. They can then be in the right place at the right time when the target company is put in play. Moreover, once a takeover looks like a success, tendering the remaining publicly held shares is almost always advisable. Small holdings of subsidiaries usually have little speculative appeal.

While some mergers actually occur, others are merely rumored. Stock prices are often influenced by these rumors. Once the real situation is known, the stock will react appropriately. If the stock is truly a target, the announcement will tend to move the price toward the level of the offer. If the rumor is incorrect, the stock will probably give back most or all of the price rise brought about by the rumor. Some investors will already own stock of a company that is rumored to be a takeover target. They would like to know whether to hold the stock until the anticipated event occurs or to sell before the rumor turns out to be merely unfounded speculation. Investors who are contemplating buying do not want to be influenced by information that turns out to be false. Clearly, for the investor to profit, he or she must know how to assess a takeover rumor.

Share Repurchases, Equity Sales, Forced Conversions, and Exchanges

Earnings retention and minor debt decisions continually alter capital structures. Other actions can appreciably alter the number of shares outstanding and/or the firm's debt ratio. These actions can dramatically affect the shareholders' expected income streams and risks. Moreover, capital structure changes that affect the relative amounts of dividend and interest payments have important tax implications. Thus, the market may well react

forced conversions

to such events as share repurchases (which decrease outstanding shares), rights offerings, and *forced conversions* (both of which increase outstanding shares). According to one study, market reactions to capital structure changes are as follows:

- Changes that affect expected taxes and/or the relative values of stocks versus bonds are associated with significant security price moves in the predicted directions.
- Different classes of security holders are often affected differently by the shift.
- Shareholders are generally adversely affected by a decrease in leverage. [12]

Other studies report that firms use share repurchases to signal their belief that their stocks are undervalued. The studies also found that common shareholders usually benefit from such repurchases and that market reaction to repurchases occurs within one day of the announcement. [13]

Share repurchases decrease shares outstanding and tend to increase per-share prices, while rights offerings and other types of equity sales may have the opposite effect. One study found a negative market reaction to the announcement and implementation of equity sales (including the sale of convertibles). [14] On the other hand, another study found that management requests to increase authorized shares had little or no impact. [15] Still another study indicated that equity carve-outs (partial sales of subsidiaries) and announcements of capital expenditures had generally positive impacts. [16]

Like sales of equity, voluntary exchanges of equity for debt and forced conversions of convertible debentures and convertible preferreds increase shares outstanding and reduce leverage. Thus, these exchanges and conversions tend to lower both per-share earnings and risk. Calling convertibles will force conversion only if the stock price has appreciated sufficiently. Therefore, the conversion value must exceed the call price by a substantial amount or owners will not willingly convert. Of course, the issuing company can force a conversion by simply calling the convertibles. Most convertibles are callable at the issuing firm's discretion. If the issuer exercises its call option to repurchase the security, the security holders generally have a month during which they may still convert. When issuers use a call, knowing that security holders will choose to convert, the issuer is said to have forced a conversion.

Voluntary and forced conversions of debt for equity have different market impacts. The announcement of the swap of stock for debt is generally associated with negative stock price performance. Subsequent performance is related to the purpose of the swap. If, for example, the swap is part of a refunding operation, subsequent performance is generally favorable. Swaps of preferreds for common stock and reversions of excess assets (from pension funds to the corporation) tend to have a favorable market impact.

According to the pecking-order theory, developed by S.C. Myers and N.S. Majluf, managers are assumed to know more about their firms than outside investors do. Existence of this information asymmetry affects firms' choice between internal and external financing and also between new issues of debt or equity securities. This leads to a pecking order, in which investments are financed first with internal funds (retained earnings), then by new issues of debt, and finally with new issues of equity. According to this theory, new equity issues are a last resort when the firm uses up its debt capacity—that is, when the costs of financial distress force creditors to restrict the firm from issuing more debt.[17]

Conversely, F. Modigliani and M. Miller contend that in a perfectly efficient capital market, any combination of debt and equity is as good as another. That is, the value of the firm is unaffected by its choice of capital structure.[18] Of course, we don't live in a perfectly efficient capital market; factors such as transaction costs, taxes, agency costs, and information asymmetry all contribute to the existence of anomalies to a perfectly efficient capital market.

Spin-Offs

A spin-off occurs when a parent company gives its stockholders shares in what had heretofore been a subsidiary of the parent firm. Clearly, such distributions create no new tangible assets. The divestiture may increase the investment's value if separating the parent from the former subsidiary enhances the subsidiary's freedom to operate effectively. Divestitures tend to have a significantly favorable impact on the seller and a modestly favorable impact on the buyer.

Cross-Correlation and Volume Effects

Investment analysts have often asserted that particular stock groups tend to lead other groups—for example, interest-sensitive stocks tend to lead the market, high-risk stocks are hit first and hardest in an economic downturn, and low-PE stocks hold up best in a down market. The existence of lead and lag relationships could facilitate useful market forecasting. An efficient market, however, should not exhibit these leads and lags.

Price trends are frequently accompanied by abnormally high volume. Volume tends to be higher on upticks than on downticks. Volume data and the applicability to technical analysis yield information that cannot be deduced from price statistics alone. Moreover, traders who use volume information tend to do better than those who do not.

Assessment of Adjustment Lags

The market appears to adjust quickly to most new information. Reactions generally occur within a day or so of the following types of announcements: earnings reports, dividend changes, additions to the S&P 500 Index, bond rating changes, allegations of corporate crimes, stock dividends, share repurchases, and rights offerings. Stock price adjustments actually tend to precede the announcement or event for splits, tender offers, mergers, and spin-offs. Thus, trading based on these relationships normally requires prior knowledge or accurate forecasts. On the other hand, revisions of earnings

---

Adjustment Time Frames

- Earnings announcements: The market reacts quickly to earnings news.
- Dividend announcements: The market reacts quickly to dividend news.
- Ex-dividend date: The stock price tends to fall by somewhat less than the amount of the payment on the ex-dividend date.
- Additions/deletions to S&P 500 Index: Stocks tend to rise when added to the index and fall when deleted.
- Bond rating changes: Price reaction is appreciable for downgrades but not for upgrades.
- Alleged corporate crime: The market reacts quickly to news of alleged illegal activity.
- Insider trading: Reports of insider trades appear to provide profitable trading signals.
- Media recommendations: There are short-term positive excess returns for recommended stocks prior to media coverage.
- Stock splits and stock dividends: The price rises before a split or dividend announcement. Price performance is negative at time of the proposal, approval, and ex-split date for reverse splits.
- Tender offers, mergers, and liquidations: Returns can be significant, but investors must anticipate the event.
- Share repurchases: Repurchases often indicate that management believes the stock is undervalued.
- Rights offerings and equity sales: Shareholders generally react negatively to announcements of rights offerings and equity sales.
- Forced conversions and debt-for-equity exchanges: Strong positive performances generally precede forced conversion and debt-for-equity exchange announcements, with negative performances afterward.
- Spin-offs: Performances are positive prior to an announcement, followed by random performances afterward.
- Cross-correlations: Some securities tend to lead, while others tend to lag the market.
- Price-volume effects: Price trends are frequently accompanied by abnormally high volume.

---

forecasts, insider trading signals, forced conversions, and possibly ex-dividend date reactions may produce usable price relationships (that is, those that take place over a long enough period to be exploited by nonmembers of the listing exchange).

speculative bubbles

Speculative Bubbles

Some analysts contend that the market has a tendency to overreact. Burton Malkiel argues that investors should seek out stocks for which a subsequent positive overreaction is likely, stressing the importance of psychological elements (as in chapter 13) in stock price determination. Individual and institutional investors are not computers that calculate warranted price-earnings multiples and print out buy and sell decisions. They are emotional human beings driven by greed, gambling instinct, hope, and fear in their stock market decisions. This is why successful investing demands both intellectual and psychological acuteness. Stocks that produce positive feelings in investors' minds can sell at premium multiples for long periods even if their growth rate is only average. Stocks not so blessed may sell at low multiples for long periods even if their growth rate is above average.

To be sure, if a growth rate appears to be established, the stock is almost certain to attract some type of following; the market is not irrational. But stocks are like people: What stimulates one may leave another cold. Moreover, a stock's multiple improvement may be smaller and slower to be realized if the stock does not have an "interesting story" and thereby does not attract Wall Street's attention.[19] Although general tests for speculative bubbles are virtually impossible, market reactions to new issues and new listings offer some guidelines.

The New Issue Market

new issues

New issues are initial public offerings (IPOs) of stocks in heretofore privately held companies. The prices of these issues often rise dramatically in the immediate postsale period. Investors might exploit such trends by buying at issue and selling quickly thereafter. However, the supplies of the most attractive new issues are rationed. Thus, only the underwriting brokers' best customers may be able to buy the issues at the offering.

Investment bankers, who are better informed than their clients, have an incentive to underprice new issues. Because the underpricing will be passed along to the issuer, the sale will be made more easily and the buyers will be happier at little cost to the underwriters. Thus, if future new issue performance is to be like the past, investors should generally follow a strategy of realizing gains soon after the initial purchase.

These abnormal short-run returns are usually followed by below-market returns for somewhat longer holding periods. A study on the long-run performance of IPOs determined that they substantially underperformed a sample of matching firms from the closing price on the first day of public trading to their 3-year anniversaries. The study found that there was significant variation in the underperformance year-to-year and across industries; firms that went public in high-volume years fared the worst. The study concluded that the pricing patterns were consistent with an IPO market in which investors are periodically overoptimistic about the earnings potential of young growth companies, and firms take advantage of these windows of opportunity.[20] A follow-up study constructed a set of matching firms based on SIC code and size of NYSE, AMEX, and NASDAQ stocks. It found that virtually all IPO underperformance occurs on Mondays and Tuesdays and that the degree of underperformance significantly differs from other days. Thus, the study concludes that a common explanation may exist for the general day-of-the-week pattern in security returns and the IPO long-run underperformance observed.[21]

new listings

New Listings

Several studies indicate that newly listed stocks typically exhibit a price pattern that is similar to that of new issues.[22] When an OTC stock gains a listing or when an AMEX stock is listed on the NYSE, its price tends to rise and then to fall back to the previous level. It can be argued that the firm and its insiders sometimes utilize the postlisting period to sell stock and, therefore, both the number of shares outstanding and the number publicly held tend to increase. This increased supply is likely to depress the price of the newly listed stock. Thus, the short-term price run-up associated with a new listing or a listing on a more prestigious exchange may offer an attractive selling opportunity. The price, however, is more likely to decline thereafter.

Assessment of Speculative Bubbles

The performance of new issues and new listings is consistent with the existence of speculative bubbles. The price rises of both new issues and newly listed issues tend to be followed by a reversal. The percentage moves of new issue prices (from offer to immediate after-market) may be large enough to yield abnormal after-commission returns. On the other hand, the difficulty of buying an issue at its initial offering price may substantially reduce the profit potential. The related price effects are generally too small for a new listing-based trading strategy to cover transaction costs.

Speculative Bubbles

- "Story" stocks: The market often gets carried away with stocks that have an attractive story.
- New issues: New issues generally appreciate in the immediate after-market, followed by a subsequent decline.
- New listings: Prices tend to rise prior to listing and subsequently decline to previous level.

Overall Assessment of Special-Situation Dependencies

All three of Smidt's hypothesized special-situation price dependencies discussed earlier in this chapter receive some support from the relevant academic research. The vast majority of the documented dependencies do not, however, provide profit opportunities for most investors. These dependencies either occur and are over with too quickly for nonexchange members to profit, or the magnitudes of the average price effects are too small for those who must pay commissions (even at a modest discount) to exploit. On the other hand, a few of the dependencies seem sufficiently large and long-lasting to yield abnormal returns, even to outsiders (nonexchange members). Specifically, tax-loss candidates, insider trading and new issues all may offer exploitable price trends. Moreover, investors who have already decided to trade may be able to take advantage of other more modest price effects. Note, however, that the reported results reflect historic average relationships. Even if these relationships continue, a large portfolio must be managed over a relatively long period to generate results close to the average.

OTHER MARKET TIMING ISSUES

Certain timing topics do not fit neatly into any of Smidt's categories. Nonetheless, we need to consider some of these topics. Accordingly, the chapter will now discuss market moves and brokerage shares, dividend reinvestment plans, and dollar cost averaging.

Market Moves and Brokerage Share Performance

Brokerage houses and investment banks (often the same firm) were long organized as partnerships or closely held corporations. Most, however, have now gone public. Their stocks reveal interesting trading patterns. Stock market volume seems to vary directly with the market averages. Brokerage profits are highly dependent on stock market volume. Thus, brokerage profits tend to be particularly strong when the market is rising and weak when it is falling. As a result, the amplitude of brokerage stock price movements tends to exceed that of the overall market.

Therefore, those who think they can call market turns may find brokerage house stocks useful trading vehicles. On the other hand, the relationship between stock volume, brokerage profits, and brokerage share prices did not follow past patterns in the late 1980s, even though it reasserted itself in the late 1990s. Again, we find that as a pattern begins to be noticed, it is particularly likely to stop working.

Dividend Reinvestment Plans

dividend reinvestment plan

Deciding whether or not to participate in a *dividend reinvestment plan*—a program in which company stockholders can reinvest their dividends directly into the company's stock—raises another timing issue. Since Allegheny Power started the practice in 1968, many nonfinancial firms have begun allowing their stockholders to reinvest their dividends directly into the company's stock. Prior to that time, a number of financial corporations had such plans. In October 1973, at least 264 nonfinancial firms offered reinvestment programs. By year-end 1980, the number had risen to over 1,102. The numbers have continued to rise throughout the 1980s and 1990s.

These plans may acquire either existing or newly issued stock. The first plans to be established relied on existing stock purchases. Typically, the corporation sends the dividends of participating stockholders to the managing bank's trust department. This bank maintains an account for each shareholder. The managing bank purchases stock on the open market. Each participant is credited with his or her shares, less brokerage fees and administrative costs. Many plans also permit additional stock purchases for cash. Large round-lot purchases by the plan tend to reduce brokerage fees. Some companies give discounts on their dividend reinvestments. Firms selling newly issued shares charge no brokerage fees on the transactions.

Dividend reinvestment plans have a number of advantages. From the firm's standpoint, the plans add to stockholder goodwill, increase demand for the firm's stock, save some dividend-related expenses, and encourage small stockholders to increase ownership. In addition, plans involving new share purchases reduce the firm's debt-to-equity ratio, provide a regular source of equity capital, and permit new equity to be sold without incurring underwriting fees or other flotation costs.

Dividend reinvestment plans also have several direct benefits to stockholders:

- They reduce, or in some cases, eliminate, brokerage costs.
- They encourage dollar cost averaging.

- The plans immediately reinvest dividend payments.
- Some plans offer a discount.
- The programs provide a form of forced savings.

The plans also have some disadvantages:

- They may adversely affect stockholder diversification.
- They reduce stockholders' liquidity.
- New share issues may cause some dilution.
- The plans may reduce individual participation.

Dollar Cost Averaging

dollar cost averaging

Most investors have little confidence in their ability to forecast market and individual security movements. To avoid the necessity of trying to time the market, an investor can engage in *dollar cost averaging*. Dollar cost averaging is the investment of a fixed amount of money at specified time intervals. Investing a fixed dollar amount per period means that investors buy more shares when prices are low than when they are high.

Unless a stock goes into a persistent decline, dollar cost averaging frequently works. It works best when the stock has an early decline and a later rise. It does not, however, protect the investor against a loss of stock values in a declining market.

When dollar cost averaging is applied to selling, it is advisable for investors with a mutual fund redemption plan to sell a fixed number of shares per period rather than a constant dollar value; the goal is to sell more shares at higher prices. No arbitrary timing system, however, can substitute for careful analysis.

SUMMARY AND CONCLUSIONS

In the first section of this chapter, which examines individual security trading strategies, we found little value in the chartist's magic. Nevertheless, some specialized dependencies associated with anxious trader effects, lags in reaction to new information, and speculative bubbles may well be profitably employed in trading decisions.

Anxious trader effects are observed in the market's reaction to block trades, tax-loss selling, secondary offerings, and intraday and overnight interactions of the bid-ask spread with the specialist's quotes. Any adjustment lags are very quick for announcements of earnings, dividend changes, additions to the S&P 500 Index, bond rating changes, share repurchases, and rights offerings. Moreover, the market tends to anticipate splits, tender offers, mergers, and spin-offs. Insider trading signals, forced conversions, and ex-dividend date reactions may produce exploitable patterns. The price effects of new issues and new listings appear to reflect the speculative-bubble phenomenon.

Overall, tax-loss candidates, insider trading, and new issues seem to offer the most exploitable price trends. The usefulness of most of the other observed dependencies is largely limited to the investor's ability to select the best times to make a particular trade that he or she might have made anyway.

The tendency of brokerage shares to magnify market moves makes them interesting trading vehicles, at least for investors with forecasting ability. Because many companies offer dividend reinvestment plans, their investors need to know the pros and cons of participation. Finally, dollar cost averaging is an alternative to trying to time individual stock purchases.

CHAPTER REVIEW

Answers to the review questions and the self-test questions start on page 774.

Key Terms

technical analysis	intraday dependencies
charting	tax-loss trading
bar chart	adjustment lags
moving average	ex-dividend date
relative strength	dividend capture
point-and-figure chart	insider trading
momentum	stock splits
resistance level	stock dividend
support level	forced conversions
head-and-shoulders formation	speculative bubbles
specialized dependencies	new issues
anxious trader effects	new listings
block trades	dividend reinvestment plan
	dollar cost averaging

Review Questions

14-1. a. Compare the positions of chartists and those who subscribe to the random walk hypothesis.

b. What is the role of the market efficiency concept in this discussion?

14-2. a. State Smidt's theory of stock pricing dependencies.

b. Briefly explain the three patterns he observed. Cite the subcategories of each.

14-3. a. How do specialists and limit orders affect intraday and overnight stock prices?

b. How can investors interpret and take advantage of this process?

14-4. a. Why should traders always ask for a price quote that includes both the bid and ask as well as the last price?

b. What other information might an investor seek when a quote is obtained? Briefly give a rationale for this request.

14-5. Discuss the profit potential and evidence for
a. tax-loss trading
b. tender offers, mergers, and liquidations

14-6. As treasurer of the Cash Rich Corporation, you now manage a portfolio containing $50 million invested in short-term government bonds. A stockbroker approaches you with a dividend capture proposal. Discuss some relevant issues to consider before making a decision.

14-7. Give a brief rationale for and the effect on stock prices of
a. stock splits and reverse splits
b. stock dividends
c. dividend reinvestment plans

14-8. a. How have brokerage stock prices tended to fluctuate with the stock market?

b. What has been the more recent experience?

14-9. Explore the effect of dollar cost averaging by performing the following calculations.
a. You purchase $100 of a $10 stock (ignore commissions). The stock's price declines to $5, whereupon you purchase another $100 worth. If the stocks' price recovers to $10, what is the value of your portfolio?
b. As before, begin with a $100 purchase of a $10 stock. When the stock price increases to $15, you purchase another $100 worth. If the stock price subsequently declines to $10, what is the value of your portfolio?

Self-Test Questions

T   F   14-1. Chart reading is a type of fundamental analysis.

T   F   14-2. The resistance level is the price level at which a significant number of investors sell their stock.

T   F   14-3. Profitable exploitation of chart reading and other technical analysis is inconsistent with the weak form of the efficient market hypothesis.

T   F   14-4.   Block trades are transactions involving 1,000 or more shares.

T   F   14-5.   Specialized dependencies justify technical analysis as a possible method of earning above-normal returns.

T   F   14-6.   Tax-loss trading is a type of specialized dependency.

T   F   14-7.   Announcements of dividend increases have been found to lead to stock price increases.

T   F   14-8.   Adjustment lags demonstrate that the stock market is not perfectly efficient in adjusting instantaneously to new information.

T   F   14-9.   Tender offers, mergers, and liquidations may present investors with attractive trading opportunities.

T   F   14-10.   Shares repurchases, rights offerings, and forced conversions all increase the number of outstanding shares of common stock.

T   F   14-11.   Speculative bubbles are increases in stock prices unrelated to proportionate increases in fundamental values, which can best be explained by emotional, rather than rational, investor behavior.

T   F   14-12.   The decision to participate in a dividend reinvestment plan raises an issue of timing.

T   F   14-13.   Dollar cost averaging consists of buying a fixed number of shares of stock at regular intervals.

NOTES

1. P. Samuelson, "Proof That Properly Discounted Present Values of Assets Vibrate Randomly," *Bell Journal of Economics and Management Science* (autumn 1973), pp. 369–374.
2. S. Smidt, "A New Look at the Random Walk Hypothesis," *Journal of Financial and Quantitative Analysis* (September 1968), pp. 235–262.
3. M. Scholes, "The Market for Securities: Substitution versus Price Pressure and the Effects of Information on Share Prices," *Journal of Business* (April 1972), pp. 179–211; and W. Mikkelson and M. Partch, "Stock Price Effects and Costs of Secondary Distributions," *Journal of Financial Economics* (June 1985), pp. 165–194.
4 M. Blume and R. Stambaugh, "Biases in Computed Returns: An Application to the Size Effect," *Journal of Financial Economics* (November 1983), pp. 387–404; W. Kross, "The Size Effect Is Primarily a Price Effect," *Journal of Financial Research* (fall 1985), pp. 169–179.
5. S. Eakins and S. Sewell, "Tax-Loss Selling, Institutional Investors, and the January Effect: A Note," *The Journal of Financial Research,* vol. 16, no. 4 (winter 1993), pp. 377–384. See also: J.R. Ritter, "The Buying and Selling Behavior of Individual Investors at the Turn of the Year," *Journal of Finance*, vol. 43, no. 3, pp. 701–717.
6. K. Nunn, G. Madden, and M. Gombola, "Are Some Insiders More 'Inside' Than Others?" *Journal of Portfolio Management* (spring 1983), pp. 18–22.
7. E. Felsenthal, "Big Weapon against Insider Trading Is Upheld," *The Wall Street Journal* (June 26, 1997), p. C1.

8. J. Pound and R. Zeckhauser, "Clearly Heard on the Street: The Effect of Takeover Rumors on Stock Prices," *Journal of Business* (July 1990), pp. 291–308.

9. P. Liu, S.D. Smith, and A.A. Syed, "The Impact of the Insider Trading Scandal on the Information Content of The Wall Street Journal's 'Heard on the Street' Column," *Journal of Financial Research*, vol. 15, no. 2 (summer 1992), pp. 181–188.

10. I. Mathur and A. Waheed, "Stock Price Reactions to Securities Recommended in Business Week's 'Inside Wall Street,' " *Financial Review*, vol. 30, no. 3 (August 1995), pp. 583–604.

11. R.M. Conroy and R.S. Harris, "Stock Splits and Information: The Role of Share Price," *Financial Management*, vol. 28, no. 3, (autumn 1999), pp. 28–40.

12. R. Masulis, "The Effects of Capital Structure Change on Security Prices: A Study of Exchange Offers," *Journal of Financial Economics* (June 1980), pp. 139–177.

13. T. Vermaelen, "Common Stock Repurchases and Market Signaling: An Empirical Study," *Journal of Financial Economics* (June 1981), pp. 139–183, L. Dann, "Common Stock Repurchases: An Analysis of Returns to Bondholders and Stockholders," *Journal of Financial Economics* (June 1981), pp. 113–138.

14. P. Asquith and D. Mullins, "Equity Issues and Offering Dilution," *Journal of Financial Economics* (January/February 1986), pp. 61–89

15. S. Bhagat, J. Brickley, and R. Lease, "The Authorization of Additional Common Stock: An Empirical Investigation," *Financial Management* (autumn 1986), pp. 45–53.

16. K. Schipper and A. Smith, "A Comparison of Equity Carve-outs and Seasoned Equity Offerings: Share Price Effects and Corporate Restructuring," *Journal of Financial Economics* (January/February 1986), pp. 153–186.

17. S.C. Meyers and N.S. Majiluf, "Corporate Financing and Investment Decisions When Firms Have Information That Investors Do Not Have," *Journal of Financial Economics* (June 1984), pp. 187–221.

18. F. Modigliani and M. Miller, "The Cost of Capital, Corporation Finance, and the Theory of Investment," *American Economic Review*, vol. 48 (June 1958), pp. 261–297; M. Miller "Debt and Taxes," *Journal of Finance* (May 1977), pp. 261–275.

19. B. Malkiel, *A Random Walk Down Wall Street* (New York: W. W. Norton, 1978), p. 273.

20. J.R. Ritter, "The Long-Run Performance of Initial Public Offerings," *Journal of Finance,* vol. 46, no. 1 (March 1991), pp. 3–27.

21. S.R. Perfect and D.R. Peterson, "Day-of-the-Week Effects in the Long-Run Performance of Initial Public Offerings," *Financial Review,* vol. 32, no. 1 (February 1997), pp. 49–70.

22. G. Sanger and J. McConnell, "Stock Exchange Listings, Firm Value, and Security Market Efficiency: The Impact of NASDAQ," *Journal of Financial and Quantitative Analysis* (March 1986), pp. 1–25; J. McConnell and G. Sanger, "The Puzzle in Post-Listing Common Stock Returns," *Journal of Finance* (March 1987), pp. 119–140.

Mutual Funds

Learning Objectives

An understanding of the material in this chapter should enable the student to

---

15-1.   Describe the various ways of organizing funds including their sales fees and whether they are open-or closed-end companies.

15-2.   Describe several types of pooled portfolio arrangements that are similar to but different from mutual funds.

15-3.   Describe the various types of mutual fund portfolios.

15-4.   Identify several mutual fund information sources.

15-5.   Describe three approaches to measuring portfolio performance that take account or risk, and explain how fund performance relates to goals, the market, and individual investor performance.

Chapter Outline

Mutual funds and similar types of investments are designed for people who want to have professionals manage some of their wealth. These pooled portfolio arrangements combine resources from many investors into a single investment medium. The average risk-adjusted performance of pooled portfolios is generally no better than that of the market averages. Nevertheless, mutual funds and the like appeal to many investors because they provide convenience, diversification, record keeping, safekeeping of securities, and portfolio management.

We begin this chapter by exploring the organizational structures of various types of pooled portfolio arrangements, including an in-depth look at selling fees. Next, the chapter discusses various types of mutual fund portfolios. A listing of some sources of information on mutual funds follows. finally, the chapter examines fund performance, paying particular attention to the difficulty funds have in outperforming the market.

DIFFERENT WAYS OF ORGANIZING FUNDS

mutual funds

Mutual funds and similar investments assemble and maintain pooled portfolios primarily for individual investors who have neither the resources nor the time to manage a portfolio of their own effectively. The ownership of these pooled portfolios is subdivided into shares or units. Each unit represents ownership of a fraction of the pooled portfolio.

Example: Each share of a fund with 10 million outstanding shares represents ownership of one 10-millionth of the fund's portfolio. Suppose that fund's portfolio has a market value of $100 million. Each share would, in effect, represent $10 worth of the portfolio. That is, a one 10-millionth share of a $100-million portfolio would be $10.

NAV

A share's pro rata ownership of the portfolio is called its net asset value *(NAV)*. If the value of the portfolio in the example above rises to $110 million, the NAV will increase to $11 (assuming that the number of shares outstanding does not change). Gains and losses in mutual fund investments largely stem from increases and decreases in their NAVs. Funds also distribute dividends and capital gains to their shareholders. These distributions reflect the shareholder's pro rata share of the portfolio's dividends and realized capital gains.

open-end investment companies

The vast majority of pooled portfolio investments are organized as mutual funds. Mutual funds are also called *open-end investment companies*: They maintain a continuous market for their shares. That is, the company that manages the fund stands willing on demand to buy and to sell the fund's shares at a price based on their NAVs.

Selling Fees on Mutual Funds

no-load funds

load funds

Mutual funds are marketed in two basic ways: The shares of *no-load funds* are generally sold directly to the fund's investors. The fund charges no sales fee on these transactions. *Load funds*, in contrast, sell their shares through an agent, such as a stockbroker or mutual fund salesperson.

Load Funds

Purchasers of load funds may incur substantial sales fees. These fees range from a maximum of 8.5 percent of the amount invested on relatively small acquisitions (under $10,000) to 1 percent on very large purchases (over $1 million). This sales fee is subtracted from the gross amount invested. The average load fund charges 3 percent to 6 percent on the minimum purchase, which typically ranges upward from $100 to $3,000. The $500 fee on a $10,000 load fund purchase leaves $9,500 for investment. A fee of 5 percent on the gross investment is equivalent to 5.3 percent on the net investment.

Example: Suppose a load fund has a NAV of $20 per share, and an investor must pay a 5 percent load. The formula for computing the price after load is as follows:

$$PL = NAV/(1 - L)$$

where:

PL = price after load
NAV = net asset value per share
L = load percentage

In this example, the NAV is 20, and the load percentage is .05. Accordingly

$$PL = NAV/(1 - L) = 20/(.95) = 21.0$$

> Thus, for an NAV of 20 and a load of 5 percent, the investor would pay $21.05 per share, or $1.05 above the NAV of $20 per share.

Although funds may charge loads of up to 8.5 percent, competition in the marketplace has forced the typical load percentage down. As of this writing, few funds charge loads of more than 5 percent. This sales fee still compares unfavorably with the 2 percent to 3 percent average commission on direct stock acquisitions (and much less with a discounter or over the Internet).

Some funds have redemption fees associated with them. These back-end loads are typically lower than front-end loads and frequently decline with the length of ownership.

Front-End Loading and Contractual Plans

front-end loading

Investors are sometimes persuaded to sign up for a plan to purchase mutual fund shares periodically over an extended period. This type of fund is called a contractual plan. For example, an individual might agree to invest $2,000 per year for the next 10 years. Perhaps the money is to be earmarked for a child's college education. The agent who sells such a plan is rewarded with an incentive commission based on the total amount of the planned purchase. Under this *front-end loading*, the purchaser pays much of this commission in the initial year of the plan. Not infrequently, however, the investor decides to cancel the program before all of the planned purchases have been made. Fees charged on front-end-loaded contractual plans can therefore be particularly costly to buyers who subsequently cancel their planned participation.

Concerns raised by the SEC spurred Congress to enact provisions for early redemption and maximum sales load percentages on monthly payments. Contractual plans have since declined in popularity.

12b-1 Funds

12b-1 funds

Some funds are permitted to charge annual 12b-1 fees (distribution and marketing fees) but are not doing so at present. Many 12b-1 funds charge less than the permitted maximum but with other added charges. With a 12b-1 plan, the selling agent is paid a commission at the time of sale but the buyer is not initially charged a fee. The SEG permits a 12b-1 fund to charge a percentage of asset value up to 1 percent, which is subtracted each year to compensate the fund for its selling expenses. Thus, the fund, in effect, advances the fee to the agent and recaptures the sum from the buyer over time (including an implicit interest charge).

Investors who redeem their 12b-1 shares before the full amount of the selling cost is recouped will generally be charged an exit fee, sometimes called the contingent deferred sales load (CDSL). Thus, 12b-1 funds are structured so as to incur very nearly the same percentage fee to buy and sell as regular load funds. Indeed, those who hold their shares for long enough may end up paying more in selling fees than if they had purchased a load fund.

Investors should carefully read a fund's prospectus to determine if a 12b-1 fee is charged. (Note that *The Wall Street Journal* quotations identify funds with a 12b-1 charge.)

What the Selling Fees Buy

The performance of the investment portfolios of no-load, and 12b-1 funds tend to be quite similar on the average. From the investor's standpoint, the principal difference among these types of funds is that those who purchase no-load funds do not incur an agent or sales fee, although, they do bear the overall selling expenses that the fund incurs. The pure no-load funds, however, have no agents to compensate. Thus, their selling expenses are relatively modest. Instead of paying a load (typically 3 percent to 6 percent), a no-load fund investor might incur selling expenses of a fraction of one percent per year.

However, the investor who buys through an agent has access to the service that the agent provides. Agents may advise their clients regarding the risks, potential returns, tax consequences, and other relevant characteristics of the funds they are able to offer through the company or companies that they represent. Mutual fund agents know the relevant features of their product. Some investors prefer, however, to find suitable no-load funds themselves with a bit of research.

Weisenberger's Investment Companies Yearbook

Prospectuses for no-load funds may be obtained by responding to advertisements in the financial press or writing to the funds listed in such guides as *Weisenberger's Investment Companies Yearbook* (an annual publication available in most libraries). Several directories are devoted exclusively to no-load funds. Published annually, they list various types of funds, along with their services, minimum investment amounts, addresses, and telephone numbers. One such guide—"Investors: Guide to Low Cost Mutual Funds and Mutual Fund Directory"—is available annually from the Mutual Fund Education Alliance (100 N.W. Englewood Road, No. 130, Kansas City, MO 64118. www.mfea.com). The *Handbook for No-Load Fund Investors* from (P.O. Box 318, Irvington-on-Hudson, NY 10533) is more comprehensive. Finally, *The Individual Investor's Guide to Low-Load Mutual Funds* is available to all members of the American Association of Individual Investors (625 N. Michigan Avenue, Chicago, IL 60611).

The list below shows the principal categories of fees and other charges embedded in mutual funds' total costs and expenses. These charges must be subtracted on a per-share basis to truly assess the return to the investor.

- **Sales Charges**
  - *Load fee* is the most obvious cost of mutual fund ownership and is the sales charge that owners of load fund shares pay. Although load fees can be substantial (as high as 8.5 percent), investors can avoid or limit the fee by buying a no-load or low-load fund. Load fees are front-end charges and are therefore paid as a deduction from the investor's initial investments.
  - *Contingent deferred sales load (CDSL)* is an alternative to a regular load. The regular load is replaced by an annual charge on all the fund's assets. To ensure that each investor pays the total load, a deferred sales load or exit fee is imposed, although the charge is reduced for each year in which the share are held.
  - *Loads on reinvestment of dividends*, also referred to as *dividend reinvestment at offering price*, are sales loads charged against the shareholder's dividends when the dividends are reinvested in the fund.

- **Redemption and Transaction Charges**
  - *Transaction fees* are paid when; the fund shares are purchased. These costs are borne by the investor making the transaction, rather than by the fund itself. If these charges are added to the fund itself, they should not be considered a sales load.
  - *Redemption charges* are paid when shares are liquidated or exchanged into shares of another fund.

- **Operating Expense Ratio**
  - The *investment advisory fee*, which is often called the *management fee*, is paid to the fund's adviser for portfolio supervision and for general management of the fund's affairs. Sometimes the fee includes an incentive/penalty provision based on the fund's performance relative to a particular benchmark.
  - *Administrative costs* are the costs of administering the portfolio, incurred largely through recordkeeping and transaction services (brokerage costs) to buy and sell securities, and are a necessary cost borne by fund shareholders.
  - *Other operating expenses* include custodial fees, legal and audit fees, and directors' fees.
  - *12b-1 distribution fees*, which are highly controversial, are fees that cover the costs of advertising, marketing, and distribution services. A fund adviser imposes these fees to increase fund assets and presumably to hire a larger, more competent staff.

- **Invisible Cost of Transactions**
  - The *invisible cost of fund transactions* is typically ignored because, as the term implies, the cost is invisible. Nevertheless, estimates suggest that it is real and significant. For example, a possible hidden cost in executing portfolio transactions is the

price pressure caused by trading a large block. Buying or selling a large block may drive the price up or down beyond what would have occurred with a smaller number of shares.

Open-End and Closed-End Investment Companies

investment company

Mutual funds are one of a broader class of investment vehicles called an *investment company*. We have already noted that mutual funds are called open-end investment companies. A mutual fund's number of outstanding shares increases or decreases with new sales and/or with redemptions.

closed-end funds

If mutual funds are open-end investment companies, what are closed-end investment companies? The answer has to do with their approach toward the sale of additional shares. The number of closed-end investment company shares outstanding almost always remains constant. *Closed-end funds* are established at a particular time with a set number of outstanding shares. Thereafter, the number of available shares will rarely change.

Unlike purchasers of mutual funds, buyers of shares in a closed-end fund do not automatically receive a prospectus when they consider a purchase. Investors buy and sell their shares in the open market much as with any other corporation. Thus, their share prices are determined by the interplay of supply and demand. The shares may sell for a premium or, more commonly, at a discount from their NAV. These discounts can often be 15 percent to 20 percent or more.

Large shareholders sometimes force closed-end funds to convert to open end. Relatively substantial resources are required to force such a reorganization. These conversions tend to be quite profitable for the fund holders, even small fund holders.

Example:	Consider a 10-million-share, closed-end fund with a per share NAV and market price of $10 and $7.50, respectively. This fund might be a takeover tempting target. Although a takeover effort would probably drive the price up, perhaps 3 million shares could be purchased over time at an average cost of $8.50. If the remaining stock is widely dispersed, 30 percent of the outstanding shares should be sufficient for control. The new control group could quickly convert to an open-end fund. By offering to buy back shares at their NAV, the fund would immediately make each holder's shares worth the $10 NAV (assuming that there was no price change while the takeover was underway).

Investment Company Quotations (Closed End)

Closed-end fund quotations can be found in *The Wall Street Journal*, *The New York Times*, and *Barron's*. Funds are grouped into a number of categories such as general equity funds, U.S. government bond funds, specialized equity funds, and convertible funds. *Investment company quotations* typically contain the following information:

- name of fund and symbol
- market where traded
- NAV
- market price
- premium or discount of stock price relative to NAV
- 52-week market return

An example is as follows:

Fund Name Symbol	Stock Exchange	NAV	Market Price	Premium Discount	2-yr Market Return
Exwhyzee (XYZ)	N	27.40	25.10	−8	16.7
Abeecee (ABC)	O	42.15	44.20	5	−3.2

Mutual Funds Quotations (Open End)

Daily price quotes for mutual funds can be found in most major newspapers. The information varies from paper to paper. Typically, individual funds are listed under the fund family. For example, funds managed by The Vanguard Group are listed under *Vanguard Funds*.

The *New York Times* Sunday edition includes the following information:

- fund family
- fund name
- type of fund
- rating
- NAV
- weekly percentage return
- year-to-date percentage return
- 1-year percentage return
- 3-year percentage return

For example, The Vanguard Index 500 Fund is listed as follows:

Fund Family							
Fund Name	Type	Rating	NAV	Wkly % Ret.	YTD % Ret.	1-Yr % Ret.	3-Yr % Ret.
Vanguard Index							
500 Idx	LB	3/4	135.22	+5.0	−0.1	+14.2	+23.2

The meaning of various symbols and footnotes is explained in the newspaper. For example, LB indicates that the fund is a domestic general stock fund that invests in a portfolio described as large blend—the company stocks are generally large capitalization and a blend of both growth and value stocks.

Redemption of Funds

Most mutual funds are set up to facilitate relatively easy redemption at their NAV. Normally, investors can call or write for a partial or full redemption and receive a speedy reply. Most funds also have arrangements for an automatic withdrawal plan. This plan can be structured to provide a monthly income for the fund holder. Thus, the investor can have a fixed sum periodically withdrawn from the fund as long as the remaining balance is sufficient to cover the withdrawal. Some funds do charge a redemption fee. Investors can, however, normally switch funds within the same group (family of funds) without incurring a load or redemption fee or even having to deal with very much paperwork. Most funds do limit the number of switches per year and charge a modest fee. Some investors try to profit from market swings by switching between a group's stock and money market funds.

Unit Investment Trusts

unit investment trusts

Unit investment trusts are similar to—but distinct from—mutual funds and other investment companies. Units of these trusts, like mutual fund shares, represent part ownership of a common portfolio but, unlike mutual funds, unit trust portfolios are unmanaged. The absence of portfolio management expenses tends to enhance the return. These trusts are typically set up and marketed by a brokerage firm that receives an underwriting fee from the proceeds of the sale. Once assembled, most debt security portfolios can be left unmanaged until they mature. The secondary market for the ownership units of these trusts is relatively inactive. Thus, unit trusts are costly to trade prior to maturity, whereas mutual funds are easy to redeem. Few investors would want to hold an unmanaged equity security portfolio. Accordingly, most unit trust portfolios are composed of debt securities. As the cash flows are received, they are paid to the trust holders (net of any administrative costs). Once all of the cash flows have been paid out, the trust is dissolved.

Variable Annuities

variable annuities

Insurance companies, banks, and brokerages sell investments called *variable annuities*. These annuities originate at insurance companies and have much in common with mutual funds, closed-end investment companies, and unit investment trusts. Each of these investment types represents pooled portfolios of assets owned by a group of investors. Unlike the other types of pooled portfolio investments, variable annuities generate a tax-deferred return. Moreover, no tax liability is incurred when funds are shifted from one annuity to another (such as from a stock to a money market annuity). On the other hand, if an individual makes withdrawals prior to age 59 ½, he or she incurs a 10 percent federal income tax penalty.

Expenses and fees tend to be higher with annuities. Thus, the annuity investor gains some tax advantages but has less flexibility than a mutual fund investor.

Also, annuities have an insurance component that guarantees an income stream for life, depending on the specifications of the annuity contract. This insurance component is funded by the insurer from the funds invested. Normally, the expected value of the payout from the annuity is less than the NAV of the underlying securities. The insurance company's actuarial calculations require consideration of the probability of the annuitant's survival, rather than the probability of his or her death.

Hedge Funds

hedge funds

Hedge funds are a type of pooled portfolio instrument organized for maximum investment flexibility. For example, they may invest in derivatives, sell short, use leverage, and invest internationally. Most hedge funds take substantial risks, seeking correspondingly large rewards. They are typically organized as limited partnerships and allow only "qualified investors" to participate. These investors must demonstrate both the sophistication and the financial resources to understand and take the risks associated with such investments.

Hedge funds can have a substantial impact on the markets. (Consider the near collapse in October 1998 of Long Term Capital Management—a large and previously high-flying hedge fund that at its height was leveraged to the tune of more than $100 billion versus a capital base of $3 billion.) Most hedge funds are organized off shore to avoid the regulations imposed on U.S. funds.

**Types of Pooled Portfolio Funds by
Organizational Structures**

- Mutual funds: open-ended; price based on NAV
  - Loan funds: sold through salesperson for a commission
  - No-load funds: sold directly without a commission
  - 12b-1 funds: sales fee assessed over time; penalty charged for early redemption
- Closed-end investment companies: corporation-owned managed portfolio; stock traded on an exchange or OTC, usually at a discount from NAV
- Unit investment trusts: unmanaged; self-liquidating; largely for debt securities
- Variable annuities: mutual fund type of instrument originating at insurance companies
- Hedge funds: typically organized as off-shore limited partnerships for qualified investors; maximum investment flexibility

---

Other Types of Pooled Portfolios: Operating Companies, Partnerships, and Blind Pools

Several other types of pooled portfolios are available to the investor. For example, some operating companies hold such large portfolios of stock that they are, in effect, investment companies in all but name. Among the better known of these firms is Berkshire Hathaway. Berkshire Hathaway was once in textiles but now is primarily an owner of stocks. Its CEO, Warren Buffett, is highly respected for his adroit portfolio management. Buffett is also a multibillionaire (the second wealthiest person in the U.S in 1999 according to *Forbes*) as a result of his investments.

Most pooled portfolios are organized as corporations either as investment companies (open-ended or closed-end) or possibly as operating companies. They may also be organized as partnerships to take advantage of the greater flexibility and tax advantages of that form of organization.

blind pool

Perhaps the most risky pooled portfolio device is the *blind pool*. With a blind pool, the investor agrees to finance a venture whose precise purposes are to be revealed later. The prospective investor will, however, be told the pool's general purpose (to finance a program of risk arbitrage, for example). Most people who invest in blind pools do so on the basis of their faith in the investor or group of investors that they are bankrolling. In some instances, the investors are given a clue, such as the intended industry or investment approach. At other times, the investors are truly blind. Blind pools may be organized as shares of stock (usually of a closed-end fund), limited partnership interests, or debt securities (often to be used in as yet undisclosed takeover attempts). Somewhat surprisingly, many people are quite willing to buy these "pigs in a poke."

Unusual Ways of Organizing Pooled Portfolios

- Operating companies: A few erstwhile operating companies hold such large portfolios that their performances are more closely related to their security holdings than to their operations.
- Partnerships: Some mutual funds choose the partnership form because of its greater flexibility and/or tax advantages.
- Blind pools: Investors bankroll enterprises whose purposes will later be revealed; these pools are sometimes involved in takeover financing.

Taxation of Pooled Portfolio Investments

The general principle of pooled portfolio taxation is that each investor is taxed as if he or she owns a portion of the pooled portfolio directly. The issue is, however, more complicated than it might seem. When shares are bought and later sold, the difference is indeed a taxable gain (long- or short-term depending on the holding period). Funds also generate taxable income (to the holder) when they earn dividends or interest on their portfolio. Similarly, taxable income for the investor results when a fund realizes capital gain on its own portfolio. To qualify as a regulated investment company under Subchapter M of the Internal Revenue Code, the fund must distribute at least 90 percent of its gross income (dividends, interest, and capital gains). Accordingly, virtually all funds comply with the income distribution requirements. The investor is liable for income taxes on these distributions, whose timing and amounts may not always be easy to predict.

DIFFERENT TYPES OF MUTUAL FUND PORTFOLIOS

Most mutual fund portfolios consist of stocks and/or bonds (including money market securities and long-term debt securities). Mutual funds can, however, be set up to manage almost any type of investable asset, including commodities, options, coins, art, and precious metals.

Bond Funds and Balanced Funds

Many different types of bond funds are available in the marketplace. Money market funds hold short-term debt security portfolios. Several categories of long-term bond funds manage portfolios of corporates, governments, or municipals. These broad categories are divided into subcategories, such as high-risk corporates and intermediate-term governments. Balanced fund portfolios combine common stocks with bonds and preferred stock. They tend to have slightly riskier portfolios with somewhat higher expected yields than comparable-maturity bond funds.

The remainder of the chapter deals with equity (common stock) mutual funds. Other types of funds will be discussed in subsequent chapters.

Different Goals of Common Stock Funds

Common Stock Funds

growth funds
income funds

Common stock funds may be classified into a number of categories that reflect their managers' stated goals. These funds differ principally in their risk orientation. *Growth funds* emphasize appreciation potential and often accept considerable risk. *Income funds* concentrate on high-dividend, low-risk stocks with modest growth potentials. Middle-of-the-road (or "blend") funds tend to place a somewhat higher premium on stability than growth funds do but less than the income funds do. A fund's initial risk orientation may be determined from its prospectus. However, many funds drift away from their original goals over the course of a year or 2 depending on the fund managers' proclivities. To provide up-to-date guidance to investors as to the general orientation of common stock funds, Morningstar and Lipper have attempted to standardize fund classification, with generally good results.

Differences in Risk Orientation of Common Stock Funds

- Growth funds: stress appreciation potential; accept considerable risk
- Income funds: focus on stocks with potential for high dividends, low risk, and modest growth
- Blend funds: place more emphasis on stability than growth funds do but less than income funds do

---

Specialized Types of Common Stock Funds

sector funds

international funds
country funds
dual funds

Specialized common stock funds include those that invest in specific industries (Chemical Fund), types of companies (Technology Fund), or regions (Northeast Fund). These types of mutual funds are sometimes called *sector funds*. They come in a variety of categories.

International funds participate in some foreign markets. *Country funds* assemble diversified portfolios from the stocks of a single country. *Dual*

swap funds
social responsibility
    funds

funds assign their portfolio's capital gains to half of the shareholders while accruing dividends for the other half. Share selections depend principally on the investor's preferences and tax status. *Swap funds* permit purchases with stock of other companies. *Social responsibility funds* restrict their portfolio to companies not involved in activities that they consider objectionable (polluters, war materials, tobacco, alcohol, and so on). Penny stock funds concentrate on low-priced stocks.

Index Funds

index fund

One of the fastest growing types of funds is the *index fund*. Index funds are structured to mimic the performance of an index. Many funds are designed to duplicate (approximately) the performance of the S&P 500 Index. Others may target the performance of some other broad-based index such as the Dow Jones Industrials or the NYSE Composite. Others may seek to emulate a narrower index, such as that for a particular industry (oils, chemicals, steel, auto, real estate, and so forth).

One strategy to managing an index fund is to purchase the securities that make up the index in the exact proportions of the index. Another approach is to purchase the most important components, hoping that the others will perform similarly. Still other methods utilize the futures markets (index futures).

Because of transaction costs, management fees, and frictions in the process, most index funds slightly underperform their indexes. On the other hand, most index funds have low or no loads and much lower fees and expenses (and very low turnover) than more actively managed funds. As a result, the average index fund has a very good chance of outperforming the average managed fund on a total expense-adjusted basis.

Recent Trends

Like many other areas of investments, the investment company industry has experienced a number of changes over the past several years. One of the most noteworthy is the huge proliferation of new funds. Several thousand different funds are now active and available to the investor. Many of these new funds are very specialized sector funds. Fidelity Select Portfolios, for example, has even established what amounts to its own little stock market. Investors can invest in one of Fidelity's sector funds and then switch from sector to sector by making a phone call and paying a modest fee. Thus, they can use Fidelity to try to catch the trends in the market without incurring the substantial commission costs that would otherwise be involved. No doubt many more investors try this strategy than succeed.

Another recent trend is the move of some funds to convert from corporations to limited partnerships. Indeed, a number of existing mutual funds have converted to the partnership form of organization to gain some flexibility and tax advantages. In a partnership, for example, interest on federal government bonds escapes the state corporate tax that could otherwise be assessed on corporate income. Furthermore, as a partnership, funds are not as restricted in their short-term trading activity. Fund holders in partnership funds become limited partners; the management firm assumes the general partnership. Some partnerships have been organized to participate in leveraged buyouts. In another ongoing trend, since 1980, mutual funds can be bought on margin, used as collateral for loans, and sold short, much like other types of securities.

Still another trend is merely a recycling of the earlier "funds of funds" concept, in which fund holders' money is invested in other mutual funds. These funds claim to shift their portfolios to catch the best-performing funds of the moment. Generally, however, they end up only imposing extra customer expenses.

Finally, a number of closed-end funds have been established, often associated with well-known names. Most of these funds are marketed with a great deal of hoopla and then promptly fall in price. Few, if any, are able to outperform the market return after allowing for flotation costs and the discount in price relative to their NAVs.

MUTUAL FUND INFORMATION SOURCES

A major mutual fund information source is *Investment Companies Yearbook*, published by Weisenberger (www.weisenberger.com). This annual publication covers more than 500 funds, with page-long descriptions on each fund's history, objectives, special services, advisers, sales charges, and 10-year performance. Every month, Weisenberger also publishes *Monthly Mutual Funds Update—A Performance Summary & Analysis*, which updates the long-term performance of more than 400 funds; *Weekly Review*, focusing on closed-end funds, is delivered by fax or e-mail.

Forbes examines mutual funds in one of its two August issues. It reports recent and 10-year returns, along with sales charges and expense ratios. Standard & Poor's surveys about 400 funds in the monthly *S&P Stock Guide*. Each issue contains data on goals, type, size, NAV, distributions, prices, and yields. *Barron's* covers mutual fund performance quarterly.

Another comprehensive source is *Morningstar* through its "Morningstar Mutual Funds," which provides a single-page evaluation of more than 1,200 mutual funds every other week. *Morningstar* also covers more than 250 closed-end funds. Finally, the Investment Company Institute (www.ici.org), 1775 K Street N.W., Washington, DC 20006, publishes the *Mutual Fund Fact Book* and articles of general interest to the industry.

MUTUAL FUND PERFORMANCE

The last section of this chapter considers mutual fund performance relative to goals, the market, and individual investor performance.

Measuring Portfolio Performance

We know that risk and return tend to be related. Higher-risk portfolios should, on the average, produce higher returns than lower-risk portfolios. Thus, any comparison of portfolio performances should take account of risk. Three primary approaches to these risk-adjusted performance measures have been devised for this purpose: the *Sharpe ratio*, the *Treynor ratio*, and the *Jensen's alpha* measure. Each seeks to measure the return performance relative to the riskiness of the portfolio.

Sharpe ratio
Treynor ratio
Jensen's alpha

The Sharpe ratio (SR) is defined as

(Equation 15-1)

$$SR = \frac{R_p - R_f}{\sigma_p}$$

The Treynor ratio (TR), in contrast, is defined as

(Equation 15-2)

$$TR = \frac{R_p - R_f}{\beta_p}$$

The Jensen measure is

$$\alpha_p = R_p - R_f - [\beta_p(R_m - R_f)] \qquad \text{(Equation 15-3)}$$

R_p = portfolio return

R_f = risk-free return

R_m = market portfolio return

σ_p = portfolio standard deviation

β_p = portfolio beta

α_p = portfolio alpha

Thus, the Sharpe measure relates excess returns (return in excess of the risk-free rate) to total risk (σ_p), while the Treynor and Jensen measures relate excess returns to market risk (β_p), with the Jensen measure calculating the percent of return above or below the "expected" or "equilibrium" return based on the estimate of β_p. The Sharpe measure is more appropriate for an investor whose total wealth is not well diversified. Both the Sharpe and Treynor measures give relative rankings, while the Jensen measure, as noted, gives an actual estimate of above or below normal return.

Fund Performance Relative to Goals

Funds usually behave in a manner that is consistent with their stated objectives. That is, funds that advertise themselves as being aggressive assemble risky portfolios and generally achieve somewhat above-average long-term returns. Funds that claim to be less risk oriented usually assemble portfolios of more stable stocks and generate lower but more secure returns. Most mutual fund performance studies find that average fund performance is indistinguishable from that of index funds.[1]

Why Mutual Funds on Average Do Not Outperform the Market

Most mutual funds do not earn abnormal risk-adjusted returns. Outperforming a relatively efficient market (such as the U.S. stock market) is difficult. Still, mutual funds do have the resources to hire the best talent, collect the most useful information, and analyze it with the most sophisticated techniques. Furthermore, their large size should facilitate operational efficiency—especially when securities are bought in quantities qualifying for commission discounts. Why then, with all these advantages, do the funds as a group so rarely outperform the market? There are several reasons:

- *Institutional investors constitute a large part of the market.* Outperforming the average would be difficult for any group of investors who make up a large part of the average. Institutions hold at least 40 percent of the total value of U.S. stocks; a still higher percentage of the larger listed issues makes up most of the market indexes.
- *Some other types of large investors have advantages similar to those of the institutions.* Each type of institutional investor (mutual funds, insurance companies, pension funds, college endowments, foundations, and bank trust departments) has access to similar managerial talent, sources of information, and types of analysis. Furthermore, private investment managers, individuals with large sums to invest, and nonfinancial corporations with large stock

portfolios all have equivalent advantages. Thus, mutual funds must compete with other similarly positioned institutional and noninstitutional investors.

- *Some investors have even greater advantages than institutional investors.* Because their abilities and resources are comparable, the various categories of institutional investors should generate similar average performances. Still other investors may have an advantage over most institutional investors. For example, companies may be particularly adept at choosing attractive times to purchase their own stock. Corporate officials, however, may sometimes take advantage of their firm's stock repurchase decision to sell their own personal holdings; insider sales may signal a price decline. While institutions sometimes trade on inside information, insiders have better access and may be able to conceal their activities more effectively. Those who use inside information to generate excess returns do so at the expense of the remainder of the market. Therefore, some noninstitutional and corporate investors have advantages that may allow them to time their trades and select their investments at least as well as, and often better than, mutual funds. Furthermore, many investors with small- to moderate-size portfolios are as sophisticated as the large institutions.

- *Unsophisticated small investors make up only a small part of the market.* The remainder of the market is made up of unsophisticated investors with small- to moderate-size portfolios. The average performance of the market represents the weighted average performances of the portfolios of the various subgroups that compromise it. The average large (or sophisticated small) investor (institutional or otherwise) can outperform the market, therefore, only at the expense of these less sophisticated small investors. This is a difficult task for several reasons. Unsophisticated small investors are a relatively minor part of the market. Thus, a substantial amount of unsophisticated, small investor underperformance (vis-à-vis the market) is required to permit any appreciable overperformance by the remainder of the market. Small, unsophisticated investor performance may, however, be largely random and thus similar to the market as a whole.

- *Mutual funds have a number of disadvantages relative to many other types of investors.* Although mutual funds offer several advantages to investors, they also have a number of disadvantages that tend to lower their return by more than any likely advantage they may have vis-à-vis small unsophisticated investors.

Mutual Fund Advantages

Mutual funds, which are currently the most popular investment vehicle in the United States, provide several valuable services to individual investors that enable them to participate in financial markets with a minimum expenditure of time and effort. *Portfolio management*, the selection and timing of securities purchases and sales to meet the fund's investment objectives, is an important function best left to professionals. *Risk reduction* is achieved through *diversification*—the careful selection of securities whose returns are not closely correlated.

Mutual funds provide convenience in a number of ways: Current income and capital gains can be reinvested automatically; amounts can be transferred from one fund to another in the fund family by wire, telephone, or on-line; some funds allow check writing to facilitate withdrawals; record keeping, especially for tax purposes, is typically available.

Advantages of Mutual Funds

- Portfolio management
- Risk reduction
- Diversification
- Convenience

Mutual Fund Disadvantages

The disadvantages of mutual funds are as follows: First, owners' returns will exceed the market return only if a mutual fund's portfolio outperforms the market by more than the fund's expenses and management fees. These fees average about 1.3 percent per year for general equity funds. Furthermore, load fund owners incur both the sales fee on purchases of the fund's shares and the commissions the fund pays when it trades. Investors who acquire stock directly or through no-load funds will, in contrast, pay commissions only on the stocks purchased. Quantity discounts on the commission on large institutional trades (which are also available to no-load funds) reduce but do not eliminate the double-commission disadvantage of load funds.

Second, funds—particularly those with large portfolios—often adversely affect the market prices of the stocks that they trade. Sizable purchases tend to be above the most recent market price and large sales below it. Small investors, in contrast, can generally purchase up to several round lots (or even more for an actively traded stock) with little or no price effect. Funds sometimes attempt to counteract this problem (as well as the control problem) by assigning portions of their portfolio to several different managerial groups. Subdividing may reduce, but is unlikely to eliminate, the adverse price effects of their large trades. Furthermore, subdividing may increase management costs.

Third, large institutions are vulnerable to certain management abuses that reduce their returns. For example, some managers may churn their accounts, producing commissions for their broker friends but reducing the fund's return. A high turnover rate may represent window-dressing dumping of "losers" before quarterly reporting, frustration with past failures, a conspiracy to milk the fund through commission payments, or a sincere belief that active trading may increase the fund's return. Fund returns are often reduced by rapid turnover, however.

Fourth, institutional investors typically restrict their analysis to a small percentage of traded stocks. Institutions frequently focus on as little as 100 to 500 companies, compared with about 5,000 listed securities and at least 20,000 traded OTC. Institutional holdings are clearly concentrated among the larger firms. The institution is reluctant either to acquire a small-dollar-value position (since it will have very little impact on the institution's overall portfolio) or to take too large a percentage position in a small company (since the institution would then risk owning too large a percentage position to be classified as a passive investor). This reluctance tends to remove a very large number of stocks from the institution's choice set. Consequently, institutional attention on the large-capitalization segment of the market may reduce the likelihood of finding undervalued stocks. Many smaller-capitalization stocks may remain misvalued because much of the market ignores them. Individual investors, in contrast to institutions, are unconstrained when it comes to investing in such stocks.

Disadvantages of Mutual Funds

- Management fees, expenses, and loads for load funds reduce their returns.
- Large investors, such as mutual funds, usually adversely affect the market when they trade.
- Institutions are vulnerable to management abuses that reduce their returns.
- Institutions usually restrict their analysis to a small percentage of traded stocks.

Mutual Fund versus Individual Performance

We have seen that institutions, including mutual funds, do not generally outperform the market. Comparable evidence on individual investor performance is limited. The average small investor's risk-adjusted return could be inferior to those of both the market and the average mutual fund.

Investors who trade in small lots generally pay full (undiscounted) commissions. Furthermore, their small portfolios are unlikely to be well diversified.

If funds do not generally outperform market averages and if accurately predicting future fund performance is very difficult, should individuals invest in mutual funds (other than index funds)? In other words, should they pay for active professional management that does not increase the risk-adjusted expected return?

Investors who choose to have a fund manage their wealth should do so with their eyes wide open. They should expect no better than average risk-adjusted performance (relative to the stock market). Investors who believe that they can outperform the market may appropriately manage their entire portfolios. Relatively modest resources (for example, $10,000) may be sufficient to construct a well-diversified portfolio. Moreover, investors who are not especially risk averse may properly choose to manage even very small portfolios. Risk-averse investors of modest means with little confidence in their investment skills and investors with limited time for investment management may wish to have a mutual fund manage part or all of their wealth.

Investors in mutual funds will find relatively few reliable selection guidelines. Clearly, investors should prefer a fund with a risk level corresponding to their preferences. Also, a small, low turnover, low-expense ratio fund with favorable past performance may generate a bit better performance than the average fund. Finally, broad-based index funds (such as the S&P 500 Index funds) were very hard to beat in the 1990s. Whether that will continue into the future, however, is unknown.

SUMMARY AND CONCLUSIONS

This chapter has considered various aspects of mutual funds and related investments. First, it explored the organizational structures of several types of pooled portfolio arrangements, looking closely at selling fees(load, no-load, and 12b-1). Different types of mutual fund portfolios were discussed next. Most mutual fund portfolios consist of stocks and/or bonds, although they can be set up to include almost any type of investable asset. Finally, mutual fund performance was discussed next. Mutual funds and similar types of investors generally fail to outperform the market for a variety of reasons: Professionally managed portfolios comprise a large part of the total market, their expenses reduce their net returns, they affect the market when they trade, they are subject to various management abuses, and they are often restricted to relatively few companies. Nonetheless, mutual funds offer a convenient and relatively cost-effective way of diversifying. Investors who do not wish to manage their portfolios may well prefer to let a mutual fund handle their investment decisions.

CHAPTER REVIEW

Answers to the review questions and the self-test questions start on page 776.

Key Terms

mutual funds	hedge funds
NAV	blind pool
open-end investment companies	growth funds
no-load funds	income funds
load funds	sector funds
front-end loading	international funds
12b-1 funds	country funds
Weisenberger's Investment	dual funds
Companies Yearbook	swap funds
investment company	social responsibility funds
closed-end funds	index fund
unit investment trusts	Sharpe ratio
variable annuities	Treynor ratio
	Jensen's alpha

Review Questions

15-1. The $$$ Mutual Fund has a portfolio valued at $650 million and 30 million shares outstanding. Suppose over the next 12 months the fund's portfolio value increases to $800 million and shares outstanding increase by 2 million.
  a. What is the initial NAV?
  b. What is the percentage increase in the NAV?

15-2. Assume that the $$$ Mutual Fund in question 15-1 is a load fund that charged a 3 percent front-end load and paid a distribution of $.70 per share over the past year. What would the one-year return for an investor in the $$$ Fund be?

15-3. Discuss the relative costs of
  a. load funds
  b. 12b-1 funds
  c. no-load funds

15-4. Compare the performance of an investment of $3,000 per year for 5 years in each of the following. Assume that each fund generates a return on its net asset value of 11 percent per year:

a. a no-load mutual fund
b. a 12b-1 mutual fund with a 1 percent fee assessed at the end of each year
c. a front-end load plan assessing an 8.5 percent commission in the first year only

15-5. Continue question 15-4 as follows: Assume that the no-load fund does generate an 11 percent return.
   a. How high must the 12b-1 fund's annual return be for it to equal the end-of-period value of the no-load fund?
   b. Would the return on the front-end load fund have to be higher or lower than the result in 15-5a? Briefly justify your answer.

15-6. The %%% Closed-End Investment Company (%CEIC) sells for $25 with a NAV of $33. Suppose 10 million shares are outstanding and the P. Boom Pekans Group proceeds to take over %CEIC. The Pekans Group pays an average of $28 for 35 percent of the stock and then converts it to an open-end fund. Suppose legal costs amount to $500,000 and commissions are 2 percent.
   a. Compute the percentage discount on the initial NAV.
   b. If the NAV is $35 at the conclusion of the takeover, what is the gross profit?
   c. What is the net return after costs and commissions are factored in?

15-7. Briefly describe and contrast
   a. open-end investment companies
   b. closed-end investment companies

15-8. a. What is meant by a sector fund?
   b. What are families of funds and what are their benefits?

15-9. The Scupper Group maintains an extensive list of no-load sector funds. Results for five of the group's funds are as follows:

Fund Name	Prior Year	Dividends	Capital Distributions	Current Year NAV
Good Good	14.29	.53	.74	13.01
Bond Bond	12.89	1.12	.47	11.98
Go Go	7.01	.03	.26	13.08
Chip Chip	16.67	.89	.78	17.57
Cash Cash	10.00	.68	.00	10.00

   a. Compute the holding period return for each fund.
   b. The market index return for the year is 22 percent. What else, in addition to return, should be considered in making the comparison?

15-10. One year's results can be misleading. A better gauge of a fund's potential performance can be obtained from an analysis of its performance over several years. Consider the fund holding period return below:

Year	Good Good	Bond Bond	Go Go	Chip Chip	Cash Cash	Market Index
Year 1	10.5	8.8	17.7	13.5	6.8	12.5
Year 2	−8.5	6.0	−21.6	−3.5	8.4	−5.3
Year 3	15.7	11.4	31.4	23.5	7.3	18.9
Year 4	14.3	9.6	23.4	17.5	5.3	16.2
Year 5	−21.3	−9.1	−32.7	−14.5	11.5	−20.2
Year 6	12.2	10.3	53.4	31.4	7.9	24.3
Year 7	9.0	11.5	−12.3	16.3	7.1	14.5

Compute the geometric mean return and standard deviation of each of the five funds and market index, using results reported for 7 years.

15-11. Calculate the Sharpe ratios for the market index and five funds in question 15-10. Use a risk-free rate of 4.7 percent.

15-12. a. Compute the Treynor ratios of the funds and index in question 15-10 for the following betas: Good Good, 1.1; Bond Bond, .6; Go Go, 1.3; Chip Chip, .9; Cash Cash, .2.
   b. Compare the results with the Sharpe ratios calculated in question 15-11. Describe your method of comparison.

15-13. What advantages and disadvantages do mutual funds have relative to other types of investors?

15-14. a. What types of investors are most likely to find mutual funds attractive?
   b. What mutual fund attributes are valuable to all investors?

Self-Test Questions

T F 15-1. Mutual funds (open-end investment companies) stand willing on demand to buy and sell the fund's shares at a price based on their net asset value (NAV).

T F 15-2. No-load mutual funds are typically sold to investors by salespeople.

T F 15-3. Most load mutual funds charge an 8.5 percent fee on the sale of shares to the public.

T F 15-4. To purchase a fund with an NAV of $20 a share and a 5 percent load, an investor would have to pay $21.05 per share.

T F 15-5. Some mutual funds are sold under a purchase plan, whereby the buyer agrees to pay a large portion of the sales charge in the first year of the plan.

T F 15-6. Funds charging 12b-1 fees are technically classified as load funds.

T F 15-7. Closed-end funds typically issue a fixed number of shares for sale to the public.

T   F   15-8.   The shares of closed-end investment companies typically sell at their net asset value (NAV).

T   F   15-9.   Closed-end funds are not permitted to convert to open-end funds.

T   F   15-10.   Unit investment trusts are typically unmanaged investment portfolios composed of debt securities.

T   F   15-11.   Variable annuities generate tax-free returns to investors.

T   F   15-12.   Hedge funds are typically organized as limited partnerships and take large risks in seeking large returns.

T   F   15-13.   Blind pools may be organized as limited partnerships or closed-end funds.

T   F   15-14.   To qualify as a regulated investment company, a fund must distribute at least 80 percent of its gross income to its owners.

T   F   15-15.   Index funds typically have lower expenses and fees than those charged by actively managed funds.

T   F   15-16.   The Sharpe ratio measures excess returns to total risk.

T   F   15-17.   The Treynor and Jensen measures relate excess returns to market risk.

T   F   15-18.   Most studies show that the average risk-adjusted performance of mutual funds usually outperforms the market.

T   F   15-19.   The risk-adjusted performance of institutional investors is no better than that of mutual funds.

T   F   15-20.   Large institutions normally trade large blocks of stocks without adverse price effects.

T   F   15-21.   Institutional investors typically focus their analysis on all traded stocks.

T   F   15-22.   Most stock mutual funds in the 1990s were able to consistently beat the returns on S&P 500 Index funds.

NOTE

1. R. Ippolito, "On Studies of Mutual Fund Performance 1962–1991," *Financial Analysts Journal*, January/February 1993, pp. 42–50.

16

Options

Learning Objectives

An understanding of the material in this chapter should enable the student to

16-1. Describe the basic terminology used by option traders, and explain the speculative appeal of options that leverage provides.

16-2. Describe the markets where option trading takes place, and explain the various factors involved in option pricing.

16-3. Explain the mechanics and basic strategies of option trading.

16-4. Explain the mechanics of trading foreign currency options, index options, and interest rate options.

16-5. Explain the tax implications of option trading, and describe institutional participation in the option markets, brokerage commissions on options, and option trading for small investors.

16-6. Describe the basic nature of rights and warrants, and explain how these options are used.

Chapter Outline

DERIVATIVES

Stocks and bonds and most other types of securities offer their investors a limited set of choices. The securities can be bought, sold, or held. They may or may not pay dividend or interest income. Stock and bond investors, however, generally have no direct way of turning their securities into anything other than what they already are.

Derivative option securities such as calls, rights, and warrants, in contrast, can be exchanged (with or without additional funds) for some other security; puts permit their owner to sell some other security for a prespecified price. In any event, their value is derived from a combination of the current and expected value of the underlying security—hence the general name *derivatives*. Calls, puts, rights, and warrants are pure options, whereas convertible bonds, convertible preferreds, Americus Trust securities, and certain other types of securities are combinations. (These securities are discussed in more detail in chapter 17.) Combination securities derive value from two sources: the potential worth of their convertibility (the option component) and the income and principal payments that they promise to make (the straight security value). Pure options' values, in contrast, are sold

derivatives

separately and are based solely on the characteristics, risks, and opportunities of the particular underlying security. Because pure option securities and combination securities constitute two classes of the family of investments called derivatives and because they are an interesting and important component of the investment scene, two separate chapters of this book are devoted to them. Futures, the third major class of derivatives, are discussed in chapter 18.

Although this chapter concentrates on pure options, it also covers several of the key ideas of all options to help make the material in chapter 17 easier to digest. The chapter begins with a discussion of puts, calls, their special terminology, and their markets. It then explores the leverage potential, quotations, valuation, and performance in various types of markets for options. This is followed by an examination of the mechanics of trading, basic and aggressive strategies, options on other assets, and other aspects of options (taxes, commissions, and so on). Finally, the chapter considers rights and warrants. Appendices A, B, and C at end of this chapter explain the Black-Scholes option formula, put-call parity, and Turov's formula. Appendix D contains profit and loss diagrams.

PURE OPTION SECURITIES

calls

Calls, rights, and warrants are all options to purchase an asset such as a stock or bond. The option itself specifies a number of matters, including the identity of the underlying security, the number of units of the security under option, the cost per unit of exercising the option, and the period (almost always limited) over which exercise is allowed. *Puts*, on the other hand, are options to sell a prespecified number of units of a prespecified security at a prespecified price over a prespecified period. A few warrants permit the investor to purchase or sell bonds or other assets. The vast majority of option securities, however, facilitate the purchase or sale of common stock.

puts

warrants
rights

Warrants and *rights* are issued by the same company as the issuer of the securities underlying the option. The issuing company almost always satisfies warrant and right exercisers by issuing additional units of its stocks. Warrants often have lengthy exercise periods (for example, 5 years). Rights, in contrast, must generally be exercised within a few weeks of their issue. Companies distribute rights to their shareholders in order to raise equity capital. Rights are usually exercisable at an appreciable discount from the stock's preoffering market price. They normally trade in the secondary market until they expire.

Unlike rights, newly issued warrants are typically exercisable at prices well above the current prices of the underlying securities. Warrants generally trade in the secondary market until their expiration and then are exercised only if doing so is profitable.

Options Clearing Corporation (OCC)

Calls and puts represent private contracts between individual buyers and sellers. Technically, the Chicago-based *Options Clearing Corporation (OCC)* (set up by the options exchanges) manages and guarantees the option contracts. Thus, each put and call buyer and seller is contracting with the corporation, rather than directly. The numbers of buyers and sellers are, however, equal. Thus, in effect, puts and calls are private contracts between buyer and seller. The OCC acts as an intermediary between the two principals in an option trade. Unlike the exercise of warrants and rights, put and call exercises do not alter the number of shares outstanding. Call writers (sellers) must be ready to supply already issued stock (either from their own portfolios or by an open market purchase). Similarly, a put writer must be prepared to purchase existing shares.

Option Terminology

Option traders have their own special vocabulary. Several key terms are defined below:

striking price

- *striking price* (strike): price at which the option is exercisable (sometimes called the exercise price)

intrinsic value

- *intrinsic value:* for a call, the amount by which the stock price exceeds the striking price, or zero if the strike is above the market price; for a put, the amount by which the strike exceeds the stock price, or zero if below

time value

- *time value:* option price less its intrinsic value

in-the-money option

- *in-the-money option:* option with a positive intrinsic value (striking price below market price for a call; above for a put)

out-of-the-money option

- *out-of-the-money option:* option with a zero intrinsic value (striking price above market price for a call; below for a put)

at-the-money option

- *at-the-money option:* option with a zero intrinsic value (striking price equal to market price for a call or a put). In practice, near-the money is a term that is more accurate when there is little deviation between the strike price and the stock price.

premium

- *premium:* the price of an option contract determined in the market, which the option buyer pays to the option writer (equal to the sum of the intrinsic and time values). Note that some people use premium to refer to the time value. At the option exchanges, however, it is used as defined here.

Understanding Stock Options[*]

The value of an option depends heavily upon the price of its underlying stock. As previously explained, if the price of the stock is above a call option's strike price, the call option is said to be *in-the-money*. Likewise, if the stock price is below a put option's strike price, the put option is in-the-money. The difference between an in-the-money option's strike price and the current market price of a share of its underlying security is referred to as the option's *intrinsic value*. Only in-the-money options have intrinsic value.

For example, if a call option's strike price is $45 and the underlying shares are trading at $60, the option has intrinsic value of $15 because the holder of that option could exercise the option and buy the shares at $45. The buyer could then immediately sell these shares on the stock market for $60, yielding a profit of $15 per share, or $1,500 per option contract.

When the underlying share price is equal to the strike price, the option (either call or put) is *at-the-money*. An option which is not in-the-money or at-the money is said to be *out-of-the-money*. An at-the-money or out-of-the money option has no intrinsic value, but this does not mean it can be obtained at no cost. There are other factors which give options value and therefore affect the premium at which they are traded. Together, these factors are termed *time value*. The primary components of time value are time remaining until expiration, volatility, dividends, and interest rates. Time value is the amount by which the option premium exceeds the intrinsic value.

Option Premium = Intrinsic Value + Time Value

For in-the-money options, the time value is the excess portion over intrinsic value. For at-the-money and out-of-the money options, the time value is the total option premium.

Generally, the longer the time remaining until an option's expiration date, the higher the option premium because there is a greater possibility that the underlying share price might move so as to make the option in-the-money. Time value drops rapidly in the last several weeks of an option's life.

Volatility is the propensity of the underlying security's market price to fluctuate either up or down. Therefore, volatility of the underlying share price influences the option premium. The higher the volatility of the stock, the higher the premium because there is, again, a greater possibility that the option will move in-the-money.

Regular cash dividends are paid to the stock owner. Therefore, cash dividends affect option premiums through their effect on the underlying share price. Because the stock price is expected to fall by the amount of the cash dividend, higher cash dividends tend to imply lower call premiums and higher put premiums.

Options customarily reflect the influences of stock dividends (e.g., additional shares of stock) and stock splits because the number of shares represented by each option is adjusted to take these changes into consideration.

Historically, higher interest rates have tended to result in higher call premiums and lower put premiums.

Premiums (prices) for exchange-traded options are published daily in a large number of newspapers. A typical newspaper listing looks as [shown below].

In this example, the out-of-the money XYZ July 115 calls closed at 3 1/2, or $350 per contract, while XYZ stock closed at 112 3/8. The in-the-money July 120 puts closed at 8 3/4, or $875 per contract.

*Source: Options Clearing Corporation, Chicago.

Option & NY Close	Strike Price	Calls—Last			Puts—Last		
		May[5]	Jun	Jul	May	Jun	Jul
XYZ[1]	105[3]	7 1/2[4]	9 1/4	10 1/8	1/4	5/8	1 1/8
112 3/8[2]	110	3	4 3/4	6 1/4	1 3/16	1 7/8	2 5/8
112 3/8	115	13/16	2 1/8	3 1/2	4	4 5/8	5
112 3/8	120	3/16	7/8	1 3/4	8 1/8	8 3/8	8 3/4
112 3/8	125	1/16	s	13/16	r	s	r
112 3/8	130	s	s	3/8	s	s	18 3/4
112 3/8							

1) stock identification	4) closing option prices
2) stock closing price	5) option expiration months
3) option strike prices	r = not traded s = no option listed

Speculative Appeal of Options: Leverage

Investors can buy options on a large number of units of the underlying security for relatively small sums. Such an option position greatly magnifies (levers) the effect of price moves in that security. A given sum of money can purchase far more options than underlying shares. For example, consider a call option. An upward stock price movement generally leads to a greater percentage gain for option holders than for stockholders. (Turov's formula in appendix C at the end of this chapter assesses this relative gain.) If, on the other hand, the stock price is below the striking price as maturity approaches, the call options quickly lose their value. An option's price can, at worst, fall to zero. Because of this upside leverage and downside loss limitation, in-the-money call options are typically priced appreciably above their intrinsic values. Moreover, options with time remaining before expiration and striking prices that are not too far below the stock's market price may also command nontrivial prices. Far out-of-the-money options and any out-of-the-money options near their expirations are, in contrast, usually almost worthless. Although it is limited to the initial purchase price, the ultimate percentage downside risk of options is still substantial, of course, at 100 percent.

The following example illustrates the relationship between a stock's price and the leverage opportunities and risk of its associated call option. Suppose a stock selling for 100 has a call to buy at 100 that sells for 10. (Striking price = 100; intrinsic value = 0; time value and premium = 10.) Figure 16-1 illustrates the relationship between the performance of the stock and call options for various stocks' near-expiration prices. The vertical axis represents the percentage return for different values of the stock measured on the horizontal axis.

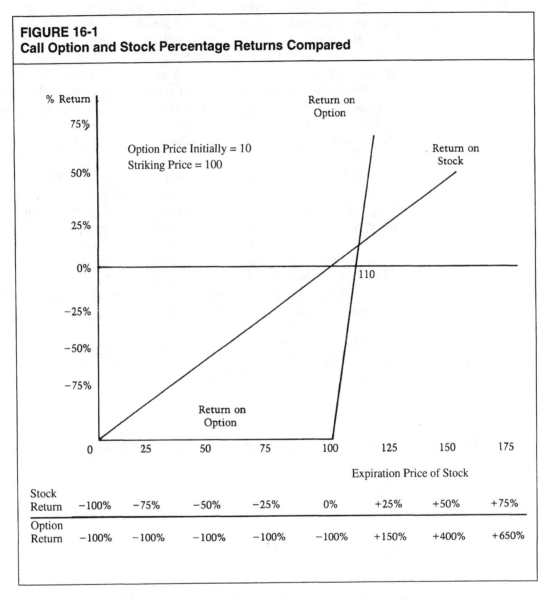

FIGURE 16-1
Call Option and Stock Percentage Returns Compared

Option Price Initially = 10
Striking Price = 100

	0	25	50	75	100	125	150	175
Stock Return	−100%	−75%	−50%	−25%	0%	+25%	+50%	+75%
Option Return	−100%	−100%	−100%	−100%	−100%	+150%	+400%	+650%

Near expiration, the call should be priced very close to its intrinsic value. For any price below 100, the call expires worthless and call holders lose their total investment. At a price of 100 to 110, the call's expiration price is less than its cost. For any stock priced above 110, the call holder makes money. Thus, when the stock is at prices below 100, the stockholder experiences a partial loss, compared with a total loss for the call holder. When the stock is at any price between 100 and 110, stockholders experience profits, while call holders experience losses. The call holder breaks even (ignoring commissions) when the stock price reaches 110.

Call holders' profits rise much faster than those of stockholders as the stock price rises above 110. For prices very slightly above 110, the stockholders' percentage returns are greater, but at somewhat higher prices, call holders' percentage returns greatly exceed those of stockholders. When the stock is at 111, for example, call holders' return is 10 percent, compared with 11 percent for stockholders (ignoring dividends). When the stock is at 112, however, call holders earn 20 percent, compared with 12 percent for stockholders.

The gain on the call rises dramatically as the price of the stock increases above the break-even level (110). A price of 120 produces a 20 percent gain for stockholders, while call holders realize a 100 percent gain. At a stock price of 150, call holders earn 400 percent, compared with 50 percent for stockholders. (Commission and dividend effects have been ignored in this analysis, but their net impact would generally be modest.) Appendix C at the end of this chapter shows Turov's formula, which gives the general method of calculating the rate of appreciation in the underlying stock that is necessary to make the call, right, or warrant a more profitable investment in percentage terms than the stock.

Note that stockholders and call holders are not in competition with each other. A rising stock price helps both; only the relative impacts are different. However, as we shall see, call option holders are in direct competition with call option writers (similarly for put holders and writers). Ultimately, the

zero-sum game options market is a *zero-sum-game*, as it is referred to by economists and other theorists, because what one party loses, another must gain.

Appendix D at the end of this chapter provides more diagrams similar to figure 16-1 showing the dollar value of profit and loss from various option and stock ownership positions and their interrelationships. These diagrams may help some readers to gain a better understanding of this material. We shall occasionally refer to these diagrams in the remainder of this chapter.

Options Markets

Actively traded rights and warrants are generally listed on a stock exchange. Most put and call trading takes place on the option exchanges. Unlisted puts and calls and less actively traded warrants and rights are traded over-the-counter.

Before listed options appeared, all option trading was in the over-the-counter market. OTC options had expiration dates and striking prices that varied greatly. Secondary market trading in OTC options was very haphazard. Virtually all option contract trading now takes place with listed puts and calls traded under rules of the OCC. Options have standardized striking prices and expire on a consistent, regular basis.

When listed option trading began in 1973, expirations were set to occur every 3 months. Three sets of expiration dates were traded at any particular time. Thus, for example, a company might have options on a January cycle. Its options would be set to expire every 3 months beginning with January. During various times of the year, it would have options expiring in January, April, July, and October. When the nearest expiration was January, the other listed options would be April and July. Once the January options expired, a new set of options would be listed for October. Other companies' options were set for February and March cycles.

Some companies' options still expire only every 3 months. Most companies with listed options, however, now have additional expirations that fill in the 2 nearest months. Consider, for example, a company with a January basic cycle. In early January, it would list expirations in January, April, and October. In addition, option expirations would also be listed for February. Thus, most companies now have a total of four options expirations. Two are in the nearest 2 months; two more distant expirations occur in the next 7-month period. Listed options are set to expire on the third Friday of their month of expiration. Their standardized striking prices and expiration dates facilitate a continuous market in identical securities.

The listed option market experienced spectacular growth throughout the latter half of the 1970s. The four exchanges (CBOE, AMEX, PHLX, and PSE) now list options on a very substantial number of stocks. The underlying values in option trading in these issues often exceed those of the underlying shares.

LEAPs®

Puts and calls are normally written for relatively short periods (9 months is typically the longest available); however, a 1990 innovation in the options market called long-term equity anticipation securities *(LEAPs®)* with expiration dates as long as 3 years—and covering both calls and puts—was introduced on the Chicago Board Options Exchange (CBOE) and the American Stock Exchange (AMEX). LEAPs® are also traded on the Philadelphia Stock Exchange (PHLX) and the Pacific Stock Exchange (PSE).

LEAPs® calls enable the investor to benefit from a stock price increase without purchasing the stock outright. In addition, the investor does not have to manage each LEAPs® position daily as a result of taking an initial LEAPs® position. LEAPs® puts provide stockowners with a hedge against significant decreases in their stocks.

LEAPs® also appeal to investors who want to take a longer-term position in some of the options they currently trade. (As mentioned above, expiration dates can be as long as 3 years.) The expiration date for LEAPs® is the Saturday following the third Friday of the expiration month. Equity LEAPs® expire in January.

Setting Strike Prices

Striking prices are initially set at levels that are divisible by 5 or 10 (or in some cases 2½) and closest to the current stock price. Thus, a stock trading at 43 would typically have options listed at 40 and 45. Similarly, a stock trading at 21 would have options listed at 20 and 22½. Stock prices, however, fluctuate over time. Options with strikes that were near the market price when initially listed will not necessarily remain near the market. As a stock price moves away from the available strikes, trading becomes unattractive in the existing options.

For example, a call with a strike of 30 on a stock selling for 50 will be priced too high to offer very much leverage. Similarly, a call with an 80 strike on a stock trading at 60 is very likely to expire worthless. Thus, these options have very little speculative appeal because one side of the market or the other has few likely buyers or sellers.

Since stock prices can move quite a bit in a few months, some strikes can differ substantially from the current quote. Accordingly, new strikes are authorized at levels close to the stock's current quote whenever its price changes appreciably. The older strike options continue to be traded but are not replaced with more distant expirations as they expire.

Black-Scholes model

Value of an Option: Black-Scholes Model

The valuation of options has long intrigued financial theorists. F. Black and M. Scholes wrote the classic theoretical option pricing work,[1] following earlier work by P. Samuelson and others. Black and Scholes began with the assumption that investors could buy the underlying nondividend-paying stock and write (sell) calls so as to maintain a fully hedged position. (See diagram G in appendix D to this chapter.) For stock price increases, writing calls can be equivalent to short-selling the stock. (See diagrams B and D in appendix D.) With such a hedge, any change in the value of the stock's price could be offset by an equivalent but opposite change in the value of the short position in calls.

Example: Suppose that a $1 change in the stock price was known to cause a $.50 change in the call price. Investors could then construct a fully hedged position by writing calls on twice as many shares as are held. Since the investor is short two calls, a $1 increase in the stock price would be matched by a $1 decrease in the value of the call position. Similarly, a $1 decrease in the stock's price would be offset by a $1 increase in the value of the call position. In fact, any small

move in the stock's price would be precisely offset
by a change in the value of the option position.

hedge ratio

As time passes and stock and call prices change, the appropriate *hedge ratio* (required ratio) will vary. For example, the required ratio of two calls to one share of stock might later change to a ratio of three calls to one share of stock. The investor can maintain a fully hedged position by adjusting the ratio of shares to calls whenever necessary. Thus, if the required ratio changes from two calls per share to three calls per share, the hedger can write (sell) an additional call for each share held. The result of this process is

riskless hedge

called a *riskless hedge*—designed to insulate the investor from market moves in the underlying stock's price. Selling the calls provides a form of insurance against the contingency of market changes in the price of the stock.

In an efficient market, an investment in the combined riskless position should earn the riskless interest rate (approximately the rate on short-term governments). Using a model based on the assumptions stated earlier, Black and Scholes developed a mathematical call valuation formula that is a function of five variables. The precise form of the model is rather complex, but the most important results are as follows: Call values *increase* with these four variables: time to maturity, interest rates, the price of the underlying stock, and volatility (or variance); they *decrease* as the fifth variable—striking price—increases.

Five Variables in Black-Scholes Model

- time to maturity
- interest rate
- price of underlying stock
- volatility
- striking price

The Black-Scholes formula is more than just an interesting theoretical exercise. Active option traders often compute Black-Scholes prices to follow a strategy of buying undervalued options (vis-à-vis the model) and writing overvalued ones. The importance of Black-Scholes and its later extensions, therefore, cannot be overstated. It provided a strong theoretical underpinning to the whole development of the derivatives marketplace since the 1970s—the most dynamic part of recent financial markets. Investors who become deeply involved in option trading should definitely learn more about the specifics of the Black-Scholes model. (See appendix A at the end of the chapter.)

On balance, the results of Black and Scholes and later studies suggest that option pricing is a relatively efficient process. No doubt, some mispricings do occur, but most seem to be relatively brief and allow profitable trades only for those who can buy and sell at minimum transaction costs. The key to most successful option trading is effective analysis of the underlying stock's potential. An investor who can somehow identify misvalued stocks may be able to magnify the profit potential with options. Options, however, are short-term assets, which can quickly lose their value or "waste" if they are not exercised or closed out properly. Investors must watch options' values closely in the financial press in order to avoid losses. Even investors who correctly analyze stock values may lose money on the stocks' options unless the market price adjusts before their options expire. All too often, the investor may be right on fundamentals but wrong on timing and lose money as a result. Remember, too, as mentioned earlier, options trading in general (and futures trading, discussed in chapter 18) is a zero-sum-game—what one party gains another must lose.

Put-Call Parity

put-call parity

The Black-Scholes model effectively deals with pricing call options. Relating call prices to put prices is another theoretical aspect of option pricing. A put-like position can be created from a call and a short position in the stock. (See diagram H in chapter 16 appendix D.) Such a *manufactured (synthetic) put* will have the same type of payoff matrix as a put. The loss on the short position from a stock price rise is limited by the call, while profits from the short position will increase as the stock's price falls. Similarly, a long position in the stock plus a put, called a *manufactured call,* has the same kind of payoff as a call. (Combine diagrams A and E and compare with diagram C in appendix D.) A loss from a decrease in stock price is limited by the put, while profits from the long position will increase as the stock's price rises. Since a put can be converted into a manufactured call and a call can be converted into a manufactured put, the prices of the two options should be related. Indeed, according to "the law of one price," whenever two assets offer equivalent payoff matrices, their prices must be identical (or within a range permitted by such arbitrage expenses as transaction costs).

manufactured (synthetic) put

manufactured call

Traders normally prefer to buy puts or calls directly, but some people choose to manufacture puts from calls, or *vice versa,* when prices get out of line. Moreover, some brokerage firms try to profit from apparent price disparities by taking offsetting positions in the manufactured and nonmanufactured puts and calls *(conversions).* This arbitrage activity (see chapter 17 for a discussion of arbitraging) tends to drive the prices back toward their proper parity.

conversions

As with the Black-Scholes formula, the precise form of the put-call parity formula is a bit too complex to discuss in this textbook. Nonetheless, serious option traders should be aware of its existence. (The explicit relationship is presented in appendix B at the end of the chapter.)

In addition to manufacturing calls from puts and puts from calls, investors can manufacture option-like positions with stock and cash. For example, buying a long stock position coupled with sufficient borrowing is equivalent to a call. The cost of the loan sets a lower bound to losses. Although it is limited by margin restrictions, this strategy can be a viable alternative when no listed call is available. But this strategy is riskier than operating in the options market because liquidating the position if the stock falls is entirely at the investor's discretion, and it could lead to large unanticipated losses or bankruptcy if the timing is wrong. The call option, on the other hand, will expire or liquidate on its own.

MECHANICS AND BASIC STRATEGIES OF OPTIONS TRADING

exercise
assignment
settlement

American-style
  options
European-style
  options

Some relatively complex mechanics come into play in the *exercise*, *assignment*, and *settlement* of an option. The following discussion is taken from a pamphlet issued by the Options Clearing Corporation titled "Characteristics and Risks of Standardized Options." This pamphlet, which covers both *American-style options* and *European-style options*, must be supplied to anyone who wishes to open a brokerage account with the right to trade options. Thus, any brokerage firm should be able to give its customers a copy.

The Mechanics of Exercise, Assignment, and Settlement[*]

EXERCISE AND SETTLEMENT

Most buyers and writers of stock options ultimately close out their options positions by an offsetting trade. Investors should nonetheless be familiar with the rules and procedures applicable to exercise. Such an understanding can help an option *holder* determine whether exercise might be more advantageous than a sale. An option *writer* needs to understand exercise procedures because of the possibility of being assigned an exercise.

HOW TO EXERCISE—An American-style option may be exercised any time until the last trading day before it expires; a European-style option may be exercised only during the established exercise period.

To exercise an option the holder must direct his or her broker to give exercise instructions to the Options Clearing Corporation (OCC). To ensure that an option is exercised on a particular day, the holder must direct his broker to exercise before the broker's cut-off time for accepting exercise instructions on that day.

A broker's cut-off time for accepting exercise instructions becomes critical on the last trading day before an option expires. An option that expires

[*] Source: Options Clearing Corporation, Chicago

unexercised becomes worthless. A holder who intends to exercise an option on the last trading day before expiration must give exercise instructions to his broker before the broker's cut-off time. Investors should determine the applicable cut-off times from their brokers.

In highly unusual circumstances (e.g., where a broker is unable to receive instructions from its customers), a broker may make an exception to its regular cut-off time. However, for an option to be exercised, the broker must pass on its customers' exercise instructions to OCC before expiration. OCC can accept exercise instructions after expiration only in the unlikely event that OCC is unable to follow its normal procedures for receiving such instructions. With that very limited exception, OCC has no authority to extend the expiration time of any option.

Once an exercise instruction is given to OCC, it cannot be revoked.

ASSIGNMENT—OCC assigns exercises in standardized lots (25 contracts or less on the date of this writing). These assignments are made in accordance with established random selection procedures to Clearing Member accounts. A description of OCC's assignment procedures is available from OCC upon request. Assignments are ordinarily made prior to the commencement of trading on the business day following receipt by OCC of the exercise instruction.

Once exercises are assigned by OCC, the broker must in turn assign them to customers maintaining positions as writers of the exercised options. Market rules require that assignment to customers be made either on a random selection basis or on a "first-in, first-out" basis. Brokers must inform their customers which method is used and how it works. Regardless of the method used, writers are subject to the risk each day that some or all of their writing positions may be assigned.

An option writer may not receive notification that an exercise has been assigned to him or her until one or more days following the date of the initial assignment to the broker by OCC. This possibility creates a special risk for writers of American-style and currently exercisable European-style calls (other than for covered writers) when the underlying stock is the subject of a tender offer, exchange offer, or similar event. A writer could fail to purchase the

underlying stock on or before the cut-off date for the offer (i.e., the expiration date, or the proration date in the case of an offer for fewer than all outstanding shares). Such a writer may learn after the cut-off date that he or she has been assigned an exercise filed with OCC on or before that date. At that point, neither a regular-way purchase of the underlying stock nor the exercise of an option (e.g., the long leg of a spread) will enable him or her to deliver the stock on the assigned exercise settlement date. But if he or she fails to make timely settlement, he or she may be held liable for the value of the offer (because the nondelivery may in turn have prevented a buyer of the stock from making timely delivery to the offeror). This risk can be avoided only by purchasing the underlying stock on or before the cut-off date for the offer. Some offers require that tendered shares be delivered less than five trading days (the normal settlement time) after the offer's expiration date or proration date. In those cases, call writers must purchase the underlying stock at an earlier point—i.e., at least five trading days before the offeror's delivery deadline—in order to protect themselves.

SETTLEMENT—Settlements between brokers or their agents on exercised stock options are routinely handled through stock clearing corporations.

The regular exercise settlement date for stock options is the fifth business day after exercise. OCC, however, has the authority to postpone settlement when it considers such action to be necessary in the public interest or to meet unusual conditions. Each broker involved in an exercise settles with its own customer.

In certain unusual circumstances, uncovered call writers may not be able to obtain the underlying stock needed to meet their settlement obligations following an exercise. This could happen, for example, in the event of a successful tender offer for all or substantially all of the outstanding shares of an underlying stock or if trading in an underlying stock were enjoined or suspended. In such situations, OCC may impose special exercise settlement procedures. These special procedures, applicable only to calls and only when an assigned writer is unable to obtain the underlying stock, may involve the fixing of cash settlement prices in lieu of delivery of the stock. In such circumstances, OCC might also prohibit the exercise of puts by holders who would be unable to deliver the underlying stock on the exercise settlement date.

When special exercise settlement procedures are imposed, OCC will announce to its Clearing Members how settlements are to be handled. Investors may obtain that information from their brokers.

After investors in options markets (or those who wish to advise them) understand the mechanics of options, they must be thoroughly grounded in the basic strategies for using options. The following section, which includes many examples, is also from the Options Clearing Corporation.

Basic Option Trading Strategies[*]

The versatility of options stems from the variety of strategies available to the investor. Some of the more basic uses of options are explained in the following examples. For more detailed explanations, contact your broker or any of the exchanges.

For purposes of illustration, commission and transaction costs, tax considerations and the costs involved in margin accounts have been omitted from the examples. These factors will affect a strategy's potential outcome, so always check with your broker and tax advisor before entering into any of these strategies. The following examples also assume that all options are American-style and, therefore, can be exercised at any time before expiration. In all of the following examples, the premiums used are felt to be reasonable but, in reality, will not necessarily exist at or prior to expiration for a similar option.

Buying Calls

A call option contract gives its holder the right to buy a specified number of shares of the underlying stock at the given strike price on or before the expiration date of the contract.

I. Buying calls to participate in upward price movements

Buying an XYZ July 50 call option gives you the right to purchase 100 shares of XYZ common stock at a cost of $50 per share at any time before the option expires in July. *The right to buy stock at a fixed price becomes more valuable as the price of the underlying stock increases.*

Assume that the price of the underlying shares was $50 at the time you bought your option and the premium you paid was 3½ (or $350). If the price of XYZ stock climbs to $55 before your option expires and the premium rises to 5½, you have two choices in disposing of your in-the-money option:

1) You can exercise your option and buy the underlying XYZ stock for $50 a share for a total cost of $5,350 (including the option premium) and simultaneously sell the shares on the stock market for $5,500 yielding a net profit of $150.

2) You can close out your position by selling the option contract for $550, collecting the difference between the premium received and paid, $200. In this case, you make a profit of 57% (200/350), whereas your profit on an outright stock purchase, given the same price movement, would be only 10%.

The profitability of similar examples will depend on how the time remaining until expiration affects the premium. Remember, time value declines sharply as an option nears its expiration date. Also influencing your decision will be your desire to own the stock.

[*] Source: Options Clearing Corporation, Chicago

If the price of XYZ instead fell to $45 and the option premium fell to 7/8, you could sell your option to partially offset the premium you paid. Otherwise, the option would expire worthless and your loss would be the total amount of the premium paid or $350. In most cases, the loss on the option would be less than what you would have lost had you bought the underlying shares outright, $262.50 on the option versus $500 on the stock in this example.

Buy XYZ 50 Call at 3½		−$350		
Underlying Stock Rises to 55 & Premium Rises to 5½			**Underlying Stock Falls to 45 & Premium Falls to 7/8**	
1)	Exercise &			
	buy stock	−$5000	Sell option	−$87.50
	Sell stock	+$5500	Cost of option	−$350.00
	Cost of option	−$350		
	Profit	+$150	Loss	−$262.50
OR				
2)	Sell option	+$550		
	Cost of option	−$350		
	Profit	+$200		

This strategy allows you to benefit from an upward price movement (by either selling the option at a profit or buying the stock at a discount relative to its current market value) while limiting losses to the premium paid if the price declines or remains constant.

II. Buying calls as part of an investment plan

A popular use of options known as "the 90/10 strategy" involves placing 10% of your investment funds in long (purchased) calls and the other 90% in a money market instrument (in our examples we use T-bills) held until the option's expiration. *This strategy provides both leverage (from the options) and limited risk (from the T-bills), allowing the investor to benefit from a favorable stock price move while limiting the downside risk to the call premium minus any interest earned on the T-bills.*

Assume XYZ is trading at $60 per share. To purchase 100 shares of XYZ would require an investment of $6,000, all of which would be exposed to the risk of a price decline. To employ the 90/10 strategy, you would buy a six-month XYZ 60 call. Assuming a premium of 6, the cost of the option would be $600. This purchase leaves you with $5,400

to invest in T-bills for six months. Assuming an interest rate of 10% and that the T-bill is held until maturity, the $5,400 would earn interest of $270 over the six month period. The interest earned would effectively reduce the cost of the option to $330 ($600 premium minus $270 interest).

If the price of XYZ rises by more than $3.30 per share, your long call will realize the dollar appreciation at expiration of a long position in 100 shares of XYZ stock but with less capital invested in the option than would have been invested in the 100 shares of stock. As a result, you will realize a higher return on your capital with the option than with the stock.

If the stock price instead increases by less than $3.30 or falls, your loss will be limited to the price you paid for the option ($600) and this loss will be at least partially offset by the earned interest on your T-bill plus the premium you receive from closing out your position by selling the option, if you choose to do so.

Buy XYZ 60 Call at 6		−$600		
Buy T-Bill at 10%		−$5,400		
Underlying Stock Rises to 65 & Premium Rises to 8			**Underlying Stock Falls to 55 & Premium Falls to 2**	
1)	Sell option	+$800	Sell option	+$200
	T-bill interest		T-bill interest	
	(6 mo.)	+$270	(6 mo.)	+$270
	Cost of option	−$600	Cost of option	−$600
	Profit	+$470	Loss	−$130
OR				
2)	Exercise &			
	buy stock	−$6000		
	T-bill interest			
	(6 mo.)	+$270		
	Sell stock	+$6500		
	Cost of option	−$600		
	Profit	+$170		

III. Buying calls to lock in a stock purchase price

An investor who sees an attractive stock price but does not have sufficient cash flow to buy at the present time can use call options to lock in the purchase price for as far as eight months into the future.

Assume that XYZ is currently trading at $55 per share and that you would like to purchase 100 shares of XYZ at this price; however, you do not have the funds available at this time. You know that you will have the necessary funds in six months but you fear that the stock price will increase during this period of time. One solution is to purchase a six-month XYZ 55 call option, thereby establishing the maximum price ($55 per share) you will have to pay for the stock. Assume the premium on this option is 4¼.

If in six months the stock price has risen to $70 and you have sufficient funds available, the call can be exercised and you will own 100 shares of XYZ at the option's strike price of $55. For a cost of $425 in option premium, you are able to buy your stock at $5,500 rather than $7,000. Your total cost is thus $5,925 ($5,500 plus $425 premium), a savings of $1,075 ($7,000 minus $5,925) when compared to what you would have paid to buy the stock without your call option.

If in six months the stock price has instead declined to $50, you may not want to exercise your call to buy at $55 because you can buy XYZ stock on the stock market at $50. Your out-of-the-money call will either expire worthless or can be sold for whatever time value it has remaining to recoup a portion of its cost. *Your maximum loss with this strategy is the cost of the call option you bought or $425.*

IV.   Buying calls to hedge short stock sales

An investor who has sold stock short in anticipation of a price decline can limit a possible loss by purchasing call options. Remember that shorting stock requires a margin account and margin calls may force you to liquidate your position prematurely. Although a call option may be used to offset a short stock position's upside risk, it does not protect the option holder against additional margin calls or premature liquidation of the short stock position.

Assume you sold short 100 shares of XYZ stock at $40 per share. If you buy an XYZ 40 call at a premium of 3½, you establish a maximum share price of $40 that you will have to pay if the stock price rises and you are forced to cover the short stock position. For instance, if the stock price increases to $50 per share, you can exercise your option to buy XYZ at $40 per share and cover your short stock position at a

net cost of $350 ($4,000 proceeds from short stock sale less $4,000 to exercise the option and $350 cost of the option) assuming you can affect settlement of your exercise in time. This is significantly less than the $1,000 ($4,000 proceeds from short stock sale less $5,000 to cover short) that you would have lost had you not hedged your short stock position.

Sell Stock Short at $40	+$4000	Sell Stock Short at $40	+$4000
		AND Buy 40 Call at 3½	−$350
If Stock Price Increases from $40 to $50:			
Cover stock at 50 Proceeds from short sale	−$5000 +$4000	Exercise call to cover stock at 40 Cost of call Proceeds from short sale	−$4000 −$350 +$4000
Loss	−$1000	Loss	−$350
If Stock Price Decreases from $40 to $30:			
Cover stock at 30 Proceeds from short sale	−$3000 +$4000	Less call expire: cost of call Cover stock at 30 Proceeds from short sale	−$350 −$3000 +$4000
Profit	+$1000	Profit	+$650

The maximum potential loss in this strategy is limited to the cost of the call plus the difference, if any, between the call strike price and the short stock price. In this case, the maximum loss is equal to the cost of the call or $350. Profits will result if the decline in the stock price exceeds the cost of the call.

Buying Puts

One put option contract gives its holder the right to sell 100 shares of the underlying stock at the given strike price on or before the expiration date of the contract.

I.   Buying puts to participate in downward price movements

Put options may provide a more attractive method than shorting stock for profiting on stock price declines, in that, with purchased puts, you have a known and predetermined risk. The most you can lose is the cost of the option. If you short stock, the potential loss, in the event of a price upturn, is unlimited.

Another advantage of buying puts results from your paying the full purchase price in cash at the time the put is bought. Shorting stock requires a margin account, and margin calls on a short sale might force you to cover your position prematurely, even though the position still may have profit potential. As a put buyer, you can hold your position until the option's expiration without incurring any additional risk.

Buying an XYZ July 50 put gives you the right to sell 100 shares of XYZ stock at $50 per share at any time before the option expires in July. This right to sell stock at a fixed price becomes more valuable as the stock price declines.

Assume that the price of the underlying shares was $50 at the time you bought your option and the premium you paid was 4 (or $400). If the price of XYZ falls to $45 before July and the premium rises to 6, you have two choices in disposing of your in-the-money put option:

1) You can buy 100 shares of XYZ stock at $45 per share and simultaneously exercise your put option to sell XYZ at $50 per share, netting a profit of $100 ($500 profit on the stock less the $400 option premium).

2) You can sell your put option contract, collecting the difference between the premium paid and the premium received, $200 in this case.

If, however, the holder has chosen not to act, his maximum loss using this strategy would be the total cost of the put option or $400. The profitability of similar examples depends on how the time remaining until expiration affects the premium. Remember, time value declines sharply as an option nears its expiration date.

If XYZ prices instead had climbed to $55 prior to expiration and the premium fell to 1½, your put option would be out-of-the-money. You could still sell your option for $150, partially offsetting its original price. In most cases, the cost of this strategy will be less than what you would have lost had you shorted XYZ stock instead of purchasing the put option, $250 versus $500 in this case.

Buy XYZ 50 Put at 4		−$400	
Underlying Stock Falls to 45 & Premium Rises to 6		**Underlying Stock Rises to 55 & Premium Falls to 1½**	
1) Purchase stock	−$4500		
Exercise option	+$5000	Sell option	+$150
Cost of option	−$400	Cost of option	−$400
Profit	+$100	Loss	−$250
OR			
2) Sell option	+$600		
Cost of option	−$400		
Profit	+$200		

This strategy allows you to benefit from downward price movements while limiting losses to the premium paid if prices increase.

II. Buying puts to protect a long stock position

You can limit the risk of stock ownership by simultaneously buying a put on that stock, a hedging strategy commonly referred to as a "married put." This strategy establishes a minimum selling price for the stock during the life of the put and limits your loss to the cost of the put plus the difference, if any, between the purchase price of the stock and the strike price of the put, no matter how far the stock price declines. This strategy will yield a profit if the stock appreciation is greater than the cost of the put option.

Assume you buy 100 shares of XYZ stock at $40 per share and, at the same time, buy an XYZ July 40 put at a premium of 2. By purchasing this put option for the $200 in premium, you have ensured that no matter what happens to the price of the stock, you will be able to sell 100 shares for $40 per share, or $4,000.

If the price of XYZ stock increases to $50 per share and the premium of your option drops to 7/8, your stock position is now worth $5,000 but your put is out-of-the-money. Your profit, if you sell your stock, is $800 ($1,000 profit on the stock less the amount you paid for the put option, $200). However, if the price increase occurs before expiration, you may reduce the loss on the put by selling it for whatever time value remains, $87.50 in this case if the July 40 put can be sold for 7/8.

If the price of XYZ stock instead had fallen to $30 per share, your stock position would only be worth $3,000 (an unrealized loss of $1,000) but you could exercise your put, selling your stock for $40 per share to break even on your stock position at a cost of $200 (the premium you paid for your put).

Buy XYZ 40 Put at 2		–$200
Buy 100 Shares at 40		–$4000

Underlying Stock Falls to 30 & Premium Rises to 11		Underlying Stock Rises to 50 & Premium Falls to 7/8	
		Sell stock	+$5000.00
1) Exercise option to sell stock	+$4000	Sell option	+$87.50
Cost of stock & option	–$4200	Cost of stock & option	–$4200.00
Loss	–$200	Profit	+$887.50

Buy XYZ 40 Put at 2		–$200
Buy 100 Shares at 40		–$4000

Underlying Stock Falls to 30 & Premium Rises to 11	
2) Retain stock position	*
Sell option	+$1100
Cost of option	–$200
Profit on option	+$900
* stock has unrealized loss of $1000	

This strategy is significant as a method for hedging a long stock position. While you are limiting your downside risk to the $200 in premium, you have not put a ceiling on your upside profit potential.

III. Buying puts to protect unrealized profit in long stock

If you have an established profitable long stock position, you can buy puts to protect this position against short-term stock price declines. If the price of the stock declines by more than the cost of the put, the put can be sold or exercised to offset this decline. If you decide to exercise, you may sell your stock at the put option's strike price, no matter how far the stock price has declined.

Assume you bought XYZ stock at $60 per share and the stock price is currently $75 per share. By buying an XYZ put option with a strike price of $70 for a premium of 1½, you are assured of being able to sell your stock at $70 per share during the life of the option. Your profit, of course, would be reduced by the $150 you paid for the put. The $150 in premium represents the maximum loss from this strategy.

For example, if the stock price were to drop to $65 and the premium increased to 6, you could exercise your put and sell your XYZ stock for $70 per share. Your $1,000 profit on your stock position would be offset by the cost of your put option resulting in a profit of $850 ($1,000 – $150). Alternatively, if you wished to maintain your position in XYZ stock, you could sell your in-the-money put for $600 and collect the difference between the premiums received and paid, $450 ($600 – $150) in this case, which might offset some or all of the lost stock value.

If the stock price were to climb, there would be no limit to the potential profit from the stock's increase in price. This gain on the stock, however, would be reduced by the cost of the put or $150.

Buy XYZ 70 Put at 1½		–$150
Own 100 Shares Bought at 60		
Which are Trading at 75		
at the Time You Buy Your Put		–$6000

Underlying Stock Falls to 65 & Premium Rises to 6		Underlying Stock Rises to 90 & Premium Falls to 1/8	
1) Exercise option to sell stock	+$7000	1) Sell stock	+$9000.00
Cost of stock	–$6000	Sell option	+$12.50
Cost of option	–$150	Cost of stock	–$6000.00
		Cost of option	–$150.00
Profit	+$850	Profit	+$2862.50
OR		OR	
2) Retain stock position	*	2) Retain stock position	*
Sell option	+$600	Sell option	+$12.50
Cost of option	–$150	Cost of option	–$150.00
Profit on option	+$450	Loss on option	–$137.50
*stock has unrealized gain of $500		*stock has unrealized gain of $3000	

Selling Calls

As a call writer, you obligate yourself to sell, at the strike price, the underlying shares of stock upon being assigned an exercise notice. For assuming this obligation, you are paid a premium at the time you sell the call.

I.   Covered call writing

The most common strategy is selling or writing calls against a long position in the underlying stock, referred to as covered call writing. Investors write covered calls primarily for the following two reasons:

1) to realize additional return on their underlying stock by earning premium income; and
2) to gain some protection (limited to the amount of the premium) from a decline in the stock price

Covered call writing is considered to be a more conservative strategy than outright stock ownership because the investor's downside risk is slightly offset by the premium he receives for selling the call.

As a covered call writer, you own the underlying stock but are willing to forgo price increases in excess of the option strike price in return for the premium. You should be prepared to deliver the necessary shares of the underlying stock (if assigned) at any time during the life of the option. Of course, you may cancel your obligation at any time prior to being assigned an exercise notice by executing a closing transaction, that is, buying a call in the same series.

A covered call writer's potential profits and losses are influenced by the strike price of the call he chooses to sell. In all cases, the writer's maximum net gain (i.e., including the gain or loss on the long stock from the date the option was written) will be realized if the stock price is at or above the strike price of the option at expiration or at assignment. Assuming the stock purchase is equal to the stock's current price: 1) If he writes an at-the-money call (strike price equal to the current price of the long stock), his maximum net gain is the premium he receives for selling the option; 2) If he writes an in-the-money call (strike price less than the current price of the long stock), his maximum net gain is the premium minus the difference between the stock purchase price and the strike price; 3) If he writes an out-of-the-money call (strike price greater than the current price of the stock), his maximum net gain is the premium plus the difference between the strike price and the stock purchase price should the stock price increase above the strike price.

If the writer is assigned, his profit or loss is determined by the amount of the premium plus the difference, if any, between the strike price and the original stock price. If the stock price rises above the strike price of the option and the writer has his stock called away from him (i.e., is assigned), he forgoes the opportunity to profit from further increases in the stock price. If, however, the stock price decreases, his

potential for loss on the stock position may be substantial; the hedging benefit is limited only to the amount of the premium income received.

Assume you write an XYZ July 50 call at a premium of 4 covered by 100 shares of XYZ stock which you bought at $50 per share. The premium you receive helps to fulfill one of your objectives as a call writer: additional income from your investments. In this example, a $4 per share premium represents an 8% yield on your $50 per share stock investment. This covered call (long stock/short call) position will begin to show a loss if the stock price declines by an amount greater than the call premium received or $4 per share.

If the stock price subsequently declines to $40, your long stock position will decrease in value by $1,000. This unrealized loss will be partially offset by the $400 in premium you received for writing the call. In other words, if you actually sell the stock at $40, your loss will be only $600.

On the other hand, if the stock price rises to $60 and you are assigned, you must sell your 100 shares of stock at $50, netting $5,000. By writing a call option, you have forgone the opportunity to profit from an increase in value of your stock position in excess of the strike price of your option. The $400 in premium you keep, however, results in a net selling price of $5,400. The $6 per share difference between this net selling price ($54) and the current market value ($60) of the stock represents the "opportunity cost" of writing this call option.

Write XYZ 50 Call at 4		+$400
Own 100 Shares Bought at 50		−$5000
Underlying Stock Falls to 40 & Premium Falls to 0		Underlying Stock Rises to 60 & Premium Rises to 10
Retain stock Call expires	* 0	Stock called away at 50	+$5000
Option premium income	+$400	Cost of stock	−$5000
		Option premium income	+$400
Profit on option	+$400	Profit on option	+$400
*stock has unrealized loss of $1000			

Of course, you are not limited to writing an option with a strike price equal to the price at which you bought the stock. You might choose a strike price that is below the current market price of your stock [such as $45 in our example] (i.e., an in-the-money option). Since the option buyer is already getting part of the desired benefit, appreciation above the strike price, he will be willing to pay a larger premium [such as $6], which will provide you with a greater measure of downside protection. However, you will also have assumed a greater chance that the call will be exercised.

Write XYZ 45 Call at 6		+$600	
Own 100 Shares Bought at 50		−$5000	
Underlying Stock Falls to 40 & Premium Falls to 0		Underlying Stock Rises to 60 & Premium Rises to 15	
Retain stock Call expires Option premium income	* 0 +$600	Stock called away at 45 Cost of stock Option premium income	+$4500 −$5000 +$600
Profit on option *stock has unrealized loss of $1000	+$600	Profit	+$100

On the other hand, you could opt for writing a call option with a strike price that is above the current market price of your stock (i.e., an out-of-the-money option). Since this lowers the buyer's chances of benefiting from the investment, your premium will be lower, as will the chances that your stock will be called away from you.

Write XYZ 55 Call at 7/8		+$87.50	
Own 100 Shares Bought at 50		−$5000.00	
Underlying Stock Falls to 40 & Premium Falls to 0		Underlying Stock Rises to 60 & Premium Rises to 5	+$5500.00 −5000.00 $87.50
Retain stock Call expires Option premium income	* 0 +$87.50	Stock called away at 5 Cost of stock Option premium income	+$5500.00 −5000.00 +$87.50
Profit on option *stock has unrealized loss of $1000	+$87.50	Profit	+$587.50

In short, the writer of a covered call option, in return for the premium he receives, forgoes the opportunity to benefit from an increase in the stock price which exceeds the strike price of his option, but continues to bear the risk of a sharp decline in the value of his stock which will only be slightly offset by the premium he received for selling the option.

II. Uncovered call writing

A call option writer is uncovered if he does not own the shares of the underlying security represented by the option. *As an uncovered call writer, your objective is to realize income from the writing transaction without committing capital to the ownership of the underlying shares of stock.* An uncovered option is also referred to as a naked option. An uncovered call writer must deposit and maintain sufficient margin with his broker to assure that the stock can be purchased for delivery if and when he is assigned.

The potential loss of uncovered call writing is unlimited. However, writing uncovered calls can be profitable during periods of declining or generally stable stock prices, but investors considering this strategy should recognize the significant risks involved:

1) If the market price of the stock rises sharply, the calls could be exercised. To satisfy your delivery obligation, you may have to buy stock in the market for more than the option's strike price. This could result in a substantial loss.

2) The risk of writing uncovered calls is similar to that of selling stock short, although, as an option writer, your risk is cushioned somewhat by the amount of premium received.

As an example, if you write an XYZ July 65 call for a premium of 6, you will receive $600 in premium income. If the stock price remains at or below $65, you may not be assigned on your option and, if you are not assigned because you have no stock position, the price decline has no effect on your $600 profit. On the other hand, if the stock price subsequently climbs to $75 per share, you likely will be assigned and will have to cover your position at a net loss of $400 ($1,000 loss on covering the call assignment offset by $600 in premium income). The call writer's losses will continue to increase with subsequent increases in the stock price.

As with any option transaction, an uncovered call writer may cancel his obligation at any time prior to being assigned by executing a closing purchase transaction. An uncovered call writer also can mitigate his risk at any time during the life of the option by purchasing the underlying shares of stock, thereby becoming a covered writer.

Selling Puts

Selling a put obligates you to buy the underlying shares of stock at the option's strike price upon assignment of an exercise notice. You are paid a premium when the put is written to partially compensate you for assuming this risk. As a put writer, you must be prepared to buy the underlying stock at any time during the life of the option.

I.   Covered put writing

A put writer is considered to be covered if he has a corresponding short stock position. For purposes of cash account transactions, a put writer is also considered to be covered if he deposits cash or cash equivalents equal to the exercise value of the option with his broker. A covered put writer's profit potential is limited to the premium received plus the difference between the strike price of the put and the original share price of the short position. The potential loss on this position, however, is substantial if the price of the stock increases significantly above the original share price of the short position. In this case, the short stock will accrue losses while the offsetting profit on the put sale is limited to the premium received.

II.   Uncovered put writing

A put writer is considered to be uncovered if he does not have a corresponding short stock position or has not deposited cash equal to the exercise value of the put. Like uncovered call writing, uncovered put writing has limited rewards (the premium received) and potentially substantial risk (if prices fall and you are assigned). The primary motivations for most put writers are:

1) to receive premium income; and
2) to acquire stock at a net cost below the current market value.

If the stock price declines below the strike price of the put and the put is exercised, you will be obligated to buy the stock at the strike price. Your cost will, of course, be offset at least partially by the premium you received for writing the option. You will begin to suffer a loss if the stock price declines by an amount greater than the put premium received. As with writing uncovered calls, the risks of writing uncovered put options are substantial. If instead the stock price rises, your put will most likely expire.

Assume you write an XYZ July 55 put for a premium of 5 and the market price of XYZ stock subsequently drops from $55 to $45 per share. If you are assigned, you must buy 100 shares of XYZ for a cost of $5,000 ($5,500 to purchase the stock at the strike price minus $500 premium income received).

If the price of XYZ had dropped by less than the premium amount, say to $52 per share, you might still have been assigned but your cost of $5,000 would have been less than the current market value of $5,200. In this case, you could have then sold your newly acquired (as a result of your put being assigned) 100 shares of XYZ on the stock market with a profit of $200.

Had the market price of XYZ remained at or above $55, it is highly unlikely that you would be assigned and the $500 premium would be your profit.

Exchange-traded options have many benefits including flexibility, leverage, limited risk for buyers employing these strategies, and contract performance under the system created by OCC's rules. Options allow you to participate in price movements without committing the large amount of funds needed to buy stock outright. Options can also be used to hedge a stock position, to acquire or sell stock at a purchase price more favorable than the current market price, or, in the case of writing options, to earn premium income.

Despite their many benefits, options involve risk and are not suitable for everyone. An investor who desires to utilize options should have well-defined investment objectives suited to his particular financial situation and a plan for achieving these objectives. The successful use of options requires a willingness to learn what they are, how they work, and what risks are associated with particular options strategies.

Strategies for Use of Options

Some of the basic strategies described in the above OCC article are listed below, along with their corresponding diagrams in appendix D at the end of this chapter:

- Buying calls: diagram C
- Buying calls to hedge short stock calls: diagrams B and C
- Buying puts: diagram E or H
- Buying puts to protect long stock position: diagrams A and E
- Covered call writing: diagram F or G
- Uncovered call writing: diagram D
- Covered put writing: diagrams B and F
- Uncovered put writing: diagram F

SOME MORE AGGRESSIVE STRATEGIES

Puts

As discussed above, a put contract enables the holder to sell 100 shares of a specific stock for a set striking price at any time up to a specified expiration date. Put holders profit if the price of the underlying stock declines sufficiently. Puts can be used in a variety of conservative strategies (as explained earlier). A speculator, however, may buy a put in the hope of profiting from a projected decline in the price of the underlying stock. On the other hand, a speculator who feels that a particular stock's price is set to rise may buy the stock and hedge the position with a put. (See diagrams A and E in appendix D at the end of this chapter.) A decline in the stock's price increases the put's value, thus largely offsetting the loss in the stock. If the stock price rises, the put is allowed to expire unexercised. The payoff matrix of this strategy is very similar to that for a call position. Indeed, this strategy is equivalent to manufacturing a call.

Speculators who believe that a stock will be stable or rise may buy the stock and sell a put on it. The cost of the stock is, in effect, reduced by the put premium. If the stock rises, the trader profits from both the put premium and the price appreciation of the stock. If it falls, however, both positions will show a loss. (See diagrams A and F in appendix D at the end of this chapter.)

Manufacturing a Put

A speculator who believes that a stock's price is about to fall can short the stock and hedge the position with a call. The resulting position is very similar to buying a put. (See diagram H in appendix D at the end of this chapter.) In general, buying a put incurs lower commissions than buying a call and shorting the stock. When only calls are listed, however, investors who want a put-like position have no alternative to manufacturing it.

Put Buying versus Short Selling

Various methods are available to investors who wish to speculate on a stock's price going down. For example, rather than hedge a short position with a call, some speculators may simply short the stock. The unhedged short seller, put buyer, and manufactured put buyer all seek to profit from an expected price decline. Buying or manufacturing a put has several advantages vis-à-vis taking an unhedged short position. On the other hand, leverage cuts both ways, and time works against the put buyer, as puts eventually expire.

Advantages of Puts Relative to Short Sales

- The risk is limited to the original put investment.
- Puts generally offer greater leverage.
- Puts involve less psychological pressure to cover.
- Puts do not require shorting of dividend payments (but manufactured puts do).
- Put commission costs are lower (but manufactured puts' commissions are not).

Exercise versus Selling in-the-Money Options

Option holders should rarely, if ever, exercise an option (put or call) whose price reflects a significant element of time value. Most options with more than a few days until expiration will have a positive time value. Thus, a put whose expiration is not imminent will almost always be more profitable to sell than to exercise.

Near-expiration puts, in contrast, are likely to be priced at or near their intrinsic values. In this case, the sell or exercise question may be a closer call. Nonetheless, as with the sale of near-expiration in-the-money calls, a near-expiration in-the-money put is generally more attractive to sell than to exercise. The alternative strategy of exercising the put and simultaneously buying the underlying stock is generally inadvisable. Not only is the single put sale transaction simpler to execute, but it also involves appreciably lower commissions. On the other hand, the put holder may already own the stock and would like to sell it. In this case, exercising the near-expiration in-the-money put is usually the most effective way of disposing of the shares. Also, if the put sells for a substantial discount from its intrinsic value, purchasing the stock and exercising the put may be more attractive than selling the put outright.

Straddles, Strips, and Straps

straddle

Simultaneously writing a put and a call in the same stock with the same exercise price and expiration date is known as a *straddle*. (See diagram J in appendix D at the end of this chapter.) This technique will provide gain only if the stock price stays quite close to the striking price. The premium that the holders pay will be the maximum gain obtainable by this straddle. Any stock price movement has the potential to generate losses to the writer (unless offsetting options are acquired to close out the position). As with other option writers, straddle writers may be covered or naked. Writing straddles against a stock position is similar to writing a covered call option. Straddle writers have some downside protection and an opportunity to profit if the stock price rises or remains constant. In return for the additional premium, however, the straddle writer undertakes to buy more stock if the put side of the straddle is exercised.

Simultaneously buying a put and a call on the same stock with the same exercise price and expiration date is also known as a straddle, and the investor is indifferent to the direction the market will take. (See diagram I in appendix D at the end of this chapter.) The investor anticipates that the underlying stock will move either up or down to such a degree that the price rise of *either* the put or the call will exceed the total cost of purchasing both options. If the particular stock or the market is highly volatile, this strategy can produce gains. When the stock's price is relatively stable, losses cannot exceed the price paid to acquire the two option premiums. The straddle buyer is looking for volatility in the stock (either up or down). On the other hand, a straddle writer will make money if the stock stays near the striking price.

strip
strap

In the prelisted option days of the old Put and Call Dealers Association, two other types of put-call combinations were frequently encountered: strips and straps. A *strip* is a combination of two puts and one call; a *strap* is two calls and a put.

Spreads

spread

Simultaneously buying a call and writing a call on the same stock with the same expiration date but with different striking prices is known as a *spread,* and it can be established either as a bear or a bull spread. Purchasing an in-the-money call and writing an out-of-the-money call create a bull spread when both options are on the same stock. Typically, the options used in this spread have the same expiration dates, although different expiration-date options are also used. In a bull spread, the investor expects the price rise of the option purchased to at least equal the price rise of the option written. If the price of the stock does rise, the investor gains on the in-the-money call but loses on the out-of-the-money option.

A bear spread involves buying an out-of-the-money call and writing an in-the-money call on the same stock. If the price falls, the investor keeps the premium paid for the call that was written but loses the premium paid for the purchased call.

In both types of spreads, the investor limits the dollar amount of potential gain and potential loss arising from the option position. The gain or loss, though, represents a high percentage return on the investment.

Option spreads can more generally be formed by any simultaneous short and long position in options on the same stock that differ either in strike, expiration, or both. Similar types of combination spread trades may also be constructed from different-delivery commodity futures contracts. (See chapter 18 for a discussion of futures.) Under this nomenclature, the two basic types of option spreads are vertical and horizontal. A vertical spread combines short and long positions of options with different striking prices. A horizontal spread, on the other hand, consists of short and long positions for options with different expirations.

Other Types of Spreads

box spread

A variety of more complicated types of spreads is also possible to construct. For example, each type of spread using call options has a corresponding spread that uses puts. Thus, the spread trader can construct both horizontal and vertical spreads with puts. A combination of a call spread and offsetting put spread is called a *box spread.* Box spreads are attractive to undertake when the put and corresponding call spreads are mispriced relative to each other.

butterfly spread

A *butterfly spread* involves positions in four contracts. The spreader writes two contracts at one strike price and simultaneously purchases one contract below and one contract that is an equal amount above that strike price. The strikes on the two purchased options are equal distances from the two that are sold.

Example:	For a stock trading at 35, the spreader might write two 35s while buying one 30 and one 40. The combined position has an initial net intrinsic position (degree or which it is in or out of the money) of zero. The two options that were written (the 35s) are at the money, and the low strike option (at 30) is in the money by the same amount that the high strike option (at 40) is out of the money. As the price moves away from 35, the net intrinsic position remains at zero. At a stock price of 40, for instance, the option with a strike of 30 has an intrinsic value of 10, while the 40 is now at the money. The two 35s (which the writer is short) have intrinsic values of 5. Thus, the net intrinsic position remains at zero [+10 − (2 x 5) ≈ 0]. No matter what happens to the price, the butterfly spread position has a net intrinsic position of zero. Risk is limited, therefore, to the relative movements in the time values of the four options.

Normally, when the two at-the-money options are written, their time values are substantial. The far in-the-money and far out-of-the-money options will, in contrast, have relatively small time values. Thus, butterfly spreads are designed to make money when the price of the underlying stock stays near the level of the central strike. As the options approach their expirations, all of the time values move toward zero. If the stock's price has not moved much from the central strike, the butterfly spreader will profit as the spreads that he or she has written (are short) have higher initial time values than those that he or she has bought (are long). If, in contrast, the underlying stock's price moves a substantial distance from the central strike, the butterfly spreader's position will show a smaller profit or possibly a small loss.

Assembling Spreads

Spreads can be bought and sold as a package or put on one side at a time. Option market makers normally quote a price that reflects the ask on the long side and the bid on the short side. The investor may use limit orders to "leg on" a somewhat better price on each side. This piecemeal approach does incur some risks, however.

To avoid putting up margin, the investor needs to purchase the spread's long side first. Once the long side is on, the price of the short side could move adversely (down) before the spread is fully established. An investor would normally close a spread position by covering the short side first (to avoid being short without a hedge).

Regardless of how they are assembled, spreads are relatively complicated trades. They are only briefly explored here. Brokers can, however, give interested investors pamphlets from the options exchanges that explain spreads and various other aspects of option trading in much greater detail.

Ratio Writing

ratio writing

Ratio writing takes spread trading to an additional level of complexity. As with writing spreads, the ratio writer takes offsetting positions in options

---

Aggressive Strategies: Some Terminology

- Straddle: simultaneously writing or buying a put and a call in the same stock with the same exercise price and expiration date
- Spread: simultaneously buying a call and writing a call on the same stock with the same expiration date but with different striking prices
  - bull spread: buying an in-the-money call and writing an out-of-the-money call on the same stock
  - bear spread: buying an out-of-the-money call and writing an in-the-money call on the same stock
- Option spreads: taking simultaneous short and long positions on the same stock that differ in strike, expiration, or both
  - vertical spread: taking short and long positions on options with different striking prices
  - horizontal spread: taking short and long positions on options with different expirations
- Box spread: combining a call spread and offsetting put spread
- Butterfly spread: taking positions in four contracts—writing two at one strike price and simultaneously purchasing one contract below and one an equal distance above the strike price
- Ratio writing: taking offsetting positions in options in the same underlying stocks but with unequal numbers of options (unlike spreads) in the offsetting positions

on the same underlying stocks. Unlike spreads, ratios contain unequal numbers of options in the offsetting positions. Thus, the ratio writer is not fully hedged or covered. The risk is greater, but so is the potential gain.

Ratio positions can be established with different ratios of short to long positions, as well as with different strikes and different expirations. Clearly, ratio writing is a complicated procedure. It does, however, allow the writer to alter the payoff matrix from that of a standard spread. One final point to consider is the need for a margin deposit on the uncovered portion of the ratio position.

OPTIONS ON OTHER ASSETS

Virtually any standardized asset can be subject to the option writing and holding process, provided enough investors are interested in trading these instruments. Assets on which standardized options are written include

- foreign currencies
- stock indexes
- industry indexes
- interest rates (Treasury securities)
- futures contracts

Discussions of foreign currency, stock index, industry index, and interest rate options follow. Futures contracts are covered in chapter 18.

Foreign Currency Options

currency options

Options for several foreign currencies trade on the Philadelphia Exchange. Price quotes for these *currency options* are in cents or fractions of a cent. No single standard number of units of all foreign currencies exists. Rather, the size of each option contract varies with the relative value of the foreign currency. For example, in early January 2000, the size of an options contract was 50,000 for Canadian dollars, 31,250 for British pounds, 250,000 for French francs, 62,500 for Swiss francs, 62,500 for German marks, 62,500 for euros, and 6,250,000 for Japanese yen.

The value of a currency option changes as the value of the dollar changes in world markets. Table 16-1 shows a typical currency options report in major financial newspapers for the euro and the Australian dollar in cents per unit. (The price of options on currencies, like those for stocks, is stated at a per-unit price.) The interpretation for the March call at a strike price of 104 cents per euro is that the last price of the call was 1.34 cents and the volume was 18,000 contracts at 62,500 euros per contract. The call entitles the holder

TABLE 16-1
Currency Trading Options—Philadelphia Exchange
(January 11, 2000, for January 10, 2000)

		Calls		Puts	
		Vol.	Last	Vol.	Last
Euro (62,500 Euro-cents per unit)					102.77
104	Jan	1	0.12	. . . .	. . . .
104	Mar	18	1.34	. . . .	. . . .
106	Jan	2	0.01	. . . .	. . . .
106	Mar	2	0.76		0.01
Australian dollar (50,000 Australian dollar-cents per unit)					65.55
60	Jan	61	5.50	. . . .	0.10

to buy 62,500 euros at a strike price of $1.04 (a total of $65,000) for a call premium of $837.50 (.0134 x 62,500). The buyer must hope that the euro will strengthen quite a bit relative to the dollar because the spot rate for the euro versus the dollar on January 11, 2000, was $1.0277, and the call is currently out of the money.

Example 1:   An option on the euro has a contract size of 62,500 euros, and both the option's strike price and the market price of euros are $1.04. If a call option for the euro is priced at $0.008 (8/10 of a cent or 0.8 cents), the premium the investor pays equals $500 ($0.008 x 62,500 euros). A rise in the value of the euro relative to the dollar means that the market price of the euro has increased in cents per euro. If the euro rises to $1.06, the intrinsic value of the call is in the money and equals $0.02 per euro, or $1,250 ($0.02 x 62,500 euros). The call's market price rises from $0.008 to a value in excess of $0.02. The actual market price depends on how investors believe the euro will move in the future. If further price increases in the euro's intrinsic value relative to the dollar seem reasonable, investors will pay a premium greater than $0.02 per euro, and the call's price on the market will exceed $0.02. On the other hand, if opinion holds that the dollar will gain relative to the euro, the call holder will either sell or exercise the call and immediately convert the euros into dollars.

Example 2:   Now assume that the call on the euro in Example 1 has a value of $0.02, and that due to foreign currency option buyers' expectations of a continued rise in the euro's value relative to the dollar, the option now sells for $0.026. The market price of the contract is now $1,625 ($0.026 x 62,500 euros). The investor who purchased the option at $0.008 realizes a dollar gain of $1,125 ($1,625 – $500). If the investor purchased the option 3 months ago, the holding period return is 225 percent [($1,125/$500) x 100%]. If the euro had not risen, the investor would have lost the $500 premium.

Some holders and writers of foreign currency options engage in the practice illustrated in the above examples to provide a hedge for their other activities. For instance, investors who have foreign currency holdings (long positions in the currency) or own foreign-denominated bonds will buy puts to protect themselves against downward price movements. Also, many U.S. multinational corporations that expect to bring dividends or profits back to the U.S. on a quarterly basis will hedge their likely need for dollars by buying puts well before the date of remittance. Investors who believe the dollar will fall will purchase puts and then exercise the options if their expectations are realized.

Stock Index Options

Mechanics of Index Options

stock index options   Users of *stock index options* are able to buy or sell an entire stock market index, such as the S&P 500 (SPX) or the NASDAQ (NDX) stock exchange index, for the premium paid for the option. Instead of selecting either an index mutual fund—whose portfolio replicates a specific stock market index—or specific stocks—with which to go long if a prolonged market rise seems imminent—the investor "buys" the market by acquiring a call option on the index. Since the gain from the rise in the market is captured for a minimal outlay, the value of the option will rise with the increase in the index. Bearish investors, on the other hand, hold puts to gain from a decline in the market index.

As with stock options, standardized expiration dates and strike prices have been established for index options. Settlement between the writer and the holder takes place on the expiration date. Strike prices are written with five-point increments on the underlying index. If the SPX (the most popular of the indexes used for option trading) stands at 1402, put and call options at 1395 and 1405 and in ± 5 or 10 increments from there could be written and traded. When the index rises to new highs or lows, options for new strike prices around those levels are written and traded—often for months to come. The options exchanges will trade index options at strike prices well beyond any recent levels of the indexes (even well above historical highs) as long as buyers and sellers can be matched. Thus, on February 16, 2000, the SPX offered strike prices ranging from March puts of 1075 all the way to March calls of 1625. The SPX index value closed at 1402 on February 15. This range of highs and lows of 50-plus percent in strike prices is not found historically for most of the stocks underlying the S&P 500 for such a short period. (Only volatile high-tech stocks tend to exhibit a similar range in offerings of standard options.)

TABLE 16-2
Excerpt from Chicago Mercantile Exchange Index Options
Published February 16, 2000 (Figures for February 15)

S&P 500 Index (SPX)				Close 1402		
	Calls			Puts		
Strike Price	Feb	Mar	April	Feb	Mar	April
1395	16	34	. . .	8	28 5/8	. . .
1400	13	39	51	9	29	41 1/2
1410	8 1/4	34	. . .	13 1/2	34	. . .
NASDAQ-100 (NDX)				Close 3997		
	Calls			Puts		
Strike Price	Feb	Mar	April	Feb	Mar	April
3980	31 3/4	247	. . .	50	207	. . .
4020	47	213 1/4	281	61 5/8	291	. . .

Table 16-2 shows an excerpt of premium quotations for the SPX and NDX options from a typical financial page. This premium quotation is multiplied by 100 to determine how much the buyer pays (or the writer receives) for the option. For example, assume that the SPX stands at 1402 and the premium asked for a March call option with a striking price of 1410 on that specific index is $34. For an index option, the normal lot is 100 units. Therefore, the price for this call option is $3,400 ($34 x 100). Since the index is 1402, this call is currently out of the money and has no intrinsic value but only a time value of $3,400.

Each stock index option trades on a specific organized exchange; the normal lot is 100 units. As with company-specific stock options, writers of index options place margin deposits with their brokers for the period of the option or until the option position is closed through purchasing an offsetting contract. Unlike the stock options in which settlement of exercised options includes the delivery of the common stocks to the call holder (or to the put writer), settlement for stock index options is made in dollars. The amount of money that will be paid on the settlement date depends on the difference between the exercise price and the index. Multiplying this difference by $100 determines the amount that will be paid by the option writer.

Example:	Referring to table 16-2, suppose on February 15, 2000, a March call on the NDX with a strike price of 3980 is purchased, and the index closes at 4020 at the end of March (third Friday)—a difference of 40 or 1.0 percent. In this case, the writer's obligation requires payment of $4,000 [($4,020 – $3,980) x 100] to the holder. If the holder acquired the call at $247 from the writer for a cost of $24,700 ($247 x 100), the buyer's loss is $20,700, and the holding period return is –84 percent ([40–247)/247] over one month. The writer, of course, gains $20,700.

A similar put option at a strike price of 3980 would not be exercised since the index value in the example above exceeds 3980. Holders of puts exercise their options only when the strike price exceeds the index value on the day the option expires. However, if the purchaser of the put had bought the put at the same time as the call buyer, the put purchaser would have paid $207 per put ($20,700) and would have lost it all (–100%). Clearly, NASDAQ index options are not for the faint of heart.

Use of Index Options

The conservative and aggressive methods that investors use to obtain gains from stock options also apply to holding and writing stock index options. These instruments are very risky, however, and the premiums for a particular option can change drastically from day to day as the underlying index changes. If the market as a whole experiences increased volatility, the risk associated with index options rises, and because premiums increase with increased volatility, the price of playing the game increases.

Despite their inherent risk, index options are often used to protect an investor's stock portfolio. The closer an investor's portfolio mirrors the index, the better the index option can protect the portfolio from downward price movements using protective puts. Of course, an investor can sell individual securities to prevent capital loss, but transaction costs must be paid, and realized capital gains are subject to federal income taxation. By purchasing an on-the-money put, the investor protects the portfolio for the life of the option. (For large portfolios, investors need to purchase several puts.) As a long-term portfolio-protection strategy, the purchase of put options becomes quite expensive, particularly since periods of upward stock price movement are longer than periods when stock prices are falling.

Example:	Suppose an investor wishes to protect her $500,000 401(k) investment in an SPX mutual fund from the risk of a market downturn. Referring to table 16-2, consider the SPX at a strike price of 1395 for February puts at $8 ($800 = $8 x 100 for one contract). Suppose the SPX is currently at 1402. To protect her portfolio's intrinsic value from falling below a strike price of 1395, this investor should buy four puts. This number is derived as follows: First, divide $500,000 by 100 to determine how many index units are in the portfolio ($500,000 ÷ 100 = 500). Then divide the portfolio's index units by the index value to determine the number of contracts to purchase. (500 ÷ 1395 = 3.58). Rounding up to 4 (a whole number is required) the cost of the protective puts is 4 x 100 x $8 = $3,200.

Industry Index Options

industry index options

Like broad stock market index options, more selective *industry index options* are also available for protecting or speculating on narrowly diversified portfolios. These indexes and their options aim at the stocks within one industry, such as international oil stocks, utility stocks, airline stocks, or computer technology stocks. Except for periods of uncertainty, such as during the 1999 oil price runup, there is only minor interest in trading these options.

Interest Rate Options

interest rate options

Puts and calls on specific U.S. Treasury securities are called *interest rate options*. When market interest rates rise, the price of bonds falls. When this occurs, the premium paid to acquire a call option decreases for exactly the same reasons that the premium paid to acquire a call option for a particular common stock or stock index decreases. The premium for a put, on the other hand, rises as investors seek the protection the put provides during a period when bond prices are declining.

Usually, these options are written on certain Treasury obligations and for a relatively large dollar amount, such as $100,000, of a particular issue. These options are based on the average yield of the most recently auctioned 7-, 10-, and 30-year U.S. Treasury bonds. Like the options on short-term interest rates, these options are exercisable only on their last trading day. One unique aspect of these options is that their duration is only one trading cycle of 3- and 6-month options. Once these expire, no new options can be written on the Treasury bonds on which these options are based. The rationale for this practice is that most of the bonds are in portfolios that are not actively traded. Sufficient secondary trading does not exist to justify a continuing market for these options.

OTHER ASPECTS OF OPTION TRADING

Tax Implications

Option trading involves a number of relevant tax implications, including these three:

- Option profits and losses are treated as capital gains or losses, provided the trader is neither a broker nor a full-time trader (that is, his or her principal income source is not from trading).
- The profit or loss on an exercised call is not realized for tax purposes until the stock is sold. Thus, the investor can carry over profits to a following year and stretch short-term gains into long-term gains.
- A call option writer whose position is exercised (this problem could have been avoided by covering prior to expiration or assignment) will have to sell stock at the striking price. If that stock was purchased at a much lower price, the writer will incur a large taxable

gain. The writer can avoid realizing this gain by purchasing the stock on the open market for delivery at the striking price. For example, the writer might have written options at 70 on stock purchased at 40. If the stock's price then rises to 80, the call is sure to be exercised. Delivery of the original stock would cause the writer to realize a profit of $3,000 per 100 shares. If taking additional capital gains this year is unattractive, the investor might prefer to cover with newly purchased stock.

Institutional Participation in Option Markets

Institutional investors, such as pension funds and bank trust departments, have become increasingly active in the options markets. These investors can write options against their large stock portfolios. Moreover, the substantial commission discounts available to institutions makes certain types of combination trades attractive. In particular, conversions (offsetting positions in calls and manufactured calls) can sometimes be structured to yield relatively attractive riskless returns for institutional investors who can trade at minimal costs.

For the investor of modest means whose preferences lean toward these instruments, some mutual funds use options as an integral part of their investment strategy. Using conservative strategies to hedge a portfolio position against an adverse market movement or to earn additional income can result in enhanced portfolio return with a minimum degree of risk. Speculating in options by using such techniques as writing naked calls should be the domain of the market professionals unless the investor can withstand large losses.

Brokerage Commissions on Options

Most brokerage firms have a separate commission schedule for options. Like the schedule for stocks, the option schedule is based on the number of units (options) and dollar volume of the trade. Option holders who exercise their calls will also pay a commission on the purchased stock, and the writer will pay a selling commission on the called-away stock. Similarly, put traders who exercise also incur commissions on the stock trades. Because the gross profits on option trades, particularly spreads, are often relatively thin, investors should pay careful attention to the impact of commissions.

Option Trading for Small Investors

Despite the large volume of option trading that takes place on a daily basis, it fails to attract the typical small investor. One reason is that in addition to the necessary expertise required for successful use of options, online computerized trading contact with these markets is essential—something the small investor generally lacks. In addition, the luxury of being able to take enough time away from his or her primary employment to actively pursue a program of trading or writing may not be feasible for the typical investor. However, the technology is changing rapidly, and as the Internet expands, even investors of modest means may have more access to and familiarity with options—especially index options. As the baby boom generation matures, many so-called small investors have substantial assets ($500,000 and up) parked in 401(k) plans and the like. Many of these assets are in index funds for convenience and safety. As Internet trading increases, knowledge about options and the opportunities they pose for hedging even relatively small risks will inevitably improve.

RIGHTS AND WARRANTS

As pure options, rights and warrants have much in common with calls. The same basic valuation principles and risk-return trade-offs are present with all three types of securities. Nevertheless, each option type has some distinctive characteristics.

Rights

A company that raises capital by offering stock to new buyers dilutes the existing stockholders' interests.

Example:	A company with 10 shareholders, each having 1,000 shares (10 percent of the company) wants to sell another 10,000 shares. Offering these shares to the highest bidder might deny them to the current shareholders and thus dilute their positions. If outsiders buy all of the new stock, the existing shareholders will see their interest reduced by half. They had each owned 10 percent of 10,000, or 1,000 shares each. Now they will each own 5 percent of 20,000 shares.

A rights offering to existing shareholders allows a company to raise additional capital and avoid diluting the current shareholders' positions. These rights, which will specify the terms for the stock purchase (price and time frame), give first refusal on the new stock to the existing shareholders. Shareholders who want to maintain their interest can simply exercise their rights. Most holders of a trivial percentage of a very large company have little or no interest in maintaining their percentage ownership. Thus, they may prefer to sell their rights on the open market. Others, however, may take advantage of the offering to increase their investment in the company.

Rights usually allow purchase of new stock at a discount from the current market price. In the terminology of puts and calls, rights are in the money. In other words, they have an intrinsic value. If the stock's price then rises further above the strike on the right, the value of the right also increases. Rights trading is, however, relatively speculative since most rights have a very short lifespan—often only a few weeks.

One right is issued for each outstanding share, typically giving the holder an option on a fraction (say, one-quarter) of a share. Thus, the holder of 100 shares of the underlying stock might receive 100 rights, which would entitle him or her to buy 25 shares. As we have seen, rights are generally issued for short exercise periods at striking prices that are far in the money. Accordingly, rights are generally priced very close to their intrinsic values (little or no time value).

Cum-Rights and Ex-Rights

cum-rights
ex-rights

As with dividends, the offering announcements of rights specify a day of record for people who own the stock to receive the rights. Up to that day is the *cum-rights* period. After that date, the stock sells *ex-rights* (no right attached). Setting the record date a few days after the ex-rights date allows time for the company's record keeping. Generally, the shares go ex-rights in the marketplace 4 business days before the record date. Table 16-3 shows the typical timing of a rights offer.

TABLE 16-3
Typical Timing of a Rights Offering

Date	Day	Event
January 15	Monday	Rights offering announced for shareholders of record on Monday, February 5
January 29	Monday	Last day to buy the shares cum-rights
January 30	Tuesday	Shares go ex-rights
February 5	Monday	Actual record date

Rights Valuation Formulas

The value of the underlying stock depends on whether it is selling cum- or ex-rights. The stock's price will generally drop on the day it goes ex-rights. Subsequent buyers will not receive the rights.

Valuation during the Cum-Rights Period. Assume that buying 10 shares of XYZ at $40 gives the buyer enough rights to buy one additional share at $38. Accordingly, the buyer can buy 10 + 1 shares of stock for $438:

$$(10 \times \$40) + (1 \times \$38) = \$438$$

The shares' average price is $438 divided by 11, or $39.82, and the intrinsic value of one right is $40 minus $39.82, or $.18. An owner of 100 shares should be able to sell the rights for $18. Thus, the intrinsic value of one right during the cum-rights period is determined by the following formula:

$$\frac{\text{Instrinsic value of one right}}{\text{during cum-rights period}} = \frac{\text{Market price of stock} - \text{Subscription price}}{\frac{\text{Number of shares needed to}}{\text{subscribe to one share}} + \text{One share}}$$

Applying this formula to the above example yields

$$\text{Intrinsic value} = (\$40 - \$38)/(10 + 1) = \$2.00/11 = \$.18$$

The market value of the right may, however, differ from its intrinsic value. That is, rights' prices may reflect some time value.

Valuation during the Ex-Rights Period. As a stock goes ex-rights, its market value usually declines slightly (as with the ex-dividend date). The adjusted formula for the intrinsic value becomes

$$\frac{\text{Intrinsic value of one right}}{\text{during ex-rights period}} = \frac{\text{Market price of stock} - \text{Subscription price}}{\frac{\text{Number of shares needed to}}{\text{subscribe to one share}}}$$

If the stock drops by $.25 to $39.75 when it goes ex-rights, the intrinsic valued of one right is as follows:

$$\frac{\$39.75 - \$38.00}{10} = \frac{\$1.75}{10} = \$.175$$

How Leverage Works with Rights. Suppose that the stock rises to $45 after it goes ex-rights but before the rights expire. The new intrinsic value becomes

$$(\$45.00 - \$38.00)/10 = \$7.00/10 = \$.70$$

Investors who bought at $.20 (a slight increment over their initial time value) and sold at $.70 would have more than tripled their money in a few weeks. Had the stock dropped below the striking price, however, these would have been a total loss. Out-of-money rights that are about to expire have very little value. Thus, trading rights can be a rather risky short-term speculation.

Decline of Preemptive Rights

preemptive rights

At one time, most corporate charters contained a *preemptive rights* clause. This clause guaranteed shareholders the opportunity to maintain their proportional ownership. Preemptive rights have been voted out of many corporate charters, however. Companies claim that they need increased flexibility to sell shares in whatever manner seems most attractive at the time of the sale. As a result, most new stock issues do not incorporate the preemptive rights clause.

Warrants

Firms that might otherwise have trouble raising capital often sell warrants in a financing package that also includes bonds. Frequently, these bonds can be used as if at par to exercise the warrant. When the bond's price is below par, exercising the warrant becomes more attractive than using cash to purchase the firm's stock.

Example: Suppose a bond is issued with warrants that permit the purchase of 50 shares of XYZ stock at 20 when the market price is 15. No one would use cash to exercise at these prices. If the bonds are selling at 60 percent of par value, however, a bond that cost $600 could be used with the appropriate number of warrants to purchase 50 shares of stock that have a market value of $750. Clearly, the warrants would have a considerable value in this circumstance.

Exercising the warrants in the above example increases the number of shares outstanding (firms almost always use Treasury stock to cover warrants and rights). Therefore, in the normal case, the market price of the outstanding shares of stock before the exercise of the warrants will tend to fall somewhat, other things equal.

Frequently, start-up firms or firms with somewhat risky (but hopeful) prospects are the main users of the warrants route to financing. Since pure debt issues would have to carry higher yields, the firm would use the bond-cum-warrants approach to lower its initial financing costs. This approach allows the bondholders to share in the firm's growth while providing a more secure return on capital if the firm does not grow. It is akin to a protective put on a long position in the stock. A takeover threat may increase the risk of warrant ownership, however, because the takeover price may be less than the exercise price with no time value remaining.

A 1971 Internal Revenue Service ruling encouraged firms to extend the life of warrants that would otherwise expire unexercised. The possibility that a warrant's life may be extended increases the danger to investors who sell warrants short. The IRS now requires firms to report as profits the sale price of any warrant that expires unexercised. Exercised warrants, in contrast, do not cause the issuer to incur a tax liability. Warrant-issuing companies occasionally try to ensure that their warrants are exercised by supporting their stock price above the warrant's strike price near expiration.

SUMMARY AND CONCLUSIONS

Option securities offer many diverse investment opportunities. Pure options such as rights, warrants, puts, and calls tend to magnify the gains or losses from price changes in the associated stock. Owners of these securities obtain substantial upside potential, while their loss exposure is limited to the cost of their positions. Put and call writers, in contrast, take the opposite side of the bet. They have limited profit potential coupled with very substantial risk exposure. Actively traded options are usually listed on an exchange, whereas more thinly traded issues trade OTC. According to the Black-Scholes valuation formula, the value of a call should increase with the underlying stock's price and volatility, time to maturity, and the interest rate, and it should move inversely with its strike price.

Options seem to be priced relatively efficiently vis-à-vis the theoretical model. Put-call parity relates the price of puts to the price of corresponding calls. Options may be bought, sold, or exercised, or the option writer may write them against owned stock (covered writing), other options (spreads or ratio positions), or nothing but sufficient assets to cover (naked writing). As with most investments, option securities are generally priced to reflect their potential. Thus, to make money with options, investors generally need to have a better idea than the market about how the price of the underlying stock is likely to move.

CHAPTER REVIEW

Answers to the review questions and the self-test questions start on page 780.

Key Terms

derivatives
calls
puts
warrants
rights
Options Clearing Corporation
  (OCC)
striking price
intrinsic value
time value
in-the-money option
out-of-the-money option
at-the-money option
premium
zero-sum game
LEAPs®
Black-Scholes model
hedge ratio
riskless hedge
put-call parity
manufactured (synthetic) put

manufactured call
conversions
exercise
assignment
settlement
American-style options
European-style options
straddle
strip
strap
spread
box spread
butterfly spread
ratio writing
currency options
stock index options
industry index options
interest rate options
cum-rights
ex-rights
preemptive rights

Review Questions

16-1.   a.   Distinguish between a put option and a call option.
       b.   Explain the writer's obligations for each.
       c.   Why is purchasing a call not equivalent to writing a put?

16-2.   a.   What kind of option activity would an investor carry out to protect a profit in a stock he or she owns?
       b.   How would such a strategy differ from simply selling the position?
       c.   What factors should an investor consider when evaluating the two strategies?

16-3.   a.   Explain the meaning of the term striking price.
       b.   How does it relate to intrinsic value, time value, or being in or out of the money?

16-4.   The ASD Company's stock sells for 32, while a 6-month option to purchase it at 35 sells for 1 5/8. (Ignore time value in a.–d. Ignore dividends in a.–c.)
       a.   What price must the stock reach within that 6 months for the option investor to break even?
       b.   At what price do the stock and option investor earn the same return?
       c.   What are the percentage gains for each if the stock rises to 45?

d.   How would all of these results change if ASD pays one dividend of $.75 during the 6-month period?

16-5.   a.   What obligation does the writer of a covered call undertake?
         b.   What are the risks and prospective returns of a covered-call-writing strategy?

16-6.   The HiDividend Corporation's stock now sells for 25. At-the-money call options for 3, 6, and 9 months sell for 1 1/2, 2 1/4, and 2 7/8. Similar options with strikes of 30 sell for 3/8, 1, and 1 1/4. Compute holding period returns for writing each of these options. Ignore time value. Assume that there is an initial required margin of 10 percent of the starting stock price. Use this as your initial investment figure.
         a.   Assume first that the stock remains at 25.
         b.   Recompute the results if the stock rises to 30 at expiration.

16-7.   a.   What is a straddle?
         b.   Under what circumstances would an investor be inclined to buy a straddle?
         c.   When would an investor be inclined to write a straddle?

16-8.   a.   Briefly explain what a spread is.
         b.   What is the motivation for holding a spread?
         c.   What are vertical and horizontal spreads?

16-9.   The QWE Corporation's stock now sells for 25 1/2. Its January 25 calls are priced at 1 3/4, while the January 30s sell for 7/8.
         a.   What is the net cost (ignore commissions and margins) of a vertical bull spread with these calls?
         b.   Discuss the potential for gain or loss.
         c.   If commissions are involved, how would your analysis change?

16-10.   Repeat question 16-9 for a vertical bear spread.

16-11.   a.   Distinguish between a warrant and a right.
          b.   Which is typically the longer term?
          c.   Which is more likely to be out of the money?

16-12.   a.   Exercising warrants increases/decreases earnings per share. Explain.
          b.   Similarly, what is the impact of exercising rights on per-share earnings?

16-13.   XYZ stock is selling cum-rights at $50. The rights entitle the holder to five shares at $47 for every 100 shares owned.
          a.   What is their theoretical value?
          b.   Compute the theoretical value assuming that during the ex-rights period, the stock price falls by the amount implied by the dilution.

Self-Test Questions

T   F   **16-1.** Stock options are written by the issuer of the stock.

T   F   **16-2.** The value of a put will decline as the price of the stock rises.

T   F   **16-3.** When the market price of the stock is less than the exercise price in the option, a call is in the money and a put is out of the money.

T   F   **16-4.** The time value of an option is the difference between an option's price and its intrinsic value.

T   F   **16-5.** The largest option premium is for those call options that have a strike (exercise) price that exceeds the market price.

T   F   **16-6.** If the underlying stock is trading at $31, the intrinsic value of a put with a striking price of $30 is –$1.

T   F   **16-7.** Warrants are standardized options issued by corporations.

T   F   **16-8.** The investment premium (or time value) on a warrant that trades at $4, carries an exercise price of $35, and has a current market stock price of $33 is $2.

T   F   **16-9.** If the market price for the stock is below the exercise price on the warrant's expiration date, the warrant is theoretically worthless (has negative intrinsic value).

T   F   **16-10.** The largest loss that the buyer of an option can suffer is the loss of the intrinsic value of the put or the call.

T   F   **16-11.** The leverage potential is greater when purchasing call options than when fully margining a long position in the stock.

T   F   **16-12.** Conventional (traditional) options place virtually no limits on the conditions of the contract, as long as the writer and buyer agree to terms.

T   F   **16-13.** Listed options have standardized expiration dates and striking prices.

T   F   **16-14.** Option users can use market, limit, and stop orders in their trading of puts and calls.

T   F   **16-15.** If an option holder elects to exercise the options, a random selection procedure under the auspices of the Options Clearing Corporation (OCC) selects the customer who has written the option to fulfill the contract.

T   F   **16-16.** Transaction costs for executing put and call trades are relatively low compared to the dollar size of the transaction itself and to the costs for similar dollar-size transactions of other securities.

T   F   **16-17.** The purchase of an out-of-the-money call when anticipating a runup in the price of a stock would be a shrewd but aggressive investment strategy.

T   F   16-18.   At its expiration, the payoff to the holder of a call option is zero if the market price of the stock is equal to the exercise (strike) price.

T   F   16-19.   An investor who anticipates a fall in the price of a stock might want to short the stock and purchase a put to protect his or her ownership interest in a particular stock.

T   F   16-20.   Writing covered calls to increase income is a conservative investment strategy.

T   F   16-21.   Buying a protective put on a stock index ensures that the owner of a diversified stock portfolio will incur only a minimum loss over the duration of the holding period.

T   F   16-22.   When the stock's price exceeds the exercise price, the payoff for the long position in the stock becomes positive, whereas the payoff for writing a naked call remains constant at the amount of the premium paid by the option buyer.

T   F   16-23.   The writer of a put expects the price to stay steady or perhaps fall in the near future.

T   F   16-24.   The risk of a short sale can be reduced by the purchase of a call on the same stock.

T   F   16-25.   A straddle combines a put and a call option on the same stock with the same exercise price but different expiration dates.

T   F   16-26.   Currency options provide an effective way to hedge a position in a foreign currency.

T   F   16-27.   When the holder of a stock-index call exercises the option, the writer must deliver a portfolio that represents the index.

T   F   16-28.   Stock index options differ from industry options in that stock options are written on broad-based portfolios of stocks intended to capture the overall behavior of the stock market, whereas industry options are written on much more narrowly defined portfolios of stocks from specific industries.

T   F   16-29.   A call option is similar to a warrant in that it gives the holder the right to purchase a specified number of shares of stock at a specified price on or before a specified date.

T   F   16-30.   The market prices of both call options and warrants rise when the price of the underlying stock falls.

T   F   16-31.   Rights give existing shareholders the opportunity to buy a new issue at a price lower than the current market price of the shares outstanding.

T   F   16-32. If four rights are needed to purchase a new share of stock, the shares are currently trading at $50, and the subscription price for a new share is $42, each right has an approximate value of $2.

T   F   16-33. Expectations of the future price of the stock and the duration of the warrant are the cause of all changes in the market price of a warrant.

T   F   16-34. Warrants earn a higher percentage return to the investor than direct ownership of the stock if the stock rises sharply in price.

NOTES

1. P. Samuelson, "Rational Theory of Warrant Pricing," *Industrial Management Review* (spring 1965), pp. 13–32; P. Samuelson, "Mathematics of Speculative Price," *SIAM Review* (January 1973), pp. 1–42; F. Black and M. Scholes, "The Pricing of Options and Corporate Liabilities," *Journal of Political Economy* (May–June 1973), pp. 637–654.
2. D. Turov, "Dividend Paying Stocks and Their Warrants," *Financial Analysts Journal* (March/April 1973), pp. 76–78.

Black-Scholes Formula

The Black-Scholes formula for call option pricing can be derived precisely, given the following assumptions:

- The capital markets are frictionless—that is, there are no transaction costs or taxes, and all information is simultaneously and freely available to all investors.
- There are no short-sale restrictions.
- All asset prices follow a continuous stationary, lognormal, stochastic process.
- There is a constant risk-free rate over time.
- No dividends are paid.
- No early exercise is permitted.

The resulting formula is as follows:

$$C_0 = S_0 N(d_1) \; - \; \frac{S\,N(d_2)}{e^{rt}}$$

$$d_1 = \frac{\ln\left(S_0 / S\right) + \left(r_f + 1/2\,\sigma^2\right)t}{\sigma\sqrt{t}}$$

$$d_1 = \frac{\ln\left(S_0 / S\right) + \left(r_f - 1/2\,\sigma^2\right)t}{\sigma\sqrt{t}}$$

and where:

C_0	=	option value
r_f	=	continuously compound riskless annual interest rate
S_0	=	stock price
S	=	strike price of option
e	=	2.718 (the Naperian or natural logarithmic constant)
t	=	time to expiration of option as a fraction of a year
σ	=	the standard deviation of the continuously compounded annual rate of return
$\ln(S_0/S)$	=	natural logarithm of S_0/S
$N(d)$	=	value of the cumulative normal distribution evaluated at d

Put-Call Parity

The formula relating the value of a put to that of a call for the same time to expiration can be written as follows:

$$C_0 = P_0 + S_0 - \frac{S}{e^{r_f t}}$$

where: C_0 = call value
P_0 = put value
r_f = risk-free rate
e = 2.718 (as above)
S_0 = initial stock price
S = striking price
t = time to expiration of the option as a fraction of the year

Appendix C

Turov's Formula

Turov's formula allows the trader to compute the rate of appreciation in the underlying stock necessary to make an option a more profitable investment than the stock. The relative attractiveness of a call (or warrant) is related to the price the stock must reach by expiration to generate equal percentage gains on the stock or option. If the stock's price is above this level, the option will show the greater gain. Otherwise, the stock will have a larger gain or lesser loss. This value equals the striking price divided by the stock price minus the current option price, as shown below:

$$f = \frac{S}{S_0 - C_0}$$

where: f = appreciation of stock necessary to generate equal gains in the stock and option

S = striking price of call or warrant

S_0 = current price of stock

C_0 = current price of call or warrant

Turov subsequently revised his formula to take account of dividends.[2] He noted, however, that in practice the impact of the adjustment was minor.

Profit and Loss Diagrams

These examples assume the following: stock price = $100; strike price = $100; call premium = $3; put premium = $2; no dividends

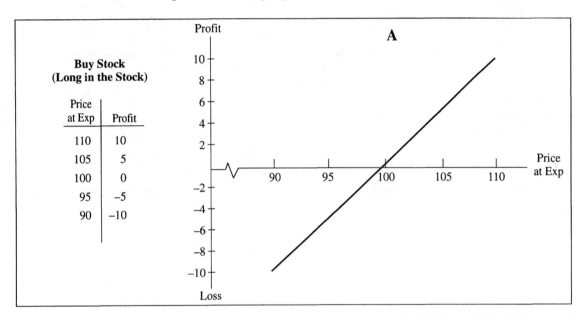

**Buy Stock
(Long in the Stock)**

Price at Exp	Profit
110	10
105	5
100	0
95	−5
90	−10

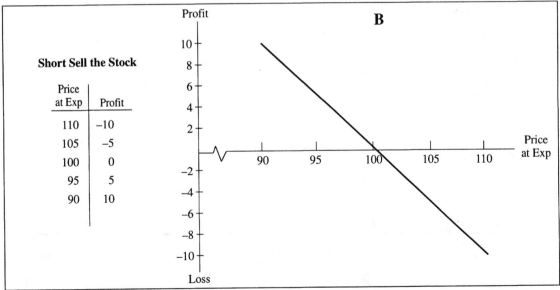

Short Sell the Stock

Price at Exp	Profit
110	−10
105	−5
100	0
95	5
90	10

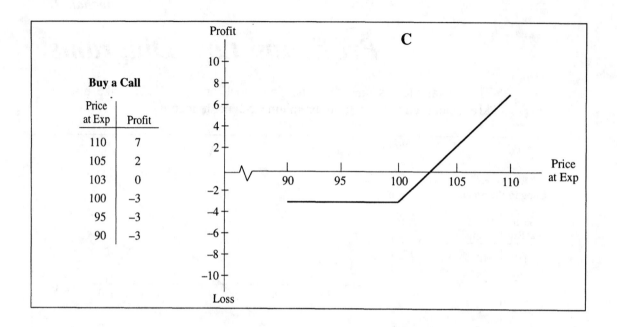

Buy a Call

Price at Exp	Profit
110	7
105	2
103	0
100	-3
95	-3
90	-3

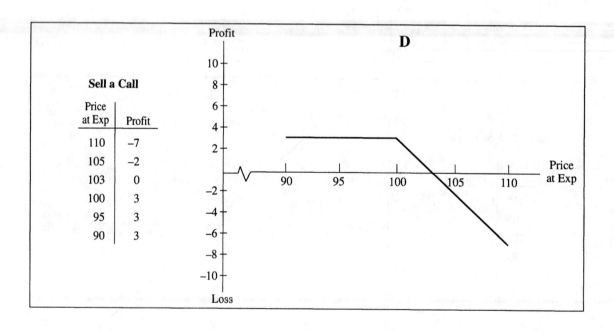

Sell a Call

Price at Exp	Profit
110	-7
105	-2
103	0
100	3
95	3
90	3

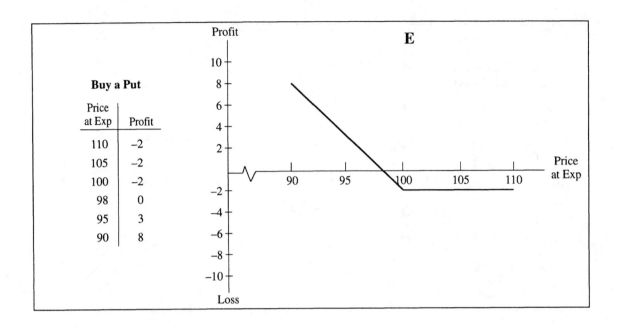

Buy a Put

Price at Exp	Profit
110	−2
105	−2
100	−2
98	0
95	3
90	8

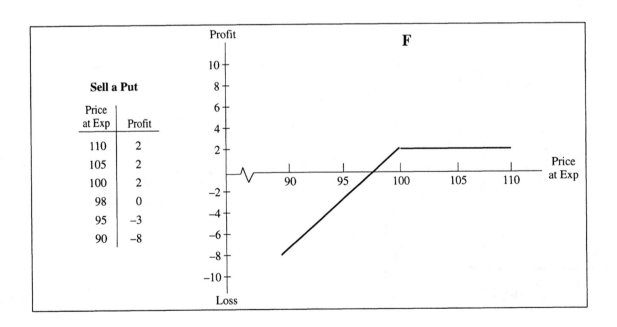

Sell a Put

Price at Exp	Profit
110	2
105	2
100	2
98	0
95	−3
90	−8

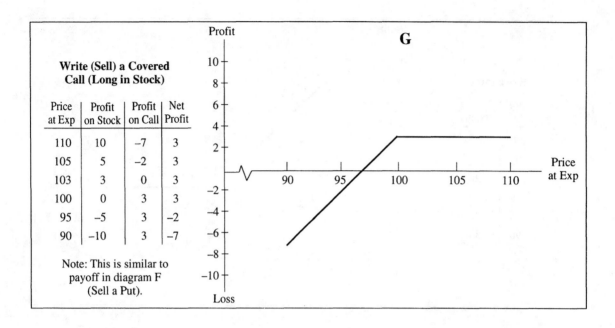

Write (Sell) a Covered Call (Long in Stock)

Price at Exp	Profit on Stock	Profit on Call	Net Profit
110	10	−7	3
105	5	−2	3
103	3	0	3
100	0	3	3
95	−5	3	−2
90	−10	3	−7

Note: This is similar to payoff in diagram F (Sell a Put).

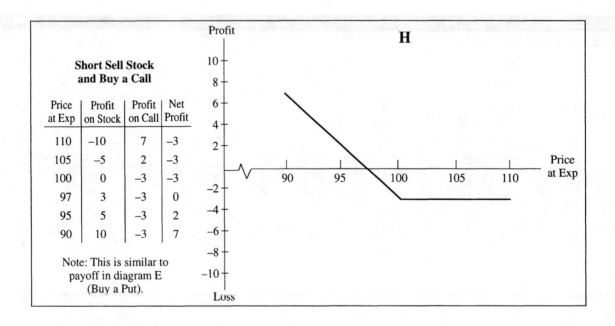

Short Sell Stock and Buy a Call

Price at Exp	Profit on Stock	Profit on Call	Net Profit
110	−10	7	−3
105	−5	2	−3
100	0	−3	−3
97	3	−3	0
95	5	−3	2
90	10	−3	7

Note: This is similar to payoff in diagram E (Buy a Put).

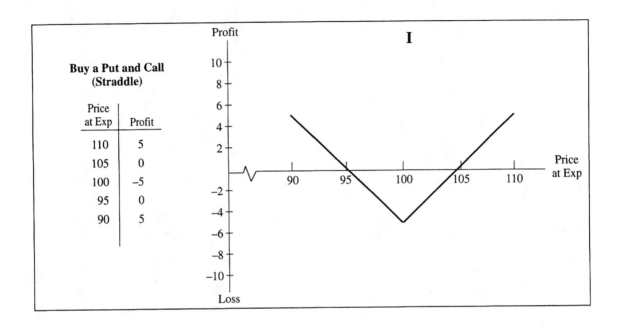

Buy a Put and Call (Straddle)

Price at Exp	Profit
110	5
105	0
100	−5
95	0
90	5

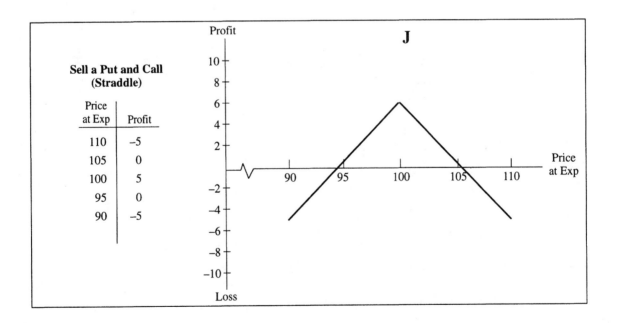

Sell a Put and Call (Straddle)

Price at Exp	Profit
110	−5
105	0
100	5
95	0
90	−5

17

Convertibles and Other Combination Securities

Learning Objectives

An understanding of the material in this chapter should enable the student to

---

17-1. Describe the characteristics of convertible bonds, including how they are valued and how their conversion premiums are determined.

17-2. Describe the characteristics of convertible preferreds, including their similarities and differences when compared to convertible bonds.

17-3. In addition to convertible bonds and convertible preferreds, describe several other types of convertible (hybrid) securities.

17-4. Explain the techniques of hedging and arbitraging as they are used in securities trading and other kinds of markets.

Chapter Outline

**convertible bonds
convertible preferreds**

After our discussion of options in chapter 16, there are, as we previously mentioned, several types of securities that combine one security, such as a bond, with characteristics similar to an option to purchase another security. These are actually another form of derivative. Two primary types of combination (hybrid) securities are *convertible bonds* and *convertible preferreds*. Other types of hybrid securities include Americus Trust securities, equity notes, liquidity yield option notes (LYONs), and commodity-backed bonds. Convertible preferred stocks are considered equity securities, whereas convertible debentures and other hybrid securities are considered debt securities. Hybrid securities can generally be exchanged for a preset number of shares of common stock. The redemption value or coupon rate of commodity-backed bonds is indexed to the price of another asset. With the exception of equity notes, conversion is at the holder of the hybrid security's option.

This chapter discusses the various types of hybrid securities, paying particular attention to convertible debentures. The chapter describes the appeal of convertible debentures to investors, and it explains convertible debentures' terminology, risk, conversion premiums, and values. There is also a brief discussion of convertible preferreds and other hybrid securities.

The chapter concludes with a discussion of hedging and arbitrage. Hedging and arbitraging involve trades that require combinations of assets or securities structured in a way to reduce risk (primarily hedging) or to make profits by taking opposite positions in two or more different assets when there are exploitable price differentials (arbitraging).

HYBRID SECURITIES

Appeal of Hybrids

Hybrid securities derive value both from their yield (interest or preferred dividends) and from their potential return as common stock. If the price of the underlying common stock rises sufficiently, it might be worthwhile for the holder of the convertible security to convert to common, thus acquiring common stock at a price below its market price. The holder might also choose to sell the convertible instrument at a profit that reflects the increase in the underlying common stock's price. A third option is to hold the convertible instrument, keep receiving periodic interest payments, and convert only when the dividends on the underlying common stock exceed the interest payments on the debt instrument, or until the debenture is about to mature (or be called). The third option gives the holder the best of both worlds—realizing both the higher interest payments on the debenture and eventually the capital gain from converting to common stock. If the stock's price does not rise sufficiently to make conversion worthwhile, the owner still receives income from the interest payments plus the face value of the debenture at maturity. Thus, convertible debentures offer a combination of the upside potential of common stock and the downside risk protection of bonds.

The conversion feature has a price, however—generally a lower coupon interest rate than that paid on straight bonds of comparable risk and maturity. In the secondary market, convertible debentures sell at a higher price than comparable bonds without the conversion feature. Also, in the event of bankruptcy, straight bonds tend to have a higher priority.

Terminology

As with pure options, there are a number of specialized terms, as defined below, with convertibles:

conversion ratio

- *conversion ratio:* number of shares into which the security is convertible

conversion price

- *conversion price:* face value of the security divided by its conversion ratio
- *conversion value:* current stock price multiplied by the conversion ratio
- *straight-debt value:* market value of an otherwise equivalent bond lacking a conversion feature

conversion premium

- *conversion premium:* bond price less its conversion value
- *premium over straight-debt value:* bond price less its straight-debt value

---

Example: Suppose a $1,000 par-value bond is convertible into 50 shares of common stock. The conversion ratio is 50. The conversion price is $1,000/50, or $20 per share. If the underlying common stock is currently trading at $15/share, the conversion value of the bond is 50 x $15 = $750, and the conversion premium is $250 ($1,000 − $750). The conversion value is a measure of what the convertible bond is worth if immediately converted into common stock.

The straight-debt value of a convertible bond is the intrinsic value of a comparable bond without the conversion feature.

Example:	Suppose the convertible bond in the example above has a coupon rate of 12 percent and 5 years to maturity, and a straight bond of comparable risk trading at par pays a coupon rate of 13.5 percent. Using a discount rate of 13.5 percent and calculating the present value, we find that the straight-debt value of the convertible bond (assuming annual interest payments) is $947.88.

Consider what happens when the price of the underlying stock rises.

Example:	Suppose the price of the stock in both examples above increases to $25 per share. The conversion value of the bond is now $25 x 50, or $1,250. The conversion value of the bond now exceeds its straight-debt value.

The market price of a convertible bond should always be at least the greater of its straight-debt value or its conversion value. This is because the holder has the option of either keeping the instrument as a bond or converting it into stock. The greater of these two amounts represents a floor below which the price of the convertible should not fall.

The market value of the convertible can, however, exceed this floor because of the time value or speculative value of the conversion option. Even if the conversion value is below the current market price of the company's stock, there is a reasonable likelihood that the price of the stock will rise sufficiently before the bond matures to make conversion worthwhile. The size of this speculative value is directly related to the time to maturity and the volatility of the price of the underlying stock, and it is inversely related to the spread between the stock's market price and the conversion price.

The difference between the market value of a convertible bond and its conversion value is called the conversion premium. The difference between the market price of the bond and its straight-debt value is called the premium over straight-debt value. The lesser of these two differentials represents the speculative value of the convertible.

Example:	Suppose in the first example above, the market value of the convertible bond is $1,000. Since its straight-debt value is $947.88 and its conversion value is $750, the speculative value of the bond is $1,000 – $947.88, or $52.12.

Advantages of Convertible Bonds

Convertible bonds offer both a fixed coupon (although generally slightly below the going rate on equivalent risk straight bonds) and the possibility of a substantial capital gain through conversion. Investors should not buy convertible bonds as fixed-income securities, since straight bonds pay a higher yield for the same level of risk. Likewise, investors should not buy them as straight equity securities, since it would be cheaper to purchase a comparable amount of common stock directly. Rather, convertibles appeal to investors who want to share in the upside potential of common stock but avoid the downside risk.

Thus, there are two principal advantages to investing in convertibles compared with common stock. First, the current yield on the convertible bond is likely to be much higher and more certain than the dividend yield on the underlying common stock. Second, the fixed interest rate gives holders considerable downside protection, since they are legally entitled to receive interest payments and the principal amount at maturity even if the company performs poorly and its stock declines in value. The straight-debt value of a convertible should remain fairly constant even if the value of the underlying common stock declines.

However, like straight bonds, convertible bonds are vulnerable to interest rate risk. If the market interest rates increase, the straight-debt value of the convertible will decline. Remember, too, that the speculative value of the convertible bond will exist only as long as there is a reasonable chance that the market price of the underlying common stock will exceed its conversion price before the bond matures.

The recent article below discusses some of the benefits of owning convertible securities in the current environment of high-flying Internet stocks.

Chicken Little Stocks*

by John Gorham

Eager to play the stock market but afraid of losing your shirt? Convertible bonds and preferred stocks may be the way to go. There are currently $140 billion worth of convertibles in the market—securities that can be converted into common stock at a predetermined ratio and that tend not to fall as far as the underlying stock in a down market.

Okay, converts don't give you as much gain in a bull market. There's no free lunch, just a way of selecting a different point on the risk-reward spectrum.

Converts offer two important advantages over the common stocks into which they are convertible. One is a higher yield (in almost all cases). The other is some protection if the issuer really falls apart. A convertible bondholder has a right to a fixed semiannual coupon and, in case of a bankruptcy, a

* Reprinted by Permission of Forbes Magazine © 2000 Forbes 1999.

claim on assets that ranks ahead of common shareholders' claims. (Preferred stocks are in between in seniority.)

Convertible returns have certainly been stellar of late. Over the past 12 months [January–December 1999] the Merrill Lynch All U.S. Convertibles Index shows a total return of 30%. While interest rates have been rising this year [1999], depressing the pure-bond value of convertibles, stocks have been strong, especially in the technology sector, which accounts for more than its share of convertible issuance.

There has been a flood of new convertibles, $33 billion (gross issuance) this year [1999], many from technology and Web companies. Says Charles Pohl, fund manager for the Putnam Convertible Income-Growth Trust: "The spigots are opened for risk capital flowing into the convert market."

So there's a lot to choose from. But how do you pick the right one? First, some basics. Convertibles tend to be issued at par—that is, at their redemption value. This price will also typically represent a 20%-to-30% premium over the underlying equity value if converted immediately. The yield on the convert will usually be better than what you could get on the common stock but worse than you would get on a nonconvertible bond.

Example: When Amazon.com issued convertible bonds in January [1999], the $1,000 bonds carried a 4.75% coupon and the right to be converted into shares of Amazon then worth $787. The $213 spread between the bond's price and the conversion value is called a conversion premium or equity premium.

When convertibles trade at or near par, an investor in high-quality companies can ideally expect a total return that captures roughly 70% of a significant upward move in the underlying stock, but suffers only 50% of the downswing if the common were to fall by a like amount. This isn't quite the giveaway to the convertible holder that it appears to be; remember that stocks are supposed to appreciate over time. In other words, in return for the reduced risk, convertible buyers are somewhat more likely to be lagging common holders than beating them over the long term.

When convertibles trade near par, they are very much a hybrid security—akin to a mix of stocks and bonds in their risks and returns. Over time, though,

the convert's price may drift far from its redemption value. And then its traits veer off toward the equity or the bond side.

America Online in November 1997 put out a 4% convertible bond due in 2002. The bond was convertible into 153.3 shares of AOL worth $714 when the convert was floated. Note the 40% conversion premium, the excess of the convertible's $1,000 par value over the $714. Since then AOL shares have exploded upward, taking the convertible along. The convertible's conversion value has climbed to $11,630, and the price of the convertible is practically the same. The conversion premium has sunk to 0.2%, while the yield on the convertible has fallen to a negligible 0.34%. The par value, lying far below the current price of the convertible, is not much of a safety net. The convertible now acts like a common stock and has almost entirely lost its fixed-income flavor. If AOL common shares go into a tailspin, they will take the convertibles with them.

At the other extreme is Federal Mogul's 7% preferred stock with a $50 par value. Issued two years ago [1997], the preferred was exchangeable into common shares then worth $40. Since then the stock has fallen apart, taking the convertible's conversion value down to $20.63. The convertible preferred hasn't fallen as far. It's down to $35. Investors figure that the conversion feature is unlikely to pay off before the preferred could be called next year; so the preferred trades on a yield basis—its current yield is now 9.8%. This is what is called a busted convert. It has lost most of its equity flavor. Note that the conversion premium has widened to 69%.

If you want something that blends the risks and rewards of stocks and bonds, look for convertibles with conversion premiums in the 15%-to-40% range, says Scott Lange, head of U.S. convertible securities research at Goldman Sachs. Another factor to consider is the payback period—how many years it takes for you to earn back your conversion premium, via a yield higher than the yield on the underlying common. To oversimplify a bit, you want a convertible with either a short payback period or a modest premium over the pure bond value. Note that convertible preferreds tend to have a higher bond premium because they are positioned lower in the capital structure.

Convertible Sweet Spot

Looking for a convertible A-list? Below are Goldman Sachs' picks of balanced convertibles: those that carry more chance of reward than risk.

Company/security	Price[1]	Current yield	Premium Over		Years to pay back
			Conversion value	Bond value	
Affiliated Computer Services/4% notes of 2005	$1,061	3.8%	21%	38%	4.6
Clear Channel Communications/1.5% notes of 2002	985	1.5	29	17	14.6
Hewlett-Packard/zero-coupon notes of 2017	620	0.0	18	11	NM
Adelphia Communications/5.5% preferreds[2]	174	6.3	25	83	3.2
AES Corp/6.75% preferreds of 2029	51	6.6	25	80	3.0

[1]As of Dec 1 [1999].   [2]Perpetual maturity.   NM: Not meaningful.   Source: Goldman Sachs.

The analysis of convertible securities can be daunting. The *Value Line Convertible Survey* ($525 a year) is helpful to serious buyers. Bloomberg quote terminals offer good analytics on convertible stocks and bonds. One helpful Web site is ConvertBond.com, which offers pricing as well as recent news.

Or, buy a fund. Over the past ten years [1989– 1999] the best-performing no-load convertible fund has been the Fidelity Convertible Securities Fund, with a 15.3% annual gain. Value Line Convertible Fund has returned 11.8%. The Putnam Convertible fund has done better, 12.6%, but carries a load of up to 5.75%.

Call Feature

During the 1980s with their high interest rates, most newly issued bonds were callable. The convertible bonds were no exception. For all the convertible bonds outstanding, the majority contain some form of call provision.

The call feature is especially relevant to holders of convertible bonds, because it can limit the bonds' upside potential. To understand, imagine that the market price of the underlying stock rises above the conversion price. As long as the interest rate on the bonds exceeds the dividend yield on the common stock, it would be cost effective to hold the bonds, continue to receive interest payments, and exercise the conversion feature just before the bonds mature. This means that the issuing company is bearing the cost of interest, while the bondholder is enjoying the potential gains from stock appreciation (with little risk), as well as receiving the interest payments.

The issuing company can effectively force conversion, however, by calling the bonds. If a convertible bond is called, the holder of the bond can either accept the bond's $1,000 face value or convert to the underlying stock. Once the last date of the call period passes, the investor no longer has the option to convert and will not earn any additional interest. Usually, corporations engage in this forced conversion when the stock value exceeds the $1,000 bond value to get the bondholders to convert. This action results in the transfer of the long-term debt account (liability) amount to the equity accounts on the balance sheet, and it permits the firm to issue a larger amount of new debt. Therefore, the corporation redresses the balance of risks by forcing conversion. Indeed, some convertible bonds are issued with variable conversion ratios—that is, the conversion ratio may decline as the convertible approaches maturity. This type of provision is a thinly disguised attempt at forced conversion before the conversion ratio is reduced.

As long as the conversion value exceeds the redemption price of the bonds (face value plus call premium), it would be logical for the bondholders to convert immediately rather than tendering the bonds for redemption. Following this logic, corporations should force conversion whenever the call price is safely below the bond's conversion value. This policy would severely limit callable convertibles' upside potentials. Thus, convertibles may offer attractive returns (vis-à-vis nonconvertibles) only if the conversion value exceeds the call price soon after the security is issued. Moreover, calling to force conversion may depress the price of the underlying stock. Most companies do not, in fact, call their convertibles as quickly as this logic would suggest.

Valuation of Convertibles

As hybrid securities, convertibles have characteristics of both bonds and stocks. The straight-debt value of convertibles is influenced by their coupon rate, default risk, maturity date, and indenture provisions. The value of the conversion feature (including its speculative value) is influenced by the firm's risk, capital structure, dividend policy, and conversion terms. Of course, the spread between the stock's current market price and the conversion price has a major impact on the value of convertibles.

When the underlying stock's price exceeds the conversion price, the resulting price movements of the convertible bond more closely resemble the price of the stock. After all, as the stock's price rises by a dollar, the bond's price rises by the conversion ratio multiplied by one dollar. The bond's price is less dependent on interest rate changes and more dependent on the success of the firm and the firm's common stock price.

This is precisely why convertible bonds, as deferred-equity instruments, are attractive to investors. Because of these dual features that favor the investor, however, the corporation can pay a slightly lower interest rate on the convertibles at their time of issue than their risk warrants. Most convertibles have been issued by firms whose bond quality rating was either at the low end of the investment grade category or the high end of the speculative category. As such, these firms might not have been able to sell debt unless there was some way for investors to share in a firm's future success while still, in the short run, having the protection of being a creditor.

Calculating the price that the stock must reach to make investments in convertibles or their associated stocks equivalent is also much more complex than with warrants. (See chapter 16 for a full discussion of warrants. Also see Turov's formula in the appendix to chapter 16.) The price must consider both the premium over conversion and the difference between interest and expected dividend income.

Usually, the total income from a convertible bond exceeds the total dividend income from the same number of shares into which the bond can be converted. Thus, the opportunity cost of buying the shares instead of the bond is the difference in current income. If the total dividend income from the shares exceeds that of the bond, investors might well convert. If the total dividends exceed the bond interest, the market price of the stock will most likely exceed the bond's $1,000 face value.

Conversion Premium

As previously mentioned, the conversion premium (bond price minus conversion value) is the amount over the underlying stock value paid for the straight-debt-value protection. Not surprisingly, the conversion premium is of considerable interest to investors. Figure 17-1 illustrates how the conversion premium changes with the price of the underlying stock. Therefore, it is important to understand the various options available to investors, depending on the stock's current market price relative to its market price at the date of issue.

The conversion price is almost always set above the current market price. If it was not, then the initial buyer of the bond would immediately either exercise the conversion option or sell the bond in the market to realize an immediate gain. Therefore, the conversion price is the minimum market price that will entice an investor to exercise the convertible option if the bond is called. The investor will not exercise this convertibility feature if the conversion price is above the market price.

Example: Suppose the conversion price is $50 and the market price is $38. The investor can take the cash—

$1,000—and buy more than the 20 shares that he or she would receive by converting the bond ($1,000/ $38 = 26.3 shares). Thus, the investor will not choose to convert the bond.

Why would the investor ever buy such a bond? The answer is because of the *upside potential* of capital gains, the *downside risk protection* of the fixed coupon, and the inherent priority of bonds over stocks.

When the underlying common stock trades at a relatively high price compared to the initial offering market price, new investors are unwilling to pay a conversion premium because of the risk that the bond might be called and conversion forced on bondholders (or they must take the call price if the option is not exercised). Thus, the bond's conversion value and its market price will tend to become equal.

Moreover, the bond cannot sell below its conversion value because arbitrageurs (see explanation of arbitraging later in this chapter) would enter the market, buy the bond, and immediately convert for an assured profit. On the other hand, the bond cannot sell below its investment value because the bond would be mispriced, which would lead investors to seize the opportunity to acquire it and earn an abnormal return relative to other bonds of comparable risk.

FIGURE 17-1
Price Behavior of Convertible Bond

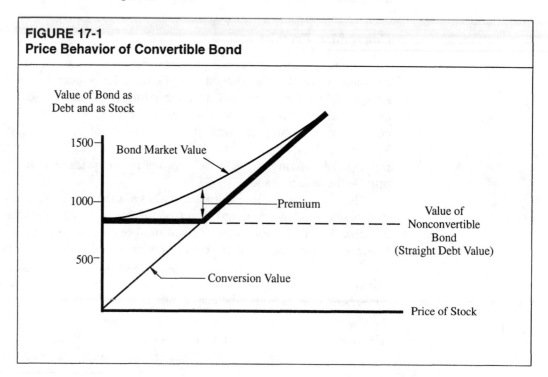

The minimum price and actual price of a typical convertible bond are indicated in figure 17-1.

When the conversion value exceeds the bond value, the minimum price is the conversion value. When the conversion value is less than the bond value, the minimum price is the bond value. At all points, however, the actual price or value exceeds the minimum value because of the conversion premium. Because convertibles are generally issued with coupons that are less than the coupons of similar bonds without the conversion feature, the bond value is usually at a discount from par value ($1,000).

Figure 17-2 illustrates how the conversion premium changes with the effect of market interest rates on the overall valuation of the underlying bond. Remember, the investment value, referred to as the issue's bond value (or price floor), is the price at which the bond would trade if the convertible option did not exist.

If market rates of interest fall below the coupon rate offered by the convertible, the floor price or bond value will increase as figure 17-2 shows. In fact, the bond value will exceed the par value of $1,000, but the conversion value will remain unchanged, and the convertible will be valued much more highly as a bond relative to figure 17-1. Also, the conversion premium will be less since the conversion value (and underlying stock values) must already be quite high before the conversion value exceeds the bond value. Figure 17-2 illustrates the result of a decline in interest rates.

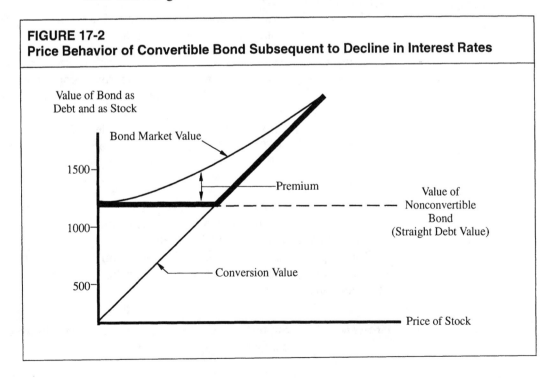

FIGURE 17-2
Price Behavior of Convertible Bond Subsequent to Decline in Interest Rates

Convertible Preferred Stock

Although they are less popular than convertible debentures, convertible preferred stock (convertible preferreds) is another type of hybrid securities. There are similarities between convertible bonds and convertible preferreds, but there are also some differences. The downside protection is less certain with convertible preferreds, since there is no legal requirement that the preferred dividends be paid. Convertible preferred stock can be converted into common stock at a specified ratio within a specified time period. After the expiration of that time period, the shares become regular preferred stock shares.

The pricing of convertible preferreds is similar to the pricing of convertible bonds. When the market price of the underlying stock is close to or above the conversion price, the conversion value influences the price of the convertible preferreds. When the market price is far below the conversion price, the price of the convertible preferreds is closer to the straight preferred stock value.

As with convertible bonds, the number of common shares that can be obtained by converting one preferred share is known as the conversion ratio. The conversion ratio can change over time. For example, an issue of convertible preferred stock may have a conversion ratio of 4:1 for the first 10 years after issue, 2:1 for the next 10 years, and become straight preferred stock thereafter.

The conversion value of convertible preferred is the market price of the common stock multiplied by the conversion ratio.

Example: If the market price of the underlying common stock is $15/share, and the conversion ratio is 4:1, then the conversion value is $60 ($15 x 4 = $60). If the market price of the convertible preferred stock is $65/share, then the conversion premium is $5 ($65 − $60 = $5).

The conversion premium is often expressed as a percentage: conversion premium divided by conversion value. In the example above, the conversion premium would be $5/$60, or 8.33 percent.

Knowing the size of the conversion premium may help an investor to determine whether the convertible preferred or the underlying common stock is the more attractive investment.

Example: Suppose the investor is choosing between a company's 10 percent (dividend) convertible preferred with a conversion ratio of 2:1 selling at $50, and its common stock with a 5 percent dividend yield selling at $20. The conversion premium is ($50 − $40)/$40, or 25 percent.

In return for the 25 percent premium in the above example, the investor receives a higher current yield and a more stable dividend, since preferred dividends must be paid before any dividends can be paid on common stock. The investor also has the upside potential inherent in the option to convert to common stock in the future. All other things being equal, however, the higher the conversion premium, the lower the likelihood that conversion will become profitable in the future, and the lower the gain even if conversion does become profitable. Remember also that, like convertible bonds, convertible preferreds are subject to call risk and interest rate risk.

Other Types of Convertibles

hybrid convertibles

Convertible bonds and preferreds are the primary types of convertible securities, but other types of combination securities also bear mentioning. Unlike traditional convertibles, *hybrid convertibles* (also called exchangeable debentures) are convertible into stock of different companies from those that issue them. Companies with substantial stock portfolios may find hybrids a useful source of funds.

Hybrids are about as attractive to investors as the underlying company's straight convertibles. The bond's default risk depends on the issuing company's financial position; the upside potential is a function of the characteristics of the company whose stock underlies the exchangeable bond. Moreover, the conversion of a regular convertible is a tax-free exchange, whereas any profit realized when a hybrid is converted is immediately taxable.

Americus Trust Securities

Americus Trust securities

Americus Trust securities, which are issued by Americus Shareowner Service Corporation, are a relatively new type of constructed security that has much in common with traditional options. Americus Trust securities divide any of a predetermined list of stocks into two parts: a low-risk component (the prime) and an option component (the score). Shares of the selected stock are deposited in a trust. Then two new securities are issued to the owner of each deposited share. The prime component entitles the owner to all dividends, voting rights, and up to some prespecified amount of end-period value. The score component, in contrast, receives the end value less the portion going to the prime. The trust's organizer receives a small fee for organizing the trust and funneling dividends to the prime holders.

Example: Suppose the stock of XYZ Corporation currently sells for $40 per share. The prime will receive the first $50 of value on a prespecified date, such as 4 years from now. The score will receive any value over that amount. If the end-period price of the stock is $80, the prime will receive $50 and all of the interim dividends; the score will receive $30.

Thus, the score's value depends largely on how much the stock exceeds the value going to the prime. It acts very much like an option with a striking price equal to the value going to the prime and an expiration date equal to the terminal date on the trust.

Equity Notes

equity notes

Equity notes (also called mandatory convertible notes) were developed to meet banks' capital needs. These notes are issued as debt instruments that yield a fixed coupon until maturity, when they are automatically converted into common stocks.

Liquidity Yield Option Notes

LYON

One of the most complex of the convertibles is the liquidity yield option note, or *LYON*. LYONs differ from ordinary convertibles primarily in being zero-coupon convertibles. In addition, they are callable and redeemable. Making the security even more complicated, both the redemption and call prices escalate through time.

Commodity-Backed Bonds

commodity-backed bonds

Commodity-backed bonds are debt instruments whose values are potentially related to the price of some physical commodity. These bonds allow the owner to speculate on a commodity price rise while earning a modest return. The bond's price will move up and down with variations in both the commodity price and market interest rates. Mexico has issued 20-year bonds with payments that depend on the price of oil. With options that specially positioned issuers can offer, commodity-backed bonds were designed to appeal to speculative investors. Additional types of innovative combination securities will probably be devised as time passes.

Types of Combination Securities

- Convertible bonds: debt securities that may be exchanged for common stock at a fixed ratio
- Convertible preferreds: preferred stock that may be exchanged for common stock at a fixed ratio
- Hybrid convertibles: debt securities of one company convertible into the common stock of another company
- Americus Trust securities: large-cap stocks reissued into two parts: the prime, which carries all dividends plus a capped end value, and the score, which carries the final end value less the portion going to the prime
- Equity notes: debt securities with a mandatory conversion to equity
- Liquidity yield option notes (LYONs): zero-coupon, convertible, callable, redeemable bonds
- Commodity-backed bonds: debt securities whose potential redemption values are related to the market price of some physical commodity, such as oil

---

HEDGING AND ARBITRAGING

As markets have become more sophisticated, security types more diverse, derivatives more commonplace, and takeover activity more widespread, hedging and arbitrage trading have risen markedly. Both brokerage firms and individual investors have gotten into the act.

hedging

Hedging involves taking opposing positions in related assets to profit (or reduce losses) from hoped-for relative price movements. For example, the hedger might buy stocks and short corresponding warrants, or *vice versa*.

arbitraging

Arbitraging, in contrast, involves simultaneously buying and selling equivalent securities in separate markets, profiting from temporary price differences. Arbitrageurs will generally take advantage of any appreciable price disparities for securities traded, say, on both the Pacific Stock Exchange and the New York Stock Exchange or any other combination of exchanges. In addition to their use in debt- and equity-related securities trading, hedging and arbitraging also take place in a wide variety of other markets, including those for currencies and commodities. Both hedging and arbitraging may be classified into risk and pure forms.

Hedging

A pure hedge is designed to reduce risk *per se*. For example, most silver mining companies have relatively stable extraction and processing costs. The risky part of their business stems from the volatility in the market price of silver. The price has, for instance, ranged from over $50 to under $5 per ounce in the past 2 decades. Establishing a price for its planned production well ahead of time would substantially reduce a silver mining firm's price-fluctuation risk. Hedge trades in the futures market would set such a price well before the silver is ready for sale. Mining companies that hedge each projected output increment largely insulate themselves from subsequent silver spot-price fluctuations. A variety of enterprises may make similar types of hedge trades. Pure hedging is often advisable whenever establishing a forward price reduces an important business risk. Pure hedges are incidental to hedgers' main spot-market business.

Risk hedges, in contrast, are designed to yield a relatively likely profit. Rather than reduce the impact of potentially adverse price moves, risk hedgers seek to profit from potentially favorable relative price movements while minimizing their exposure to potentially adverse moves. Put and call spreads and ratio positions (discussed in chapter 16) are examples of risk hedges.

Arbitraging

Pure arbitrageurs assume opposite positions on equivalent (or convertible to equivalent) assets when prices in separate markets diverge sufficiently. Pure arbitrage produces a quick certain profit. Risk arbitrageurs, in contrast, take offsetting positions in *potentially* equivalent securities. The shares of an acquisition candidate and its proposed acquirer are the primary types of potentially equivalent securities. The arbitrageur may or may not hedge an exchange for debt or equity securities. A tender for cash does not require the arbitrageur to make an offsetting trade, however.

A proposed merger involving an exchange of shares will generally leave the relative prices of the two stocks somewhat out of line with the merger terms.

Example:	XYZ may offer two of its shares for each share of UVW Corporation. If preoffer prices of XYZ and UVW are 50 and 75, immediate postoffer prices may move to 52 and 85. At these levels, the UVW stock will still be underpriced relative to the XYZ offer. Assuming the merger agreement takes effect, the UVW stock will be worth 104 (two times the per-share price of XYZ). That is, the arbitrageur will buy in the ratio of one share of UVW at 85, while shorting two shares of XYZ for a total of 104. The net result is a gain of 19 (104 − 85) multiplied by the

number of shares of UVW purchased.

The current price of two shares of XYZ (104) represents a premium of 22.4 percent over the current market price of one share of UVW (85)—that is, 19/85 = 22.4 percent. The arbitrageur can profit from this discount by buying UVW and shorting twice as many XYZ shares. The investment required for the arbitrage includes the amount to be paid for the UVW stock plus the margin percentage required to short the XYZ stock. Normally, 50 percent of the dollar value of the short position is required for margin. Thus, the arbitrageur needs to invest the cost of the UVW shares (85) plus half of the cost of the XYZ shares (104 x .5 = 52) for a total cost of 137 for each share of UVW purchased.

As the example above shows, the gross gain (ignoring commissions) on the transaction is, in fact, 19. A gain of 19 on an investment of 137 amounts to 13.9 percent. If the acquisition is completed in 6 weeks and commissions amount to 5 percent, the arbitrageur will earn an 8.9 percent profit (13.9 percent – 5 percent – 8.9 percent) in 6 weeks. This rate of profit is equivalent to approximately 77 percent per annum. An arbitrageur who is able to generate profits at that rate more or less consistently will do well indeed. These profits, however, depend on the proposed merger's taking place as planned.

In general, when a proposed merger falls through, the acquisition candidate's stock will decline, and it may decline all the way to its preoffer level. The acquiring company's stock could, in contrast, remain largely unchanged. Thus, the arbitrageur will be forced to incur a considerable loss to reverse the trade.

Example: Suppose, in the example above, the merger proposal falls through and the prices return to their premerger proposal levels. The arbitrageur who bought UVW at 85 will have to sell at 75 for a loss of 10. The short position in XYZ at 52 will be covered at 50 for a gain of 2. This gain corresponds to 4 (2 x 2) for the two shares shorted per purchased share of UVW.

The net effect of unwinding the failed risk arbitrage trade is –6 (4 – 10) per share of UVW purchased. This amounts to a loss of 6, relative to an investment of 137, or 4.4 percent. That loss plus commissions of 5 percent amounts to a total loss of 9.4 percent.

Clearly, the risk arbitrageur does not want to be involved in too many takeover plays that are not consummated. The overall profit from a risk arbitrage program should allow for a combination of profitable trades, failed arbitrages, and periods when no suitable trades are available.

Merger proposals can fall through for a number of reasons. Antitrust problems, shareholder opposition, or management reassessment can block a proposed deal. In other cases, a hostile takeover attempt can be derailed by insufficient tenders or the target firm's defensive maneuvers. At still other times, a bidding contest or actions of the target firm's management or shareholders can result in an improved offer. In any case, many large sophisticated investors have generated substantial profits through risk arbitrage. This game is not, however, for the faint of heart.

Most hedge and arbitrage trades are designed to produce relatively modest short-term profits (in percentage terms). Very nimble movements and minimum commissions are needed, since profits often depend on obtaining favorable overall prices in both markets. Few amateur investors have sufficient funds, time, expertise, and courage to undertake serious arbitrage plays. Even professionals have to move quickly when profitable price relationships open up. Hedging is somewhat less demanding than arbitraging. Thus, it is more suited to amateur traders.

Types of Hedges and Arbitrages

- Pure hedging: reducing the risk of an exposed asset position by making an offsetting trade
- Risk hedging: taking offsetting positions in related assets in the hope of profiting from relative price moves
- Pure arbitraging: simultaneously buying and selling identical assets on different markets at price differences that guarantee a profit
- Risk arbitraging: taking offsetting positions in the securities of an acquisition candidate and its proposed acquirer at prices that guarantee a profit if the takeover succeeds

---

SUMMARY AND CONCLUSIONS

Convertible debentures and convertible preferred stock are the most common types of combination (hybrid) securities. Other more obscure types of hybrid securities include exchangeable bonds, Americus Trust securities, equity notes, LYONs, and commodity-backed bonds. Each of these securities combines a fixed-income security with an option (or in the case of equity notes, an obligation) to convert the security into common stock or another asset whose future price is uncertain. As such, these securities offer both upside potential and downside protection by combining a more volatile security (such as common stock) with a more stable one (such as a bond).

Hybrid securities are priced to reflect their upside potential (conversion premium) and their downside protection (straight-debt value). Therefore, convertible bonds usually have a lower interest rate than comparable straight bonds do. Likewise, the dividend yield on convertible preferred stock is likely to be lower than the dividend rate on straight preferred stock of comparable risk.

Convertible securities generally have a call feature, which limits their upside potential since it enables the issuing company to force conversion when the market price of the stock exceeds the conversion price. This prevents the holder from receiving the higher interest rate on the bond and converting just before the bond matures. Convertible securities are also subject to interest rate risk and default risk. In the event of bankruptcy, straight debt generally takes precedence over convertible debt.

In short, convertible securities combine the upside potential of common stock with the downside protection of fixed-income securities. This combination of benefits, however, is not free. It generally carries an implicit price in the form of a lower interest rate on the convertible bond than is available on straight debt of comparable risk and maturity.

Hedging involves both pure and risk types of trades. The pure type requires offsetting positions in equivalent assets in order to reduce or eliminate risk. Options (discussed in chapter 16) and futures (discussed in chapter 18) are frequently used in hedging programs. Risk hedgers seek to profit from favorable price movements while minimizing exposure to adverse movements.

Pure arbitraging assumes opposite positions on equivalent assets when prices in separate markets (or for separate assets) diverge. Risk arbitraging takes offsetting positions in potentially equivalent assets. The former produces a quick certain profit. The latter may not, depending on certain elements of risk involved in the forecasts of expected price movements.

CHAPTER REVIEW

Answers to the review questions and the self-test questions start on page 784.

Key Terms

convertible bonds	Americus Trust securities
convertible preferreds	equity notes
conversion ratio	LYON
conversion price	commodity-backed bonds
conversion premium	hedging
hybrid convertibles	arbitraging

Review Questions

17-1.   a.   Why is call risk particularly relevant to convertibles?

   b.   Under what circumstances are convertibles particularly likely to be called?

17-2.   a.   Discuss the various factors that affect a convertible's premium over conversion value.

   b.   How does the premium over conversion value relate to the time value on an a call option?

17-3.   The SOM Company convertible debentures sell for 105, while its common stock is priced at 4. The convertible's conversion ratio is 20; its annual coupon rate is 10 percent. Its estimated straight-debt value is 90. The stock pays a dividend of $.20 per share per year. The bonds mature in 2007 and are callable at 107.

   a.   Compute the convertible's
   - conversion price
   - conversion value
   - conversion premium
   - premium over straight-debt value
   - current yield

   b.   If you purchased the bonds at par ($100) and the stock subsequently rose to 5 1/2, what is the minimum profit per bond (ignore the impact of commissions and coupon payments)?

   c.   Assuming dividend payments are maintained at the current level and the bonds are called to force conversion in 5 years, what price must the stock have reached for an investment in the stock and the bonds to have produced equivalent percentage profits? (Ignore the impact of commissions and the time-value of money. Assume that the convertible was purchased at the beginning of 2000 at par and that all five payments are received.)

17-4.   a.   For the SOM convertibles in question 17-3, to what would the price of the bond fall if the stock price declined to 3? Assume the market interest rates do not change and the premium over conversion value remains unchanged in percentage terms as at the start of this question.

    b. Now suppose that the stock price rose to 6 1/2 and the bonds were called. What would the convertibles sell for after the calling, assuming conversion was still possible?

17-5. A share of convertible preferred selling at $100 may be exchanged for two shares of common stock, trading at $40. What is the conversion premium?

17-6. a. In the example in question 17-5, what should the convertible preferred sell for if the common goes to $60?

      b. What assumption is required in order to derive a price?

17-7. What do convertible bond investors obtain and what do they sacrifice relative to investors in straight bonds and relative to investors in the underlying stock?

Self-Test Questions

T   F   17-1. The term *conversion premium* refers to the difference between the market price of the bond and its par value.

T   F   17-2. The investment value or bond value of a convertible is defined as the price at which the convertible would trade if it were nonconvertible and valued at (or near) the prevailing market yields of nonconvertible comparable issues.

T   F   17-3. Convertible bonds offer the issuer the opportunity to initially offer common stock at a price above the stock's current market price.

T   F   17-4. Convertible bonds that are called may be either converted into stock or redeemed at the call price.

T   F   17-5. Because of their risk, convertible bonds carry a higher interest rate than comparable bonds without the conversion option.

T   F   17-6. Most convertible bonds are callable.

T   F   17-7. All convertible bonds are convertible until maturity; however, there may be an initial waiting period.

T   F   17-8. An investor would never be wise to convert a bond when called if the underlying stock was trading at a price less than the conversion price.

T   F   17-9. There is little correlation between returns on convertible bonds and returns on the stock market.

T   F   17-10. A convertible's conversion premium is directly related to the price of the underlying common stock.

T   F   17-11. Assuming that the stock price rises above the conversion price, eventually the conversion value and the market price of a convertible bond will equal each other because of the risk that the bond might be called.

T   F   17-12. A convertible bond will sell at a price not less than the larger of its bond investment value or its conversion value.

T   F   17-13. Convertible bonds have greater price sensitivity to changes in interest rates than nonconvertible bonds do.

T   F   17-14. A pure hedge is always less risky than not hedging.

T   F   17-15. Selling one security short and buying another security long is unlikely to be a technique used by arbitrageurs.

T   F   17-16. Risk arbitrage is different from pure arbitrage in that the former usually makes a profit, whereas the latter rarely makes a profit.

18

Futures

┌───┐
│ **Learning Objectives**   │
│ *An understanding of the material in this chapter should enable the student to* │
├───┤
│ 18-1. Describe the characteristics of futures contracts, and explain how they are used in trading commodities like agricultural products, materials, and minerals. │
│   │
│ 18-2. Describe the different kinds of financial futures markets, and explain what is meant by program trading. │
└───┘

Chapter Outline

Commodities are a bit off the beaten path, compared to more traditional investables (stocks and bonds). But futures markets are an important investment area for several reasons. The dollar value of futures contracts traded, including both commodities and financial futures, substantially exceeds that of securities. Moreover, the futures market's dramatic price swings appeal to many speculators. Finally, futures prices reflect anticipated market conditions in many important industrial goods (meat, grain, sugar, silver, lumber, and gasoline) and financial services (interest rates, currencies, and stock market indexes).

The futures markets challenge even the most skillful traders. Nonetheless, investors need some understanding of the market to decide intelligently whether or not to participate. This relatively brief introduction is not designed to equip investors to trade something as complex and risky as futures. It should, however, provide sufficient background for the interested reader to study the topic in greater depth later if desired.

COMMODITIES AND FUTURES

The word commodity is primarily used to refer to deferred-delivery contracts traded on a futures exchange. A commodity futures contract obligates one side (the seller) to deliver a specific quantity of a specific type of asset (wheat, silver, T-bills, and so on) on a prespecified date to a prespecified location or set of locations. The other side (the buyer) promises to pay for the asset upon delivery.

The production of agricultural products to be sold in near and distant markets inspired the practice of commodity trading. As in earlier years, at any given moment, a supply of products is available in the market for delivery immediately. In modern terminology, negotiations that end with immediate delivery of a commodity are concerned with the *spot (cash) market*. For these transactions, the product must be currently available for delivery. In the *futures market,* a commodity must be available at a prearranged future date.

spot (cash) market

futures market

Who would be interested in buying products for delivery at some distant date? The obvious answer is a manufacturer whose finished product requires the commodity and who wants to be assured that a supply will be coming to its factory. This reduces the manufacturer's necessity to store raw materials until needed. Since contracts for future delivery establish the delivery price, the commodity producer (seller of the contract) and the manufacturer (buyer of the contract) can make plans based on a knowledge of how much each will receive or pay. In this manner, revenues and costs are predictable.

Futures versus Options

Futures and option contracts are sometimes confused. Both involve subsequent events. An option holder has a right but not an obligation to buy or sell a specified quantity of some asset at a specified price over a specified time period. The holder of a futures contract, in contrast, has the obligation to accept and pay for a specified quantity of some asset at a specified price at a specified time. Thus, those who own options have a right, whereas those who own futures have an obligation to do something in the future.

Difference between Futures Owner and Option Holder

- Futures owner has the obligation to accept and pay for a specified quantity of an asset at a specified price at a specified time.
- Option holder has the right—but not an obligation—to buy or sell a specified quantity of an asset at a specified price over a specified time period.

Forward Contracts versus Futures Contracts

forward contract

A *forward contract* is a unique contractual agreement between parties to accept delivery (buy) and to deliver (sell) a specified commodity or financial instrument at an agreed-upon price, settlement date, quantity, and location. The terms of this contract result from direct negotiations between the parties, and the parties accept the terms of the contract. Because these contracts are nonstandard ones, there is no organized exchange for trading forward contracts.

futures contract

A *futures contract* is divided into two contracts—one to buy and one to sell—and it contains standardized features that cover the same commodity covered in the forward contract. Since the terms are standardized, active secondary markets exist. Indeed, most futures contracts trade on an organized exchange that sets the standards for the contracts, provides the location for their trading, and monitors their settlements.

Futures contracts allow those who expect later to have or need that asset to establish a price and quantity ahead of time. Standardizing the contract's terms (grade, quantity, delivery location, and date) facilitates active trading. That is, a large number of interested parties can trade the same (standardized) contract.

Futures may be used to hedge spot (that is, immediate delivery) positions or to speculate on commodity price changes. Rather than make or take physical delivery, most hedgers and speculators eventually close their positions with offsetting trades. Spot and futures market prices that move too far out of line, however, do encourage some traders to make or take delivery. Indeed, the threat of such arbitraging activity generally drives spot and near-delivery futures prices together.

Most futures can be traded with margins (earnest money) of from 5 percent to 15 percent of the contract's value. Thus, even a small change in the price of a contract can produce a very substantial profit or loss. Margin percentages are generally set just high enough to limit default risk.

> **Differences between Forward Contracts and Futures Contracts**
>
> - Forward contract: a nonstandardized (unique) contract between parties to accept delivery (buy) and deliver (sell) a specified commodity or financial instrument at an agreed-upon price, settlement date, quantity and location. There is no organized exchange for trading forward contracts.
> - Futures contract: a standardized contract divided into two contracts—one to buy and one to sell—a specified commodity or financial instrument. Most futures trade on an organized exchange that sets contract standards, which establish price, quantity, delivery location, and date.

Different Types of Commodities

Listed futures contracts exist for three basic classes of delivery vehicles: agricultural, mineral, and financial commodities. The principal foods include cattle, hogs, chickens, wheat, oats, corn, soybeans, barley, sugar, potatoes, coffee, orange juice, and cocoa. The commodity exchanges also trade nonfood agricultural items such as lumber, plywood, cotton, and wool. The minerals traded on futures exchanges include crude oil, natural gas, gasoline, heating oil, copper, zinc, gold, silver, platinum, tin, palladium, and lead. Such financial futures as those for federal funds, Treasury bills, long-term government bonds, several stock market indexes, and various currencies have grown increasingly popular.

The prices of all these items are quite volatile, reflecting their underlying supply and demand variability. No legal or theoretical barriers prevent futures trading in rhubarb or peppermint, but interest would probably be insufficient to justify these listings. Commodity exchanges do, however, frequently try to establish futures trading in new commodities. For example, contracts for turkeys, shrimp, apples, and diamonds were tried and failed, while live cattle, pork bellies, rice, oats, lumber, plywood, heating oil, and a number of financial futures have been more successful. Many other items such as steel reinforcing bars (re-bars), scrap aluminum, returnable drink bottles, uranium, milk, butter, coal, cement, cinder blocks, sulfur, and nails might or might not support futures trading.

Predicting which futures contracts will succeed is quite difficult. Successful contracts have, however, generally possessed most or all of the following characteristics:

- a relatively competitive spot market
- a meaningful standardized contract
- storability or its equivalence (a call on production)

- sufficient price volatility to attract (or require) speculative and hedging interest

Characteristics of Futures Contracts

Different Instruments

If AT&T issues a series of 7 percent bonds that mature in 2000, these bonds are a different investment instrument than a series of 7 percent AT&T bonds that mature in 2001. Similarly, a futures contract for wheat to be delivered next September is different from one for wheat to be delivered next October. Despite the fact that both bond issues and both wheat futures have many common characteristics, each has different market performance characteristics and thus is a distinct investment instrument reported separately in the financial press.

Required Delivery and Acceptance

When investors purchase stocks or bonds, they anticipate taking delivery of the certificates. With futures contracts, acceptance and delivery of the commodity must be made at the settlement date. Most buyers and sellers of futures contracts, however, do not expect either to take or make delivery. Rather, they plan to close out their position by purchasing an offsetting contract. That is, if a futures holder has a September wheat future buy order, the holder will purchase a September wheat future delivery order. Since the investor holds contracts on both sides of the transaction, the contracts cancel each other out. The exchange on which these contracts trade records the closing out of the position.

The same procedure is followed for the holder of a delivery order who closes out the position. Although offsetting transactions are made, it does not follow that neither a gain nor a loss is realized. This would be the case only if the buy and sell prices of September wheat specified in the futures contracts were equal.

Large Dollar Value

Although stocks and bonds normally trade in round lots of 100 shares or five bonds, the dollar value of most buy and sell orders is not all that large. One hundred shares of a $75 stock have a value of $7,500 plus transaction costs, and five bonds total about $5,000 plus transaction costs. But the standard futures contract for wheat, for example, contains 5,000 bushels. If wheat is priced at $5 per bushel, the contract has a market value of $25,000. (The size of a futures contract for Treasury bills is $1 million, and, for example, on January 10, 2000, a March contract traded for $945,000.) Unlike stocks or bonds, the standardized futures market does not trade in odd lots or contracts of less than standard size. Thus, each futures contract has a high dollar value and controls a sizable quantity of a commodity or financial instrument.

Gains and Losses

long transaction
short transaction

Buying a contract for future delivery of a commodity is referred to as a *long transaction*; selling a contract for future delivery is called a *short transaction*. In a long transaction, the buyer expects the future price of the commodity to be higher than that specified in the contract so that the value of the future contract will increase. If this occurs, the buyer gains and the seller (shorter) losses. The reverse occurs if the price of the product falls by or on the delivery date of the contract. Aside from commissions, gains and losses are always equal. Economists describe this as *zero-sum market*.

zero-sum market

Long Transaction versus Short Transaction

- Long transaction: buying a contract for future delivery of a commodity. Buyer expects future price of the product to rise.
- Short transaction: selling a contract for future delivery of a commodity. Seller expects price of the product to fall.

Commissions

round-trip fee

As described above, investors in future contracts can close out their position without having to deliver or accept delivery of the futures commodity or financial instrument. *Delivery actually takes place in only one percent of all futures contracts.* Since the standard procedure is to close out the position by acquiring an offsetting contract, the transaction cost paid at the formation of a long or short futures contract is a *round-trip fee* that covers the commission at both ends of the transaction. The size of the commission varies, depending on the commodity or financial futures contract and the number of contracts being traded.

Margin Deposits

Investors can purchase stocks and bonds by paying in full at the time of purchase or by using a margin transaction in which the investor places the initial margin requirement (percentage of purchase price) with the broker and borrows the remainder. When the investor wants to acquire the stock (or bond) in his or her name, the borrowing (the margin loan) must first be paid

earnest money

off. In the futures market, all purchases are made with a margin deposit. This deposit is *earnest money* (security) to guarantee the performance by the buyer or the seller of the futures contract. The transaction does *not* involve any borrowing. The margin deposit stays with the broker through whom the order is placed until the contract is either completed or closed out.

mark-to-market

Like margin accounts with stocks and bonds, these margin deposits have initial and maintenance requirements established for each commodity or financial instrument. For example, the wheat future with a market value of $25,000 requires an initial deposit of $1,500 and a maintenance deposit of $1,000. Using a procedure called *mark-to-market,* the futures contract is valued at the close of business each day, and the investor's deposit (mark) is adjusted for the day's gain or loss. Under this procedure, losses reduce the investor's deposit, and a margin call is made if the deposit falls below the maintenance amount for that particular futures contract. If the investor fails to meet the margin call, the broker will close out the account by purchasing an offsetting transaction, and the investor must then settle any loss on the account with the broker. If the mark-to-market procedure results in a gain to the contract holder, the deposit is increased by the gain. The investor can use the gain, if sufficient in amount, as the initial deposit on additional futures contracts, thus pyramiding his or her holdings in exactly the same manner as used in margin accounts for stocks and bonds.

Trading of Futures

Trading of all stocks and bonds on an organized exchange takes place from midmorning until late in the afternoon, with extended trading hours recently implemented by the New York Stock Exchange. In the futures market, however, investors have only a short period of time—an hour or two each day—in which to conduct trading in any specific futures contract. Furthermore, because of two unique rules established by the exchanges—the daily price limit and the maximum daily price range—on some days no trading of a particular futures contract occurs at all. The exchanges designed these two rules to prevent wide fluctuations in contract prices because of rumors, events, or undue speculation.

**daily price limit
(interday limit)**

The first rule, the *daily price limit* (sometimes called the *interday limit*), prevents more than a specific amount of difference between the closing price (price of last trade) of the previous day and the opening price (price at which the first trade takes place) the next day.

Example: Assume that the daily price limit for wheat is $0.25 and that September wheat futures closed at $5 yesterday. Today's opening price for September wheat futures can be neither lower than $4.75 nor higher than $5.25, no matter what new information might have come to the market between the closing and the opening times. For instance, suppose that during the night, a severe storm ravaged the wheat-growing section of the Midwest and early reports describe widespread damage to wheat crops. This information would make many individuals and businesses seek to immediately acquire wheat futures contracts for September delivery in anticipation of sizable price increases. Without the daily price limit, the price of wheat would skyrocket—perhaps unnecessarily—to as high as $6, but the daily price limit fixes the opening contract at $5.25. Although buyers of September delivery wheat futures would be numerous, sellers would be scarce. If no contract can be formed at $5.25, the exchange closes for the remainder of the day's trading period. The following day, the upper limit of the opening price is $5.50 (lower limit $5). Again, if no contracts are formed, the exchange closes, and the following day's opening price can rise to $5.75. Following this procedure, the market will eventually open. After a day or so to assess the damage, it may be discovered that the initial information about the storm overstated the crop damage and that wheat will be in greater supply than previously anticipated. In this case, the daily price limit prevented the price of wheat from rising rapidly at first and then falling sharply after a less hasty assessment of the situation.

Each different type of futures contract has a different daily price limit, depending on the price per unit of the underlying commodity or financial instrument. (*Note:* No such procedure exists on the securities exchanges. The specialist will stay at the trading post until a transaction is consummated, and as many as 2 or 3 hours might elapse before a stock or bond opens. Also, there is no limit on the change in dollars or percentage of selling price between the first transaction price and the prior day's closing price.)

The second rule concerning futures contracts is the *maximum daily price range* restriction. This rule precludes the formation of any contract that falls outside a range around the opening price of twice the interday limit.

Example:

Assume that wheat closed at $5.75 yesterday and opened at $5.80 today. The maximum daily price range is twice the daily price limit. After wheat opens at $5.80, trades can take place only at $5.80 ± $0.25 ($5.55 to $6.05). (*Note*: No such restriction applies to stocks and bonds; their prices can change from a few pennies to $20 or $30 in a single day.)

Although a $0.25 change in the price per bushel of September wheat seems small, the change in the value of the contract is large. Five thousand bushels of wheat at $0.25 translates to a $1,250 change in the contract's price. An adverse price change equal to the daily price limit can almost eliminate the total amount of an investor's initial $1,500 deposit for wheat.

Open Outcry

open outcry

The stock exchanges use specialists to maintain an orderly market in the securities, and the auction system is used to match buy and sell orders. By contrast, futures trading uses a system called *open outcry*. In this system, traders shout out their desire to sell (or buy) a contract. In addition to shouting their preferences, traders also use a system of hand and finger signals to indicate the number of contracts they wish to sell (or buy) and how much (in fractions of a cent) they are willing to accept or pay above or below the last-traded full-cent price. When someone acknowledges a willingness to trade at those terms, the contract is formed and recorded. If this sounds somewhat chaotic, it is!

Differences between Commodities and Securities Markets

As discussed above, the commodities and securities markets differ in a number of important respects. Since futures terms rarely exceed 18 to 24 months, long-term commodities investment is restricted to traders who are willing to take possession and pay storage. Because very few traders are prepared to do this, almost all futures trades are short run. Futures have maximum daily trading limits that prevent prices from moving up or down by more than a set amount. The inability to trade once the price has reached its daily limit may delay a timely coverage of an exposed position. Holding near-delivery futures positions risks having to make or take delivery. Margins are much lower on commodities than on securities; 15 percent or less is common, compared with 50 percent (in 1999) for stocks.

Security market short-selling restrictions (short sales must not be on a downtick) do not apply to the commodities market. Short interest in securities is usually a small fraction of long interest, while commodity short positions and long positions are numerically equal. Unpaid commodity margin balances do not incur interest since actual payment takes place only at delivery. The futures market has no specialist system. Certain types of commodity transactions receive commission discounts. No similar discounts apply to securities transactions. Commodity and option positions must be closed with the brokerage firm that handled the initial transaction. Stocks and bonds may, in contrast, use different brokerage firms to buy and sell.

Differences between Commodities and Stocks

Commodities	Stocks
• Limited term	• Unlimited term
• Maximum daily price moves	• No limit on daily price moves
• Delivery possible	• Never becomes spot
• Margins of 5% to 15%	• Margins of 50% or more
• Long interest equal to short interest	• Short interest usually small fraction of long interest
• No short selling restrictions	• Short sales not permitted on a downtick
• No interest charged on unpaid margin	• Interest incurred on margin debt
• Market has no specialist system	• Market making by specialists
• Commission discounts on special types of trades	• No commission discounts for trades
• Positions must be opened and closed with same brokerage firm	• No restriction on opening and closing positions with different firms

Different Types of Commodity Traders

A substantial fraction of commodities traders are professionals. For example, large firms in commodity-related industries (mining, baking, meat packing, grain, and so on) often maintain representatives on the relevant exchanges. These particular professionals seek to provide a future supply or market for their companies' products. They make it their business to have access to and a detailed understanding of the latest information relevant to their particular commodities. For instance, they may be following the latest crop estimates, cost comparisons, weather reports, possible government policy changes, trade figures and the international economy, and a host of other useful data. Access to all of the relevant and available knowledge tends to give these professionals a decided advantage over less-informed traders.

Several additional classes of professional commodity traders bear mentioning. They include scalpers, day traders, position traders, and arbitrageurs. Like stock exchange floor traders and specialists, these traders usually have seats on the exchange and trade for their own accounts. Scalpers seek to buy at slightly below or to sell at slightly above the previous price. They hope to close out their positions within a short time at a modest profit. Scalpers do not plan to maintain their positions for long; an hour is a relatively long time. They are not required or expected to make a market, but their activity does help keep trading more orderly. Scalpers provide buying or selling interest even when relatively few other traders are available.

Day traders usually close their positions by the end of each day. They trade somewhat less frequently than scalpers but also hope to profit from modest price movers. Unlike scalpers and day traders, position traders seek to profit from fundamental or technical forces that may manifest themselves over several days. Finally, arbitrageurs try to exploit relative prices that vary from expected relationships.

Types of Professional Futures Market Traders

- Firm representatives: hedge needs or outputs of commodity-related firms
- Scalpers: seek to take advantage of very short-run imbalances in supply and demand
- Day traders: short-run traders who close their positions each day
- Position traders: may hold positions for several days based on fundamental or technical factors
- Arbitrageurs: seek to exploit departures from expected relative price relationships

---

Trading Futures Contracts

The individuals or firms that generate the majority of the trading in futures contracts do so for the following reasons: hedging, speculating, or spreading.

hedging

Hedging

Many manufacturers purchase commodities and then convert the raw materials into finished products. These firms expect to earn profits from the production and sale of the finished product. The prices of raw materials used in the production process, however, can change significantly from the time they are purchased to the time the finished product is sold to the manufacturer's customer. In many cases, the spot market price at the time the finished good is sold strongly influences that product's selling price. If the spot price falls between the time the raw material is purchased and the time the finished product is sold, the finished product will most likely sell for less than the manufacturer had anticipated. Thus, an unexpected loss will result from holding the commodity during the production cycle. (A gain will occur if the spot market price rises and the finished product can be sold at a price that is higher than expected.)

To protect against this loss, the manufacturer buys the commodity in the spot market as a raw material for a finished product and simultaneously sells (shorts) the commodity for delivery at the time the finished product will be sold. When the finished product is ready for sale, the manufacturer will close out the short position. If the commodity is then selling for less than the price paid for it as a raw material, a gain will be realized when the manufacturer covers the short position, but less will be realized from the sale of the finished product (*vice versa* if the commodity is selling for more than the price paid for it).

In an absolutely effective hedge, the gain from covering the short is exactly equal to the loss from the sale of the finished product at a lower price. Likewise, the loss from covering the short position due to an increase in the spot price equals the gain that arises from the unanticipated increase in the selling price of the finished product. When used in this manner, most hedges do not provide matching gains and losses, but they do capture most of the adverse price changes and thereby reduce the risk to the manufacturer.

Other manufacturers might have a contract to deliver a finished product at a specified price and date but have no desire to purchase and hold the needed raw material until the time that production starts. To assure the cost of the needed raw material, buying a future contract that specifies delivery when the raw materials are needed gives the manufacturer the desired protection against adverse price changes of the ingredient.

The strategy of hedging with futures can be used with financial futures for stock indexes, foreign currencies, or interest rate futures, as well as for commodities.

Speculating

speculating

Individuals who use *speculating* as an investment tactic anticipate that the price of a commodity or financial future will change during the duration of the option, and they hold a contract that will benefit from the price movement. Expecting the price to rise, speculators purchase futures contracts (go long). If the market price of the commodity or financial instrument rises, the investor can sell the contract for a profit. Since the margin deposit is relatively small, the profits can be quite impressive. For example, if an investor pays $1,500 for a wheat contract, a $.25 rise in the price of a bushel of wheat will result in a gain of $1,250 ($.25 x 5,000 bushels) and a holding period return of 83.33 percent ($1,250/$1,500). Of course, if the price of wheat falls, the loss can be just as spectacular.

A speculator who expects the price to fall sells (shorts) the future and gains if the price does as expected. The loss from a rise in the price of the commodity or financial instrument can be virtually unlimited if the speculator is unable to close out the open position during the upward price movement and ultimately has to purchase in the spot market so that delivery can be made.

Spreading

spreading

Users of *spreading* as an investment tactic buy one futures contract (go long) and sell a second futures contract (go short) that has different terms. In spread positions, the most likely result is that one contract will gain and the other will suffer a loss. This tactic, being both long and short, limits the loss that can result. It also reduces the potential gain. The net result tends to be small gains or losses, but the investor faces less risk than the speculator faces.

Hedge Trading Results

Another question relating to the futures markets is, Who on balance makes and who loses money? In particular, do those who hedge generally have to pay for the risk reduction that they obtain?

Hedging is akin to purchasing insurance. Thus, those who facilitate hedge trading (speculators) might well be expected to earn a risk premium. Testing this proposition requires identifying those who are seeking to hedge and separating them from those who are speculating. Discriminating between risk takers and hedgers from aggregated data, however, is relatively difficult. Nevertheless, the results of several studies over past years that have attempted such desegregation are as follows:

- Small traders lose slightly more on short positions than they make on long positions.
- Large speculators profit at the expense of hedgers; the greatest profits are made in large active markets.
- Hedgers tend to do well in low-volume markets; the profits of large speculators in high-volume markets come mainly from the small speculator.

Thus, professionals may profit at the expense of small traders, and small speculators do not seem to receive a risk premium for their risk taking. More recent studies also find evidence of rewards (profits to risk takers) for speculators.[1]

Disadvantages of Commodity Trading for Amateurs

Professional traders have better access to relevant information, lower trading costs and/or quicker executions than the vast majority of amateurs. Most small inexperienced investors should be discouraged by this state of affairs. No one wants to compete in a market in which he or she is at a significant disadvantage relative to a large part of the market's participants. Moreover, the number of listed commodities is much smaller than the number of actively traded stocks. Thus, each commodity receives proportionately more attention. Presumably, such attention leads to relatively well-informed pricing, thereby increasing the difficulty of finding misvalued contracts.

In addition, unlike the securities market, each specific futures contract (such as July wheat) has equal numbers of short and long contracts. If the price declines, the shorts gain what the longs lose, and *vice versa*. If the professionals make money on balance, the amateurs must lose. Furthermore, both losers and winners must pay commissions.

FINANCIAL FUTURES MARKETS

Commodity futures have long been traded on agricultural and mineral physicals. New types of commodity contracts have accounted for much of the market's growth, however. In particular, currency, interest rate, and, more recently, stock market futures have grabbed the spotlight.

Transactions in financial futures deal with contracts for foreign currencies, debt securities (commonly called interest rate futures), and stock indexes (index futures). Although the standard size and dollar value of these contracts vary, many of the characteristics and trading concepts of commodity and financial futures are identical. Except for stock index futures, settlement in all other futures contacts is either by taking delivery or delivering. Prior to expiration, all futures positions can be closed out by purchasing the other side of the contract.

Futures on Indexes and Cash Settlement

Traditionally, futures contracts have specified delivery of some specific asset. Although most contracts may have been closed out with offsetting trades, those few still in force at contract expiration result in the long taking and the short making delivery. This same practice continues with many of the newer financial contracts.

For some contracts, however, the delivery instrument does not exist and would be relatively difficult, expensive, or inconvenient to establish. Specifically, futures contracts on various market indexes present a potential problem with delivery. Rather than settling by delivery of a physical asset, index contracts are settled with cash. That is, the buyer and seller determine the difference between the price when they institute the trade and the index value at contract expiration. The loser pays the winner that difference. These cash settlements are used with index futures based on stock, bond, and commodity indexes.

Interest Rate Futures

While money lending has gone on for about as long as trading in such futures-related items as wheat and gold, no one gave much thought to a debt instruments futures market until the early 1970s. Many individuals and institutions do, however, have a stake in and/or an opinion on the future level of interest rates. Just as similar circumstances had long fostered futures trading in other commodities, *interest rate futures* trading looked like a good bet.

interest rate futures

Trading in financial futures began with the Chicago Board of Trade's Government National Mortgage Association (GNMA) futures contracts and the Chicago Mercantile Exchange's T-bill contract. The market subsequently expanded to include long-term Treasury bonds, one- and 5-year Treasury notes, municipal bonds, CDs, and Eurodollars. Most of the recent trading has been in Eurodollars, T-bills and Treasury bonds. GNMA futures are no longer actively traded.

Like all futures contracts, interest rate futures call for delivery of a specific amount of the relevant commodity at the contract's expiration. For example, the Treasury bond contract specifies the delivery of $100,000 face amount of Treasuries. Price fluctuations in the contract reflect variations in the expected bond interest rate. Eight percent as the benchmark yield has been set for some time. If market rates are lower, then the appropriate discount rate for the $100,000 instrument is lower, and the spot and futures prices are appropriately set higher.

Institutions that plan to borrow at some later time can use interest futures to hedge against adverse interest rate moves. Similarly, financial institutions with future sums to invest may use the market to establish the rate that they will earn on the investment. Finally, those whose expectations differ from the market may speculate in interest rate futures. A number of researchers have explored the productive use of interest futures in hedging and managing interest rate risk.

currency futures

Currency Futures

The major foreign currencies are traded on futures exchanges and in over-the-counter forward contracts. Futures and forward contracts differ primarily in two ways: First, almost all futures contracts are traded on a futures exchange; all forward contracts are traded over the counter. Second, futures contracts require margin deposits; no margin is required for forwards. Otherwise, the two types of contracts are quite similar. Both envision future delivery at a price negotiated at the time of the trade. Both offer international traders an opportunity to hedge their foreign exchange risks. Some spot speculation in foreign exchange also uses travelers checks, foreign bank accounts, and securities denominated in foreign currencies. (Many others trade currency options, as discussed in chapter 16.)

Foreign-exchange speculators bet on the relative movements in exchange rates. Thus, an investor who expects the yen to appreciate relative to the dollar can buy yen or deferred-delivery yen (either futures or forward contracts) with dollars. If the investor's analysis is correct, the position can subsequently be covered at a profit. If exchange rates move adversely, however, the position will produce a loss. Currency futures and forward contracts have been widely traded since the floating of the dollar in the 1970s. Table 18-1 replicates a typical futures listing for the euro for January 10, 2000.

TABLE 18-1
Currency Future Prices Reported January 11, 2000
(for January 10, 2000)

EURO FX (CME) Euro 125,000; $ per Euro

	Open	High	Low	Settle	Change	Lifetime High	Lifetime Low	Open Interest
Mar	1.0348	1.0348	1.0263	1.0304	−.0028	1.1242	1.0089	56,056
June	1.0384	1.0389	1.0350	1.0375	−.0028	1.1077	1.0166	166
Sept	.....	......	.....	1.0440	−.0028	1.1136	1.0226	97

Est vol 11,105; vol Fri 11,914; open int 56,323, −177.

The table shows the March futures price for the euro traded on the Chicago Mercantile Exchange (CME) in contracts of 125,000 euros each. It opened at 1.0348 and closed at 1.0304, a change versus the prior day of −.0028—meaning that there is an expectation that the value of the euro will be lower by 2.8 cents compared with the prior day's close. Open interest (number of open contracts available to trade) from the prior day was 56,056, and the volume traded on January 10 was 11,105 contracts.

Stock Market Index Futures

stock market index futures

The successful introduction of debt instrument futures spurred interest in equity futures. Today, the most popular *stock market index futures* are the Chicago Mercantile Exchange's S&P 500 Index and the Chicago Board of Trade's (CBT) Dow Jones Industrial Average index. Several European indexes are traded on European futures markets, and the Nikkei 225 stock average of blue-chip Japanese stocks is traded on the CME. The CME also trades the Russell 2000 and the NASDAQ 100. The Russell 2000 provides a vehicle for speculating or hedging in relatively small-capitalization stocks; the NASDAQ 100 is heavily influenced by large and small technology stocks. These equity contracts offer a variety of ways to speculate or hedge on the stock market's movement. In particular, the contracts are an ideal way for portfolio managers to hedge either their anticipated funds needs or their portfolios against anticipated market reversals.

Example:

Suppose a large common stock portfolio manager anticipates a market decline. To liquidate and later reinvest the portfolio would be costly (spreads, commissions, and so forth). The stock index futures market provides a relatively simple way to neutralize the portfolio from market moves. First, the manager determines his or her portfolio's beta and then uses the following formula to determine the number of contracts to short:

$$\frac{\text{Number of contracts}}{\text{needed for hedge}} = \frac{\text{Portfolio value}}{\text{Contract value}} \times \frac{\text{Weighted average}}{\text{beta of portfolio}}$$

Consider a portfolio with a weighted average beta of 1.14 and market value of $20 million. The S&P futures contract value is $250 multiplied by the S&P Index future value:

S&P futures contract value = $250 (S&P Index future value)

Assume the S&P Index future is 1460. Thus, a single contract would be worth $365,000 ($250 x 1460).

Accordingly, the number of contracts needed to short is as follows:

$$\begin{array}{c}\text{Number of contracts} \\ \text{needed for hedge} \\ \text{(short)}\end{array} = \left(\dfrac{\$20,000,000}{\$365,000}\right) \times 1.14$$

$$= 62.5 \text{ (rounded up to 63} \\ \text{whole contracts)}$$

Thus, selling 63 contracts should approximately neutralize the portfolio from market fluctuations. That is, the fluctuations in the value of 63 S&P Index futures contracts should closely approximate those of a $20 million stock portfolio that has an average beta of 1.14. If the portfolio's value declines, a short position in the S&P futures contracts should rise by an offsetting amount. Similarly, an increase in the portfolio's value should be offset by a fall in the value of the futures position.

Futures Options

futures option

A commodity option, or *futures option,* is an option on a futures contract. As such, it is an abstraction on an abstraction. The futures contract is itself a deferred-delivery agreement that trades and has a life of its own. An option on such an agreement represents the right but not the obligation to take or make delivery on such a contract. Thus, a call option on a futures contract is a right to buy such a contract at a prespecified price over a prespecified period. Similarly, a put is an option to sell such a futures contract.

The unique feature of options on futures is that they give the investor the opportunity to make a small dollar investment that can control a sizable position in a particular futures commodities or financial instrument. These puts and calls give the holder the right to sell or buy a specific commodity or financial futures contract for a specified period of time and for a given striking price. Unlike futures contracts in which delivery and acceptance must be made at the expiration of the contract (unless an offsetting position has been taken), the buyer can walk away from the transaction; therefore, the largest possible loss on futures options is the acquisition price paid. Like other options, the price behavior of futures options moves with the underlying asset. A call future option on a foreign currency rises in value when the price of that currency relative to the U.S. currency increases. (A put futures option falls in price.)

Options on Futures Contracts

- Call: the right—but not the obligation—to buy a futures contract at a prespecified price over a prespecified period
- Put: the right—but not the obligation—to sell a futures contract at a prespecified price over a prespecified period

---

The mechanics of futures options are similar to those for puts and calls on stocks. If the underlying futures price rises sufficiently, the price of the commodity call will also rise. A decline in the futures price will, at worst, cost the owner only the purchase price of the call. The relationships are similar for puts, except that the holder profits from a price decline and incurs limited risk for an upward move. Those who own (or are short) futures contracts outright incur a much greater loss liability. Thus, commodity options offer upside leverage and downside protection. A rather hefty premium is required to induce option writers to assume the risks inherent in the contract's sell side.

Listed option trading was prohibited in the United States in the 1930s. Accordingly, traders had to seek a market outside the United States or trade in an over-the-counter market. In either case, up-to-date price quotes were difficult to obtain, and the market was relatively imperfect. Some major commodity option scandals occurred in the absence of an active U.S. exchange market. Notwithstanding this, the commodity option instrument itself has a legitimate role. Indeed, the commodity exchanges resumed listed commodity options trading in 1982. Currently, futures options are listed on a number of agricultural, mineral, and especially financial assets. Such trading and the increased flow of information that it generates reduce the abuses that once resulted from OTC commodity options trading. A number of pricing models similar to those for stocks have been developed and tested.

Because of their potential for high rates of return and because the loss is limited to the amount paid for the option, these options pose less dollar risk than trading directly in futures contracts. Nevertheless, the investor must have a thorough knowledge and understanding of the products and markets for commodities and financial futures before any purchase or writing of futures options.

Program Trading

program trading

The advent of stock index futures and options has facilitated the rise of a type of trading that generally uses the indexes: *program* (or programmed) *trading*. In a general sense, program trading refers to any large-volume, mechanical trading system. This trading is generally based on some computerized model of theoretically appropriate price relationships.

Normally, a program involves the simultaneous execution of trades in a number of stocks. The large-capitalization stocks that are members of one of the major indexes, such as the S&P 500, are particularly likely to be involved. These trades also often involve the use of stock index futures or options on these index futures. Program trades for stocks listed on the New York Stock Exchange are facilitated by their *DOT* (designated order transfer) and *SuperDOT* systems. These two systems allow the near simultaneous execution of large trades of a number of stocks. The orders are submitted directly to the system and then transmitted electronically to the specific stock trading posts of each of the securities.

DOT

SuperDOT

By far, the most popular types of program trading are portfolio insurance and index arbitrage. Both involve the use of index contracts (futures or options on futures), and both are primarily used by large institutional investors and traders, including some brokerage firms trading for their own accounts.

Portfolio Insurance

The index futures example above illustrates an increasingly popular strategy of portfolio managers. Portfolios, particularly large portfolios, can be managed to limit their exposure to market downturns. The process of limiting a portfolio's market exposure is called *portfolio insurance*. This insurance can be structured to reduce greatly the possibility that losses will exceed some prespecified limit. At the same time, the portfolio will still retain an opportunity to profit from a rising market. The portfolio insurer can use various types of contracts, including index futures, options on index futures, and options on individual stocks.

portfolio insurance

Under one form of downside protection, the insurer closely monitors the market. When the stock market suffers a significant pullback, the client's portfolio is hedged. Usually, the insurer sells an appropriate number (for the portfolio's size and beta) of index futures contracts. Alternatively, the insurer may purchase an equivalent number of stock index puts. Either approach largely neutralizes the impact of further down moves in the market. For example, a short position in index contracts would appreciate as the value of the portfolio declines. Similarly, the index puts would place a floor on losses in the portfolio.

Both of these approaches to portfolio insurance (futures or options hedges) generally protect the portfolio against a downturn. Protection, however, has a cost. In addition to the relatively modest direct costs (insurer's fee, commission, and forgone interest on margin deposits), the investor sacrifices some potential gains. Purchasing puts incurs the premium paid for the option, while selling index futures contracts shifts any profits from a stock market rise to the purchaser of the contracts. Moreover, the implementation of the strategy requires the availability of sufficient potential supply of/demand for (at reasonable prices) the hedging contracts. A substantial drop in stock prices may create a major imbalance in the supply-demand relationships for these contracts. Everyone cannot abandon ship at once. The supply of available lifeboats is limited.

In short, portfolio insurance can provide some protection against market downturns. It is not, however, always possible to implement, and when it is possible to apply, a portfolio insurance strategy may reduce potential profits from subsequent upturns.

Index Arbitrage

index arbitrage

The existence of stock index futures has facilitated and stimulated another relatively new type of trading. *Index arbitrage* is a strategy designed to take advantage of disparities between index futures prices and the cash market prices of the securities that make up the index.

Suppose, for example, the futures contract on the S&P Index is priced appreciably above the current value of the index itself. The final settlement price of an index futures contract is the closing value of the underlying index. Thus, at the expiration of the index future, the index and the futures contract on the index must have the same value. Accordingly, a long position in the stocks that make up the index, coupled with a short position in futures on that index, will produce a gain that is approximately equal to the difference between the cost of the two positions. Some adjustments must be made for the impacts of commissions, bid-ask spreads, and dividends on the underlying stocks. The precise amount of dividends and the level of prices after deducting trading costs are not known at the outset. Moreover, the index programs must be initiated quickly when price disparities open up. Still, when the futures price exceeds the corresponding index, something close to a guaranteed trading profit is possible. If such a profit is attractive compared with alternative risk-free returns, an index arbitrage trade is indicated.

Similar index arbitrage opportunities are available when the futures contract is priced somewhat below the index. In this circumstance, the index arbitrageur sells the underlying stocks short while purchasing the futures contract. This type of program trade is profitable only if the difference in the two prices is sufficient to offset the trading costs (commissions and bid-ask spreads) and dividends on the shorted stocks.

Program Trading, the Brady Commission, and the Crash of 1987

Program trading—particularly index arbitrage—was subject to a substantial amount of criticism in the wake of the stock market's 1987 crash. The exchanges' regulators (and others) have studied the causes of the crash. The best-known of these studies was sponsored by Congress and generally referred to as the Brady Commission (named after the commission's chairman Nicholas Brady, later Secretary of the Treasury). Studies were also sponsored by the New York Stock Exchange, Securities and Exchange Commission, Commodity Futures Trading Commission, Chicago Mercantile Exchange, and General Accounting Office. Prominent personalities who testified on the subject include Alan Greenspan, Federal Reserve Board chairman; and Donald Regan, formerly CEO at Merrill Lynch, Secretary of the Treasury, and Reagan Chief of Staff. Many financial commentators and some of the committee reports blamed the crash, at least in part, on financial futures trading. Index arbitrage and portfolio insurance received special attention. More generally, trading in financial futures was blamed for the apparent increase in stock market volatility. The commissions, regulators, financial commentators, stock exchanges of New York, and the futures exchanges of Chicago argued vigorously over this and related issues. No one contends that financial futures have no impact on the markets for the underlying financial instruments. Whether the impact is relatively minor, short run, and perhaps stabilizing or is more serious, longer run, and destabilizing remains controversial.

One potential scenario involves the interaction of index arbitrage and portfolio insurers in a (crash) market downturn. As the stock market starts to drop, the portfolio insurers enter the market, selling index futures to hedge their clients' portfolios. According to many observers, these sales tend to enter the market just as its decline is accelerating. The selling tends to push the futures index price below the spot market price of the index as reflected in the price of the underlying stocks. As futures prices fall below the prices in the stock market itself, index arbitrageurs enter the market. These traders buy index futures and simultaneously short the stocks making up that index. Their short selling pushes stock prices down further, perhaps bringing on more portfolio insurance selling of the index futures. The process may drive the market down substantially and even create a panic.

Such a scenario may well have been one of the factors contributing to 1987 crash or at least exacerbating the market's decline. Most critics of program trading concede that fundamental factors (rising interest rates, concern about inflation and the dollar, and so on) were largely responsible for the 1987 stock market drop. Thus, some sort of decline and perhaps a crash might have happened anyway. On the other hand, these critics attribute the swiftness of the decline and panic of October 19, 1987, largely to the massive amount of program-induced selling pressure.

This analysis is based on the allegations of those who blame the stock market crash (at least in part) on the financial futures market. Another of their principal concerns relates to the limited amount of capital available to most specialists' firms. To date, these allegations remain just that— allegations. Not surprisingly, the various constituencies have rather different perspectives.

Most critics of the present system would like to restrict index arbitrage, program trading, or, in some instances, financial futures. One possibility is to impose some margin requirements on financial futures. Another proposal seeks to stop any panic by the installation of so-called circuit breakers, whereby both stock and financial futures trading would stop briefly if the market moves more than some predetermined amount. In fact, circuit breakers were implemented in the late 1980s and then, more recently, scaled back. Other analysts assert that any attempt to restrict or ban financial futures or cash-market trading on U.S. exchanges will simply shift the markets overseas. No doubt, this debate will long continue.

Hedge Funds

hedge funds

Some mutual funds called *hedge funds* use trading futures options contracts as their main investment strategy. These funds—and some professionally managed portfolios—typically require minimum investments of $25,000, $100,000, or more. Therefore, they are not available to the investor with modest means. Indeed, some of the wealthiest investors, such as George Soros, are prominently connected with hedge funds. To this point, these funds are unregulated because it has long been believed that since small investors are not likely to be involved, there is no need for regulations. A recent episode with a hedge fund has widened the debate, however.

The Long Term Capital Management (LTCM) hedge fund near-debacle in late September 1998 reveals both the power and risks of hedge fund performance and behavior. LTCM was funded by many of the largest investment firms and commercial banks on Wall Street and abroad. In the summer of 1998, the fund managers and partners assumed that abnormal interest rate spreads between U.S. government debt instruments and other debt securities, which were widening, would narrow sooner rather than later. Thus, they bet on this principle by buying options, futures, and other derivatives on the non-U.S. debt instruments.

The widening worsened dramatically, however, after the Russian government's default on its foreign debt and the spill-over effect on Latin American financial markets. This led to a worldwide investor "flight to quality," which meant even more investors fleeing to U.S. government instruments. This, in turn, greatly exaggerated the spread and required the fund managers to cover their positions with even more capital. At the time, they had leveraged some $98 billion of exposure with $4.8 billion of capital. By the end of September, capital had dwindled to some $600 million.

The managers went to their lead lenders and asked for more capital. Enough of the lenders balked that it became necessary to force a bailout masterminded by the head of the New York Federal Reserve Bank. In the end, the lenders (under duress) invested $3.6 billion of new capital, and the original partners' share in the company dwindled to 10 percent.

moral hazard

Debate then raged as to whether the original investors' punishment fit the risks and losses they had caused. The major issue was *moral hazard*—the assumption of risks by one party that causes widespread costs that are not fully borne by that one party, thereby forcing other parties to bail them out.

systematic risk

The Fed was criticized and blamed for its role in the crisis, even though no direct taxpayer funds were ever at risk. The Fed argued that *systematic risk* of an LTCM bankruptcy would have been too destabilizing to the U.S. and world economies. Most observers probably agreed. In any event, the Fed still had to step in and make further Fed funds rate cuts to restore confidence in financial markets.

Critics have continued to argue that the Fed's moves in sum created the conditions for further unwarranted euphoria in financial markets in 1999 and thereafter. Others in Congress have called for tighter regulation of hedge funds to prevent their excesses. The consensus opinion to date is that both the hedge fund investors and the funds lenders should be the watchdogs on hedge fund managers. This debate will also continue.

SUMMARY AND CONCLUSIONS

A large dollar volume of futures trading takes place on the various futures exchanges. Standardized commodity futures contracts in grade, size, location, and delivery date facilitate substantial hedge and speculative trading. The relatively low percentage margins required to trade futures allow investors to magnify greatly the profits and losses generated by a given price move in the underlying physical. Financial futures markets have grown rapidly because of the opportunity to hedge (and speculate) on the basis of securities in other financial markets and because of the introduction of a variety of new types of contracts. To succeed in the futures market, a contract requires a basis with sufficient competition, standardization, and price volatility to establish an active trading market.

Financial futures differ from stock options in a number of ways, including term, trading limits, delivery possibility, margin percentages, short restrictions, interest on margin, specialists, commission structure, and opening and closing positions with the same broker. Because of their relatively independent (not related to the stock market) volatility, financial futures contracts may be useful in diversification, but their own volatility limits their appeal to amateurs.

Several different types of professional futures traders compete with the amateur speculator: Scalpers trade on the floor of the exchange, seeking very quick turns; day traders close their positions at the end of each day; position traders may hold for several days; arbitrageurs seek profits from disequilibrium price relations; firm representatives trade for the accounts of firms that deal in the underlying physical.

Most commodity and financial futures contracts result in some (albeit small) loss to the traders. In contracts that do realize gains, however, the gains are substantial. It is the allure of the substantial gains that creates the interest in these contracts. Because of the expertise and time needed to devote to these contracts, they are not the province of the casual investor. They also encourage new forms of speculation and other practices, such as index arbitrage and hedge fund arbitrage, that have the potential to adversely affect volatility in financial markets as a whole.

As with options, futures trades may be based on fundamental and technical analysis. Combination trades involve offsetting positions in related contracts with the hope of hedging against adverse price changes or profiting from relative price moves.

Financial futures instruments include currency, interest, and stock market index futures. These new instruments are increasingly important and provide new opportunities to make markets more efficient and to reduce (or spread) risks.

CHAPTER REVIEW

Answers to the review questions and the self-test questions start on page 785.

Key Terms

spot (cash) market	speculating
futures market	spreading
forward contract	interest rate futures
futures contract	currency futures
long transaction	stock market index futures
short transaction	futures option
zero-sum market	program trading
round-trip fee	DOT
earnest money	SuperDOT
mark-to-market	portfolio insurance
daily price limit (interday limit)	index arbitrage
open outcry	hedge funds
hedging	moral hazard
	systematic risk

Review Questions

18-1.　Compare commodity trading with stock market trading.

18-2. Suppose you start with $5,000 that you invest in silver futures at $5 per ounce, putting down margin equal to 10 percent. A month later, silver rises to $6 per ounce. When your account is marked to market, you use the excess in your margin account to buy more silver up to the maximum. A month later, silver rises to $7 per ounce. You again buy the maximum amount of silver futures. When silver hits $8 per ounce, you liquidate your position.
    a. How much have you made?
    b. What is the holding period return?

18-3. Suppose that in question 18-2, you had not liquidated your position and that you would receive a margin call when your account fell to 5 percent of the value of your positions.
    a. At what price of silver would you receive a margin call?
    b. Suppose you then sold enough silver to bring your equity up to 10 percent. How much further must silver fall for you to get another margin call?

18-4. What characteristics are needed for a commodity contract to be traded actively on a futures exchange?

18-5. Explain the motivations and advantages that each type of professional commodity trader possesses.

18-6. What factors have led to the recent growth of futures markets?

18-7. a. How do interest rate futures work?
    b. What are some of the debt securities underlying such contracts?

18-8. a. How do stock index futures work?
    b. How can they be used to hedge a stock portfolio?

18-9. Compute the number of contracts needed to neutralize a $50 million stock portfolio having a beta of 1.07. Assume the S&P Index future is at 1450.

18-10. Explain what a commodity option is.

18-11. Discuss the theorized role of program trading in the stock crash of October 19, 1987.

Self-Test Questions

T   F   18-1. The buyer of a futures contract is required, if the contract is held at its expiration, to take delivery of the item covered by the contract.

T   F   18-2. Only the number of contracts and the price (per unit) are negotiable between buyers and sellers of commodity futures contracts for a specified commodity.

T   F   18-3. In contrast with stocks and bonds, margin is often used in commodity futures contracts.

T   F   18-4.   The margin requirement for futures contracts is considered a down payment against the total costs of the contract.

T   F   18-5.   The margin required for futures transactions is a specified dollar amount that varies according to the type of contract and is the amount an investor borrows when making margin transactions.

T   F   18-6.   Like investors in stocks and bonds, investors in futures contracts must meet two types of margin (or deposit) requirements.

T   F   18-7.   Futures contracts are marked to the market on a daily basis.

T   F   18-8.   Recognizing the volatile nature of commodities contracts, the exchanges impose daily price limits and maximum daily price ranges for each of the commodity contracts traded on the exchanges.

T   F   18-9.   An investor who holds a portfolio of bonds and plans to sell the bonds within a 6-month period could now sell a futures contract against this portfolio as a short hedge.

T   F   18-10.   An investor who expects interest rates to decline in the near future would profit by selling interest rate futures.

T   F   18-11.   If a speculator anticipates that interest rates will rise in the future, he or she might consider buying (going long) interest rate futures to make a profit if interest rates do rise.

T   F   18-12.   A short hedge that involves selling a stock index future while holding a portfolio of stocks enables the investor to offset most of a decline in the value of the portfolio should the market fall.

T   F   18-13.   The buyer of a futures option has no additional obligation to the seller and is not subject to a margin call as occurs with a futures contract.

T   F   18-14.   The biggest difference between a futures option and a futures contract is that the option limits the investor's loss exposure to the price of the option.

T   F   18-15.   Index arbitrage seeks to profit by exploiting differences in the prices of stock index futures and the stock index underlying the contract.

NOTE

1. E. Chang, "Returns to Speculators and the Theory of Normal Backwardation," *Journal of Finance* (March 1985), pp. 193–208; E. Fama and K. French, "Commodity Futures Prices: Some Evidence on Forecast Power, Premiums, and the Theory of Storage," *Journal of Business* (January 1987), pp. 55–73.

19

Real Estate Investments

Learning Objectives

An understanding of the material in this chapter should enable the student to

---

19-1. Describe the characteristics of people who invest directly in real estate, and identify 10 basic principles of real estate investing they should know.

19-2. Explain three different ways of estimating real estate values.

19-3. Describe several aspects of the real estate transaction including bargaining, financing, and refinancing.

19-4. Describe various types of direct real estate investments including an apartment building, condominiums, and land.

19-5. Describe several indirect methods of investing in real property indicating the pros and cons of each method.

Chapter Outline

Many investment courses do not cover investments in real estate. Neglecting this important investment medium seems unfortunate. Even investors who prefer other media need some exposure to the subject to make an informed decision. This chapter gives the reader just such an exposure.

First, the chapter explores real estate's role in the economy. Then it examines real estate's investment suitability and discusses specific guidelines and parameters. Next, it considers 10 basic principles of real estate investing, followed by illustrations of three approaches to real estate valuation (market, cost, and income). In the process, the chapter discusses such topics as bargaining, loan negotiation, property management, and refinancing. It then considers various types of real estate investments: apartments, land, condominiums, recreational property, and commercial property. Finally, the chapter examines the pros and cons of investing in different types of real estate companies and tax shelters.

ROLE OF REAL ESTATE IN THE ECONOMY

Real estate ownership is a large and profitable part of the economy. Because most real estate trades in relatively small localized markets, its size and importance are often underrated.

Two-thirds of all dwelling units are owner occupied. Thus, a large percentage of the population is in one way or another involved in real estate investing. Real estate investing has proved quite profitable in the past. Indeed, at times, average real estate returns have exceeded average stock returns. The past, however, is no guarantee of the future. That is, high average returns on real estate in the past do not ensure attractive returns on specific real estate investments in the future.

REAL ESTATE AS AN INVESTMENT

Who Should Invest in Real Estate?

In spite of the real estate market's importance, size, and profitable history, far more people are well positioned to invest in stocks or bonds than in real estate (other than their own homes). Anyone who is serious about becoming a real estate investor should be able to answer yes to each of the following five questions:

direct investments in real estate

- Can the investor tie up the necessary capital for a minimum of several years? Small investors with only a few hundred to a few thousand dollars to invest are unlikely to find very many real estate investments in their price range. *Direct investments in real estate* often require the owner to have access to additional funds for emergencies, such as unexpected repairs or uncovered damage to the property. Furthermore, individual items of real estate are difficult to sell on short notice. Thus, the investor should be prepared to hold properties for an appreciable period (perhaps a minimum of several years).
- Is the investor likely to remain in the same geographic area for the foreseeable future? Real estate investments usually require frequent attention. Therefore, investors need to be near enough to their properties to supervise them properly.
- Does the investor have the time and talent to manage property effectively? Rental property often requires a substantial amount of maintenance. New tenants must be found periodically. Rents must be collected. Records must be kept and bills must be paid. Even if others are contracted to do these tasks, someone still must hire the managers and monitor their work. Moreover, investors who do the tasks themselves enhance their returns relative to those who hire the work out. However, the time and energy spent managing real estate means that the investor gives up the income that could have been earned in other pursuits.

low liquidity

- Can the investor assume the substantial risk inherent in real estate investing? High leverage and *low liquidity* both add to real estate's risk. Only those positioned to absorb these risks should expose themselves to them. High leverage means that the investor will put down a small percentage of the purchase price and borrow the rest.

Low liquidity refers to the long time required to turn a real estate investment back to cash.

- Does the investor have the credit standing necessary to borrow on attractive terms? Most successful real estate investors use extensive leverage. The investor who is unable to make effective use of borrowed funds may find real estate relatively unprofitable. Since real estate loans are usually secured by the property values themselves, most people can answer yes to this question.

Only investors who can answer each of these questions affirmatively are properly suited for real estate investing. No doubt, one or more of these five criteria will rule out a large number of prospective investors. Many of these people should, however, still learn more about the topic. Some who are not now positioned to invest in real estate may eventually be better able to do so. Many of those not well situated for general real estate investing may still be prospective homeowners. Still others may prefer the stocks of real estate-oriented companies. The following discussion is addressed to all such investors.

Real Estate Investing Principles

The preceding discussion introduced real estate investing and considered its investor suitability. Now we turn to some specific aspects of real estate-investing, beginning with 10 investment principles.

Principle 1

Real estate values are determined by their highest and best (that is, most profitable) uses. Potatoes could be grown in midtown Manhattan and a flea market operated on Miami beachfront property. These locations will, however, almost certainly be put to much more profitable uses. The Manhattan land would earn more as a site for office buildings, apartments, hotels, department stores, or even parking lots. The Miami beachfront parcel should yield a much higher return as a hotel site.

Investors have a strong incentive to acquire and upgrade underutilized property. Bidding prices up to their most productive use values tends to maximize each property's productivity. Potential buyers and sellers should always evaluate real estate in terms of its most productive use. Poorly informed sellers may sometimes price their property below its highest use values. An efficient investment market should, however, make such bargains relatively rare. On the other hand, an investor never wants to sell real estate for less than its most productive use value. Thus, determining realistic values is a key aspect of real estate investing.

Principle 2

The supply of land is largely fixed, while demand tends to increase over time. Heretofore worthless (for human usage) land may sometimes be made useful by draining, clearing, grading, or irrigating. In rare instances, air rights (the right to build over someone else's property) may substitute for high-priced land. Increasing the supply of usable land is relatively expensive and may encounter environmental (for example, preservation of the wetlands) objections, however.

A growing population and increasing affluence have tended to raise land values. Similarly, rising materials and labor prices have tended to increase construction costs. Since these trends seem likely to persist, real estate values should continue to rise, at least in the long run.

Principle 3

As with almost any investment, short-run individual price moves may differ substantially from the long-run aggregate trend. During the 1930s, real estate values plunged, along with the price of almost every other investment asset. Much of the property bought in the 1920s remained below its purchase price until well into the 1940s. Some property bought in the Florida land boom of the 1920s is still worth less than the inflated sums paid at the peak of the hysteria.

Principle 4

Careful comparison shopping is a useful first step in identifying real estate values. As with all investing, shopping around and bargaining is advisable. Paying more than is necessary or selling for less than top dollar reduces returns. Comparative fundamental analysis of an assortment of available properties is an important aspect of real estate investing. Similarly, obtaining properties at attractive prices usually requires information on alternative real estate opportunities. Few fortunes have been made with hasty, half-baked decisions.

Principle 5

Effective real estate investing almost always involves a careful but extensive use of leverage. Few investors have the resources to buy very much real estate for cash. Moreover, property that earns more than the cost of financing yields a positive differential. Therefore, investors should use the collateral value of their property to borrow heavily whenever the projected return safely exceeds the borrowing cost.

Banks, savings and loan associations, and other financial intermediaries are quite willing to lend a substantial percentage (usually up to 75 percent to 80 percent) of the purchase price of developed property. The interest expense is tax deductible, and any unrealized price appreciation on the property is tax deferred. The lower the down payment of a particular purchase, the more of the buyer's funds that remain available for investment in other properties. Borrowers must normally make a large enough down payment to protect the lenders in case they default.

Principle 6

Just as they comparison shop for an attractive purchase price, investors should shop around and bargain for the best financing terms. While the amount borrowed, length of repayment, and interest rate (or formula for a variable rate mortgage) are all important, other factors such as repayment flexibility should not be overlooked. Since an interest rate decline may make refinancing attractive, the absence of a prepayment penalty is especially desirable. Moreover, *closing costs*, insurance arrangements, and property tax escrow accounts should all be considered in negotiating a loan.

closing costs

Closing costs include fees paid to the lender for granting the loan (points), lawyers' fees, and title search expenses. A *point* is 1 percent of the loan principal. Lawyers charge fees for both drawing up the purchase and sales agreements and for searching and guaranteeing the title. A number of loan provisions are designed to protect the lender from specific contingencies. For example, lenders will normally require fire and casualty insurance on any developed property and perhaps borrower's life insurance equal to the outstanding loan principal. Any unpaid property taxes are assessed against the property. Thus, the lender may require that an *escrow account* be established for property taxes and insurance and that the pro rata expected property taxes and insurance premiums be added to the mortgage payment. Property taxes are due at specific times (once or twice) during the year. Borrowers who are not required to make escrow payments have full use of the funds until the due date.

point

escrow account

The initial payments of real estate mortgages (usually monthly) are primarily devoted to covering the interest charge. At first, only a small portion of the monthly payment is available for principal repayment. Over time, however, the amount of the debt is reduced so that less of the fixed payment is required for interest and more is available for principal repayment.

ARMs

At one time, almost all residential real estate mortgages had fixed terms and interest rates. Economic uncertainty and increasingly volatile interest rates in the 1970s led most lenders to prefer to make variable or adjustable rate mortgages (*ARMs*). Since ARMs' terms can differ substantially, the investor still needs to shop around and negotiate.

Many ARMs, for example, start with a set rate for the first year and limit how much the rate can vary per period and how high it can go (a cap on the rate). One lender might offer a 6 1/2 percent first-year rate, a rate in subsequent years that varies annually, and a 12 1/2 percent maximum rate. Another might start at 5 1/2 percent and raise the rate no more than 1 percent each year with no cap on the rate over the life of the mortgage. In some mortgages, the monthly payment is fixed, with the variation in the rate affecting the number of payments. In most cases, however, the amount of the payment fluctuates with the interest rate.

Several innovative financing methods reduce the amount of the monthly payments for the buyer. One of these is the appreciation mortgage. In exchange for a lower interest rate, the appreciation mortgage lender receives a portion of the gain that is realized when the property is sold. The lender in effect bets that the property will appreciate by more than enough to offset the difference in interest rates. Other types of mortgages include growing equity and graduated payment. Both types begin with relatively low mortgage payments that increase over time.

Knowledge of the available range of interest rates or rate formulae, minimum down payment percentages, point charges, escrow terms, available maturities, prepayment penalties, and the like should help the investor to select the most attractive place to begin negotiations. Moreover, the terms of different lenders will be more attractive in some respects than in others (for example, a lower interest rate but a higher down payment). Persistent negotiation with several lenders may afford the best of each world.

Principle 7

Real estate investors should seek to limit all spending on improvements and maintenance to projects that are cost effective. For example, they should not automatically replace a deteriorating roof, repaint the exterior of a faded duplex, or remodel the interior of a now out-of-date office complex. The additional rents the better-maintained property generate may not be worth the higher costs. The expected payback, rather than the physical need, should justify any spending on maintenance and remodeling. Rental rates that are depressed by rent control or a deteriorating neighborhood encourage the investor to realize what is possible with minimal maintenance and eventually to abandon the property. On the other hand, perfectly functional structures may at times be substantially altered or torn down if a different structure would earn enough to justify the conversion.

Principle 8

An investor should never purchase real estate without a careful on-site inspection and comparison with the relevant alternatives. Some companies use a free dinner and slide show to sell Sunbelt property to people living in other areas—especially the Snowbelt. There is no substitute, however, for an on-site inspection. These inspections may reveal a drainage problem; unpleasant odors from nearby factories, sewage treatment facilities, or garbage dumps; neighboring developments that limit land values; more attractively priced nearby property; and many other unexpected factors. Investors should consider investing only in property that is near enough to inspect. The following are some relevant characteristics to consider in any proposed property purchase:

- location. What changes are taking place? Will they work to the property owner's benefit? Consider road access, utilities and services, and neighboring property development. If property is being bought for business purposes, do surrounding businesses complement it? Are suppliers nearby? Is parking adequate? Would the owner be able to expand to adjacent property if need be?

- competition. What nearby properties have similar uses? Does this choice have any particular advantages or disadvantages? Will competitive moves in the area affect the owner?

- facilities and maintenance. Does the physical quality of the buildings compare favorably with neighboring properties? Do the structures have multifaceted use? Are costly repairs likely to be required? If so, does the asking price reflect these projected costs? That is, would the combination of the cost of purchase and the cost of any needed repairs still make the property an attractive investment?

- financing. Can the property be financed by both the current buyer and a subsequent buyer? How committed is the original lender to financing the rest of the development? Would other area lenders consider financing the property? If not, why not?

- operating expenses. How stable are the expenses for taxes, management, utilities, and insurance? Might they rise substantially? Would the new owner be adversely affected by rising energy costs? Are the figures provided consistent with the experience of owners of similar buildings? Do long-term leases provide sufficient additional revenues to cover these projected cost increases?

- income. If the property provides rental income, can rents be increased? How do the rents compare with those for similar property? Is the tenancy likely to be stable? What lease terms can the owner offer?

- price asked. How does the price compare with that paid by other property buyers? Could the same dollar commitment buy attractively priced property in a more established area? If the property is income producing, does the price permit a positive cash flow after taxes and mortgage payments? How firm is the asking price?

Principle 9

Owners of real estate should strive to minimize the use of expensive professionals. Real estate investors often require the services of lawyers, realtors, appraisers, architects, accountants, contractors, property managers, and several other types of professionals. These professionals are sometimes well worth their cost. At other times, however, the property owner may effectively perform the task and save the fee.

Realtor commissions are normally set at 6 percent to 7 percent on developed property and 10 percent or more for land. Thus, the sale of a $150,000 house generates a $9,000 to $10,500 fee. Suppose the owner attempts to sell the house directly. He or she might reduce the price by $2,500 and spend $300 on classified advertising. If the effort is successful, the owner would save $6,000 to $7,500. Some buyers also prefer to purchase properties directly. Owners who personally market the property can afford to sell for less.

Most owners can also handle such jobs as bookkeeping, appraising, and property management. Some professional services, however, are practically unavoidable. For example, few nonlawyers know how to do a title search, and the lender is unlikely to accept the work of those who do. Similarly, few laypersons can design and contract major construction. Moreover, an independent appraisal of a very large parcel might be well worth the cost. Similarly, large property holdings may benefit from professional management and accounting. The issue really boils down to how highly the investor values his or her time and talent.

Principle 10

Investors should continually keep abreast of relevant local, state, and federal agency policies and proposed policies. For example, moving quickly to secure property near new government projects, such as an interstate highway interchange or rapid transit terminal, may yield large profits. Other state or local government actions (for example, rent control) can appreciably depress real estate values. Accordingly, we will now explore the impacts of such factors as major government and nongovernmental construction, legalized gambling, rent control, the environmental movement, national credit trends, and property tax levels.

Major Government and Nongovernmental Construction. Developable property near successful shopping centers usually appreciates in the period immediately following leasing the space in the center. Since local zoning board approval is one key to shopping center development, real estate investors should keep up-to-date regarding the issues coming before these agencies.

Federal installation constructions also offer profit opportunities. Private enterprise is expected to provide support services for the new facility's employees. Since suppliers, restaurants, and shop owners will need space, nearby land will usually appreciate. Recreational land values near expanding government installations may also rise. For example, a planned dam that creates lakefront property or a new access road to some scenic or recreational attraction almost always increases nearby property values. To learn about proposed projects, investors should follow the activities of legislative agencies and their parks and public works committees. Many of these proposals are easily approved. On the other hand, those that are likely to reduce nearby land values are generally hotly contested. For example, proposals for nuclear power plants, sewage treatment facilities, prisons, and airports tend to be carefully scrutinized.

Legalized Gambling. Legalizing casino gambling caused Atlantic City real estate values to soar. Property suitable for hotel casinos rose dramatically, but even many residential property values quadrupled. The Atlantic City example illustrates the profit potential of anticipating and taking quick advantage of such an event. On the other hand, those who waited too long got hurt. Atlantic City was soon overbuilt, causing many property values to decline appreciably.

Rent Control. Laws that constrain rent increases can appreciably reduce an investment's return. Accordingly, real estate investors should closely monitor rent control efforts. Local media generally report this issue thoroughly. Landlords may even take a leaf from the tenants' book and organize themselves.

The Environmental Movement. While its relative importance may vary over time, the environment has clearly become one of the nation's major social concerns. Controlling real estate development constitutes an important aspect of the environmental movement.

Environmentalists view with alarm the conversion of urban residential property to commercial use, the residential development of what had been agricultural land, the planned development of new towns, and even individual homeowner's preferences for dwellings with investment potential. Their basic thesis seems to be that profit-oriented real estate development has been harmful. They propose that the government plan and control real estate development in ways that would greatly restrict profit opportunities. Such controversial views involve many debatable value judgments. In effect, they question the capitalistic approach to economic activity.

Regardless of an investor's own opinion, disregarding antidevelopment sentiment is hazardous. These views are popular, particularly with those who do not own rental or investment real estate. Land use and zoning regulation may require environmental impact findings, limit the owner's ability to subdivide property or convert apartments to condominiums, force expensive improvements such as buried telephone and transmission cables, and require that a major part of the land be left in its natural state. These restrictions clearly limit the land's desirability and investment potential. Even if current legislation does not constrain development, restrictions may be imposed before the purchaser has time to realize a profit.

National Credit Trends. National credit trends also affect real estate investors. When the high cost of mortgage loan money threatens real estate profits, investors should be particularly cautious. The opportunities and risks are correspondingly higher at such times. Investors should not, however, overlook the attractive opportunities that high interest rates create. No doubt, high rates burden real estate buyers. On the other hand, burdensome carrying costs may force some property owners to sell at distress prices. Particularly well-positioned investors may find a tight credit/weak real estate market an excellent time to buy.

10 Principles of Real Estate Investing

- Remember that the value of a property is determined by its most profitable uses.
- Keep in mind that land supply is fixed, while prices may rise with population and affluence.
- Understand that, in the short run, real estate prices often fall.
- Shop around and bargain for the best possible price on property.
- Use leverage extensively where profitable.
- Shop for attractive terms on interest, down payment, maturity, closing cost, insurance, points, escrow accounts, and so on.
- Justify all expenses by expected incremental returns.
- Never buy property sight unseen.
- Minimize the use of professionals, whenever it is possible to do so.
- Be mindful of the impacts of government actions.

Property Taxes. A shrinking tax base can adversely affect local real estate values. Similarly, an area that spends heavily on government services must finance that spending. High real estate taxes may reduce returns and thereby decrease potential price appreciation. Thus, the investor should proceed cautiously when local tax rates are high. On the other hand, a high level of government services may enhance property values sufficiently to offset the taxes required to provide them.

DETERMINING REAL ESTATE VALUES

The 10 real estate investment principles summarized above constitute a useful set of ad hoc advice for novice investors. They do not, however, come directly to grips with the basic issue of real estate valuation. Accordingly, we shall now explore three different ways of estimating real estate values: the market approach, the cost approach, and the income approach.

market approach

Market Approach

Most people would agree that an item is worth what it will sell for. The value of a particular property should not differ greatly from realistic asking prices and recent sale prices of similar real estate. Thus, a check of the market and recent transactions should give some guide to what a particular property is worth. No two properties are precisely equivalent, however. Every property has a different location, and other characteristics (size, condition, and so on) will usually vary, often substantially. Furthermore, a property's market value may differ appreciably from its worth to a particular investor. Therefore, investors should not rely exclusively on the market approach. On the other hand, a price that is above the comparable alternatives is surely too high, while a price that is below the competition is at least worth further consideration.

cost approach

Cost Approach

Real estate values may also be based on the cost of equivalent land and construction. The construction cost should include the cost of funds tied up while the property is being built, and it should allow for the differential values of new versus used structures. When replacement costs are below market prices, investors are encouraged to build rather than to buy. Developed property selling for less than its replacement cost may, depending on demand, be either a bargain or severely outdated or mislocated. Thus, valuations based on replacement costs provide a much better ceiling than a floor on true values.

income approach

Income Approach

Just as common stock values are related to expected future dividend payments, real estate values are strongly influenced by their expected future rental (or other) income.

Example:	Suppose an apartment building yields annual rentals of $10,000, is to be purchased for cash (no mortgage), and has expected annual expenses (maintenance, property taxes, insurance, and so on) of $3,000. To simplify the computations, assume that depreciation, income taxes, and resale value changes are offsetting. Thus, the property is expected to generate a net annual cash inflow of $7,000.
	The present value of a constant income stream is simply 1/r times the income stream (where r is the appropriate discount rate). Discounted at 14 percent, then the property's expected income stream is worth $50,000.

An even simpler approach utilizes the multiples of gross rents.

Example:	If the property in the example above is valued at five times its gross rents, this approach would also value the hypothetical property at $50,000 (5 x $10,000 = $50,000).

The appropriate multiple in this approach will, of course, vary with market interest rates. Investors might also take some account of other factors such as risk, leverage potential, net cash flow, and opportunities to upgrade the property.

These very rough-and-ready uses of the income approach can provide a cursory evaluation of a particular property. The potential investor can simply estimate rental income and direct expenses (exclusive of mortgage payments and income taxes) to find the gross income of the real estate. Dividing this sum by the appropriate discount rate will produce a "first pass" value estimate. Such an approach can help separate obviously unattractive opportunities from those deserving further study.

A much more detailed analysis is needed, however, before the investor can make a final decision. Specifically, the investor should consider the cash flows after loan payments and income taxes are paid, should take account of the property's expected market price change, and should relate the net return to the actual outlay (down payment) rather than the total cost.

Determining the Present Value of Real Estate

Valuing real estate by the income approach is just another application of capital budgeting. In this instance, the cash flows relate to real estate rather than, for example, to a piece of equipment or a new product. The actual implementation of the income approach involves the following six steps:

1. Determine the appropriate discount rate r.
   a. Ascertain the current market cost of borrowing funds to finance the contemplated real estate purchase.
   b. Estimate the highest alternative low-risk return that might otherwise be earned on the funds required for the down payment.
   c. Determine the weighted average cost of funds: Multiply the percentage to be borrowed by the borrowing rate; multiply the percentage of the down payment by its alternative rate; then add the two values.
   d. Add a risk premium to this weighted average cost of funds. The size of the premium depends on the project's risk. A very low-risk project might warrant a 1 percent premium, whereas a higher-risk investment could deserve 4 percent.
2. Forecast future rental income. An established property's current rental rates are known. Rates on similar units provide a guide for newly constructed projects. Forecasting future rates is more difficult. In some cases, the anticipated future rates may be built into the lease. Rental rates on comparable property, vacancy rates, construction costs, and building activity are all relevant factors in rent determination. The investor should usually forecast rent increases conservatively.
3. Forecast the future expenses associated with maintaining the property, including taxes, repairs, renovations, and management costs. Knowledge of the building's structural soundness would be helpful in estimating some of these costs. Current expenses might be projected to rise with inflation. Some adjustments may be required for anticipated needs (such as a new furnace). Note, however, that even experts have difficulty predicting future inflation rates. Since inflation's effects on rents and maintenance costs tend to be offsetting, the investor can at least assume consistent increases for both. Mortgage loan payments should be added to the other expense estimates to forecast the before-tax cost of maintaining the property. The property's taxable income must be determined before income taxes can be calculated.

4. Forecast the property's holding period and value at the time of sale. Again, the investor should try to be consistent. The property's sale price should not normally be expected to rise faster than its ability to produce income.

5. Use these figures to estimate the real estate's value.
   a. Subtract expected costs for each year from anticipated revenues to obtain expected net cash flow.
   b. Use a present-value table or financial calculator to compute the discounted value of each year's expected net income for the selected r.
   c. In like manner, find the present value of the property's expected sale price.
   d. Add the present value of the expected net income to the expected sale price to obtain the present value of the total.

6. Compare the present value of the expected income stream plus future sales price (the income-approach valuation) with the price of the property. The higher the income approach valuation relative to the price, the more attractive the potential investment.

Income Approach: An Example

Now consider a brief application of the income approach procedure:

1. Determine r. (Note that in some market environments these rates may seem high—or perhaps low. They are not meant to be representative of a particular current situation.)
   Borrowing cost: 10%
   Alternative yield on low-risk investment: 6%
   Percent down payment required: 25%
   Weighted average cost of capital: .75 x 10% +.25 x 6% = 9%
   Risk premium: 4%
   Total cost of capital (r): 9% + 4% = 13%

2. Estimate current and future rental income. (To be conservative, use the current amount for future years.)
   Current rental income: $2,000 per month, or $24,000 per year

3. Estimate current and future property expenses.

Property taxes	$4,000 per year
Repairs	400 per year
Miscellaneous	600 per year
Total	$5,000 per year

4. Forecast the expected holding period and selling price.
   Expected holding period: 5 years

Expected selling price: $164,000 (a modest increase over the current asking price of $160,000)

5. Use figures to estimate the real estate's value.

    a. Net income per year – annual property expenses:
        $24,000 – $5,000 = $19,000

    b. Discounted value of each year's expected net income (determined using HP 12C calculator):

Year	Income	Present Value (Discounted at 13%)
Year 1	$19,000	$16,814
Year 2	$19,000	14,880
Year 3	$19,000	13,168
Year 4	$19,000	11,653
Year 5	$19,000	10,312
		Total: $66,827

    c. Present value of expected sales price: $164,000 received at the end of year 5 = $89,013

    d. Present value of expected net income plus expected sales price:
        $66,827 + $89,013 = $155,840

6. Compare present value of d. above with asking price. Since the present value is less than the asking price ($155,840 versus $160,000), the property seems relatively unattractive. If we could justify using a lower discount rate, however, the estimated value would increase. Similarly, a higher projected income stream would increase the value estimate. Finally, the seller might accept a lower price.

Note that while we used greater detail in the example above than in the earlier simplified example, this procedure still focuses on the whole project's return. The return on the investor's contribution, a more meaningful figure, will be discussed in greater detail later in the chapter.

Three Approaches to Valuing Real Estate

*   Market approach: bases value on asking and sale prices of comparable properties
*   Cost approach: bases value on cost of constructing equivalent property
*   Income approach: bases value on present value of expected future net income stream

Combining the Three Valuation Approaches

Attractive real estate opportunities are priced below their market, cost, and income valuations. Real estate priced above any one of these three "values" is probably an unwise investment. If, for example, the price is above either the market or replacement values, more attractively priced properties should be available elsewhere. A price that is high relative to the income-approach valuation suggests that other investments (perhaps outside of real estate) offer higher returns. An investment's attractiveness varies inversely with its price, however. Moreover, real estate asking prices are often flexible.

THE REAL ESTATE TRANSACTION

Bargaining

Unlike most other investments, real estate transactions often involve some bargaining. Thus, investors should bargain with the seller in an effort to purchase potentially attractive investment possibilities as cheaply as possible. Sellers generally expect to receive less than their asking price. Investors should seek to buy at the lower end of the realistic range.

The investor should begin the bargaining process with an offer high enough to be taken seriously but well below what is likely to be accepted. An offer of about 20 percent below the asking price (or 10 percent below a realistic market price) would normally be viewed as low but not ridiculously so. The appropriate level for an initial offer is difficult to prespecify in the abstract, however.

Some properties are so overpriced that an offer of two-thirds or even one-half of the asking price is realistic. In other cases, an offer 20 percent below the asking price might be insulting. The offer should be high enough to elicit a counteroffer but leave the potential buyer maximum flexibility to continue the bargaining process. Unless the market is particularly strong, the seller will usually counter a noninsulting offer. The seller might, for example, drop 5 percent off the price. Then the investor could come back with a 5 percent to 10 percent increase in the offer. Once the investor's offer and the seller's asking price are close, one of the parties will usually suggest splitting the difference.

Uninformed sellers can pose both opportunities and difficulties. A seller who wants cash in a hurry or does not fully recognize the property's value may set too low a price. On the other hand, a seller who has an exaggerated vision of property values may try the buyer's patience. Examples of potential uninformed sellers include the following: an out-of-town heir who needs to pay estate taxes, a longtime owner who has not kept up with current prices, the owner of a run-down property who does not realize that much greater rents could be charged if the property was rehabilitated.

While some uninformed sellers may not know how much their property is worth, others may not know how little it should sell for. Some novice sellers may believe that the real estate market is so strong that eager buyers will meet almost any asking price. Perhaps having the property on the market for a few months will persuade these sellers to be more reasonable.

When an uninformed seller overestimates a property's value, the interested investor can look elsewhere or try out a reasonable offer. The investor might, for example, offer 5 percent to 10 percent below the property's full market value and then not budge until the seller is willing to negotiate. Alternatively, the investor might try out a very low price—for example, one-third below the property's market value. Who knows? The seller just might accept.

seller financing

Seller Financing

Real estate investors may also use the seller to help finance the purchase. For example, a seller who desires a steady income might take back a below-market-rate mortgage on the old property. Most people are unable to earn secure returns on their own investments as high as the rates paid to mortgage lenders. Thus, the opportunity to earn a relatively low (compared to the market) mortgage rate may still seem attractive to them. The seller who receives partial payment in the form of a mortgage will earn a steady monthly income and qualify the transaction as an installment sale, which may reduce taxes for a cash-basis taxpayer.

A buyer who knows the seller's circumstances may be able to work out financing arrangements that are beneficial to both. For example, the buyer might make a 20 percent down payment, assume the seller's existing low-interest mortgage, and give the seller a 5-year note for the remaining debt. The principal will, however, need to be refinanced or paid off well before a long-term mortgage would come due. Interest rates may or may not then be lower. Therefore, the buyer who relies on seller financing may only be postponing the inevitable.

While seller financing is helpful to buyers who need a few years to prepare for higher interest rates and mortgage payments, it should not be viewed as permanent financing. Indeed, borrowers frequently have difficulty paying off short-term seller financing.

The seller should also understand the advantages and disadvantages of entering into a financing arrangement. On the plus side, providing seller financing helps market the property. On the minus side, the buyer's note almost always bears a below-market interest rate. As a "second," it should yield more than a first mortgage. Thus, if first mortgage rates are 10 percent, the market rate on a second mortgage should be 12 percent or more. A lower rate on a second mortgage is, in effect, a hidden price reduction. Moreover, a buyer who has difficulty paying off the note may pressure the seller into extending the loan. Clearly, seller financing is no panacea for either party.

Negotiation through Intermediaries

Third parties such as realtors or lawyers are frequently brought into real estate negotiations. This approach helps to avoid potential personality conflicts from direct buyer-seller contact. For instance, the seller may become defensive if the buyer directly notes the property's negative factors.

The agent earns a commission only if the buyer and seller come to terms. Accordingly, he or she has an incentive to convey the buyer's concerns in a tactful manner. Thus, the agent should be able to comment effectively on the property's condition, location, and/or price relative to that of similar properties. While agents may pressure both the seller and the buyer to improve their offers, buyers are usually better able to resist. They almost always have alternative investment opportunities. Sellers, in contrast, often have only one sale to make.

Buyers should never tell an agent their maximum possible offer until they are ready to make that offer. An intermediary who knows the top figure may not be sufficiently vigorous in seeking a still better price from the seller. The negotiating agent should, however, be given some reasonable explanation for the size of the offer, particularly if it is low. Experienced sellers know not to expect top dollar for second-rate property. Once the buyer's position is clarified, the seller will often make significant concessions.

Closing the Deal

If bargaining reaches an apparent impasse, the would-be buyer should consider low-cost concessions that might push a close negotiation to a conclusion. Offering to agree to an early closing date, for instance, might elicit additional flexibility from a seller who is concerned about timing. An early closing means that the seller will promptly receive the proceeds from the sale.

Similarly, relenting on some original demands, such as ignoring certain small problems, offering to buy some of the seller's personal property, or working out a payment plan suitable to the seller, could all clinch a deal at minimum expense to the buyer. If, however, negotiations proceed to differing figures that seem firm for both sides, the would-be buyer must decide whether to pay more or look elsewhere.

Negotiating the Loan

Once a price that is satisfactory to both the buyer and seller has been established, the next step is obtaining financing. Finding financing is up to the investor.

Example: Consider this scenario: The investor begins the financing process by making preliminary inquiries at a local bank and/or thrift institution. The savings and loan institution is short of mortgage money, but since the buyer is a long-time depositor, the bank is willing to consider an application. The buyer then applies for a $100,000 loan (80 percent of the purchase price). The bank is willing to make a 20-year loan at 10 percent, plus two points. The bank had earlier quoted 9.5 percent but now notes that the rate was a month-old figure that applied to loans with 25 percent down payments. The bank then offers a $98,000 20-year loan at 10 percent with no points. The borrower asks for and receives an option to repay any time after 3 years without penalty, as well as the right to handle property tax and insurance payments without an escrow account. The borrower is required to purchase a term life insurance policy equal to the face value of the mortgage loan.

When both parties are satisfied with the financing arrangement, the loan negotiations are complete.

Completing the Transaction

Once the financing has been arranged, the present owner's clear title must be established (via a title search). The transaction also needs to be registered and taxes paid in the proper locality. At the closing, the buyer, the seller, an officer of the mortgage loan-granting institution, and their attorneys meet and pass the final papers and funds.

Refinancing

refinancing

Refinancing is a useful option in many real estate investment situations. Assume that an apartment building was purchased 5 years ago for $900,000. The buyer borrowed $720,000 and made a $180,000 down payment. Now the property has appreciated, and amortization has reduced the mortgage principal to $650,000. The owner could sell the property for a substantial gain, but significant drawbacks of a sale are that a large part of the proceeds would have to be paid as taxes and subsequent appreciation would be forgone. Thus, the owner may prefer to extract some funds by refinancing. If, for instance, a reappraisal establishes $2 million as the property's fair market value, the bank should now be willing to increase the loan by about $950,000 (to $1.6 million, or 80 percent of $2 million).

Although refinancing may seem to be an attractive way to obtain additional funds, there are some potential pitfalls:

- First, an existing loan might have to be refinanced at a higher rate.
- Second, there are some additional fees and penalties associated with refinancing (for example, a prepayment penalty, title search, and points).
- Third, the new loan will require an increase in the loan payments.
- Fourth, in extreme cases, a refinancing will be viewed by the IRS as a quasi-sale, and taxes will be assessed on the apparent gain.

Rather than a complete refinancing, then, the investor might take out a second mortgage loan. The investor would thus retain the existing mortgage loan while paying the new (higher) rate only on the new loan. Depending on the relative loan size and rates involved, obtaining a second loan may be a less costly and more flexible way of extracting additional principal.

DIRECT REAL ESTATE INVESTMENTS

An Apartment Building (Example)

Most real estate investors start small. They are likely to begin with duplexes or single-unit properties. After some years of investing in small-size properties, a successful real estate investor who has been able to accumulate sufficient funds might next consider investing in an apartment building. Both the problems and the profit potential increase with the scale of investment.

In this example, assume the investor is looking for an old but solidly built structure in an established neighborhood that is close to transportation routes. The investor requires a 10 percent minimum initial return. (Note that the minimum acceptable return should vary with market interest rates. If government bonds are yielding 9 percent, for example, 10 percent would be too low.)

After reviewing the various possibilities, the investor chooses an established section in his or her locality. The investor then contacts various real estate brokers and explains his or her objectives. Market conditions, while not ideal, are considered acceptable. Most available properties are either run-down or high priced. After 3 months, however, a new listing for a 24-unit apartment building looks promising. Since the property meets the desired physical objectives, the investor carefully examines its financial picture.

The seller's fact sheet shows gross income of $450,000, operating expenses of $350,000, and net cash flow of $100,000. A cash flow of 25 percent on the $400,000 down payment seems suspiciously high. In fact, it is too good. After careful examination, a more realistic picture emerges, as shown in table 19-1. For example, the first year's cash return is 5 percent instead of 25 percent. Clearly, the potential investor should always seek to determine the true story.

TABLE 19-1
Financing and Cash Flow for 24-Unit Apartment Building

Financing		
First mortgage, 13% due 2017		$1,000,000
Second mortgage, 15% due 2007 (10-year amount)		600,000
Down payment required		400,000
Total price (after negotiations)		$2,000,000
Annual cash flow		
Gross income		$ 450,000
Operating expenses:		
Fuel	$ 8,610	
Utilities	5,350	
Taxes	52,000	
Insurance	2,750	
Maintenance	17,500	
Superintendent (part-time)	12,580	
Management	64,500	
Vacancy (3%)	10,000	
Total operating expenses	$173,290	
Interest, first mortgage	$129,345	
Interest, second mortgage	88,125	
Principal, first mortgage	11,245	
Principal, second mortgage	28,035	
Total loan payments	$256,750	
Gross cash outflow		$ 430,040
Net cash flow		$ 19,960
Cash return on investment: 5.0%		
Return prior to principal repayment (+ $39,280): 14.8%		

Assume, in our example, that the buyer has decided to use a small local company to manage the property. Its fee is based on the gross income of the apartment complex. Since the management company will look after the property's problems, why not get it into the act early? The buyer might well have the management company evaluate the building's price and general condition. The fee for this service should be modest.

The buyer and seller eventually agree to a price of $2 million. The investor is now an apartment owner. What about the risks involved with the neighborhood and its environment? What safeguards does the investor have?

Often, an apartment building's superintendent is given a rent-free apartment for keeping an eye on things and doing odd jobs. Thus, such tasks as simple plumbing, carpentry, and electrical repairs will be up to the superintendent. Perhaps a share of profits would increase his or her interest. Beyond that, management problems will be the management company's responsibility. An occasional visit by the owner will reveal if the management company is handling its work smoothly and demonstrate that the investor is more than just an absentee landowner.

If the management company selects responsible tenants and maintains the property well, the occupancy rate should be relatively high. Furthermore, if rents are reasonable for the area, turnover should be low. Tenants may be encouraged to fix up their own apartments. Costs will be low (no charge for labor), and the tenants will be happier with units that they can alter to suit themselves.

How can profits be increased? Perhaps buying quality furnishings for some of the apartments and renting them as furnished units would allow a rent increase of $150 a month. In 2 or 3 years, the furniture would be paid for, but it would probably last 5 or 6 years. Converting 12 of the 24 apartments to furnished units over several years could thus increase annual income by a few thousand dollars.

Condominiums

Apartments, duplexes, and single-unit houses are not the only types of residential real estate available to investors. Indeed, a substantial investment market has developed for condominiums. The rent on the unit usually covers most of the investor's out-of-pocket costs. Moreover, in addition to deducting interest and property taxes, the owner may also deduct depreciation (a noncash expense). The investment may therefore show a loss for tax purposes while producing a positive cash flow. Moreover, condominium investments require only limited management, and maintenance is covered by a monthly assessment to the owner's association. Some parents even purchase condominiums for their children to live in while attending college. Their goal is to provide their children with superior housing and eventually earn a profit on the investment.

Condominium investors have earned high returns in some areas. Growth in the singles and older populations has helped boost condominium prices. Since the apartment shortage has added to the strength of the rental market, condominium investors have frequently received excellent rents while they wait to sell their units at attractive prices. As with all investments, however, condominiums are far from a sure thing.

Although some financial institutions prefer borrowers who intend to live in their units, they will usually agree to lend to condominium investors when money is less tight. On the other hand, many communities have strictly limited the conversion of existing apartments to condominiums. Thus, potential government restrictions are one major factor to consider before buying an apartment building for condominium conversion.

Land

Land ownership appeals to many investors because of its high profit potential and because, in a sense, land costs less than developed property. Relatively large land parcels are often available for less than $50,000, whereas most developed real estate sells for far more.

The attractiveness of undeveloped real estate is enhanced by a cash return, which can cover at least part of the cost of carrying the property (taxes, insurance, financing, and so on). Some types of land are suitable for farming, grazing cattle, timber, hunting, or fishing. On the other hand, holding land for subsequent development can also be quite profitable. The investor should, however, be prepared to wait years before the growth of a city, the construction of a highway or shopping center, or some other nearby activity makes development attractive. Once such an event takes place, however, the land's value might multiply many times.

Unlike loans for developed real estate, land loans are generally limited to 50 percent of the value of the undeveloped property. Moreover, the taxes and mortgage loan payments will, at best, be only partially covered by the land's modest return (if any). Land investors must be prepared to service the loan and pay the property taxes, largely from other sources.

Attractive land parcels are likely to have one or more of the following characteristics:

- The property is the next step or the second step beyond the area's most recent development.
- The property is already zoned for development, and the local government might allow even higher-density residential, commercial, or industrial use.
- A nearby property owner might soon want to add the land to his or her own parcel.

- Developers or other knowledgeable real estate entrepreneurs are buying or about to start buying in the area.
- A public or private development has been announced for the area.
- The land is producing an attractive yield from farming, grazing, or some other activity, helping to offset holding costs.

Note, however, that even under the most attractive circumstances, raw land is a relatively risky investment. Moreover, as with other investments, largely overlooked land investment opportunities may be the most profitable.

Recreational Property

At some times, sites that offer recreational opportunities, especially those near water, are hotly sought after. At other times, the high price and occasional scarcity of gasoline severely depress the recreational real estate market. Thus, investors should consider how potential owners would reach their property. On the other hand, many city dwellers still want to get away to fish, hunt, boat, hike, grow something, or just relax. Well-located recreational properties, therefore, will always be marketable. Moreover, the transportation outlook can change or a population center might grow up near a heretofore isolated area. As with other types of real estate investing, predictions and generalizations are hazardous. Isolated out-of-the-way spots might suddenly seem much closer to civilization if an interstate highway is built or oil is discovered nearby.

Commercial Property

An investor could become a silent partner in a car wash, distributorship, or shopping center. That, in effect, is what commercial property investors are. These investors do have the security of owning the property, however. If one tenant does poorly, perhaps another will be more successful. Since location is a very important aspect of profitable commercial operations, potential investors should carefully evaluate main traffic arteries and exits, parking, and the proximity of competitors.

Investors in commercial property can normally borrow up to 75 percent of the property's price. Usually a 5- or 10-year lease obligates the tenant to pay all operating costs except for mortgage loan service, property insurance, and major renovations. The proposed tenant's credit rating should be carefully examined before executing a lease. The investor should expect to earn at least several percentage points above the current inflation rate. Some owners charge a percentage of sales rather than a flat rental fee. Renters thus pay less in poor years and more in good years. Assuming this added risk should generally increase the owner's return. Rents can also be structured as a flat amount plus a percentage of sales.

REAL ESTATE STOCKS AND TAX SHELTERS

Many investors are not well situated to own, manage, and assume the risks involved with direct real estate ownership. Yet the returns that property has generated in the past seem attractive. These investors may want to consider other ways of participating in the real estate market. Real estate investment trusts, real estate development companies, real estate tax shelters, real estate sales companies, and companies with substantial property holdings all represent indirect ways of investing in property. Each offers the opportunity to participate in the market without having management responsibility. Most of these investments are publicly traded companies that own, develop, manage, or sell real estate.

Real Estate Investment Trusts (REITs)

REITs assemble and manage portfolios of real estate and real estate loans. They are organized like and their shares trade in the same markets as those of corporations. They are not, however, assessed corporate profits taxes if they pay out 95 percent or more of their income as dividends.

REITs create portfolios of real estate investments with the proceeds from the sale of stock to the public and borrowed funds. Investors purchase shares of the investment portfolio the real estate investment trust holds. By law, at least 75 percent of REIT assets must be invested in real estate, and no less than 75 percent of its income must be attributed to real estate.

REITS offer investors who want to diversify their portfolio to include real property and mortgages an opportunity to make such investments without having to actively manage assets. Investors take a passive role, receive professional management, and since the REIT's shares are actively traded, have a marketable asset that they can sell quickly. Direct investments in real estate require active management and are illiquid.

As with all equity investments, returns from REITs vary greatly from year to year, causing them to fall periodically from favor with investors. Investors should evaluate REITs by applying the same methods they would use to evaluate any stock prior to purchase.

REITs are essentially closed-end investment companies with stated investment objectives that fall into one of three general categories:

equity REITs
- *Equity REITs* invest in office buildings, apartments, hotels and shopping malls.

mortgage REITs

hybrid REITS

- *Mortgage REITs* are in the business of making both construction loans and mortgage loans.
- *Hybrid REITs* are a combination of equity and mortgage REITs.

Equity REITs are typically the most popular type with investors who want to participate in the growth of real estate values. Dividends should rise if rents increase, and share prices generally reflect changes in property values.

Mortgage REITs, however, are similar to bonds: Like all interest rate-sensitive investments, their prices will rise when interest rates fall, and fall when interest rates rise.

Hybrid REITs, since they invest in a combination of equities and mortgages, must be evaluated differently. To the extent that they invest in property directly, their returns will be similar to those of equity REITs; to the extent of their mortgage holdings, their returns will be similar to those of mortgage REITs.

Real Estate Tax Shelters

Many companies make a business of selling investments structured primarily as tax shelters. These investments are designed to appeal to people in high (or at least above average) tax brackets. Tax shelters are often built around wildcat oil wells, cattle farms, equipment leases, and real estate. Under the Tax Reform Act of 1986, losses on such shelters are generally classified as passive. Passive losses can only be used to offset passive income.

Real estate tax shelter syndicates were once very popular. They were generally formed to finance a construction project or the acquisition of existing properties. Subtracting depreciation, operating expenses, and interest from rental income produced a tax loss. Once rents rose sufficiently to generate a profit (in perhaps 5 years), the property was sold for a gain (so the tax was deferred until the sale). Thus, the shelter was designed to produce tax losses for a number of years. To be an attractive investment, the gain on the sale had to exceed the operating loss total.

Often, an investment that seems attractive on paper does not produce the desired results. Promoters sometimes organize these shelters primarily to pay themselves unreasonably high sales and management fees. These expenses come off the top of any returns the shelter may generate. In other instances, inefficient management and real estate sales reduce the return. Inflated prices are frequently paid to acquire the shelter's property, thereby reducing any chance for a gain. Investments in most tax shelters are not very marketable. Moreover, the IRS will eventually disallow part or all of the tax loss deduction on abusive tax shelters. Investors are charged interest and a penalty on the resulting tax underpayment. Furthermore, tax laws may change and thus eliminate or substantially reduce the projected tax advantage of a particular type of deal. While tax shelters are ill suited to most small investors, the wealthy may still find the tax advantages worth the effort.

Real Estate Limited Partnerships (RELPs)

real estate limited partnerships

Real estate limited partnerships, or RELPs, are specialized securities that provide investors with an interest in a portfolio of real estate properties. Organized as a limited partnership, these securities have much in common with corporations. Each investor's liability is limited to the amount that he or she initially invests. The management function rests with a group of hired managers. The securities may be freely bought and sold. The principal difference from a corporation is in the way the partnership's income is taxed.

A corporation is an entity that is subject to tax in its own right. The dividends that it pays are taxed a second time as income to the owners (assuming that they are subject to an income tax). A partnership is viewed as a conduit for transferring income to the owner. Thus, the full amount of any partnership income is subject to the investor's income tax. No additional tax is assessed at the partnership level. Therefore, the partnership's income is taxed only once. Accordingly, the combination of limited liability and favorable tax treatment makes the RELP an ideal vehicle for individual participation in the real estate market.

A number of brokerage firms have sponsored the issuance of RELPs through public offerings. Others have been offered by the syndicator sponsor who is slated to manage the partnership once it is established. All limited partnerships must have a general partner who assumes general liability. Usually, the sponsor takes on this role.

The principal drawbacks to RELPs are their relatively limited secondary markets and their relatively high overhead structure of fees and expenses. Such investments are generally difficult to sell prior to their scheduled liquidation. Moreover, the sponsoring syndicate usually structures the deal so that much of the profits go to the sponsor, while most of the risks are borne by the investors. Average returns for RELPs have not thus far been particularly impressive.

REIT Mutual Funds

Another way to invest in real estate is to purchase the shares of a mutual fund that invests in REITs, typically equity REITs. This approach enables the small investor to reduce risk through diversification.

Especially attractive in this area are REIT index funds. Rather than trying to select REITs that will outperform the sector, index funds purchase the shares of REITs that are included in the Morgan Stanley REIT Index. Investor returns should equal those of the index, minus fund expenses. As with any mutual fund investment, low expenses give the investor a head start.

Index equity REITs are generally considered aggressive investments: They concentrate investment in a sector that can be rather volatile. Investors should expect wide price fluctuations.

The main sources of risk are as follows:

- market risk. Regardless of the success of individual REITs, they are common stocks that are subject to price fluctuations as the stock market fluctuates. If the overall market trend is down, the prices of REITs will probably decline.
- industry risk. The value of the properties that individual REITs own can decline due to such factors as decreasing rental income caused by overbuilding or tax law changes.
- interest rate risk. The value of income-producing properties can be adversely affected by rising interest rates.
- concentration risk. Any "sector fund" essentially concentrates its investments in a small part of the overall market. Thus, the fund is diversified only within that sector, not across the economy. If the particular sector falls from favor with investors, investments in that sector can underperform the market over an extended period.

Companies with Real Estate Holdings

In addition to the real estate-related investments, a number of other types of companies have substantial property holdings. In most instances, their properties are related to their primary business, but in others, the companies own the real estate. Among the real estate holders are the following:

- paper and forest products companies. These firms often have substantial land holdings from which they obtain timber and wood pulp. Some of this land may be worth far more as homesites, for example. Other property may be worth a good deal just as timberland.
- railroads. Many railroads, particularly those located in the West, own substantial tracts of land, much of which goes back to 19th century government land grants. Other railroads own valuable downtown property near their terminals. Railroads with poor prospects as transport companies are often quite depressed. If their landholdings are ever liquidated, however, the profits to shareholders could be substantial.

- ranch and farm companies. Some agricultural operations with substantial landholdings are organized as corporations. Frequently, this property is carried on the books at very low historical costs. The liquidation values of these firms are often well above the market prices of their stock.
- oil and mining companies. Generally, their most valuable holdings are their mineral resources, but often these companies, too, own some real estate. As with the other types of firms, the stock price may not fully reflect the property's liquidation value.
- manufacturers. Most manufacturers own only the plants that they operate. Some, however, own valuable office buildings and attractive landholdings that are often overlooked by the market.
- insurance companies. Life insurance companies have huge sums to invest. While most of their funds go into bonds, mortgages, and other loans, some are invested in real estate. Moreover, in many instances, the market seems to undervalue that property.
- movie companies. While most moviemakers have sold off their real estate, some still have valuable studio property in Hollywood. This property may or may not be recognized in the stock's price.
- retailers. Many large retailers have valuable real estate in the form of the store buildings in which they operate. Others have long-term leases at rental rates that are far below the current market levels.

The investment attractiveness of companies with substantial real estate holdings depends both on the extent to which their stock price reflects the holdings and on the likelihood that the property will be sold in the relatively near future.

SUMMARY AND CONCLUSIONS

Real estate investing entails a number of aspects. A prospective real estate investor should first determine his or her suitability for such investing. Can he or she afford to tie up sufficient funds for several years? Is the investor likely to remain in the same geographic area for the foreseeable future? Are the talents needed to manage real estate present? Is the investor willing and able to accept the risks?

Among the 10 basic principles of real estate investing are principles that relate to the determination of the price of a given parcel of land by its most valuable uses, the fixed supply of land, the possibility of adverse price moves, the importance of shopping around, the use of leverage, the control of expenses, the inspection of prospective real estate, the use of professionals, and the impact of government actions.

The three approaches to real estate valuation are the market approach, the cost approach, and the income approach. Real estate transactions also usually involve some bargaining, loan negotiation, property management, and refinancing.

In addition to single-unit houses, duplexes, and apartment buildings, other real estate investments include land, condominiums, recreational property, commercial property, REITs, RELPs, and companies that own substantial amounts of real estate.

CHAPTER REVIEW

Answers to the review questions and the self-test questions start on page 788.

Key Terms

direct investments in real estate
low liquidity
closing costs
point
escrow account
ARMs
market approach

cost approach
income approach
seller financing
refinancing
equity REITs
mortgage REITs
hybrid REITs
real estate limited partnerships

Review Questions

19-1.   What issues should be considered when determining the suitability of real estate investment?

19-2.   Briefly explain the following methods of real estate valuation:
a.   market approach
b.   cost approach
c.   income approach

19-3.   How might the results of the three approaches discussed in question 19-2 best be used?

19-4.   You are considering the purchase of a home for $179,000. Your local banker will lend you 80 percent of the purchase price. You must, however, pay three points for the loan and a $500 loan application fee. Title insurance in your area costs $700, and inspections for structural soundness cost $250. Transferring the title will cost you 0.5 percent of the sale price. You must deposit 12 months' property taxes and insurance into an escrow account; property taxes are set at about 2 percent of the sale price. Insurance rates in your community are $4 per $1,000 of protection, and the bank requires that you insure your property for 100 percent of the initial mortgage balance. Having a lawyer represent you at the closing will incur a fee of $200. Hooking up various utilities will require fees of $340 and deposits of another $500.

   a. What is the total payment for acquiring and occupying the house?
   b. Other than the bank loan, how much cash must you raise in order to occupy the house?
   c. If we consider the difference between the total payment and purchase price to be transaction costs, what percentage do transaction costs represent of the purchase price?

19-5. A duplex is for sale for $180,000. After expenses, it offers a net rental income (after deducting all out-of-pocket expenses except financing costs) of $28,000 per year. The rents, expenses, and market value of the property are expected to remain constant for the foreseeable future. The borrower may borrow up to 90 percent of the purchase price at 11 percent. The seller agrees to deduct any closing costs from the purchase price. What is your assessment of the merit of this purchase?

19-6. You are considering the purchase of a parcel of land for $45,000. You can borrow up to 50 percent of the purchase price at a rate of 10.5 percent. Long-term government bonds are yielding 6.5 percent. Briefly discuss the factors that are relevant in determining the cost of capital.

19-7. What alternatives are available to the small investor who likes the general prospects of real estate but is put off by some of the problems of direct real estate investing?

19-8. Suppose that you purchase 100 acres for a cemetery. You estimate that there is room for 1,000 graves per acre. Yearly sales will likely number 800 at $1,000 per sale. Of this amount, $300 will go for preparation and selling expenses and $600 will go into a maintenance trust. The remainder will be profit.

   a. Using a 14 percent discount rate, what is the present value of this business?
   b. How much would the value change if an 11 percent discount rate is used and the maintenance trust requires only $550 per grave?

Self-Test Questions

   T   F   19-1. Direct investments in real estate require the owner to provide for management services.

   T   F   19-2. High leverage is seldom used in direct investments in real estate.

   T   F   19-3. Direct investments in real estate are highly liquid.

T   F   19-4. A point is one percent of the purchase price of the property.

T   F   19-5. Lenders may require an escrow account for property taxes and insurance.

T   F   19-6. Many adjustable rate mortgages have a cap limiting how high the rate may increase over the life of the mortgage.

T   F   19-7. Realtor commissions are normally the same for developed property as they are for raw land.

T   F   19-8. The market approach to estimating real estate values relies on an evaluation of the cost to replace the structure.

T   F   19-9. The total cost of capital is found by adding the risk premium to the weighted average cost of capital.

T   F   19-10. The present value of $20,000 received one year from today is greater than the present value of $20,000 received 3 years from today.

T   F   19-11. When seller financing is employed, the rate of interest on the buyer's note is usually above the market interest rate.

T   F   19-12. Refinancing an existing mortgage is a way to obtain additional funds without selling the property.

T   F   19-13. REITs do not have to pay corporate profit taxes if they distribute at least 95 percent of their income as dividends.

T   F   19-14. A REIT is an open-end mutual fund that redeems its shares when investors sell.

T   F   19-15. Hybrid REITs invest exclusively in office buildings, apartments, and shopping malls.

T   F   19-16. All income a real estate limited partnership (RELP) earns is taxable to the partners.

T   F   19-17. Index REITs are not subject to market risk because they offer a diversified investment portfolio.

T   F   19-18. Purchasing stock in paper and forest products companies is a way for investors to get an equity position in those companies' vast land holdings.

Glossary

12b-1 fund • a type of mutual fund that does not charge a load but does take out a selling fee on an annual basis

AAII • *See* American Association of Individual Investors.

absolute priority of claims principle • the principle in bankruptcy law that each class of liability claims is repaid in full before the succeeding category receives even partial payment

accelerated depreciation • writing off assets faster than proportional to their pro rata life expectancy

acceptance • *See* banker's acceptance.

accrued interest • the pro rata interest obligation on a bond or other debt instrument that has accumulated since the last payment date. Most bonds trade at a price that reflects their net market price plus accrued interest. Defaulted and certain other bonds, however, trade "flat."

acid ratio test • cash and accounts receivable divided by current liabilities; used to measure short-term liquidity (also called quick ratio). It differs from the current ratio by not including inventory in the numerator.

actuarial tables • tables reporting particular age groups' probabilities of death. These tables are based on past experience with separate tables for men and women and certain hazardous occupations.

adjustable rate mortgage • type of mortgage in which the interest rate is periodically adjusted as market rates change

adjusted beta • a statistical correction to beta forecast estimates due to the tendency for historically estimated beta to drift toward 1.0 as later data are gathered. *See also* beta and mean reversion.

adjusted gross income • an interim figure that is reached on the way to computing tax liability. It consists of total income less allowed adjustments, which include such items as moving expenses, IRA and Keogh contributions, and employee business expenses. Taxable income then results from subtracting deductions and the allowance for exemptions from adjusted gross income.

adjustment lag • the time it takes for stock prices to react appropriately to new information

ADR • *See* American depository receipt.

advance-decline pattern • technical indicator showing ratio or difference between number of stocks advancing versus number of stocks declining in a particular period (usually one day) on a particular exchange

advisers' sentiment index • a technical market indicator based on a composite of investment advisers' forecasts. Index users believe that bullish advisers' sentiment forecasts a market decline.

after-tax cash flow • the difference in the actual cash income and outgo for an investment project after taking account of the tax impact

after-tax return • the rate of return an investor receives after adjusting for taxes. Thus, a 10 percent before-tax return corresponds to a 7.2 percent after-tax return for an investor in the 28 percent marginal tax bracket.

agency problem • the conflict of interests and disparity of goals between corporate managers and shareholders

agency security • a debt security issued by federal agencies such as the FNMA, GNMA, or Freddie Mac

AGI • *See* adjusted gross income.

all-or-nothing order • an order that must be executed in its entirety or not at all

alpha • the intercept term in the market model that provides an estimate of a security's return, given a zero market return.

alternative minimum tax • tax that may be applicable to those with large amounts of otherwise sheltered income (preferences) such as accelerated depreciation deductions; applies when the tax liability computed by disallowing these preferences exceeds the liability when the tax is computed the normal way

Altman Z score • a scoring technique used to identify bankruptcy candidates

amalgamation • combining two or more firms into a single firm

American Association of Individual Investors • organization designed to help and promote the interests of small investors

American depository receipt • a U.S.-traded security representing stock in a foreign corporation

American Stock Exchange • an organized stock exchange tending to deal in small to mid-capitalization stocks. Merged with NASDAQ. *See* New York Curb Exchange.

American Stock Exchange Index • a value-weighted index of AMEX stocks

American-style option • an option that may be closed out or exercised at any time prior to or at its expiration date

Americus Trust security • a type of security that divides the ownership of certain stocks into two categories of instruments. The primes receive dividends and are entitled to a liquidation value equal to the price of the stock at termination or a predetermined value, whichever is lower. The scores are entitled to the remaining termination values.

AMEX • *See* American Stock Exchange.

amortization • the process of writing off the value of an asset or liability, particularly a paper asset or liability

AMT • *See* alternative minimum tax.

analyst neglect • *See* neglected firm effect.

annual percentage rate • the yield to maturity on a fixed-income investment or the interest rate charged on a loan, computed using a compounding factor reflecting the balance still due

annual report • a yearly report to shareholders containing financial statements (balance sheet, income statement, changes in financial position statement, and flow of funds statement), auditor's report, president's letter, and various other information

annuity • an asset that usually promises to pay a fixed amount periodically for a predetermined period, although some pay a sum for an individual's lifetime. Certain values of annuities are variable, depending on the issuer's investment experience. Most are sold by insurance companies.

anomalies • conditions in the security markets that appear to allow for persistent abnormal returns on a consistent basis after adjusting for risk. *See also* market imperfection.

antidilution clause • a provision in a convertible bond or other security indenture restricting new share issues

anxious trader effects • short-run price distortions caused by sales or purchases of impatient large traders

appreciation • increase in the value of an investment over time

appreciation mortgage • a mortgage in which the lender is given the rights to a percentage of any price appreciation derived when the property is sold. In exchange for giving up part of the profit potential, the borrower usually receives a more attractive rate than that charged on a standard loan.

APR • *See* annual percentage rate.

APT • *See* arbitrage pricing theory.

arbitrage (pure) • simultaneously buying in one market and selling equivalent assets in another for a certain riskless profit. *See also* risk arbitrage.

arbitrage pricing theory • a competitor to the capital asset pricing model that introduces more than one factor in place of (or in addition to) CAPM's market index

arbitrageurs • investors who take advantage of arbitrage opportunities

arbitraging • *See* arbitrage.

arithmetic mean return • the simple average return found by dividing the sum of the separate per-period returns by the number of periods over which they were earned

ARM • *See* adjustable rate mortgage.

arrearage • an overdue payment, as in unpaid preferred dividends. If the dividends on the senior security are cumulative, arrearage must be made up before common dividends are resumed.

ask • the lowest price at which a security is currently offered for sale that may emanate from a specialist (exchange), market maker (OTC), or unexercised limit order

asset • any item of value, often income producing, that appears on left side of balance sheet

asset allocation (financial planning) • the principal method of portfolio management by financial planning advisers utilizing tools of optimal (efficient) asset allocation theory (Markowitz model), and modern portfolio theory (MPT).

asset allocation (market trading) • a compromise approach to market timing. The asset allocator divides his or her portfolio among a number of categories such as low-risk stocks, high-risk stocks, short-term bonds, and long-term bonds. The percentage of the portfolio invested in each of these categories will be varied depending on whether the asset allocator's outlook is positive or negative. *See* market timing.

asset play • when a firm's underlying assets are worth substantially more (after deducting the firm's liabilities) than the market value of its stock

asset turnover • ratio of sales to assets. In fundamental analysis of the firm, it is a measure of the "productivity" of assets used by the firm.

assignment • selection of a particular option broker's trades for exercise by the OCC (Options Clearing Corporation)

at-the-close order • an order that must be executed near or at that day's close

at the money • when the current stock price is the same as the strike price

at-the-money option • an option whose strike price is equal to the current market price

at-the-opening order • an order that must be executed at that day's opening

auditor's statement • a letter from the auditor to the company and its shareholders in which the accounting firm certifies the propriety of the methods used to produce the firm's financial statements

back testing • trying out a proposed investment strategy on prior-period data to see if it would have been profitable to employ in the past. Successful back testing does not necessarily prove that the tested rule will work (be profitable) in the future; the past experience may not reflect the future market environment.

balanced fund • a mutual fund that invests in both stocks and bonds

balance of payments • the difference between a country's international payments and its international receipts

balance of trade • the difference between a country's expenditures on imports and its income from exports

balance sheet • a financial statement providing an instant picture of a firm's or individual's financial position that lists assets, liabilities, and net worth (equity)

balloon payment • a final large principal payment on a debt instrument whose interim payments either incompletely amortized or did not amortize the initial principal at all

banker's acceptance • a money market instrument (also called acceptance) usually arising from international trade and made highly acceptable by a bank's guarantee or acceptance

bankruptcy proceeding • a legal process for dealing formally with a defaulted obligation; may result in a liquidation or reorganization. *See also* Chapter VII bankruptcy and Chapter XI bankruptcy.

bankruptcy trustee • the person who takes legal title to the property of the debtor and holds it "in trust" for equitable distribution among the creditors

bar chart • in technical analysis, a type of graph that plots the price over time and typically contains data on the high, low, and volume

Barron's • a major weekly investment periodical published by Dow Jones & Co., Inc.

Barron's Confidence Index • a technical indicator based on the yield differential between high-grade and average-grade corporate bonds, with a small differential signifying confidence in the future and a large differential signaling a lack of confidence

basis (commodity) • the difference between the spot price and the futures price

basis (taxable) • the acquisition cost of an asset less any capital distributions. The difference between the basis and the sale proceeds is the taxable gain.

basis point • one-hundredth of one percentage point; primarily used with interest rates

basis risk • the risk that the basis of a commodity contract will move adversely

BCI • *See* Barron's Confidence Index.

bear • one who expects a declining market

bearer bond • an unregistered bond whose ownership is determined by possession

bear market • a declining market

bear raid • an attempt to drive prices down by selling short

benefactor • a person named to receive property or other resources as in a will or insurance policy

best-effort basis • an order to sell (or buy) according to the best available price offered in the market

beta • a parameter that relates stock or portfolio performance to market performance. For example, an x percent change in the market, a stock, or a portfolio will tend to change by x percent times its beta.

bid • the highest currently unexercised offer to buy a security that may emanate from a specialist (exchange), market maker (OTC), or limit order

bid-ask spread • the price difference between the bid price and the ask price for an asset

Big Board • a popular term for the New York Stock Exchange, the largest U.S. stock exchange

bills • government debt securities issued on a discount basis by the U.S. Treasury for periods of less than one year

black knight • a potential acquirer opposed by existing management and to which management would prefer to find an alternative (that is, a white knight)

Black-Scholes model • an option pricing formula based on the assumption that a riskless hedge between an option and its underlying stock should yield the riskless return. The model gives an option's value as a function of the stock price, strike price, stock return volatility, riskless interest rate, and length of time to expiration.

blind pool • a form of mutual investment venture in which the precise purposes of the venture are not revealed until later to the pool of investors

block trade • a trade involving 10,000 shares or more, usually handled by a block trader

block trader • one who assembles the passive side of a block trade

Bloody Monday • *See* Crash of 1987.

blue chip stock • shares of a large, mature company with a steady record of profits and dividends and a high probability of continued earnings

blue sky laws • state laws designed to protect investors from security frauds

Blume adjustment • a method of adjusting estimated betas toward unity to improve their general accuracy

boiler room operations • high-pressure selling programs often associated with investment scams such as Ponzi schemes. These programs are characterized by aggressive sales forces utilizing banks of telephones to extract investments from unsophisticated individuals for risky and often worthless ventures.

bond • a debt obligation (usually long term) in which the borrower promises to pay a set coupon rate until the issue matures, at which time the principal is repaid; sometimes secured by a mortgage on a specific property, plant, or piece of equipment. *See also* debenture, collateral trust bond, and equipment trust certificate.

bond rating • a rating of a bond's investment quality and default risk, usually provided by a rating agency such as Standard & Poor's, Moody's, or Fitch

bond swap • a technique for managing a bond portfolio by selling some bonds and buying others, possibly to achieve benefits in the form of taxes, yields, maturity structure, or trading profits

book value per share • the total assets of an enterprise minus its liabilities, minority interests, and preferred stock at par, divided by the number of outstanding common shares

borrower life insurance • an insurance policy on the borrower's life equal to the outstanding loan principal and naming the lender as the beneficiary

Boston Consulting Group • a consulting firm that does strategic planning and is famous for its growth-share matrix

box spread • a type of option spread in which the investor assembles a vertical spread with calls and a similar but offsetting spread with puts

Brady Commission • one of a number of commissions set up by the U.S. Congress that studied the causes for the stock market crash of October 19, 1987. It was named after Nicholas Brady, former New Jersey senator and U.S. Secretary of the Treasury.

breakup value • the sum of the values of a company's individual assets if sold separately (also called liquidation value)

broker • an employee of a financial intermediary who acts as an agent (not a dealer) in buying and selling securities for customers

brokerage firm • a firm that offers various financial services such as access to the securities markets, account management, margin loans, investment advice, and underwriting

broker call-loan rate • the interest rate charged by banks to brokers for loans that brokers use to support their margin loans to customers (usually scaled up for the margin loan rate)

bull • one who expects a rising market

bullion • gold, silver, or other precious metals in the form of bars, plates, or certain coins minted to contain a specific unit of weight (bullion coins)

bull market • a rising market

business cycle • the pattern of fluctuations in the economy

Business Week • a major business periodical published weekly by McGraw-Hill, Inc.

butterfly spread • a type of spread in which two calls are sold at one strike price, and one call each is purchased at strike prices above and below the sold calls

buying power • the dollar value of additional securities that can be purchased on margin with the current equity in the account

call • an option to buy stock or some other asset at a prespecified price over a prespecified period

callable bond • a bond for which the issuing company has an option to repurchase the securities at a set price over a prespecified period (prior to maturity)

call-loan rate • *See* broker call-loan rate.

call premium • *See* premium (option) and premium (bond).

call price (premium) • the price at which a bond, preferred stock, warrant, or other security may be redeemed prior to maturity; usually begins at a significant premium to the face value and then the premium declines as the instrument approaches its stated maturity (also called redemption price)

call protection • an indenture provision preventing a security (usually a bond or preferred stock) from being redeemed earlier than a certain time after its issue. For example, a 20-year bond might not be callable for the first 5 years.

call provision • a provision in a bond indenture that gives the issuer the option of redeeming the bond prior to maturity.

call risk • the danger that a callable bond or preferred stock will be redeemed early (called) by the issuer

capacity effect • the tendency of inflationary pressures to accelerate when the economy approaches the full employment level

capacity utilization • the percent of utilization of existing productive resources (capital and labor) as measured by the Federal Reserve Board for industrial (nonservice) activities in the total economy

capital asset • virtually any investment asset. To qualify as a capital asset (subject to long-term capital gains treatment), an asset must be held as an investment rather than in inventory as an item of trade.

capital asset pricing model • the theoretical relationship that seeks to explain returns as a function of the risk-free rate and market risk

capital distribution • a dividend paid out of capital rather than from earnings. Such distributions are not taxed when received but do reduce the investment's basis (also called liquidating dividend).

capital gains (losses) • the difference between the basis and sales price of an investment asset held for a period specified by the IRS

capitalization • *See* market value.

capitalizing of expenses • placing current business expenses on the balance sheet and writing them off over time

capital market line • the theoretical relation between an efficiently diversified portfolio's expected return and risk derived from the capital asset pricing model

CAPM • *See* capital asset pricing model.

carry • the cost of holding a physical commodity until it is deliverable on a futures contract (primary components being storage and financing costs)

cash cow • a company or its subsidiary that in the normal course of operations generates a substantial cash surplus

cash flow • reported profits after taxes plus interest, depreciation, depletion, amortization, and other noncash expenses minus noncash receipts

cash management account • an individual financial account that combines checking, credit card, money fund, and margin accounts to maximize returns and minimize interest charges on transaction balances

cash market (spot market) • a market in which physical commodities (spot) are traded for cash

CBOE • *See* Chicago Board Options Exchange.

CBOT • *See* Chicago Board of Trade.

CD • *See* certificate of deposit.

Center for Research in Security Prices (at the University of Chicago) • a data source tape containing daily stock price information

Central Certificate Service • an organization that allows clearing firms to effect security deliveries with computerized bookkeeping entries

central market • a proposal for a complete linkup of the various markets trading securities. *See* Composite Order Limit Book.

central unemployment rate • the unemployment rate for males in the 25-to-45 age group or some similar high-employment grouping

certificate of deposit • special redeemable debt obligation issued by a bank and other depository institution

CFTC • *See* Commodity Futures Trading Commission.

changes in financial position statement • an accounting statement that reports on a firm's cash inflows and outflows (formerly called sources and uses of funds statement)

Chapter VII bankruptcy • a formal, detailed, and usually lengthy bankruptcy proceeding

Chapter XI bankruptcy • an informal, less costly, and shorter procedure than Chapter VII; allowable only upon the agreement of creditors

characteristic line • the relationship between a security's expected return and the market return as defined by the security's α (intercept) and β (slope parameter)

charting • an attempt to forecast stock price changes from charts of past price and volume data

chartist • technical analyst who practices chart reading in order to forecast prices

Chicago Board of Trade • the largest of the commodity exchanges; lists futures in a variety of physical commodities, including wheat, corn, oats, soybeans, plywood, and silver, as well as financial futures in stock indexes, interest rates, and currencies

Chicago Board Options Exchange • the largest of the option exchanges, as well as the originator and promoter of organized options trading

Chicago Mercantile Exchange (the Merc) • the second largest commodity exchange that lists futures in a variety of commodities, including cattle, hogs, pork bellies, fresh broilers, lumber, stock indexes, currencies, and debt securities

churning • overactive trading of customer accounts designed to generate commissions for the manager/broker

circuit breakers • a procedure for stopping trading when a market move reaches a prescribed threshold. For example, stock trading might be halted for 30 minutes whenever the market moves 300 points on the Dow Jones Industrial Average during a single day.

classified common stock • different categories of stock, including nonvoting and nondividend receiving

clearing house • an intermediary organization that keeps track of and guarantees fulfillment of futures contracts or options contracts

CLOB • *See* Composite Limit Order Book.

closed-end fund • a type of investment company organized as a corporation with its stock traded in the same markets as other stocks (the price fluctuates from the fund's net asset value)

closing costs • expenses associated with obtaining a real estate loan and completing the purchase. These costs may include title search, points, transfer taxes, and various other fees.

CMO • *See* collateralized mortgage obligation.

coefficient of determination (R^2) • a parameter that measures how much of the variance of a particular time series or sample of a dependent variable is accounted for (explained by) the movement of the independent variable(s) in a regression analysis

Coffee, Sugar and Cocoa Exchange • a commodity exchange located in New York City that lists futures contracts for coffee, sugar, and cocoa

collateral • asset pledged to assure repayment of debt. The lender may take ownership of the collateral if the loan is not repaid as promised.

collateralized mortgage obligation • multiclass mortgage pass-through security that reduces uncertainty about prepayments by specifying time of repayment; a secured bond that is backed by the mortgage payments on real estate

collateral trust bond • a secured bond; for example, an equipment trust certificate secured by such collateral as railroad rolling stock or airplanes

collectibles • any of a variety of specialized assets, such as dolls, toys, coins, stamps, and antiques, that have value based on their intrinsic value to collectors

combination security • an asset combining characteristics of more than one type of security, including convertible bonds, convertible preferred stocks, hybrid convertibles, equity notes, and commodity-backed bonds

commercial paper • short-term, usually low-risk debt issued by large corporations with very strong credit ratings

commingled real estate fund • in effect, a self-liquidating unit investment trust with a managed portfolio of real estate

commissions • fees charged by brokers for handling investment transactions such as security or real estate trades

commodity • in general, any article of commerce; in investments, any of a select group of tangible items traded on one of the commodity exchanges, either spot (for immediate delivery) or in the futures market (for delivery at a prespecified future date). Commodities differ from other spot and futures investments since they are tangible and have practical as well as investment value.

commodity-backed bond • debt security whose potential redemption value is related to the market price of some physical commodity such as silver

commodity board • an electronic sign in the trading room of a commodity exchange that displays current market statistics

Commodity Futures Trading Commission • the federal regulator of the futures markets

commodity option • a put or call option to purchase or sell a futures contract

common stock • stock that represents proportional ownership of an incorporated enterprise. Common stockholders are the residual claimants for earnings and assets after all holders of debt and preferred stock have received their contractual payments.

company analysis • evaluation of the strengths and weaknesses of a company and its investment appeal vis-à-vis its markets and competitors (also called firm analysis)

Composite Limit Order Book • a proposal that would list all orders on all stock exchanges in one composite list that, with free order flow, would allow all orders to be executed in any market where the security is traded

compounding • growth of an asset's value due to adjustment of the initial value by each period's rate of return to produce an end-period value

compound interest • interest earned on interest as a result of reinvesting one period's income to earn additional income the following period. (Compounding may take place as frequently as daily.) For example, compounded annually, $100 earning 9 percent will yield $9 the first year. In the following year, the 9 percent will be applied to $109, for a return of $9.81. In the third year, the principal will have grown to $118.81 (100 + 9 + 9.81), and another 9 percent will add about $10.62. This process continues with the interest rate being applied to a larger and larger principal. In general, when interest rate r is compounded for t periods, the original investment is multiplied by $(1 + r)^t$.

compound value • the end-period value of a sum earning a compounded return

Compustat data tape • a data source containing balance sheet, income statement, and other information on a substantial number of companies for the most recent 20 years; owned by McGraw-Hill

concentrated position • a margined portfolio having most of its value represented by one or a few securities that may also have a higher margin maintenance percentage than that set by brokerage firms for more diversified accounts

conditional forecast • a forecast based on some exogenous factor such as a stock performance forecast relative to market performance

Conference Board • an organization that compiles quarterly capital appropriations statistics and reports them in Manufacturing Industrial Statistics; also compiles monthly statistics on business cycle indicators (leading, lagging, coincident) and procedures a consumer confidence survey

conglomerate • a company with a diversified portfolio of business units, particularly one formed through a merger of a diverse array of formerly independent companies

consol • a perpetual debt instrument that pays interest but never matures and thus never returns principal

constant growth model • form of the dividend discount model (DDM); used to evaluate the intrinsic value of an asset based upon the assumptions of a constant growth rate g of cash flow or dividends and a known discount rate k, where k>g

consumer credit • personal debt as represented by credit card loans, finance company loans, or similar debts

consumer durables • long-life assets such as furniture or appliances

consumer price index • a monthly cost-of-living index prepared by the Bureau of Labor Statistics, U.S. Department of Labor

consumption expenditures • spending by individual consumers on final goods and services

contingent liability • a potential claim against a company or other entity. For example, a lawsuit claiming damages would represent a contingent claim against the defendant.

contrarian indicators • technical market indicators that are interpreted "contrary to" conventional market analyses

contrary opinion • an investment approach that concentrates on currently out-of-favor securities that may be desirable in the future

conversion premium • the difference between the market price and the conversion value of a convertible

conversion price • the face value of a convertible bond divided by the number of shares into which it is convertible

conversion ratio • the number of common shares into which a convertible bond or preferred stock may be converted

conversion value • the market price of a stock multiplied by the number of shares for which the convertible may be exchanged

convertible • a bond or preferred stock that may be exchanged for a specific number of common shares

convertible bond • *See* convertible.

convertible debenture • a debenture that may for the bond's life be exchanged for a specific number of shares of the issuing firm's common stock

convertible preferred • a preferred stock that may be exchanged for a specific number of shares of the issuing company's common stock

corner • the act of acquiring a large, often controlling interest in a security issue or other specific type of asset that raises the market price significantly and restricts supply. This process is especially damaging to short positions held by investors who may need to cover at very disadvantageous prices.

corporate bond fund • a mutual fund that holds a diversified portfolio of corporate bonds

corporates • corporate bonds

correlation coefficient • a measure of the comovement tendency of two variables, such as the returns on two securities

cost approach • a method of evaluating the value of a real estate investment in terms of the replacement costs of the property or the cost of equivalent land and construction

country fund • a type of mutual fund that assembles and manages a portfolio of securities in a single country, such as the Japan Fund or the Mexico Fund

coupon bond • a bond with attached coupons that must be clipped and sent in to receive interest payments

coupon clipping • claiming income on coupon bonds by detaching each physical coupon and presenting it for payment when due

coupon effect • the price impact of differential yield components derived from coupon versus price appreciation as a bond moves toward maturity. Thus, a deep-discount, low-coupon bond will offer a yield to maturity that includes a substantial component of tax-deferred capital gains. Such a bond's price will usually be affected favorably by the coupon effect.

coupon-equivalent yield • yield on an investment computed to correspond with a bond that trades at par and pays a semiannual coupon

coupon rate • the stated dollar return of a fixed-income investment

covariance • the covariance of variables x and y is: $Cov = E[x - E(x)] [y - E(y)]$, where $E(z)$ is the expected value of z. If x and y tend to be above their means simultaneously and below their means simultaneously, the covariance is positive. If one is above when the other tends to be below, the covariance is negative. If they are independent, the covariance is zero.

covered writing • writing options against existing stock holdings

covering • repurchasing securities or other assets sold short

CPI • *See* consumer price index.

crack • combination commodity trade in which the trader buys crude oil futures and sells corresponding amounts of heating oil and gasoline futures

Crash of 1987 • the largest one-day percentage decline in stock market history. On October 19, 1987, the Dow Jones Industrial Average dropped 508 points, which corresponded to 23 percent of its value the previous close.

credit balance • a positive balance, as in a brokerage account

credit union • a cooperative association in which the members' pooled savings are available for loans to the membership

Creditwatch • one of several short-term credit analysis services. (A bond in danger of being downgraded would be likely to be placed on S&P's Creditwatch list once some degree of trouble is spotted.)

CREF • *See* commingled real estate fund.

crown jewel option • antitakeover defense in which the most sought after subsidiary of a target firm is spun off

crush • a combination trade, especially a commodity trade in which soybean futures are bought and corresponding amounts of soybean oil and meal futures are shorted

cum-rights • the time prior to the day of record that determines when shareholders receive a rights distribution. Securities that sell cum-rights will reflect the imputed value of the rights to be distributed.

cumulative • a preferred stock for which dividends in arrears must be paid before common dividends can be resumed

cumulative voting • a method of voting for corporate directors that gives each shareholder votes equal to the product of the number of shares held times the number of director slots. This method allows a group of shareholders with a substantial but minority position to concentrate their votes on one or a few candidates and thereby elect at least their proportional share of directors.

Curb Exchange • now known as the American Stock Exchange, which until 1953 was called the New York Curb Exchange

currency • any form of money accepted by a country and in actual use within that country as a medium of exchange

currency futures • a commodity futures contract calling for delivery of a certain quantity of a currency's units at a certain price per unit in terms of dollars

currency options • options on currency contracts bought and sold on selected options exchanges such as the Philadelphia Options Exchange

current assets • assets that are expected to be used up or converted to cash within the next year or next operating period, whichever is longer (include primarily cash, accounts receivable, and inventory)

current liabilities • liabilities that will become due and payable in the next year or the next operating cycle, whichever is longer (include accounts payable, short-term bank loans, the current portion of long-term debt, and taxes payable)

current ratio • the ratio of current assets to current liabilities (often a measure of short-term liquidity)

current yield • a bond's coupon rate divided by its current market price or a stock's indicated dividend rate divided by its per-share price

daily price limit (interday limit) • the rule established by the futures exchanges for the maximum range of price movement permitted between the closing price of the previous day and the opening price of the next day of trading for any given commodity. Once the limit is reached, trading must stop until the next trading session.

day of record • the date on which ownership is determined for that quarter's dividends or for the issuance of some other distributions, such as rights

day order • an order that is canceled if it is not executed sometime during the day that it was entered

day trader • a commodity trader who closes all of his or her positions by the end of the day; thus all transactions are opened and closed on the same day

DDM • *See* dividend discount model.

dealer • a security trader who acts as a principal rather than as an agent and who is considered a specialist or a market maker, not a broker (brokers are agents)

debenture • a long-term debt obligation that, unlike a collateralized bond, gives the lender only a general claim against the borrower's assets. In a default, the debenture holder has no claim against any specific assets.

debit balance • a negative balance in a margin account

debt-equity ratio • the ratio of total debt to total equity

debt margin • *See also* leverage and margin account.

debt securities • bonds and similar securities that call for the payment of interest until maturity and principal at maturity. A firm that defaults on its interest or principal obligations may eventually be forced into bankruptcy.

deduction • in tax computation, an amount that may be subtracted from the adjusted gross income to determine taxable income. For example, the taxpayer may choose to itemize state income taxes, charitable contributions, mortgage interest expenses, and certain other costs.

deep-discount bond • a bond selling for substantially less than its par value

default • failure to live up to any of the terms in a bond indenture or other credit agreement

default risk • the risk that a debt security's contractual interest or principal will not be paid when due

defeasance • the process whereby a debtor offsets the impact of a portion of its debt by purchasing high-quality debt instruments (usually government paper) whose payments cover the payment obligations of the debt issue

deflation • an increase in the purchasing power of the dollar or some other currency unit (the opposite of inflation)

depletion • the writing off of assets, particularly mineral assets such as oil or natural gas, as they are exploited

depository trust company • a firm that facilitates exchange members' securities trading with one another by using bookkeeping entries rather than physically delivering the stock certificates

depreciation • a deduction from income that allocates the cost of fixed assets over their useful lives (a noncash expense)

depression • an economic collapse with high unemployment and negative growth

derivative • *See* derivative security.

derivative security • a security whose intrinsic value is derived from the value of another security or combination of other securities; for example, options, futures, rights, and warrants

differential return • the difference in returns between security A and security B, or the difference in returns between a security and the market as a whole

dilution • issuance of additional shares and thereby reduction of proportional ownership of existing shareholders

direct investments in real estate • direct ownership by the investor of real estate property, as distinct from ownership of shares in a real estate company or REIT

discount brokers • brokers who charge below-retail commission rates and usually offer a more limited set of investment services

discount loan • a loan from the Federal Reserve System to a member bank to cure a temporary reserve deficiency

discount rate (for Fed members) • the interest rate charged by the Federal Reserve System on loans to member banks

discount rate (for income stream) • the interest rate applied to an income stream or expected income stream in estimating its present value; the risk-free rate plus the risk premiums for that particular source of income (such as a stock or bond)

discount yield • a yield computation in which the return is based on the final value of the asset. Thus, a bill that sells for $100 - x$ and matures in one year for 100 has a yield of x percent.

disinflation • a slowing in the rate at which prices increase

disintermediation • the tendency of high interest rates to draw funds out of thrift institutions and therefore away from the mortgage market

diversifiable risk • firm-specific or industry-specific risk. Such risks tend to offset one another and thus average out in an efficiently diversified portfolio.

diversification • the technique of spreading an investment portfolio over different industries, companies, investment types, and risks for the purpose of reducing risk

dividend • the payment by a stock corporation to its shareholders on a per-share basis (either common stock dividend or preferred stock dividend)

dividend capture • a strategy in which an investor purchases securities in order to own them on the day of record and then quickly sells them to capture the dividend but avoid the risk of a lengthy hold

dividend discount model • a process of evaluating stocks on the basis of the present value of their expected stream of dividends. Under circumstances where the expected growth rate of dividends is constant at a rate g, and the appropriate discount rate is k (with k>g), the basic formula is $P = d_1/(k - g)$, where P = current stock price, d_1 = initial year dividend, k = appropriate discount rate, and g = expected growth rate.

dividend reinvestment plan • a company program that allows dividends to be reinvested in additional shares, which are often newly issued and may be sold at a discount from the current market price

dividend restriction • the limitation placed on dividend payments in a bond indenture

dividends • payments made by companies to their stockholders that are usually financed from profits

dividend yield • the ratio of annual dividends per share to price per share

divisor • the number divided into the sum of Dow Jones 30 stock prices to determine the average. The divisor is adjusted to preserve consistency when any of the components is split.

dollar cost averaging • a formula investment plan requiring periodic (such as monthly) fixed-dollar amount investments. This practice tends to "average" the unit purchase cost of an investment made over time.

DOT (designated order transmission) • a system on the New York Stock Exchange in which orders are routed electronically to the trading posts where the securities are traded (often used by program traders)

Dow • *See* Dow Jones Industrial Average.

Dow Jones Inc. • the firm that publishes *The Wall Street Journal* and *Barron's* and also compiles Dow Jones stock indexes

Dow Jones Industrial Average • the most commonly referred to index of stock prices (also known as the Dow); computed as the sum of the prices of 30 leading industrial firms divided by a divisor that is adjusted to reflect splits of its components. Dow Jones indexes are also computed for utilities and transportation companies.

downtick • a transaction that takes place at a lower price than the immediately preceding price

Dow theory • a charting theory originated by Charles Dow (Dow Jones Inc.). According to Dow theory, a market uptrend is confirmed if the primary market index (such as the Dow Jones Industrial Average) hits a new high that is soon followed by a high in the secondary index (such as the Dow Jones Transportation Index). A downtrend is signaled in a similar fashion.

draft • a check-like instrument that calls for payment upon receipt

dual fund • a type of closed-end investment company that divides its returns between dividend-receiving fund holders and capital-gains holders

dual listing • a security listed for trading on more than one exchange

Dun & Bradstreet • a firm that rates the creditworthiness of many borrowers and generates financial ratios on many industry groups

Dupont formula • a profitability relationship that relates return on equity to several components: ROE = (net income/sales) x (sales/assets) x (assets/equity), where ROE is return on equity. The formula is used for trouble shooting; by breaking return on equity into its component parts, individual ratios can be analyzed to assess a firm's condition.

duration • the time-weighted average rate of return of a bond's principal and interest divided by the discounted present value of the bond; used as a measure of a bond's sensitivity to interest rate changes; a superior index of the payback rate compared to length to maturity, which ignores returns prior to principal repayment

earnest money • the margin deposit that serves as a security to guarantee the performance of the contract by the buyer or the seller of a futures contract

earnings multiplier • the ratio of market price per share to earnings per share. *See also* PE ratio.

earnings per share • the net income of a company, minus any preferred dividend requirements, divided by the number of outstanding common shares; provides the investor or potential investor with information on the stability of dividends and capital gains potential; considered one of the most important indications of the value of common stock

earnings surprises • the difference between actual reported earnings and anticipated earnings as measured by the consensus estimates of analysts who make such earnings forecasts

econometric model • a model based on an analysis of economic data, particularly models of the economy

econometrics • the statistical analysis of economic data

efficient frontier • a set of expected risk-return tradeoffs, each of which offers the highest expected return for a given risk. *See* Markowitz model and modern portfolio theory.

efficient market hypothesis • the theory that the market correctly prices securities in light of the known relevant information. In its weak form, the hypothesis implies that past price and volume data (technical analysis) cannot be profitably used in stock selection. The semistrong form implies that superior manipulation of public data is impossible. Thus, such data cannot be used to improve stock selection over what is possible through random selection. In the strong form of the hypothesis, even inside (nonpublic) information is thought to be reflected accurately in prices.

efficient portfolio • any portfolio on the efficient frontier that offers the highest expected return for that risk level

EMH • *See* efficient market hypothesis.

employee stock ownership plan • a program in which a corporation contributes newly issued company stock worth up to 15 percent of employee payrolls into what amounts to a tax-sheltered profit-sharing plan

EPS • *See* earnings per share.

equipment trust certificate • a type of bond collateralized by equipment, particularly railroad rolling stock or airplanes

equity • also used to describe the ownership interest in a firm composed of stock holdings in comparison with debt holdings of a firm by creditors. Equity is used interchangeably with stock by most authors. *See* net worth.

equity accounting • partially consolidating income and equity of affiliates that are 20 percent or more owned by the parent firm

equity kicker • a sweetener designed to make a debt issue more attractive by giving its owner an opportunity to benefit from the borrower's success

equity note • debt security that is automatically converted into stock on a prespecified date at a specific price or one based on a formula that is prespecified (also called mandatory convertible note)

equity REIT • a REIT that invests in office buildings, apartments, hotels, and shopping malls

escrow account • in general, an account designed to hold a sum of money for a specific purpose and in particular, concerning real estate, the fund for monthly deposits of the expected pro rata real estate taxes

ESOP • *See* employee stock ownership plan.

Eurobonds • bonds that may be denominated in dollars or some other currency but must be traded internationally. They are denominated in a currency other than that of the country in which they are issued.

Eurodollar deposits • dollar-denominated deposits held in banks based outside the United States, mostly in Europe, but some in Asia and other areas

Euromarkets • financial markets that operate outside any national jurisdiction and deal in securities that may pay unusually high interest rates. The securities are usually based on deposits of large international corporations or governments of nations involved in extensive foreign trade.

European-style option • an option that may be exercised only during a specified period before it expires, usually exercisable only on its expiration date

ex ante facto • before the fact. Thus, it refers to a procedure that consistently identifies attractive investments by relying on prior data and generally facilitates a profitable trading strategy.

ex-dividend date • the day after the day of record. Purchases completed on or after the ex-dividend date do not receive that period's dividend even if the stock is held on the payment date.

exemption • a dollar sum per dependent that may be used to reduce an individual's taxable income

exercise • closing out an option of futures position by purchase and sale of the underlying security or commodity, usually accomplished through clearing houses or exchange markets

exercise price • *See* strike price.

expected return • the highest probability return; typically calculated as the arithmetic average of historical returns over a chosen past period

expected value • the sum of the probabilities multiplied by their associated outcomes; the arithmetic mean or average value

expense deferral • an accounting technique whereby expense recognitions are spread over time

expiration date • in stock options markets, the Saturday following the third Friday of the stated month

explanatory notes • additional information in the form of notes; keyed to stock and bond quotations by letter symbols

ex post facto • after the fact. Thus, it refers to a procedure that identifies attractive investments but relies on ex post data to do so and would not by itself facilitate a profitable trading strategy.

ex-rights • the time subsequent to the day of record for a rights distribution

extraordinary gain (loss) • an unusual nonrecurring gain (loss)

extrapolation • a projection or forecast technique based upon the simple extension of growth or change in the past that assumes the trend will continue at the same rate

face value • the maturity value of a bond or other debt instrument; sometimes referred to as the bond's par value

factor model • *See* arbitrage pricing theory (APT).

Fama-French hypothesis • the theory that book value of the firm relative to market value of the firm, and firm relative size are sufficient to explain differential security returns relative to the market; that beta is not necessary. This controversial conclusion violates the central conclusion of the capital asset pricing model (CAPM) that returns are systematically related to risk as measured by beta.

FASB • *See* Financial Accounting Standards Board.

FDIC • *See* Federal Deposit Insurance Corporation.

Fed • *See* Federal Reserve System.

Federal Deposit Insurance Corporation • a federal agency that insures deposits at depository institutions up to $100,000 per depositor

federal funds market • the market where banks and other financial institutions borrow and lend immediately deliverable reserve-free funds, usually on a one-day basis

federal funds rate • the interest rate charged in the federal funds market

Federal Home Loan Mortgage Corporation • a government agency that assembles pools of conventional mortgages and sells participations in a secondary market; called "Freddie Mac"

Federal Housing Administration • a federal government agency that insures home mortgages

Federal National Mortgage Association • a corporation, now privately owned, that operates a secondary market in mortgages and issues its own debt securities to finance its mortgage portfolio; called "Fannie Mae"

Federal Open Market Committee • the Federal Reserve Board committee that decides on open market policy (consists of all seven of the Federal Reserve Board Governors plus five of the presidents of the regional Fed banks, including the president of the New York bank)

Federal Reserve Board of Governors • the governing body of the Federal Reserve System, composed of seven members appointed by the President for long and staggered terms

Federal Reserve System • the federal government agency that exercises monetary policy through its control over banking system reserves (also called the Fed)

Federal Savings and Loan Insurance Corporation • a former federal government agency that insured deposits at savings and loan associations up to $100,000 per depositor (replaced by FDIC)

FHA • *See* Federal Housing Administration.

FIFO (first in, first out) • an inventory valuation method whereby items taken out of inventory are assumed to have cost the amount paid for the earliest unused purchase

fill-or-kill order • a type of security market order that must be canceled unless it can be filled immediately

filter rules • any mechanical trading rule, such as a rule to buy stocks when their PE ratio falls below some predetermined value or to trade whenever a particular price pattern is observed

Financial Accounting Standards Board • an accounting organization that establishes rules for preparing financial statements

financial ratio • a ratio such as the debt/equity or times-interest-earned designed to reflect a firm's financial strength

firm analysis • *See* company analysis.

firm commitment basis • futures contracts that are undertaken with margin requirements sufficient to allow futures brokers to guarantee fulfillment of the contracts

fiscalist • a type of economist who believes that fiscal (not monetary) policy is the primary economic tool

fiscal policy • government tax and spending policy that affects the economy

Fitch Investors Service • a bond-rating service that is considerably less well known than Moody's or Standard & Poor's

fixed assets • tangible assets with a relatively long expected life (greater than a year) that are not intended for resale and that are used in the operations of the business. These assets include plant and equipment but not inventories or accounts receivable.

fixed costs • costs that do not vary with the firm's output in the short run

fixed-income security • any security that promises to pay a periodic nonvariable sum, such as a bond paying a fixed coupon amount per period

fixed-rate mortgage • a mortgage having a constant interest rate for the life of the debt

flat • a term used to describe a type of trade wherein bonds trade for a net price that does not reflect any accrued interest

flight-to-quality effect • the tendency of investors to rapidly sell off their positions in risky investments and shift toward less risky investments when disturbing news is disseminated (such as news of a war or of a major bankruptcy)

flipping • the act of quickly selling a recently acquired investment. Thus, an investor who subscribed to a new issue and then sold in the immediate aftermarket could be described as a flipper.

floating rate preferred • a type of preferred stock whose indicated dividend rate varies with market rates

floating rate security • a type of debt security whose coupon rate varies with market interest rates

floor trader • one holding a seat on an exchange who trades for his or her own account (also called registered competitive market maker [RCMM])

flower bonds • government bonds that may be used at their par value for estate tax payments

flowthrough • a method of handling investment tax credits in which benefits are taken into income statements as they are incurred, rather than spread over the acquired asset's life (normalization)

FNMA • *See* Federal National Mortgage Association.

focal point • a round number value that is generally agreed upon or recognized

FOMC • *See* Federal Open Market Committee.

footnotes (to a financial statement) • notes that explain or expand upon entries and that are an integral part of a financial statement

Forbes • a twice-monthly popular investment periodical famous for its Forbes lists, such as the net-net list

forced conversion • the calling of a convertible security that effectively forces the holder to exercise the conversion option

forecast • a statement or numerical estimate of an event or level of a variable that is expected to occur in the future. A forecast is typically based on past values of the variable in association with other observable variables. A conditional forecast is based upon stated assumptions about certain conditions that are expected to remain in order for the forecast to be true.

Form 10K • a detailed annual report that must be submitted to the SEC, to the listing exchange, and to any shareholders who request it

Form 10Q • a detailed quarterly report that must be submitted to the SEC and the listing exchange and may be sent to shareholders who request it

Form 13D • a required SEC filing of any individual or group owning 5 percent or more of any public corporation. The form must disclose a number of matters, including the actual ownership percentage, its cost, the intentions of the owner, and any relevant agreements of the owner with any other party.

forward contract • a unique, nonstandard contractual agreement to accept delivery (buy) and to deliver (sell) a specified commodity or financial instrument at an agreed-upon price, settlement date, quantity, and location

four-nine position • a holding of approximately 4.9 percent of the outstanding shares of a company, which is about the limit for a quiet holding. At 5 percent, the holder must file a Form 13D with the SEC revealing his or her position.

fourth market • direct trading of listed securities between institutions

Freddie Mac • *See* Federal Home Loan Mortgage Corporation.

front-end loading • taking a large portion of the sales fee from the early payments of a long-term purchase contract

front running • an illegal trading strategy in which the trader (usually an employee of a brokerage firm) learns that a large trade is about to take place (usually placed by a substantial customer) and runs ahead of that trade to place an order at the pretrade price. If the large trade causes a major price change, the position can be reversed at a nice profit. In effect, the front runner is trading on inside information (knowledge of the forthcoming trade).

FSLIC • *See* Federal Savings and Loan Insurance Corporation.

full employment • the unemployment rate that is thought to be the minimum level before inflationary pressures accelerate and the maximum level the public will view as reasonable. Opinions on this level have varied over time from about 4 percent to 6 percent.

full faith and credit • the promise backing a debenture or other type of uncollateralized debt instrument. The borrower promises to pay and pledges its full faith and credit.

fundamental analysis • the evaluation of firms and their investment attractiveness based upon the firms' financial strength, competitiveness, earnings outlook, managerial strength, and sensitivity to the macroeconomy and to specific industry effects

futures contract • a standardized deferred-delivery commodities or security contract or promise to deliver a certain quantity of a commodity or security at a specified price at a specified future date; a contract derived from the underlying value of a commodity or security contract

futures market • regulated commodity exchange market where standardized futures contracts are bought and sold. *See* Chicago Board of Trade, Chicago Mercantile Exchange, and Commodity Futures Trading Commission.

futures options • call and put options on futures contracts

GAAP • *See* generally accepted accounting principles.

gambler's ruin • the wiping out of an individual's original capital by a series of adverse events; often used in the context of the risk of gambler's ruin

gamma factor • the number of years of above-average growth at a rate equal to that of the recent past that is necessary to justify the current PE multiple on growth stocks

GDP • *See* gross domestic product.

general creditor • a creditor whose loan is not secured (uncollateralized) by any specific assets. Debts are secured by the full faith and credit of the borrower.

generally accepted accounting principles • a set of accounting principles that are supposed to be followed in preparing accounting statements

general mortgage bond • a bond having a generalized claim against the issuing company's property

general obligation • a municipal bond secured by the issuer's full faith and credit

geometric mean return • the value of the compounded per-period average rate of return of a financial asset determined during a specified time

GIC • *See* guaranteed interest contract.

gilt-edge security • a very secure bond or other asset

give up • a now-prohibited practice whereby brokers making trades for a mutual fund were directed to pay a portion of their commission fees to brokers who had sold the fund's shares

Glass-Steagall Act • (1933 Bank Act) a 1933 federal act that required the separation of commercial and investment banking; prevented competition between financial institutions in the banking, insurance, and securities industries and established the framework for federal deposit insurance; repealed in November 1999 by the Gramm-Leach-Bliley Act

GMR • *See* geometric mean return.

GNMA (Ginnie Mae) • *See* Government National Mortgage Association.

go-go fund • a type of mutual fund popular in the late 1960s that sought short-term trading profits (also called a performance fund)

going private • the process of a company's buying back all of its publicly held stock so that ownership rests with a few owners and it becomes a privately held company

going public • the process of a start-up or heretofore private firm selling its shares in a public offering

golden handcuffs • an employment agreement that makes the departure prior to normal retirement age of upper-level managers very costly as they may lose attractive stock options

golden handshake • a provision in a preliminary merger agreement in which the target firm gives the acquiring firm an option to purchase its shares or assets at attractive prices or to receive a substantial bonus if the proposed takeover does not occur

golden parachute • a very generous termination agreement for upper management that takes effect if control of their firm shifts

good-'til-canceled order • a type of order that remains in effect until executed or canceled

goodwill • the amount by which a firm's going-concern value exceeds its book value

Government National Mortgage Association • a government agency that provides special assistance on selected types of home mortgages. Securities are backed both by GNMA mortgage portfolios and by the general credit of the government.

governments • U.S. government bonds issued by the Treasury Department and backed by the full faith and credit of the federal government

grace period • time period in which legal action is stayed until a defaulting debtor has an opportunity to cure the default

Graham (Benjamin) and Dodd (David) approach • a type of securities analysis that stresses fundamentals. Its originator, Benjamin Graham, coauthored the investment text that dominated the market from the 1930s to 1950s (also called Graham approach).

Gray approach • an investment-timing device that seeks to identify overvalued and undervalued market phases on the basis of interest rates relative to market PE ratios

Great Crash • the most severe stock market decline, when large company stock prices on average declined approximately 86 percent from August 1929 to June 1932 and small company stocks declined approximately 89 percent during the same period

greater fool theory • the tongue-in-cheek view that a still "greater fool" will come along to bail out a foolish investment

greenmail • the practice of acquiring a large percentage of a firm's stock and then being bought out at a premium after threatening to take over the firm

gross income • total income, either actual or estimated

gross margin • the net sales of an enterprise minus its cost of goods sold

gross domestic product • the sum of market values of all final goods and services produced annually in the economy of a country

growth fund • a common stock mutual fund that seeks price appreciation by concentrating on growth stocks

growth investing • investing in stocks that have above-average PE ratios or above-average price-to-book value per share

growth share matrix • a relationship popularized by the Boston Consulting Group that seeks to explain most interfirm profit differences as due to the combined impacts of market share and growth

growth stock • the shares of a company that is expected to achieve rapid growth (often carries above-average risks and PE ratios)

GTC order • *See* good-'til-canceled order.

guarantee bond • a bond with a guarantee from a company other than the issuer

guaranteed interest contract • an investment sold by insurance companies that offers high yields plus the opportunity to earn similar returns on additions to the plan

guarantee preferred • a preferred stock with a guarantee from a company other than the issuer

head-and-shoulders formation • a technical pattern that looks like a head and shoulders and is said to forecast a price decline

hedge fund • a type of mutual fund that seeks to offset some of its long positions with short positions, particularly to offset the effects of exchange-rate risk on foreign assets

hedge ratio • in the Black-Scholes model, that ratio of number of written calls that would exactly offset the stock price movement of a number of shares of the underlying stock held. Any small move in the stock's price would be precisely offset by a change in the value of the option position with such a ratio of number of calls to number of shares of stock.

hedging • taking opposite positions in related securities in the hope of profiting from relative price movements (risk hedging) or of reducing an existing risk (pure hedging)

histogram • a discrete probability distribution display

holding company • a company set up to maintain voting control of other business enterprises

holding period return • the rate of return over some specific time

holding period return relative • the end period compound value for a specific holding period; that is, the holding-period return plus one (1)

horizontal spread • short- and long-option positions on the same security with the same strike price but different expiration dates

HPR • *See* holding period return.

HPRR • *See* holding period return relative.

Hulbert Financial Digest • a publication containing ratings of investment advisory services

hybrid convertible • a complicated type of convertible security. *See* Americus Trust security, equity note, LYON, and commodity-backed bond.

hybrid REIT • a REIT that is a combination of equity and mortgage REITs

hypothecation • the pledging of securities as loan collateral

IMM • *See* International Monetary Market.

immunization • the process of minimizing the interest rate risk on a bond portfolio by maintaining a portfolio with a duration equal to an investor's planning horizon

inactive post • NYSE trading post for inactively traded securities

in and out • the purchase and sale of the same security within a short period

income anticipation • an accounting practice whereby a profit is reflected in the income statement before it is received

income approach • valuing real estate or some other asset as the discounted value of its expected income stream

income bond • a bond on which interest is paid only if the issuer has sufficient earnings

income fund • a common stock mutual fund that concentrates on stocks that pay high dividends

income statement • a financial statement of interim earnings that provides a financial accounting of revenues and expenses during a specified period—that is, 3 months, one year, and so on

income stock • a stock known for its high dividend rate (payments)

incorporation • the forming into a legal body endowed with various rights and duties

indenture (bond) • the contract or statement of promises the company makes to its bondholders, including a commitment to pay a stated coupon amount periodically and return the face value (usually $1,000) at the end of a certain period (such as 20 years after issue). A trustee, such as a bank, is charged with overseeing the issuing firm's commitments.

indenture trustee • the independent trustee (usually a bank or trust company) that is named to oversee the issuance of the bonds, to collect and pay interest and principal, and to protect the bondholder's rights as specified in the indenture

independence (statistical) • the relationship between two variables if knowledge of one's value does not help explain the other's value. Thus, if IBM and AT&T stock returns are totally unrelated, knowing that AT&T stock returned x percent over the most recent 12 months would not help explain IBM stock's return over the same period. In general, if changes in two variables are unrelated, the variables are independent.

index arbitrage • a trading strategy involving offsetting positions in stock index futures contracts and the underlying cash market securities (stocks making up the index). If, for example, the index futures is priced above the stocks making up the index, the arbitrageur would buy the stocks and sell the index. If, in contrast, the index was priced below its corresponding stocks, the arbitrageur would short the stocks and buy the index.

index fund • a mutual fund that attempts to duplicate the performance of a market index such as the S&P 500

industry analysis • the evaluation of an industry's position and prospects as they relate to its component firms' investment attractiveness

industry index option • option on stock index tailored to reflect the stocks of a particular industry sector

inflation • the rate of increase in the overall price level. For example, if on the average, $1.06 will buy what $1 would buy a year earlier, inflation has equaled 6 percent.

inflation hedge • an asset whose value varies directly with the price level

informal workout • an approach to dealing with a troubled firm that seeks to avoid the problems of a bankruptcy proceeding by obtaining sufficient lender concessions to allow the company to continue

in play • the status of being an actively pursued takeover candidate

input-output model • a model that relates various industries' outputs to their derived demands from other industries

insider trading • the buying or selling by traders or investors with access to relevant nonpublic information relating to the company in question. This practice is illegal if the information is material and used at the expense of other shareholders.

insolvency • insufficient liquid assets to meet financial obligations that are currently due

installment sale • in general, any sale that calls for payments to be made over time. In real estate transactions, an installment sale may reduce and postpone the tax liability if the payments are stretched out over a sufficiently long period.

instinet • an automated communications network among block traders

institutional investor • an organization that invests the pooled assets of others, such as pension funds, mutual funds, bank trust departments, insurance companies, and other investment companies

intercorporate dividend • dividend payment from one corporation to another, 70 percent of which is not subject to the corporate income tax

interday limit • *See* daily price limit.

interest • the amount a borrower pays for the use of a lender's funds, frequently expressed as an annual percentage of the principal balance outstanding and compounded on a monthly, quarterly, annually or some other periodic basis

interest rate futures • a commodity futures contract calling for delivery of a debt security, such as a T-bill or long-term government bond

interest rate option • an option on the current market price of government securities based on the assumption of a coupon rate of 8 percent

interest rate risk • the risk that an interest rate rise will take place, thereby reducing the market value of fixed-income securities

international fund • a mutual fund that invests in securities of firms based outside the fund's home country

International Monetary Market • a futures exchange associated with the Chicago Mercantile Exchange that trades futures contracts on gold, T-bills, Eurodollars, CDs, and several foreign currencies

Internet • the national and international networks of computers, communications systems, and software that are linked by common network signals and software requirements, and used by businesses and households to communicate text, data, video, and audio messages (also called packet switching network)

in-the-money option • an option whose strike price is more favorable to option holders than the current market price of the underlying security: for calls, when the current stock price is higher than the strike price and for puts, when the current stock price is lower than the strike price

intraday dependencies • nonrandom price movements of transactions taking place over the course of a single day

intrinsic value (call, right, warrant) • the price of the associated stock less the strike price of the option, or zero if the difference is negative. *See* in-the-money and out-of-the money option(s).

intrinsic value (option) • *See* intrinsic value (put) and intrinsic value (call).

intrinsic value (put) • the strike price of a put less the price of the associated stock, or zero if the difference is negative. *See* in-the-money and out-of-the-money option(s).

intrinsic value (stock) • the underlying value that a careful evaluation would produce; generally takes into account both the going-concern value and the liquidation or breakup value of the company. An efficient market would always price stocks at their intrinsic values; an inefficient market would not necessarily do so.

inventory turnover ratio • the ratio of the cost of goods sold to average yearly inventory

inverted market • a futures market in which the futures price exceeds the spot

inverted yield curve • a yield curve showing short-term interest rates higher than long-term rates, reflected by a downward sloping yield curve

investment banker • a firm that organizes a syndicate to underwrite or market a new issue of securities

investment company • a company that manages pooled portfolios for a group of owners. The owners may be either a closed-end company, whose fixed number of shares outstanding are traded like other shares, or an open-end company (mutual fund), whose shares outstanding change by the amounts bought and sold.

Investment Company Institute • an organization of mutual funds and other institutional investors that publishes *Mutual Fund Forum*

investment manager • one who manages an investment portfolio

Investor's Daily • a national business newspaper that competes with *The Wall Street Journal*

irrational exuberance • a phrase used by Alan Greenspan, chairman of the Federal Reserve Board, on December 5, 1996, in questioning current stock market values ("How do we know when irrational exuberance has unduly escalated asset values?")

itemizing • one of two basic approaches to filing income taxes that involves taking deductions for specific allowed expenses. Taxpayers who do not itemize take a standard deduction.

January effect • an anomaly detected in past studies of stock market performance that asserts that the buying into the small cap stock market in January tends to produce above-normal returns

January indicator • a technical timing device utilizing the assertion that as January goes, so goes the year

Jensen's alpha • *See* alpha.

junk bonds • high-risk bonds usually promising a very high coupon rate coupled with a substantial default risk

Kansas City Board of Trade • a futures exchange listing wheat and Value Line stock index futures

Krugerrand • a South African gold coin containing one ounce of gold that is often traded by gold speculators and is now prohibited from importation into the United States

kurtosis • the degree to which a distribution departs from normal. *See also* platokurtosis and leptokurtosis.

lagging indicators • conference board-compiled data series whose movements are identified as tending to follow turns in the overall economy

law of one price • the principle that whenever two assets offer identical payoffs, their prices must be identical

LBO • *See* leveraged buyout.

leading indicators • conference board-compiled data series whose movements are identified as tending to precede turns in the overall economy

leakages • funds that "leak" into savings, import purchases, or taxes during each round of stimulatory spending or tax reduction, thus reducing the impact of fiscal policy

LEAPs® • *See* long-term equity anticipation securities.

learning curve • a relationship popularized by the Boston Consulting Group that hypothesizes that manufacturers are able to reduce costs substantially as they increase their cumulative volume. In one formulation, costs are said to decrease by 20 percent with each doubling of cumulative volume.

least squares regression line (analysis) • a statistical construct that uses a technique of minimization of the squares of the deviations from the line of best fit through a scatter diagram of two variables to create a linear relationship between the two variables

legal lists • lists of stocks authorized by various states for fiduciary investing

leg on • the process of assembling a spread or other combination position one side at a time

leptokurtosis • the degree to which a distribution differs from the normal by having more probability in the peak and less probability in the tails

lettered stock • newly issued stock sold at a discount to large investors in a private placement prior to a public offering of the same issue. In accordance with SEC Rule 144, buyers agree not to sell their shares for a prespecified period.

leverage • using borrowed funds or special types of securities (warrants, calls) to increase the potential return (usually increases both risk and expected return)

leveraged buyout • the takeover of a company financed largely by debt secured by the acquired firm's own assets

liabilities • debts that appear on the right side of a balance sheet

LIFO (last in, first out) • an accounting method that for income reporting purposes values items that are taken out of inventory at the most recent unused invoice cost

limited liability • property that under most circumstances limits shareholders' liabilities for their corporation's debts to their initial investments

limited partnership • a form of business organization that is used by investors in projects that have a finite life and that involve a limited liability partnership as the form of organization in order to avoid SEC registration requirements

limit order • an order to buy or sell at a prespecified price

linear model • a method of estimating portfolio risks that requires only alpha and beta estimates of the components; more generally, a model that assumes a linear relationship between two or more variables

line of credit • prearranged agreement from a lender to supply up to some maximum loan at prespecified terms

liquidation • the process of selling all of a firm's assets and distributing the proceeds first to creditors and then to shareholders

liquidation value • the value of a going concern's assets if sold piecemeal

liquidity • the ease with which an investment can be converted to cash for approximately its original cost plus its expected accrued interest

liquidity preference hypothesis • the term structure of the interest rates hypothesis that asserts that most borrowers prefer to borrow long and most lenders prefer to lend short (implies that long-term rates generally exceed short-term rates)

liquidity ratio • a ratio (for example, current or quick) of a firm's short-run financial situation that is a measure of the firm's ability to meet short-term obligations

liquidity risk • the risk that an asset cannot be quickly converted to cash at its fair market value

listed stocks • stocks approved for trading by one or more of the stock exchanges

listing • the act of obtaining exchange approval for trading

listing requirements • the qualifications that a company must meet in order to be listed on an exchange

load • the selling fee applied to a load mutual fund purchase

load fund • a type of mutual fund sold through agents who receive fees that are typically 8.5 percent on small purchases and somewhat less on trades above $10,000

lock-up agreement • an agreement between an acquirer and a target that makes the target unattractive to any other acquirer; similar to a golden handshake

long interest • the number of futures or options contracts outstanding (owned and sold)

long position • the ownership of stocks or other securities as opposed to a short position, in which the investor has sold securities that are not owned

long-term assets • *See* fixed assets.

long-term capital gain (loss) • gain (loss) on a capital asset held for at least 6 months

long-term equity anticipation securities • options sold on the CBOE permitting long-term call or put positions up to 2 years in the future.

long-term liabilities • liabilities that are not due in the next year or next operating period, whichever is shorter; usually include outstanding bonds, debentures, mortgages, and term loans

long transaction • the purchase or sale of a long position

loss • net revenues minus costs when costs exceed revenues

low liquidity • the difficulty with which an investment can be converted to cash in a short period of time

low PE stocks • stocks with low price-earnings ratios that are sought out by value-oriented investors

low-price effect • an alleged anomaly to the efficient market hypothesis that is characterized by the tendency for low-priced stocks to earn above-normal returns

LYON • a complicated type of zero coupon convertible debt security that is both callable and redeemable at prices that escalate through time

M1 • the basic money supply that includes checking deposits and cash held by the public

M2 • a broader-based money supply definition than Ml that includes everything in M1 plus most savings and money market deposit accounts

M3 • a still broader-based money supply definition than M2 that includes everything in M2 plus large certificates of deposit and money market mutual funds sold to institutions

macroeconomic analysis • an evaluation of a firm's or market's investment potential within its macroeconomic (economy-wide) setting

management control • a situation in which no group or individual owns enough of the firm's stock to exercise control and effective control is thus held by the managers

management-oriented company • a firm that is largely run in the interest of management as opposed to that of the shareholders

mandatory convertible note • *See* equity note.

manufactured (synthetic) call • a call-like position generated by a combination put and long position in the underlying stock; position with a similar payoff matrix to a call

manufactured (synthetic) put • a put-like position generated by a combination of a call and short position in the underlying stock; position with a similar payoff matrix to a put

margin account • borrowing to finance a portion of a securities purchase; regulated by the Fed. For example, if a 60 percent margin rate is set, $10,000 worth of stock may be purchased with up to $4,000 of borrowed money. Only securities of listed and some large OTC companies qualify for margin loans.

marginal tax rate • the percentage that must be paid in taxes on the next income increment

margin call • a demand by a brokerage firm for more collateral or cash to support existing margin debt. A call is required when the borrower's equity position falls below a preset percentage (for example, 35 percent) of the value of margined securities.

margin maintenance • the minimum percentage that an equity account must maintain to avoid a margin call

margin rate • the percentage of the cost of a purchase of marginable securities that must be paid for with the investor's own money

marketability • the ease with which an investment can be bought or sold without appreciably affecting its price. For example, blue chip stocks are usually highly marketable because they are actively traded.

market anomaly • an exception to what is expected in an efficient market

market approach • estimating the value of properties (particularly real estate) based on the sale price of similar properties

market imperfection (anomaly) • the condition that exists whenever any group of investors can consistently earn risk-adjusted returns that are above market returns after considering transaction costs, taxes, and so on

market indexes • an average of security prices designed to reflect market performance. The Dow Jones Industrial Average, the best known and most closely followed, is calculated by adding the market prices of 30 leading industrial companies and dividing by a divisor. The divisor is changed periodically to reflect stock splits. Dow Jones Inc. also compiles averages for utility and transportation stocks. Standard & Poor's Investor Services, the NYSE, NASD, and AMEX all compute their own indexes. Indexes are also compiled for bonds, commodities, options, and various other investment types.

market indicator • *See* technical market indicator.

market maker • one who creates a market for a security by quoting a bid and ask price

market model • relating the price of individual security returns to market returns with a linear equation of the form $R_{it} = \alpha_i + \beta_i(R_{mt})$, where R_{it} = return of security i for period t; R_{mt} = market return for period t; and α_i and β_i are firm i parameters

market-on-close order • an order that is to be held until just before the close and then executed

market order • an order to buy or sell at the market price that requires immediate execution

market portfolio • a hypothetical portfolio representing each investment asset in proportion to its relative weight in the universe of investment assets

market price • the current price at which willing buyers and willing sellers will make trades

market risk • the return variability associated with general market movements and not diversifiable within the market (also called systematic risk)

market segmentation hypothesis • the theory that there are separate markets for bonds of different maturities, so the interest rates on bonds of one maturity should not be affected by the interest rates on bonds of another maturity

market timing • the effort by portfolio managers to time their allocations of funds in the market as between, say, stocks, bonds, and money market funds in order to take advantage of perceived differential expected performance among the different assets (asset classes)

market value • a term used to describe the estimated total value of an asset in the market derived by multiplying the number of units of the asset (for example, shares of common stock) by the current market price per unit (share) of the asset, sometimes called capitalization or market capitalization

Markowitz model • the model created by Harry Markowitz in 1956 that relates the expected mean (average) of security market returns to the expected variance of returns; modern portfolio theory (MPT)

mark-to-market • practice of recomputing equity position in a margin account (stock or futures) on a daily basis

master limited partnership • a method of organizing a business that combines some of the advantages of a corporation with some of the advantages of a limited partnership. Shares of ownership trade much like corporate stock, yet the MLP is taxed like a partnership; that is, profits are imputed to the owners and taxed only once.

matched and lost • term applied to the outcome for the loser when two traders simultaneously arrive at the relevant trading post with equivalent orders, only one of which may be filled within the current market situation as determined by a coin toss

maturity • the length of time until a security must be redeemed by its issuer

maturity date • the date at which a security's principal must be redeemed

mean • the average or expected value of a sample or distribution

mean return • the average return of a sample distribution of returns

mean reversion • the tendency of an historical average return to revert to the mean (average) return in the market as the sample period grows larger

me-first rules • restrictions in a bond's indenture that limit a firm's ability to take on additional debt with similar standing to that of the bond in question

merger wave (merger activity) • a widespread tendency to combine two or more firms into a single company

MGIC • *See* Mortgage Guarantee Insurance Corporation.

middle-of-the-road fund • a mutual fund that invests in a balanced portfolio of stocks (some blue chips and some more speculative)

MLP • *See* master limited partnership.

mode • the high point or most likely outcome of a distribution. For a symmetrical distribution, the mode and mean (average value) are identical.

modern portfolio theory • the combination of the capital asset pricing model (CAPM), efficient market hypothesis (EMH), and related theoretical models of security market pricing and performance

modified duration • an adjusted measure of duration used to estimate the interest rate sensitivity of a bond

momentum • tendency for movement to continue in the same direction, such as a rising trend in stock prices

Monday–Friday stock pattern • the observed tendency of stock prices to decline on Mondays and rise on Fridays

monetarist • one who emphasizes the economic role of monetary (as opposed to fiscal) policy

monetary asset • an investment that is denominated in dollars

monetary policy • government policy that utilizes the money supply to affect the economy and that is implemented by the Fed through its control of bank reserves and required reserves

money fund • *See* money market fund.

money illusion • failure to take account of inflation's impact. Thus, an individual who received a 10 percent raise and thought his or her financial situation had improved would suffer from money illusion if prices had risen by 20 percent.

Money Magazine • a monthly personal finance periodical published by Time Inc.

money market • the market for high-quality, short-term securities, such as CDs, commercial paper, acceptances, Treasury bills, short-term tax-exempt notes, and Eurodollar loans

money market account • a type of bank or thrift institution account that offers unregulated money market rates, requires a minimum deposit of $1,000 (many banks require $2,500), and limits withdrawals to six per month, only three of which may be by check

money market fund • a mutual fund that invests in short-term, highly liquid securities (also called money fund)

money multiplier • the ratio of a change in reserves to the change in the money supply. Thus, a money multiplier of five would imply that a $1 billion increase in reserves would result in a $5 billion increase in the money supply.

money supply • generally defined as the sum of all coin, currency (outside bank holdings), and deposits on which check-like instruments may be written. *See* M1, M2, and M3.

mood indicators • technical market indicators designed to reflect the market's pessimism or optimism

Moody's Industrial Transportation, Utility and Finance Manual • annual publication containing detailed historic information on most publicly traded firms organized by type

Moody's Investor Service • a firm that publishes manuals containing extensive historical data on a large number of publicly traded firms. Moody's also rates bonds.

moral hazard • a firm's or individual's incurrance of risks whose full costs are avoided by that firm or individual. Thus, for example a firm may invest in risky ventures without telling all of its investors, or an individual may hide dangerous activities from a life insurance company.

mortgage • a loan collateralized by property, particularly real estate. The lender is entitled to take possession of the property if the debt is not repaid in a timely manner.

mortgage-backed security • a debt instrument representing a share of ownership in a pool of mortgages (for example, GNMA pass-throughs) or backed by a pool of mortgages (for example, FNMA bonds)

mortgage bond • debt security for which specific property is pledged

mortgagee • the lender under a mortgage loan

Mortgage Guarantee Insurance Corporation • one of a group of companies that, for a fee, guarantee the timely payment of a portion of certain mortgages' obligations

mortgage REIT • a REIT that is in the business of making both construction loans and mortgage loans

mortgagor • the borrower under a mortgage loan

moving average • average amount over a specified period of time (for example, average daily stock price over previous 60 days)

MPT • *See* modern portfolio theory.

multi-index model • a method of estimating portfolio expected return that utilizes a market index and indexes for various market subcategories

multiplier • the ratio caused by a change in government spending to the change in the GDP (also called fiscal multiplier)

municipal bond fund • a mutual fund holding a portfolio of municipal bonds

municipals • tax-free bonds issued by state and local governments

mutual fund • a pooled investment in which managers buy and sell assets with the income and gains and losses accruing to the owners; may be either load (with sales fee) or no-load (no sales fee); stands ready to buy back its shares at their net asset value

mutual fund cash position • a technical market indicator based on mutual fund liquidity. High fund liquidity is said to be associated with subsequent market rises.

NAIC • *See* National Association of Investment Clubs.

naked option writing • writing options without owning the underlying shares. The naked writer satisfies the contract with the option holder, if it is exercised, by buying the required shares on the market. Writing naked options is very risky because there is no limit to how high the market price of the underlying stock may rise.

NASD • *See* National Association of Securities Dealers.

NASDAQ • *See* National Association of Securities Dealers Automated Quotations.

NASDAQ Composite Index • a value-weighted index of OTC issues

NASDAQ National List • the secondary list of OTC issues carried in many newspaper stock quotations that are not sufficiently active for the NASDAQ list

NASDAQ National Market System List • the primary list of OTC issues carried in most newspaper stock quotations. Membership is determined by criteria similar to the AMEX listing.

NASDAQ Supplemental List • the tertiary list of OTC stocks carried in some newspaper stock quotations (stocks not active enough for the two major NASDAQ lists)

National Association of Investment Clubs • organization that fosters and assists in the setting up of investment clubs

National Association of Securities Dealers • the self-regulator of the OTC market

National Association of Securities Dealers Automated Quotations • an automated information system that provides brokers and dealers with price quotations on securities that are traded over the counter

National Bureau of Economic Research • a private nonprofit research foundation that dates business cycles and sponsors economic research

national market issues • selected NASDAQ securities that represent the largest firms listed on the quotation system

NAV • *See* net asset value.

near money • assets such as savings accounts and Treasury bills that can quickly and easily be converted into cash

neglected firm effect • an alleged anomaly to the efficient market hypothesis that is characterized by the tendency for security analysts to overlook small or obscure firms in their security evaluations

net asset value • the per-share market value of a mutual fund's portfolio

net margin • gross profit margin on sales, adjusted for depreciation and taxes to obtain net profit margin on sales

net-net • a stock whose market price is very low relative to the value of its liquid assets; more specifically, a stock whose per-share price is less than the company's per-share liquid assets after subtracting the pro rata amount of both short- and long-term debt

net worth • the dollar value of assets minus liabilities; that is, the stockholders' residual ownership position (also called equity)

new issue • an initial stock sale, usually of a company going public (also an initial bond sale)

new listing • a stock that has recently been listed on an exchange that may be the company's first listing on the particular exchange or first on any exchange

New York Curb Exchange • the former name for what is now called the American Stock Exchange

New York Futures Exchange • a futures exchange associated with the NYSE that lists futures and option contracts on the NYSE Composite Index

New York Stock Exchange • the largest organized stock exchange based on Wall Street in New York City. Stocks listed tend to be large to mid-capitalization stocks. *See also* Big Board.

New York Stock Exchange Index • a value-weighted index of NYSE stocks

nifty fifty • a list of about 50 companies, with high multiples and rapid growth rates, that were preferred by many institutional investors in the early 1970s

NMI • *See* national market issues.

no-load fund • a fund whose shares are bought and sold directly at the fund's NAV. Unlike a load fund, no agent or sales fee is involved.

nominal interest rate • the stated interest rate on a bond or other debt instrument that is the sum (approximately) of the real risk-free rate, inflationary expectations premium, and the risk premium of the debt instrument

nonmarket risk • individual risk not related to general market movements. The total risk of an investment may be decomposed into that associated with the market and that which is not (also called unsystematic risk).

non-normal distribution • a distribution, such as a skewed distribution of returns, that differs from the normal shape. *See* leptokurtosis and platokurtosis.

nonparticipating insurance • a type of insurance sold by a stockholder-owned company, as opposed to participating insurance, which is sold by an insurance company owned by its policyholders (mutual)

normal distribution • a distribution corresponding to the shape of the normal (bell) curve

normalization • spreading the benefits of investment tax credit or other types of credits across the life of an asset. *See also* flowthrough.

notes • intermediate-term debt securities issued with maturity dates of one to 5 years

NOW (negotiable orders of withdrawal) accounts • a special type of deposit account that draws interest and allows check-like instruments to be written against it

NYFE • *See* New York Futures Exchange.

NYSE • *See* New York Stock Exchange.

NYSE Composite Index • a value-weighted index of all NYSE-listed securities

OCC • *See* Options Clearing Corporation.

odd-lot activity • measure of the amount of odd-lot purchases or sales; said to reflect activity by less sophisticated investors. *See* odd-lot trade.

odd-lot short ratio • a technical market indicator based on relative short trading by small investors. When such trading is heavy, the market is said to be near a bottom.

odd-lotter • one who trades in odd lots

odd-lot trade • a transaction involving less than one round lot of stock, usually 100 shares, although a few stocks are traded in 10-share lots

off-board trading • trading that takes place off an exchange, particularly OTC trading in NYSE-listed securities. NYSE Rule 390 restricts such trading by member firms.

one-decision stocks • a now largely discredited concept of the early 1970s that certain high-quality growth stocks should be bought and held

open-end investment company • a mutual fund or other pooled portfolio of investments that stands ready to buy or sell its shares at their NAV (or NAV plus load if the fund has a load)

open interest • the number of option or commodity contracts outstanding (analogous to shares outstanding for stock)

open market operations • Federal Reserve transactions in the government bond market that affect bank reserves and thereby influence the money supply, interest rates, and economic activity

open outcry • organization of futures trading on the futures exchanges in which traders shout their desire to buy (sell) a contract, often using hand and finger signals

option • a put, call, warrant, right, or other security giving the holder the right but not the obligation to purchase or sell a security at a set price for a specific period

Options Clearing Corporation • the clearing house for listed options that facilitates options trading by guaranteeing execution of trades between options brokers and traders

ordinary least squares • a method of estimating regression parameters by choosing linear coefficients that minimize the square of the residuals. *See* least squares regression line (analysis).

organizational slack • wasted firm resources due to managerial deadwood, lack of aggressiveness, carelessness, and so on

OTC • *See* over the counter.

out-of-the-money option • an option whose strike price is less attractive than the current market price of its underlying stock; for calls, when the current stock price is lower than the strike price; for puts, when the current stock price is above the strike price; such an option has no intrinsic value, but has time value based on potential stock price movements prior to the option's expiration

overbought • an opinion that the market has risen too rapidly and is therefore poised for a downward correction

oversold • an opinion that the market has fallen too rapidly and is therefore poised for an upward correction

over the counter • the market in unlisted securities and off-board trading in listed securities

paper • *See* commercial paper.

paper loss • an unrealized loss

paper profit • an unrealized gain

par (bond) • the face value at which the issue matures

par (common stock) • a stated amount below which per-share equity (net worth) may not fall without barring dividend payments

par (preferred stock) • the value on which the security's dividend and liquidation value is based

parking • the illegal practice of holding a security for another in an attempt to conceal the owner's true identity. Sometimes stock is parked during the period prior to launching a takeover attempt.

par ROI equation • an empirically estimated profitability equation of the Strategic Planning Institute

participating bond • bond that may pay extra coupon increment in years in which the issuing firm is especially profitable

participating preferred • preferred stock that may pay an extra dividend increment in years in which the issuing firm is especially profitable

passed dividend • the omission of a regular dividend payment

pass-through • a share of a mortgage pool whose interest and principal payments are flowed through to the holders

payback period • the length of time until an original investment is recaptured

payout ratio • dividends per share as a percentage of earnings per share

PE • *See* price earnings ratio.

penny stock market • a market for low-priced stocks (under $1 per share), especially active in Denver

penny stocks • low-priced stocks usually selling for under $1 per share, normally issued by small speculative companies

PE ratio • price earnings ratio or the share price of a stock divided by its actual or anticipated earnings per share

PE ratio model • a model designed to use PE ratios to identify undervalued or overvalued stocks

percentage order • a market or limit order that is entered once a certain amount of stock has traded

performance fund • *See* go-go fund.

per-period return • the return earned for a particular period

physical • the underlying physical delivery instrument for a particular futures contract

pink sheets • quotation source for most publicly traded OTC issues

pink sheet stocks • OTC stocks not traded on the NASDAQ system, issued by very small, obscure, and often speculative companies

pit • the name of the physical location where specific commodity contracts are traded

planning horizon (portfolio management) • the time frame in which a portfolio is managed that reflects the length of time before the funds are expected to be needed to meet projected expenses

platokurtosis • the degree to which a distribution differs from the normal by having less of the distribution concentrated at the peak and more at the tail; sometimes called fat-tailed

point (stocks and bonds) • pricing unit. For stocks, a point represents $1 per share; for bonds, a point is equivalent to $10.

point-and-figure chart • a technical chart that has no time dimension. An x is used to designate an up move of a certain magnitude, while an o denotes a similar size down move. The xs are stacked on top of each other as long as the direction of movement remains up. A new column is begun when direction changes.

points (real estate) • a fee charged for granting a loan, especially for a mortgage on real estate, with a point being one percent of the amount of the loan

poison pill • antitakeover defense in which a new diluting security is issued if control of the firm is about to shift

Ponzi scheme • an investment scam promising high returns that are secretly paid out of investor capital; usually exposed when incoming funds are insufficient to cover promised outpayments. The scam depends upon fresh investor capital to pay its promised return.

pooling of interest accounting • a type of merger accounting in which an acquired firm's assets and liabilities are transferred to the acquiring firm's balance sheet without any valuation adjustment

portfolio • a holding of one or more securities by a single owner (institution or individual)

portfolio insurance • a service in which the "insurer" endeavors to place a floor on the value of the "insured" portfolio. If the portfolio value falls to a prespecified level, the insurer neutralizes it against a further fall by purchasing an appropriate number of index puts or selling an appropriate number of index options.

portfolio optimization • a mathematical and statistical technique, using modern portfolio theory, of finding the most efficient (least risk for maximum return) portfolios among the available or feasible set of portfolios

portfolio risk • risk that takes account of the diversifying impact of portfolio components

portfolio variance • a statistical parameter that measures portfolio risk

position trader • a commodity trader who takes and holds futures positions for several days or more

post • one of 18 horseshoe-shaped locations on the NYSE floor where securities are traded (also called trading post)

postponable expenditures • purchases of long-term assets such as consumer durables

PPR • *See* per-period return.

preemptive rights • shareholders' rights to maintain their proportional share of their firm by subscribing proportionally to any new stock issue

preferred habitat • one of four hypotheses for explaining the term structure of interest rates based on a tendency for borrowers and lenders to gravitate toward their preferred loan lengths

preferred stock • shares whose indicated dividends and liquidation values must be paid before common shareholders receive any dividends or liquidation payments. Unlike common stock, the amount of preferred dividends is fixed and specified upon issue.

premium (bond) • the amount by which a bond's price exceeds its par or face value

premium (option) • the market price of an option

premium over conversion value • the amount by which a convertible's price exceeds its conversion value

premium over straight-debt value • the amount by which a convertible's price exceeds its value as a nonconvertible debt security

prepayment penalty • the fee assessed for early liquidation of an outstanding debt

present value • the value of a future sum or sums discounted by the appropriate interest rate or discount rate

price dependencies • price movements that are related to past price movements

price earnings ratio • for trailing earnings, the stock price relative to the most recent 12-month earnings per share; for ex ante earnings, the stock price relative to the next 12-month expected earnings

price floor • the support level of a convertible bond provided by its straight-debt value

price risk • the risk of a bond's price changing in response to unknown future interest rate changes. If rates increase after a bond is purchased, the realized price for the bond in the secondary market would be below expectations, whereas if rates decrease, the realized price would be above expectations. Because the direction of future interest rates is unknown, there is uncertainty about the bond's future price.

price stability • the absence of inflation or deflation

pricing points • *See* point.

primary distribution • the initial sale of a stock or bond (new issue)

primary market • the market for initial sales of securities that are later traded in the secondary market

prime • one of the two component securities created when appropriate shares are deposited into an Americus Trust. The prime receives the stock's dividends and up to some prespecified liquidation payment at the termination date. The score receives any value in excess of the amount assigned to the prime.

prime rate • the borrowing rate that banks advertise as their best (although some very secure borrowers may receive a still lower rate)

principal (in a trade) • the person or institution for whom the broker acts as an agent

principal (of a bond) • the face value of a bond

private placement • a direct security sale to a small number of large buyers without the registration requirements of a public offering

probability distribution • a display of possible events along with their associated probabilities

profit • net revenues minus costs and expenses

profitability models • models designed to explain company profit rates

profitability ratio • a ratio such as return on equity and return on sales designed to reflect the firm's profit rates

profit and loss statement • *See* income statement.

programs • the actual trades instituted by a program trader. Market watchers might, for example, see a series of large trades in stocks making up the S&P 500 and conclude that programs are moving the market in a particular direction.

program trading • a type of mechanical trading in large blocks by institutional investors that usually involves both stock and index futures contracts as, for example, in index arbitrage or portfolio insurance (also called programmed trading)

proprietorship • the condition of ownership of a business entity, usually referring to sole ownership

prospectus • an official document that all companies offering new securities for public sale must file with the SEC. It spells out in detail the financial position of the offering company, what the new funds will be used for, the qualifications of the corporate officers, risk factors (such as competition), and any other material information.

proxy • a shareholder ballot

proxy fight •a contest for control of a company

proxy material • a statement of relevant information that the firm must supply to shareholders when they solicit proxies

public offering • a security sale made through dealers to the general public and registered with the SEC

purchase accounting • a type of merger accounting in which the net assets of the merged firm are entered on the books of the acquiring firm at amounts that add up to the firm's acquisition price. The purchase price of the acquired firm minus its net worth is recorded as "goodwill" by the acquiring firm.

pure arbitrage • an arbitrage that involves no element of risk

pure hedge • a hedge whose purpose is to reduce the risk on an existing position

pure risk • *See* pure risk premium.

pure risk premium • the portion of the expected yield above the riskless rate that is due to pure risk aversion, as opposed to the expected default loss. In other words, the risk premium represents compensation to investors for the anxiety associated with uncertainty about future cash flows from an investment.

put • an option to sell a stock at a specified price over a specified period

put bond • a bond with an indenture provision allowing it to be sold back to the issuer at a prespecified price

put-call parity • a theoretical relation between the value of a put and a call on the same underlying security with the same strike and expiration date

quarterly earnings • profits, usually per-share profits, for a 3-month period

quarterly report • a report to shareholders containing 3-month financial statements and other relevant information

quick ratio • *See* acid ratio test.

raider • a hostile outside party that seeks to take over a company against the wishes of that company's management

rally • a brisk general rise in security prices usually following a decline

random walk • the random motion of stock prices that are as likely to move in one direction as another, regardless of past price behavior. This type of behavior is called Brownian motion in the physical sciences. It is consistent with the weak form of the efficient market hypothesis (EMH).

rate of return • a rate that takes into account both dividends and capital appreciation (increases in the price of the security). For example, a 9 percent rate of return implies that the owner of $100 worth of stock will earn a total of $9 in dividends and capital appreciation over the forthcoming year.

rating (bond) • a quality or risk evaluation assigned by a rating agency such as Standard & Poor's or Moody's

ratio analysis • balance sheet and income statement analysis that utilizes ratios of financial aggregates to assess a company's financial position

ratio writing • a complex form of option spread in which the writer takes offsetting positions in the same underlying security but with unequal numbers of options in the offsetting positions. One part of the position is therefore uncovered.

RCMM (registered competitive market maker) • *See* floor trader.

real estate investment trust • companies that buy and/or manage rental properties and/or real estate mortgages and pay out more than 95 percent of their income as dividends. No corporate profit taxes are due on their income.

real estate limited partnership • a type of investment organized as a limited partnership that invests directly in real estate properties

real estate sales company • a firm that sells property, especially at marketing events such as complimentary dinners. The property is often in a distant location and part of a projected retirement or vacation development.

real interest rate • nominal interest rate adjusted for inflation

real return • a return on an investment adjusted for changes in the price level. For example, if the nominal rate of return were 7, a 3 percent inflation rate would reduce the real return to 4 percent. This amount equals the increase in purchasing power resulting from saving or investing money.

rebate • a return of a portion of a payment

recession • an economic downturn categorized as a recession by the National Bureau of Economic Research. In the past, two successive quarters of decline in real GDP have been the standard gauge for a recession.

record date • the shareholder registration date that determines the recipients of that period's dividends

redemption fee • a charge sometimes assessed against those who cash in their mutual fund shares

redemption price • *See* call price.

refinancing • the selling of new securities to finance the retirement of others that are maturing or being called

regional exchange • a U.S. stock exchange located outside New York City

registered bond • a bond whose ownership is determined by registration as opposed to possession (bearer bond)

registered competitive market maker • *See* floor trader.

registered representative • an employee of a registered brokerage firm who is qualified to serve as an account executive for the firm's customers

registered trader • an exchange member who trades stocks on the exchange floor for his or her own account (or an account in which he or she is part owner)

registrar • a company, such as a bank, that maintains the shareholder records

registration statement • a statement that must be filed with the SEC before a security is offered for sale and that must contain all materially relevant information relating to the offering. A similar type of statement is required when a firm's shares are listed; it generally contains more detailed information than the prospectus.

regression • an equation that is fitted to data by statistical techniques. Computers are often used to perform the calculations. In the simplest case, a regression would have one variable to be explained (dependent variable) and one variable to explain it (independent variable), and it would take the form: $x_t = a + by_t$ (where x_t = dependent variable; y_t = independent variable; and a and b are parameters selected by the computer that best fit the data). Graphically, one can envision a scatter diagram relating x_t and y_t with a line drawn through the points (close to the line on the average) as the regression line. The "a" is the intercept and "b" the slope coefficient of this line. More complicated regression equations of the form $x_t = a + by_t + cz_t + dwy_t + ev_t$ ... containing more than one explanatory variable may also be estimated. Again, the computer can be used to select the best values of a, b, c, and so on. *See* least squares regression line (analysis).

regression toward the mean • the tendency of many phenomena to migrate toward the average over time. *See* mean reversion.

regulated investment company • a company, such as a mutual fund or closed-end fund, that qualifies for exemption from federal corporate income tax liability as a result of meeting the requirements set forth in Subchapter M of the Internal Revenue Code

Regulation Q • a Fed rule that at one time limited interest rates that banks and thrifts could pay on certain types of deposits/investments (rendered ineffective by deregulation)

Regulation T • a Fed rule that governs credit to brokers and dealers for security purchases

Regulation U • a Fed rule that governs margin credit limits

reinvestment rate risk • the risk associated with reinvesting coupon payments at unknown future interest rates. The yield to maturity (YTM) is generally computed on the assumption that coupons will be reinvested at the same rate as the bond's current YTM. If rates decrease after a bond is purchased, the coupon payments will be reinvested at rates below the promised YTM, and the return will be below expectations, whereas if rates increase, the coupon payments will be reinvested at rates above expectations. Because the direction of future rates is unknown, there is uncertainty about the rates at which coupon payments will be reinvested.

REIT • *See* real estate investment trust.

relative PE ratio • a technical indicator of relative overvaluation or undervaluation of stock

relative strength criterion • a technical analysis concept based on an assumption that stocks that have risen relative to the market exhibit relative strength, which tends to carry them to still higher levels. Tests of the concept are largely negative.

RELP • *See* real estate limited partnership.

reorganization • restructuring a firm's capital structure and operating facilities in the face of a default, near-default, or bankruptcy

replacement cost approach • the valuing of real estate or other assets on the basis of the cost of producing equivalent assets

repo • *See* repurchase agreement.

repurchase agreement • a type of investment in which a security is sold with a prearranged purchase price (repo) and the date is designed to produce a particular yield—in fact, an indirect form of borrowing

required rate of return • the rate of return on an investment required by the market in order to justify the degree of risk incurred. Using modern portfolio theory, it is the rate of return determined by the capital asset pricing model, which incorporates the relationship between market risk and return, resulting in a standardized methodology for identifying a security's unique required rate of return (discount rate).

reserve requirement • the percentage of reserves the Fed requires each bank to have on deposit for each increment of demand or time deposits

resistance level • a price range that, according to technical analysis, tends to block further price rises

retained earnings • reflected on the income statement as annual after-tax profits less dividends paid, and on the balance sheet as the sum of annual retained earnings to date

return on assets • profits before interest and taxes as a percentage of total assets (also called return on investment)

return on equity • profits after taxes, interest, and preferred dividends as a percentage of common equity

return on sales • profits as a percentage of sales

return (reward) to variability • *See* Sharpe ratio.

return (reward) to volatility • *See* Treynor ratio.

revenue bond • a municipal bond backed by the revenues of the project that it finances

reverse crush • a commodity trade that involves buying oil and meal and selling soybean futures

reverse split • a security exchange in which each shareholder receives a reduced number of shares but retains the same proportional ownership. Thus, a 10-for-1 reverse split would exchange 10 new shares for each 100 old shares.

riding the yield curve • a bond portfolio management strategy of taking advantage of an upward-sloping yield curve by purchasing intermediate term bonds and then selling them as they approach maturity

right • a security allowing shareholders to acquire new stock at a prespecified price over a prespecified period, generally issued in proportion to the number of shares currently held and normally exercisable at a specified price that is usually below the current market price. The new shares offered are usually made available from the firm's treasury stock. Rights generally trade in a secondary market after they are issued.

rights offering • an offering of rights by a firm wishing to raise additional equity capital while avoiding dilution of existing shareholders' relative ownership

risk • the variance of the expected return; that is, the degree of uncertainty associated with the expected return

risk-adjusted return • the return from an asset adjusted for the degree of market risk associated with the asset. Using the market model, this return is equal to the risk-free-rate + beta x (market return – risk-free rate). *See* security market line.

risk arbitrage • the taking of offsetting positions in the securities of an acquisition candidate and the would-be acquirer when the combined position should show a profit, provided the merger takes place

risk arbitrageurs • those who engage in risk arbitrage

risk averse • the property of preferring certainty and demonstrating a willingness to sacrifice expected return to achieve a more secure yield

risk aversion • the degree of preference for less risky, lower yields versus more risky, higher yields

risk-free rate • the interest rate on a riskless investment such as a Treasury bill

risk hedge • a hedge position undertaken from scratch that seeks to profit from relative price moves in the underlying positions—for example, spreads

riskless hedge • a hedge position without risk due to exactly offsetting returns in both directions of price movement of the associated underlying security(ies)

riskless investment • an investment having an expected return that is certain. A riskless asset, for example, expected to yield 6 percent, has a 100 percent chance of a 6 percent return.

risk neutrality • the property of preferring the highest return with indifference to risk

risk premium • the expected return in excess of the risk-free rate that is compensation for the investment's risk

risk-return trade-off • tendency for more risky assets to be priced to yield higher expected returns

risk-reward ratio • a measure of the amount of risk assumed in seeking a specific level of expected return

risk tolerance • the degree of preference for more risk, higher-return yields versus less risk, lower-return yields. *See* risk aversion.

ROA • *See* return on assets.

Robert Morris Associates • an organization of bankers that compiles averages of financial ratios for various industry groups

ROE • *See* return on equity.

rollover • a change from one type of investment to another

ROS • *See* return on sales.

round lot • the basic unit in which securities are traded, consisting usually of 100 shares, although some stocks trade in 10-unit lots

round-trip fee • the total commission costs of executing a transaction in the futures market paid at the time of formation of the contract

Rule 144 • an SEC rule restricting the sale of lettered stock

Rule 390 • a NYSE rule (repealed in 1999) restricting members from off-board trading (not on an exchange)

Rule 415 • an SEC rule allowing shelf registration of a security that may then be sold frequently over a 2-year period without separate registrations of each part

run • an uninterrupted series of price increases or decreases

Sallie Mae • *See* Student Loan Market Association.

saturation effect • the impact on revenues and profits when a heretofore rapid growth firm or industry largely satisfies its market's demand

savings bonds • low-denomination Treasury issues designed to appeal to small investors

scalper • a commodity trader who seeks to profit from very short-run price changes

scorched-earth defense • an antitakeover tactic in which the defending company's management engages in practices designed to reduce the firm's value to such a degree that it is no longer attractive to the potential acquirer

S corporation • *See S*ubchapter S corporation.

screening • data-analysis technique commonly used by stock market analysts to screen out (or screen in) certain stocks on the basis of their achievement of various numerical or technical criteria—for example, "pick all stocks that rose more than 15 percent last year and whose PE ratios are below 20"

seasoning • the process of new issues acquiring market acceptance in after-issue trading

seat • a membership on an exchange

SEC • *See* Securities and Exchange Commission.

secondary distribution • a large public securities offering made outside the usual exchange or OTC market. Those making the offering wish to sell a larger quantity of the security than they believe can be easily absorbed by the market's usual channels. A secondary offering spreads out the period for absorption.

secondary market • the market for already issued securities that may take place on the exchanges or OTC

secondary stocks • relatively obscure stocks favored by individual investors (not favored by institutional investors) that may trade on the AMEX, NASD, regional exchanges, or as smaller companies listed on the NYSE market

second mortgage • a mortgage debt secured by a property's equity after the first mortgage holder's claim has been subtracted from the pledged asset's value

sector fund • a type of mutual fund that specializes in a narrow segment of the market—for example, an industry (chemicals), region (Sunbelt), or category (small capitalization)

securities • paper assets representing a claim on something of value, such as stocks, bonds, mortgages, warrants, rights, puts, calls, commodity contracts, or warehouse receipts

Securities Amendment Act of 1970 • an act restricting the front-end loading fees that mutual funds can charge

Securities and Exchange Commission • the federal government agency with direct regulatory authority over the securities industry

Securities Investor Protection Corporation • a federal government agency that guarantees the safety of brokerage accounts up to $500,000, no more than $100,000 of which may be in cash

securitization • the process of turning an asset with poor marketability into a security with substantially greater acceptability—for example, a security that looks like a standard bond but is derived from real estate mortgage loans, auto loans, or credit card balances

security market line • the theoretical relation between a security's market risk and its expected return. The equation form is as follows: $R_i = R_f + \beta_i(R_m - R_f)$ where R_i is the risk-adjusted expected return, R_f is the risk-free return, β_i is the beta measure for security i, and R_m is the market return.

segmented markets hypothesis • a theory that explains the term structure of interest rates as due to the supply and demand of each maturity class

selection (survivor) bias • the tendency for standard stock market indices to incorporate only surviving and successful firms in their measurement, ignoring the effect of nonsurviving, less successful firms

self-tender • a firm tendering for its own shares and often used as an antitakeover defense

seller financing • a procedure in which the real estate seller finances part of the purchase price

selling short • the act of borrowing and selling a security that belongs to someone else. The short seller covers by buying back equivalent securities and restoring them to the original owner.

semistrong form of the efficient market hypothesis • the view that market prices quickly and accurately reflect all public information, suggesting that fundamental analysis applied to publicly available information and data is useless

semiweak form of the efficient market hypothesis • the view that market prices cannot be successfully forecast with technical market indicators

senior debt • debt that has priority over other (subordinate) debt in the event of bankruptcy

separation theorem • the hypothesis (due to James Tobin) that the return to any efficient portfolio and its risk can be completely described by an appropriate weighted average of two separate parts: the risk-free rate and the return to the market portfolio

serial bond • a bond issue in which portions mature at stated intervals rather than all at once

serial correlation • correlation between adjacent time series data for the same variable

settlement • the cash settlement of an exercised option or future

shark repellent • antitakeover provisions such as a poison pill

Sharpe ratio • a measure of risk-adjusted performance of an asset, calculated as the ratio of the asset's rate of return minus the risk-free rate divided by the asset's standard deviation

shelf registration • an SEC provision allowing preregistration of an amount of a security to be sold over a 2-year period without specific registration of each sale (as permitted by SEC Rule 415)

short against the box • the short selling of stock that is owned, usually to extend the date of realizing a gain

short covering • buying an asset to offset an existing short position

short interest (commodities and options) • the number of futures or options contracts written and outstanding

short interest (stocks) • the number of shares sold short; sometimes used as a technical market indicator of an anticipated market decline (if short interest is believed to reflect well-founded professional traders' opinions) or as an indicator of anticipated market rise if covering of short interest is expected (contrarian indicator)

short (position) • *See* short selling.

short selling • selling an asset that is not owned in the hope of repurchasing it later at a lower price

short squeeze • the result when powerful forces driving up the price of a stock have the effect of squeezing a substantial short interest

short-swing profit • a gain made by an insider on stock held for less than 6 months. Such gains must be paid back to the company.

short-swing rule • a tax rule that prevents a trader from realizing a tax loss on a sale and immediately repurchasing the issue in question. Stock must be held at least 30 days before the sale, and repurchase must be delayed at least 30 days after the sale to qualify for a tax loss.

short-term gains (losses) • gains (losses) on capital assets held less than 6 months

short-term trading index • a technical market indicator based on the relative percent of advancing versus declining stocks

short-term unit trust • a unit investment trust made up of an unmanaged portfolio of short-term securities (usually self-liquidating within 6 months of issue)

short transaction • the purchase or sale of a short position

simple interest • interest paid and computed only on the principal

single-index model • a method of estimating portfolio return and risk that utilizes only the market index and the market model (beta) for each security in the portfolio, as opposed to the full variance-covariance matrix of returns among all securities in the portfolio

single-premium deferred annuity contract • an annuity with a defined future value that is sold by insurance companies

sinking fund • an indenture provision requiring that a specific portion of a bond issue be redeemed periodically; required by many bond indentures so that all of the debt will not come due simultaneously

SIPC • *See* Securities Investor Protection Corporation.

skew distribution • a nonsymmetrical statistical distribution that is spread out more on one side of its mode than the other

skewness • the degree to which a distribution is skewed. *See* skew distribution.

SMA • *See* special miscellaneous account.

small firm effect • an alleged anomaly to the efficient market hypothesis that is characterized by the tendency for small firms to earn above-normal rates of return after risk adjustment

smokestack companies • companies in basic industries whose profits and sales are cyclical with the economy

social responsibility fund • a type of mutual fund that avoids investments in allegedly socially undesirable companies, such as those involved with tobacco, alcohol, natural pollution, armaments, and so forth

source and application of funds statement • an accounting statement reporting a firm's cash inflows and outflows (now called changes in financial position statement)

specialist • an exchange member who makes a market in listed securities

specialized dependencies • predictable return patterns related to some specific type of event, such as a new issue or tax-loss trading

special miscellaneous account • a sum associated with a margin account; normally equal to the account's (margin) buying power. The account is increased when stock is sold and decreased when stock is purchased. At times, the SMA of an account can become inflated (above the account's buying power) when the equity of the account is near or below the minimum for margin maintenance.

special offering • a large block of stock offered for sale on an exchange with special incentive fees paid to purchasing brokers (also called spot secondary)

speculating • the act of committing funds for a short period at high risk in the hope of realizing a large gain

speculative bubble • large increase in stock prices that can best be explained by emotional, rather than rational, investor behavior

speculative risk • high risk associated with speculation

split • an exchange of securities whereby each shareholder ends up with a larger number of shares representing the same percentage of the firm's ownership. For example, in a two-for-one split, a shareholder with 100 old shares would receive an additional 100 shares.

spot (cash) market • the market for immediate delivery of some commodity, such as wheat or silver

spot secondary • *See* special offering.

spread (bid-ask) • the difference between the bid and the ask price

spread (trade) • a type of hedge trade, such as a vertical or horizontal spread (options) or some comparable combination trade in the futures market, that offsets positions taken in similar securities in the hope of profiting from relative price moves

spreading • creating a spread trade

Standard & Poor's (S&P) Corporation • an important firm in the investment area that rates bonds, collects and reports data, and computes market indexes

Standard & Poor's Corporation Records • an investment periodical containing quarterly analyses of most publicly traded firms

Standard & Poor's Equity Investor Services • an important firm in the investment area that primarily rates bonds and also computes market indexes, compiles investment information, and publishes various investment periodicals

Standard & Poor's Index 500 (S&P Index 500) • the most commonly used index of stock prices for comparison purposes with individual stocks; composed of the top 500 (by capitalization) stocks in U.S. markets (from NYSE, NASDAQ, and AMEX) with weights according to market capitalization of each stock

Standard & Poor's Stock Market Encyclopedia • a book containing analyses of S&P 500 stocks

Standard & Poor's Stock Guide • a monthly publication with a compact line of data on most publicly traded corporations

standard deviation • a measure of the degree of compactness or spread of a distribution. About two times out of three, the actual value will be within one standard deviation on either side of the mean value. About 19 out of 20 times, it will be within two standard deviations. One standard deviation is the square root of the variance. *See* variance.

standstill agreement • a reciprocal understanding between a company's management and an outside party that owns a significant minority position in the company's stock, with each party giving up certain rights in exchange for corresponding concessions by the other party. For example, the outside group may agree to limit its ownership position to some prespecified level. In exchange, management may agree to minority board representation by the outside group.

Stein estimators • statistical techniques for estimating a variable that assume a regression toward the mean tendency

stock certificate • a document of ownership of a share or shares of stock in a corporation

Stock Clearing Corporation • NYSE subsidiary that clears transactions for member firms

stock dividend • a dividend paid in the form of a corporation's additional stock; similar to a stock split, although the distribution consists of proportionately less new stock

stock exchange • an organization for trading a specific list of securities over specific trading hours, usually at a single location

stockholder-oriented company • a company whose management is particularly responsive to the interest of its stockholders. A large ownership group may exercise effective control, or management itself may own a large block of the stock.

stock index futures • a commodity futures contract that does not require delivery of the underlying stock index but is instead settled in dollars according to the difference between the strike price and the actual price of the index

stock index option • option on the value of stock indexes stated as units of 100

stock market index futures • *See* stock index futures.

stock market overreaction • an analyst term used to describe the alleged tendency for the stock market to react more than is warranted to news, whether good or bad.

stock split • the division of a company's existing stock into more shares (say, 2 for 1, or 3 for 1), usually reducing the price per share in the hope of improving the shares' marketability

stop-limit order • an order to implement a limit order when the market price reaches a certain level

stop-loss order • an order to sell or buy at market when a certain price is reached

straddle (in commodities) • another name for a spread, where offsetting positions are taken in similar contracts, such as adjacent expirations of the same commodity future contract

straddle (in options) • a combination put and call on the same stock at the same strike price

straight-debt value • the value of a convertible bond as a straight-debt (nonconvertible) bond

straight-line depreciation • a method of writing off assets at a constant dollar rate over their estimated lives

strap • a combination of two calls and a put, each having the same strike and expiration date

Strategic Planning Institute • a consulting group known for its models of business profitability

street name • securities held in customer accounts at brokerage houses but registered in the firm's name.

strike price (exercise price) • the price at which the option holder can exercise the option to buy (call) or sell (put) shares, thereby fixed for the life of the option (also called strike; sometimes called striking price)

strip • a combination of two puts and a call, each having the same strike and expiration date

strip bond • a coupon bond (with its coupons removed) that returns only principal at maturity and thus is equivalent to a zero-coupon bond

strong form of the efficient market hypothesis • the view that market prices quickly and accurately reflect all public and nonpublic information (suggests that inside information is useless in security selection)

Student Loan Market Association • a federal government agency that sells notes backed by government-guaranteed student loans

Subchapter M • the section of the Internal Revenue Code that sets forth the criteria for a regulated investment company. *See* regulated investment company.

Subchapter S • the section of the Internal Revenue Code that sets forth the criteria for a Subchapter S corporation

Subchapter S corporation • an arrangement whereby a corporation may be taxed as a partnership under the provisions of the Internal Revenue Code

subordination • *See* subordination provisions.

subordination provisions • bond indenture provisions that give an issue a lower priority than other issues

sum of the years' digits depreciation • a method of accelerated depreciation that assigns depreciation equal to the ratio of the number of years remaining to the sum of the years in the asset's estimated life

SuperDOT • *See* DOT (designated order transmission).

superNOW account • an interest-bearing checking account with no set maximum interest rate. Most banks require a $2,500 minimum balance.

support level • a floor price that, according to technical analysis, tends to restrict downside price moves

Survey Research Center • research institute at the University of Michigan that surveys and publishes statistics on consumer sentiments

swap fund • a type of mutual fund that allows purchases with shares of other companies at their market prices

sweep fund • a type of bank account that daily sweeps the portion of the balance exceeding some preassigned minimum into a money fund where rates are not limited by Fed restrictions

syndicate • a group of investment bankers organized to underwrite a new issue or secondary offering

systematic risk • *See* market risk.

takeover bid • a tender offer designed to acquire a sufficient number of shares to achieve working control of the target firm

tangible investments • a broad group of commodities that includes precious metals, gemstones, artifacts, and some types of collectibles

tangibles • *See* tangible investments.

tax credit • amounts applied against computed taxes on a dollar-for-dollar basis, reducing the amount otherwise due

tax-equivalent yield • the yield on state and local debt instruments after adjustment for the fact that the debt holder is not liable for federal income tax; calculated as $r_t = r_{s\&l}/(1-t)$ where r_t is tax-equivalent yield, $r_{s\&l}$ is nominal yield on state and local debt, and t is marginal federal tax rate of the investor

tax-exempt bond fund • a mutual fund that invests in municipal bonds, offering tax-free income to its holders

tax-loss carryforward • unutilized prior-period losses that may be employed to offset subsequent income

tax-loss trading • year-end selling of depressed securities designed to establish a tax loss

tax-managed fund • a type of investment company that, prior to IRS rulings disallowing such a practice, sought to convert dividend income into capital gains. Such funds organized themselves as corporations rather than as mutual funds and reinvested their portfolios' dividends.

tax shelter • an investment that produces deductions from other income for the investor with a resulting savings in income taxes. The Tax Reform Act of 1986 severely restricted most types of tax shelters.

tax swap • a type of bond swap in which an issue is sold to yield a tax loss and replaced with an equivalent issue

T-bill • *See* Treasury bill.

TEBF • *See* tax-exempt bond fund.

technical analysis (broad form) • a method of forecasting general market movements with technical market indicators

technical analysis (narrow form) • a method of evaluating securities based only on past price and volume behavior

technical market indicator • a data series or combination of data series said to be helpful in forecasting the market's future direction (market indicator)

Templeton approach • a fundamental approach to investment analysis, named after renowned mutual fund manager John Marks Templeton, that emphasizes a global view to finding undervalued issues

tender offer • an offer to purchase a large block of securities made outside the general market (exchanges, OTC) in which the securities are traded (often as part of an effort to take over a company)

term structure (of interest rates) • a pattern of yields for differing maturities (risk controlled). *See also* segmented markets hypothesis, unbiased expectations hypothesis, and liquidity preference hypothesis.

term to maturity • the length to maturity of a debt instrument

tertiary stocks • the most obscure group of stocks that are much less popular than even the secondary stocks and trade on the pink sheets

thin market • a market in which volume is low and transactions relatively infrequent

third market • the over-the-counter market in listed securities

thrift institutions • institutions other than commercial banks that accept savings deposits, especially savings and loan associations, mutual savings banks, and credit unions

thrifts • *See* thrift institutions.

tick • the minimum size price change on a futures contract

ticker symbols • symbols for identifying securities on the ticker tape and quotation machines as listed in the *S&P Stock Guide* and several other publications

ticker tape • a device for displaying stock market trading

Tigers (Treasury Investment Growth Receipts) • zero-coupon securities assembled by Merrill Lynch and backed by a portfolio of Treasury issues

tight money • restrictive monetary policy

times-interest-earned ratio • before-tax, before-interest profit (net operating income) divided by interest expense (a ratio used to detect possible risk of default)

time value (option) • the excess of an option's market price over its intrinsic value

time value (present value) • the value at the present time of (expected) future cash flows

timing • *See* market timing.

title search • a process whereby the validity of a title to a real estate parcel is evaluated

TOLSR • *See* total odd-lot short ratio.

top-tier stocks • established growth stocks preferred by many institutional investors

total odd-lot short ratio • a technical market indicator that relates odd-lot short selling to total odd-lot trading

total return • dividend return plus capital gains return

total risk • the sum of market and nonmarket risk

trading post • *See* post.

trailing earnings • most commonly used by the financial press in calculating PE ratios, the use of recent past earnings relative to current price. Academic studies frequently attempt to use the ratio of anticipated earnings in calculating current PE ratios.

transfer agent • the agent who keeps track of changes in shareholder ownership

transfer tax • a New York State tax on the transfer of equity securities

Treasury bill • government debt security issued on a discount basis by the U.S. Treasury

Treasury stock • previously issued stock reacquired by the issuing company

Treynor ratio • a measure of risk-adjusted performance of an asset calculated as the ratio of the asset's rate of return minus the risk-free rate divided by the asset's beta value; sometimes called the return (reward) to volatility ratio

trust • a property interest held by one person for the benefit of another

trustee • a bank or other third party that administers the provisions of a bond indenture

turnover • trading volume in a security or the market

Turov's formula • a formula for computing the amount by which a stock price must change to produce equivalent returns on its options

two-tier tender offer • takeover tactic in which one offer (usually cash) is made for the controlling interest of the target firm and a second offer (usually securities) is made for the remainder

UIH • *See* uncertain information hypothesis.

unbiased expectations hypothesis • a theory explaining the term structure of interest rates as reflecting the market consensus of contiguous future short rates

uncertain information hypothesis • the hypothesis that uncertain information will tend to make investors perceive a higher risk to the firm. Even though the information itself may be positive, the net effect upon the firm's stock may be negative due to increased risk perception.

underwrite • to agree to buy all or part of a new security issue, planning to sell the securities to the public at a slightly higher price

underwriter • an investment dealer who agrees to buy all or part of a new security issue and plans to sell the securities to the public at a slightly higher price

underwriting fee • the difference between the price paid and the selling price on an underwritten issue

unemployment rate • the percentage of those actively seeking employment who are actually out of work

unit investment trust • a self-liquidating unmanaged portfolio in which investors own shares; a concept similar to a closed-end fund but with a specified liquidation date

unit labor costs • the ratio of total employee compensation (wages plus benefits) to total real output; frequently used as an indicator of pressure on prices, since labor costs are the dominant part of total costs for a firm

Unlisted Market Guide • an investment publication that periodically covers small companies that are not found in larger periodicals, such as Value Line and Standard and Poor's

unlisted security • a security that trades only in the OTC market

unsystematic risk • *See* nonmarket risk.

uptick • a transaction that takes place at a higher price than the immediately preceding price

urgent selling index • a technical market indicator based on the relative volume in advancing and declining issues

VA • *See* Veterans Administration.

value investing • *See* value-oriented investor.

Value Line • a firm that publishes quarterly analyses on firms and compiles the *Value Line Index*

Value Line Index • an unweighted, broadly based stock price index

value-oriented investor • an investor who seeks to assemble a portfolio of stocks that sell at low prices relative to their underlying values, such as their earnings, cash flows, book values, breakup values, and liquid assets

variable rate mortgage • a mortgage in which the interest rate is allowed to vary with market rates

variance • the expected (average) value of the square of the deviation from the mean: variance of $X = E(X - X)^2$ where R is the mean of X, and E is the expected value

variance-covariance model • a method of estimating portfolio risk that utilizes the variances and covariances of all of the potential components

venture capital • risk capital extended to start-up companies or small going concerns that usually requires an ownership interest as distinct from a pure loan

versus purchase order • sale order that specifies the purchase date of securities to be delivered for sale

vertical spread • short and long option positions on the same security with the same expiration but different strike prices

vested benefits • pension benefits that are retained even if the individual leaves his or her employer

Veterans Administration • a federal government agency that, among other services to veterans, guarantees the mortgage loans of veterans

volume • the number of shares traded in a particular period

Wall Street Journal, The • a business/investments newspaper published 5 days a week by Dow Jones Inc.

Wall Street Week • a popular and long-running weekly business news television program hosted by Louis Rukeyser

warrants • certificates offering the right to purchase stock in a company at a specified price over a specified period. Unlike options, warrants are issued by the same company that issues the underlying stock.

wash sale • a sale and repurchase made within 30 days, thereby failing to establish a taxable loss

weak form of the efficient market hypothesis • the view that market prices move randomly with respect to past price return patterns; implies that the broad form of technical analysis is useless

Web site • a site on the Internet that offers entertainment, culture, information about services, products, news, and so on

Weisenberger • a major publisher of mutual fund investment information, including *Investment Companies Yearbook*

Weisenberger's *Investment Companies Yearbook* • *See* Weisenberger.

when issued • trading in as yet unissued securities that have a projected future issue date

white knight defense • finding an alternative and presumably more friendly acquirer than the immediate takeover threat

white squire defense • finding an important ally to purchase a strong minority position of the firm now controlled by existing management but threatened by an outside group. Presumably, the white squire will oppose and, ideally, block the efforts of the outsider to take control of the vulnerable company.

Wilshire 5000 Equity Index • a value-weighted stock index based on a large number of NYSE, AMEX, and OTC stock

wire house • an exchange member electronically linked to an exchange

working capital (gross) • the sum of the values of a firm's short-term assets

working capital (net) • a firm's short-term assets minus its short-term liabilities

working control • the ownership of sufficient shares to elect a majority to the company's board of directors

writer (of an option) • one who assumes the short side of a put or call contract and therefore stands ready to satisfy the potential exercise of the long side; in effect, a seller of options

yield • the return of an investment expressed as a percentage of its market value

yield (current) • current income (dividend, coupon, interest, rent, and so on) divided by the current price of the asset

yield curve • a graphic representation of the relationship between yield to maturity and term to maturity (or duration) for equivalent-risk debt securities

yield to earliest call • the holding period return for the assumption that the issue is called as soon as the no-call provision expires

yield to maturity • the yield that takes account of both the coupon return and the principal repayment at maturity

YTM • *See* yield to maturity.

zero-coupon bond • a bond issued at a discount that matures at its face value and makes no interest payments prior to maturity

zero sum game • *See* zero sum market.

zero-sum market • a market such as the derivatives and futures markets where the net gains and losses of buyers and sellers sum to zero after all transactions and expirations of contracts. Also, for each long position, there must be a corresponding short position, which means that the net gains and losses for both parties sum to zero.

zero tick • a transaction immediately preceded by a transaction at the same price

Answers to Review Questions and Self-Test Questions

Chapter 1

Answers to Review Questions, pp. 35–36

1-1. *Return* is the gain or loss in value that results from an investment. When we are looking to the future, we are likely speaking of expected return. An expected return is considered to be the most likely outcome or term ending value. The range of other possible returns represents risk, which is the possibility that a return will be different from the expected return.

1-2. *Holding period return relative* (HPRR) is the ratio of the final value (including any intermediate payments) divided by the initial value. The time period can be of arbitrary length.

Holding period return (HPR) is HPRR – 1, which is the percentage change from the initial value.

Per-period return (PPR) is the standardized version of HPR. The length of time is defined by the context of the situation. PPR may differ from HPR when the time frames do not match.

Annualized return is an HPR or PPR that has been converted to a one-year statistic, often for comparison.

Compound interest is interest that accrues to a preceding period's interest. With compound interest, a return is earned on both the initial investment and previous interest payments.

Arithmetic mean (average) return (AMR) is a single number that is representative of a group of numbers. It is calculated by adding the group's components, which are multiplied by their respective weights. In the simplest case, the weight is 1/n where n is the number of components.

Geometric mean (average) return (GMR) incorporates compounding when calculating the representative statistic. Calculating multiperiod returns using the GMR will yield accurate results. Using the AMR may lead to inaccurate results because it omits compounding.

1-3. a. HPRR = $7,000 / $5,000 = 1.4
   HPR = 1.4 – 1 = .4 = 40%
   b. HPRR = $3,000 / $1,800 = 1.667
   HPR = 1.667 – 1 = .667 = 66.7%
   c. HPRR = $228,500 / $195,000 = 1.17
   HPR = 1.17 – 1 = .17 = 17%

1-4. Since the holding period is one year, the HPR is the same as the annual return for all parts of question 1-4.
   a. Total value = $11.00 + $0.30 = $11.30
   HPRR = $11.30 / $10 = 1.13
   HPR = 1.13 – 1 = .13 = 13%
   b. .07 / 4 = .0175 (quarterly rate)
   HPRR = (1.0175 x 1.0175 x 1.0175 x 1.0175) / 1 = 1.07186
   HPR = 1.07186 – 1 = .07186 = 7.186%
   c. First, we need to compute the coupon income. Eight percent of $1,000 is $80. Half of this amount, or $40, would be received at midyear. At 9 percent (the approximate yield on the bond), that coupon payment would earn another $1.80. At year-end the bond would produce another $40 payment. Thus, the total coupon income would be approximately $81.80. The bond price fell by $40 so the net profit would be about $41.80 ($81.80 – $40).

The current value of the investment would be $931.80 ($850 + $81.80). Thus,

$$HPRR = \$931.80 \,/\, \$890 = 1.0470$$
$$HPR = 1.0470 - 1 = .0470 = 4.7\%$$

1-5. Annually $= 1.1 \times 1.1 = 1.21$
Semiannually $= (1 + .10 \,/\, 2)^4 = 1.2155$
Quarterly $= (1 + .10 \,/\, 4)^8 = 1.2184$
Monthly $= (1 + .10 \,/\, 12)^{24} = 1.2204$

1-6. a. Arithmetic mean return:

$$(7.8\% + 9.3\% + 4.5\% + 11.5\%) \,/\, 4 = 8.275\%$$

b. If the amounts were in the proportions of .2, .3, .4, and .1, the mean return would be

$$.2 \,(7.8) + .3 \,(9.3) + .4 \,(4.5) + .1 \,(11.5) = 7.30 = 7.3\%$$

1-7. a. We must begin by determining the holding period return relative (HPRR).

$$GMR + 1 = (HPRR)^{1/n}$$
$$HPRR = (1.056)\,(1.089)\,(1.100)\,(1.077)\,(1.130) = 1.539496$$
$$GMR + 1 = (1.539496)^{1/5} = 1.090; \; GMR = .090 = 9\%$$

b. $AMR = (5.6\% + 8.9\% + 10\% + 7.7\% + 13\%) \,/\, 5 = .0904 = 9.04\%$

1-8. a. It is a general characteristic of the marketplace that prices are determined that are appropriate for the expected return and risk level of a particular investment. As the risk of an instrument increases, its price declines, thereby increasing its expected rate of return.

b. Not all high-risk investments offer high returns. This may be due to a market valuation based on reasons in addition to risk—for instance, humanitarian motives.

1-9. a. Both liquidity and marketability deal with the ease of selling an instrument. The distinction lies in the selling price. If the market price at which an instrument is sold is at or above the purchase price, the investment is liquid; if it is below, the investment is merely marketable. Therefore, liquid investments are a subset of marketable assets.

b. All liquid instruments are marketable (unless there are external restrictions such as contractual penalties), but not all marketable investments are liquid.

1-10. Investments require varying degrees of attention and effort. For example, selecting and managing some types of investments require little or no special knowledge, facilities, or time commitment, while investments in other assets, such as real estate or soybean futures, require very special knowledge, talent, and/or facilities. Likewise, some types of investments may be maintained with little or no effort (bonds), whereas others require constant management (an apartment complex).

1-11. Minimum investment levels can range from a few dollars to open a savings account to millions of dollars for some select mutual funds. Investors should assess the minimum investment level along with appropriateness and affinity. Some investors screen their investments in order to hold only the assets that are associated with products or services that reflect or do not conflict with their belief systems. They may therefore sacrifice return for peace of mind.

1-12. Federal taxes on investments are generally at the ordinary income level (marginal rate) or the long-term capital gains rate. Investments taxed at the marginal rate include interest income (excluding state and municipal securities), rents, royalties, dividends, and short-term capital gains (assets held for less than one year). Long-term capital gains are taxed at a maximum rate of 20 percent. Capital distributions are not taxable but alter the basis that is used in capital gains calculations.

1-13. a. Using the 2000 tax tables gives us a standard deduction (SD) of $7,350 for a married couple filing jointly:

Total income $= \$29,000 + \$750 + \$500 + \$1,200 = \$31,450$
(municipal interest is nontaxable at the federal level)
Personal and dependency exemptions (PE) $= 4 \times \$2,800 = \$11,200$
Taxable income $=$ Total income $-$ SD $-$ PE
$$= \$31,450 - \$7,350 - \$11,200 = \$12,900$$

As evidenced by table 1-1, taxable income falls within the 15 percent marginal tax bracket. Therefore, the tax owed = .15 ($12,900) = $1,935.

b. Since this taxpayer is in the 15 percent marginal tax bracket—the lowest bracket—the average tax rate (based on taxable income) is the same as the marginal tax rate.

Taxable income = $12,900
Tax owed = $1,935
Average tax rate = $1,935/$12,900 = 15%

1-14. a. Total income = $90,000 + $3,000 = $93,000
Personal and dependency exemptions (PE) = 3 x $2,800 = $8,400
Itemized deductions (ID) = $9,000 + $6,500 + $800 = $16,300
Taxable income = Total income – ID – PE = $93,000 – $16,300 – $8,400 = $68,300
As evidenced by table 1-1, taxable income falls within the 28 percent marginal tax bracket. Therefore, the tax owed = $6,577.50 + 28% of the amount over $43,850, or $24,450 = $6,577.50 + $6,846 = $13,423.50.

b. Based on taxable income of $68,300, this taxpayer is in the marginal tax bracket of 28 percent.

Taxable income = $68,300
Tax owed = $13,423.50
This taxpayer's average tax rate is computed as follows: $13,423.50/$68,300 = 19.7%, which is considerably lower than the marginal rate of 28%.

Answers to Self-Test Questions, pp. 36–37

1-1. True.
1-2. False. Marketable assets can usually be bought and sold in quantity at the current market price while those investments that can be quickly converted into cash at little cost or risk are considered to be liquid.
1-3. True.
1-4. False. An asset's PPR is defined as the sum of that period's income payments and price appreciation divided by its first-of-period price.
1-5. True.
1-6. True.
1-7. False. Insurance companies are in the business of selling protection from pure risk. Pure risks involve only the chance of loss or no loss, whereas speculative risks involve the chance of loss, no loss, or gain.
1-8. False. The more distant the redemption date (that is, the longer until its maturity), the less liquid the investment is considered to be. Thus, long-term debt securities are generally not very liquid.
1-9. True.
1-10. False. Itemizing deductions is only advantageous to the taxpayer if allowable deductions exceed the standard deduction.
1-11. False. Deductions are allowed for many types of taxes but not sales taxes.
1-12. True.
1-13. True.
1-14. False. State and local government bond interest typically is untaxed at the federal level.
1-15. False. The basic rule is that short-term capital gains are taxed as ordinary income.
1-16. True.
1-17. True.
1-18. False. The higher of the regular tax or the AMT is the tax amount that must be paid.
1-19. True.
1-20. False. Decisions made by a group tend to be riskier than individual decisions.

Chapter 2

Answers to Review Questions, pp. 60–62

2-1. a.

	Dimensions						
Types	Risk	Return	Liquidity	Marketability	Min. Size	Effort	Ethical Appeal
Savings deposits	L	L	H	H	L	L	N
Savings bonds	L	L	H	H	L	L	N
Money market funds	L	L	H	H	L	L	N
Treasury bonds	L	L	L to H	H	M	L	N
Corporate bonds	L to H	L to H	L to M	L to M	M	L	L
Municipal bonds	L to H	L to M	L to M	L	M	M	N

   b. Interest payments of Treasury issues are free from state and local taxes. Municipal bond interest is free of federal taxation and also free of state and local taxes within the issuing state.

2-2. Bond commissions are generally set at or about $5 per bond with a $50 minimum (10 bonds).
   a. Commission = 7 x $5 = $35 for a purchase of 7 bonds, but the $50 minimum applies.
   b. Commission = 15 x $5 = $75 for a sale of 15 bonds.
   c. Commission = 3 x $5 = $15 for a purchase of 3 bonds, but the $50 minimum applies.

2-3. a. The bond price of 70 (points) = $700.
       Total purchase = 7 x $700 = $4,900
       Commission percentage = $50/$4,900 = .01 = 1%
   b. The bond price of 105 (points) = $1,050
       Total purchase = 15 x $1,050 = $15,750
       Commission percentage = $75/$15,750 = .005 = .5%
   c. The bond price of 56 (points) = $560
       Total purchase = 3 x $560 = $1,680
       Commission percentage = $50/1,680 = .03 = 3%

2-4. a.

	Dimensions						
Types	Risk	Return	Liquidity	Marketability	Min. Size	Effort	Ethical Appeal
Common stock	M to H	L to H	L	H	L	L	L
Preferred stock	L to M	L	L	H	L	L	L

   b. The tax treatment of common and preferred stock is split between dividends and capital gains. Dividends are taxed at ordinary income rates, and capital gains classified as short-term are taxed at ordinary income rates, while those classified as long-term are taxed at the maximum rate of 20 percent.

2-5. a. *Limited partnerships* combine the benefits of a corporation's limited liability with the single taxation advantage of a partnership. A single general partner, who is usually the organizer and may be a corporation, *does* have unlimited liability. The limited partners, however, are not liable for the partnership's debts and obligations beyond their initial capital contributions.

    b. Most limited partnerships have one major drawback: Because they are relatively small, their ownership units trade in very thin markets. The master limited partnership (*MLP*) is designed to overcome this drawback. Most MLPs are relatively large (compared to limited partnerships). Their ownership units are designed to trade actively in the same types of markets as stocks.

2-6.   The after-tax yield can be computed from the formula for tax equivalent yield found in chapter 1. In this case, C is actually the after-tax yield. Keep in mind that only 30 percent of dividends are taxable for corporations.

$$\text{Solving for C: } C = TE (1 - T)$$
$$C_{Individual} = .075 (1 - .28) = .054 = 5.4\%$$
$$C_{Corporation} = .075 (1 - .36 (.30)) = .067 = 6.7\%$$

2-7.   a. Since there is only a single holding period, the overall return is simply the arithmetic mean (average) return:

$$AMR = (80 - 25 - 15 + 12 + 105 - 80 + 350 - 100 + 0) / 9 = 36.33\%$$

    b. The geometric mean return (GMR) is calculated as follows:

$$GMR = (AMR + 1)^{1/5} - 1 = (1.3633)^{1/5} - 1 = .064 = 6.4\%$$

2-8.   a. The percentage holding period return for an investment in a stock purchased at 20 and sold for 30 is

$$HPRR = 30 / 20 = 1.5$$
$$HPR = HPRR - 1 = .5 = 50\%$$

    b. If call options were bought with a strike price of 20 for a price of 2 and exercised when the stock reached 30 and the resulting stock position then sold, the holding period return would be determined as follows:

$$Profit = (30 - 20) - 2 = 8$$
$$HPR = 8 / 2 = 4 = 400\%$$

2-9.   a. *Warrants*, like calls, permit their owner to purchase a particular amount of stock at a prespecified price within a prespecified period. Unlike calls, warrants are generally exercisable for relatively long periods, such as several years. Furthermore, warrants are issued by the company whose stock underlies the warrant. If the warrant is exercised, the issuing company simply creates more shares. In contrast, existing shares are used to satisfy the exercise of a call. Thus, warrants are company-issued securities whose exercise results in additional shares and generates cash for the issuer. Calls are contracts between individual investors that do not involve the underlying company.

    b. Both rights and warrants are company-issued options to buy stock, and both are traded in the same markets that trade the stocks that underlie them. However, rights differ from warrants in two ways: First, rights are issued for very short-run periods. They expire in a few weeks or at most a few months from the time of their issue. Second, rights are generally exercisable at a price that is substantially less than the current market price of the stock. The issuer sets a low enough price to make immediate exercise attractive. Most rights are exercised, therefore, while the exercise of warrants is more uncertain.

2-10. a. First determine the cost of purchase. The front-end load involves a charge of $0.85; the total purchase price is $10.85:

$$HPRR = \$12/\$10.85 = 1.11$$
$$HPR = 1.11 - 1 = .11 = 11\%$$

    b. If the fund is no-load, the calculations are

$$HPRR = \$12/\$10 = 1.2$$
$$HPR = 1.2 - 1 = .2 = 20\%$$

2-11. Real estate investors have several reasons for being cautious:

- The more debt (leverage) used to finance real estate purchases, the greater the risks.
- The one-of-a-kind nature of individual real estate investments makes such properties relatively difficult and costly to buy and sell. Having to sell real estate on short notice can result in a substantial sacrifice.
- Determining a fair value for a prospective real estate investment requires considerable expertise.
- Managing improved property is a time-consuming task.
- Real estate commissions are considerably higher than those on securities.
- Most real estate purchases require a relatively large initial investment (down payment).

2-12. a. The investor must have at least 10 percent of the value of the futures contract in his or her margin account. Since the futures contract has a value of $150,000, the investor needs at least $15,000 in the margin account.

b. As determined in a, the amount originally invested in the position is $15,000. If the initial value of the futures contract is $150,000 and it rises to $200,000 when it is closed out, the investor has a $50,000 gain. The gain as a percentage of the amount invested is [HPR = Gain/Initial Investment = $50,000/$15,000 = 3.33 = 333%] 333 percent. This is the holding period return or HPR.

Answers to Self-Test Questions, pp. 62–63

2-1. False. Depository institutions are no longer subject to maximum rate limitations on their accounts and certificates. Now they are allowed to pay whatever rates the competitive situation calls for.

2-2. True.

2-3. True.

2-4. True.

2-5. False. Only 23 percent of U.S. households own stock directly, but many more participate indirectly.

2-6. False. Stock prices generally fluctuate much more than bond prices.

2-7. False. Preferred stock is not particularly liquid, but it is generally marketable.

2-8. True.

2-9. True.

2-10. False. Calls are contracts between individual investors that do not involve the underlying company.

2-11. True.

2-12. False. Mutual funds are classified as open-end investment companies, which may issue new shares as well as redeem outstanding shares.

2-13. True.

2-14. False. Commissions on commodity trades are only a tiny fraction of the potential gains or losses.

2-15. True.

Chapter 3

Answers to Review Questions, pp. 117–118

3-1. Congress set up the Security Investors Protection Corporation (SIPC) patterned after the Federal Deposit Insurance Corporation (FDIC) that protects deposits in banks. SIPC protects brokerage customers against losses that would otherwise result from the failure of their brokerage firm. Of course, customers are not protected against losses due to market fluctuations. SIPC liquidates troubled firms at the SEC's request. Customers are insured up to $500,000, not more than $100,000 of which may be in cash. Any claims above those sums are applied against the firm's available assets during liquidation. Most brokerage firms, however, have purchased additional insurance.

3-2. The National Daily Quotation Service reports the bid and ask prices for all actively traded OTC issues (about 6,000 NASDAQ and 22,000 other issues). These price quotations appear daily in the *Pink Sheets*, copies of which are available at most brokerage firms. Investors who want a current quotation of a Pink Sheet stock need to have their brokers call one or more of the firms listed as making a market in the stock for a price. The phone numbers of these firms are listed in the Pink Sheets.

3-3. a. The commission on a single trade of 1,500 shares at $7 per share is
Purchase value = 1,500 ($7) = $10,500
Commission = $30 + 1.25% ($10,500) + $80 + $5.50 (15) = $323.75

b. The commission on 15 separate 100-share trades at $7 per share is
One-trade purchase value = 100 ($7) = $700
One-trade commission = $9 + 2.75% ($700) = $28.25 (which is below the $35 minimum)
15-trade commission = 15 ($35) = $525

c. Of the two commissions in a. and b., that of the single trade is lower.

3-4. a. Purchase value = 500 ($81) = $40,500
Commission = $210 + .60% ($40,500) + $8(5)
= $210 + $243 + $40 = $493
   b. Purchase cost = $40,500 + $493 = $40,993
   c. Spread = Difference between bid and ask price
Spread for 80–81 is 1
   d. Percentage spread is 1/80 = 1.25%
3-5. Sale value = 500 ($90) = $45,000
Commission = $210 + .60% ($45,000) + $8(5)
= $210 + $270 + $40 = $520
Sale revenue = Value of stock minus the commission
= $45,000 – $520 = $44,480
Gain = $44,480 – $40,993 = $3,487 or 8.5% of initial purchase cost of $40,993
3-6. A *market order* requires an immediate execution at the best available price. A *limit order* stipulates the minimum (sell) or maximum (buy) price acceptable for a trade to take place. A *stop-loss order* requires an immediate market trade if the specified price is reached. A *stop-limit order* activates a limit order if a specified price is reached.
3-7. a. The investor's basis in the 700 shares normally is determined under a first-in, first-out (FIFO) approach. This requires that the shares purchased earliest be recorded as the ones sold first. Therefore, the first 700 shares were bought at $15 (300 shares), $18 (300), and $31 (100):
Normal basis = $15 (300) + $18 (300) + $31 (100) = $13,000
   b. Under a specified versus purchase order, the investor can specify which block of stock that he or she holds is to be sold. Therefore, the 700 shares can be allocated to the blocks priced at $40, $31, and $23 per share as follows:
Highest basis = $40 (300) + $31 (300) + $23 (100) = $23, 600
3-8. a. (1) If relevant news is expected to affect the price, speed of execution is essential. Therefore, set the limit price near the current price.
(2) When no imminent development dictates the trade, set the limit price near the expected low (high) for a buy (sale).
(3) Set the limit price near but not at a focal point. This will increase the likelihood of execution.
   b. These rules are beneficial when the investor has the time to try to maximize price. If this is not the case, a market order should be used.
3-9. The *third market* is the trading of listed stocks in the over-the-counter (OTC) market. It came about as a rebellion against the formerly high fixed commissions of the NYSE. Direct trading between institutions is termed as taking place in the *fourth market*. The benefit of this method is that prices can be negotiated and commissions bypassed (although there may be a finder's fee for the party bringing the institutions together).
3-10. a. A house call is made when the equity percentage falls below the minimum maintenance level set by the brokerage firm. A Fed call occurs when the equity percentage falls below the maintenance level set by the Federal Reserve Board for margin accounts.
   b. A margin call may be satisfied in any of the following ways:
   • adding more money to the account
   • adding more marginal collateral to the account
   • selling stock from the account and using the proceeds to reduce the margin debt
3-11. After 23 months' experience with the Up Up Corporation stock, Jo Ann's position is as follows:
   a. She owns 4,583 shares.
   b. Her stock is valued at $229,150.
   c. She owes $68,740 in margin.
   d. Her equity position is $160,410.

Month	Price	Shares	Value	Net Equity	Margin
0	$10	1,000	10,000	5,000	5,000
1	$15	1,000	15,000	10,000	5,000
5	$20	1,500	30,000	25,000	5,000
	Bought	1,000	20,000		
		2,500	50,000	25,000	25,000
11	$30	3,125	93,750	68,750	25,000
	Bought*	1,458	43,740		
		4,583	137,490	68,750	68,740
23	$50	4,583	229,150	160,410	68,740

*Only whole shares are purchased

3-12. When the share price isn't specified during a margin call, it must be calculated. With the information we have, we must first determine the portfolio value: Value = Margin/(1 – equity %). Next, Share price = Value/shares owned. Last, the number of shares that must be sold to restore 50 percent equity = (Equity – margin)/share price.

Thus, when Joe liquidates his position in the Down Down corporation stock after the third margin call, he has only $7,806 left out of his original $50,000 investment.

Month	Price	Shares	Value	Beginning Equity	Ending Equity	Margin
0	$50	2,000	100,000	50,000	50,000	50,000
6	$38.46	2,000	76,923	50,000	26,923	50,000
	Sold	600	23,077			(23,077)
		1,400	53,846		26,923	26,923
8	$29.59	1,400	41,420	26,923	14,497	26,923
	Sold	420	12,426			(12,426)
		980	28,994		14,497	14,497
9	$22.76	980	22,303	14,497	7,806	14,497

3-13. The $53,000 balance corresponds to the call rate plus ¾ percent or 9 ¼ percent. This rate is equivalent to a monthly rate of 9.25/12 = 0.771%. The first month's charge is $53,000 (0.771%) = $408.54. The second month's charge is ($53,000 + $408.54) (0.771%) = $411.69. Continuing with a. and making the necessary adjustments for b. and c. (with relevant rates of 10 ¼ percent and 10 ¾ percent respectively):

a.	Month	Charge	b.	Month	Charge	c.	Month	Charge
	1	$ 408.54		1	$230.63		1	$ 62.71
	2	411.69		2	232.59		2	63.27
	3	414.86		3	234.58		3	63.84
	4	418.06			$697.80		4	64.41
	5	421.28					5	64.99
	6	424.53					6	65.57
		$2,498.96					7	66.16
							8	66.75
							9	67.35
							10	67.95
								$653.00

3-14. The investment banker may choose to act as an agent for the issuing firm, in which case the job is taken on a best-effort basis. Most underwriting, however, is done on a firm-commitment basis, which means the investment banker buys the securities from the issuer and then resells them to the public.

3-15. The drive for centralization will link disparate markets into one large marketplace. Linkage should lead to greater efficiency with benefits such as narrower spreads and a greater ability to absorb trading volume. In addition, information will flow quickly through the market, allowing for more accurate pricing and thereby limiting arbitrage opportunities.

3-16. a. Debt allows firms to leverage their shareholders' equity positions. In addition, the interest payments on debt are tax deductible so the effective cost to the issuing firm can be relatively low. If the operating profits earned with the borrowed funds exceed the cost of the loan, the return attributable to the owners (shareholders) is enhanced. Shareholders, therefore, will benefit from an effective use of debt.

   b. A borrower firm is contractually obligated to make principal and interest payments on its debt. In addition, a high debt ratio tends to increase the interest rate on all the company's borrowings and the discount factor applied to all future earnings. Moreover, if the borrowing rate exceeds the return on the additional investment, debt will depress the firm's earnings.

3-17. Current book value = $60,000,000/5,000,000 = $12 per share
New net worth = $60,000,000 + 750,000 ($18) (1 – .15) = $71,475,000
New book value = $71,475,000/5,750,000 = $12.43 per share

3-18. a. Stock prices of poorly managed firms often do not fully reflect their potentials. These undervalued situations attract investors who may try to take control, put in more effective managers, and profit from the improved operations. Sometimes the mere threat of a takeover is enough to motivate better management.

   b. While takeovers have many motivations, almost all stem at least in part from the acquirer's belief that the current market price of the proposed acquisition is undervalued relative to its potential. This potential can best be exploited (even in a friendly takeover) by bringing in fresh ideas, resources, and faces. Takeovers and potential takeovers, therefore, help weed out deadwood and keep managers on their toes.

   c. Because the value of stock option packages tends to increase with a firm's growth potential, the options of promising firms may help attract managerial talent that other firms could hire only with higher salaries. Start-up companies, especially high-tech start-up companies, are particularly likely to use option packages to attract new management.

Answers to Self-Test Questions, pp. 119–121

3-1. True.

3-2. True.

3-3. False. The SIPC protects brokerage customers against losses that would otherwise result from the failure of their brokerage firm.

3-4. False. The NYSE has only about 2,500 listed companies and about 3,000 listed securities, including preferred shares.

3-5. True.

3-6.   False. Institutional trading makes up a much larger part of NYSE volume than that of either the AMEX or NASDAQ.

3-7.   True.

3-8.   True.

3-9.   False. Since May 1975, each brokerage firm has set its own commission rate schedule, rather than fixing commissions by agreement.

3-10.   False. Spreads tend to represent a smaller percentage of the price for higher priced and more actively traded stocks.

3-11.   False. A limit order transaction must await an acceptable price since this type of order is executable only at the limit price or better.

3-12.   True.

3-13.   False. The total commission on such a stretched-out trade would appreciably exceed that on a single transaction of the same number of shares.

3-14.   False. An all-or-nothing order can be executed only when sufficient volume is simultaneously available since the order must trade as a unit. However, the order does not have to be executed immediately. It can wait until sufficient volume exists for a single transaction. The type of order that must be either executed immediately or canceled is a fill-or-kill order.

3-15.   True.

3-16.   True.

3-17.   False. In 1999, only 10 such floor traders remained.

3-18.   False. Between 75 percent and 85 percent of all transactions utilize market orders that require immediate execution at the current level.

3-19.   True.

3-20.   False. Listed stocks are generally more marketable than those traded over the counter.

3-21.   False. The third market involves over-the-counter trading of listed stocks. Informal arrangements for direct trading between institutions are referred to as the fourth market.

3-22.   True.

3-23.   False. As of 1999, the margin requirement on stocks was set at 50 percent.

3-24.   True.

3-25.   True.

3-26.   True.

3-27.   False. Using short sales to drive a stock's price down is considered an illegal attempt to manipulate the market. If the last price change was a decline, a would-be short seller must wait until the price begins to rise again before implementing a short sale.

3-28.   True.

3-29.   True.

3-30.   False. Investment bankers generally agree to sell a new issue on a firm-commitment basis, which means that they buy the security from the issuer and then sell it to the public.

3-31.   True.

3-32.   False. In 1921, the New York Curb Exchange did indeed go indoors, but it changed its name to the American Stock Exchange in 1953.

3-33.   False. Off-exchange member trading of listed securities is no longer prohibited *per se,* but restrictions still discourage such activity.

3-34.   True.

3-35.   False. Retained earnings supply most equity capital for most firms over most time periods. Stock sales generate only a modest portion of total new equity funds.

3-36.   False. Debt security sales average about 10 times the amount of new capital raised from new stock sales.

3-37.   True.

3-38.   True.

3-39.   False. Proxy fights have become popular because, compared with tender offers, they are generally less costly for the acquirer.

3-40.   True.

Chapter 4

Answers to Review Questions, pp. 139–140

4-1. An investment entails a current outflow of cash and an expected future inflow. The expected inflow must be greater than the initial; this is compensation for the investor forgoing current use of funds. The value of an investment is, therefore, time dependent. This aspect of investment is defined as *time value*. Future cash flows can be valued in current terms (*present value*) if time and risk are taken into account via a discount factor. *Compounding* takes valuation in the other direction; it projects cash flows forward to valuation as of some future date.

4-2. a. The present value of $50 annually, forever discounted at 10 percent is as follows:

PV = $50/.10 = $500

b. The PV of $1 received annually for 20 years and discounted at 20 percent is $4.87. Therefore, the PV for $200 annually for 20 years, discounted at 20 percent is as follows:

PV = 4.87 x $200 = $974.00

c. The PV of $1 received annually for 12 years and discounted at 16 percent is $5.197; $1 to be received in 12 years and discounted at 16 percent is $0.168. Therefore, the PV of a bond with $150 annual coupon for 12 years, maturing at $1,070, discounted at 16 percent is as follows:

PV = (5.197 x 150) + (0.168 x 1,070) = $779.55 + 179.76 = $959.31

d. The present values of $1 received in years 1, 2, 3, and 4 and discounted at 8 percent are $0.926, $0.857, $0.794, and $0.735, respectively. Therefore, the PV for a payment stream of $200 in year 1, $300 in year 2, $400 in year 3, and $500 in year 4 is as follows:

PV = (0.926 x $200) + (0.857 x $300) + (0.794 x $400) + (0.735 x $500) = $1,127.40

4-3. a. The PV of $1 received annually for 20 years and discounted at 7 percent is $10.594. The PV of $1 received in 20 years and discounted at 7 percent is $0.258:

PV = (10.594 x $100) + (0.258 x $1,000) = $1,317.40

b. The PV of $1 received annually for 20 years and discounted at 9 percent is $9.128. The PV of $1 received in 20 years and discounted at 9 percent is $0.178:

PV = (9.128 x $100) + (0.178 x $1,000) = $1,090.80

c. The PV of $1 received annually for 20 years and discounted at 10 percent is $8.514. The PV of $1 received in 20 years and discounted at 10 percent is $0.149:

PV = (8.514 x $100) + (0.149 x $1,000) = $1,000.40

d. The PV of $1 received annually for 20 years and discounted at 11 percent is $7.963. The PV of $1 received in 20 years and discounted at 11 percent is $0.124:

PV = (7.963 x $100) + (0.124 x $1,000) = $920.30

e. The PV of $1 received annually for 20 years and discounted at 13 percent is $7.024. The PV of $1 received in 20 years and discounted at 13 percent is $0.087:

PV = (7.024 x $100) + (0.087 x $1,000) = $789.40

4-4. a. According to the time value theory—all other things being equal—early cash flows are more valuable than later ones. Cash flow A has most of its flows toward the end of the 5-year period; therefore, it has the lowest present value. The opposite is true of B, thereby gaining cash flow B the highest value.

b. The present value of the income streams A, B, and C discounted at 12 percent is as follows:

$$PV_A = \frac{\$100}{(1+.12\ )} + \frac{\$200}{(1+.12)^2} + \frac{\$300}{(1+.12)^3} + \frac{\$400}{(1+.12)^4} + \frac{\$500}{(1+.12)^5} = \$1,000.18$$

$$PV_B = \$1,162.69$$

$$PV_C = \$1,077.76$$

c. With an interest rate of zero, there is no time value, and all cash flows are priced at face value. Each of the cash flows is therefore worth $1,500.

4-5. The price of Bond A is computed as follows:

$$PV_A = \sum_{i=1}^{10} \frac{\$80}{(1+.12)^i} + \frac{\$1,000}{(1+.12)^{10}} = \$773.99$$

Similarly, the prices of Bonds B, C, and D are as follows:

PV_B = $1,226.01
PV_C = $ 932.40
PV_D = $1,368.67

4-6. Two factors must be determined when calculating the present value of a future payment. An examination of the relevant risk leads to a discount interest rate. Once the timing of the payment has been determined, the present value can be calculated. This process is repeated for each cash flow until all are accounted for. Their sum is the total present value of the investment.

4-7. The difference in selling price is due to the interest rates employed in discounting the cash flows. A higher discount rate results in a lower price. In a similar manner, lower discount rates lead to higher valuations. The discount rates that would lead to valuations of $600 and $1,200 would have to be of vastly different magnitudes, corresponding to a radically different interest rate environment or changes in the bond's risk.

4-8. a. Default risk is an assessment of the probability that an entity will not pay all or a portion of an asset's cash flows.

   b. Interest rate fluctuations are changes in the general interest rate environment. The cause may be viewed as economy-wide; thus all rates are affected to some degree.

   c. The pure risk premium is an aggregation of all other risks exclusive of default (for example, foreign exchange, early call, and so on).

4-9. Inflation affects a bond's price via the discount rate. This occurs through direct and indirect avenues. Inflation is a component of the risk-free rate (the direct avenue). Companies are affected to varying degrees by interest rate changes. Large rate changes can cause operational difficulties that endanger cash flows and ultimately the solvency of the company. These difficulties are priced in the marketplace by adjustments to the risk premium.

Answers to Self-Test Questions, pp. 140–141

4-1. False. For the vast majority of bonds, the periodic interest payment is fixed at a set amount called the coupon rate.

4-2. False. Any bond with a coupon rate below the discount rate is worth less than its face value.

4-3. True.

4-4. True.

4-5. False. Market interest rates vary inversely with the relative supply of loanable funds.

4-6. False. The prices of longer-maturity debt issues are much more sensitive to interest rate shifts than are the prices of shorter-term debt issues.

4-7. True.

4-8. True.

4-9. False. Nominal interest rates are stated in current dollar terms, and real interest rates are stated in inflation-adjusted terms.

4-10. True.

4-11. False. The risk premium set by the market is directly observable as the difference between the bond's yield to maturity (YTM) and the risk-free rate.

4-12. True.

4-13. False. The decomposition of the risk premium into two components cannot be observed directly.

Chapter 5

Answers to Review Questions, pp. 182–183

5-1.   The equivalent yield for a one-year T-bill priced at 95 is as follows:

$$\text{Equivalent yield} = \frac{\text{discount}}{\text{price}} = \frac{500}{9500} = 5.26\%$$

5-2.   To compute the equivalent yield for a 180-day T-bond strip priced at 97.31, we must convert the quote to decimal form as follows: 97 31/32 => .979688. The equivalent yield is 4.20 percent, as determined below:

   Price = $10,000 (.979688) = $9,796.88

   Discount = $10,000 – $9,796.88 = $203.12

$$\text{Equivalent yield} = \frac{203.12}{9,796.88}\left(\frac{365}{180}\right) = 4.20\%$$

5-3.

	Advantages	Disadvantages
Treasury bills	Low risk, liquid, tax-advantaged, competitive yields	High denominations, competitive yields
Commercial paper	Higher rates	Higher risk, high denominations
Federal funds	Low risk	Available only to banks
Money market funds	Variable rates, liquid, added functions, variety of types	Rates not as high as direct investment, variable risk

5-4.   New price = $9,796.88 + $10 = $9,806.88

   Discount = $10,000 – $9,806.88 = $193.12

$$\text{Equivalent yield} = \frac{193.12}{9,806.88}\left(\frac{365}{180}\right) = 3.99\%$$

   The yield has declined .21 percent.

5-5.   a.   Government bonds include both those issued by the federal government and its agencies (sponsored and not). Risk varies from the essentially riskless Treasuries to low-risk, nonsponsored agencies. Maturities extend from 10 to 30 years. Liquidity ranges from extremely high (Treasuries) to low (agencies). Trading costs vary inversely with liquidity. Most of these securities are tax advantaged in some way. Agencies typically pay higher rates than Treasuries, but the spread can vary by issuer and time. Most trading of government issues occurs in the OTC market.

   b.   State and local governments raise funds through the issuance of *municipal bonds*. Either a specific revenue source or general taxing authority backs these bonds. The variety of issuers is immense. Because of this, risk and promised return can vary greatly. Risk is occasionally ameliorated by the issuer's purchase of a credit enhancement. A prime feature of these securities is their tax-advantaged status. This feature results in lower yields than would be expected if only risk was considered.

   c.   Corporations are the third major source of debt securities. Since firms lack taxation powers, their bonds are inherently more risky than Treasuries. Beyond this, the range of risk levels is quite varied. *Corporate bonds* are either secured (unlike Treasuries) or debenture. Some issues add convertibility options. Most trading of corporates takes place in the OTC market.

5-6.   a.   Securitization involves pooling individual securities (for example, mortgages) in order to create a new asset. The new security may possess very different attributes from the underlying assets. This may be due to the pooling (for example, diversification) or financial engineering (for example, carving up the cash flows).

    b.   Pooling assets can lessen undesirable attributes, such as poor marketability, and accentuate positive ones, such as steady cash flow. Securitization benefits the original issuer by freeing it from risk and maintenance costs. This releases resources, thereby expanding their capacity. By extension, this gain translates to greater marketplace capacity, increased liquidity, and a greater variety of instruments. The individual investor benefits from greater choice of instruments and decreased risk due to diversification.

5-7.   Municipal bonds are able to offer lower yields because they are exempt from local, state, and federal taxes. Ignoring risk, the attractiveness of a particular municipal's yield depends on an investor's unique tax profile. The investor's marginal tax rates and place of domicile determine the degree of benefits to be derived. This process can be quantified with the proper inputs into the tax-equivalent yield calculation. Yields can then be compared because taxes have been adjusted for.

5-8.   a.

Marginal Tax Rate	Tax-Equivalent Yield
15%	6.75%
28	5.72
31	5.48
36	5.08
39.6	4.80

    b. $.0794 (1 - X) = .0541$
        Solve for the marginal tax rate X:
          $X = .319 = 31.9\%$

5-9.   a.   *Income bonds* are primarily (but not always) associated with firms that are experiencing financial difficulty. Because of payment uncertainty, income bond prices are much lower than those of unstressed companies are. Investors may find the potential for high returns sufficient to offset higher risk.

    b.   *Floating-rate securities* offer variable coupons that compensate for inflation. This feature leads to a stable real return (nominal return minus inflation) and prices. When contemplating these securities, the investor should consider how the rate is calculated, what it is pegged to, and, as always, what the default risk is.

    c.   A *zero-coupon bond* is one that offers no coupon. The only payment is the face value at maturity. Purchase prices are well below face value because of the lack of intermediate payments. A discount bond's single cash payment can provide safety, in addition to locking in interest rates. These features can be a problem if a sale occurs before maturity. An investor should be aware that the discount from face value leads to an imputed annual tax liability. Some zero-coupon bonds are derived from coupon bonds through the process of stripping.

5-10. a.   Investors receive many benefits from the existence of *Eurobonds*. Prime examples are greater instrument choice and portfolio diversification. A prospective Eurobond investor should address idiosyncratic characteristics, such as taxes and foreign exchange implications, prior to purchase.

    b.   *Private placements* are large blocks of stock that are sold to corporations, closed-end funds, and wealthy investors (bypassing the market). Therefore, unless investors are very wealthy, closed-end funds offer the only avenue for participation in private placements.

    c.   *Preferred stock* is a hybrid of bonds and common stock. The purchase of preferred stock provides the investor with a more stable cash flow than that associated with common stock. The preferred owner has a higher priority of claim on the firm's assets than the common stockholder does in the event of corporate bankruptcy. In some cases, missed payments may entitle the owner to voting rights and/or bonus dividends. The individual investor is not entitled to tax breaks that corporations have for owning preferred stock.

5-11. Mutual funds and unit trusts are alternative options. In some cases (for example, closed-end funds and private placements), these are the only choices. Funds and trusts may confer additional benefits, such as lower minimum investment levels, diversification, and tax protection. Investors should pay close attention to fees and operating costs because of their diminishing effect on returns.

Answers to Self-Test Questions, pp. 183–185

5-1.   False. T-bills are issued at a discount and mature at par or face value.

5-2.   True.

5-3.   True.

5-4.   False. Bids may be entered on either a competitive or noncompetitive basis. All noncompetitive bids are accepted by the Treasury, and buyers who enter these bids agree to pay the average price of all competitive bids that are accepted.

5-5.   True.

5-6.   True.

5-7.   False. Commercial paper is secured only by the issuer's good name.

5-8.   False. Commercial paper issuers are generally able to pay slightly less than the prime rate on their borrowings.

5-9.   False. The principal of negotiable CDs issued by bank and thrift institutions is covered by up to $100,000 of government deposit insurance.

5-10. True.

5-11. True.

5-12. True.

5-13. False. Since Eurodollar deposits are liabilities of banks located in Europe or anywhere else outside the United States, disputes must be settled without reliance on the protections of the U.S. legal system.

5-14. True.

5-15. True.

5-16. False. Because money market funds concentrate on very liquid short-term instruments, adverse interest rate moves are unlikely to affect the fund's share prices significantly.

5-17. True.

5-18. False. Short-term unit investment trusts are unmanaged and mature.

5-19. False. Yields on existing units will not increase when market interest rates rise. The trustholder must wait until the units mature and then reinvest at the higher rate available in the market.

5-20. False. Small-denomination CDs issued by banks are generally nontransferable. However, holders can redeem them prior to maturity but will forfeit some interest.

5-21. True.

5-22. False. U.S. Treasury notes are issued with maturities from one to 10 years, while Treasury bonds have maturities greater than 10 years at the time of issuance.

5-23. False. Treasury note and bond price quotations are expressed in 32nds, while T-bill quotes are in hundredths.

5-24. False. All newly issued Treasury notes and bonds are in registered form. Prior to mid-1983, some notes and bonds were issued in bearer form.

5-25. True.

5-26. True.

5-27. False. Treasury securities are not subject to state and local taxes.

5-28. True.

5-29. True.

5-30. True.

5-31. False. Freddie Mac purchases conventional, not government-backed, mortgages for its pools.

5-32. True.

5-33. False. The category of municipal bonds known as revenue bonds is backed by revenues from a designated project, authority, or agency or by the proceeds from a specific tax. General-obligation municipal bonds are backed by the general taxing power of the issuing government.

5-34. False. Corporate bonds known as debentures are backed only by the issuer's full faith and credit.

5-35. True.

5-36. False. Income bonds pay interest only if the issuer earns it. Specific indenture provisions indicate when earned income is sufficient to require an interest payment.

5-37. True.

5-38. False. A bond separated from its coupons is known as a strip bond.

5-39.   False. Zero-coupon bonds have precisely identifiable maturity values.

5-40.   False. Even though zeros pay no coupons, they nevertheless impose an annual tax liability on their owners.

5-41.   True.

5-42.   True.

5-43.   True.

5-44.   False. Even though preferred stockholders are residual claimants behind all creditors, their claims still have a higher priority than the claims of common stockholders.

5-45.   False. Since preferred dividends are not tax deductible to the issuer, all other things being equal, corporations would generally prefer to issue bonds rather than preferred stock.

5-46.   False. Discount yields work with a 360-day year and assume that the interest is deducted at the outset.

5-47.   True.

Chapter 6

Answers to Review Questions, pp. 227–228

6-1.   Fundamental provisions delineate maturity date, principal, and coupon levels. The investor should also pay close attention to the details of sinking fund and call provisions. Both can affect the existence or timing of cash flows; they therefore are factors in overall bond pricing. While always important, subordination is of greater significance with higher-risk issues. Its provisions might determine what, if any, funds the investor receives from a faltering firm.

6-2.   A firm is considered to be in technical default if it has failed to fulfill any of its indenture provisions (in any of its issues). Most defaults are signals of minor financial difficulties and do not result in bankruptcy. However, the investor should actively monitor subsequent events because they may result in the indenture agreement's being altered and cash flows threatened. Default in some cases is just the first event in a worsening situation that subsequently leads to bankruptcy. Markets are therefore very sensitive to defaults. Their reactions can be severe and can exacerbate the company's problems. Firms should therefore deliberate very seriously before defaulting.

6-3.   Once liquidation of a company's assets begins, claims are paid according to the *absolute priority of claims principle*. This method assigns claims to classes, each of which is in a strict hierarchy. The firm's remaining assets are then paid out, beginning with the highest class. The process continues until funds are exhausted. The last class to be paid might receive only partial payment. If this is the case, all claimants within the class are treated equally, therefore receiving proportional payments. In most bankruptcies, some claimants and or classes receive no payment.

6-4.   a.   Ratings agencies satisfy a clear need, given the vast quantity of financial information. Their function is to sift and analyze the information to derive an accurate assessment of default risk.

        b.   Standard & Poor's and Moody's are the best known of bond rating agencies.

        c.   First, rating methodology is not transparent; the investor must trust the agency for accuracy and the appropriateness of models. Second, ratings may lag in volatile times, leaving the investor with inadequate time to react.

6-5.   a.   Financial theory states that investors should be compensated for taking on additional risk. When the theory is applied to bonds, we would expect that riskier bonds offer higher yields. This is, in fact, what we see in the marketplace.

        b.   Studies have shown that spreads between risk levels are greater than is justified. This could be due to investment constraints, such as investment guidelines. Whatever the rationale, investors may be able to capitalize by constructing diversified portfolios, thereby taking advantage of the market's inefficiencies.

6-6.   The *market segmentation theory* posits that investors and borrowers have preferred time horizons; therefore, they each occupy a distinct segment along the yield curve. This theory, when it is applied to the normal, upward-sloping yield curve, means that there are fewer people interested in investing in longer time periods; higher yields must therefore be offered to entice investors to lend (as opposed to holding cash).

      The *preferred habitat theory* modifies market segmentation with the provision that investors can be induced to leave their preferred segment by the offer of higher yields. In this case, the upward-sloping curve is explained by rate premiums being offered to entice investors to move from short to long.

Under the *liquidity preference theory*—all other things being equal—investors prefer their money now rather than later. To combat this tendency, borrowers must offer interest rates that increase with the length of the loan. This theory best explains a rising yield curve.

The *unbiased expectations theory* explains that the yield curve is constructed of the market's expectations of short-term rates that will occur in the future. Each rate is, in essence, a geometric average of short-term rates. With a rising yield curve, the market must be expecting that future short-term rates will be higher than today's.

6-7.   As expected, both durations declined, but the $100 coupon bond declined .53 years as opposed to .46 for the $60 coupon bond.

Bond A			
Year	Cash Flow	Present Value at 20%	Year x Present Value (Column 1 x Column 3)
1	$ 60	$ 50.00	$ 50.00
2	60	41.67	83.34
3	60	34.72	104.16
4	60	28.94	115.76
5	60	24.11	120.55
6	60	20.09	120.54
7	1,060	295.83	2,070.81
Total	$1,420	$495.36	$2,665.16

Duration = $2,665.16/$495.36 = 5.38

Bond B			
Year	Cash Flow	Present Value at 20%	Year x Present Value (Column 1 x Column 3)
1	$ 100	$83.33	$ 83.33
2	100	69.44	138.88
3	100	57.87	173.61
4	100	48.23	192.92
5	100	40.19	200.95
6	100	33.49	200.94
7	1,100	306.99	2,148.93
Total	$1,700	$639.54	$3,139.56

Duration = $3,139.56/$639.54 = 4.91

6-8.   Duration Bond A = 4.27
       Duration Bond B = 7.10
       Duration Bond C = 8.95

6-9.   a.   Investors in higher tax brackets often prefer their investment gains in the form of capital gains—as opposed to dividends—because the rate is lower than that associated with ordinary income. Low-coupon, deep-discount bonds are ideal for this situation. Because of this, these investors bid up prices, causing corresponding yields to decline. This tax-induced deviation from expected behavior is called the *coupon effect*.

b. *Immunization* attempts to protect portfolio value against interest rate changes. In practice, this might entail matching cash inflows with outflows or simply matching a bond's maturity with the investor's horizon. More sophisticated methods involve constructing a portfolio with the desired duration. This may include the use of interest rate futures.

6-10. Portfolio duration is the weighted average of the individual durations ($D_A = 4.27$; $D_B = 7.10$; $D_C = 8.95$). The individual weights must be solved for algebraically.

$$W_C = .6 \qquad W_B = 1 - W_C - W_A = .4 - W_A$$
$$8 = .6D_C + (.4 - W_A)D_B + W_AD_A$$
$$W_A = \frac{8 - .6D_C - .4D_B}{D_A - D_B} = .07 \quad W_B = .33$$

The portfolio return is the weighted average of the individual yields:

$$W_C = .7 \qquad \text{Return} = W_C(9.5) + W_B(8.5) + W_A(7.5) = 9.03\%$$
$$8 = .7D_C + (.3 - W_A)D_B + W_AD_A$$
$$W_A = .14 \qquad\qquad W_B = .16$$
$$\text{Return} = .7(9.5) + .16(8.5)\ .14(7.5) = 9.06\%$$

The portfolio consisting of 70 percent Bond C has the higher return.

6-11. $\quad W_A = .5 \qquad\qquad 6 = .5D_A + (.5 - W_C)D_B + W_CD_C$
$$W_C = .17 \qquad\qquad W_B = .33$$
$$\text{Return} = .5(7.5) + .33(8.5) + .17(9.5) = 8.17\%$$
$\quad\quad W_A = .6 \qquad\qquad 6 = .6D_A + (.4 - W_C)D_B + W_CD_C$
$$W_C = .32 \qquad\qquad W_B = .08$$
$$\text{Return} = .6(7.5) + .08(8.5) + .32(9.5) = 8.22\%$$

The portfolio made up of 60 percent of Bond A has the higher yield.

Constructing a portfolio with a shorter duration requires that we use relatively more of Bonds A and B. Correspondingly, the portfolio return drops.

6-12. a. *Marketable* issues have lower spreads, thereby lowering trading costs and raising prices.

b. *Seasoned* issues are priced higher than new issues.

c. *Call protection* protects future cash flows, which generally enhances a security's value.

d. *Sinking funds* reduce the probability of default, enhancing value.

e. An investor should first evaluate whether he or she wants a bond that has one or more of these characteristics. The investor should then determine whether he or she finds the factor's pricing is fair in relation to what the investor is willing to pay.

6-13. a. Investors should evaluate their needs in relation to such factors as risk, return, maturity/duration, taxes, diversification, and liquidity. Decisions on these factors will determine the makeup and management of their portfolios.

b. Selling and buying components alters a bond portfolio; this process is termed *bond swapping*. It is through this method that a portfolio can be maintained or changed.

c. Transaction costs include commissions, bid-ask spreads, and accrued interest. While generally low, these vary with the type of bond and the timing of the transaction.

Answers to Self-Test Questions, pp. 228–230

6-1. True.

6-2. False. The coupon rate is the contractually stated rate on a bond.

6-3. False. The yield to maturity is based on the market price of the bond as well as the coupon rate. Therefore, it is possible for the yield to maturity to be higher or lower than the coupon rate.

6-4. True.

6-5. False. Aside from general credit conditions, the most significant factor that influences the coupon rate of a bond is the risk of default.

6-6. True.

6-7. True.

6-8. False. Debentures do not have specific property serving as collateral but are backed by the full faith and credit of the issuer.

6-9. True.

6-10. False. A call provision gives the issuer the option of redeeming the bonds prior to maturity.

6-11. True.

6-12. False. In the case of bankruptcy, unsecured creditors have priority over preferred stockholders.

6-13. False. A bond with a rating of A has less risk of default than one with a rating of B.

6-14. True.

6-15. True.

6-16. False. Under the liquidity preference hypothesis, investors prefer to invest in short-term debt securities, while borrowers tend to prefer to borrow long term.

6-17. True.

6-18. False. Duration is a better measure of a bond's sensitivity to interest rate changes.

6-19. True.

6-20. True.

6-21. True.

6-22. True.

6-23. True.

6-24. False. Interest payments on municipal bonds are not taxable, but capital gains are.

6-25. True.

6-26. False. Compared to commissions on common stock transactions, those on bond trades are relatively low as a percentage of the principal amount involved.

6-27. True.

6-28. True.

Chapter 7

Answers to Review Questions, pp. 246–248

7-1. a. Over the 5-year period, dividends will be paid out at the rate of $3.25, $3.50, $3.75, $4.00, and $4.25. At the end of 5 years, the stock will sell for 12 x $4.25 = $51. Thus, we need to compute the present value of the income stream: $3.25, $3.50, $3.75, $4.00, and $4.25 + $51. At a discount rate of 8 percent, the present value factors are 0.926, 0.857, 0.794, 0.735, and 0.681:

PV = (0.926 x $3.25) + (0.857 x $3.50) + (0.794 x $3.75) + (0.735 x $4.00) + (0.681 x $55.25) = $49.55

b. At a discount rate of 10 percent, the present value factors are: 0.909, 0.826, 0.751, 0.683, and 0.621:

PV = (0.909 x $3.25) + (0.826 x $3.50) + (0.751 x $3.75) + (0.683 x $4.00) + (0.621 x $55.25) = $45.70

c. At a discount rate of 12 percent, the present value factors are: 0.893, 0.797, 0.712, 0.636, and 0.567:

PV = (0.893 x $3.25) + (0.797 x $3.50) + (0.712 x $3.75) + (0.636 x $4.00) + (0.567 x $55.25) = $42.25

d. At a discount rate of 15 percent, the present value factors are: 0.870, 0.756, 0.658, 0.572, and 0.497:

PV = (0.870 x $3.25) + (0.756 x $3.50) + (0.658 x $3.75) + (0.572 x $4.00) + (0.497 x $55.25) = $37.69

e. At a discount rate of 18 percent, the present value factors are: 0.847, 0.718, 0.609, 0.516, and 0.437:

PV = (0.847 x $3.25) + (0.718 x $3.50) + (0.609 x $3.75) + (0.516 x $4.00) + (0.437 x $55.25) = $33.76

f. With a stable dividend of $3.00 and a discount rate of 8 percent:

PV = (0.926 x $3.00) + (0.857 x $3.00) + (0.794 x $3.00) + (0.735 x $3.00) + (0.681 x $39.00) = $36.50

7-2. Over the 5-year period, dividends will be paid out at the rate of $1.10, $1.20, $1.30, $1.40, and $1.50. At the end of 5 years, the stock will sell for 6.5 x $1.50 = $9.75. Thus, we need to compute the present value of the income stream: $1.10, $1.20, $1.30, $1.40, and $1.50 + $9.75. At a discount rate of 16 percent, the present value factors are 0.862, 0.743, 0.641, 0.552, and 0.476:

PV = (0.862 x $1.10) + (0.743 x $1.20) + (0.641 x $1.30) + (0.552 x $1.40) + (0.476 x $11.25) = $8.80

7-3. a. With a discount rate of 10 percent:

PV = (0.909 x $1.10) + (0.826 x $1.20) + (0.751 x $1.30) + (0.683 x $1.40) + (0.621 x $11.25) = $10.91

    b. With a discount rate of 20 percent:

$$PV = (0.833 \times \$1.10) + (0.694 \times \$1.20) + (0.579 \times \$1.30) + (0.482 \times \$1.40) + (0.402 \times \$11.25) = \$7.70$$

7-4. a. This problem uses the constant growth case of the dividend discount model:

$$S = d / (k - g) = \$1 / (0.12 - 0.10) = \$50$$

    b. $S = \$2 / (0.12 - 0.11) = \$200$

    c. $S = \$1.50 / (0.12 - 0.08) = \$37.50$

7-5. a. Payout percent = d / e => e = d / (payout percent). With a dividend of $1 and a payoff percent of 0.55 we have

$$e = \$1 / 0.55 = \$1.82 \qquad PE = \$50 / \$1.82 = 27.47$$

    b. $d = \$2 \qquad e = \$2 / 0.55 = \$3.64 \qquad PE = \$200 / \$3.64 = 54.95$

    c. $d = \$1.50 \qquad e = \$1.50 / 0.55 = \$2.73 \qquad PE = \$37.50 / \$2.73 = 13.74$

7-6. a. As the survey of research demonstrated, analysis does not generally result in accurate pricing. Relative pricing is an alternative that *may* lead to some success. This is accomplished by deriving prices for a group of stocks. A comparison is then made with market pricing of these same assets. Disagreements in ordering between the two assessments may signal a potentially profitable mispricing by the market.

    b. A thorough analytical evaluation depends on a realistic model and accurate forecasts and data. The reliability of price forecasts is jeopardized by factors such as faulty earnings predictions, inappropriate discount rates, and insensitivity to risk changes.

7-7. To compute the market-implied long-term growth rate,

    a. rearrange the PE formula as follows: PE = p / (k – g) => g = k – p / PE = 0.12 – 0.40 / 8 = 0.07

    b. $g = 0.12 – 0.50 / 10 = 0.07$

    c. $g = 0.12 – 0.60 / 15 = 0.08$

7-8. a. $PE = p / (k – g) = 0.25 / (0.12 – 0.07) = 5$

$$g = k – p / PE = 0.12 – 0.25 / 8 = 0.089$$

Therefore, g must rise 1.9 percent to justify a PE of 8.

       A market adjustment of price due to a higher retention of earnings is most likely. Converting retained earnings to a much higher growth rate is difficult and hard to predict with any accuracy; therefore, it is much less likely.

    b. $PE = 0.75 / (0.12 – 0.07) = 15$

$$g = 0.12 – 0.75 / 8 = 0.026$$

Therefore, g must decline 4.4 percent to justify a PE of 8.

       Although it is easy to lower growth rates, it is still much easier for the price to be adjusted in the market; therefore, it is more realistic for the PE ratio to change.

7-9. Firms are reluctant to adjust dividend rates because of the anticipated negative reaction in the marketplace. The other component of earnings is funds that are retained for reinvestment in the firm. Optimal use of retained earnings can enhance the growth of the firm and thereby increase future profitability. Since focusing on dividends can be misleading and ignoring retained earnings results in an incomplete picture, analysis of earnings is by consensus considered to be the best valuation proxy.

7-10. Early studies indicated that *analysts' predictions* offered little advantage over simple computational models. Later studies moved to a more positive assessment. Analysts have proven much more accurate forecasting sectors than individual firm performance. On the other hand, predictions have tended to be excessive in cases of high or low performers. *Management predictions* have been as good as or slightly better than those of analysts, but this conclusion is based on a very small sample. Predictions based on *quarterly earnings* have proven of little merit. Sophisticated extrapolations based on *past earnings* have exhibited substantive predictive accuracy but are in line with other methods in order of magnitude.

       All of the discussed methods have shown some predictive accuracy in short-term forecasting. *Integration* of the various methods and increasing sophistication may lead to better forecasting. Keep in mind, however, that theoretical pricing formulas have an infinite time horizon; therefore, forecasting, as it is practiced, is of little use in accurate valuation. Its value may lie in comparing relative, as opposed to absolute, pricing.

Answers to Self-Test Questions, pp. 248–249

7-1. False. The capital gain a shareholder can reasonably expect when selling a stock is based on the discounted value of the stock's expected future cash flows.
7-2. True.
7-3. True.
7-4. False. Dividend payments on stock tend to increase over time.
7-5. True.
7-6. True.
7-7. False. When using the constant growth model, the price of a stock should equal *the next period's dividend* divided by (k – g).
7-8. True.
7-9. True.
7-10. True.
7-11. False. A security identified as undervalued may not necessarily earn a superior return for its owners.
7-12. True.
7-13. True.
7-14. True.
7-15. False. Past earnings growth has not been found to be an accurate predictor of future earnings growth.

Chapter 8

Answers to Review Questions, pp. 291–293

8-1. The difference between the popular and the financial definition of risk has more to do with rigor than any substantive differences. The financial definition attempts to build a concise definition of risk. All possible outcomes are explored in order to construct a quantitative description. By moving risk into the statistical realm, risk can be modeled and predictions made.

8-2. a. Mean = (–5% + 0% + 5% + 10%)/4 = 2.5%
Variance = [(–5% – 2.5%)^2 + (0% – 2.5%)^2 + (5% – 2.5%)^2 + (10% – 2.5%)^2]/4 = .3125%

Standard Deviation = $\sqrt{\text{Variance}}$ = 5.59%

  b. Mean = [.1(0%) + .15(5%) + .25(10%) + .25(15%) + .15(20%) + .1(25%)] = 12.50%
Variance = [.1(0% – 12.5%)^2 + .15(5% – 12.5%)^2 + ...+ .1(25% – 12.5%)^2] = .5125%
Standard Deviation = 7.16%

  c. Mean = 10% / 1 = 10%
Variance = (10% – 10%)^2/1 = 0 and Standard Deviation = 0

8-3. a. The formula for two-asset risk is as follows:

$$\sigma_p^2 = X^2\sigma_x^2 + 2XYC_{xy} + Y^2\sigma_y^2$$

This formula demonstrates that the risk of a two-asset portfolio consists of the assets' individual risk and the risk associated with their related price movements.

  b. Covariance is a quantification of how the two assets' prices move in relation to each other. Covariance can range from negative to positive.

  c. Weights are the proportion that each asset represents of the portfolio. Asset weights can be adjusted to produce portfolios with varying risks and returns.

  d. If the covariance is sufficiently negative, it is possible to adjust the weights to produce a risk-free portfolio. The greatest portfolio risk occurs when the two assets move in perfect lockstep (high positive covariance).

  e. As the number of assets increases, the formula gains terms so that all possible pairs of covariance are incorporated.

8-4. $\overline{X} = (.03 + .05 - .01 + .10 + 0 + .01)/6 = .03$ and, similarly, $\overline{Y} = .017$

$$C_{xy} = \sum_{i=1}^{6} \frac{(X_i - \overline{X})(Y_i - \overline{Y})}{6} = .0014$$

8-5.   a $\sigma_p^2 = X^2 \sigma_x^2 + 2XYC_{xy} + Y^2 \sigma_y^2 = (.5)^2(.05) + (.5)^2(.05) = .025$

       b. $\sigma_p^2 = .36$

       c. $\sigma_p^2 = .04$

8-6.   As the number of assets in a portfolio increases, the covariance pairs become the dominant source of risk. Analysis of an asset's covariability with a market portfolio leads to the creation of the *beta* statistic. Beta is the slope component of the *market model* that can be used to make predictions of future returns. Beta calculation entails significantly less computation than that of a variance-covariance matrix. The market model, using specific assumptions, can be modified to produce the *capital asset pricing model*.

       Creation of beta and the two associated models was a significant step forward in financial theory, a byproduct of which was a reduction in necessary computing power.

8-7.

Expected Returns for Three Stocks						
		Market Returns				
α	β	0.05	0.1	0.15	−0.05	−0.1
0.01	0.7	0.045	0.08	0.115	−0.025	−0.06
0.05	1.1	0.105	0.16	0.215	−0.005	−0.06
−0.02	1.5	0.055	0.13	0.205	−0.095	−0.17

8-8.   In the market model, alpha is the return when the market's return is zero; beta is the slope of the regression line. Under CAPM, alpha is the return on a risk-free asset, and beta is the slope of the line linking the risk-free asset and the market portfolio. The lines graphically represent the expected asset return for a given market return and excess market return for the market model and CAPM, respectively. Covariability becomes increasingly important as the number of assets increases. Beta is a proxy for covariance. It is therefore very useful in portfolio risk determination (due to linearity, portfolio risk is the weighted average of the individual betas). Beta in conjunction with alpha is also used to predict future returns.

8-9.   The market model is the outcome of a statistical regression of an asset's return with the return of a market portfolio. The linear equation that results has a y-intercept alpha and slope beta. The alpha is the asset's return when the market return is zero. The CAPM, by contrast, is based on strict theoretical assumptions. It is functionally different in that alpha is the return on a risk-free asset and beta is multiplied by the market portfolio's excess return over the risk-free asset (as opposed to the market's return in the market model).

8-10. a.   Market risk encompasses macroeconomic factors that affect all firms. These include interest rate volatility, inflation, and taxation. Nonmarket risks are idiosyncratic to a firm or industry. Examples are management performance, labor shortages, legal issues, and funding problems.

       b.   Nonmarket risk decreases as diversification increases. This is because the idiosyncratic risks tend to offset each other. As diversification increases, nonmarket risk diminishes to the point where, for all intents and purposes, only market risk remains (which can't be eliminated). In this ideal scenario, two-thirds of the total risk will have been eliminated.

8-11. a.   By varying the weights assigned to assets, we can draw a curve in risk-return space. At each point on the curve, no better return can be achieved for a given risk level, and no lower risk is possible for a specific return. Thus, from an investing standpoint, the curve is efficient. When a risk-free asset is introduced, the efficient frontier becomes a straight line connecting the risk-free asset and the market portfolio (which consists of all assets in their exact value-weighted proportions). To hold a portfolio along this line is to hold both the risk-free asset and the market portfolio in varying proportions (points to the right of the market portfolio involve borrowing to purchase more than 100 percent of the market portfolio).

    b. If only lending is possible, the efficient frontier consists of the line connecting the risk-free asset and the market portfolio. To the right, the frontier is once again the risky asset curve.

    c. If borrowing occurs at a rate higher than the risk-free rate, the line to the right of the market portfolio will be lower and have less slope than in the previous case. This is because borrowing costs diminish returns.

8-12. Since we know that the market portfolio always has a beta of 1.0, we can use the formula $R_i = R_f + \beta_i (R_m - R_f)$ to obtain the return for each of the portfolios.

Expected Returns for Efficient Portfolios						
		β				
Risk-free	Market	0.7	1	1.3	1.6	
0.07	0.14	0.119	0.14	0.161	0.182	
0.09	0.16	0.139	0.16	0.181	0.202	
0.05	0.1	0.085	0.1	0.115	0.13	

Answers to Self-Test Questions, p. 293

8-1. False. It is the expected return from an investment that is subject to uncertainties.

8-2. False. Return by itself is insufficient to properly assess and compare the performance of different investments. Risk must also be considered.

8-3. False. In the field of investments, risk is the chance that the actual outcome will differ from the expected outcome. It can be thought of as uncertainty, as the range of possible outcomes, or as the dispersion of possible outcome from the expected outcome. Mathematical measures of risk include the standard deviation and the range (highest minus lowest possible outcome).

8-4. True.

8-5. False. A portfolio of securities is less risky than its component securities. This is why diversification is a very important investment strategy.

8-6. False. A portfolio's return is the *weighted average* of the returns of its assets. The average assumes that each asset has an equal weight in the portfolio, which could be the situation when the portfolio was first established. But as relative prices change, the relative weights or influence of each asset on the portfolio return also change. Therefore, using an unweighted average would result in an inaccurate measure of portfolio return.

8-7. False. A perfectly negative correlation (−1) of the returns between two assets would reduce the variability or risk of the portfolio. This would reduce the standard deviation of the returns to the portfolio. In fact, it would be possible to construct a risk-free portfolio by combining two assets whose returns have a correlation of −1. However, the weighted return of the portfolio would not change.

8-8. True.

8-9. True.

8-10. True.

8-11. True.

8-12. False. If a portfolio is on the capital market line, it is a well-diversified portfolio.

8-13. False. The required return for this investment is 10.6 percent. The market risk premium (10 percent − 4 percent = 6 percent) is multiplied by the stock's beta (1.1) and is then added to the risk-free rate (4 percent) for an expected rate of return of 10.6 percent (6.6 percent + 4 percent).

Chapter 9

Answers to Review Questions, pp. 322–323

9-1. *Fundamental analysis* involves researching factors (for example, earnings, dividends, sales, costs, and capital requirements) that affect a firm's future income stream. The resulting valuation is then compared with the current market price to assess likely future price movement. *Technical analysis* takes place at a more superficial level and seeks less to understand than predict; investor sentiment is more important than theoretical justification. Technical analysis can take into account factors such as price, volume, and market indicators.

9-2. The weak form of EMH implies that historical price behavior can't be used to predict future prices. If true, this view negates the efficacy of technical analysis. Research has indicated that this form of EMH holds. Under the semistrong form, all publicly available information is already incorporated into an asset's price; therefore, both technical and fundamental analysis are useless for price anticipation. Evidence supporting this version is mixed. The implication is that insiders and astute fundamental analysts may in some cases be able to anticipate price changes. Under the strong form of EMH, all information is incorporated into asset prices; therefore it is not possible to predict price movement. Financial research has generally not found substantial evidence supporting this version of EMH.

9-3. As the table below demonstrates, the 5 percent threshold is not met for any of the three criteria.

Previous Price	New Price	% Change	Previous High	Low	% Change from Previous High	Low
51	51.25	0.49%	51	51	0.49%	0.49%
51.25	52	1.46	51.25	51	1.46	1.96
52	51.5	−0.96	52	51	−0.96	0.98
51.5	50.875	−1.21	52	51	−2.16	−0.25
50.875	49	−3.69	52	50.875	−5.77	−3.69
49	48.25	−1.53	52	49	−7.21	−1.53
48.25	49	1.55	52	48.25	−5.77	1.55
49	50.5	3.06	52	48.25	−2.88	4.66
50.5	52	2.97	52	48.25	0.00	7.77
52	52.75	1.44	52	48.25	1.44	9.33
52.75	53	0.47	52.75	48.25	0.47	9.84
53	53.875	1.65	53	48.25	1.65	11.66
53.875	55	2.09	53.875	48.25	2.09	13.99
55	57	3.64	55	48.25	3.64	18.13
57	56.5	−0.88	57	48.25	−0.88	17.10
56.5	57.875	2.43	57	48.25	1.54	19.95
57.875	58.5	1.08	57.875	48.25	1.08	21.24
58.5	60	2.56	58.5	48.25	2.56	24.35
60	62	3.33	60	48.25	3.33	28.50
62	61.5	−0.81	62	48.25	−0.81	27.46
61.5	59	−4.07	62	48.25	−4.84	22.28
59	57	−3.39	62	48.25	−8.06	18.13
57	58.5	2.63	62	48.25	−5.65	21.24
58.5	59	0.85	62	48.25	−4.84	22.28

9-4. Referring to the table in question 9-3, the following actions are taken because of the noted price changes:

3% Filter Rule Based on Price Change From		
Previous Price	Previous High	Previous Low
Sell: 50.875 – 49	Buy: 55 – 57	Sell: 50.875 – 49
Buy: 49 – 50.5	Buy: 60 – 62	
Buy: 55 – 57		
Buy: 60 – 62		
Sell: 61.5 – 59		
Sell: 59 – 57		

9-5. It is possible that the sheer magnitude of data may obscure relevant information. This may delay or prevent prudent investor action. To achieve efficient markets requires ease of access. In practice, investors may not have the resources or understanding (in the case of exotic assets or methods) to act upon information. Investors may lack the desire to undertake investment research; in other words, other activities may take precedence. It is possible that the economy is, for the most part, efficient, but efficiency does not extend to the fringes. For example, the information of small firms may be difficult to obtain, thereby making valuation more fraught with error.

9-6. a. According to modern portfolio theory, nonmarket risk can be diversified away and therefore should be irrelevant to pricing. Market studies have not found this to be the case.

    b. Possible causes are as follows: Market participants are unable, for various reasons, to effectively diversify; investors, on occasion, act irrationally; bad investment luck impairs resources and thus precludes diversification; if the borrowing rate is higher than lending, this serves as a barrier to diversification; statistical errors result in the perception of nonmarket risk where, in fact, none exists; and statistical misspecification leads to incorrect models, therefore making interpretation invalid.

9-7. The theoretical market portfolio is made up of assets of all possible types. This includes international assets, real estate, insurance, and personal assets. Diversification on this scale is not possible for most investors. Intermediaries such as mutual funds can serve as vehicles toward this end. But portfolio management entails administrative costs that lower return. In light of these and other factors, diversification is a goal that is difficult to fully implement.

9-8. a. Portfolio theory is predicated on asset returns being normally distributed. Some researchers have argued that if this is not the case, it is of strong enough consequence to invalidate the models.

    b. Research into historical returns has found that daily returns are leptokurtic and skewed, whereas lengthening the observation period results in more normally distributed returns.

    c. Investigations into investor preferences indicate that the desired distribution is skewed (offering the possibility of high returns).

9-9. a. To do the calculations, it must be assumed that the possible returns are discrete—for example, that the first possible return is 5 percent, instead of less than 5 percent.

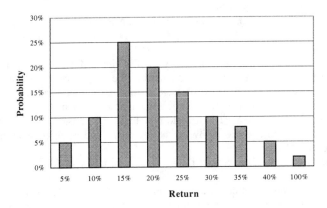

    b. The mean is 22.55 percent; the variance is 2.01 percent; the standard deviation is 14.17 percent.

    c. The distribution is skewed to the right (in other words, it has a fat tail on the right).

9-10. a. Betas are generally calculated by regressing an asset's historical returns on those of a market portfolio.

    b. As with many financial statistics, betas tend to be more reliable when applied to a wider perspective—that is, to portfolios as opposed to individual assets. The inaccuracy of individual betas may be due to errors in estimation or an inherent instability of the statistic.

    c. Many academics have suggested beta adjustments to correct for the tendency to regress toward the average beta of one. Others have added more input information into the beta calculation. Some researchers hope to improve prediction by examining and revising the assumptions underlying modern portfolio theory. Despite all of this tinkering, prediction with betas leaves much to be desired.

9-11. Note that the Blume betas are all closer to one. This reflects the desired mean reversion.

Unadjusted Beta	Blume Beta
1.34	1.26
.57	.74
.78	.88
1.2	1.17
1.47	1.35
1.73	1.53
.45	.66
1.44	1.33
.89	.96
.95	1
1.8	1.57
1.11	1.1
.69	.82
.87	.94
1.15	1.13

9-12. a. An implication of modern portfolio theory is that an ideal portfolio is internationally diversified. In comparison to a domestically based one, an international portfolio may in fact be more efficient, providing higher returns with less risk.

b. The investor has many available avenues for international investing, including international mutual funds, U.S.-based multinational corporations, and American Depository Receipts. There are, however, many problems associated with international investing: Information is more difficult to obtain; regulation varies greatly; there can be legal impediments, political risk, higher transaction costs, and foreign exchange risk. Despite increasing international integration and the previously mentioned problems, there are still strong benefits to be derived from diversifying internationally.

9-13. a. Problems have arisen with both the theory and application of MPT. These include the following: Markets have not proven to be as efficient as the theory requires, nonmarket risk occurs in valuation, and forecasts have proven unreliable.

b. The main rival to MPT is the arbitrage pricing theory. APT begins with similar assumptions, but it deviates by extending what drives returns to many risks, as opposed to the single-market risk of MPT. APT's flexibility and complexity are appealing, but a major obstacle is that the number and identity of variables are not specified. This has inspired a great deal of theoretical and empirical research; no consensus has materialized. Finally, statistical comparisons with MPT have yielded ambiguous results.

9-14. a. The maximum expected return is achieved by purchasing only the diversified stock portfolio. The expected return of this portfolio is 15 percent.

b. Purchasing only the short-term debt securities results in the minimum risk portfolio with an expected return of 8 percent.

c. A portfolio of bonds and short term debt can't possibly have a beta over .3, so we can restrict our search to stock/bond and stock/short-term debt combinations. To compare the expected returns, the relative weights must be calculated. The weights are then used to estimate returns.

Stock and Bond Portfolio
$.5 = X (1) + (1 - X) (.3) = X + .3 - .3X = .7X + .3$
$.7X = .2$
$X = .2/.7 = .29$

Return $= .29 (15) + .71 (11) = 12.16\%$

Stock and Short-Term Debt Portfolio

$.5 = X (1) + (1 - X) (.1) = X + .1 - .1X = .9X + .1$

$.9X = .4$

$X = .4/.9 = .44$

Return $= .44 (15) + .56 (8) = 11.08\%$

Therefore, the maximum return of a .5 beta portfolio consists of 29 percent of the stock portfolio and 71 percent of the long-term bond portfolio. The expected return is 12.16 percent.

Answers to Self-Test Questions, pp. 323–324

9-1. True.

9-2. True.

9-3. False. The efficient market, as the term is used in investments, is one in which the prices of all securities fully reflect all known information quickly and, on average, accurately.

9-4. True.

9-5. True.

9-6. False. The semistrong form of the EMH holds that all publicly available information (including past market data) is reflected in stock prices. However, it does not hold that nonpublic information is also contained in stock prices.

9-7. True.

9-8. False. The semistrong form of the EMH states that neither technical nor fundamental analyses will lead to excess profits.

9-9. False. The RVAR assesses a portfolio performance by measuring the excess return per unit of total risk. This is accomplished by dividing the excess return (portfolio return less the risk-free rate) by the portfolio's total risk (its standard deviation). Therefore, this measure does not assess total return.

9-10. False. This measure assesses the excess return of the portfolio relative to its beta.

9-11. False. Fund rankings may differ depending on which measure is chosen.

9-12. True.

9-13. False. Several studies of corporate insiders found that they earned abnormal returns on their stock transactions.

9-14. True.

9-15. False. Money managers need not only be concerned with diversification and risk of the securities, but must also consider transaction costs and taxes in the design and management of the portfolios.

9-16. True.

9-17. True.

Chapter 10

Answers to Review Questions, pp. 368–370

10-1. Economic analysis entails the evaluation of the current economic environment and its effect upon market, industry, and company fundamentals. The level of economic activity has a major impact on company sales and prices. A detailed analysis of the historical relationships between the economy, industry, and company should determine the sensitivity of profits to economic activity, inflation, interest rates, and so on. For example, this information along with a forecast of GDP (a proxy for overall economic activity) could lead to a prediction of market sales. This figure is modified by estimates of depreciation and taxes to yield a net profit and earnings-per-share forecast. A new PE forecast results from estimating each of the variables in the PE formula. A prediction of market price is the outcome of the product of the earnings-per-share and PE forecasts. This example illustrates the general process of forecasting the future price level. Whether a simpler or more complicated model is used, most proceed from a macroeconomic proxy to profit projection to price level prediction. The primary difficulty is deriving accurate estimates of the relationships between intermediate variables.

10-2.   a.   PE = p/(k − g) = .5/(.13 − .09) = 12.5
        b.   PE = .45/(.13 − .09) = 11.25
        c.   PE = .5/(.13 − .11) = 25
             An increase of 2 percent in the growth rate is unlikely except in cases of unstable or young companies.
        d.   PE = .5/(.1 − .09) = 50
             A decrease of 3 percentage points in the required rate of return, in a short period of time, is an extremely unlikely occurrence.

10-3.   Economic analysis when applied to an industry uses a similar methodology to that used to predict market performance (see answer to question 10-1). Unless the investor has unlimited time and resources, an index is adequate as representative of the industry. The process begins with a macroeconomic forecast, such as GDP or personal disposable income. This leads to a prediction of sales and ultimately earnings. The earnings forecast combined with PE yields a price estimate for the index.

10-4.   a.   When the index's sales growth is expected to be 1.7 times that of GDP's 6 percent, XYZ High Tech Index per-share sales would be as follows:
             Index sales growth = (.06) 1.7 = 10.2% and Sales forecast = $500 (1.102) = $551
        b.   If the GDP actually falls 3 percent, per-share sales would be as follows:
             Index sales growth = (−.03)1.7 = −5.1% and Sales forecast = $500 (1 − .051) = $474.50

10-5.   A similar methodology as that employed for market and industry forecasts (see answers to questions 10-1 and 10-3) can be used to forecast company performance. A top-down process is appropriate; market and industry forecasts result in predictions of company sales, earnings, and finally stock price. At the company level, there are an infinite number of variables that can be used as inputs to the pricing algorithm. The art is in determining relevant influences and their effects. A caveat is that the calculated price should be judged relative to that of other companies.

10-6.   A company's competitive position directly bears upon its future growth and profits. The latter is generally of prime concern to investors. Larger firms can, in many cases, achieve economies of scale allowing them to produce goods more cheaply than their rivals. These economies can extend to other areas, such as distribution and marketing. Competitive position may, in some instances, dictate directions for corporate expansion (vertical, horizontal, or for diversification purposes). But size can bring inefficiencies and management ineffectiveness. Company size and actions may spark government scrutiny. Antitrust activity often varies with the political climate. This variation does not necessarily correlate with actual market conditions.

10-7.   To estimate the PE ratio for the High Tech Index, we can use the relationship PE = p/(k − g). The growth rate of sales is, in fact, equivalent to the dividend growth rate. We therefore have all the information we need:
             g = 10.2%;   PE = .5/(.13 + .02 − .102) = 10.42
             g = −5.1%;   PE = .5/(.13 + .02 + .051) = 2.49

10-8.   a.   For the implied growth rate we use the rearranged formula in the answer to question 10-7 as follows:
             g = k − p/PE = .18 − .2/(35/1.25) = 17.3%
        b.   We can next calculate the earnings per share and PE in 5 years:
             EPS = 1.25 (1 + .25)^5 = 3.81
             PE = p/(k − g) = .4/(.16 − .10) = 6.67
             The stock price = EPS (PE) = 3.81 (6.67) = 25.41

10-9.   The quality of management is difficult for most investors to judge. Investors are primarily dependent upon the media for profiles and data. Companies out of the spotlight—the vast majority—receive almost no coverage. When information is available, investors should pay attention to research and development, marketing, management style, innovation, and responsiveness to shareholder concerns. The psychological element should not be discounted; the value of much of the news is not in the details but rather in the market reaction to them.

10-10. The *balance sheet* lists assets and liabilities; it provides a glimpse of how the assets were financed. The debt side of the ledger yields the debt-to-equity ratio that can be used to assess whether the firm is taking on too much risk. The *income statement* begins with total revenues, then details the expenses that are deducted to reach the final earnings figure. This statement reveals expenses and their relation to each other, and it puts them into a historical perspective. The *change in financial position statement* furnishes financial data that reveal cash flows. The firm's liquidity position can be determined from this information.

10-11. a. *Liquidity ratios* measure the firm's ability to meet its short-run obligations (cash, inventory, accounts receivable, and so on.) *Debt ratios* give an indication of the firm's financial position (leverage) and its future prospects. *Profitability and efficiency ratios* reflect the company's productivity. *Other ratios,* such as PE, relate the company's stock price to marketplace profitability. Book value is a current accounting valuation of the firm as opposed to the stock price's current and future orientation.

       b. Ratios derive their usefulness by their relation to past figures; the historical perspective confers intelligibility. Ratios provide a quick but superficial view of the state of the firm. If used with this in mind, they are of great value. Deeper inferences about a company's performance and future prospects should be derived from closer examination and analysis.

10-12. a. Too much debt can produce short-term growth but saddle the firm with crippling future payments. Diverting cash flows can catalyze growth but often only for a short time because the original target may eventually need the cash flow and, possibly, retroactive flows. Generally, high growth rates resulting from increased debt, higher capacity utilization, accounting changes, or price increases are not sustainable. A company's reliance on any single area for growth commonly results in ephemeral growth. Sustainable growth is usually derived from a balanced approach.

       b. Investment analysis can help detect whether a company is resorting to quick fixes or a comprehensive strategy.

10-13. Applying the equation ROE = ROS x assets turnover x debt margin to Firms A, B, C, D, and E using the 1999 figures results in the following returns on equity:

       Firm A: ROE = (5m/50m)(50m/11m)(11m/8m) = 62.5%

       Firm B: ROE = (5m/50m)(50m/17m)(17m/10m) = 50%

       Firm C: ROE = (5m/30m)(30m/10m)(10m/7m) = 71.4%

       Firm D: ROE = (5m/30m) (30m/10m) (10m/7m) = 71.4%

       Firm E: ROE = (5m/51m)(51m/17m)(17m/12m) = 41.7%

Answers to Self-Test Questions, pp. 370–371

10-1.   False. Profits are more variable than almost all the components of the GDP.

10-2.   False. The assumptions are essentially identical. Indeed, the payout ratio must also be assumed in order to apply the PE (earnings multiplier) approach.

10-3.   True.

10-4.   True.

10-5.   False. Using the dividend discount model, the higher the expected growth rate of dividends are, the higher the PE will be.

10-6.   True.

10-7.   True.

10-8.   True.

10-9.   False. The basic balance sheet equation is as follows: Assets – liabilities = net worth.

10-10. False. The quick ratio of current assets minus inventories over current liabilities is used to assess the firm's liquidity condition.

10-11. False. The intrinsic value of the firm's stock could be raised or lowered depending on the growth and risk assessment of the firm after the debt-equity ratio is raised.

10-12. False. Using the Dupont formula (ROE = ROS x asset turnover x debt margin), it is clear that raising the debt margin would raise return on equity, all other things equal. The risk characteristics of the firm would be affected, however.

10-13. False. Fully diluted earnings per share are calculated after assuming convertible debt has been converted into shares of stock in order to establish a conservative estimate of earnings for PE ratio calculation purposes.

10-14. True.

Chapter 11

Answers to Review Questions, pp. 406–408

11-1. a. GRO EPS$_{5years}$ = \$1 $(1.1)^5$ = \$1.61
New GRO price = New PE (GRO EPS$_{5years}$) = 20 (\$1.61) = \$32.2
   b. Asset Play EPS$_{5years}$ = \$1 $(1.1)^5$ = \$1.61
New Asset Play price = New PE (Asset Play EPS$_{5years}$) = 15 (\$1.61) = \$24.15
   c. GRO HPR = \$32.2/\$25 −1 = 28.8%

GRO annualized return = $\sqrt[5]{1.288}$ −1 = 5.2%

Asset Play HPR = \$24.15/\$8 −1 = 201.9%

Asset Play annualized return = $\sqrt[5]{3.019}$ −1 = 24.7%

11-2. a. GRO EPS$_{5years}$ = \$1 $(1.05)^5$ = \$1.28
New GRO price = New PE (GRO EPS$_{5years}$) = 12 (\$1.28) = \$15.36
Asset Play EPS$_{5years}$ = \$1 $(1.05)^5$ = \$1.28
New Asset Play price = New PE (Asset Play EPS$_{5years}$) = 6 (\$1.28) = \$7.68
   b. GRO HPR = \$15.36 / \$25 − 1 = −38.6%

GRO annualized return = $\sqrt[5]{.614}$ −1 = −9.3%

Asset Play HPR = \$7.68 / \$8 − 1 = −4%

Asset Play annualized return = $\sqrt[5]{.96}$ − 1 = −.8%

11-3. a. GRO: p = .13, k = .13, PE = 25
PE = p/(k − g) => g = k − p/PE
g_{GRO} = .13 − .13/25 = 12.5%
   b. Asset Play: p = .5, k = .12 PE = 8
$g_{Asset\ Play}$ = .12 − .5/8 = 5.75%

11-4. During the 1975–1995 period, investing in low-PE stocks resulted in a 2.5 percent superior return to a strategy of investing in growth stocks. The relationship has reversed in the last 4 years, with growth stocks experiencing a 4 percent greater return.

11-5. Many econometric studies have found that the PE effect disappears when also accounting for the *small firm effect*. Various causes for the small firm effect have been hypothesized; these include misspecification of CAPM, higher rewards for incomplete information, underestimated risk, or thin markets. Research that controls for these factors has not been able to eliminate the effect.

11-6. A lack of information and strong price sensitivity have caused many investors to shy away from low-priced stocks. This *neglected firm effect* is an attempt to explain the low price effect and as such could be a rationale for underpricing. The *low price effect* appears to be stronger than the PE and size effects. Possible causes are greater or mismeasured risk, higher trading costs, or general aversion. If returns are higher due to nonmarket risk, this could be diversified away, thereby generating superior returns. In addition, trading costs are minimized over long holding periods.

11-7. Identifying takeover candidates is desirable because acquisition generally occurs at a premium over the pretakeover price. Early identification allows the investor to enjoy the subsequent price appreciation.

11-8. Valuation of Cash Cow Corporation can be done by using cash flow (CF) in the dividend formula with CF = \$3 million, k = 12%, and g = 5%:
$$P = CF/(k − g) = [1.05 (\$3\ \text{million})]/(.12 − .05) = \$45\ \text{million}$$
Note that we increased the present cash flow by 5 percent to comply with the formula's required next period cash flow. Also remember that cash flow is not the same as long-term dividends and that this result is only a rough gauge of the value of Cash Cow Corporation.

11-9.   a.   The principal components of the Altman bankruptcy formula are as follows:
A = working capital/assets (assures enough capital to meet most needs)
B = retained earnings/assets (indicates that the firm is investing in prospects for the future)
C = pretax earnings/assets (indicates healthy earnings)
D = sales/assets (indicates adequate revenue)
E = market value of equity/liabilities (indicates healthy market capitalization or low liabilities)

   b.   A company's health is positively correlated with each of the variables in a. above. Investment opportunities are identified by company Altman scores and stock prices within a peer group. Good candidates are firms whose numbers are anomalous. If, for example, a firm has a low Altman score, the investor can capitalize on this information by either shorting the stock or purchasing put options. If the stock price falls as predicted, the investor will profit.

11-10.

| Company | Ratios | | | | | Altman Score |
	1.2A	1.4B	3.3C	D	.6E	
A	0.02	.22	.99	1.00	0.10	2.33
B	0.02	.17	.66	1.20	0.04	2.09
C	0.01	.02	.08	1.13	0.04	1.28
D	0.03	.04	.37	1.11	0.60	2.15

Firm C exhibits the highest risk.

11-11.

Company	EPS	PE
A	4.10	2.44
B	1.40	3.57
C	0.21	14.29
D	2.10	11.90

11-12.   Stockholders are primarily concerned with stock price—theoretically based on the present value of all dividends into infinity. The stockholder is therefore interested in management's taking a long-term perspective that maximizes return while minimizing risk. A manager's self-interest may clash with this goal. Management might undertake a short-term strategy that enhances its image in order for the manager to secure higher pay or a more lucrative position at another firm. Managers might also seek power, resulting in a large, inefficient company. When management and stockholders differ in their goals, the stock price will likely suffer. If this condition persists, stockholders may pressure or replace management. Management can resist by attempting to gain ownership through methods such as a leveraged buyout.

11-13.   a.   A large body of research has investigated the case of management's having a short-term philosophy and its adverse impact on shareholder wealth. Findings include the following: A short-term focus often leads to low R&D investment; owner-controlled firms have relatively more income and return; mergers have a negative impact on profitability; management-controlled monopolies have significantly lower profit rates; firms that align management and shareholder interests enhance shareholder wealth.

   b.   The implication is that the investor should look for firms in which management and shareholders have the same goals. Positive signals include management ownership of shares, low turnover at the executive level, and cost cutting. Negative signals include high merger activity, excessive compensation, low dividend yield, and low growth rates.

Answers to Self-Test Questions, p. 408

11-1.   True.
11-2.   True.

11-3.   False. Low PE stocks do tend to perform better than expected on a risk-adjusted basis, but *on average*, there is not sufficient evidence that they perform enough better to warrant the extra effort and costs associated with investing in them. Many, if not most, of the low-PE stocks are small-company stocks that have special characteristics. In other words, the low-PE effect is commingled with the size effect, and it is too early to judge this as an anomaly.

11-4.   False. Analyst neglect arises largely because institutional investors are less interested in small firms with low capitalizations. All publicly held corporations must publish their results.

11-5.   True.

11-6.   False. Altman's Z score is used to identify potential bankruptcy candidates, not takeover candidates.

11-7.   False. The agency problem is inherent in modern corporations in which stock ownership is usually separated from management control. Therefore, the firm might not operate as efficiently as it could, regardless of executive pay levels.

11-8.   True.

11-9.   True.

Chapter 12

Answers to Review Questions, pp. 441–443

12-1.   Econometric and leading indicator models have shown little success in predicting market prices. The shortcomings of econometric models include infrequent updating and the inability to supply information that has not already been incorporated into the market price. On the other hand, leading indicators have shown predictive ability but only of the economy as a whole. Some indicators are more successful at predicting economic upturns; others are better at predicting downturns. The stock market itself appears to be a leading indicator of the economy. Poor track records have not prevented ongoing investment and research.

12-2.   The government can act on the economy either through direct transfers (tax cuts or cash payments/vouchers) or indirectly through programs or projects. Government expenditures are occasionally aimed at increasing production. The theory is that the fruits of increased spending and production trickle through the economy, resulting in an overall output increase. Offsetting this effect is the funding mechanism; taxes and borrowing decrease privately available funds for investment. The tools for spurring the economy are spending and tax cuts. Tax increases and reduced government spending tend to restrain the economy. Keynesians believe that government spending is more effective than tax cuts for economic stimulation. Two caveats should be observed: (1) Spending and its funding work at cross-purposes, thereby partially nullifying each other, and (2) the effect of governmental action depends on the current state of the economy; if the economy is near capacity, inflation may be the only result.

12-3.   The Federal Reserve influences the economy via the credit markets. Its primary weapons are reserve requirements, open market operations, and the discount window. Changing the reserve requirement is a very powerful but seldom used tool. The discount window is also rarely employed and has proven of limited influence. Open market operations alter total banking reserves that, in turn, affect the level of lending. For the most part, this has been the Fed's chosen economic weapon. When the Fed embarks upon an economic policy shift, it signals its intention by announcing a target for the federal funds rate. It then proceeds to alter aggregate reserves through open market transactions. The federal funds rate is determined by supply and demand of loanable funds, but these are, in turn, strongly influenced by Fed activity in its open market operations.

12-4.   Reasons for following monetary policy include the following: It has a unique influence on the economy; its effects are easier to model and predict than those attributable to fiscal initiatives; influential economists tout the primacy of monetary policy; interest rate changes have effects throughout the economy. Monetary policy's effect on the stock market occurs through pricing models (via the federal funds rate); rate changes alter the relative attractiveness of various securities; margin costs modify the ability to support the market through borrowing. A sophisticated model of the stock market should include both fiscal and monetary drivers, but as with most models, the devil is in the details. The recent trend among market prognosticators has been to minimize the effect of fiscal policy on the economy. Research has shown that the stock market is relatively efficient in pricing (capitalizing) the effects of monetary action. Opportunity may arise from effective implementation of market expectations as opposed to mechanical rules.

12-5. a. With lower interest rates comes easier credit, which—all other things being equal—should serve as a catalyst for the economy. The stock market should therefore rise.

b. These actions are consistent with each other and positive with respect to the economy; a rise in stock prices should be expected.

c. The moratorium signals turmoil in the credit markets that will likely be received poorly by the stock market.

12-6. Inflation can affect stock prices directly and/or indirectly through economy-wide developments. In theory, stock prices adjust and reflect the general price level. This may, in fact, be the case if firms can adapt their operations to ratchet up profits, thus nullifying inflation. Many studies contradict this view and therefore predict a short-term fall in stock prices. In the long run, stock prices have offered a real return that is well in excess of inflation. If investors with a long-term horizon make decisions based upon this information, stock prices should adjust.

12-7. a. Expected inflation = $.1(2) + .3(4) + .4(6) + .2(8) = 5.4\%$

Expected Returns
Stocks = 8%
Short-term bonds = 3 + inflation = 8.4%
Long-term bonds = 5 + .3(inflation) = 6.62%

To maximize expected returns, you should purchase 100 percent short-term bonds.

b.

Nominal and Real Returns for Each Possible Inflation Rate				
	Inflation Rate			
	2	4	6	8
Stocks	8 (6)*	8 (4)	8 (2)	8 (0)
Short-term bonds	5 (3)	7 (3)	9 (3)	11 (3)
Long-term bonds	5.6 (3.6)	6.2 (2.2)	6.8 (.8)	7.4 (–.6)
Real estate	3.4 (1.4)	5.8 (1.8)	8.2 (2.2)	10.6 (2.6)
*Real return in parentheses				

Only short-term bonds offer a real return greater than 2 percent at all of the inflation rates shown. You should purchase only these securities if this is your concern.

12-8. If the investments are perfect inflation hedges, their return in a stable price environment (no inflation) is their real return. Returns in inflationary environments are shown in the table below:

		Inflation			
	Real	2	4	6	10
A	3	5	7	9	13
B	5	7	9	11	15
C	2	4	6	8	12
D	6	8	10	12	16
E	10	12	14	16	20
F	7	9	11	13	17

12-9. Long-term studies indicate that stock prices more than nullify the effects of inflation. However, short-term studies offer mixed results. Sensitivities have been shown to unanticipated inflation and accelerating/decelerating rates. If investors have long-run horizons, they can invest in stocks confidently. Investors with short horizons cannot depend on a catchall pronouncement.

12-10. Returns are as shown in the table below:

Nominal (Real) After-tax Returns				
	2	4	6	10
A	3.5 (1.5)	4.9 (.9)	6.3 (.3)	9.1 (−.9)
B	4.9 (2.9)	6.3 (2.3)	7.7 (1.7)	10.5 (.5)
C	2.8 (.8)	4.2 (.2)	5.6 (−.4)	8.4 (−1.6)
D	5.6 (3.6)	7 (3)	8.4 (2.4)	11.2 (1.2)
E	8.4 (6.4)	9.8 (5.8)	11.2 (5.2)	14.0 (4)
F	6.3 (4.3)	7.7 (3.7)	9.1 (3.1)	11.9 (1.9)

12-11. Returns where b = .3, .5, .7, and .9 are as follows:

Nominal (Real) After-tax Returns				
0.3	2	4	6	10
A	2.5 (.5)	2.9 (−1.1)	3.4 (−2.6)	4.2 (−5.8)
B	3.9 (1.9)	4.3 (.3)	4.8 (−1.2)	5.6 (−4.4)
C	1.8 (−.2)	2.2 (−1.8)	2.7 (−3.3)	3.5 (−6.5)
D	4.6 (2.6)	5.0 (1)	5.5 (−.5)	6.3 (−3.7)
E	7.4 (5.4)	7.8 (3.8)	8.3 (2.3)	9.1 (−.9)
F	5.3 (3.3)	5.7 (1.7)	6.2 (.2)	7 (−3)

Nominal (Real) After-tax Returns				
0.5	2	4	6	10
A	2.8 (.8)	3.5 (−.5)	4.2 (−1.8)	5.6 (−4.4)
B	4.2 (2.2)	4.9 (.9)	5.6 (−.4)	7 (−3)
C	2.1 (.1)	2.8 (−1.2)	3.5 (−2.5)	4.9 (−5.1)
D	4.9 (2.9)	5.6 (1.6)	6.3 (.3)	7.7 (−2.3)
E	7.7 (5.7)	8.4 (4.4)	9.1 (3.1)	10.5 (.5)
F	5.6 (3.6)	6.3 (2.3)	7 (1)	8.4 (−1.6)

Nominal (Real) After-tax Returns				
0.7	2	4	6	10
A	3.1 (1.1)	4.1 (.1)	5 (−1)	7 (−3)
B	4.5 (2.5)	5.5 (1.5)	6.4 (.4)	8.4 (−1.6)
C	2.4 (.4)	3.4 (−.6)	4.3 (−1.7)	6.3 (−3.7)
D	5.2 (3.2)	6.2 (2.2)	7.1 (1.1)	9.1 (−.9)
E	8 (6)	9 (5)	9.9 (3.9)	11.9 (1.9)
F	5.9 (3.9)	6.9 (2.9)	7.8 (1.8)	9.8 (−.2)

Nominal (Real) After-tax Returns				
0.9	2	4	6	10
A	3.4 (1.4)	4.6 (.6)	5.9 (−.1)	8.4 (−1.6)
B	4.8 (2.8)	6 (2)	7.3 (1.3)	9.8 (−.2)
C	2.7 (.7)	3.9 (−.1)	5.2 (−.8)	7.7 (−2.3)
D	5.5 (3.5)	6.7 (2.7)	8 (2)	10.5 (.5)
E	8.3 (6.3)	9.5 (5.5)	10.8 (4.8)	13.3 (3.3)
F	6.2 (4.2)	7.4 (3.4)	8.7 (2.7)	11.2 (1.2)

12-12. Bonds appear to offer some short-term protection against anticipated inflation. Part of this is due to reinvestment opportunity at maturation. Long-term returns on bonds are historically poor in relation to stocks. Some researchers have pointed to commodities as possible inflation hedges. Generally, commodities are of greater risk and require specialized knowledge relative to stocks and bonds. The same can be said of real estate.

12-13. a. A profit of $2 million and sales of 500,000 at $40 per unit imply that TUV's total revenues and total costs were $20 million and $18 million, respectively. Total variable costs are the product of sales and per-unit variable costs: 500,000 ($20) = $10 million. Thus, fixed costs must be $8 million. If TUV absorbs the higher inputs costs, it can expand sales by 20 percent with existing capacity. Under these circumstances, its profits will be determined as follows:

Sales revenues = $40 [500,000 (1.2)] = $24,000,000
Total variable costs = $25 (600,000) = $15,000,000
Total fixed costs = $8,000,000
Total costs = Total variable costs + total fixed costs = $23,000,000
Profits = Sales revenues − total costs = $1,000,000

b. If TUV raises its price to cover the increased variable costs, its profit will be as follows:

Sales revenues = $45 [500,000 (.8)] = $18,000,000
Total variable costs = $25 (400,000) = $10,000,000
Total fixed costs = $8,000,000
Total costs = Total variable costs + total fixed costs = $18,000,000
Profits = Sales revenues − total costs = $0

Under these circumstances, holding the line on prices and absorbing the cost increase would be the more profitable strategy. Note, however, that such a strategy depends on the existence of sufficient capacity to service the additional demand.

Answers to Self-Test Questions, pp. 443–444

12-1. False. Both micro- and macroeconomic data are typically used to forecast economic activity.

12-2. True.

12-3.   False. Increases in government spending stimulate the economy (spur growth); tax increases have a restraining effect on the level of economic activity.

12-4.   False. After leakages are taken into account, a $1 increase in government spending increases the GDP by less than $2.

12-5.   False. The Federal Reserve System has primary authority over monetary policy.

12-6.   True.

12-7.   True.

12-8.   False. Checkable deposits are by far the largest component of M1.

12-9.   True.

12-10. False. The federal funds rate is the rate that banks charge each other for the overnight use (loan) of excess reserves.

12-11. False. The tools of fiscal policy are changes in tax rates and the level of government spending.

12-12. True.

12-13. False. The primary goals of both monetary policy and fiscal policy are the same—full employment and price stability.

12-14. False. Price stability is the absence of either a rising or falling trend in overall prices. We want the price level (average) to remain stable, while individual prices fluctuate to reflect changing supply and demand conditions for individual goods and services.

12-15. True.

12-16. True.

12-17. False. Restrictive monetary policy raises interest rates and limits credit availability to stronger credit risks, thereby affecting the allocation of funds away from financially weaker borrowers.

12-18. True.

12-19. True.

12-20. False. Only if the after-tax cost of the loan is below the rate of return earned on the investment will the use of leverage enhance an investor's nominal return.

12-21. True.

12-22. False. Treasury bills provide the greatest short-term inflation protection but offer the least long-term real return.

Chapter 13

Answers to Review Questions, pp. 471–472

13-1.   The market was bullish until the weekend before the crash. The subsequent precipitous fall doesn't speak well of market efficiency. Panics highlight an emotional element that is difficult to reconcile and incorporate into financial theory.

13-2.   a.   Stock A: $PE_A = 15$ and $\Delta g_A = .09$

$$PE_{Market} (1 + \Delta g_A)^{gamma_A} = PE_A$$

$$gamma_A = \frac{\ln(PE_A) - \ln(PE_{Market})}{\ln(1 + \Delta g_A)} = \frac{\ln(15) - \ln(10)}{\ln(1 + .09)} = 4.705 \text{ years}$$

b.   Stock B: $PE_B = 30$ and $\Delta g_B = .20$

$$gamma_B = \frac{\ln(30) - \ln(10)}{\ln(1 + .20)} = 6.026$$

13-3.   a.   From question 13-2, $PE_A = 15$, $\Delta g_A = .09$, and $gamma_A = 4.705$. If the PE_{Market} changes with all other information remaining the same:

$$gamma_{New} = \frac{\ln(15) - \ln(8)}{\ln(1 + .09)} = 7.294$$

If the original gamma declines 20 percent to 3.764 (a more realistic assumption):

New $PE_A = 8(1.09)^{3.764} = 11.065$ (a decline of 26.23 %)

b. $PE_B = 30$, $\Delta g_B = .20$, and $gamma_B = 6.026$:

$$gamma_{New} = \frac{\ln(30) - \ln(8)}{\ln(1+.20)} = 7.250$$

A 20% decline in the original gamma results in

New $PE_B = 8(1.20)^{4.821} = 19.267$ (a decline of 35.78%)

13-4. Use of equilibrium company or market PEs as predictive signals has produced poor results. Many rationalizations have been offered for their failure: accounting distortions, company manipulation of figures, industry differences, and the use of historical versus forecasted earnings. Attempts to rectify these shortcomings have not resulted in any noteworthy improvements.

13-5. Gray's approach is based on the relationship between interest rates and prices. According to this theory, there is an equilibrium relationship that signals price changes by deviations from the norm. A possible implementation is to monitor the spread between bond yields and total stock returns. For example, if the spread narrows because bond yields are very high (low prices), this could be interpreted as signaling that stock prices are too high and should subsequently fall. There has been little empirical testing of Gray's theory.

13-6. The PE equation: $PE = \dfrac{p}{k-g}$ is equivalent to: $\dfrac{P}{E} = \dfrac{D/E}{k-g}$

$\Rightarrow \quad k - g = \dfrac{D/E}{P/E} = \dfrac{D}{E}\dfrac{E}{P}$

$\Rightarrow \quad k = \dfrac{D}{E}\dfrac{E}{P} + g$ (Gray's equation)

13-7. Public pronouncements are generally assessed according to who the speaker is and whether the pronouncement is a deviation from prior expectations. Statements by people such as the Chairman of the Federal Reserve and the Secretary of the Treasury are accorded great weight. Evidence on stock repurchase announcements has been mixed at best. This is at least partially due to the multitude of motivations for the repurchases. In sum, announcements that are truly useful in predicting the future prices are relatively rare because of informational efficiency.

13-8. The use of short trading data is often motivated by the belief that short traders have superior market insight. Implementation of this doctrine requires that their actions be mimicked in anticipation of price declines. A philosophical spin-off is the contrarian belief that short pressure will likely lead to higher demand, thus driving up prices; investors should, therefore, buy when short volume increases. Studies have refuted both of these strategies. Other theorists focus on odd-lot traders and their perceived poor market timing. It is thought that contrary positions should produce profits. Research has found that some positive gains may have been achievable in the 1950s and 1960s, but more recently, this is not the case.

13-9. a. odd-lot short ratio $= \dfrac{\text{odd-lot short sales}}{\text{total odd-lot sales}} = \dfrac{.07}{1.3} = .0538$

$TOLSR = \dfrac{\text{odd-lot short sales}}{\text{odd-lot purchases/odd-lot sales}} = \dfrac{.07}{1.6/1.3} = .0569$

b. odd-lot short sales = .24 million

odd-lot short ratio $= \dfrac{.24}{1.3} = .185$ and $TOLSR = \dfrac{.24}{1.6/1.3} = .195$

13-10. a. Many assume that specialists have superior market insight. This belief dictates following specialists short-selling. Evidence on the results of doing so is unclear.

b. A similar market timing method entails monitoring mutual funds' cash position. If the cash position becomes large, a significant market upswing is possible. The implication is that the fund is waiting for the right buying opportunity. Mutual funds have generally not been successful with their cash management strategies.

c. Some investors view the bond market as offering clues about future moves of the stock market. A low value of a statistic such as the Barron's Confidence Index (BCI) indicates that the rate spread between high-grade and speculative bonds is wide, thus revealing that investment is shifting away from speculative bonds. This demonstrates pessimism and does not bode well for the stock market. Results using this method have not been encouraging.

13-11.   Barron's Confidence Index = high-grade rates / average-grade rates

$$BCI_A = \frac{5.67}{6.01} = .943 \qquad\qquad\qquad BCI_B = \frac{7.89}{8.85} = .892$$

$$BCI_C = \frac{9.50}{11.78} = .806 \qquad\qquad\qquad BCI_D = \frac{10.34}{13.89} = .744$$

13-12.   a.   The *advance-decline ratio* has been shown to have some persistence. In other words, advances (declines) tend to extend beyond one trading day (sometimes termed momentum).

b.   The *short-term trading index* uses the ratio of average decline volume to average advance volume. Traders using this statistic have claimed positive results.

c.   The *January effect* comes in two forms. First, if the market rises in January, there is a high chance it will continue to do so for the rest of the year. The second form is based on the observation that small stocks consistently outperform the market for the first several weeks in January. This effect may be due to tax implications and has diminished in recent years.

d.   The *advisers' sentiment indicator* is a contrarian approach to short-term market moves. When adviser consensus is most bullish (bearish), the market is expected to decline (rise).

e.   Some studies have found that there is a disparity between price changes on Monday and Friday. Prices are apt to fall on Monday and rise on Friday.

Answers to Self-Test Questions, pp. 472–473

13-1.   False. The weak form of the EMH allows for random overreaction as a part of the noise in the data.

13-2.   False. The return attributed to market timing was shown to be one-half or less of the return attributed to stock selection in the Brinson, Singer, and Beebower study.

13-3.   False. Most of the timing studies or techniques use trailing accounting earnings in the denominator of the PE ratio, whereas the PE ratio that is stipulated in the earnings multiplier model projects next year earnings (forward).

13-4.   True.

13-5.   True.

13-6.   False. The Dow theory seeks to confirm if a primary trend, either upward or downward, has emerged. The theory relies on the secondary moves for this purpose.

13-7.   True.

13-8.   True.

13-9.   True.

13-10.   False. If mutual fund managers are holding more of their assets in the form of cash, this is a bullish indicator.

13-11.   True.

13-12.   True.

13-13.   True.

Chapter 14

Answers to Review Questions, pp. 498–499

14-1.   a.   The basic premise of chartism is that future prices can be predicted based upon observation of past prices. Supporters of the random walk hypothesis believe that this is not possible, that there is no link between past and future price patterns. From this perspective, price movements can be viewed as random.

b.   The belief in the separation of past and future prices is a subcategory of the weak form of the efficient market hypothesis. This theory states that a stock's current price incorporates all previously available information. This precludes profit opportunities because price adjustments occur too quickly.

14-2.   a.   Smidt theorized that there are patterns in the movement of stock prices due to anxious traders, informational lags, and speculative bubbles.

b. First, predictable price movements may result from supply and demand imbalances. These come under Smidt's *anxious trader* heading and may be attributed to block trades and secondary offerings, intraday price dependencies related to order clustering and specialist trading, price movement caused by informed traders who have nonpublic information, and year-end selling in order to establish tax losses.

Second, prices take time to adjust to new information. The existence of *adjustment lags* is evidence that markets are not perfectly efficient. Specific instances cited are earnings and dividend announcements; ex-dividend behavior and dividend capture strategies; composition changes to the S&P 500 Index; bond rating changes and corporate crime disclosures; insider trading; media recommendations; stock splits, reverse splits, and dividends; tender offers, mergers and liquidations; share repurchases, equity sales, forced conversions, and exchanges; spin-offs; and cross-correlation and volume effects.

Third, price movements that result from *speculative bubbles* can be attributed to psychological drivers. Evidence for this theory is difficult to reconcile with the cold rationality of the efficient markets theory. Examples are "story" stocks, the new issue market, and new listings.

14-3. a. Orders in a specialist's book tend to bunch at certain levels (for example, whole numbers). This bunching can cause price movements to stall and then accelerate. In addition to being disjointed, price movements can become exaggerated. Various researchers have postulated that specialists amplify price changes in the overnight market. The specialist moves prices by trading from his or her account. In this way, limit prices are triggered and still more trades result. The implication is that the specialist is moving the market to generate commissions.

b. An investor should view the current price and determine likely cluster points for limit orders. This information and a preconception of price direction could signal an opportunity to capitalize on a potentially significant price move. A key factor in the decision process should be the accumulated order volume. With this in mind, the investor should request order sizes in addition to bid-ask prices.

14-4. a. Information on the bid-ask price and last price can give an indication of pricing pressure. The prices should be viewed in relation to each other. For instance, a wide spread could be a sign of lukewarm investor interest. If the last price is very low relative to the bid-ask prices, this may indicate that future price movement will be upward.

b. Order size can also help to determine pricing pressure. A large number of orders on the bid side might indicate an imminent price rise.

14-5. a. Tax-loss trading primarily involves the stock of small firms at year-end. Price decreases are occasionally dramatic. Evidence for this anomaly is strong.

b. Tender offers, mergers, and liquidations all offer significant profit opportunities. There can be a significant run-up in the stock's price if a firm is the target of any of these actions. A significant decline may be expected if the action is canceled or proven to be only a rumor. While this trading strategy can be dangerous, it may also present a profit opportunity. Research indicates that companies in these situations often experience price movements well before announcements are made, indicating some insider behavior. The average investor may therefore find that timely action is extremely difficult.

14-6. The present portfolio is low risk, low return, and free from federal taxation of dividends. The proposed portfolio will likely have higher risk and possibly higher returns. Federal tax savings on dividends may range from 70 percent to 100 percent, depending on the number of shares purchased. There may be additional profit opportunities resulting from pricing anomalies associated with the ex-dividend date. All of these factors should be taken into account when comparing likely returns for each portfolio. Returns should be adjusted by their associated risks.

14-7. a. A common management belief is that there is an optimal range of prices for their stock to trade in. Stock splits and reverse splits attempt to implement this philosophy. The marketplace reacts differently to the directions of splits—rising for splits and declining for reverse splits. These price movements tend to occur prior to announcements (some studies add that price volatility follows the announcement). This may be due to insider information or simply to a market consensus that the current price level impels a split.

b. The rationale for stock dividends is similar to that expressed in a. above. Stock dividends are often viewed as signals that management has a very optimistic outlook. The market reacts positively to these, with price increases correlated with the size of the dividend.

c. Dividend reinvestment plans have benefits for both management and stockholders. Increased demand for stock and lower administrative costs benefit management. Stockholders benefit from lower transaction costs. Reinvestment plans are generally viewed in a positive light, thereby contributing to stock value. On the other hand, newly issued shares dilute the market, thus creating downward price pressure.

14-8. a. Brokerage profits generally have an indirect correlation with the stock market's overall price level. Market volume rises with price upturns and *vice versa*. Since brokerage commissions are based on volume, the profit relationship is a logical one. Price swings in brokerages' stock prices typically exceed those of the market. Investors should be aware of this and may be able to turn this to their advantage.

b. The profit pattern did not hold in the 1980s. Record profits in the late 1990s reasserted this theory's relevance.

14-9. a. The value of your portfolio is determined as follows:

P = $10, buy 10 shares; total shares = 10   Portfolio = 10 ($10) = $100
P = $5, buy 20 shares; total shares = 30   Portfolio = 30 ($5) = $150
P = $10   Portfolio = 30 ($10) = $300

b. The value of your portfolio is calculated as follows:

P = $10, buy 10 shares; total shares = 10   Portfolio = 10 ($10) = $100
P = $15, buy 6.67 shares; total shares = 16.67   Portfolio = 16.67 ($15) = $250
P = $10   Portfolio = 16.67 ($10) = $166.67

Answers to Self-Test Questions, pp. 499–500

14-1. False. Chart reading is a type of technical analysis.
14-2. True.
14-3. True.
14-4. False. Block trades are transactions involving 10,000 or more shares.
14-5. True.
14-6. True.
14-7. True.
14-8. True.
14-9. True.
14-10. False. Rights offerings and forced conversions increase the number of outstanding common shares, but share repurchases decrease the number of outstanding shares of common stock.
14-11. True.
14-12. True.
14-13. False. Dollar cost averaging consists of spending a fixed amount of money on stock purchases at regular intervals.

Chapter 15

Answers to Review Questions, pp. 524–526

15-1. a. The initial NAV of the $$$ mutual fund is $21.67, calculated as follows:

$$\text{Initial NAV} = \frac{\$650,000,000}{30,000,000} = \$21.67$$

b. The increase in the NAV is 15.37 percent, as shown below:

$$\text{New NAV} = \frac{\$800,000,000}{32,000,000} = \$25.00$$

$$\text{Percentage increase} = \frac{\$25.00}{\$21.67} - 1 = 15.37\%$$

15-2. Suppose the investor purchases one share. The one-year return can be determined as follows:

$$\text{Cost} = \frac{\text{NAV}}{1-\text{L}} = \frac{\$21.67}{1-.03} = \$22.34$$

Final value = Final NAV + Distributions = $25.00 + $.70 = $25.70

$$\text{Return} = \frac{\$25.70}{\$22.34} - 1 = 15.04\%$$

15-3. a. Load funds can be either front end or back end. Front-end loads can be up to 8 1/2 percent and are deducted upon purchase. Back-end loads occur upon redemption. They are lower than front-end loads and frequently decrease as the ownership period lengthens.

b. An alternative to loading is to spread out sales fees by charging an annual 12b-1 fee. Averaging one percent, this fee is low relative to loading, but the investor should be aware that this ongoing fee will perpetually affect fund performance.

c. No-load funds greatly lower selling costs by marketing directly to investors. This type of fund has no purchase or redemption fees. No-load funds incur selling costs, but they are typically much lower than those associated with 12b-1 funds.

15-4. a. The best way to proceed is to examine each year's investment. The performance of the no-load mutual fund can therefore be determined as shown below:

$$\text{Year } 1 = \$3,000 \, (1.11)^5 = \$5,055.17$$
$$\text{Year } 2 = \$3,000 \, (1.11)^4 = \$4,554.21$$
$$\text{Year } 3 = \$3,000 \, (1.11)^3 = \$4,102.89$$
$$\text{Year } 4 = \$3,000 \, (1.11)^2 = \$3,696.30$$
$$\text{Year } 5 = \$3,000 \, (1.11) = \$3,330.00$$
$$\text{Final value} = \$20,738.57$$

b. To calculate the performance of the 12b-1 mutual fund with a 1 percent fee at the end of each year, we can proceed as in 15-4a., but a little algebra will make things simpler. The rate of increase can be combined with the 12b-1 fee to arrive at a single annual rate as follows:

$$\text{Annual rate} = (1 + \text{return}) \, (1 - \text{fee}) - 1 = (1.11) \, (.99) - 1 = 9.89\%$$
$$\text{Year } 1 = \$3,000 \, (1.0989)^5 = \$4,807.42$$
$$\text{Year } 2 = \$4,374.76$$
$$\text{Year } 3 = \$3,981.03$$
$$\text{Year } 4 = \$3,622.74$$
$$\text{Year } 5 = \$3,296.70$$
$$\text{Final value} = \$20,082.65$$

c. To determine the performance of the front-end load with an 8.5 percent commission in the first year only, we can use the figures from a. after adjusting the first year's figure as follows:

$$\text{Year } 1 = \$3,000 \, (1 - .085) \, (1.11)^5 = \$4,625.48$$
$$\text{Final value} = \$20,308.88$$

15-5. a. Assume that the unknown annual rate is r. The 12b-1 fund's annual return must be 12.12 percent to equal the no-load fund's end-of-period value, as calculated below:

$$(1 + r) \, (1 - \text{fee}) = 1.11$$
$$(1 + r) \, (.99) = 1.11$$
$$1 + r = 1.11 \, / \, .99$$
$$r = (1.11 \, / \, .99) - 1 = 12.12\%$$

b. The answer to question 15-4 tells us that the final value with a front-end load is higher than that associated with a 12b-1 fee. The annual rate can therefore be lower.

15-6. a. The percentage discount on the initial NAV is determined as follows:

$$\text{Discount} = (33 - 25) / 33 = 24.24\%$$

     b. Pekans Group purchased 35 percent of the 10 million shares. These 3.5 million shares were purchased at an average per-share cost of $28. With a final price of $35, the gross profits are $24.5 million, as calculated below:

$$\text{Gross profits} = 3,500,000 \ (\$35 - \$28) = \$24,500,000$$

     c. Since this is a takeover, we can assume that only purchase commissions are involved. The net return, therefore, is 22.49 percent, computed as follows:

$$\text{Commissions} = .02 \ [\$28 \ (3,500,000)] = .02 \ (\$98,000,000) = \$1,960,000$$
$$\text{Total costs} = \text{Legal costs} + \text{Commissions} = \$500,000 + \$1,960,000 = \$2,460,000$$
$$\text{Net return} = \frac{\text{Gross profits} - \text{Total costs}}{\text{Outlay for stock}} = \frac{\$24,500,000 - \$2,460,000}{\$98,000,000} = 22.49\%$$

15-7. a. Mutual funds are examples of open-end investment companies. Open-end companies have a flexible number of shares that can expand or shrink with demand. The price of open-end shares is determined by the value of the underlying shares—in other words, NAV.

     b. Closed-end companies have a fixed number of shares that are determined at the inception of the fund. The share price of a closed-end fund is determined by supply and demand; it is therefore generally disconnected from the NAV. Purchase of closed-end shares occurs in the open market, unlike the purchase of open-end shares, which ultimately come from the issuing company. Closed-end companies can decide or be forced into becoming open-end companies. Force is usually through shareholder pressure. Transformation into open-end companies results in shares selling at NAV. Since this usually involves a price increase, the incentive for transformation is clear.

15-8. a. The stocks in a sector fund generally have a unifying theme. The number of sector funds is vast, as are the variety of themes. Examples of sectors include such themes as industry, geographical region, and investment philosophy.

     b. A single investment company manages families of funds. By offering a variety of funds, the investment company hopes to appeal to as wide an audience as possible. Exchanges between family funds generally have much lower transaction costs than exchanges outside the family. In this way, the investment company hopes to attract and retain customers.

15-9. a. The holding period return for Good Good is computed as follows:

$$\text{Good Good} = \frac{13.01 + .53 + .74}{14.29} - 1 = -.07\%$$

Thus, the holding period returns for the remaining four funds are as shown below:

Bond Bond = 5.28%
Go Go = 90.73%
Chip Chip = 15.42%
Cash Cash = 6.8%

     b. Returns should never be viewed in isolation. Return has no meaning unless it is "explained" by the risk incurred. Investors should also consider fees and taxes.

15-10. The geometric mean return and standard deviation for the five funds and the market index are as follows:

	Mean Return	Standard Deviation
Good Good	3.67%	12.97%
Bond Bond	6.70%	6.77%
Go Go	4.43%	29.27%
Chip Chip	11.00%	14.68%
Cash Cash	7.74%	1.77%
Market Index	7.62%	14.60%

15-11. The Sharpe ratios for the five funds and the market index using a risk-free rate of 4.7 percent are as follows:

	Sharpe Ratio
Good Good	−.079
Bond Bond	.295
Go Go	−.009
Chip Chip	.429
Cash Cash	1.715
Market Index	.200

15-12. a. Using the betas shown for each fund and the market index, the Treynor ratios and Sharpe ratios are as shown in the following:

	Beta	Treynor Ratio	Rank	Sharpe Ratio	Rank
Good Good	1.1	−0.009	6	−0.079	6
Bond Bond	0.6	0.033	3	0.295	3
Go Go	1.3	−0.002	5	−0.009	5
Chip Chip	0.9	0.07	2	0.429	2
Cash Cash	0.2	0.152	1	1.715	1
Market Index	1	0.029	4	0.2	4

   b. Treynor ratios and Sharpe ratios are not directly comparable since the formulas are different. Probably the best method of comparison is by ranking the ratios (putting them in the order of their magnitude). For both measures the rankings are the same.

15-13. Mutual funds compete with other similarly equipped institutions such as banks. It is in comparison to individual investors that disparities become pronounced. For example, funds have lower trading costs, superior analytical means, and vast credit resources. An additional benefit is lowered risk through diversification. On the other hand, individuals are exempt from the costs associated with fund management and enjoy total freedom in asset choice. In addition, the individual always has the alternative of co-opting mutual funds as an investment weapon.

15-14. a. Investors of modest means are probably the greatest beneficiaries of the existence of mutual funds. Funds can be found that allow small initial and/or continuing contributions. Participating in a large pool of investments lowers risk. The small investor can also achieve tax and retirement benefits depending on the fund.

   b. All mutual fund investors receive the benefits mentioned in 15-14a. Additional benefits include time savings, record keeping, and choice of risk level and fund specialization.

Answers to Self-Test Questions, pp. 526–527

15-1. True.
15-2. False. No-load mutual funds are typically sold directly to the public without the aid of a sales force.
15-3. False. Few funds charge a front-end load of 8.5 percent of the purchase price of the shares. Most front-end-loaded funds charge less than 5 percent, with the majority in the 3-percent-to-4½ percent range.
15-4. True.
15-5. True.
15-6. False. Since no initial selling fee is charged, funds that levy 12b-1 fees are classified as no-load funds.
15-7. True.
15-8. False. The shares of closed-end investment companies are sold in the open market at prices determined by supply and demand. They may sell at a premium or discount to their net asset value.
15-9. False. Large shareholders can force closed-end funds to convert to open-end status by electing people to the board of directors who favor the move.
15-10. True.
15-11. False. Variable annuities allow funds to grow and accumulate tax deferred. During the distribution phase, however, all gain is taxed as ordinary income.
15-12. True.
15-13. True.

15-14. False. At least 90 percent of gross income must be distributed to shareholders for the fund to qualify as a regulated investment company.

15-15. True.

15-16. True.

15-17. True.

15-18. False. On average, mutual funds underperform the market.

15-19. True.

15-20. False. Large block trades by institutions often result in adverse price effects.

15-21. False. Typically, institutional investors restrict their analysis to a small percentage of traded stocks.

15-22. False. In the 1990s, few mutual funds were able to consistently beat the returns on S&P 500 Index funds.

Chapter 16

Answers to Review Questions, pp. 570–571

16-1. a. A call involves the right to buy (from the writer) at the strike price, whereas a put grants the right to sell (to the writer) at the strike price. Calls participate in the underlying security's price appreciation; puts participate in its depreciation.

   b. A call writer must deliver the promised asset at the specified price if the call is exercised prior to expiration. Similarly, the put writer must purchase with exercise.

   c. A call derives its value gains from those of the underlying asset. The call owner's loss is capped by the call's price if the asset's value is unchanged or declines. A put writer's profit is capped at the put premium. Increases in the price of the underlying asset do not affect this. The put writer's loss increases as the underlying asset's price decreases. The lack of equivalency between purchasing calls and put writing is demonstrated by the differences in profit patterns. (See diagrams C and F in appendix D to this chapter.)

16-2. a. Purchase of a put will protect the investor from decreases in the stock's value and allow the investor to continue to receive dividends.

   b. Selling the stock protects the investor from price decreases, but the investor forgoes dividends and any profits from subsequent price increases.

   c. If the put was free, its ownership is clearly the superior strategy. This strategy's value varies inversely with the put's price. The investor should also consider transaction costs and the time horizon (puts expire).

16-3. a. The striking price is the price at which a transaction in the underlying asset will take place if an option is exercised.

   b. The intrinsic value for calls is the maximum of (1) the difference between the price of the underlying asset and the strike price or (2) zero. In the case of puts, (1) is modified to be the result's absolute value. Time value is the difference between the option's intrinsic value and the market price of the option. The strike price determines whether an option is in or out of the money. If the price of the underlying asset is above the strike price, a call is in the money and a put is out of the money. If the underlying asset's price is below the strike price, the positions are reversed.

16-4. a. The investor breaks even when the call's intrinsic value (C_1) is equal to its purchase price (C_0):

$$C_1 = S_1 - S$$
$$S_1 = C_1 + S = C_0 + S = 1.625 + 35 = 36.625$$

   b. The returns are equal when the stock's and call's HPRRs are equal:

$$\frac{S_1}{S_0} = \frac{C_1}{C_0} \text{ (substitute } C_1 = S_1 - S \text{ and solve for } S_1)$$

$$S_1 = \frac{-S_0 S}{C_0 - S_0} = 36.87$$

   c. $\text{HPR}_{\text{Stock}} = (45/32) - 1 = 40.63\%$
   $\text{HPR}_{\text{Call}} = [(45 - 35) / 1.625] - 1 = 515.38\%$
   Turov's formula (see appendix C to this chapter) provides an alternative solution method.

    d. The dividend must be added to the stock's price when calculating the stock's returns in b. and c. above. This is not the case with the call's calculations; only the market price is used.

16-5. a. In exchange for the premium, the writer is obligated to turn over the stock (receiving payment at the strike price rate) if the call is exercised.

    b. Covered call writers receive dividends but forego any future gains from stock price appreciation. Stock price gains are canceled out by losses on the call (assuming exercise). Writers retain the risk of price declines. As is evident, call writers desire that stock prices remain stable or rise; this optimal result allows retention of the premium and any dividends that were received. (See diagram G in appendix D to this chapter.)

16-6. a. Calculating the returns of written calls is somewhat different from conventional calculations. At first glance, there appears to be no initial outlay, only incoming funds. In practice, the incoming funds—or premiums—are held as margin by the brokerage. In addition, an extra margin is required to initiate the transaction. In this case, the required margin (M_0) is 10 percent, or $2.50 per share of written calls. This figure should be used as the basis for calculations of returns. The HPR formula becomes

$$HPR = \frac{C_0 - C_1}{M_0}$$

where C_0 is the initial call premium and C_1 is the call's final value. With a final stock price of $25 ($S_1$), C_1 is zero for both strike prices:

           S = \$25   S = \$30

$$HPR_{\text{3-month}} = \frac{1.5 - 0}{2.5} = 60\% \qquad\qquad HPR_{\text{3-month}} = \frac{.375 - 0}{2.5} = 15\%$$

    $HPR_{\text{6-month}} = 90\%$ $HPR_{\text{6-month}} = 40\%$

    $HPR_{\text{9-month}} = 115\%$ $HPR_{\text{9-month}} = 50\%$

    b. $S_1 = \$30$ and a strike of $25 makes $C_1 = 30 - 25 = \$5$:

$$HPR_{\text{3-month}} = \frac{1.5 - 5}{2.5} = -140\% \qquad\qquad HPR_{\text{6-month}} = -110\%$$

    $HPR_{\text{9-month}} = -85\%$

    If $S = \$30$, $C_1 = 30 - 30 = 0$, and the HPRs are as in 16-6a.

16-7. a. A straddle is simultaneously holding or writing a put and call. A written straddle may be covered or uncovered. (See diagrams I and J in the appendix to this chapter.)

    b. Straddle buyers are anticipating price movement in the underlying asset. The straddle begins to pay off whether prices move up or down and can therefore be viewed as insurance against price changes.

    c. Investors who feel that the underlying asset's price is stable are likely straddle writers. If their predictions are realized, all or most of the premium is retained.

16-8. a. The holder of a spread possesses a call and writes a call on the same security. The calls have the same expiration date and different strike prices.

    b. A spread holder expects the call's value to rise faster than that of the written call. If the calls both decline, the premium provides an offset. The two positions can be seen as a form of insurance that limits gains and losses. (See diagrams C and D in the appendix to this chapter.)

    c. A vertical spread has different strike prices; hence, it is really just the basic spread. A horizontal spread has different expiration dates.

16-9. a. Net cost: −1.75   Call purchase at strike 25

                  <u>+.875</u>   Call premium at strike 30

                  −.875   Cost per share, or $87.50 per pair of contracts

    b. The bull spread holder hopes that the value of the call purchased rises faster than his or her commitment to the written call. If this is the case, there is no theoretical limit on potential gains. In practice, profit is limited since gains are not infinite and the holder captures only a fraction of every point rise in the call's value. If the out-of-the-money call's value rises faster than the in-the-money's, losses are theoretically limitless. This scenario is not likely and is offset by the premium.

    c. Commissions are incurred with call writing, purchase, and cancellation of position. The investor also has to consider that the call may be exercised. This outcome also involves commissions, not to mention a potential large temporary outlay to purchase the stock. All of these costs have to be weighed when assessing the profit potential of a bull spread.

16-10. a. Net cost: −.875 Call purchase at strike 25

                     +1.75 Call premium at strike 30

                    +.875 Profit per share, or $87.50 per pair of contracts

    b. The bear spread holder is betting that the underlying asset declines in value. In this case, the premium more than offsets the loss on the purchased call. A less likely profit opportunity occurs when the out-of-the-money call appreciates faster than the written in-the-money call. Losses result if the opposite transpires, with the premium providing an offset.

    c. The commissions discussion is similar to that for question 16-9c.

16-11. a. A right is essentially an option. The shareholder receives one right per share that entitles him or her to an additional fractional share. The stated price is frequently below market levels. Rights can be traded. Warrants can also be traded but are usually tied to bonds, rather than equity. Warrants are also similar to options; the owner is entitled to convert bonds into shares. Warrant owners are likewise granted a form of discount by allowing exercise at the bond's face value. The degree of discount depends on the bond's purchase price below par and the stock's market value.

    b. Warrants are generally much longer term than rights.

    c. Rights are commonly issued in the money; warrants are not. This is due in part to the long-term nature of warrants and the different motivation for issuance—to raise long-term debt capital rather than equity capital without diluting current shareholders' interest.

16-12. a. New shares are issued when a warrant is exercised. By definition, per-share earnings must decrease if earnings remain constant and shares increase.

    b. Rights also increase the number of shares outstanding, thereby decreasing per-share earnings.

16-13. a. Initial stock price $= S_0 = \$50$

        Subscription price $= S = \$47$

        Number of shares required $= N = 20$

$$\text{Cum - right } \frac{S_0 - S}{N+1} = \frac{50-47}{20+1} = \$.14$$

    b. The number of shares increases 5 percent $[(21/20) - 1]$. This implies that the new share price (S_1) should be 20/21 of what it was previously (S_0):

$$S_1 = S_0\left(\frac{N}{N+1}\right) = 50\left(\frac{20}{21}\right) = \$47.62$$

$$\text{Ex - right} = \frac{S_1 - S}{N} = \$.03$$

Answers to Self-Test Questions, pp. 572–574

16-1. False. Options are written by investors and sold to other investors.

16-2. True.

16-3. False. If the market price were in excess of the strike price, the call would be in the money and the put would be out of the money. When the market price of a stock is below the strike price, a call option is out of the money but a put option is in the money.

16-4. True.

16-5. False. A call option whose strike price exceeds the market can expire without the market ever reaching that price. But one with an exercise price below the prevailing market price has intrinsic value, since the underlying stock can be purchased at a price less than market. Therefore, the option premium will be much higher for the one with a strike price less than the current market. This price relationship holds true, regardless of the expected growth in the price potential of the underlying stock.

16-6. True.

16-7. False. Although warrants are issued by corporations, usually attached to a bond issue to make that bond more attractive, each warrant issue is unique. Warrants trade on the same secondary market as the corporation's stock.

16-8. False. The intrinsic value of the warrant is determined as follows: Value of warrant = ($33 – $35) x 1 = –$2. Since the stock is currently trading at a price below the exercise price, the intrinsic value is –$2. Apparently, however, the market feels that there is a reasonably good chance that the stock will appreciate to a price where the warrant can be profitably exercised before it expires. Consequently, the warrant is selling at $4, which is $6 above its intrinsic value. Therefore, the warrant premium is $6.

16-9. True.

16-10. False. The maximum amount that can be lost is the price paid for either option. Since an option typically sells for more than its intrinsic value, the loss can be greater than the intrinsic value.

16-11. True.

16-12. True.

16-13. True.

16-14. True.

16-15. False. When an option is exercised, the OCC randomly selects a broker who is obligated to randomly select one of the firm's customers who has written the option to fulfill the commitment.

16-16. False. In relation to the number of shares of common stock controlled (100 share per option), the transaction costs are relatively low. That is, the transaction costs involved in buying one option are less than the cost of buying 100 shares of stock. However, on a dollar-amount basis, the costs are fairly high. For example, to purchase 100 shares of stock costing $50 per share—a $5,000 transaction—the commissions might be about $85. To purchase one option on those 100 shares of stock, assuming the option premium is $2.50 (a $250 transaction), the commission would be about $27 or about one-third of the commission cost on the stock transaction. However, a dollar investment in the options equal to that of the stock ($5,000) would entail commission costs of about $220, or over 2 ½ times the commission cost for the $5,000 stock transaction.

16-17. True.

16-18. True.

16-19. False. An investor anticipating a drop in the price of a stock might want to short the stock but would not use a put to hedge the position. If a hedge is desired, the investor might purchase a call that would allow the purchase of stock to replace the short at a known price should the stock price not move as anticipated. In this way, the investor could set a definite upper limit on potential losses.

16-20. True.

16-21. True.

16-22. False. In this situation, the writer of the uncovered (naked) call would suffer a dollar-for-dollar loss as the market price of the stock subject to the call rose. The result described in the question would occur had it been a covered call. Then the writer would have retained the option premium but would have forgone any further gain on the long position in the stock.

16-23. False. The writer of a put expects the price either to stay steady or to rise so that the option holder will not exercise the right to sell the shares.

16-24. True.

16-25. False. The statement describes a spread rather than a straddle. With a straddle, the stock, exercise price, and expiration date are identical. The investor does not care in which direction the stock moves, provided it moves by a sufficiently large amount. More can be gained on a stock rise with a call (or with a call and a put) than will be lost on the identical put (call). The investor who uses a straddle loses if the stock's price does not change by an amount sufficient to compensate the investor for the premiums paid for both the call and the put.

16-26. True.

16-27. False. With the exercise of any index option, the settlement is made in dollars, not in actual delivery of the securities. This settlement is $100 for each point difference between the stock index close and the strike price of the option on the index.

16-28. True.

16-29. True.

16-30. False. The price of a warrant or a call option will rise when the market price of the underlying stock rises.

16-31. True.

16-32. True.
16-33. True.
16-34. True.

Chapter 17

Answers to Review Questions, pp. 606–607

17-1.　a.　The call provision gives the issuing company the power to limit conversion value. This limitation of upside potential reduces the value of the convertible.

　　　b.　Convertibles are more likely to be called when the conversion value passes the call price. This likelihood is slightly lower in the period immediately after issuance. This is because companies are reluctant to terminate securities so soon after being created.

17-2.　a.　The conversion premium decreases as the stock price rises, as shown in figure 17-1. This is primarily due to the fact that as the stock price rises, the market price of the convertible takes on more of the characteristics of the stock and less of the characteristics of the bond—there is ultimately no difference in the price of the convertible and the stock as stock price continues to rise. This effect is even greater for convertible bonds with a call feature (the majority of such bonds are callable). This is because a call becomes more likely as the stock price rises, and will result in the certain loss of the premium. A drop in interest rates will raise the bond portion's value. With this comes a decrease in the conversion premium. This is due to the conversion option's becoming relatively less valuable, thereby decreasing the "extra" amount investors are willing to pay for the premium. A rate rise causes the opposite result.

　　　b.　As figures 17-1 and 17-2 demonstrate, the time value of call options and the conversion premium of convertibles are similar in appearance. Both are the difference between market price and intrinsic value and have similar relationships to stock value.

17-3.　a.　The computations are as follows:
　　　　　●　Conversion price = 100 / 20 = $5
　　　　　●　Conversion value = 4 (20) = $80
　　　　　●　Conversion premium = 105 – 80 = $25
　　　　　●　Premium over straight-debt value = 105 – 90 = $15
　　　　　●　Current yield = coupon/price = 10 / 105 = 9.52%

　　　b.　In this case, the minimum value is the conversion value because the option is in the money. The profit could be even greater because of the conversion premium. Conversion value = 5.5 (20) = $110; profit = $110 – $100 = $10.

　　　c.　At the time of call, the bond investor will have received $50 in coupons. The stock investor will have received $1 in dividends. For equal profit percentages the following relationship must hold:

$$\text{Convertible HPRR} = \text{Stock HPRR}$$

$$\frac{107 + 5(10)}{100} = \frac{S_1 + 5(.20)}{4}$$

$$S_1 = \frac{4[107 + 5(10)]}{100} - 5(.20) = \$5.28$$

17-4.　a.　The new convertible price is the higher of straight debt value ($90) or conversion value plus premium. In question 17-3, the conversion premium was 31.25 percent of the conversion value. This leads to a new conversion value plus premium of 60 (1.3125) = $78.75. Since this is lower than the straight-debt value, $90 is the convertible's new price.

　　　b.　The investor has the choice of converting or receiving the $107 call offer. Conversion value = 6.5 (20) = $130. The market would logically gravitate to this higher price.

17-5.　The conversion premium is as follows:

$$\text{Preferred price} - \text{Common price (ratio)} = 100 - 40 (2) = \$20$$

17-6.　a.　If the common stock rises to $60, we can rearrange the equation as follows to derive the price at which the convertible preferred should sell:

$$\text{Preferred price} = \text{Conversion premium} + \text{Common price (ratio)} = 20 + 60 (2) = \$140$$

b. It is assumed that the conversion premium remains unchanged.

17-7. The owner of a convertible bond gains an option to exchange the bond for a predetermined number of shares of common stock. This option gives the bond stock-like attributes. Convertibles offer lower coupon rates because of the option. From the straight bondholder's perspective, convertibles offer more upside potential, but a call feature often limits this potential. From the stockholder's viewpoint, convertibles offer more downside protection because of the bond portion. Offsetting this is the accompanying interest rate and default risk.

Answers to Self-Test Questions, pp. 607–608

17-1. False. The term *conversion premium* refers to the difference between the market price of the bond and its conversion value.

17-2. True.

17-3. True.

17-4. True.

17-5. False. The conversion option is a feature that is favorable to the bondholder. As such, it gives the issuing corporation the opportunity to sell the bonds for their face value, while at the same time paying a slightly lower interest rate than would be the case for comparable bonds that lack the potential gain from convertibility.

17-6. True.

17-7. False. There is no waiting period. The conversion period typically extends for the life of the bond. In some cases, however, the issuing corporation may wish to limit the conversion period. At the end of the conversion period, the convertible reverts to a straight-debt issue with no conversion privilege.

17-8. True.

17-9. False. The performance of convertibles is heavily dependent on stock market activity.

17-10. False. The conversion premium tends to be greater when the price of the stock is lower. As the price of the underlying stock rises above the conversion price, the conversion premium declines; the value of the convertible becomes increasingly equivalent to the value of the underlying stock and decreasingly dependent on its bond value. In essence, the conversion premium represents the amount the investor is willing to pay to have downside security (provided by the bond value) while retaining upside potential. As the conversion value further exceeds the bond value, the downside protection becomes less important. Therefore, the conversion premium declines.

17-11. True.

17-12. True.

17-13. False. Due to the presence of the equity option, convertible bonds typically are less sensitive to interest rate changes than nonconvertible bonds are.

17-14. True.

17-15. False. Risk arbitrageurs frequently use this technique to take advantage of stock price differentials between two stocks of potential merger candidates.

17-16. False. Pure arbitrageurs make a quick certain profit due to existing price differentials between two different markets for the same or equivalent securities or assets.

Chapter 18

Answers to Review Questions, pp. 633–634

18-1. Commodity market trading hours are much more restricted than those of equity markets. Commodity exchanges restrict price movements. Equity markets also do this, but there are no hard and fast rules, and occurrences in which prices are restricted are rare. Commodity price changes can trigger a shutdown in trading. Again, this is extremely rare in equity markets.

18-2.   a. You have made $92,144, as calculated below.

$5/oz.	Portfolio = $50,000	Loan = $45,000
	Equity = $5,000	Ounces = $50,000 / $5 = 10,000
$6/oz.	Portfolio = $60,000	Loan = $45,000
	Equity = Portfolio – Loan = $15,000	Ounces = 10,000
Buy:	Portfolio = $150,000	Loan = Portfolio – Equity = $135,000
	Equity = $15,000	Ounces = 10,000 + ($90,000 / $6) = 25,000
$7/oz.	Portfolio = $175,000	Loan = $135,000
	Equity = $40,000	Ounces = 25,000
Buy:	Portfolio = $400,000	Loan = $400,000 – $40,000 = $360,000
	Equity = $40,000	Ounces = 57,143
$8/oz.	Portfolio = $457,144	Loan = $360,000
	Equity = $97,144	Ounces = 57,143

Profit = final equity – initial equity = $97,144 – $5,000 = $92,144

b. The holding period return is calculated as follows:

$$HPR = \$92,144 / \$5,000 = 1,842.88\%$$

18-3.   a. You receive a margin call when the loan value increases to 95 percent of the portfolio value—in other words, your equity has fallen to 5 percent. The new price of silver is calculated by using the new portfolio value and the number of ounces owned. The equations below indicate that you would receive a margin call when the price of silver is $6.63 per ounce.

$$.95 \text{ Portfolio} = \text{Loan}$$

$$\text{Portfolio} = \frac{\text{Loan}}{.95} = \frac{\$360,000}{.95} = \$378,947.37$$

$$\text{Silver} = \frac{\text{Portfolio}}{\text{Ounces}} = \frac{\$378,947.37}{57,143} = \$6.63/oz.$$

b. You must sell enough silver to bring your equity up to 10 percent. To double your equity percentage, you must halve the portfolio value. This is because all proceeds reduce the loan value while leaving your equity unchanged:

$$\text{Portfolio} = \frac{\$378,947.37}{2} = \$189,473.69$$

and

$$\text{Loan} = .9\ (\$189,473.69) = \$170,526.32$$

To accomplish this you must sell half (ounces = 57,143/2 = 28,572) of your holdings. As in 18-3a, you must calculate a new portfolio value that will trigger a new margin call. The corresponding silver price can be determined as follows:

$$\text{Portfolio} = \frac{\text{Loan}}{.95} = \frac{\$170,526.32}{.95} = \$179,501.39$$

$$\text{Silver} = \frac{\$179,501.39}{28,572} = \$6.28/oz.$$

18-4.   An initial condition is an active and competitive spot market. Another good attribute is a standardized contract that reduces trading costs. Price volatility will attract participants who want price protection (hedging) and those who speculate. These participants make for a deeper market. Some commodity futures are predicated on the existence of storage. In these cases, storage must be available at a reasonable cost.

18-5.   *Firm representatives* are active traders who seek either to promote the market for their firm's output or to obtain good prices on inputs; they are generally knowledgeable and experienced. *Scalpers* move in and out of the market quickly, seeking to take advantage of ephemeral price anomalies created by supply and demand imbalances; they usually have seats on the exchange, are knowledgeable, and benefit from lower trading costs. *Day traders* are similar to scalpers but trade less frequently and try to close all positions at each day's end. *Position traders* rely on fundamental analysis and are not tied to any specific time frame. *Arbitrageurs* are also analytical but concentrate on relative prices; they search for deviations from historical pricing patterns between commodities or contracts.

18-6. Much of the recent growth in futures markets can be attributed to the creation of innumerable new types of financial futures. Interest rates have a direct effect on financial institutions and, to a lesser degree, a vast number of other markets. Rapid futures innovation has attempted to satisfy demand for hedging and speculation in this area. Global trade and corporate expansion have increased the need for currency futures. Booming investment in stocks and other financial assets has sparked demand for instruments, such as index futures. These are just a few examples that are fueling the growth in financial futures.

18-7. a. Interest rate futures are similar to other futures in that they lock in a future price for a commodity—in this case, debt instruments. Setting prices for a date in the future is equivalent to locking in interest rates (via the dividend discount model). This basic relationship is augmented by the variety of underlying instruments. Bets can be made on interest rate spreads (different yield curves associated with different classes of instruments—for example, corporate securities and municipals), a foreign country's rates, and credit card rates, to name just a few.

     b. Some of the underlying debt securities are Treasuries, municipals, CDs, and Eurobonds.

18-8. a. Stock index futures are comparable to other futures except that there is no delivery of the underlying commodity. This cash settlement makes stock futures similar in some ways to options.

     b. With perfect immunization, writing index futures essentially locks in the current portfolio price. A decline in portfolio value is offset by an increase in the future's value. In a similar manner, increases in portfolio value are canceled out by money owed on the futures. (This analysis ignores the premiums that are received for writing the futures.)

18-9. The number of contracts needed to neutralize a $50 million stock portfolio with a beta of 1.07 is as follows:

$$\text{Number of contracts} = \frac{\text{Portfolio}}{\text{Contract value}}(\text{Beta}) = \frac{50{,}000{,}000}{500(1{,}450)}(1.07) = 74$$

18-10. A commodity option is an option on a futures contract. The owner, therefore, possesses the right but not obligation to buy (sell) futures contracts at a specified price within a prescribed time limit. This instrument gives the owner a great deal of leverage and means that the owner risks only the premium. Prospective owners should be aware that determining whether the option's price is fair is difficult because a commodity option is a derivative of a derivative; any errors in the input statistics compound the error in the resulting price.

18-11. The theory of program trading's role in the October 1987 crash is as follows: Portfolio managers seek insurance to protect their portfolios against further price declines. The portfolio insurance is principally in the form of written index futures. The managers want to ensure that there are buyers of their index futures; they therefore price them slightly below the actual index prices. Arbitrageurs spot the price differential and enter the market to take advantage of it. They buy the underpriced futures and short the higher-priced stocks. Shorting the stocks pressures a further decline in prices and accordingly the indices. This, in turn, begins a new cycle of futures writing. The effect of this cycle is accelerated and magnified by the automation of program trading. Program trading is used primarily by large institutions with huge portfolios. Scale and automation can turn a small decline into a large decline that leads other investors into panicked trading. In a worst case scenario, a crash ensues.

Answers to Self-Test Questions, pp. 634–635

18-1. True.

18-2. True.

18-3. False. In fact, all commodity futures are traded on margin.

18-4. False. Margin, as used in futures contracts, is a good faith deposit (earnest money) made by both the buyer and the seller to ensure the completion of the contract. It is akin to a performance bond.

18-5. False. The margin required on commodity futures transactions usually ranges from 2 percent to 10 percent of the value of the contract, depending on the commodity. However, the investor is not required to borrow the remaining balance to complete the transaction. Margin on futures transactions is actually a deposit (or earnest money), since the commodity is not actually bought or sold until the contract expires. (Most futures contracts are closed out before the contract expires. Therefore, most commodities futures contracts never involve the actual purchase or sale of the commodity.)

18-6. True.

18-7. True.

18-8.   True.

18-9.   True.

18-10. False. If the investor follows this tactic and interest rates fall as expected, the investor will need to either close out his or her position or deliver the securities. In either case, with the decline in interest rates, the prices of the futures contracts will have risen, and there will be a loss on the transaction. If an investor expects interest rates to decline substantially in the near future, it might be advisable to purchase interest rate futures.

18-11. False. When interest rates rise, the price of bonds (or other fixed-return instruments) falls. If interest rates are expected to rise, the speculator would sell (go short) these futures contracts, since the actual instrument being contracted for is a bond or loanable funds whose price will *decline* if interest rates rise. If interest rates do, in fact, fall, then an offsetting contract can be purchased at a price less than that realized for the contract involved in the short portion. As a consequence, the speculator would gain.

18-12. True.

18-13. True.

18-14. True.

18-15. True.

Chapter 19

Answers to Review Questions, pp. 669–670

19-1.   The potential investor should first determine whether he or she has the necessary capital and credit. Risks and related financial liabilities for the life of the investment should be added to this assessment. Some real estate investments entail management and necessitate a location near enough for easy access. These and the likely length of involvement are all factors for consideration.

19-2.   a. The *market approach* involves researching the current ask and recent sales prices of comparable properties. Careful attention should be paid to similarities and dissimilarities; it is often from these that a unique price estimate can be determined.

        b. *Cost approach* valuation takes into account what the costs will be if land is purchased and a new building constructed. This estimate is usually used as a ceiling on what should be paid for an existing property.

        c. If the investor desires a more analytical method, the *income approach* may be the most appropriate. This method involves determining all cash inflows, outflows, and future property values. The present values are then added to ascertain the overall project value and return. A number of alternative methods give rough approximations of this technique.

19-3.   Properties that are valued above the results using the three approaches in question 19-2 should be examined very thoroughly since they are probably overpriced. A price above that yielded by the income approach is a signal that there are most likely alternative investments that offer higher returns for comparable risk. Prices above the market and replacement figures should prompt consideration of other properties. These assessments should always take into account possible further bargaining concessions.

19-4.   a. Total costs are $190,833.80, as shown below.

House Cost	$179,000.00
Other Costs	
Loan points	4,296.00
Loan application fee	500.00
Title insurance	700.00
Inspections	250.00
Title transfer	895.00
Escrow	4,152.80
Lawyer	200.00
Utility fees	840.00
Total:	$190,833.80

        b. Your funding responsibility is $47,633.80, determined as follows:

            $190,833.80 – $143,200.00 = $47,633.80

c. Transaction costs represent 6.61 percent of the purchase price, calculated as follows:
$$(\$190,833.80 - \$179,000)/\$179,000 = 6.61\%$$

19-5. You are given enough information for a rough back-of-envelope calculation using the income approach:
Value = Income stream/Discount rate = $28,000/.11 = $254,545.45
The calculated value is much higher than the asking price; therefore, this transaction definitely merits further investigation.

19-6. The weighted average cost of capital (WACC) is .5(10.5%) + .5(6.5%) = 8.5%. The desired discount rate (cost of capital) should then add a risk premium to the WACC. The premium can be somewhat arbitrary but should at least cover that of the loan. Therefore, the absolute minimum risk premium and total cost of capital are 2 percent and 10.5 percent, respectively. The actual premium and discount rate should be comfortably above these figures.

19-7. Investors can choose from a wide variety of REIT mutual funds, many of which have low minimum investments. REIT funds offer the added benefit of diversification, especially in the case of index funds. Investors can also search for individual companies that have significant real estate holdings. They should assess whether the stock's price adequately reflects the holding's value and whether sales are imminent.

19-8. a. The present value is $571,428.57, calculated as shown below.
Costs = $300 + $600 = $900/grave
Per-grave profit = Sales price − Costs = $1,000 − $900 = $100
Annual profit = (Per-grave profit) (Number of graves sold) = ($100) (800) = $80,000
Present value = Annual profit/Discount rate = $80,000/.14 = $571,428.57

b. The value has increased $519,480.52, determined as shown below.
Costs = $300 + $550 = $850/grave
Per-grave profit = $1,000 − $850 = $150
Annual profit = $150 (800) = $120,000
Present value = $120,000/.11 = $1,090,909.09

Answers to Self-Test Questions, pp. 670–671

19-1. True.

19-2. False. High leverage is typically employed because investors desire to put as little of their own cash in the investment and borrow as much as possible.

19-3. False. Direct investments in real estate offer investors low liquidity. The investments may take a long time to sell at a fair price, depending on market conditions.

19-4. False. A point is one percent of the loan principal. If a property is purchased for $100,000 and the buyer takes out an $80,000 mortgage that requires 3 points, the cost of the points would be $2,400 ($80,000 x .03. = $2,400).

19-5. True.

19-6. True.

19-7. False. Commissions for raw land and undeveloped property are usually higher than commissions for developed real estate—10 percent versus 6 percent.

19-8. False. The market approach simply relies on an analysis of recent sales of similar properties to estimate the current value of a particular property.

19-9. True.

19-10. True.

19-11. False. The rate of interest is typically below market.

19-12. True.

19-13. True.

19-14. False. A REIT is essentially a closed-end investment company whose shares trade on an exchange or OTC.

19-15. False. In addition to direct investments in property, hybrid REITs also make construction and mortgage loans.

19-16. True.

19-17. False. Index REITs are subject to market risk. If investor interest moves away from the real estate sector, the prices of the individual REIT stocks included in the index will decline.

19-18. True.

Index

Note: A lowercase f following a page number refers the reader to a figure on that page; a lowercase n indicates a note (thus, "38n2" refers to note 2 on page 38); a lowercase t indicates a table.